Desolation Wilderness (p391), California

Yellowstone National Park (p218), Wyoming

Toolkit

Storybook

SUZIE DUNDAS FOR LONELY PLANET

Yosemite National Park (p388), California

WESTERN USA

THE JOURNEY BEGINS HERE

Countries have national birds, flowers and even dishes. And while the notion of a national compass direction is definitely not a thing, if it was, USA's would be west. In the literal sense, western expansion is a chapter in the history books that has, and continues to, inform our national identity – for better and worse.

Then there's the symbol of the West. Not just the tall tales of cowboys and desperadoes, but also the accounts of self-reliance, opportunity and freedom. It's why dude ranches continue to be popular among vacationers and Hollywood keeps serving up stories of ranchers and wranglers. There's something about the West that stokes an insatiable curiosity in us, even today.

Lean into that curiosity. Embark on a journey into the West, even for a week or a weekend. Wrangle your ski poles, tame a mountain-bike trail, or ride an unruly Pacific Ocean wave. Go West, young traveler!

My favourite experience
A road trip once took me across Texas, the Southwest and California. I'll never forget seeing the ocean after having traversed so many dramatically different landscapes. Eye candy is selling it short. It was an eye feast.

Amelia Mularz

@ameliamularz

Amelia is a Midwest-born, LA-based writer who loves to tell stories about travel and design.

WHO GOES WHERE

Our writers and experts choose the places which, for them, define Western USA

W TIMOTHY SCHAIFF/SHUTTERSTOCK

Driving the **Peter Norbeck Scenic Byway** (p118) in the Black Hills of South Dakota is a blast. The Iron Mountain Rd section loop-de-loops through the pines while the 14-mile Needles Hwy leg twists passes otherworldly granite spires. And oooh, those sketchy one-way tunnels!

Amy C Balfour

@AmyCBalfour

Amy is a writer and guidebook author covering travel, food and adventure. She wrote the sections on Iowa, North Dakota and South Dakota.

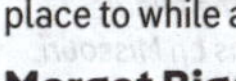

DAVID BUZZARD/SHUTTERSTOCK

Growing up in Portland, Oregon, there were so many things I took for granted, from easy access to old-growth forests to **Powell's City of Books** (p471), the largest new-and-used bookstore in the country, covering three floors and an entire city block. I can't think of a better place to while away a rainy day.

Margot Bigg

@margotbigg

Margot is a travel writer and essayist from Portland, Oregon. She wrote the Toolkit and the History of the Western USA in 15 Places.

REFRINA/SHUTTERSTOCK

The **Ballard Locks** (p454) quickly became one of my favorite places in Seattle. At first glance, it doesn't look like all that much, but there's so much to see if you look around – feats of engineering, seasonal salmon jumping out of the water, blooming blossoms, and even the occasional harbor seal.

Sarah Etinas

sarahetinas.com

Sarah is a freelance travel writer and editor. She wrote the Pacific Northwest chapter.

Hiking the Rim Trail in **Bryce Canyon National Park** (p318), I had one of those moments that only seems to happen in the parks of this remarkable state. All of a sudden, the Earth fell silent, there was no-one else around, and it felt like this special landscape was holding its breath. I stood still, doing the same, looking around me in wonder. And then, somewhere high on the rock walls, a single chickadee started to sing.

DIBROVA/SHUTTERSTOCK

Anthony Ham

@AnthonyHamWrite

Anthony Ham writes about the wild places of our planet, from the deserts of Africa and the Arctic to the Amazon. He curated the Southwest USA chapter.

Nothing feels more like coming home than setting foot in the **Tallgrass Prairie National Preserve** (p70) in Kansas. When I was a kid, we took a road trip around Kansas, and this landscape has stuck with me ever since. When I listen to the whispering wind, the chirping meadowlarks and the snorting bison, it roots me right back here, no matter how long I've been away.

SPUTNIK ALOYSIUS/SHUTTERSTOCK

Lauren Keith

@noplacelike_it

Lauren is a guidebook author who grew up in Kansas. She's often found somewhere between the Midwest and the Middle East. She wrote the sections on Missouri, Kansas, Oklahoma and Nebraska.

I'm not sure what I expected to find as I headed to **Craters of the Moon National Monument** (p246) in Idaho. But standing in the middle of a blackened lava field, small volcanoes dotting the horizon, I felt like I was on the Big Island in Hawai'i. Until it started to snow. It was surreal, this volcanic landscape dusted in white, a reminder of just how wildly diverse the Rocky Mountain region is.

LIZA PRADO FOR LONELY PLANET

Liza Prado

@liza.prado

Liza is a corporate lawyer turned travel writer and the author of over 60 books. She researched the Rocky Mountains chapter.

CHRIS LABASCO/SHUTTERSTOCK

Entering **Sacramento** (p406), I always have the feeling that I'm entering a city and a forest at the same time. The city has more than a million trees, cooling walkers on sweltering summer days, meeting in grand arches across the streets and framing the 1920s wooden Craftsman homes and flamboyant midtown Victorians. There are even city center redwoods. Sacramento is a city of government, but the trees turn it into a green dreamscape.

Helena Smith

@helenasmithpix

Helena loves to write about eco travel, community and the outdoors. She researched the California chapter.

FOTOLUMINATE LLC/SHUTTERSTOCK

Texas' wild places have always captivated me: the long seacoast, parched canyons and western mountains. They make a fine counterpoint to the cities, which are packed with urban intrigue. Then there are places like the **Hill Country** (p146) that straddle two worlds. I love going for hikes along rugged trails, followed by a dip in a swimming hole. By evening, it's on to an old dancehall for live music and drinks under the pecan trees.

Regis St Louis

@regisstlouis

The son of two Coloradans, Regis has spent half a lifetime exploring remote corners of the world for Lonely Planet. He wrote the chapter on Texas.

CONTRIBUTING WRITERS

Brett Atkinson
Alexis Averbuck
Alison Bing
Dale Blasingame
Celeste Brash
Jade Bremner
Esther Carlstone
Suzie Dundas
Brandon Fralic
Nicole Hagg
Ashley Harrell
Anita Isalska
George Joe
Sarah Kezele
Dylan Lalanne-Perkins
Alex Leviton
Stephen Lioy
Becky Ohlsen
Lisa Park
Christopher Pitts
Britany Robinson
Margot Seeto
Meena Thiruvengadam
Priscilla Totiyapungprasert
Julie Tremaine
Ryan Ver Berkmoes
Wendy Yanagihara

Seattle
Eat your way through the legendary Pike Place Market (p446)
Columbia River Gorge
Hike, bike and windsurf in a canyon famous for waterfalls (p486)
Wine Country
Soak up valley views while sipping in Napa and Sonoma (p371)
Zion National Park
Explore slot canyons and take in towering sandstone cliffs (p320)
Las Vegas
Try your luck and let loose in mega-resorts and casinos (p256)
Los Angeles
Hit the beach then a Hollywood studio tour (p409)
Grand Canyon National Park
Get a load of one of the Seven Natural Wonders of the World (p273)
Saguaro National Park
See the nation's largest cacti, plus ancient petroglyphs (p300)
CANADA
Delta
Bellingham
Seattle
Riverside
WASHINGTON
Olympia
Mt Rainier (14,411ft)
Spokane
Portland
Columbia River Gorge
Sheridan
St Paul
Eureka
Missoula
Cascade Range
OREGON
IDAHO
Springfield
Mitchell
Bend
Grants Pass
Medford
Burns
Ontario
Boise
Brookings
Klamath Falls
Goose Lake
Mountain Home
Trinidad
Eureka
Twin Falls
Pocatello
Burley
Redding
Winnemucca
Wells
Chico
Elko
Wine Country
Reno
Stillwater
Salt Lake City
Santa Rosa
Lake Tahoe
Austin
UTAH
Sacramento
Carson City
Eureka
NEVADA
Ely
San Francisco
Columbia
San Jose
Tonopah
Fresno
Yosemite National Park
Caliente
CALIFORNIA
Huron
Zion National Park
Morro Bay
Bakersfield
Death Valley National Park
Mesquite
Las Vegas
Grand Canyon National Park
Los Alamos
Las Cruces
Santa Barbara
ARIZONA
Kingman
Barstow
Flagstaff
Channel Islands National Park
Los Angeles
Palm Springs
Riverside
Prescott
Sedona
Carlsbad
San Diego
Phoenix
Saguaro National Park
Tucson
500 km
250 miles

Yellowstone National Park
Visit the home of over 60% of the world's geysers (p218)
Badlands National Park
Peep bison, big horn sheep and a fossil or two (p110)
Rocky Mountain National Park
Explore the crown jewel of Colorado's national parks (p190)
Santa Fe
Wander through adobe neighborhoods and go gallery hopping (p327)
Austin
Jam out in the Live Music Capital of the World (p130)
Branson
Hit up an Old West–themed amusement park for family fun (p66)
Havre
Minot
Lawton
NORTH DAKOTA
Sidney
Douglas
Buffalo
Valentine
MONTANA
Dickinson
Bismarck
Buffalo
Buffalo
Columbia
SOUTH DAKOTA
Yellowstone National Park
Sheridan
Spearfish
Grand Teton National Park
Buffalo
Gillette
Pierre
Huron
Brookings
St Paul
Medford
Austin
Rocky Mountains
Mitchell
Douglas
Chadron
Valentine
Yankton
WYOMING
Alliance
NEBRASKA
Scottsbluff
Rawlins
North Platte
Broken Bow
Cheyenne
Fort Collins
Sidney
Ogallala
Sidney
Delta
Mountain Home
Rocky Mountain National Park
Boulder
Denver
Springfield
Aspen
COLORADO
Delta
Colorado Springs
Kearney
Columbia
Jefferson City
Abilene
Moab
Montrose
Gunnison
Portland
Pueblo
KANSAS
Bluff
Durango
Alamosa
Trinidad
Springfield
Dodge City
Kingman
Wichita
Buffalo
Bismarck
Springfield
Raton
Mesa Verde National Park
Medford
Branson
Taos
Enid
Stillwater
Tulsa
Winslow
Mountain Home
Los Alamos
TEXAS
Santa Fe
Las Vegas
Cheyenne
Oklahoma City
Albuquerque
Santa Rosa
Amarillo
Little Rock
Broken Bow
Clovis
Lawton
San Antonio
Ardmore
NEW MEXICO
Wichita Falls
Roswell
Lubbock
Texarkana
Riverside
Fort Worth
Mesquite
Las Cruces
Carlsbad
Abilene
Midland
Barstow
Waco
Buffalo
Baton Rouge
Bakersfield
College Station
Valentine
MEXICO
Mountain Home
Austin
San Antonio
Dickinson

BIG NATURE

Mother Nature certainly didn't slack when it came to decorating the West. Coastal California and the Pacific Northwest are home to wild waters, dramatic cliff formations and lush forests – some touting redwoods, the world's tallest trees. The region's interior is dotted with deserts, and beyond that, the Great Plains resemble a sea where waves are formed by gorgeously undulating grasses. Then there are the Rocky Mountains, which deserve every hyperbole uttered by awe-struck admirers. Awesome. Epic. Just wow.

FROM LEFT: MICHELE VACCHIANO/SHUTTERSTOCK, STEFLAS/SHUTTERSTOCK, OLEG KOVTUN HYDROBIO/SHUTTERSTOCK

Dinosaur Tracks

In Moab, fossilized dino footprints are part of the scenery. At the **Mill Canyon Dinosaur Tracksite** (pictured; p311) visitors can check out prints from at least 10 species.

Endangered Ecosystem

North America was once home to 170 million acres of tallgrass prairie, but less than 4% remains. Head to the **Tallgrass Prairie National Preserve** (pictured; p70) to see some of what's left.

Why Are the Rocks Red?

Rocks of the Southwest get their distinctive hue from iron-rich minerals, like hematite, which oxidize – essentially rusting – when exposed to air and water.

Garden of the Gods (p207), Colorado

BEST NATURE EXPERIENCES

Drive, hike or bike past sandstone arches, windows, fins and a precariously balanced rock in ❶ **Arches National Park** (p314).

Explore the ❷ **Grand Canyon** (p276), where a 277-mile river cuts through two-billion-year-old rocks, whose geological secrets are revealed within a mile-high stack.

See why photographers and sand sledders alike have been mesmerized by the ripples of chalk-white dunes at ❸ **White Sands National Park** (p337).

Take in Washington's powerful volcanoes by hiking around ❹ **Mt Rainier** (p458) or visiting **Mt St Helens** (p467) to learn about its mighty 1980 eruption.

Gawk at mesmerizingly gorgeous 300ft rock formations at Colorado's ❺ **Garden of the Gods** (p207), where grasslands meet mountain forests.

Mendocino coastline (p376), California

ROMANTIC GETAWAYS

Whether you're on your honeymoon or simply treating your sweetie, the West is where it's at for romance. Bed down in a Victorian B&B or in a tent under a canopy of stars. Clink glasses in a winery bistro or at a mountaintop picnic. Surrender to R&R in a chic spa or hike out to an isolated forest cabin.

Vineyard Love

Let wine country do the wooing at cozy vintage accommodations like **Blackbird Inn** (p438), a 1902 cottage in Napa, or **An Inn 2 Remember** (p438), a Victorian-style stay in Sonoma.

Going to the Chapel

Looking to elope? The **Little Church of the West** (p257) is one of the oldest of the many wedding chapels in Las Vegas. And, yes, they have an Elvis option.

BEST ROMANTIC EXPERIENCES

Heed the call of romance in ❶ **Mendocino** (p376), with cottages and quiet country inns.

Snag a hotel room with a hot tub, take to the slopes and try some pairs skating in snow-covered ❷ **Jackson Hole** (p221).

Take a long walk on the beach in sparkling ❸ **Malibu** (p419), built for cozy cuddling and oceanside strolls.

Indulge in couples' spa treatments, go for sunset hikes and do some serious stargazing in ❹ **Sedona** (p281).

Go on a gondola ride together, then grab a bottle of wine and cozy up to a fireplace in ❺ **Telluride** (p203).

FROM GRAPE TO GLASS

Though Napa and Sonoma have garnered a good amount of fame (and for good reason), California isn't the only wine-productiong state in the region. Find Tuscany in Texas, wine galore in Washington and tasting rooms with ogle-worthy views in Oregon, too. And in California, don't miss out on wine areas farther downstate, like the Santa Ynez Valley near Santa Barbara.

FROM LEFT: TERRI BUTLER PHOTOGRAPHY/SHUTTERSTOCK, VIOLET MULLINS/SHUTTERSTOCK

Cheers, Y'all!

Wine in Texas? Absolutely. Texas Hill Country is actually the third-largest AVA in the country, covering over 9 million acres with more than 100 wineries.

Organic vs Biodynamic

Organic means grapes aren't exposed to chemical fertilizers, pesticides or herbicides. Biodynamic means integrated farming intended to sustain healthy ecosystems.

Cider & Beer Too

California is tops for more than wine: it has the most craft breweries in the nation and a killer cider game, with heritage apple orchards throughout.

BEST WINE EXPERIENCES

Wear your cowboy hat to the winery in ❶ **Texas Hill Country** (p147), known for its tempranillo, cabernet sauvignon and mourvèdre.

Sample some of America's best wines in ❷ **Napa Valley** (p373), where you can even sip while riding a wine train or wine gondola.

Sip riesling, zinfandel and even cider (for when you're wine'd out) in ❸ **Tin City** (p402), a cluster of post-industrial-cool tasting rooms in Paso Robles.

Take your pick of tasting rooms in downtown ❹ **Walla Walla** (p468), touted for its top-notch cabernet sauvignon and syrah.

Grab a seat in a hilltop tasting room and whet your whistle with vibrant pinot noirs in the ❺ **Willamette Valley** (p484).

HISTORICAL HOTSPOTS

Museums? Save 'em for later. First you'll want to climb a wooden ladder into a cliff dwelling, poke around the ruins of a Pony Express Station, or simply join the congregation inside a 1700s Spanish mission. What else is there to explore in the West? Crumbling forts and trading posts. Abandoned ghost towns. Adobe pueblos. Wander historic sites like these for up-close, evocative links to the region's rich, multilayered past.

Historic Routes

Opportunity, gold and religious freedom sent hundreds of thousands of settlers west on the Oregon, California and Mormon trails, all of which traverse multiple states.

California's Missions

Stretching from San Diego to Sonoma, 21 missions built between 1769 and 1823 tell the story of religious conversion and Spanish colonialism in California.

Meramec Caverns

An Osage guide led French colonist Philip Renault to the Missouri caverns in 1720, and Jesse James is said to have hidden out in them in the 1870s.

FROM LEFT: ZACK FRANK/SHUTTERSTOCK, NEVADA.CLAIRE/SHUTTERSTOCK, BRYAN MULLENNIX/GETTY IMAGES

Mesa Verde National Park (p200), Colorado

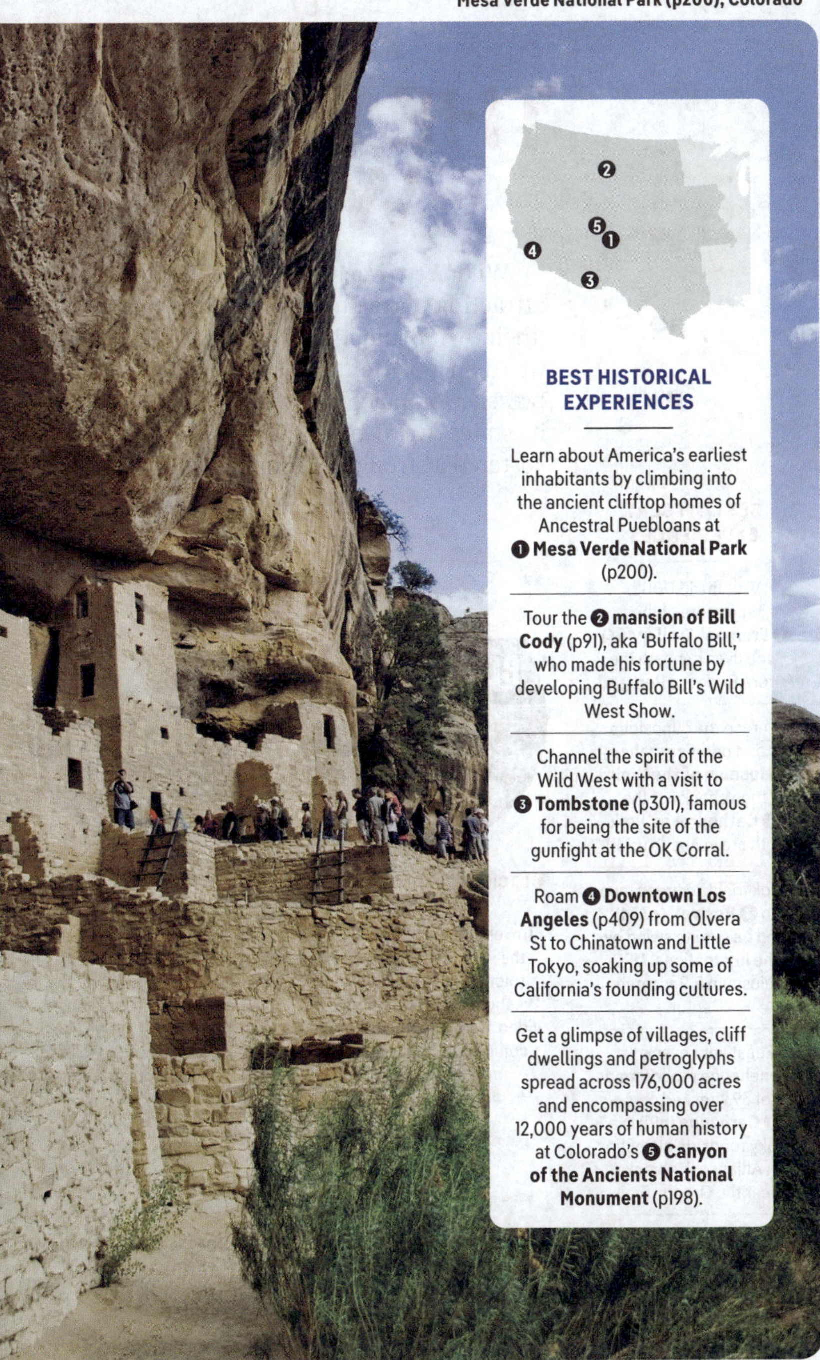

BEST HISTORICAL EXPERIENCES

Learn about America's earliest inhabitants by climbing into the ancient clifftop homes of Ancestral Puebloans at ❶ **Mesa Verde National Park** (p200).

Tour the ❷ **mansion of Bill Cody** (p91), aka 'Buffalo Bill,' who made his fortune by developing Buffalo Bill's Wild West Show.

Channel the spirit of the Wild West with a visit to ❸ **Tombstone** (p301), famous for being the site of the gunfight at the OK Corral.

Roam ❹ **Downtown Los Angeles** (p409) from Olvera St to Chinatown and Little Tokyo, soaking up some of California's founding cultures.

Get a glimpse of villages, cliff dwellings and petroglyphs spread across 176,000 acres and encompassing over 12,000 years of human history at Colorado's ❺ **Canyon of the Ancients National Monument** (p198).

THE WACKY WEST

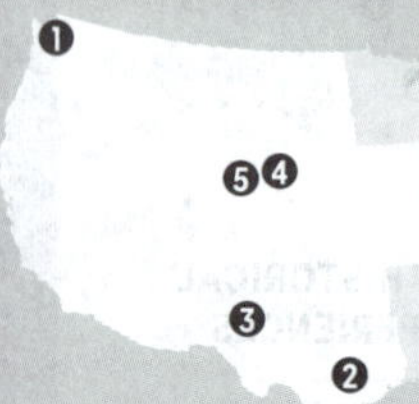

Wild? Yes. Wacky? Also yes. Known for attracting residents who march to the beat of their own drum, the West proudly serves up weird on a platter to tourists. Add to that, the presence of major highways stretching across its states (we're lookin' at you, Route 66) have fostered a strong tradition of kooky roadside attractions.

BEST OFFBEAT EXPERIENCES

Visit the 13,000lb sculpture of the ❶ **Fremont Troll** (p453), who lives beneath the Aurora Bridge in Portland.

Peruse the curiosities and oddities at the ❷ **Museum of the Weird**, then check out the ❷ **Cathedral of Junk**. Both are in Austin (p131).

Look for little green men in ❸ **Roswell** (p334) and be sure to swing by the International UFO Museum & Research Center.

Feast your eyes on a Stonehenge replica made of 39 wrecked cars. ❹ **Carhenge** (p91) is a kooky roadside attraction in Alliance, Nebraska, near the Oregon Trail.

Get a load of dozens of ❺ **8ft-tall cowboy boots** (p212) – painted by local artists – that tell the history of Cheyenne and Wyoming.

FROM LEFT: QUIGGYT4/SHUTTERSTOCK, JOSHUA RAINEY PHOTOGRAPHY/SHUTTERSTOCK

Blockbuster Still Exists

Travel back in time by visiting the very **last Blockbuster** (pictured; p489). This final vestige of the popular 1990s video store is in Bend, Oregon, complete with packages of microwave popcorn.

The Capital of Weird

Texans use the slogan 'Keep Austin Weird,' while in the Pacific Northwest they say 'Keep Portland Weird.' Austin was the original, but we like to think there's enough weird to go around.

High Jinks on Route 66

The Mother Road is famous for quirky roadside attractions, especially its retro-style diners. In Seligman, Arizona, **Delgadillo's Snow Cap** (p294) still serves over-the-counter pranks alongside burgers.

Las Vegas (p256), Nevada

BRIGHT LIGHTS, BIG CITIES

Tiny towns and rural stretches give the region its rugged reputation, but the West's major cities are an integral part of its character, too. Plus, they'll give you a chance to kick the dirt off your hiking boots and indulge in a multicourse meal, catch a concert or explore a network of noteworthy museums.

BEST CITY EXPERIENCES

Hit the wonderland that is ❶ **Los Angeles** (p409), visiting everything from Hollywood dives to the Getty Museum.

Listen to live music, see the Pacific Northwest Ballet and shop at an iconic food market – all in ❷ **Seattle** (p446).

Investigate ❸ **Portland**'s (p471) food obsessions, wander a handicraft market and get lost in the world's largest independent bookstore.

Indulge in trendsetting food, social movements, art and technology in ❹ **San Francisco** (p346).

See if lady luck is on your side in any of the ❺ **Las Vegas** (p256) casinos.

Sin-tillating City

Las Vegas is one of the brightest places on Earth when viewed from space, thanks to the sheer number of shimmering lights on the Strip.

Huge Cultural Hub

While visiting the Bay, be sure to swing by San Francisco's Chinatown, the oldest and largest Chinatown in North America, and the second-biggest outside Asia.

COASTAL PLEASURES

For road trippers, the coast is the classic end to an epic journey. But don't call it quits just because you ran out of land. The Pacific Coast, from SoCal all the way up to northern Washington, is where the fun really begins. Even if you're not big on sunbathing or swimming, there's plenty to do, like taking a captivating joy ride around Big Sur, whale watching from an archipelago off Washington and exploring maritime history in San Diego.

FROM LEFT: CK FOTO/SHUTTERSTOCK, JOANNA SZYPULSKA/SHUTTERSTOCK, CHRISTIANA ANGOTTO/SHUTTERSTOCK

Beach Scenes

In California, endless summers are fueled by Ferris wheels and carnival games, coupled with soul-stirring sunsets in Santa Monica (pictured), Venice Beach and Santa Cruz.

Can You Swim near Seattle?

Yes...kind of. Alki Beach Park (pictured) in West Seattle is popular among sunbathers. You can get in the water, but the temp ranges from 46-56°F so it'll be refreshing.

Iconic Big Sur

That coastline in all those car commercials? Definitely Big Sur. Cradled by redwood forests, the coast is a place of hidden waterfalls and heart-hammering bridges.

Orca, San Juan Island (p464), Washington

BEST COASTAL EXPERIENCES

Kayak the coastline and walk sandstone cliffs and dunes in dreamy, often fog-filled ❶ **Half Moon Bay** (p369).

Peep fluffy tufted puffins taking refuge on Haystack Rock, a 235ft-tall, 17-million-year-old Oregon icon located in ❷ **Cannon Beach** (p491).

Ooh and ahh at the sight of offshore orcas from Lime Kiln Point State Park (aka 'Whale Watch Park') on ❸ **San Juan Island** (p464).

Dig for razor clams, a classic Washington activity, just before low tide on ❹ **Long Beach**. Many hotels even provide digging equipment (p465).

Tour the USS Midway Museum, located on a decommissioned aircraft carrier, and meander the Maritime Museum of San Diego to see historic ships – both in ❺ **San Diego** (p433).

REGIONS & CITIES

Find the places that tick all your boxes.

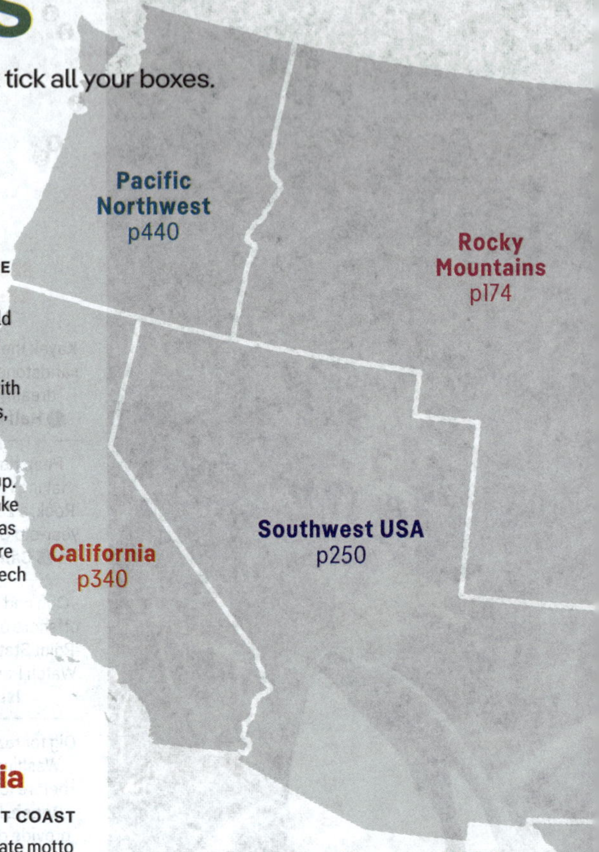

Pacific Northwest
p440

Rocky Mountains
p174

Southwest USA
p250

California
p340

Pacific Northwest

AN UNBEATABLE NATURE ESCAPE

Breathe air so fresh it should be bottled, hike to hidden waterfalls and explore innovative cities sprinkled with food carts, microbreweries, coffee connoisseurs and entrepreneurs ready to launch the next great startup. Washington and Oregon make up this region, which is just as famous for its alluring nature trails as its groundbreaking tech industries.

p440

California

THE LEISURELY LEFT COAST

Eureka! It's a fitting state motto for a place teeming with cultural and geographical treasures just waiting to be discovered. Southern California's dreamy beaches, palm-tree-dotted skyline and glamorous nightlife understandably get a lot of buzz. But don't sleep on the Central Coast's surf towns or Northern California's enchanting redwood forests.

p340

Southwest USA

ONE OF AMERICA'S GRAND EPICS

The American Southwest – which includes Nevada, Arizona, Utah and New Mexico – lures adventurous travelers with red-rock canyons and Wild West legends. Reminders of the region's Native American heritage also abound, with centuries-old cliff dwellings as well as more modern adobe architecture and art galleries stocked with distinctive pottery, weaving and jewelry.

p250

Rocky Mountains

EPIC BEAUTY MEETS OUTDOOR ADVENTURE

Prepare to feast your eyes on one of the most beautiful mountain ranges on Earth. In the Rocky Mountains – spread across Colorado, Wyoming, Montana and Idaho – picking your jaw up off the ground after taking in the dramatic landscapes is practically a sport in itself. There's climbing, hiking, mountain biking and fishing galore, too.

p174

The Great Plains
p48

The Great Plains

SURPRISING CITIES AND PRISTINE PRAIRIE

Don't let the 'plain' part fool you. This region is home to seven states – Missouri, Kansas, Oklahoma, Nebraska, Iowa, South Dakota and North Dakota – that are stacked with quietly cool cities. And for nature lovers, this anything-but-ordinary area has the two longest rivers in the country, the Missouri and the Mississippi.

p48

Texas
p124

Texas

BIG SKIES AND OPEN ROADS

Like they say, everything's bigger in Texas, including the possibilities for having a good time. This sweeping state is the second largest in the country by land area. You'll find two sprawling national parks, bustling cities, beaches, historic towns and a thriving music scene – all in the Lone Star State.

p124

ITINERARIES

Southwest on 66

Allow: 7 days **Distance**: 1030 miles

Get your kicks – and enjoy some kitsch – on Route 66. Though it's only a fraction of the Mother Road, this route is still chock-full of charming roadside attractions. Work up a sweat in the desert, passing through New Mexico, Arizona and Eastern California, then cool off on the coast.

1 SANTA FE 1 DAY

The day before embarking on your Southwestern sojourn, stretch your legs by wandering **Santa Fe** (p327) and checking out its distinctive Pueblo Revival–style architecture. Fill up on Frito Pie (pictured) and enchiladas smothered in red and green 'Christmas' salsas and brush up on your map-reading skills by hitting the town's Margarita Trail. Get a good night's rest and you're ready to tackle this historic route.

2 ALBUQUERQUE 1 DAY

If you went too hard on Santa Fe's Margarita Trail, no worries. Your first day's drive is an easy 90 minutes to **Albuquerque** (p325). Enjoy the views of the Sandia Mountains (pictured) on the way, then make time for a couple of only-in-Albuquerque attractions, like the Anderson-Abruzzo Albuquerque International Balloon Museum and a visit to the 18th-century (allegedly haunted) High Noon Saloon.

3 FLAGSTAFF 1 DAY

From Albuquerque, it's about 2½ hours to the Arizona border, then another 45 minutes to the **Petrified Forest National Park** – a superb spot to get some fresh air, with a side of surreal Painted Desert landscapes (pictured). Continue west and roll into **Flagstaff** (p287) to take a self-guided public mural tour.

Detour: *Feeling ambitious? Head north to* ***Grand Canyon National Park*** *(p273) for a half-day of hiking.*

FROM LEFT: FOOD IS LOVE/SHUTTERSTOCK, NAYADADARA/SHUTTERSTOCK, ANDREA CHIOZZI/SHUTTERSTOCK

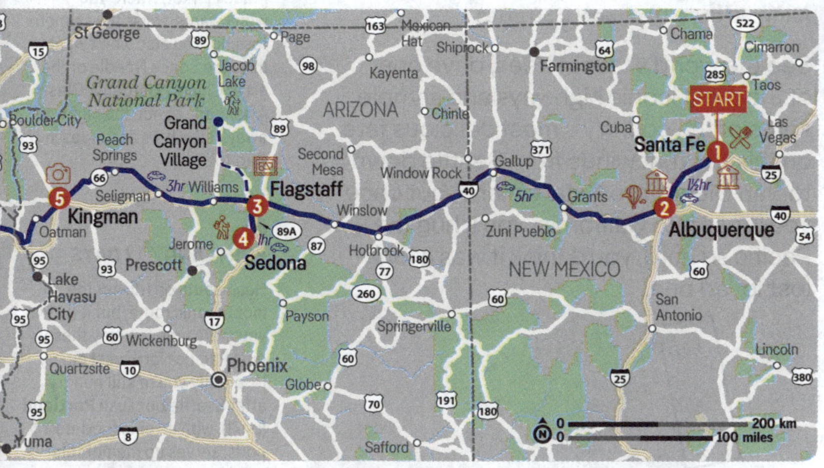

4

SEDONA 1 DAY

White technically not on Route 66, **Sedona** (p281) is a quick one-hour drive south of Flagstaff and well worth the detour. Hike trails with towering red-rock buttes, visit a vortex or two and take part in every new-agey spiritual practice you've ever dreamed of (shop for healing crystals, meet with a psychic, get a photo of your aura, your psychic's aura, etc).

5

KINGMAN 1 DAY

Here's where you pay homage to the historic route you've now been traveling for days. In **Kingman** (p293), visit the Route 66 Museum and swing by the Kingman Visitor Center for the ultimate photo op: a pic with the drive-thru Route 66 sign. And don't leave town before dining at Mr D'z Route 66 Diner, a retro restaurant covered in turquoise paint and a neon glow.

6

LOS ANGELES 2 DAYS

Final stop: the Golden State. Route 66 enters California in Needles (pictured) and cuts across the Mojave Desert before passing San Bernardino and the San Gabriel Valley. You'll enter **Los Angeles** (p409) in Pasadena, where you'll be tempted to veer off and explore the city's Old Town, but stay the course to feel the satisfaction of reaching Route 66's end at Lincoln and Olympic in breezy, beachside Santa Monica.

FROM LEFT: DUSTY ROADS/SHUTTERSTOCK, CARLA GLOBETROTTER/SHUTTERSTOCK, ALLARD ONE/SHUTTERSTOCK

ITINERARIES

Pacific Coast Cruising

Allow: 10 days **Distance**: 1650 miles

See the world's tallest trees, drive one of the most iconic highways and sample some of the country's most delicious fare on this trip that winds from Seattle down to San Diego. You'll start inland, but once you cross into California, you'll hug the Pacific so hard, you'd think it was a long-lost loved one.

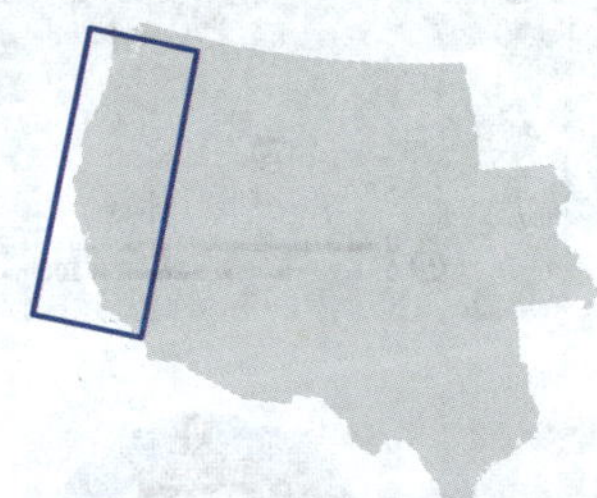

Pike Place Market (p450), Seattle

1
SEATTLE 2 DAYS

Get well caffeinated by spending two days in the country's coffee capital, **Seattle** (p446). Pair your java with any of the multitude of munchies available at Pike Place Market, where you won't want to miss the salmon tossing. You also won't want to miss the Space Needle or the art at Chihuly Garden & Glass. After dark, dance the night away at the bars and clubs in Capitol Hill.

2
PORTLAND 2 DAYS

Head south on I-5; not the most scenic route, but it'll give you more time to enjoy these dual Pacific Northwest cities. Hopefully you're still hungry after Seattle because **Portland** (p471), with its epic food-cart pods, serves up memorable meals, too.

Detour: *Drive east for an afternoon of hiking and waterfall watching along the* ***Columbia River Gorge*** *(p486).*

3
REDWOOD NATIONAL & STATE PARKS 2 DAYS

From Portland, set your GPS for Crescent City, California, and continue south along I-5. Crescent City is near **Redwood National and State Parks** (p381), a system of four public parks that sit along a 50-mile driving route on Hwy 101 (roughly Crescent City to Orick). Spend your time hiking through fern-covered canyons, hunting for agates on wild beaches and ogling redwoods – the tallest trees on earth.

ALEX CIMBAL/SHUTTERSTOCK

4

MENDOCINO 1 DAY

In case you didn't realize it, up in Redwood National and State Parks you officially linked up with the world famous Pacific Coast Hwy (PCH). Called Hwy 101 up north, PCH becomes Hwy 1 near Leggett. About 50 miles south of there, you'll hit **Mendocino** (p376), a dreamy historic timber town built on a bluff. Hike the Mendocino Headlands and sample the fine dining in the village.

5

SAN FRANCISCO 2 DAYS

Take your time getting down to **San Francisco** (p346), passing through charming oceanside towns (like Jenner and Bodega Bay) along the PCH. Once you've arrived, spend your time riding cable cars, watching sea lions at Fisherman's Wharf and admiring the Victorian architecture around the city. To refuel, head to Chinatown for family-style feasts.

Detour: *Hop over to Berkeley, across the Bay Bridge, to eat at legendary farm-to-table restaurant Chez Panisse.*

6

SANTA BARBARA 1 DAY

South of San Francisco you'll cruise some of the most gobsmackingly gorgeous stretches of the PCH, particularly around Big Sur. A few hours south, you'll land in **Santa Barbara** (p397). Nicknamed the American Riviera, Santa Barbara has long been a weekend escape for Californians living in more urban areas. Soak up all the Mediterranean-inspired architecture and chill, beach-town vibes, then toast to an epic road trip completed.

ZACK FRANK/SHUTTERSTOCK

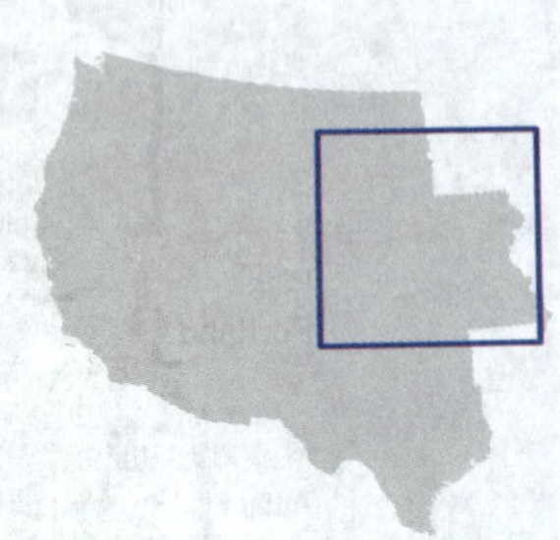

Chimney Rock National Historic Site (p92), Nebraska

ITINERARIES

Great Plains & Historic Trails

Allow: 5 days **Distance**: 860 miles

A combo of truly great Great Plans cities and legendary trails make this route, which passes through Iowa and Nebraska, especially appealing to history buffs. Spend time in a former hub for the fur trade, get a feel for the Oregon Trail, and Lewis and Clark expedition route, and pay homage to the travelers of yesteryear.

FROM LEFT: PIXEL PERFECT PIX/SHUTTERSTOCK, BERGMANND/GETTY IMAGES, EWY MEDIA/SHUTTERSTOCK

1

DUBUQUE 1 DAY

Begin in Iowa's oldest city **Dubuque** (p95), once a hub for the fur trade and known for its boat-building industry. Today, the woodworking factories in the Millwork District have been transformed into restaurants and shops. On your way out of town, stop in Dyersville, just 30 minutes west off US-20, to visit the Field of Dreams.

Detour: Set out for an afternoon of cave exploration in **Maquoketa Caves State Park** *(p96), about 30 miles south of Dubuque on US-61.*

2

SIOUX CITY 1 DAY

For one member of the Lewis and Clark expedition, a stop in **Sioux City** (p104) was especially fateful. Learn about Sergeant Charles Floyd and the rest of the crew at the Lewis & Clark Interpretive Center. For you, however, there's no need to worry. A day here should be all about leisurely exploring the waterfront and trying a Tastee sandwich at Tastee Inn & Out.

3

OMAHA ½ DAY

Welcome to Nebraska. Stop in **Omaha** (p86) for a lunch and grab a Reuben or a runza (pictured) – two sandwiches created in the Husker State (the latter is a rectangle of yeast-dough bread filled with ground beef and onions). Afterward, shop at the Old Market, a neighborhood with cobblestone streets and revitalized 19th-century warehouses to get a feel for the city's history.

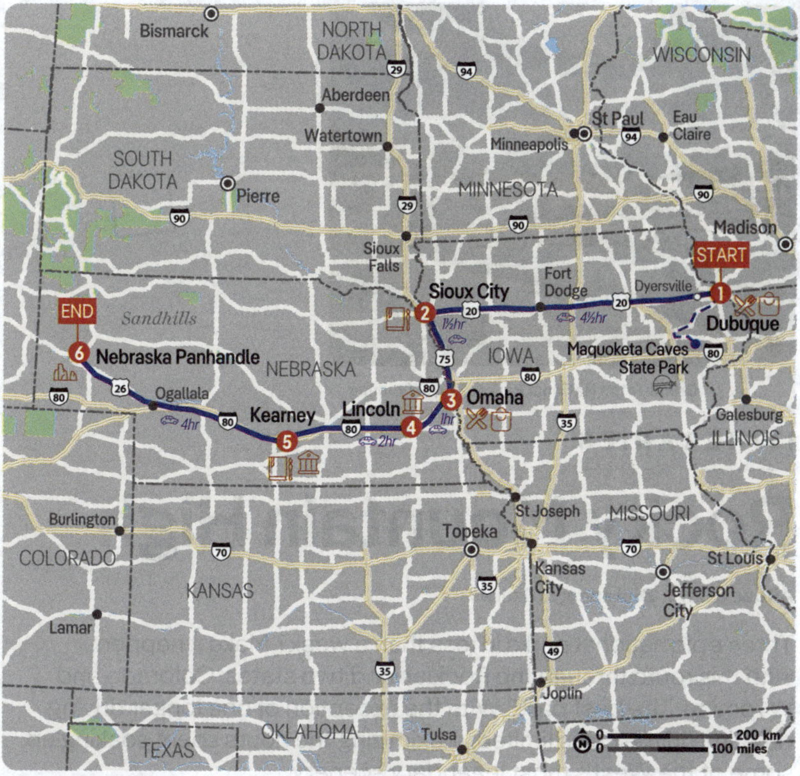

4

LINCOLN ⏱ ½ DAY

The history lesson continues in Nebraska's capital, **Lincoln** (p88), southwest from Omaha on I-80. Educational institutions in this university town include the Nebraska History Museum, International Quilt Museum and Lincoln Children's Museum. Making your way down to Lincoln also sets you up to head west along I-80 and follow the path of the Oregon Trail, with landmarks along the way.

5

KEARNEY ⏱ 1 DAY

Before you hit **Kearney** (p90), you'll pass Fort Kearny, just off I-80. The post was built in 1848 to protect travelers on the California and Oregon Trails. Also nearby, visit the Archway Museum. Just past Kearney, in Gothenburg, step inside an original log-built 1860 Pony Express station. About 45 minutes northwest of there, visit Buffalo Bill Ranch State Historical Park.

6

NEBRASKA PANHANDLE ⏱ 1 DAY

Your final destination is filled with natural wonders and roadside attractions. The **Nebraska Panhandle** (p92) is home to the Chimney Rock National Historic Site, where you can spot a 300ft spire rising from the earth. Scotts Bluff and Agate Fossil Beds (pictured) national monuments, along with Carhenge, are also in the area.

FROM LEFT: FAINA GUREVICH/SHUTTERSTOCK, MELISSAMN/SHUTTERSTOCK, LAIMA SWANSON/SHUTTERSTOCK

FIIPHOTO/SHUTTERSTOCK

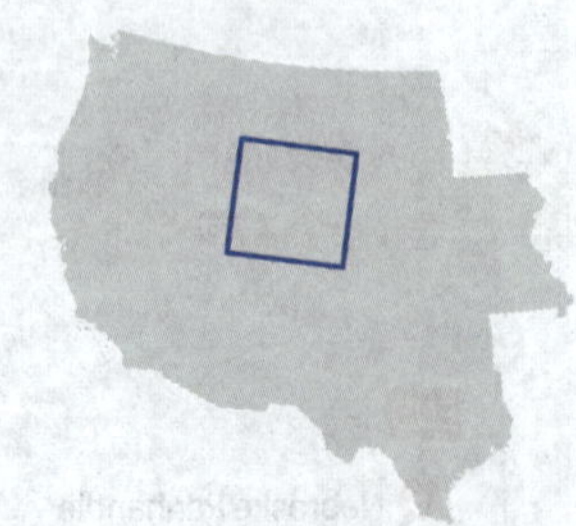

Grand Teton National Park (p222), Wyoming

ITINERARIES

Rocky Mountain High

Allow: 6 days **Distance**: 670 miles

Three epic national parks in less than a week? Make it happen with this route through the Rockies and two states: Colorado and Wyoming. The best part? With the exception of one longer driving day, time in the car is limited, maximizing the hours spent soaking up some of the West's most legendary scenery.

1

DENVER 1 DAY

Denver (p184) is an ideal place to kick off a road trip, as it's home to the only major international airport in the Rocky Mountain region. But before you gas up your rental car and hit the road, spend a day refueling yourself by bopping around the shops and restaurants at the city's iconic Beaux-Arts-style Union Station (pictured), or catching a show at the Denver Performing Arts Complex.

2

BOULDER 1 DAY

Heading northwest on US-36, it's a quick drive to **Boulder** (p188), which will give you time to hit the hiking trails in Chautauqua Park (pictured) once you arrive. A paradise for both trekkers and climbers, the park has 15 trails to choose from and is home to Boulder's iconic Flatirons – 1000ft red-rock slabs rising up out of the earth. Afterward, toast to your favorite trail at one of the town's many craft-beer spots.

3

ROCKY MOUNTAIN NATIONAL PARK 1 DAY

Now your hiking boots are warmed up, it's time to hit **Rocky Mountain National Park** (p190). Get a front-row view of dramatic glacial valleys and granite summits by heading to the Bear Lake and Glacier Gorge Junction trailheads. If you have kids in tow, stop at the Junior Ranger Headquarters in Hidden Valley for kid-friendly discovery activities.

FROM LEFT: GERALD A. DEBOER/SHUTTERSTOCK, PAGE LIGHT STUDIOS/SHUTTERSTOCK, HAVESEEN/SHUTTERSTOCK

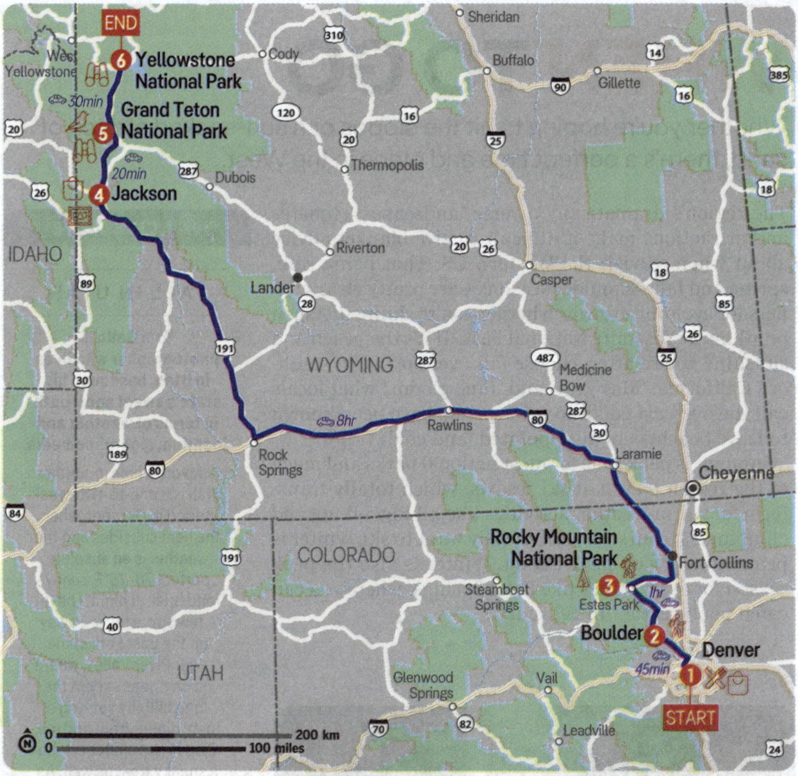

4

JACKSON ⏱ 1 DAY

After the longest drive of the trip, by far – crossing state lines from Colorado to Wyoming, then heading a few hundred miles northwest – you deserve some R & R in downtown **Jackson** (p217). Wander the Town Square's galleries and shops, and pause for a photo op under the iconic arches made of elk antlers (pictured). Then cozy up to a cut of steak at Gun Barrel Steak and Game House.

5

GRAND TETON NATIONAL PARK ⏱ 1 DAY

With such a short drive from Jackson, you can get up early and head to Oxbow Bend, Willow Flats or Moose-Wilson Rd at dawn for your best chance of spotting moose, elk, grizzlies and bald eagles in **Grand Teton National Park** (p222). Afterward, hit the water by either renting kayaks at Jenny Lake, or taking a scenic rafting ride along the Snake River.

6

YELLOWSTONE NATIONAL PARK ⏱ 1 DAY

If you stay in Colter Bay Village in Grand Teton National Park, it's only a half-hour drive to the southern entrance of **Yellowstone National Park** (p218). Round out your trip by gawking at geysers. And, don't miss the overlook at Artist Point. You'll get panoramic views of the Grand Canyon of the Yellowstone and the Lower Yellowstone Falls – the perfect finale for your adventure.

FROM LEFT: MISHELLA/SHUTTERSTOCK, BLUEBARRONPHOTO/SHUTTERSTOCK, SERGE YATUNIN/SHUTTERSTOCK

WHEN TO GO

Whether you're hoping to hit the slopes or a sun-soaked stretch of sand, there's a perfect time and place in the West.

The region's dramatically diverse landscapes, climates and attractions make it difficult to give blanket advice about when to visit the Western US. That being said, spring and fall – shoulder seasons – are pretty clear winners for avoiding crowds, whether you're skiing in Aspen or hiking at Yosemite National Park. If it's the beach and sunshine you're after, choose fall over spring in southern California. 'May gray' and 'June gloom,' what locals call the overcast conditions in spring, have been known to leave beachgoers disappointed (and cold).

Summer is peak time for most national parks and much of the region – even at ski resorts, which totally transform for warm-weather activities like hiking, biking and climbing. Of course, if you actually want to ski, winter is prime time for on-piste action. Winter is also the peak season for desert cities like Palm Springs, where you can catch pool weather in February.

I LIVE HERE

FALL IN UTAH

Tom Gallo, a photographer who lives in Utah, has found his state's sweet spot, both in terms of weather and location. @ghprimemedia

My favorite time in southern Utah is a one-to-two-week period in October, when the heat subsides and the weather is an absolute perfect 70–75°F, sunny and brisk at night. I have a few spots tucked away up the East Fork of the Sevier River Valley, where no one goes except the lone hillbilly seeking a tasty dinner trout and me. Zion in November can be a sneaky treat as well. As the crowds dissipate, the leaves change and snow sporadically covers the red, rocky peaks.

FROM LEFT: SARAH_XIE7/SHUTTERSTOCK, JOHN P KELLY/GETTY IMAGES

Yosemite National Park (p388), California

SKI SEASON

Peak time in the mountains is generally December through March. That's when conditions are optimal for winter sports, but rates are higher and resorts are more crowded. Early season (November) and late season (April) sometimes come with lower prices.

Weather through the Year

JANUARY	FEBRUARY	MARCH	APRIL	MAY	JUNE
Avg daytime max: **48°F**	Avg daytime max: **49°F**	Avg daytime max: **58°F**	Avg daytime max: **65°F**	Avg daytime max: **73°F**	Avg daytime max: **86°F**
Days of rainfall: 2	Days of rainfall: 3	Days of rainfall: 3	Days of rainfall: 5	Days of rainfall: 6	Days of rainfall: 4

BEST FOR THE BEACH

Contrary to what many would think, late spring and early summer are not the best time for hitting the beach in Southern California. What locals call May Gray and June Gloom create cool, overcast conditions. Instead, aim for July through September.

The Big Festivals & Parades

Ring in the Lunar New Year with fireworks, drumlines and a 200ft dragon at the **Chinese New Year Parade** (p357) in San Francisco. **February**

South by Southwest (SXSW; p137), held annually in Austin, is a conference and series of festivals that celebrate tech, film, music, education and culture. **March**

Acoustic music aficionados and nature appreciators spend four days camping and jamming out during the **Telluride Bluegrass Festival** (p203) in Colorado. **June**

Wanna know what cowboys are up to these days? See it all – including bull riding, barrel racing and big names in country music – at **Cheyenne Frontier Days** (p211). **July**

Tens of thousands of free spirits descend on the Nevada desert, creating an art-filled makeshift metropolis called Black Rock City, for **Burning Man Festival** (p266). **August/September**

Lesser-Known But Just as Fun

Over five days in early spring, indie music lovers descend on downtown Boise for the **Treefort Music Festival** (p239), which also includes a slew of creative themed spaces or 'forts.' **March**

In a celebration of pure joy for a fictional character plagued by a gloomy outlook, Austinites celebrate **Eeyore's Birthday Party** (p135) each year to raise money for nonprofits. **April**

Watch competitive fence painting, frog jumping and a look-alike concert at the **National Tom Sawyer Days** (p65) in Hannibal, Missouri, the childhood hometown of Mark Twain. **July**

Have a fun time with fungi at the **Telluride Mushroom Festival** (p204), which includes talks from world-famous mycologists, live music, crafts and a parade. **August**

At the **Great Reno Balloon Race** (p264), see a kaleidoscope of colors as more than 100 hot-air balloons race across the desert over the course of three days. **September**

I LIVE HERE

SUMMER IN COLORADO

Boulder resident Christine Boothroy, a wellness specialist and founder of Become Boulder, relishes summer in Colorado. @becomebouldercо

I love Colorado midsummer! It's ideal for music festivals, thanks to its stunning natural landscapes at outdoor venues such as Red Rocks and Planet Bluegrass. There is nothing better than listening to incredible music while enjoying a dip in the river or a hike to your favorite viewing spot.

Red Rocks Amphitheater (p187), Colorado

IN THE DESERT

Spring and fall bring the most pleasant weather in desert climates, with daytime temps ranging from mid-60s to high 80s. Summer is aggressively hot, but if you're hanging in, say, Las Vegas, you'll be comfortable in the air-conditioned casinos and hotel rates are at their lowest.

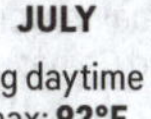

JULY	AUGUST	SEPTEMBER	OCTOBER	NOVEMBER	DECEMBER
Avg daytime max: **92°F**	Avg daytime max: **90°F**	Avg daytime max: **83°F**	Avg daytime max: **68°F**	Avg daytime max: **57°F**	Avg daytime max: **48°F**
Days of rainfall: 5	Days of rainfall: 4	Days of rainfall: 4	Days of rainfall: 3	Days of rainfall: 2	Days of rainfall: 2

FROM LEFT: BILLY MCDONALD/SHUTTERSTOCK, AJ PICS/ALAMY

Lake Tahoe (p391), California

GET PREPARED FOR THE WESTERN USA

Useful things to load in your bag, your ears and your brain.

Clothes

Diverse landscapes and a wide range of climates mean you might pack snow pants or a sundress depending on where, specifically, you're headed within the region – even during the same time of year. In general, you'll be fine with casual clothes in most places in the West, including in big cities like Austin and LA. Layers, however, are key across the board, from the desert to the mountains, in both summer and winter. Desert climates can be deceiving, as temperatures drop dramatically at night. And coastal areas often call for sweaters when marine fog rolls in.

As for footwear, always opt for comfort, especially if you'll be hiking. Cowboy boots (and hats!) are genuinely worn in places like Texas, Oklahoma, Montana and Wyoming. Save room in your suitcase and buy a souvenir pair during your trip.

Words

English, with regional nuances ('howdy, y'all!'), is the most widely spoken language in the West. A few words to keep an ear out for: 'pop' (what folks in the Great Plains call 'soda'), 'Coke' (what they call 'soda' in Texas and Oklahoma, regardless of the beverage's brand), 'reckon' (a synonym for 'think' in Texas) and 'stoked' ('excited' for Californians).

After English, Spanish is the most common language. In Texas, for example, about 29% of people speak Spanish at home, and that number is about 31% in California. Other top languages include German (especially in the Rocky Mountains), Vietnamese (especially in Texas and Oklahoma), Navajo (in New Mexico and Arizona) and Chinese (in California and the Pacific Northwest).

READ

Bury My Heart at Wounded Knee (Dee Brown; 1970) Heartwrenching account of westward expansion and crimes against Native Americans.

The Grapes of Wrath (John Steinbeck; 1939) One fictional family's journey from Oklahoma to California during the 1930s Dust Bowl.

Close Range: Wyoming Stories (Annie Proulx; 1999) Eleven short stories set in rural Wyoming, including award-winning 'Brokeback Mountain.'

Taco USA: How Mexican Food Conquered America (Gustavo Arellano; 2012) Tasty tales of how Mexican food became a hit among Americans.

Manners

Greetings A smile and a nod go a long way. Shake hands on more formal occasions.

Tipping At restaurants, a 20% tip is standard for table service. Tipping isn't required for counter service, but 10% is nice. At bars, $1 or $2 will suffice for a beer or simple drink, while 15% to 20% is more common for complex cocktails when you're running a tab.

Smoking Lighting up indoors is illegal in most places. In outdoor spaces, like patios at restaurants or bars, it's always best to ask first before reaching for your lighter.

Cannabis Laws vary state by state, with some allowing both medicinal and recreational cannabis use, and others not allowing either. One thing to note if you'll be road-tripping: federal law prohibits carrying cannabis across state lines, even if it's legal in both states. So stick to buying in the state you're in and using it up before moving on.

Photography Always ask before taking anyone's photo, especially when visiting Native American reservations, where photography and cell phone use may be restricted.

Hats Remove any hats when entering a home or restaurant, as well as during the national anthem at sporting events.

WATCH

True Grit (Ethan and Joel Coen; 2010) A teen hires a rough-and-tumble US Marshal to avenge her father's murder.

Butch Cassidy and the Sundance Kid (George Roy Hill; 1969) Paul Newman and Robert Redford play bank robbers in 1890s Wyoming.

City Slickers (Ron Underwood; 1991) Facing middle age, a group of urbanites take a trip to the Southwest for a cattle drive.

Field of Dreams (pictured; Phil Alden Robinson; 1989) An Iowa farmer who builds a baseball diamond discovers, 'if you build it, they will come.'

LISTEN

Waylon & Willie (Waylon Jennings and Willie Nelson; 1978) Two Texan legends warn 'Mammas Don't Let Your Babies Grow Up to Be Cowboys.'

John Denver's Greatest Hits (John Denver; 1973) New Mexico–born Denver delivers 'Take Me Home, Country Roads' and 'Rocky Mountain High.'

All Eyez on Me (2Pac; 1996) Tupac Shakur's last album features the song 'California Love' and West Coast stars like Dr Dre and Snoop Dogg.

Amor Prohibido (Selena; 1994) Tejano singer-songwriter Selena Quintanilla's genre-bending, history-making album, featuring the bop 'Bidi Bidi Bom Bom.'

COLIN D. YOUNG/SHUTTERSTOCK

Rocky Mountain National Park (p190), Colorado

TRIP PLANNER

NATIONAL PARKS

The US has a total of 63 national parks, and 39 of them are in the West. With the lion's share of prized and protected landscapes, the region practically begs visitors to lace up their hiking boots. Here's how to make it happen, with highlights from particularly outstanding parks.

YOSEMITE NATIONAL PARK

Thunderous waterfalls tumble over sheer cliffs. Climbers scale the enormous granite domes of El Cap and Half Dome. Hikers walk beneath ancient groves of giant sequoias, or meander through wildflower-strewn meadows in valleys carved by rivers and glaciers. It's all business as usual in this anything-but-ordinary park (p388).

GRAND CANYON NATIONAL PARK

The sheer immensity is what grabs you at first. The canyon (p276) is 277 miles long, about a mile deep on average, and made up of colored layers of rock that tell a geological history about two billion years in the making. To explore the park, take your pick of adventures: hiking, biking, rafting or mule riding. Or simply grab a seat along the Rim Trail and watch the earth change colors before you.

ZION & BRYCE CANYON NATIONAL PARKS

Towering red cliffs hiding graceful waterfalls, narrow slot canyons and hanging gardens dominate Zion National Park (p320). As an added bonus, private vehicle access is limited, making for an especially tranquil experience. Or, try Bryce Canyon National Park (p318), only 80 miles away. There, expect a hypnotic, Tolkienesque place where pastel-colored rock spires shimmer like trees in a magical forest of stone.

YELLOWSTONE NATIONAL PARK

The world's first national park (p218) is a hotbed (quite literally) of geothermal and wildlife wonders. Yellowstone is home to

NATIONAL PARK PACKING LIST

General Clothing
- Quick-dry short-sleeved shirt and pants or shorts
- Additional layers (quick-dry long-sleeved shirt and/or sweatshirt) and extra socks
- Hiking shoes or boots and gaiters
- Waterproof rain jacket
- Hat and sunglasses
- Swimsuit

Cold-Weather Clothing
- Down parka
- Fleece jacket or vest
- Beanie, gloves and wool hiking socks
- Leggings or long underwear
- Waterproof outer pants

Hiking Gear
- Backpack
- Reusable water bottle
- Trekking poles
- First-aid kit
- Sunscreen and insect repellent
- Portable charger

Camping Gear
- Tent, sleeping bag and mat
- Flashlight, headlamp and lantern
- Towel
- Multi-tool
- Propane stove, plates, bowls, utensils and cup
- Trash bags and bear bag

over half of the world's active geysers, plus hot springs, mudpots, and fumaroles. It's also home to grizzlies, black bears, wolf packs, elk, bison and moose, roaming across some 3500 sq miles of wilderness.

ROCKY MOUNTAIN NATIONAL PARK

With hiking boots laced and the trail unfurling beneath your feet, this park's (p190) majestic, untamed splendor becomes unforgettably personal. From epic ascents along the Longs Peak Trail and Continental Divide to family-friendly Calypso Falls, there's a vista for everyone.

GLACIER NATIONAL PARK

Montana's sprawling national park (p232) is a million times worthy of an in-depth visit. Road warriors can maneuver the thrilling 50-mile Going-to-the-Sun Road; wildlife watchers can scan for elk, wolves and grizzlies; and hikers have 700 miles of trails to explore.

GALYNA ANDRUSHKO/SHUTTERSTOCK

Glacier National Park (p232), Montana

TOP NATIONAL PARK TIPS

Budget for Fees
- National park entry averages $10 to $35, with some charging per vehicle and others charging per person (usually applicable to those entering by foot or bike). Also, keep an eye on the calendar for Free Entrance Days *(nps.gov/findapark/feefreeparks.htm)*.

Consider an Unlimited Pass
- If you'll be visiting multiple national parks during your trip – or over the course of the next 12 months – consider an America the Beautiful pass *($80)*. It covers unlimited admission to national parks, national forests and other federal recreation lands for one year.

Be Prepared with Permits
- Often required for overnight backpackers and extended day hikes, wilderness permits are issued at ranger stations and park visitor centers. Daily quotas may be in effect in peak periods (usually late spring through early fall).

Know Your Limits
- Keep in mind that you may not be fully acclimated to the local altitude or temperature, and that weather conditions change throughout the day – especially in the desert where the mercury rises substantially with each passing hour.

Designate a Meeting Spot
- Cell service is often limited in parks, so if you're exploring with a group, pick a designated meeting spot in case someone gets separated. If you're hiking alone, it's wise to let someone know where you're headed and when you expect to return.

GIMAS/SHUTTERSTOCK

Taos Pueblo (p330), New Mexico

TRIP PLANNER

ART & ARCHITECTURE

Dwellings carved into cliffs, entire neighborhoods of perfectly preserved mid-century modern homes, and oversized sculptures crafted in concrete and displayed under the Texas sun; the West is wonderfully unique when it comes to showing off its creative side. Learn about its standout architecture, distinctive galleries and prominent painters.

Indigenous Structures

As exciting as it is to see an early 19th- or 20th-century building, taking in architecture that's 1000 years old is downright extraordinary (especially in the US). Make it happen in New Mexico at **Taos Pueblo** (p330), a UNESCO World Heritage site made up of adobe structures, some believed to date as far back as 1000 CE. Though the pueblo is still a living Native American community, travelers are welcome to visit during designated times.

In southwest Colorado, **Mesa Verde National Park** (p200) is home to fascinating cliff dwellings carved into the San Juan Mountains. The dwellings were inhabited by Ancestral Puebloans for over seven centuries, until they mysteriously abandoned the site in the 14th century. Visitors can take ranger-led tours of certain sites, or see the dwellings on their own from various overlooks.

A Modernist Movement

While the architecture of **Palm Springs** (p422) is notably newer than that of Taos Pueblo and Mesa Verde, it stands out for its preservation as well. The city has the largest concentration of preserved mid-century modern architecture in the world. The winning combination of favorable weather and passionate local preservationists has helped keep buildings intact. That's good news for anyone who appreciates

GREAT PAINTERS OF THE GREAT PLAINS

Get to know three artists who have helped shape a vision of the West, in dramatically different ways. See works by all of them at the National Cowboy & Western Heritage Museum in Oklahoma City (p80).

Albert Bierstadt
A 19th-century German-American painter, Bierstadt tagged along on multiple journeys of the Western Expansion to capture luminous landscapes.

Charles Marion Russell
Russell was nothing if not prolific. He created over 2000 paintings of cowboys, Native Americans and landscapes set in the West.

T.C. Cannon
Known for combining traditional American Indian and modern American cultures, Cannon is described as one of the most influential Native American artists of the 20th century.

architecture. Wander the city's sun-soaked neighborhoods and you can see works from industry icons like Richard Neutra, Donald Wexler and William Cody.

Outdoor Galleries

When your landscapes are so gorgeous, why not incorporate them with the art? While the West has plenty of traditional art museums, it also takes advantage of its wide open spaces and breathtaking backdrops to showcase art in more innovative ways. Take, for example, Donald Judd's striking concrete works, set in an open field on an abandoned army base in **Marfa, Texas** (p168). Then there are the famous **Venice Beach Art Walls** (p422) in Venice Beach, California, set among the sand and palm trees right on the Pacific. In **Dubuque, Iowa** (p95), the city itself is the gallery, with over 40 murals painted on the exteriors of historic brick buildings.

JON BILOUS/SHUTTERSTOCK

Palm Springs (p422), California

TIPS ON BUYING NATIVE AMERICAN ART

Jewelry, pottery, rugs and baskets – a visit to the region brings ample opportunity to invest in one-of-a-kind pieces from Indigenous artists. Here's what to know before you shop.

Do Your Research
Get to know the pieces you like, what tribe makes them and the signatures of the style. If, for example, you're keen on collecting pottery, you might fall for Hopi pieces from Arizona, noted for their intricate designs and earthy colors, including black, dark orange and white. Understanding what you like not only helps you browse, it might also help you catch an inauthentic piece if something is wildly off.

Shop Direct
Buying directly from the artist is the best way to know what you're getting; it also ensures they're paid fairly. Artist collectives and reputable galleries with knowledgeable employees – found all over cities like Santa Fe, Phoenix and Tucson – are also a good way to go.

Ask Questions
If a piece says it's handmade but doesn't spell out by who, ask the salesperson. They may fess up that it is handmade, but not in the US.

Look for Hallmarks
When buying Native American jewelry, always look for hallmarks, the artist's initials or signature stamped on the piece. This can prove authenticity and origin, as online databases offer a list of established hallmarks and tribal affiliations.

FOODGRAPHY39/SHUTTERSTOCK

Reuben sandwich (p40)

THE FOOD SCENE

Bring your appetite and a culinary curiosity for multicultural meals, microbreweries and a multitude of food festivals.

The western part of the United States enjoys a wealth of food cultures, thanks in part to geography (as you'll see below Mexican cuisine plays a major role), climate (warm weather keeps farmers markets stocked year-round in much of the region) and an openness to trying new things (fusion cuisines are still all the rage in LA, where you can get green-chili chutney on your pizza and ramen noodles on your burger).

Speaking of trying new things, the food scene is evolving in places like the Great Plains, where stereotypes would tell you that meat and potatoes, and maybe a casserole, are the only things on the menu. Instead, restaurants are embracing ingredients native to the prairie and reigniting an interest in Indigenous recipes and cooking techniques.

Locally sourced, seasonal ingredients have long been a gastronomical go-to in California, a state that also provides plenty to pair with your food, thanks to several robust wine regions. You'll also find top-notch wines in the Pacific Northwest, famous in its own right for salmon, oysters and Dungeness crab.

Mexico's Culinary Influence

If you've ever dug into chili con carne, devoured beef enchiladas or sat electrified as a plate of sizzling fajitas made their way across a restaurant to your table, you've been part of a grand cultural exchange. All of the foods above are Tex-Mex, the culinary tradition that developed in Texas, particularly in San Antonio, in the late 1800s as cooks fused traditional Mexican cooking with ingredients that appealed to American palates.

Texas wasn't the only place to experience Mexico's massive gastronomical influence. New Mexico felt it too, in its own unique way. There, the red and green chilies that grew in the area took center stage. Ordering enchiladas 'Christmas style' (with both red- and green-chili salsa) is still a staple in New Mexican restaurants.

In Arizona, the influence came largely from Sonora, which is why the Copper State is the birthplace of the Sonora hot dog – a frankfurter wrapped in bacon and topped with pinto beans, jalapeño salsa, tomatoes and onions.

Meanwhile, health-conscious Californians have emphasized fresh, seasonal ingredients in Cal-Mex cuisine. And the gastronomical evolution continues with more recent riffs, like Korean-style bulgogi tacos and Middle Eastern falafel tacos, becoming a hit in SoCal.

Land of Microbreweries

Microbreweries – or small-batch beer producers – are a specialty of the West, and you'll find at least one good brewery in outdoorsy towns from Missoula to Moab. Though usually closely identified with their home towns, these popular watering holes share a few commonalities: boisterous beer sippers, deep-flavored brews with locally inspired names, and cavernous tap rooms that smell of hops, sweat and adventure.

Hiking, biking or climbing near Boulder? Celebrate post-adventure with a saison, sour or stout on tap at Mountain Sun (p188). Heading to Mount Rushmore? Stop off at either Harriet & Oak or Independent Ale House in Rapid City, South Dakota (p115). Three Mile Brewing Company (p407) in Davis, California, is another good one.

CAROL M. HIGHSMITH, NO RESTRICTIONS, VIA WIKIMEDIA COMMONS

FOOD & DRINK FESTIVALS

Paso Wine Fest (p402) Splurge on the Grand Tasting and get access to sips from over 120 of Paso Robles' best wineries in Central California in May.

Iowa State Fair (p100) In August, indulge in deep-fried Twinkies, then feast your eyes on sculptures made of butter (pictured).

Gravenstein Apple Fair (p375) Dig into pie and fritters galore, and wash it all down with cider in Sonoma County in August.

Kelseyville Pear Festival (p379) Pick your favorite pear-flavored treat – including pies, shakes and ice cream – in Northern California in September.

Oktoberfest (p148) Toast to Fredericksburg's German heritage at Texas' largest Oktoberfest and be sure to try the schnitzel.

Austin Food & Wine Festival (p135) Hang with pitmasters, chefs and wine connoisseurs, and come hungry in November.

KENIPELAI/SHUTTERSTOCK

New Mexico chile

Specialties

Cioppino Fish stew in a rich tomato broth, invented by Italian fisherfolk who had emigrated to San Francisco.
Chimichanga Deep-fried burrito created in Arizona that's part of the Tex-Mex tradition.
Sopapillas Fried pastry created in New Mexico, sometimes drizzled with honey and sprinkled with cinnamon.
California Roll Sushi roll invented in 1960s LA using crab, avocado and cucumber. It's a fusion of Japanese culinary methods and American palates.
Frybread Flat, doughy bread fried in oil created as Native Americans were forced from their homes and forced to live on rations.
Frito Pie Chili and cheese piled on a bed of corn chips. Its origins are hotly debated, but likely invented in either Texas or New Mexico.
Green Chile Stew A classic and comforting New Mexico stew made with Hatch green chiles, grown exclusively in the state's Hatch Valley.
Barbecue Kansas City, St. Louis and the entire state of Texas are all particularly proud of their BBQ brisket, pulled pork and ribs.
Reuben Sandwich Corned beef, Swiss cheese, sauerkraut and Thousand Island dressing on rye bread. One theory says it was invented at the historic Blackstone Hotel in Omaha.
Chili Said to be invented in the Lone Star State (many New Mexicans disagree), it's Texas's official state dish.

Green chile stew

MEALS OF A LIFETIME

Skogen Kitchen (p119) Pick from a toppings menu that includes lobster and caviar, and add it to your Wagyu in Custer, South Dakota.
Joël Robuchon (p257) Live it up in Las Vegas with a French meal, featuring seasonal tasting menus, from a legendary chef.
Coyote Cafe (p326) Feast on upscale Southwestern cuisine, like peppered elk tenderloin, and leave room for the dessert tamale in Santa Fe.
Chez Panisse (p367) In Berkeley, California, dine at the place that put food trends like farm-to-table on the map.
Ltd Edition Sushi (p452) Savor a seasonally inspired omakase experience at an intimate eight-person sushi bar in Seattle.

THE YEAR IN FOOD

Spring

In the Pacific Northwest, seafood lovers can feast on salmon, dungeness crab, halibut and spot prawns – all in season. It's also primetime for morel mushroom hunting in places like Wyoming, Montana and Oklahoma.

Summer

From Sioux City to San Diego, farmers markets are bursting with locally grown bounty. Pick up sweet corn and heirloom tomatoes in Iowa, perfectly juicy peaches in Colorado and high-quality avocados in SoCal.

Fall

Calling all oenophiles for harvest in wine countries such as Sonoma and Napa in California, the Willamette Valley in Oregon and Walla Walla Valley in Washington. Plus, pick apples in the Plains.

Winter

Cozy up with bowls of chili con carne and green chile stew. In ski towns, dunking bread into ooey-gooey cheese fondue is comforting, and a date shake – a Palm Springs specialty – is refreshing in the desert.

TOP: FANFO/SHUTTERSTOCK; FROM LEFT: BARMALINI/SHUTTERSTOCK, VDB PHOTOS/SHUTTERSTOCK, JUANCAT/SHUTTERSTOCK, 5PH/SHUTTERSTOCK

OSTRANITSA STANISLAV/SHUTTERSTOCK

Cioppino (fish stew)

FROM LEFT: DANITA DELIMONT/SHUTTERSTOCK, MICHAEL BARAJAS/SHUTTERSTOCK

Ice Park (p202), Ouray, Colorado

THE OUTDOORS

Ride a horse, mule, coaster, hot-air balloon or wave. The region's diverse geographies and cultural pastimes make for an interesting mix of alfresco activities.

Whoever came up with the phrase 'the great outdoors' had surely visited the West. It's here that you get every landscape imaginable – mountains, plains, deserts, glaciers, ocean, lakes and rivers – and extraordinary opportunities to enjoy them all.

While it's nearly impossible to pick the area's top outdoor pursuit – who are we to prize kayaking over mounting a mule? – skiing, surfing and hiking stand out as exceptional. That's because the West has some of the most spectacular slopes, swells and long-haul trails.

Skiing & Snowboarding

Outdoor fun doesn't stop when temperatures drop (in some places, it actually revs up), thanks to the West's exceptional snow. Top ski resorts in the region can be found in Colorado, Wyoming, Montana, Idaho, Utah, New Mexico and California.

Detailing every remarkable resort and run in the region could be an entire book in itself. Highlights of some key destinations include: **Vail**, **Colorado**, the largest resort in the state; **Aspen**, **Colorado**, with four mountains that live up to the hype; **Jackson Hole**, **Wyoming**, with some of the steepest terrain in the US; **Big Sky**, **Montana**, offering over 5800 acres of terrain and the world's longest eight-person chairlift; **Sun Valley**, **Idaho**, the country's first destination ski resort; and **Lake Tahoe**, **California**, with over 14 ski areas within a 100-mile radius.

Adrenaline Sports

WHITE-WATER RAFTING
Go white-water rafting on the Snake River just outside **Jackson, Wyoming** (p217).

ROCK CLIMBING
Try beginner belaying, intermediate crack climbing or advanced anchoring at **Yosemite National Park** (p388) in California.

ICE CLIMBING
There's more than one way to climb in the West. Kick your crampons into vertical ice in **Ouray, Colorado** (p202).

FAMILY ADVENTURES

Loop-de-loop on rides at **Disneyland** (p428), the **Santa Monica Pier** (p418) and the **Santa Cruz Beach Boardwalk** (p406) in California.

Crouch and wiggle through underground nooks at **Maquoketa Caves State Park** (p96) in Iowa.

Kayak below ancient quartzite formations along Split Rock Creek at **Palisades State Park** (p112) in South Dakota.

Skywalk through the towering redwoods at **Sequoia Park Zoo** (p380) in Eureka, California.

Splash around a 3-acre spring-fed swimming spot at **Barton Springs Pool** (p133) in Austin, Texas.

Ride a mule around a majestic canyon rim at **Grand Canyon National Park** (p273).

Go snow-tubing in the Wasatch Mountains at **Park City Mountain Resort** (p307) in Utah.

Wherever you go, find the best deals by purchasing multiday tickets or, even better, a season pass. Ski and snowboard packages that include airfare, hotel and lift tickets can also save you some cash. Find them through resorts, travel agencies and online travel-booking sites.

Surfing

California is one of the best places to ride the swell, not just in the West, but in the country as a whole. In San Francisco, more experienced surfers can give **Ocean Beach** a go (though don't forget your wetsuit – this is Northern California, after all). About 30 miles north, the bohemian beach town of **Bolinas** has another popular surf break.

In Central California, **Santa Cruz** – home to iconic spots such as Steamer Lane, Pleasure Point and Mavericks – is a legendary surf city. But even beginners can get in on the action, especially with a lesson at **Cowell's Beach**, which has predictable waves in a sheltered cove. And down the coast, **Santa Barbara's Rincon**, aka the 'Queen of the Coast,' is a beloved spot.

SoCal is jam-packed with places to catch a wave, from **Malibu** to **San Diego**, roughly 150 miles south. In between, **Huntington Beach** is the quintessential surf capital, with perpetual sun and a 'perfect' break, particularly during winter when the winds are calm.

Surfer, Santa Cruz (p403), California

Walking & Hiking

There's no shortage of hiking trails in the West, with most metropolitan areas having at least one large park with paths. The region is also home to more than three-dozen national parks, offering options for both lengthy adventures and short rambles, as well as strenuous treks and easy strolls. For extreme hiking adventures, consider the 2650-mile **Pacific Coast Trail**, which passes from Mexico to Canada through California, Oregon and Washington; or the 3100-mile **Continental Divide Trail**, which is a route through the Rocky Mountains.

HOT-AIR BALLOONING
Soar through the sky in a hot air balloon with Rainbow Ryders in **Albuquerque, New Mexico** (p325).

BIOLUMINESCENT PADDLING
Embark on a nighttime kayaking adventure and see glowing waters in **Bellingham Bay, Washington** (p461).

HORSEBACK RIDING
Do as the cowboys do by hopping on horseback at a dude ranch in **Bandera, Texas** (p147).

MOUNTAIN BIKING
Power up steep slickrock and barrel through woodsy trails – all while on two wheels – in **Moab, Utah** (p308).

ACTION AREAS

Where to find Western USA's best outdoor activities.

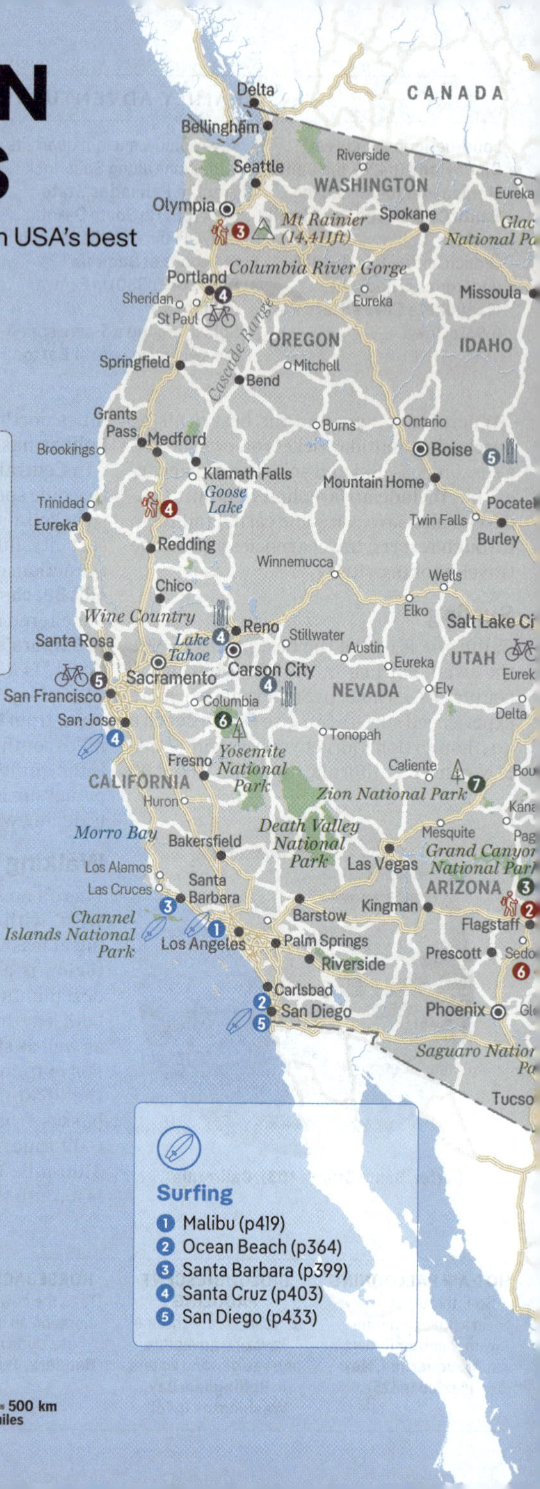

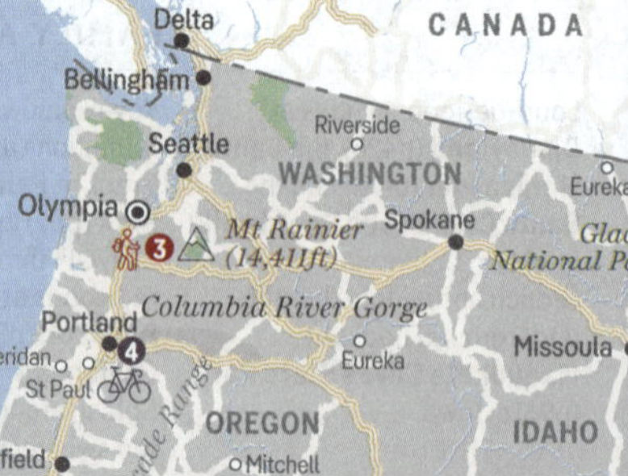

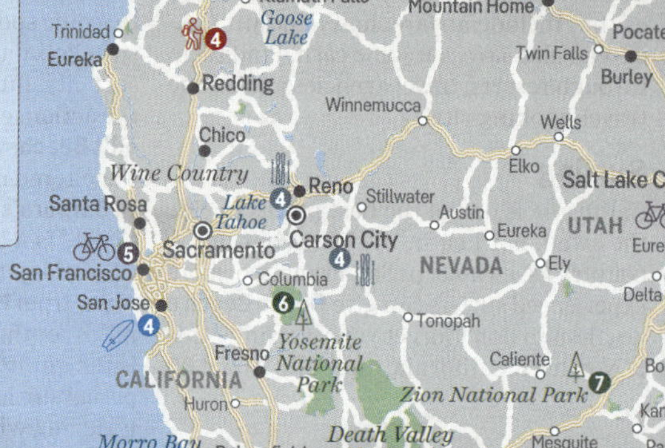

Cycling

1. Boulder (p188)
2. Moab (p308)
3. Park City (p307)
4. Portland (p471)
5. San Francisco (p346)

National Parks

1. Badlands National Park (p110)
2. Big Bend National Park (p168)
3. Grand Canyon National Park (p273)
4. Rocky Mountain National Park (p190)
5. Yellowstone National Park (p218)
6. Yosemite National Park (p388)
7. Zion National Park (p320)

Surfing

1. Malibu (p419)
2. Ocean Beach (p364)
3. Santa Barbara (p399)
4. Santa Cruz (p403)
5. San Diego (p433)

0 500 km
0 250 miles

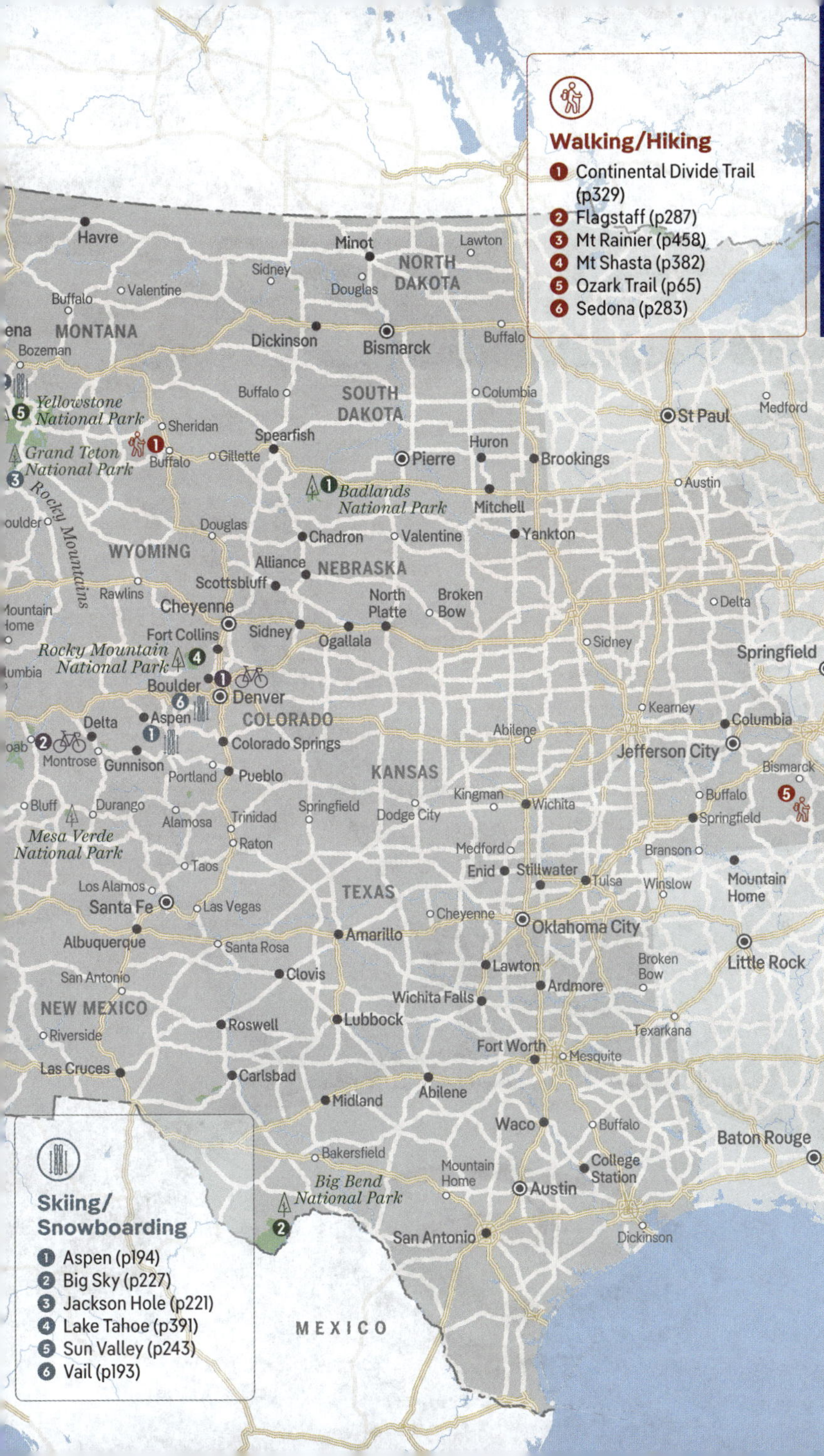

Walking/Hiking
1 Continental Divide Trail (p329)
2 Flagstaff (p287)
3 Mt Rainier (p458)
4 Mt Shasta (p382)
5 Ozark Trail (p65)
6 Sedona (p283)
Skiing/ Snowboarding
1 Aspen (p194)
2 Big Sky (p227)
3 Jackson Hole (p221)
4 Lake Tahoe (p391)
5 Sun Valley (p243)
6 Vail (p193)
MONTANA
NORTH DAKOTA
SOUTH DAKOTA
WYOMING
NEBRASKA
COLORADO
KANSAS
TEXAS
NEW MEXICO
MEXICO
Havre
Minot
Lawton
Sidney
Douglas
Valentine
Buffalo
Bozeman
Dickinson
Bismarck
Yellowstone National Park
Grand Teton National Park
Rocky Mountains
Sheridan
Gillette
Spearfish
Pierre
Huron
Brookings
Columbia
St Paul
Medford
Austin
Badlands National Park
Mitchell
Yankton
Chadron
Alliance
Scottsbluff
Rawlins
Cheyenne
North Platte
Broken Bow
Delta
Fort Collins
Sidney
Ogallala
Rocky Mountain National Park
Boulder
Denver
Aspen
Springfield
Kearney
Columbia
Jefferson City
Abilene
Delta
Montrose
Gunnison
Colorado Springs
Portland
Pueblo
Bismarck
Durango
Alamosa
Trinidad
Springfield
Dodge City
Kingman
Wichita
Buffalo
Springfield
Mesa Verde National Park
Raton
Medford
Branson
Taos
Enid
Stillwater
Tulsa
Winslow
Mountain Home
Los Alamos
Santa Fe
Las Vegas
Cheyenne
Oklahoma City
Albuquerque
Santa Rosa
Amarillo
Lawton
Broken Bow
Little Rock
San Antonio
Clovis
Ardmore
Wichita Falls
Roswell
Lubbock
Riverside
Texarkana
Fort Worth
Mesquite
Las Cruces
Carlsbad
Abilene
Midland
Waco
Buffalo
Baton Rouge
Bakersfield
Mountain Home
College Station
Big Bend National Park
Austin
San Antonio
Dickinson

WESTERN USA

THE GUIDE

Chapters in this section are organised by hubs and their surrounding areas. We see the hub as your base in the destination, where you'll find unique experiences, local insights, insider tips and expert recommendations. It's also your gateway to the surrounding area, where you'll see what and how much you can do from there.

Painted Desert (p292), Arizona

WIRESTOCK CREATORS/SHUTTERSTOCK

Researched and curated by
Lauren Keith and Amy Balfour

The Great Plains

SURPRISING CITIES AMID PRISTINE PRAIRIE

The Great Plains are happy to transition you between east and west, but don't you dare dismiss this as flyover country.

If you slow down, the Heartland invites you in and shares some of the country's finest history, scenery and adventure. Each of its seven states has enough to stop you in your tracks; the only hard part is figuring out how to experience as much as possible in this vast region that makes up 15% of the country.

The USA's two longest rivers, the Missouri and the Mississippi, cut through the Plains, and many of the region's cities got their start along these mighty routes. Dams have tamed them since then, but wild – and federally protected, thanks to their outstanding scenery – waterways can still be found in Missouri's Ozarks and Nebraska's Niobrara Valley. Other gripping landscapes include the dreamy colors of the badlands in the Dakotas and the bison-studded prairies also found there, as well as in Kansas and Oklahoma. Meanwhile, the Great Plains cities are quietly cool and self-confident – many have been undergoing a renaissance as they spruce up former warehouse districts and embark on new infrastructure projects that make it easier to travel here.

Does this region have the national parks of Utah, the coastline of California or the big cities of the East? No, but if you've come this far, you know that's not why you're here. Open your mind in these wide-open spaces, and you're bound to be captivated by what you discover.

RIVERNORTHPHOTOGRAPHY/GETTY IMAGES

THE MAIN AREAS

MISSOURI
The Show Me State has a ton to show off. **p54**

KANSAS
Wide open spaces and unexpected attractions. **p67**

OKLAHOMA
Deep Native history and cool Route 66 cities. **p74**

NEBRASKA
Still at the heart of travelers' trails. **p84**

For places to stay in the Great Plains, see p122

ALEX CIMBAL/SHUTTERSTOCK

Bison, Custer State Park (p119)

IOWA
Heartland beauty and a cycling hot spot. **p94**

NORTH DAKOTA
Explore the grasslands that inspired Theodore Roosevelt. **p105**

SOUTH DAKOTA
Mt Rushmore, bison and badlands. **p109**

Find Your Way

Distances in the Great Plains are vast, and having your own wheels is the best way to rack up the miles. Interstates crisscross the region; the smaller state and federal highways are slower but more scenic.

TRAIN

Amtrak *(amtrak.com)* runs four long-distance routes across the Great Plains. Arriving by train (particularly from the hub city of Chicago) is an option, but getting around is not, with the exception of the *Missouri River Runner* between St Louis and Kansas City.

CAR

A car is essential for getting around the Great Plains, as well as within its cities, which lack comprehensive public transport networks. Car rental companies usually have locations in airports and downtown districts.

AIR

The major cities in each of the Great Plains states have airports, including **St Louis**, **Kansas City**, **Omaha**, **Oklahoma City** and **Des Moines**. However, they generally connect to larger hubs like Denver, Chicago and Dallas instead of one another.

North Dakota, p105
Find the celebrity woodchipper in Fargo, mingle with dinosaurs in Chamberlain, and hike the landscapes that Theodore Roosevelt called 'the romance of my life.'

South Dakota, p109
Squint at presidents at Mt Rushmore then drive past shaggy bison, granite spires and ponderosa pines in the Black Hills. National parks spotlight caves and badlands.

Iowa, p94
Admire architectural treasures in Des Moines and Mason City, cycle statewide trails, follow Lewis and Clark, and soak up the bucolic scenery that inspired American Gothic.

Nebraska, p84
Trace routes taken by the travelers of yore along the Oregon Trail and return to modernity in the Cornhusker State's culture-filled cities.
Kansas, p67
Slow down and let the understated beauty of the Sunflower State speak to your soul through its whispering tallgrass prairie and laid-back towns.
Oklahoma, p74
Native stories are woven into Oklahoma's fabric like few other places in the USA. The long stretch of Route 66 calls to road trippers.
Missouri, p54
Sandwiched in by riveting St Louis and Kansas City, the most populous state in the region also has a stunning natural side.
NEBRASKA
KANSAS
OKLAHOMA
MISSOURI
IOWA
COLORADO
TEXAS
NEW MEXICO
Scotts Bluff National Monument
Mitchell
Chimney Rock National Historic Site
Nebraska National Forest
North Platte
Kearney
Grand Island
Lincoln
Lawrence
Yankton
Vermillion
Norfolk
Fremont
Blair
Omaha
Council Bluffs
Plattsmouth
Nebraska City
Ames
Ankeny
Marshalltown
Cedar Rapids
Iowa City
Davenport
Dubuque
Edmond
Minneapolis
Topeka
Kearney
Kansas City
Lawrence
Olathe
Tallgrass Prairie National Preserve
Jefferson City
Gateway Arch National Park
Bismarck
Cape Girardeau
Dodge City
Wichita
Rita Blanca National Grassland
Fargo
Bartlesville
Tulsa
Greenwood Rising
Muskogee
Oklahoma City
Amarillo
Blair
Lawton
Fort Worth
Dallas
0
400 km
0
200 miles

Plan Your Time

The Great Plains cover a huge expanse of the country. Be strategic about how much you can bite off and how much time you want to spend in the car.

KIT LEONG/SHUTTERSTOCK

Meramec Caverns (p57)

A Long Weekend

- Arrive in **St Louis** (p54) and ride the 1960s tram to the top of the **Gateway Arch** (p60). Unleash your inner child (or actual children) at **City Museum** (p54) and check out the museums and family-friendly attractions dotted around **Forest Park** (p58).

- Drive or take Amtrak's *Missouri River Runner* to **Kansas City** (p61) to go full glutton on some **barbecue** (p61). When you're full up, dig into the trenches of history at the **National WWI Museum** (p61) and peruse the galleries of the **Nelson-Atkins Museum of Art** (p61). After dark, head to the historic Black district of **18th and Vine** (p63) for drinks and jazz.

- If time allows, add on a trip to **Omaha** (p86) or **Des Moines** (p100), both about a three-hour drive from KC.

SEASONAL HIGHLIGHTS

This region mostly hibernates in winter (November to February). Other times of the year bring out vibrant, only-here festivals that highlight the quirks and culture of the Great Plains.

FEBRUARY

Bird-watchers flock to Nebraska's Platte River to witness half a million honking sandhill cranes make a stop on their northerly migration. Conservation organizations in Grand Island and Kearney run **tours** (p90).

MARCH

Tornado season starts, but we hope the only whirlwind you see is the inside of a Lawrence, Kansas, sports bar, cheering on the University of Kansas Jayhawks basketball team during **March Madness** (p23).

MAY

Truman Day (May 8) is a Missouri state holiday, and entry to the **Harry S Truman Presidential Library** (p64) in Independence is free. Some bars and restaurants offer a third off your bill in honor of the 33rd president.

A Week in the Plains

- After a few days in **St Louis** (p54), snake up the Mississippi River to Iowa along the **Great River Road**, stopping in **Dubuque** and **Davenport** (p95). Pause in the folksy **Amana Colonies** (p98), established as 19th-century German religious communes, with a museum, shops and a boutique hotel.

- Take the back roads or hop on I-80 to **Des Moines** (p100) for art and architecture. Cross the state line to **Omaha** (p86) to explore shops, bars and restaurants in the **Old Market** (p86).

- Leave city life behind on your way to **Badlands National Park** and **Mt Rushmore** (p118) in South Dakota, stopping in Nebraska to float the Niobrara River near **Valentine** (p93) or just having lunch at **Monowi Tavern** (p93), run by the town's sole resident.

Route 66

- Marking its 100th anniversary in 2026, Route 66 is one of the USA's most iconic road trips. The Mother Road clocks up many miles through three Plains states. Spend a week or more checking out the cool cities and oddball small towns along the way.

- After seeing the sights of **St Louis** (p54), have a concrete at Ted Drewes (p57) and hit the road. **Meramec Caverns** (p57), the largest commercial cave in Missouri, is a classic stop.

- **Kansas** (p67) contains just 13 miles of the Mother Road but has diversions aplenty.

- Budget most of your time for Oklahoma. Stop at roadside attractions like the **Blue Whale** (p78) and get waylaid in **Tulsa** (p74), the 'capital of Route 66,' then carry on through **Oklahoma City** (p80) toward Texas.

JUNE

School's out, and summer fun is starting. Get weird on the water at Wichita's **Riverfest** (p69), celebrate **Pride** in cities across the region and mark **Juneteenth** on Tulsa's Black Wall Street (p74).

JULY

Road-tripping families scoot across Missouri, Kansas and Oklahoma along historic Route 66, while cyclists set off on **RAGBRAI** (p104), a weeklong non-competitive 470-mile bike ride that traverses Iowa.

AUGUST

The **Iowa State Fair** (p100) in Des Moines is legendary, even inspiring a Broadway musical. More than a million visitors come to eat deep-fried Twinkies, coo over farm animals and check out the famous butter sculptures.

OCTOBER

Admire prismatic fall foliage along the **Great River Road** (p100), which traces the Mississippi River along Iowa's eastern edge through quaint waterfront towns. Peak leaf-peeping times are in mid- to late October.

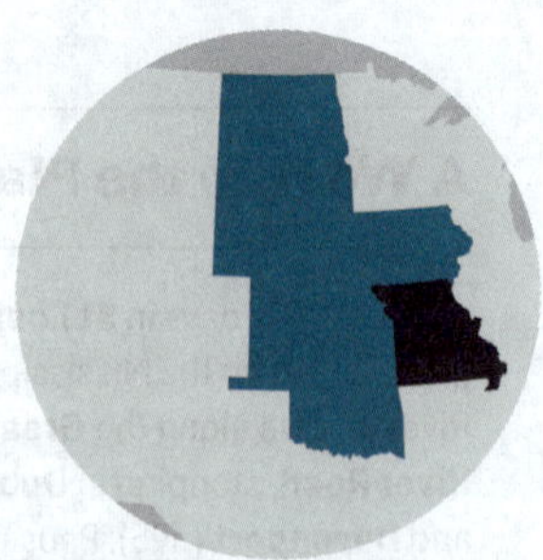

Missouri

FINGER-LICKING BARBECUE | COOL MUSEUMS | WILD RIVERS

Places

With more forest and fewer farm fields than neighboring states, Missouri might not seem like a natural fit in the Great Plains. Limestone canyons, more caves than anywhere else in the country and glacial-blue springs that feed undammed rivers aren't what many travelers expect, but the Show Me State deserves to brag about its outdoor attractions, as well as its cities.

The most populous Plains state likes to mix things up. St Louis (STL) and Kansas City (KC) are on opposite ends of the state, both with excellent museums, must-devour foods, and diversions for music fans and sports nuts. Expect to spend at least a few days soaking up the sights in each.

From St Louis, Route 66 cuts its way diagonally across the state, delivering hokey roadside detours. No matter where you go, you're sure to find an adventure worthy of Missouri native Mark Twain as you explore the state.

TOP TIP

Which state is Kansas City in? Well, both Kansas (KCK) and Missouri (KCMO). Don't get it wrong like many national politicians and musicians shouting it on stage. We include Kansas City in Missouri in this book, but we've noted when places are on the Kansas side of the state line.

St Louis

Run wild at the City Museum

City Museum *(citymuseum.org; $20)*, perhaps St Louis' most boring-sounding attraction, is one of the coolest things to do in the entire region, so don't you dare let the dull name put you off. The Ferris wheel and school bus on the roof surely hint at the hilarity inside this museum gone maximalist.

GETTING AROUND

International airports in Kansas City and St Louis bookend Missouri, making the state the easiest entry point by air into the Great Plains. You can travel between these two cities aboard Amtrak's *Missouri River Runner*, but if you're going further afield, you'll need a car.

Often congested, I-70 connects St Louis and Kansas City, while I-44 paved over much of Route 66 between St Louis and the Kansas–Oklahoma border. Roads in the Ozarks are often scenic, winding, two-lane roller coasters.

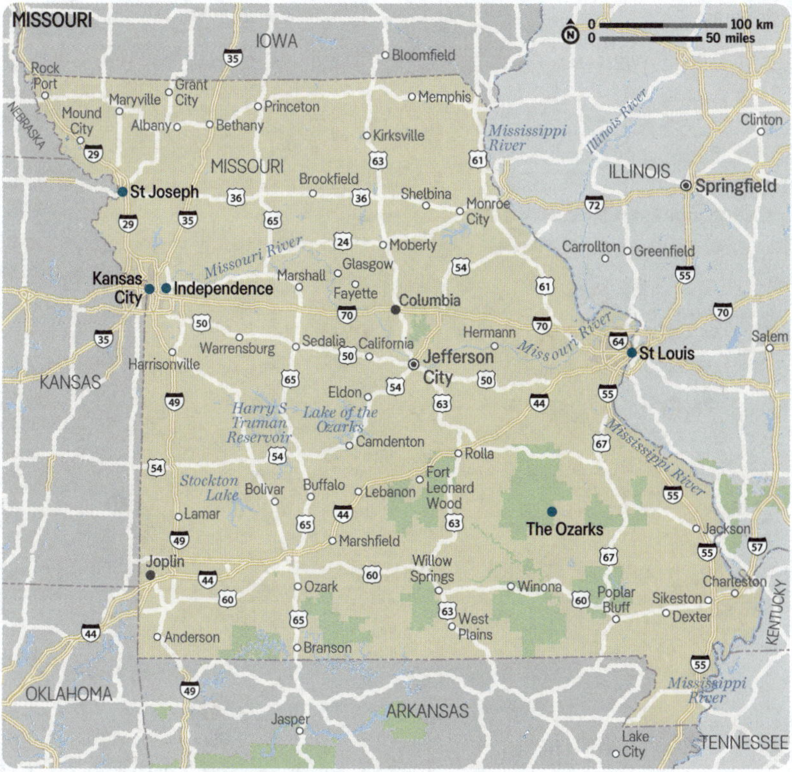

Part playground, part architectural salvage, part art installation, this fun house is a wild ride – literally. Seven- and 10-story slides cascade through the industrial building, a century-old former warehouse for the International Shoe Company. Relics from demolished buildings – many designed by architect Louis Sullivan, the 'father of skyscrapers' and mentor to Frank Lloyd Wright – are portals to other floors (and maybe even other worlds).

It costs $8 extra to visit the roof, but it's worth it. The modern art is sure to crack a smile, from a 'sausage man' made of bronze to *Bop Bear,* a punching bag resembling a bear-shaped honeypot that first debuted at Burning Man and is now a hit with kids.

EATING IN ST LOUIS: OUR PICKS

City Foundry: Upscale food hall with 17 globe-trotting stalls, plus shops, mini-golf and escape rooms, in an old motor factory. *10am-9pm* **$$**

Blood & Sand: This former members-only club has opened to us commoners with a signature tasting menu and killer cocktails. *5-11pm Mon-Sat* **$$$**

Broadway Oyster Bar: Suck down crawfish and other Cajun treats at this New Orleans–style joint that's part bar, part live-music venue, but all restaurant. *11am-10pm* **$$**

Katie's Pizza & Pasta: Phenomenal Italian food right outside Busch Stadium in Ballpark Village. *11am-10pm Mon-Thu, from 10am Sat & Sun* **$$**

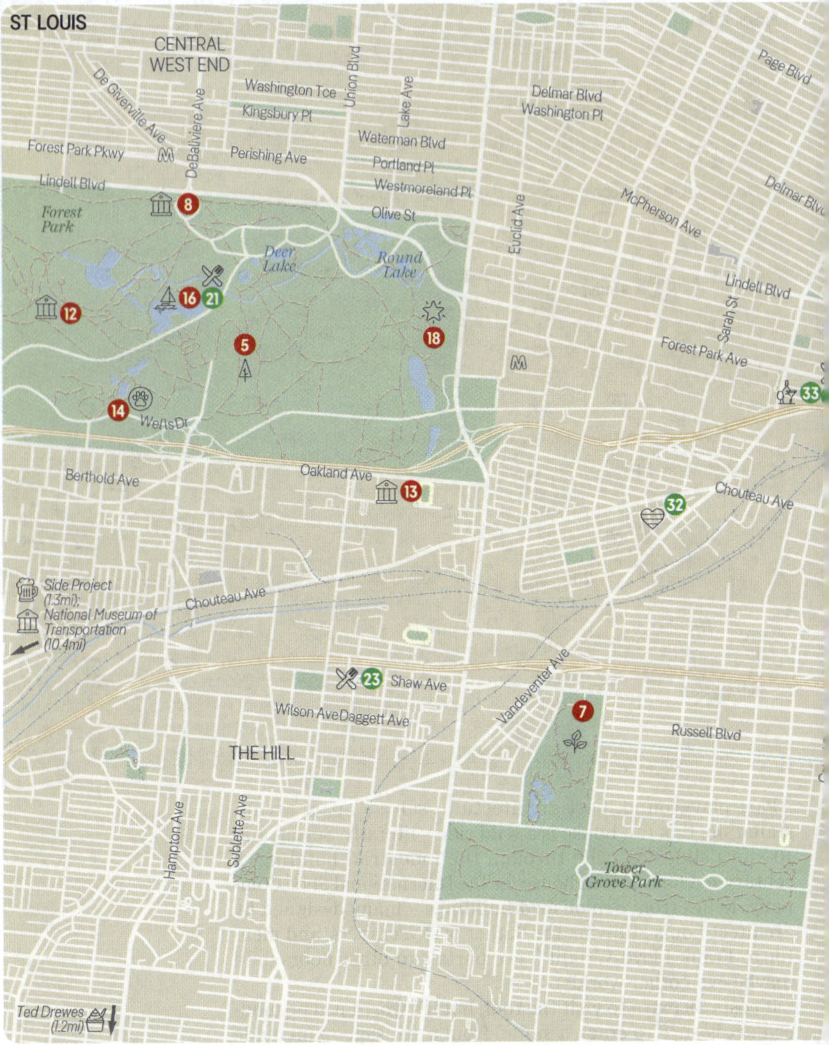

ST LOUIS

HIGHLIGHTS
1 City Museum

SIGHTS
2 Busch Stadium
3 Energizer Park
4 Enterprise Center
5 Forest Park
6 Gateway Arch National Park
7 Missouri Botanical Garden
8 Missouri History Museum
9 Museum at the Gateway Arch
10 National Blues Museum
11 Old Courthouse
12 St Louis Art Museum
13 St Louis Science Center
14 St Louis Zoo
15 Union Station

ACTIVITIES
16 Big Muddy Adventures
17 Gateway Arch Riverboats
18 Steinberg Skating Rink

SLEEPING
19 St Louis Union Station Hotel

EATING
20 Blood & Sand
21 Boathouse at Forest Park
22 Broadway Oyster Bar
23 Charlie Gitto's
24 City Foundry
25 Imo's
26 Katie's Pizza & Pasta
27 Pappy's Smokehouse
28 Park Avenue Coffee

DRINKING & NIGHTLIFE
29 4 Hands Brewing Co
30 Anheuser-Busch Brewery
31 Blueprint Coffee at High Low
32 Just John Club
33 None of the Above

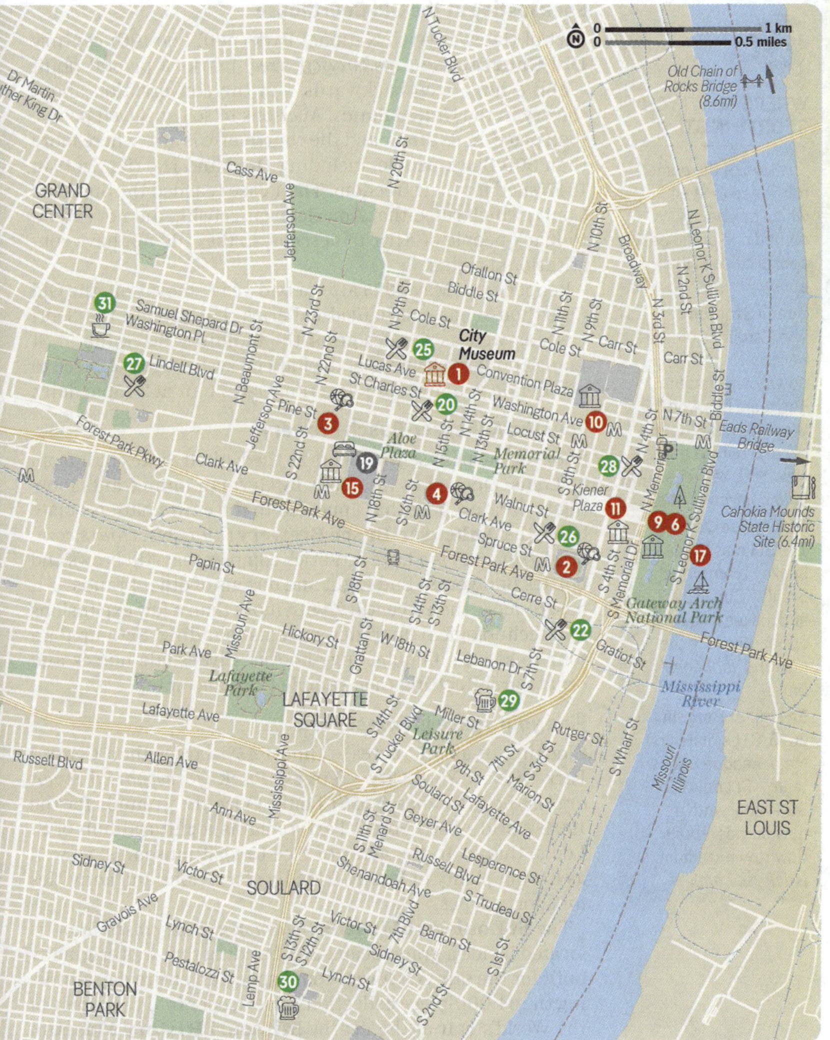

ROUTE 66 STOPS IN MISSOURI

Old Chain of Rocks Bridge: Now open only to pedestrians and cyclists, this mile-long span over the Mississippi River north of St Louis opened in 1929.

Ted Drewes: Save room for a concrete, a cup of thick frozen custard, invented at this St Louis institution in 1959. *(teddrewes.com)*

Meramec Caverns: Hugely popular and totally corny, these caves are filled with stalactites and Civil War history. *(americascave.com; adult/child $29.50/16)*

Uranus Fudge Factory: No pun is left unexcreted at this shameless roadside attraction. *(uranusgeneralstore.com)*

WHERE TO WATCH SPORTS IN STL

The love of the game runs deep in St Louis, which has been named one of the best sports cities in the country.

Busch Stadium: The Cardinals play baseball in this fun downtown stadium. The team has won the World Series 11 times, second only to the New York Yankees. *(mlb.com/cardinals)*

Enterprise Center: The St Louis Blues hockey team won the Stanley Cup in 2019 and makes frequent appearances in the playoffs. *(nhl.com/blues)*

Energizer Park: In 2023, STL got its first Major League Soccer team – St Louis City SC – along with a new purpose-built downtown stadium. *(stlcitysc.com)*

Seek justice at the Old Courthouse

Part of Gateway Arch National Park (p60), the 19th-century **Old Courthouse** *(nps.gov/jeff; free)* marks a pivotal point – and a huge step backwards – in the conversation about slavery in the United States. Auctions to sell enslaved people took place on its steps, and the courthouse is also where more than 300 Black people, including Dred and Harriet Scott in 1847, sued for their freedom. Their case reached the Supreme Court, which ruled that American citizenship did not extend to Black people of African descent, so they did not have constitutional rights.

Reopened in May 2025 after a two-year renovation, the Old Courthouse has overhauled galleries that explain the Scott case, as well as the design of the building, Black life in St Louis and the relevance of the judicial system. You are free to wander on your own or join a ranger-led tour at 2:15pm daily.

Tour the Anheuser-Busch Brewery

Some of the best-selling beers in the United States hail from St Louis. Opened in the 1850s by German immigrants looking to create a beer that appealed to the entire nation's taste buds, the **Anheuser-Busch Brewery** *(budweisertours.com; tours from $15)* is a huge red-brick complex that still brews and bottles Budweiser, Bud Light and dozens of other brands as it has for more than a century, with more than a few expansions and technological upgrades since its founding. Sign up for a tour to see the famous huge-hooved Clydesdale horses and ornate architecture, then sample the suds on tap.

Find your space in Forest Park

Clocking in at 1371 acres – almost 45% larger than Central Park in New York City – **Forest Park** *(forestparkforever.org)* is the green heart of St Louis. Once the grounds for the 1904 World's Fair, Forest Park remains a cultural hub of St Louis, thanks to the array of free-to-visit museums, as well as having plenty of family-friendly attractions and activities for sporty types.

The **St Louis Art Museum** *(slam.org; free; closed Mon)* is located inside a grand beaux-arts building that was originally built for the fair. Art lovers could spend an entire day admiring the 34,000-piece collection. Dive deeper into the legacy of the World's Fair at the nearby **Missouri History Museum** *(mohistory.org; free; closed Mon)*, whose showcase exhibit is

EATING IN ST LOUIS: ICONIC STL FOODS

Charlie Gitto's: Said to be the spot that invented toasted ravioli in 1947 when a chef dropped them in oil instead of water. *5-9pm Sun-Thu, to 10pm Fri & Sat* $$$

Imo's: This local chain is a prolific purveyor of St Louis–style pizza: cracker-thin, square-cut crust topped with Provel cheese. *10am-11pm or later* $

Park Avenue Coffee: Treat yourself to a slice of gooey butter cake. This cafe does them in several flavors, such as red velvet and pumpkin caramel. *7am-2pm Mon-Fri* $

Pappy's Smokehouse: Food Network called these the best BBQ ribs in the country, and our sticky fingers agree. *11am-4pm or later Wed-Mon* $

RN PHOTO MIDWEST/SHUTTERSTOCK

Forest Park

a scale model of the 1904 grounds. The museum's gift shop is one of the best places in town for STL souvenirs you never knew you needed, like a toasted ravioli fridge magnet.

Kids will be more drawn in by the critters at the **St Louis Zoo** *(stlzoo.org; free)* and the interactive displays and demonstrations at the **St Louis Science Center** *(slsc.org; free; closed Tue & Wed)*. From mid-November to early March, lace up your ice skates to glide on the **Steinberg Skating Rink** *(steinbergrink.com)*, the largest in the Midwest.

Fuel up for a big day out at the **Boathouse at Forest Park** *(boathousestl.com)*, the park's waterside cafe, where you can dine outdoors next to the ducks. Next door, rent paddle boats, canoes, kayaks, stand-up paddleboards – or bikes for landlubbers – from **Big Muddy Adventures** *(paddleforestpark.com)*.

MORE STL SIGHTS

Missouri Botanical Garden: Walk around a 14-acre Japanese garden, a Victorian-style hedge maze and the geodesic Climatron. *(missouribotanicalgarden.org; adult/child $16/free)*

National Blues Museum: Explore the deep history of this influential music genre. *(nationalbluesmuseum.org; adult/child $15/10)*

National Museum of Transportation: Huge railroad locomotives, historic cars cooler than your rental and more that moves. *(tnmot.org; adult/child $16/8)*

Union Station: Family-friendly attractions in this former train station include a 200ft-tall Ferris wheel, a shark-filled aquarium and a ropes course. Adults can watch the light show in the Grand Hall, now a hotel bar (p122). *(stlouisunionstation.com)*

DRINKING IN ST LOUIS: OUR PICKS

4 Hands Brewing Co: STL's largest craft brewery is down the road from big brother Bud, with a lively taproom. *11am-10pm or later Mon-Sat, to 8pm Sun*

Side Project: Hopheads must visit this suburban brewery that's been ranked as one of the best in the world multiple times. *4-8pm Mon, Wed & Thu, from 1pm Fri-Sun*

None of the Above: Sleek speakeasy below City Foundry (p55) started by a James Beard–winning chef. Look for the red light. *5pm-1am Wed-Mon*

Blueprint Coffee at High Low: This 'literary cafe' serves live music, art exhibitions and a creative atmosphere alongside coffee and pastries. *8am-4pm*

TOP EXPERIENCE

Gateway Arch National Park

The world's largest arch soars 630ft above the smallest national park in the United States. Set within a green space near the Mississippi River, long an unofficial divider between east and west, the Arch is a symbol of St Louis, promoting the city's historic role as the 'Gateway to the West.' The museum presents nuanced views on manifest destiny and white western migration.

FIIPHOTO/SHUTTERSTOCK

TOP TIPS

- Save $3 on tram tickets with the **America the Beautiful** national park pass. Combo tickets for cruises also net small savings.
- Going through airport-style security is required to visit the museum and take the trams.
- Tram tickets often sell out; book online in advance.

PRACTICALITIES

- gatewayarch.com; nps.gov/jeff
- museum free; tram ride from $12
- museum and tram open 9am-6pm; grounds 5am-11pm

Museum at the Gateway Arch

The fascinating, free-to-visit **Museum at the Gateway Arch** will take up the majority of the time you spend at this national park. It's filled with interactive exhibits that detail the history of St Louis, provide updated perspectives on westward expansion, and dive into the architectural and engineering feats required for the arch's construction.

Tram to the Top

A visit to the Gateway Arch isn't complete without whizzing to the top in one of the small trams that feel like 1960s space capsules straight out of *The Jetsons*. They take four minutes to trundle to the top, releasing passengers into a narrow viewing area with windows that provide unbeatable views over the city.

Gateway Arch Riverboats

Churn up the 'Big Muddy' (the Mississippi River) on replica 19th-century steamboats on a narrated cruise with **Gateway Arch Riverboats**. Unfortunately, this stretch of river isn't particularly scenic, but it's still a fun way to see the city, and it's the only way to get on the fast-flowing water of the country's most fabled river.

Kansas City

Remembering the Great War

The United States' congressionally designated national museum of the Great War isn't in Washington, DC, but in the heart of the country in Kansas City. Enter the impressive, modern **National WWI Museum** *(theworldwar.org; adult/child $19.50/11.50; closed Mon Sep-May)* on a glass walkway over a field of red poppies, the symbol of remembrance of WWI. Through detailed and engaging displays, learn about a war that is almost forgotten by many Americans.

Outside, the **Liberty Memorial** towers nearly 270ft above the lawn, and you can ride an elevator to the top (for an extra $6) to see the city from on high. The view of Union Station (p59) from the top of Liberty Memorial and the courtyard below is the most photographed angle of Kansas City. The courtyard is free for all to access – you don't have to visit the museum.

Artsy outing at Nelson-Atkins

One of the top galleries in the region, the **Nelson-Atkins Museum of Art** *(nelson-atkins.org; free; closed Tue & Wed)* is a cherished city treasure and a must-visit for culture vultures. The globe-trotting collection spans continents, showing off ancient Egyptian coffins, Chinese bronzes and works by European masters (including pieces by Monet and Caravaggio).

But the most iconic pieces aren't in the museum at all – they are outside on the lawn. Four 18ft-tall badminton shuttlecocks playfully plunge into the grass on either side of the museum building, which represents the net, and they feature on countless KC souvenirs.

Nearby, the smaller **Kemper Museum of Contemporary Art** *(kemperart.org; free; closed Mon & Tue)* has edgy rotating exhibitions and an excellent cafe.

Track down KC's best barbecue

Kansas City was once home to some of the largest stockyards in the country, second only to Chicago, and smoked meat is still big business. KC's status as one of the best places in the USA to eat barbecue is thanks to Henry Perry, a Black pitmaster who opened a restaurant in the early 1900s. Although Perry's restaurant no longer exists, he trained apprentice pitmasters who carried on his craft at the thriving institutions of **Gates Bar-B-Q** *(gatesbbq.com)* and **Arthur Bryant's** *(arthurbryantsbbq.com)*.

WHERE TO WATCH SPORTS IN KC

Kansas City is the smallest city to host the 2026 World Cup games. To say that this place is sports mad is an understatement.

Arrowhead Stadium: Even before Taylor Swift, the Kansas City Chiefs were hitting the headlines, winning the Super Bowl three times between 2020 and 2024. *(chiefs.com)*

Kauffman Stadium: The Royals baseball team hits homers at The K. *(mlb.com/royals)*

CPKC Stadium: The first arena in the world purpose-built for a professional women's sports team opened for the KC Current's soccer stars in 2024. *(kansascitycurrent.com)*

Children's Mercy Park: Sporting KC, the men's soccer team, plays on the Kansas side. *(sportingkc.com)*

EATING IN KANSAS CITY: OUR PICKS

Antler Room: Local ingredients go global in seasonal small plates, which might include fresh pasta, potato gyoza or grilled octopus. *5-10pm Wed-Sun* $$

Baba's Pantry: Nowhere else in town does hummus, falafel and chicken shawarma as good as this Palestinian-American deli. *11am-7pm Mon-Sat* $

Green Dirt on Oak: The charcuterie boards are works of art and mostly sourced from its own farm in Weston, about 30 miles northwest. *10am-10pm Wed-Sun* $$

Corvino: Sit in the darkened dining room for a decadent New American dinner, starting with the signature seaweed doughnuts. *5-10pm Sun-Thu, to 11pm Fri & Sat* $$$

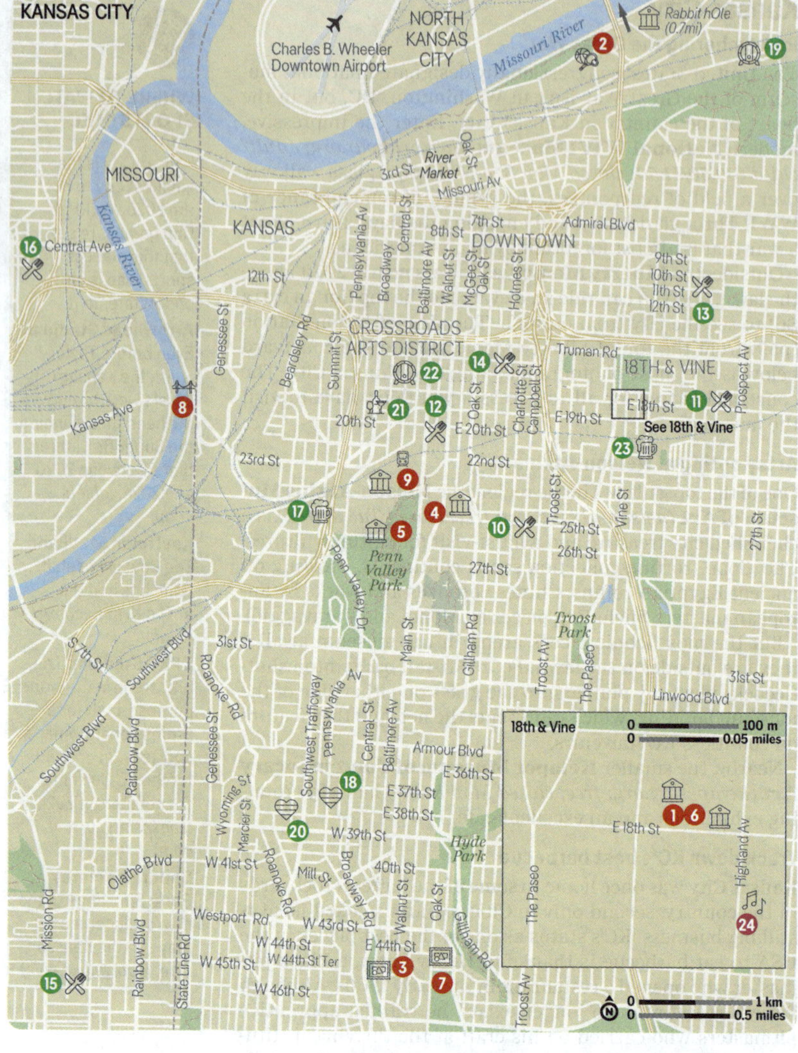

SIGHTS

1 American Jazz Museum
2 CPKC Stadium
3 Kemper Museum of Contemporary Art
4 Museum of BBQ
5 National WWI Museum
6 Negro Leagues Baseball Museum
7 Nelson-Atkins Museum of Art
8 Rock Island Bridge
9 Union Station

EATING

10 Antler Room
11 Arthur Bryant's
12 Corvino
13 Gates Bar-B-Q
14 Green Dirt on Oak
15 Joe's Kansas City Bar-B-Que
16 Slap's BBQ

DRINKING & NIGHTLIFE

17 Boulevard Brewery
18 Hamburger Mary's
19 J Rieger
20 Missie B's
21 Swordfish Tom's
22 Tom's Town
23 Vine Street Brewing Co

ENTERTAINMENT

24 Mutual Musicians Foundation

Kansas City barbecue has deep roots but continues to evolve, with a new generation of pitmasters firing up the smokers for their own takes on tradition. The Z-Man sandwich (sliced brisket, smoked provolone cheese and onion rings on a Kaiser roll) from **Joe's Kansas City Bar-B-Que** *(joeskc.com)* holds legendary status, best devoured at its original location in a gas station on the Kansas side of the state line. Vegetarians should try the version with portobello mushroom. Elsewhere in KCK, **Slap's BBQ** *(slapsbbqkc.com)*, well, slaps. (Its name is actually an acronym that stands for 'Squeal Like a Pig.') Burnt ends – the fatty charred ends of brisket, like smoked beef crackling – are a Kansas City invention and a must-order here and at any spot worth its sauce.

Before you fill your stomach, feed your mind at the world's first **Museum of BBQ** *(museumofbbq.co; $12)*, opened in March 2025. It dissects the history of KC barbecue and other major regional styles. More importantly, it has a 'bean' ball pit.

Feel the soul of Black Kansas City

The historic Black district of **18th and Vine** was a cradle of jazz music and is still a focal point of Black culture in KC.

Learn about musicians – including Kansas City native Charlie 'Bird' Parker – instruments and styles at the **American Jazz Museum** *(americanjazzmuseum.org; adult/child $10/6)*, which also has an jazz club called the **Blue Room** for live performances throughout the week, some of which are free. Jazz-loving night owls should head to **Mutual Musicians Foundation** *(themutualmusiciansfoundation.com; midnight-5am Fri & Sat)*. When performers wrap up their evening shows elsewhere, they head to Mutual Musicians to jam. Sessions don't get going until midnight or later, and Mutual Musicians is the only place in the entire state that's allowed to sell alcohol all night, thanks to a special exemption from the Missouri legislature.

Next to the American Jazz Museum, the **Negro Leagues Baseball Museum** *(nlbm.com; adult/child $10/6; closed Mon)* covers the lesser-known history of Black teams, such as the KC Monarchs and New York Black Yankees, that flourished until baseball became fully integrated.

Vine Street Brewing Co *(vinestbrewing.com; closed Tue)*, Missouri's first Black-owned brewery, opened in 2023 and is already a neighborhood staple. Sip a pint of Jazzman, a black lager that's the brewery's signature pour, at its premises in a graffitied limestone former public-works building.

This district has been undergoing major and much-needed improvements, including a new pedestrian plaza for better

KC WITH KIDS

Rabbit hOle: Tumble into the magic of children's literature at this one-of-a-kind art-filled celebration of kids' books. *(rabbitholekc.org; $16)*

Union Station: It's still a working train station, but it also contains Science City, a planetarium and a five-story-tall movie screen. *(unionstation.org)*

Kansas City Zoo & Aquarium: Colorful fish, sharks and a giant Pacific octopus fill a 650,000-gallon aquarium opened in 2023. *(kansascityzoo.org; from $20)*

Wonderscope: Children's museum best suited for under-10s. *(wonderscope.org; $16)*

Deanna Rose Children's Farmstead: Pet farm animals and bottle-feed baby goats in the Kansas-side suburb of Overland Park. *($5)*

DRINKING IN KANSAS CITY: OUR PICKS

Swordfish Tom's: KC's best cocktail bar is hiding down an alleyway. Descend the stairs into a darkened basement boiler room. *4pm-1:30am Tue-Sat*

J Rieger: This historic distillery was closed during Prohibition but resurrected a century later by the founder's great-great-great-grandson. *3-10pm Wed-Sat*

Tom's Town: Distillery named for a 1930s political boss with an art deco-style bar and a weekend-only speakeasy. *4-10pm or later Mon-Fri, noon-midnight Sat*

Boulevard Brewery: A conglomerate now owns KC's original craft brewer, but locals still love sipping Boulevard Wheat. *noon-9pm Mon-Sat, 10am-6pm Sun*

INDEPENDENCE TO THE FRONTIER

Nicknamed the 'Queen City of the Trails,' Independence was a major launching point for the Santa Fe, California and Oregon Trails.

National Frontier Trails Museum: This free museum covers the history of the three main trails, as well as the Mormon Trail. Mormons still have a major presence in Independence, which church leader Joseph Smith declared as Zion. *(ci.independence.mo.us/nftm)*

SantaCaliGon Days: Named after the three trails, this late-summer fun fair brings amusement park rides and food vendors to Independence's historic square. *(santacaligon.com)*

Pioneer Trails Adventures: Tour the main sites of Independence in a covered wagon. *(pioneertrailsadventures.com)*

walkability, renovations of the century-old Boone Theater – set to become a Black Movie Hall of Fame – and a planned expansion of the Negro Leagues Baseball Museum to include more exhibit space, a seven-story hotel and rooftop bar.

Independence

Get to know the only president from Missouri

Harry Truman, the 33rd US president, grew up in **Independence**, a suburb east of Kansas City. Reopened in 2021 after a $29 million update, the **Harry S Truman Presidential Library and Museum** *(trumanlibrary.gov; adult/child $12/5; closed Sun)* is a behind-the-scenes look at his life, legacy and the world at large in the 1940s and '50s. Exhibits include somber artifacts, such as the safety plug from the atomic bomb dropped on Nagasaki, Japan, to more lighthearted items like the famous 'The Buck Stops Here!' sign.

Join a National Park Service ranger on a tour of the **Harry S Truman National Historic Site** *(nps.gov/hstr; free; 9am-4pm Wed-Sun)* to see the simple life Harry and his wife, Bess, lived in their basic but charming wood house. The former president lived here from 1919 to 1972, and it's furnished with their original belongings. Visits are by a 30-minute tour only, and you must pick up a first-come, first-served free ticket from the **Harry S Truman National Historic Site Visitor Center**, about half a mile away.

St Joseph

From the Pony Express to psychiatry

St Joseph (usually abbreviated to St Jo) was another major departure point for westward-bound 19th-century pioneers headed for the goldfields of California or the Oregon territory. No matter their origin or final destination, travelers converged in St Jo, once the westernmost American city accessible by rail and a river port for steamboats.

As the eastern terminus of the Pony Express, which first set off from here in April 1860, St Jo served as a lifeline that connected east and west. The **Pony Express National Museum** *(ponyexpress.org; adult/child $10/5)* is located in the stables from which the horse riders once departed. Time your visit for June for the annual **Re-Ride**, when riders gallop along the historic route and still carry letters in a leather mochila.

Nearby, the imposing 1858 **Patee House** *(ponyexpressjessejames.com; adult/child $8/5)* was a luxury hotel and the Pony

EATING & DRINKING IN INDEPENDENCE: OUR PICKS

Dixon's Famous Chili Parlor: Open since 1919, Dixon's is a diner that served Truman; wonder if he got the chili or all-you-can-eat tacos. *10am-9pm Mon-Sat* $

Clinton's Soda Fountain: Little has changed from when Truman got his first job. Come for ice cream and phosphate sodas. *11am-5pm Tue-Sat* $

3 Trails Brewing: This welcoming brewery is a hub for the community and hosts lots of events. *4-10:30pm Wed & Thu, to midnight Fri, noon-midnight Sat, to 7pm Sun*

Sentinel Room: Top-notch cocktail bar with a huge whiskey selection in a former newspaper office. *3-10pm Tue-Thu, to midnight Fri, noon-midnight Sat*

MATT FOWLER KC/SHUTTERSTOCK

Ethnic Enrichment Festival

Express headquarters. It now showcases the city's rich story with exhibits full of historic memorabilia. Behind it is the modest house of notorious outlaw **Jesse James** *(extra $5/3)*. He was murdered here, and the bullet hole is still visible in the wall.

Continue the dark tourism trend at the **Glore Psychiatric Museum** *(stjosephmuseum.org; adult/child $12/8)*. Housed in the former State Lunatic Asylum No 2, this museum gives a frightening and fascinating look at lobotomies, the 'bath of surprise' and other discredited mental health treatments.

The Ozarks

Hike the hills and float in wild rivers

Ozark hill country spreads across southern Missouri and extends into northern Arkansas and eastern Oklahoma. Flashy Branson receives the lion's share of tourists, but the region's true charms lie not in town but further afield in the rolling hills and deep clefts where spring-fed rivers carry legions of happy campers floating downstream.

Two wild rivers, the Current and the Jacks Fork, wind through 80,000 acres of raw natural beauty in the **Ozark National Scenic Riverways** *(nps.gov/ozar; free)*, the first national park established to protect a waterway. Numerous natural springs feed the river; the most famous and accessible is **Big Spring**, which releases some 286 million gallons a day. **Blue Spring** is harder to get to but even more stunning, with surreal cerulean waters that almost look glacial. Swimming in the springs isn't allowed, but you can jump in the river nearby.

Another scenic swimming spot is **Johnson's Shut-Ins State Park** *(mostateparks.com; free)*, where the Black River swirls through canyon-like gorges (shut-ins). Find outfitters and rental services for river activities in the towns of **Van Buren** and **Eminence**. Summer weekends get busy and boisterous.

Hikers can tackle portions of the 430-mile **Ozark Trail** *(ozarktrail.com)*, parts of which follow the Current River. For a good half-day hike, head to **Taum Sauk Mountain State Park** *(mostateparks.com; free)*, where you can scale the state's

BEST MISSOURI FESTIVALS

National Tom Sawyer Days: Head to Hannibal, the childhood hometown of Mark Twain, to watch competitive fence painting and more in July. *(hannibaljaycees.org)*

Mardi Gras: The second-largest Mardi Gras celebrations in the country take place in the St Louis neighborhood of Soulard. *(stlmardigras.org)*

Ethnic Enrichment Festival: Diverse clubs in KC set up booths to share their food and culture in August. *(eeckc.org)*

Birthplace of Route 66 Festival: The nation's largest celebration of the Mother Road takes place every August in Springfield. *(route66 festivalsgf.com)*

Maifest: Celebrate spring in the German-heritage town of Hermann in May. *(maifesthermann.org)*

LGBTIQ+ MISSOURI

In 2024, Missouri ranked last – along with 23 other states – in a Human Rights Campaign survey of LGBTIQ+ equality, but that doesn't necessarily mean queer travelers should avoid the state.

St Louis and Kansas City have the most welcoming attitudes and dedicated gay bars. Try **Hamburger Mary's** *(hamburgermarys.com)* and **Missie B's** *(missiebs.com)* in KC, and **Just John Club** *(justjohnnightclub.com)* and other nearby LGBTIQ+ bars in the Grove neighborhood of STL. The college town of Columbia, home to the University of Missouri, was the first Missouri city to ban conversion therapy for LGBTQ+ youth. These three cities, along with Springfield, have Pride festivities in June.

LAUREN KEITH

Blue Spring **(p65)**

highest peak, 1772ft Taum Sauk Mountain (a flat walk from the already elevated parking lot) and see the state's tallest waterfall, 132ft Mina Sauk Falls.

See Branson's artificial and natural amusements

Hokey, family-friendly **Branson** is an unabashedly shameless tourist resort. The main attractions are **Silver Dollar City** *(silverdollarcity.com; 1-day pass adult/child $92/82)* – a huge Old West–themed amusement park – and the more than 45 theaters hosting country music, magic and comedy shows. **Branson's Famous Baldknobbers** *(baldknobbers.com; adult/child from $46/23)* is the musical comedy show that started it all in 1959. Three generations of the Mabe family – and a lot of 'friends' – cover country and gospel tunes, dance and offer up cornball comedy.

Drive just a few minutes out of town and you'll find yourself close to the Ozark wilderness again, though in a more manicured form. Man-made **Table Rock Lake** is a popular destination for boating and fishing, and you can rent motorboats and pontoons from multiple marinas. Much of the conserved land around Branson is thanks to Johnny Morris, the Missouri-born CEO of Bass Pro Shops. **Top of the Rock** *(bigcedar.com/top-of-the-rock; adult/child from $45/20)* lets you drive a golf cart along limestone cliffs and into a cave (which, of course, has a bar inside), while **Dogwood Canyon** *(dogwoodcanyon.org; adult/child from $19/14)* offers opportunities for hiking, cycling, horseback riding, fishing and hopping onto a trailer for nature tour.

EATING IN BRANSON: OUR PICKS

Keeter Center: Staffed by students at the College of the Ozarks, this country-chic farm-to-table restaurant gets top marks. *10:30am-8pm Mon-Sat* $$

Gettin' Basted: Grilled by award-winning pitmasters, brisket, pulled pork and burnt ends are the stars at one of the best places to eat on Branson's '76 Strip.' *11am-9pm* $

Full Throttle Distillery: Devour barbecue and comfort food at this motorcycle-themed spot that makes its own moonshine. *7am-10pm or later* $$

Pie Safe: Kitschily charming Victorian-styled cafe serving miniature pies and other baked goods alongside flavored lattes. *10am-6pm Mon-Sat* $

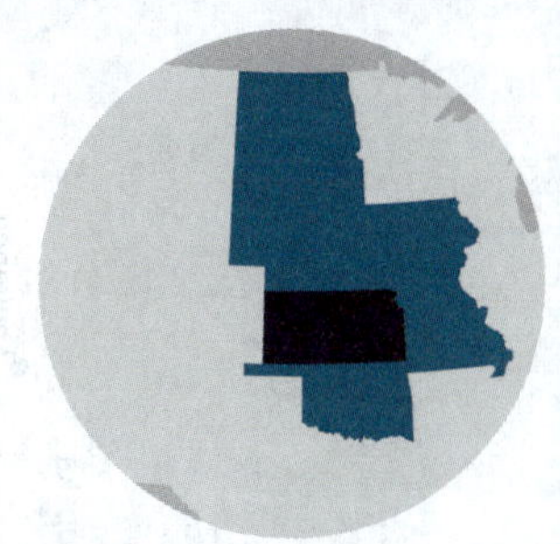

Kansas

PRESERVED PRAIRIE | AVIATION HISTORY | OUTSIDER ART

Wicked witches, yellow-brick roads and tornadoes powerful enough to erase entire towns are popular images of Kansas, but visions of amber waves of grain spreading as far as the eye can see are closer to reality.

What Kansas might lack in mind-boggling scenery, it makes up for in quirky, soul-stirring stops. The rolling hills and limitless horizons have an evocative, understated beauty, particularly evident in places like the beguiling Tallgrass Prairie National Preserve. Gems abound, from the superb space museum in Hutchinson to the college-town cool of Lawrence.

The largest city in the state is Wichita, a 19th-century cow town that became the 'Air Capital of the World' as a major aircraft manufacturer. This transformation is emblematic of how the whole state continues to reinvent itself in weird and wonderful ways while still drawing on history and tradition – no matter where you go in Kansas, it's unlikely to be at all what you expected.

Places

TOP TIP

For discounts on tolls on the Turnpike, request a free K-TAG online *(ksturnpike.com)* before your trip, which will be mailed to you. Toll tags from some other states, such as Best Pass, Pikepass, EZ TAG and SunPass, can also be used here. Tolls cannot be paid with cash.

Atchison

Birthplace of America's finest female aviator

Famed flier Amelia Earhart broke many barriers and records. She was the first female pilot to fly solo nonstop across the Atlantic, and she disappeared in 1939 attempting to become the

GETTING AROUND

You need a car to get around Kansas. Two interstates cross the state in different directions, coming together near Kansas City: I-35, linking Wichita and Kansas City; and I-70, which shoots through Lawrence, Topeka and points west. Sections of both interstates are toll roads, called the Kansas Turnpike.

Wichita Dwight D Eisenhower National Airport is the busiest airport in Kansas (Kansas City's airport is in Missouri) and has services from regional hubs, such as Dallas, Denver and Chicago. Amtrak's *Southwest Chief,* which runs from Chicago to Los Angeles, stops in Lawrence, Topeka and Dodge City.

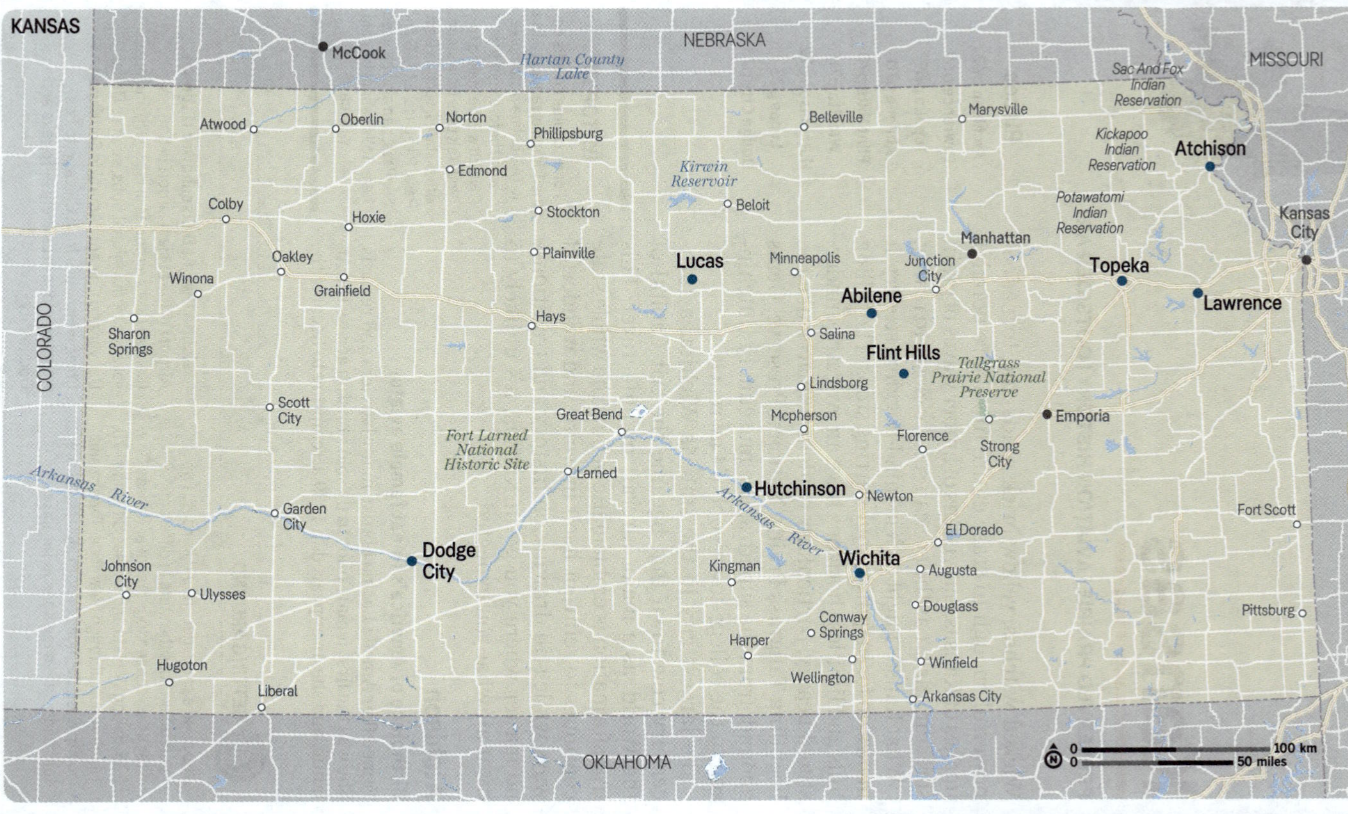
KANSAS
NEBRASKA
MISSOURI
COLORADO
OKLAHOMA
McCook
Harlan County Lake
Sac And Fox Indian Reservation
Kickapoo Indian Reservation
Potawatomi Indian Reservation
Atchison
Kansas City
Topeka
Lawrence
Manhattan
Junction City
Abilene
Flint Hills
Tallgrass Prairie National Preserve
Emporia
Strong City
Florence
Atwood
Oberlin
Norton
Phillipsburg
Edmond
Belleville
Marysville
Kirwin Reservoir
Beloit
Colby
Hoxie
Stockton
Plainville
Lucas
Minneapolis
Oakley
Winona
Grainfield
Hays
Salina
Sharon Springs
Lindsborg
Scott City
Great Bend
Mcpherson
Fort Larned National Historic Site
Larned
Hutchinson
Newton
Arkansas River
Garden City
Dodge City
Johnson City
Ulysses
Kingman
Wichita
El Dorado
Augusta
Douglass
Fort Scott
Pittsburg
Conway Springs
Harper
Wellington
Winfield
Arkansas City
Hugoton
Liberal
0 100 km
0 50 miles

first woman aviator to circumnavigate the globe. She championed gender equality and women pursuing male-dominated careers in engineering and science. Her body and plane were never found, which fuels speculation to this day.

Aptly located at Atchison's tiny airport, the **Amelia Earhart Hangar Museum** *(ameliaearharthangarmuseum.org; adult/child $15/8; closed Mon & Tue)* opened in 2023 and shows off *Muriel,* the only surviving Lockheed Electra 10-E plane, exactly like the one Earhart flew on her final voyage.

You can also visit the **Amelia Earhart Birthplace Museum** *(ameliaearhartmuseum.org; guided/self-guided tour $15/12),* the 1861 Gothic Revival home where she grew up.

Lawrence

College-town vibes in Kansas' coolest city

Lawrence has been an island of progressive politics since its inception. Founded by East Coast abolitionists in 1854, it became a battlefield in the clash between pro- and antislavery factions. The city's free-thinking spirit continues, fueled in no small part by the huge student body at the University of Kansas (KU). It's one of the country's most vibrant college towns.

The appealing downtown centers on **Massachusetts St** (abbreviated to Mass), lined with historic buildings home to the city's best restaurants, coffee shops, bars and stores. It's an excellent place to spend an afternoon shopping and bar-hopping.

The KU campus is at the top of Mt Oread, aka 'the Hill,' and it's worth stopping by the **Spencer Museum of Art** *(spencerart.ku.edu; free; closed Sun & Mon)* to check out the exhibitions, and globe-trotting and century-spanning works.

Topeka

The push to desegregate public schools

Kansas' vital role in the country's race relations is documented in the otherwise humdrum state capital of Topeka. Set in the former Monroe Elementary School, one of Topeka's four segregated primary schools for Black students, **Brown v Board of Education National Historical Park** *(nps.gov/brvb; free; closed Sun & Mon)* tells the story of the famous 1954 Supreme Court case that threw out the 'separate but equal' doctrine, in the context of the wider Civil Rights movement.

BEST KANSAS FESTIVALS

Riverfest: Wichita's biggest festival includes a city-wide scavenger hunt, 'cowboy bathtub' races and a cardboard boat regatta in June. *(wichitariverfest.com)*

Walnut Valley Festival: This September bluegrass festival near Winfield draws more visitors than the town's population. *(wvfest.com)*

Water Wars: Everyone in Humboldt participates in a town-wide water fight in August. *(facebook.com/waterwars.humboldt)*

Lawrence Busker Festival: Fire breathers, dancers, magicians and other street performers take over downtown Lawrence in May. *(lawrencebuskerfest.com)*

Louisburg Ciderfest: Celebrate all things apple in late September. *(louisburgcidermill.com)*

EATING & DRINKING IN LAWRENCE: OUR PICKS

Free State Brewing: Opened in 1989 as the first brewery in Kansas since Prohibition, with pints and pub grub. The cheddar ale soup is classic. *11am-9pm* **$$**

715: Classy but laid-back Italian-influenced restaurant with a neighborhood feel on Mass St. A happy hour favorite. *3-9pm Tue & Wed, to 10pm Thu-Sat* **$$**

Barker: Out-of-this-world pastries from a James Beard–nominated chef. Go early lest they sell out. *7am-8pm Mon-Fri, 8am-2pm Sat & Sun* **$$**

John Brown's Underground: The best cocktail bar in town is named for the famed abolitionist and Kansas hero. *5pm-midnight Wed-Sat*

BEST KANSAS SMALL TOWNS

Humboldt: A brewery, a boutique hotel with a cool cocktail bar, and lakeside cabins have put tiny Humboldt on the map in a big way. *(abolderhumboldt.com)*

Lindsborg: Its Swedish heritage shines with events like Våffeldagen (Waffle Day) and a Midsummer's Festival. *(visitlindsborg.com)*

Nicodemus: Formerly enslaved people founded Nicodemus in 1877 as the first Black town west of the Mississippi. The National Park Service has restored the town hall and church. *(nps.gov/nico)*

Council Grove: Main St was the Santa Fe Trail, and historic businesses, including Hays House, the oldest continuously operating restaurant west of the Mississippi, line the route. *(councilgrove.com)*

Climb to the top of the Kansas State Capitol

The grand **Kansas State Capitol** *(kansashistory.gov/capitol; free; closed Sun),* made of state-sourced limestone, took 37 years to complete after its cornerstone was laid in 1866. You can take a guided or self-guided tour of the building – either way, don't miss *Tragic Prelude* on the east side of the 2nd-floor rotunda. This fiery mural by Kansas-born artist John Steuart Curry depicts a raging, oversized John Brown, a famous abolitionist who was later convicted of treason, holding a Bible in one hand and a rifle in the other. Brown stands in front of sparring Union and Confederate Civil War soldiers with a tornado and a prairie fire engulfing the background. Guided tours depart on the hour between 9am and 3pm, except at noon, Monday to Friday, and 10am, 11am, 1pm and 3pm on Saturday.

The Kansas Statehouse is one of the few where you can climb up into the huge copper dome on a guided tour. Brace yourself for the 296 steps; there's no elevator. Dome tours take place at 15 minutes past the hour.

Abilene

Make like Ike in Eisenhower's childhood home

In the late 19th century, Abilene was a rowdy cow town at the end of the Chisholm Trail. Today, its compact core of historic brick buildings and well-preserved neighborhoods seems perfectly appropriate for the birthplace of Dwight D Eisenhower, the 34th president.

The **Dwight D Eisenhower Presidential Library and Museum** *(eisenhowerlibrary.gov; adult/child $20/15)* includes Ike's boyhood home, a museum and library, and his and his wife's graves. Interactive exhibits cover the Eisenhower presidential era (1953–61) and his role as the Supreme Allied Commander in Europe in WWII. Don't miss the original script for his landmark 1961 speech in which he famously warned of the military-industrial complex.

Flint Hills

Pieces of the last surviving tallgrass prairie

Prairie once covered more than 30% of North America – some 170 million acres – but was decimated by agriculture and urban development. Only a tiny sliver remains today, mostly in Kansas' Flint Hills, which were never plowed because the soil is too rocky.

Run by the National Park Service, the 11,000-acre **Tallgrass Prairie National Preserve** *(nps.gov/tapr; free; buildings 8:30am-4:30pm, trails 24hr)* protects one of the last stands of this ecosystem that's symbolic of the center of the country. Walking trails meander along gently rolling hills, including through a pasture where reintroduced bison roam, as well as to the **Lower Fox Creek School**, a one-room limestone schoolhouse that drew in students from 1882 to 1930.

Near the visitor center, the impressive 1881 **Spring Hill Ranch House** was surprisingly sophisticated for its remote

LAUREN KEITH

Tallgrass Prairie National Preserve

location in the rural countryside, built in Second Empire style with a mansard roof, a grand walnut staircase, and ornate woodwork and ceiling medallions. Find the preserve 2 miles northwest of tiny Strong City or 23 miles west of Emporia, a larger city that sits on I-35. A scenic way to get here is on the **Flint Hills National Scenic Byway**, where grasses and wildflowers wave you on through the timeless landscape that looks much the same as it did when the Native Kaw, Osage, Pawnee and Wichita people called it home.

If you're driving I-70 through Kansas, a closer option is the **Konza Prairie Biological Station** *(nature.org; free)* near the college town of Manhattan, home to Kansas State University. It's smaller and doesn't have bison, but its three looped hiking trails are just as evocative. Remember that these areas are grassland, so you won't find shade from trees. Sun protection and timing your hikes for cooler parts of the day are musts.

In March or April every year, prescribed burns set 2.2 million acres of the Kansas prairie on fire. This process, now started by humans instead of naturally by lightning, preserves the ecosystem and is a sight to see.

Wichita

A family-friendly, history-filled day out

The **Museums on the River** district could occupy a day or more of your time in Wichita. Note that here the name of the Arkansas River is pronounced 'OUR-Kansas,' not like the state of Arkansas.

A hit with kids and history-lovers, the **Old Cowtown Museum** *(oldcowtown.org; adult/child $12/10; closed Mon & Tue)* recreates the Wild West. This mini city is complete with dirt

ROUTE 66 IN KANSAS

The Sunflower State holds a mere 13 miles of the Mother Road (less than 1% of the total), but it still has a lot to see. It's also the only part of Route 66 that hasn't been overwritten by the interstate.

Entering from Missouri, you pass through mine-scarred **Galena**, where a rusty old tow truck inspired Pixar animators to create the character Mater in *Cars*. Look for the original outside **Cars on the Route** *(facebook.com/CarsOnTheRoute)*, a restored gas station.

West of Galena, stop at the red-brick **Old Riverton Store** *(oldrivertonstore.com)* and stock up on sandwiches and Route 66 memorabilia. Continue to the 1923 **Rainbow Bridge** and then to the **Kansas Route 66 Visitor Center** *(baxtersprings museum.org)* in **Baxter Springs**.

MORE WICHITA ATTRACTIONS

Frank Lloyd Wright's Allen House: Completed in 1918, with more than 30 pieces of Wright-designed furniture and original art glass windows. *(flwright wichita.org; $22)*

Original Pizza Hut Museum: In 1958, two Wichita State University students borrowed $600 to start a pizza restaurant. A few exhibits are inside the tiny building. *(free)*

Kansas Aviation Museum: This museum inside the city's first airport shows off aviation artifacts and aircraft such as the 1920 Laird Swallow, the first built in Wichita. *(kansas aviationmuseum.org; adult/child $10/6)*

Hatman Jack's: Famed hat shop that's outfitted Hollywood celebrities. *(hatman jacksict.com)*

streets and a significant number of authentic 1800s buildings from Wichita and around Kansas, which were saved from demolition and relocated here. Don't miss the opportunity to sip a sarsaparilla in the saloon. From April to October, costumed cowboys, blacksmiths, newspaper printers and schoolmarms wander the grounds to bring history to life, and gunfights are known to break out.

Another kid favorite is **Exploration Place** *(exploration.org; adult/child from $12/10),* an architecturally striking children's museum that has no end of cool exhibits, including a tornado chamber where you can feel 75mph winds and a sublime erosion model that shows water creating a new little Kansas. A 6-acre playground is set to open in spring 2026.

On the other side of the river, the **Mid-America All-Indian Museum** *(theindianmuseum.org; adult/child $7/3; closed Sun & Mon)* features Native art from its 3000-piece collection, particularly those of Kiowa-Comanche artist Blackbear Bosin – his 44ft-tall **Keeper of the Plains sculpture** stands outside at the river confluence. The Keeper is an icon of the city, and every night a 'ring of fire' is lit around the base of the statue for 15 minutes, starting at 9pm in spring and summer and 7pm in fall and winter.

For a dose of culture and color, head to **Botanica** *(botanica.org; adult/child $12/10),* the city's botanical gardens including a children's area with a carousel, and the **Wichita Art Museum** *(wam.org; free; closed Mon & Tue),* which greets you with the vibrant glasswork of Dale Chihuly.

Hutchinson

Below ground and above the atmosphere

About 50 miles northwest of Wichita, Hutchinson has two incredible sights that are worth a detour.

Possibly the most surprising sight in the state, the amazing **Cosmosphere** *(cosmo.org; adult/child $16.50/13.50)* captures the race to the Moon better than any other museum on the planet. Absorbing displays and artifacts such as the *Apollo 13* command module and entire rockets will enthrall you for hours. You'll come to realize why the museum is regularly called in to build props for Hollywood movies portraying the space race, including *Apollo 13.*

Speaking of Hollywood props, a surprising number are stored nearby at **Strataca** *(underkansas.org; adult/child from $25/18; closed Mon),* a salt mine 650ft underground,

EATING & DRINKING IN WICHITA: OUR PICKS

Doo-Dah Diner: A model for diners everywhere; regularly named Wichita's favorite restaurant. *7am-2pm Tue-Fri, from 8am Sat & Sun* $

Georges French Bistro: Wichita's first appearance on a James Beard list came in 2025 thanks to this classy spot. *11am-10pm Mon-Sat, 10am-2pm Sun* $$$

Central Standard Brewing: Our favorite brewery in town is this chilled-out spot with mid-mod furniture. *3-10pm or later Mon-Fri, noon-midnight Sat, to 5pm Sun*

Lava & Tonic: Speakeasy-style tiki bar with drinks in appropriately retro ceramicware. *5-11pm Wed & Thu, 4pm-12:30am Fri & Sat, 4-10pm Sun*

including the original camera negatives of *Gone with the Wind,* and Batman and Mr Freeze costumes. Why are they here? Stable temperatures, low humidity and the fact that salt doesn't catch on fire. Visits are by tour, which includes a tram ride through some of the 150 miles of tunnels.

Lucas

Get weird in the grassroots art capital of Kansas

Nothing is too off the wall for tiny Lucas, population 333, a hub of 'outsider' art made by self-taught creators.

If you only have time for a bathroom break, **Bowl Plaza** is the place to stop. These public restrooms have a toilet-shaped entrance and are covered in mosaics and trinkets.

Also on Main St are the **Grassroots Art Center** *(grassrootsart.net; adult/child $9/5),* an intriguing collection of 'outsider' works, and the **World's Largest Collection of the World's Smallest Versions of the World's Largest Things** *(worldslargestthings.com; free),* a museum that perfectly encapsulates the spirit of Lucas.

A few blocks east is the **Garden of Eden** *(gardenofedenlucas.org; adult/child $9/4),* the former home of Civil War veteran SP Dinsmoor, who decorated his yard with kooky concrete sculptures of bankers, politicians and biblical figures. He even prepared his own mausoleum, where you can see his moth-munched remains under a glass-topped coffin.

Dodge City

Relive the cowboy days in the 'queen of the cow towns'

Dodge City – where famous lawmen Bat Masterson and Wyatt Earp tried, sometimes successfully, to keep law and order – had a notorious reputation during the 1870s and 1880s. The **Boot Hill Museum** *(boothill.org; adult/child $20/14)* brings it roaring back to life with gunslingers and cancan dancers along reconstructed Front St, Dodge City's historic main street, with some original buildings, including the 1865 Fort Dodge jail.

Today, Dodge City is still a cow town, but of a different sort. Along with nearby Garden City and Liberal, Dodge City is home to multiple cattle slaughterhouses, which 'process' up to 5800 cows a day each. The stench might make you want to get the hell out of Dodge, but if you want a view over the enormous cattle pens, visit the **Feed Yard Overlook** off Wyatt Earp Blvd.

SIGHTS ON THE SANTA FE TRAIL IN WESTERN KANSAS

Unlike the later California and Oregon Trails, the Santa Fe Trail (1821–80) was primarily for commerce, not emigration. On this route, traveling traders moved goods between Missouri and Mexico.

Santa Fe Trail Tracks: See evidence of the thousands of 50in wooden prairie-schooner wagon wheels that carved their way through the Plains about 10 miles west of Dodge City, off US 50.

Fort Larned National Historic Site: A remarkably well-preserved 1860s fort in an evocative setting. It's well worth the trip, about 60 miles northeast of Dodge City, to learn about the turbulent history of the Indian Wars era. *(nps.gov/fols; free)*

EATING & DRINKING IN DODGE CITY: OUR PICKS

Central Station Bar & Grill: Dine on steak or Mexican food in an extension of the train station or an old railroad car. *11am-10pm Mon-Fri, from 4pm Sat* **$$**

Gollo Grande: About 65% of Dodge City's residents are of Hispanic descent, and this is one of the top Mexican joints. *10:30am-9pm or later Wed-Mon* **$**

Boot Hill Distillery: Three farmers run and supply the grains at this soil-to-sip distillery. Ask about the prickly ash bitters. *3-11pm Wed-Sat*

Dodge City Brewing: Southwest Kansas' first craft brewery serves its own excellent beers plus brick-oven pizza. *4-10pm Wed-Fri, from 11am Sat, 11am-8pm Sun*

Oklahoma

NATIVE STORIES | COWBOY LORE | COOL CITIES

Places

Oklahoma gets its name from Choctaw words meaning 'brave people.' With 39 tribes located in the state – many forcibly relocated to the unwanted 'Indian Territory' in the 19th century – it remains a place of deep Native heritage that has withstood the onslaught of centuries of assimilation and erasure that the word brave hardly begins to cover.

On the other side of the Old West coin, cowboys also figure prominently in the Sooner State, and there's still a great sense of the open range, interrupted only by urban Oklahoma City and Tulsa. Both cities, but Tulsa in particular, feel as if they are on the up, with so many new attractions, restaurants, breweries and bars that you're destined to find yourself adding extra days to your itinerary.

Oklahoma's share of Route 66, the second-longest of any state, links some of the Mother Road's iconic highlights and atmospheric old towns.

TOP TIP

If you're in Oklahoma to visit its hard-hitting, top-notch museums, leave your visit for later in the week. Many are closed on Mondays or Tuesdays – or both.

Tulsa

Remembering Black Wall Street

On May 30, 1921, a Black male teenager and a white female teenager were alone in an elevator in downtown Tulsa when she screamed. The how and why have never been answered, but the incident sparked three days of race riots that engulfed the neighborhood of Greenwood, nicknamed 'Black Wall Street'

GETTING AROUND

Highways crisscross the state, including Route 66 (mostly overtaken by I-40 west of OKC). Several of the US highways and interstates are toll roads that can't be paid for with cash. It's worth ordering a Pikepass *(pikepass.com)* in advance for discounts of up to 50%. Passes used for toll roads in Kansas (K-TAG; *ksturnpike.com)* and Texas (EZ TAG, TollTag, TxTag) are also valid on Oklahoma highways.

Parking is paid in downtown Tulsa and OKC. Download ParkMobile *(parkmobile.io; $1/hour)* in Tulsa and Flowbird *(flowbirdapp.com; $2/hour)* for OKC.

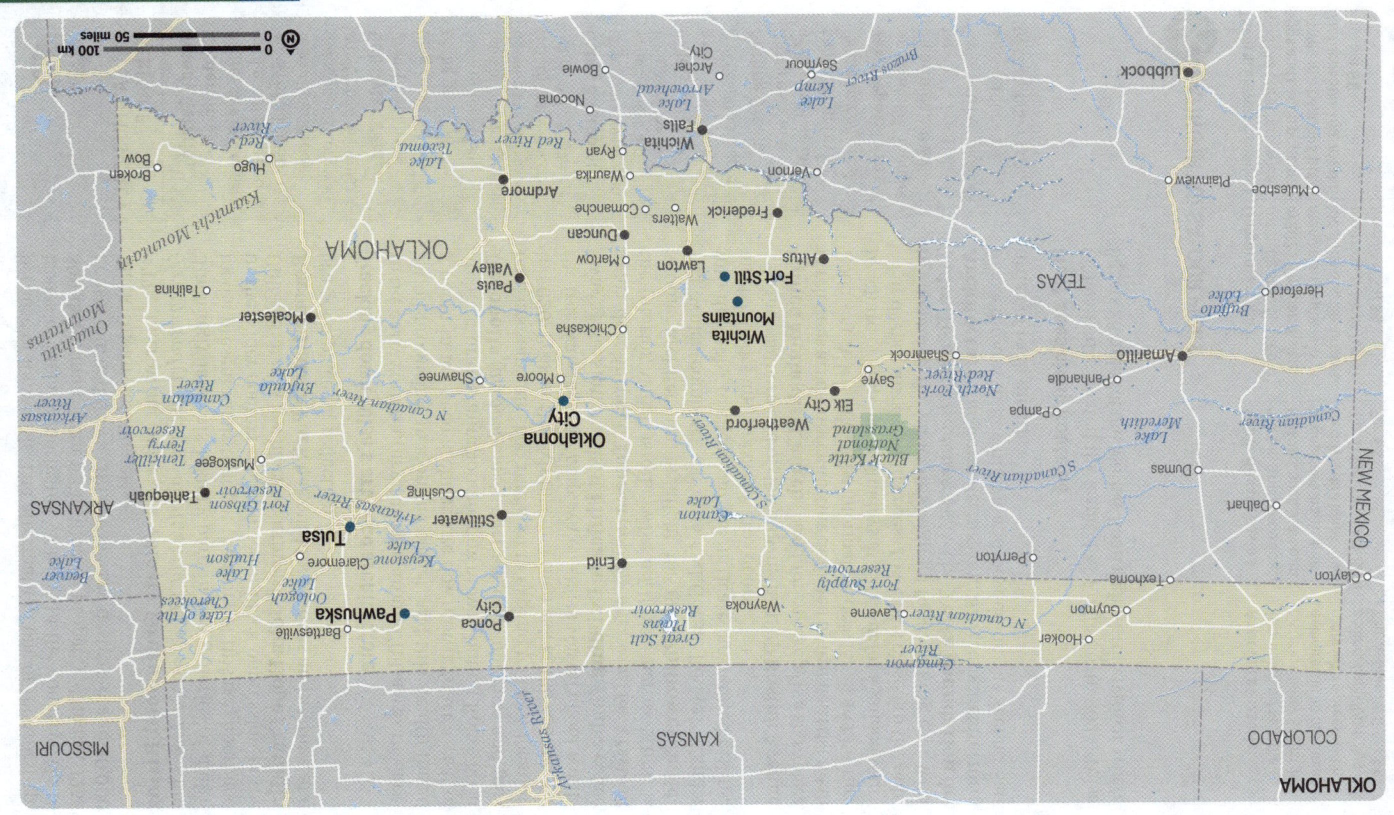
OKLAHOMA
COLORADO
KANSAS
MISSOURI
ARKANSAS
NEW MEXICO
TEXAS
OKLAHOMA
Oklahoma City
Tulsa
Pawhuska
Bartlesville
Ponca City
Stillwater
Enid
Cushing
Claremore
Tahlequah
Muskogee
Mcalester
Shawnee
Moore
Chickasha
Pauls Valley
Ardmore
Duncan
Marlow
Comanche
Waurika
Ryan
Walters
Lawton
Fort Still
Wichita Mountains
Frederick
Altus
Weatherford
Elk City
Sayre
Shamrock
Waynoka
Laverne
Hooker
Guymon
Texhoma
Perryton
Clayton
Dalhart
Dumas
Pampa
Panhandle
Amarillo
Hereford
Muleshoe
Plainview
Lubbock
Vernon
Seymour
Wichita Falls
Archer City
Nocona
Bowie
Talihina
Hugo
Broken Bow
Arkansas River
Cimarron River
N Canadian River
S Canadian River
Canadian River
North Fork Red River
Red River
Brazos River
Great Salt Plains Reservoir
Canton Lake
Fort Supply Reservoir
Black Kettle National Grassland
Keystone Lake
Oologah Lake
Lake of the Cherokees
Lake Hudson
Fort Gibson Reservoir
Tenkiller Ferry Reservoir
Eufaula Lake
Lake Texoma
Lake Arrowhead
Lake Kemp
Lake Meredith
Buffalo Lake
Beaver Lake
Ouachita Mountains
Kiamichi Mountain
0 50 miles
0 100 km

TULSA'S MUSICAL HERITAGE

Woody Guthrie Center: This impressive museum explains the life and music of this 1930s folk artist. *(woodyguthriecenter.org; adult/child $12/free)*

Bob Dylan Center: Walk through the long career of one of the greatest songwriters of all time at this museum, opened in 2022. *(bobdylancenter.com; adult/child $15/free)*

Cain's Ballroom: Legendary live music venue where Sid Vicious of the Sex Pistols punched a hole in the wall. *(cainsballroom.com)*

Guthrie Green: Urban park with a full schedule of concerts and events. *(guthriegreen.com)*

Jazz Depot: Tulsa's Union Station is under renovation but will feature a Jazz Hall of Fame and live gigs when it reopens. *(jazzdepotlive.com)*

because of its wealth. The aftermath of one of the worst episodes of racially motivated violence in the country? Up to 300 dead, more than $2 million in property damage, 1256 houses burned down, 191 businesses destroyed and 10,000 Black Tulsans left homeless.

The harrowing but extraordinary **Greenwood Rising** *(greenwoodrising.org; adult/child $15/8; closed Mon)* unflinchingly lays this history bare in five galleries of multimedia presentations that put the story of this neighborhood in the wider context of centuries of Black oppression in the United States. A few blocks northwest, **John Hope Franklin Reconciliation Park** has outdoor plaques and statues, and is a good place for reflection.

Tracking down Tulsa's art deco architecture

In the early 20th century, the land around Tulsa was the largest oil-producing area on the planet, and this wealth fueled a boom in art deco architecture downtown. Start a visit of architectural admiration not downtown, but on Route 66 at **Decopolis** *(decopolis.net),* part art deco museum and part bonkers souvenir shop that's set to expand to a new location in 2026. Peek at the exhibits and then ask at the counter for the free walking-tour map, which starts you off about a mile away at the stunning 1931 **Philcade Building**. Grab a coffee at art-deco-inspired **Topeca** *(topecacoffee.com)* for a taste of the interior, which is otherwise off limits. Across 5th St is another architectural highlight, the 1928 **Philtower Building**, which combines art deco and Gothic Revival. Wander into the lobby to check out the intricate fan-vaulted ceiling, marble floors and brass elevator doors.

At the southern end of downtown, the 1929 **Boston Avenue United Methodist Church** *(bostonavenue.org)* is a showpiece of religious art deco architecture designed by female artist Adah Robinson. Ask inside at the information desk for an architecture brochure or stop by on Sundays at 12:15pm for a guided tour.

For deeper insights and access to lobbies closed to the public, including the Philcade's, sign up for a walking tour with **Tulsa Tours** *(tulsa.tours; $45)*. The **Tulsa Foundation for Architecture** *(tulsaarchitecture.org; $20)* runs architecture-focused tours in downtown and beyond on the second Saturday of each month.

Must-sees along Route 66

Officially designated the 'capital of Route 66' in 2024, Tulsa boasts 28 miles of the Mother Road right through town, where

EATING IN TULSA: OUR PICKS

Tavern: Elevated comfort food like sriracha devilled eggs and bacon popcorn served in a beautiful pub. *11am-1pm Sun-Thu, to 1am Fri & Sat* $$

Daigoro: Romantic riverside spot opened in 2025. The pan-Asian menu also peppers in local flavors, like brisket fried rice. *5-10pm Tue-Fri, from 11am Sat* $$

Vault: Brunch, pasta and more in a mid-mod space that was once the world's largest 'autobank' with six drive-thru lanes. *11am-10pm Mon-Sat, 10am-3pm Sun* $$

Andolini's Pizzeria: Top-notch pizza in the historic Cherry St District delivered in an old dining room with a pressed-tin ceiling. *11am-10pm Sun-Thu, to 11pm Fri & Sat* $$

SIGHTS
1 Bob Dylan Center
2 Center of the Universe
3 Greenwood Rising
4 Guthrie Green
5 Jazz Depot
6 John Hope Franklin Reconciliation Park
7 Meadow Gold Mack
8 Meadow Gold Sign
9 Philcade Building
10 Philtower Building
11 Woody Guthrie Center

ACTIVITIES
12 Tulsa Foundation for Architecture
13 Tulsa Tours

SLEEPING
14 Mayo Hotel

EATING
15 Ike's Chili
16 Tavern
17 Vault
18 Wildflower Cafe

DRINKING & NIGHTLIFE
19 Saturn Room
20 Soundpony Lounge
21 Topeca

ENTERTAINMENT
22 Cain's Ballroom

SHOPPING
23 Buck Atom's Cosmic Curios on 66
24 Decopolis

TOP ROUTE 66 STOPS IN OKLAHOMA

Oklahoma has more miles of the original alignment than any other state.

Blue Whale: One of the most photographed Route 66 landmarks is the 80ft-long Blue Whale, the centerpiece of a long-gone water park in Catoosa.

Pops 66: A 66ft LED soda bottle near Arcadia lures you into buying some of the hundreds of varieties of pop from around the world. *(pops66.com)*

Oklahoma Route 66 Museum: If you take time for just one museum, make it this engagingly designed exhibition in Clinton. *(okhistory.org/sites/route66; adult/child $7/4)*

Pony Bridge: The 38-truss, 0.75-mile-long Pony Bridge crosses the Canadian River in rhythmic style.

it's called 11th St. The **Meadow Gold District** *(meadowgolddistrict.com)* is one of the most interesting stretches, so called because of the 1930s neon-lit **Meadow Gold sign**. Originally a promo for a dairy company, this Route 66 landmark was saved from demolition by preservationists and moved a few blocks from its original location. It now sits atop an open brick structure built specifically for it.

Look nearby for the three 20ft-tall 'muffler men' sculptures – **Meadow Gold Mack** *(meadowgoldmack.com)*, the friendly lumberjack; and space cowboy Buck Atom and gunslinging cosmic cowgirl Stella Atom outside **Buck Atom's Cosmic Curios on 66** *(buckatomson66.com)*, a teeny former gas station turned souvenir shop.

For more neon nostalgia, the glowing beacon of the **Route 66 Neon Sign Park** *(free)* is on the way out of town if you're driving west to Oklahoma City.

Take the family to the country's favorite city park

The 66-acre **Gathering Place** *(gatheringplace.org)* is a model for parks worldwide – since it opened in 2018, it's ranked at the top of lists of the best green spaces in the USA. Multiple themed playscapes designed for different age groups include a 5-acre adventure playground and Slide Vale (which has a slide that goes underground), plus a skate park and courts for pickleball, basketball, volleyball and street soccer.

Parents, don't hold back – you can join in the fun, too. The boathouse, with views of downtown and the Arkansas River, rents out free pedal boats and canoes, and tons of events take place on the huge lawn and stage.

Accessibility is built into the park so that kids of all abilities can enjoy it. It's fully ADA-compliant and offers quiet spaces, sensory bags, and free wheelchairs to rent.

Nearby, **Discovery Lab** *(discoverylab.org; $14)*, a huge science-centric children's museum, is an ideal indoor alternative when the weather isn't cooperating for a park visit.

Arty attractions

South of town, the **Philbrook Museum of Art** *(philbrook.org; adult/child $18/8; closed Mon & Tue)* is housed in an oil magnate's converted 1920s Italianate villa that's just as much a work of art as the pieces it contains. It displays fine Native American works, and classic and contemporary international art.

Northwest of downtown, the superb **Gilcrease Museum** *(gilcrease.org)* is another gem in Tulsa's cultural crown, but it's undergoing a huge renovation and reconstruction project and is

EATING IN TULSA: OUR PICKS ON ROUTE 66

Tally's Good Food Cafe: Let the neon signs lure you into this bustling chrome-and-vinyl diner dishing up Americana on a plate. *6am-11pm* $

Ike's Chili: Serving chili for more than 110 years. Get it straight, in a Frito pie (a Midwest fave), or atop a hot dog, fries or spaghetti. *10am-2:30pm Mon-Sat* $

Mother Road Market: This sprawling food hall attracts joyous groups who feast on the plethora of creative offerings. *11am-9pm Tue-Sun* $

Wildflower Cafe: A brunch staple with made-from-scratch waffles, biscuits and gravy, and a line out the door on weekends. *7am-3pm* $

Meadow Gold sign

set to open in fall 2026. It's named for Thomas Gilcrease of the Muscogee (Creek) Nation, who discovered oil on his allotment.

Pawhuska

Hear Osage stories

The Hollywood spotlight shone on the Osage Nation (Ni Okašką, 'People of the Middle Waters') in a big way with the 2023 release of *Killers of the Flower Moon*, detailing the true story of a series of murders after oil was discovered on their reservation. The town of Pawhuska was the center of the movie's production. Its historic main street, Kihekah Ave, was covered in dirt, and the old brick storefronts were restored to their original looks, traces of which remain. Stop for a 'cowboy coffee' (dark roast with sarsaparilla syrup) or a bite to eat at **Pioneer Woman Mercantile** *(themercantile.com)*, started by Food Network star Ree Drummond.

At the **Osage Nation Visitors Center** *(osageculture.com; closed Sat & Sun)*, staff can help you plan your visit, and you can browse a few history and art exhibits. The small **Osage Nation Museum** *(free; closed Sun & Mon)* is in an old stone chapel and is the country's oldest tribal museum.

Get a sense of the land's majestic sweep and what many Osage must have seen at the **Joseph H Williams Tallgrass Prairie**

BEST OKLAHOMA FESTIVALS

Red Earth Festival: A three-day celebration of Native culture in OKC, with an art market, tribal dance performances and a powwow in March. *(redearth.org)*

Paseo Arts Festival: This late-May event shows off the galleries and restaurants of its namesake neighborhood in OKC. *(thepaseo.org)*

Fried Onion Burger Day Festival: Watch the world's largest fried onion burger – 850lb – get cooked, and feast on this Depression-era classic in El Reno in May. *(facebook.com/elrenoburgerday)*

Tulsa Juneteenth Festival: Experience this federal holiday that marks the end of slavery in Greenwood (p76), Tulsa's Black Wall Street, with food trucks, vendors and games. *(tulsajuneteenth.org)*

DRINKING IN TULSA: OUR PICKS

American Solera: Sip award-winning craft beer in this brewery's laid-back industrial-mod space. *4-9pm Mon-Thu, noon-10pm Fri & Sat, to 6pm Sun*

Soundpony Lounge: A sticker-covered dive bar par excellence with welcoming bartenders, live music and karaoke nights. *3pm-2am*

Saturn Room: Find the 'tropics of Tulsa' at this adorable tiki bar with a light-strung patio. It pours knock-out drinks with just the right amount of rum and fire. *4pm–2am*

Pump Bar: A 1960s gas station morphed into a kitschy vintage bar with great drinks and snacks like 'trashy tots.' *11am-10pm Tue-Thu & Sun, to midnight Fri & Sat*

Preserve *(nature.org; free)*, the world's largest remaining protected area of its kind that's home to 2500 free-range bison. Enthusiastic staff can talk you through the nature exhibits in the small visitor center, and you can get out into nature on three looped hiking trails, ranging from a half-mile to 2 miles.

TRAIL OF TEARS

In the 1830s, white farmers in the southeastern US wanted to expand onto land occupied by more than 125,000 Native people. President Andrew Jackson used the army to remove tribes from their homelands and forced them to walk upwards of 1000 miles to Indian Territory, present-day Oklahoma.

Tens of thousands of people from the Cherokee, Chickasaw, Choctaw, Muscogee (Creek) and Seminole nations – the 'five civilized tribes' – made the journeys. A third are thought to have died along the way. Don't miss the **Five Civilized Tribes Museum** *(fivetribes.org; adult/child $6/3)* in Muskogee or the many museums in **Tahlequah**, the capital of the Cherokee Nation since 1839.

Oklahoma City

Myths and truths about the American West

Oklahoma has the highest proportion of Native people of any state (14.2% of residents), and the **First Americans Museum** *(famok.org; adult/child $15/5; closed Tue)* tells the stories of the 39 tribes that call this place home – many because of forced government migration along the Trail of Tears. With a collection largely sourced from the storage rooms of the Smithsonian's National Museum of the American Indian in Washington, DC, this museum, opened in 2021, is perhaps the best Native cultural institution in the country. The 2nd floor shows off the Smithsonian's goods, on long-term loan and returned to Oklahoma for the first time in a century, while the ground floor details the long history of Native life on this land, moving through deceitful US government 'deals' and laws, and into the present, explaining it all from a Native perspective in evocative multimedia displays. Outside, the free-to-visit 90ft-high mound is reminiscent of Cahokia in Illinois, and one of the three daily docent-led tours heads there. Save time for a meal made with traditional ingredients, such as bison, chokecherries and hominy, at **Thirty-Nine Restaurant**, the museum's on-site eatery, helmed by Loretta Barrett Oden, a member of the Citizen Potawatomi Nation.

Native history is often overshadowed by white cowboys and romantic – and unrealistic – Westerns, but the **National Cowboy and Western Heritage Museum** *(nationalcowboymuseum.org; adult/child $20/12)* does a more multifaceted deep dive into this background. It has some displays of Native artifacts, along with an excellent collection of historic and contemporary paintings and sculptures depicting life in the West, including works by underrepresented Native and female artists. Kids love walking through the mock cow town and running amok in the huge outdoor playground with recreated Native cliff dwellings, tipis and sod houses.

Get a combination ticket to visit both museums for $30, saving $5.

Remembering the 1995 OKC bombing

The story of the United States' worst incident of domestic terrorism is laid out in sobering hour-by-hour detail at the poignant **Oklahoma City National Memorial and Museum** *(memorialmuseum.com; adult/child $18/15)*. Outside is a free-to-visit area with 168 empty chair sculptures, one for each of the people killed in the attack; the 19 small ones are for the children who perished in the daycare center.

Park at the Memorial Parking Garage at the northeast corner of 6th and Harvey for free parking with a museum ticket purchase.

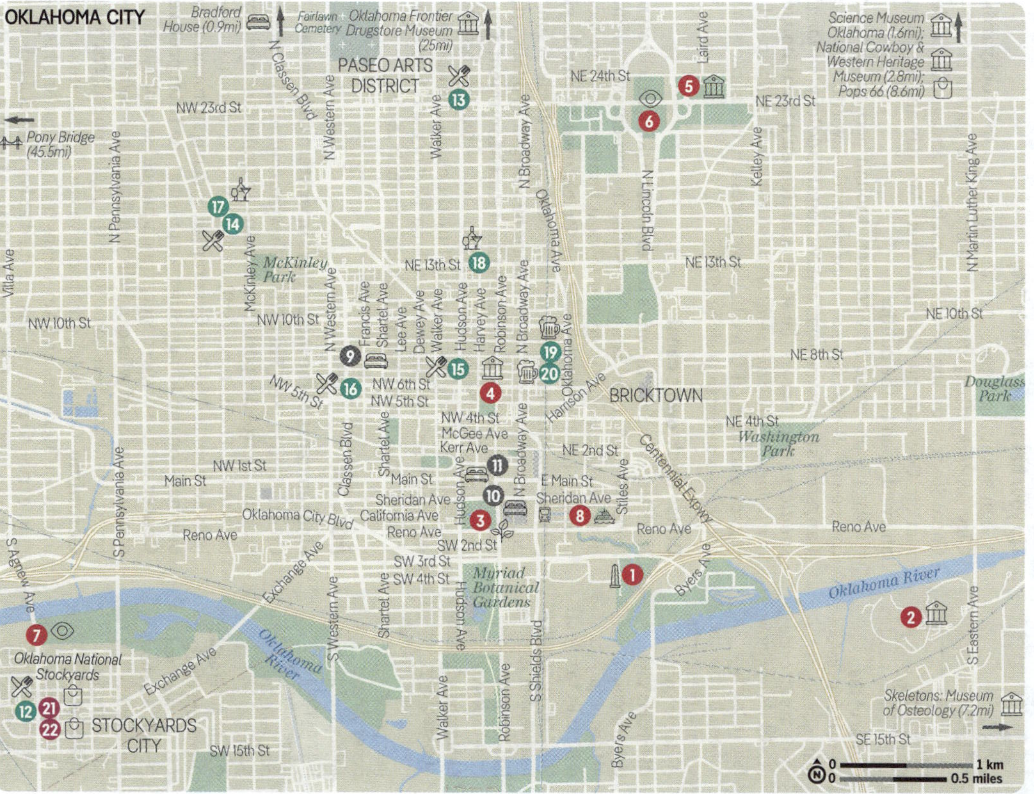

SIGHTS

1 Centennial Land Run Monument
2 First Americans Museum
3 Myriad Botanical Gardens
4 Oklahoma City National Memorial & Museum
5 Oklahoma History Center
6 Oklahoma State Capitol
7 Stockyards City

ACTIVITIES

8 Bricktown Water Taxi

SLEEPING

9 Classen Inn
10 Colcord Hotel
11 The National

EATING

12 Cattlemen's Steakhouse
13 Cheever's Cafe
14 Ma Der Lao Kitchen
15 Nonesuch
16 Sunnyside Diner

DRINKING & NIGHTLIFE

17 Good for a Few
18 Later Bye
19 Prairie Artisan Ales
20 Skydance Brewing Co

SHOPPING

21 Langston's
22 National Saddlery

ODDBALL OKLAHOMA

Center of the Universe: It's said that noise made inside this 8ft circle of bricks in downtown Tulsa is loudly echoed, but people standing outside the circle can't hear it.

Oklahoma City Underground: Art and history exhibits line a mile of color-coded corridors below downtown OKC. *(downtownokc.com/underground)*

Skeletons: Museum of Osteology: Flesh-eating beetles help prepare the bones of dead animals for a new life on display. *(skeletonmuseum.com; adult/child $14/12)*

Oklahoma Frontier Drugstore Museum: A kooky museum in Guthrie that shows the remedies (like jars of leeches) offered at an Old West pharmacy. *(drugmuseum.org; adult/child $5/4)*

Tip your hat to Stockyards City

A sign spanning Agnew Ave welcomes you to **Stockyards City** *(stockyardscity.org)*, still home to the Oklahoma National Stockyards, the world's largest feeder and stocker cattle market. Cows are auctioned off every Monday and Tuesday, an event open to the public.

Most people come here to shop, though perhaps not for live cows – Western-wear shops abound. Favorites include **Langston's** *(langstons.com)* and **National Saddlery** *(nationalsaddlery.com)*. Across the street, **Cattlemen's Steakhouse** *(cattlemensrestaurant.com)* is the oldest continually operating restaurant in OKC, feeding cowpokes and city slickers big breakfasts and steaks since 1910.

Cruise Bricktown's canal

Modeled after San Antonio's **River Walk**, OKC's **Bricktown** *(bricktownokc.com)* is an industrial-turned-entertainment district. Much of it is geared toward families and can feel touristy, but it's worth a wander. **Bricktown Water Taxi** *(bricktownwatertaxi.com; adult/child $15/12)* runs hour-long boat trips on the canal past historic buildings and public art, culminating at the **Centennial Land Run Monument**. Covering the size of a football field, 45 larger-than-life bronze horsemen and wagon drivers capture the chaos and drama of the 1889 land rush that settled a large part of the future state – and dispossessed Native people from their lands.

Fort Sill

Find remnants of the Indian Wars in western Oklahoma

Constructed in 1869, **Fort Sill** *(sill-www.army.mil; free; closed Sun)* was a frontier post that remains an important military base today. The history is still on display for visitors, particularly around the Old Post Quadrangle, which is surrounded by original stone buildings. Start your visit at the **Interpretive Center** on its southern side, which has old-school museum displays and staff who can help you find other points of interest. Many travelers come to see the eagle-topped **grave of Geronimo** (Goyahkla), an Apache warrior and shaman who fought the Mexicans and Americans trying to confine his nomadic tribe to reservations. He died at Fort Sill as a prisoner of war in 1909. The **US Army Artillery Museum** is another draw for those interested in historic and modern weaponry.

EATING IN OKC: OUR PICKS

Nonesuch: Slide into one of just 22 seats for a foodie adventure in Oklahoma flavors via a multicourse tasting menu. *5:30-9pm Tue-Sat* **$$$**

Ma Der Lao Kitchen: A Laotian restaurant in OKC? Yes, and a damn good one, too. The crispy rice salad is a must-order. *11am-10pm Tue-Thu, to 11pm Fri & Sat* **$$**

Cheever's Cafe: Upscale cafe in an art deco former flower shop with excellent Southwestern-style fare. *11am-9pm Mon-Thu, to 10pm Fri-Sun* **$$**

Sunnyside Diner: This cheerful cheapie doles out the best breakfasts in town, from fresh blueberry pancakes to Okie poutine. *6am-2pm* **$**

ZACK FRANK/SHUTTERSTOCK

Bison, Wichita Mountains Wildlife Refuge

Fort Sill is still an active Army base, so visitors without a Department of Defense license require a background check before entering. Speed up the process by giving your details on the Visitor Pre-Registration System online in advance. Non-US citizens aren't allowed on base unless they know someone stationed there.

Wichita Mountains

Hiking and wildlife-watching off the grid

West of Oklahoma City, the state opens into expansive prairies, nowhere as beautifully as in the Wichita Mountains. The 59,020-acre **Wichita Mountains Wildlife Refuge** *(fws.gov/refuge/wichita-mountains; free)* protects bison, elk, longhorn cattle and prairie dogs.

Displays at the **visitor center** highlight the refuge's flora and fauna, and it has large picture windows for views of prairie grasslands. For elevated views, drive to the top of **Mt Scott**, the highest peak in the refuge at 2464ft. For a short but scenic hike, try the **Kite Trail**, which climbs above the West Cache Creek and has access points to small waterfalls. Your best bet for food and accommodations is in **Medicine Park**.

MORE OKC ATTRACTIONS

Myriad Botanical Gardens: Elaborate landscapes with thousands of plants right in the city center. The IM Pei–designed conservatory holds a tropical wonderland. *(myriadgardens.org; grounds free, conservatory adult/child $10.50/5.50)*

Oklahoma State Capitol: Built in 1917, the Capitol building has stained-glass windows, rotating art exhibits and even on-site oil wells. Free walk-up tours at 11am and 1pm weekdays.

Science Museum Oklahoma: Family-friendly galleries filled with planes, dinos and a planetarium *(sciencemuseumok.org; adult/child $23/18)*.

Oklahoma History Center: Focuses on the people of the Sooner State through interactive exhibits; good Native galleries *(adult/child $12.50/9)*.

DRINKING IN OKC: OUR PICKS

Prairie Artisan Ales: Craft-beer spot run by a fourth-generation brewer in the Automobile Alley district. Bomb, a stout, is its flagship pint. *11am-10pm*

Skydance Brewing Co: Only 0.4% of craft breweries are Native-owned, and Skydance showcases Indigenous stories. *noon-10pm Sun-Thu, to midnight Fri & Sat*

Good for a Few: Magic mixologists pour incredible creations in this moody cocktail bar, semi-hidden in a burger restaurant. *4pm-midnight Wed-Sat*

Later Bye: This cozy 31-seat neighborhood cocktail bar can do no wrong. Pair drinks with Italian or Spanish small plates. *3pm-midnight Mon-Thu, to 1am Fri & Sat*

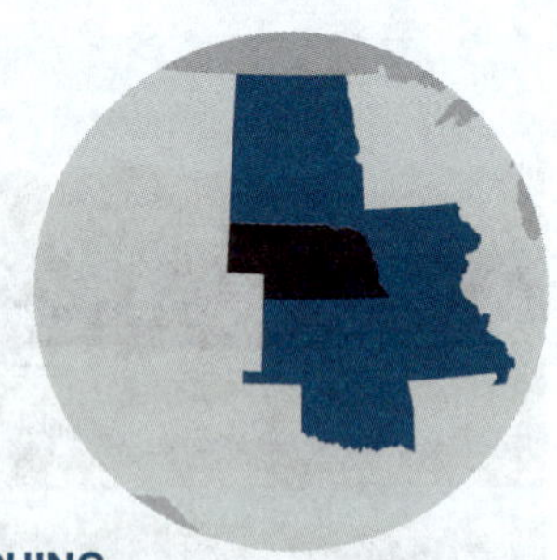

Nebraska

PIONEER TRAILS | FRONTIER FORTS | BIRD-WATCHING

Places

TOP TIP

Nebraska ranks second in the country (after Texas) as the state raising the most cattle, so if you're an omnivore, sampling the steak is a must. Committee Chophouse (p88) in Omaha is a top pick. Its summer-only 'steak flights' offer four perfectly prepared slabs sourced from Nebraska ranches.

Travelers have traversed Nebraska for millennia: Native tribes; transcontinental settlers coming by covered wagon, railroad and automobile on the USA's first country-belting routes; thousands-strong flocks of sandhill cranes on their seasonal migration; and dinosaurs and other extinct prehistoric wildlife. You can still follow their trails, but do more than just make tire tracks through the Cornhusker State.

Alongside the state's sprinkling of cute towns, Nebraska's two main cities are culture-driven and artful. Omaha, the state's biggest urban center, is home to the brick-street Old Market district of revamped warehouses, a booming riverfront, and several museums and family-friendly attractions. Just an hour's drive away, the state capital of Lincoln is anything but stuffy, thanks to the students at the University of Nebraska who know how to have a good time.

Nature calls in the remote Nebraska Panhandle, where stark rock formations stand sentinel over the prairie, and in the lush Niobrara Valley, a federally protected scenic river.

GETTING AROUND

You need a car to get around Nebraska. I-80 is the state's main access point by car, and Nebraska's biggest cities are dotted along it.

The interstate allows you to zip across Nebraska for 455 miles at 75mph, but the real way to enjoy the countryside is to take the smaller roads. Some I-80 alternatives include US 6 between Omaha and Lincoln, US 30 between Omaha and Grand Island, and US 34 between Grand Island and Lincoln. US 30, the Lincoln Hwy, is particularly historic. Opened in 1913, it was the first transcontinental highway specifically for cars.

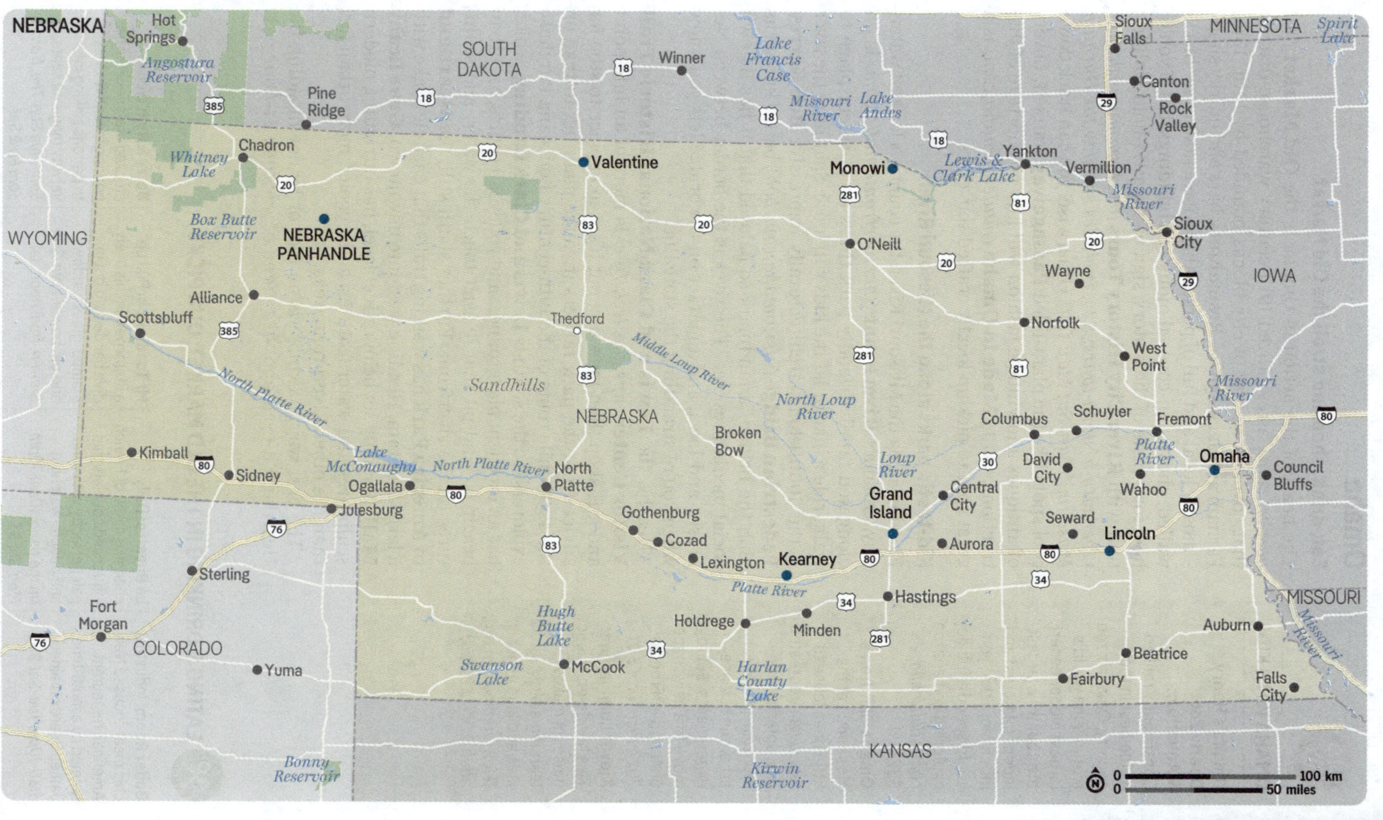
NEBRASKA
Hot Springs
Angostura Reservoir
SOUTH DAKOTA
Winner
Lake Francis Case
Missouri River
Lake Andes
Sioux Falls
MINNESOTA
Spirit Lake
Canton
Rock Valley
Pine Ridge
Chadron
Whitney Lake
Valentine
Monowi
Lewis & Clark Lake
Yankton
Vermillion
Missouri River
Box Butte Reservoir
NEBRASKA PANHANDLE
WYOMING
Sioux City
O'Neill
Wayne
IOWA
Alliance
Scottsbluff
Thedford
Middle Loup River
Norfolk
West Point
Sandhills
North Loup River
Missouri River
North Platte River
NEBRASKA
Broken Bow
Columbus
Schuyler
Fremont
Platte River
Omaha
Council Bluffs
Kimball
Sidney
Lake McConaughy
North Platte River
North Platte
Ogallala
Loup River
David City
Wahoo
Grand Island
Central City
Julesburg
Gothenburg
Cozad
Seward
Lincoln
Aurora
Lexington
Kearney
Sterling
Platte River
Hastings
MISSOURI
Fort Morgan
Hugh Butte Lake
Holdrege
Minden
Auburn
COLORADO
Missouri River
Yuma
Swanson Lake
McCook
Harlan County Lake
Beatrice
Fairbury
Falls City
KANSAS
Bonny Reservoir
Kirwin Reservoir
100 km
50 miles

OMAHA WITH KIDS

Omaha's Henry Doorly Zoo & Aquarium: Consistently ranked as the best in the country, Omaha's zoo features the world's largest indoor desert, the country's largest indoor rainforest and much more that you could spend a full day exploring. *(omahazoo.com; adult/child $32/25)*

Omaha Children's Museum: Let the little ones loose to take over a recreated city, splash in the fountains, create art or run science experiments. Set to move to a new space on the RiverFront in 2027. *(ocm.org; $17)*

Kiewit Luminarium: This hands-on science museum makes learning a blast for kids and kids at heart. *(kiewitluminarium.org; adult/child $25/20)*

Omaha

Eat, drink, shop and stroll the Old Market

The heart of the action in Omaha is the **Old Market** *(oldmarket.com)*, a revitalized 19th-century warehouse district that covers a square of city blocks bounded by 10th, 13th, Farnam and Jackson Sts. Restaurants, bars and quirky shops – mostly local and full of personality – have taken over brick-walled, ghost-sign-covered industrial buildings, but if you're here for a taste of the history, sign up for a 1½-hour walking tour with **River City History Tours** *(durhammuseum.org/river-city-history-tours; $26, includes entry to the Durham Museum; 10am Sat May-Oct)*. Otherwise, you can track down cool spots like the plant-filled **Passageway** yourself. Lovers of antiques and vintage fashion will find no shortage of distractions, while **Made in Omaha** *(madeinomaha.com)* is a great spot to pick up locally crafted souvenirs.

Kid-tastic parks along the Missouri River

Flowing along the Missouri River, the country's longest waterway, Omaha's **RiverFront** *(theriverfrontomaha.com)* is an elongated family-friendly park that's an excellent place to walk, ride a bike or let the kids run loose. Spanning the river is the 3000ft-long, architecturally impressive **Bob Kerrey Pedestrian Bridge** *(visitomaha.com/bob)*, better known as 'Bob the Bridge,' a landmark so beloved that it has its own social media presence. The river is the border between Nebraska and Iowa, and a marker on the bridge lets you know when you're straddling the state line.

Nearby, the **Lewis and Clark National Historic Trail Visitor Center** *(nps.gov/lecl; free)* is more of an info point and gift shop than museum, but it's a good place to stop for advice from the park rangers if you're planning to take on the 4900-mile route of the 19th-century Louisiana Purchase explorers. To the south is **Lewis and Clark Landing**, which has an excellent playground, sand volleyball courts, an 'urban beach' (a sand pit that doesn't touch the water) and sculptures on the riverfront. Further south still, the **Heartland of America Park** has walking trails that encircle a lake with a large fountain. Heading west into downtown, **Gene Leahy Mall**, partially set below street level, has intriguing modern sculptures and water features, and a cooler, more urban feel than the other RiverFront areas.

The best way to explore is on foot or by downloading the Heartland B-cycle app *(heartland.bcycle.com; 24-hour pass*

EATING & DRINKING IN THE OLD MARKET: OUR PICKS

Boiler Room: Industrial chic meat-focused New American restaurant helmed by a multi-time James Beard nominee. *5:30-10pm Tue-Sat* **$$$**

La Buvette: Daily changing menu of French-influenced specials that pair perfectly with wine and people-watching on the patio. *10am-10pm Mon-Sat* **$$**

Mr Toad's Pub: Pull up a literal pew in this lively dive bar decked out in stained-glass windows and old books. *2pm-2am Sun-Fri, from noon Sat*

Berry & Rye: Well-stocked craft cocktail bar pouring inventive drinks to patrons sinking into velvety magenta seats. *5pm-2am Sun-Thu, from 3pm Fri & Sat*

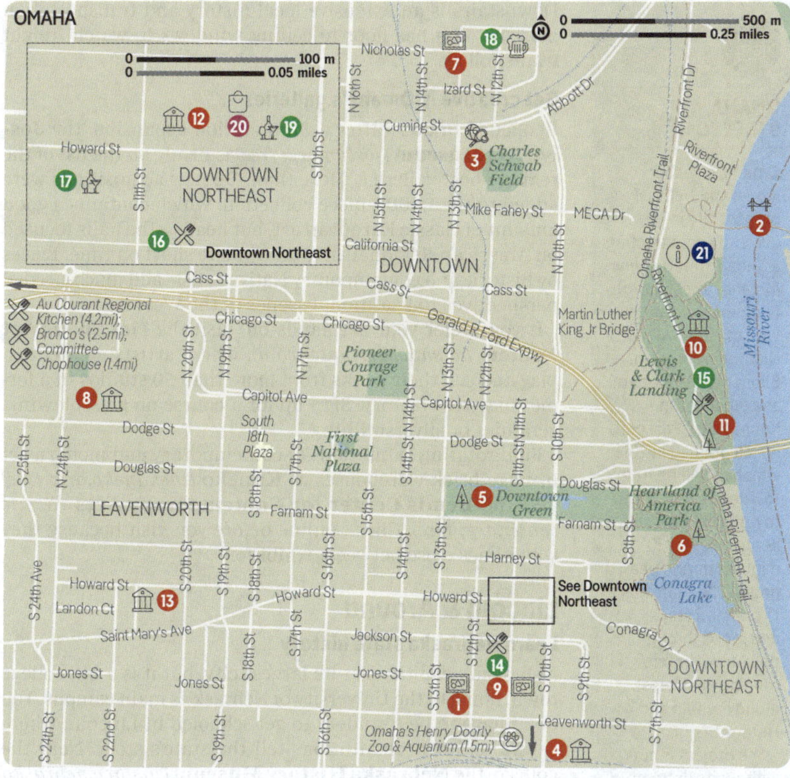

SIGHTS

1 Bemis Center for Contemporary Arts
2 Bob Kerrey Pedestrian Bridge
3 Charles Schwab Field
4 Durham Museum
5 Gene Leahy Mall
6 Heartland of America Park
7 Hot Shops Art Center
8 Joslyn Art Museum
9 Kaneko
10 Kiewit Luminarium
11 Lewis & Clark Landing
12 Old Market Passageway
13 Omaha Children's Museum

EATING

14 Boiler Room
15 Fig
16 La Buvette

DRINKING & NIGHTLIFE

17 Berry & Rye
18 Kros Strain Draft Works
19 Mr Toad's Pub

SHOPPING

20 Made in Omaha

INFORMATION

21 Lewis & Clark National Historic Trail Visitor Center

$16.05) and checking out one of the docked e-bikes. Bicycles are allowed in most RiverFront areas, while e-scooters are not. Fuel up first at **Fig** *(figomaha.com)*, a sun-filled cafe overlooking the river.

All aboard for history at the Durham Museum

Though trains no longer stop here, Omaha's soaring art deco Union Station, now the **Durham Museum** *(durhammuseum.org; adult/child $15/8)*, is a sight to behold with its cathedral windows, geometric chandeliers, ornate ceilings and reliefs of railroad workers carved into the facade. Admire it from the old-school soda fountain while drinking a phosphate pop.

OMAHA STREETCAR

Omaha is on the move, and Nebraska's biggest city is currently constructing a 3-mile streetcar line *(omahastreetcar.org)* to connect downtown with the Blackstone District in Midtown. Similar to the modern streetcar line in Kansas City, Missouri, which opened in 2016, Omaha's will be free to ride. It's scheduled to open in 2028, with services every 10 minutes during peak hours. The route has 13 planned stops and loops through downtown before running east–west along Farnam and Harney Sts.

The project is not without its detractors, including Warren Buffett, Omaha's most famous resident and the fifth-richest man in the world, who said that the $306 million plan is too expensive and that residents deserved to vote on it.

Downstairs is an extensive local history and transportation museum that has floor-to-ceiling windows to watch freight trains roll by.

Get creative in Omaha's galleries

Reopened in 2024 after a $100 million expansion, the **Joslyn Art Museum** *(joslyn.org; free)* is firmly on the list of the region's best galleries. More than 100 new acquisitions were added to the 12,000-piece collection, which contains a good amount of classic European art, but head to the halls focused on American Regionalism first if you're short on time. Pieces by historic and contemporary Native artists add much-needed perspectives to traditional scenes of the West.

If you prefer your art hands-on, visit the **Hot Shops Art Center** *(hotshopsartcenter.com)*, where artists create, display and sell their works from more than 50 studios in a former mattress factory. Sign up for a course on glassblowing, ceramics or silversmithing.

Find rotating exhibitions of contemporary and modern art in huge brick warehouses at **Kaneko** *(thekaneko.org; free)* and the **Bemis Center for Contemporary Arts** *(bemiscenter.org; free)*. Check online before you visit because they sometimes close between exhibitions.

Lincoln & Around

Learn Nebraska state history

Nebraska's capital isn't its largest city, but it is a big college town, home to the University of Nebraska's main campus. You don't have to be a student to get schooled in Lincoln, where several cultural institutions tell the state's story. Near the college, the **Nebraska History Museum** *(history.nebraska.gov/museum; adult/child $5/3; closed Sun and Mon)* begins the narrative 13,000 years ago, and its three floors of displays carry on to the present.

Less than a mile south, the 400ft-high **Nebraska State Capitol** *(capitol.nebraska.gov; free)* is architectural eye candy. Completed in 1932, its art deco interiors could be mistaken for a soaring cathedral. For deeper insights, join the free guided tours that depart from the north end of the 2nd floor on the hour *(9am-4pm Mon-Fri, from 10am Sat, from 1pm Sun)*, or you can wander up on your own to the 14th-floor observation deck.

EATING & DRINKING IN OMAHA: OUR PICKS

Committee Chophouse: The summertime 'steak flight' from Nebraska ranches is an indulgent treat at this suave, low-lit steakhouse. *5-10pm* **$$$**

Bronco's: Classic 1950s local fast-food joint with an iconic neon sign. Burgers are made from state-sourced ground beef. *9am-10pm* **$**

Au Courant Regional Kitchen: Farm-fresh artful plates of New European cuisine in the Benson neighborhood west of downtown. *5-10pm Thu-Sun* **$$**

Kros Strain Draft Works: Sip the flagship Fairy Nectar IPA inside the industrial taproom in a former furniture warehouse or on the patio. *hours vary; closed Mon*

Joslyn Art Museum

Back to school at UNL

The University of Nebraska has its main campus in the middle of Lincoln. Nebraska doesn't have any major-league sports teams, so everyone in the state pins their hopes on the Huskers. In fall, football games kick off at **Memorial Stadium** *(huskers.com)*, and the 85,000 seats often sell out.

A pigskin throw away, the **University of Nebraska State Museum** *(museum.unl.edu; adult/child $12.50/6.75; closed Mon)* has fascinating, though somewhat dated, displays of dinos, many of which were found in the Agate Fossil Beds (p91) in the Nebraska Panhandle. The museum's icon is Archie, the world's largest Columbian mammoth skeleton, which stands 15½ft tall. The newer top-floor Cherish Nebraska exhibit details the state's ecology and changing environment.

On the East Campus, agriculture majors hand-make and sell cheese and ice cream at the **UNL Dairy Store** *(dairystore.unl.edu)*. Cones come in more than a dozen delicious seasonal flavors, including sweet corn and white chocolate lavender.

MORE ATTRACTIONS IN & AROUND LINCOLN

International Quilt Museum: Elevates the humble quilt to an exquisite art form. *(internationalquiltmuseum.org; adult/child $8/4)*

Sunken Gardens: In the 1930s, a former neighborhood dump was transformed into this pocket park.

Lincoln Children's Museum: Kids can run free in this 23,000-sq-ft space with prairie dog–style tunnels, a three-story climbing structure and even a miniature Runza (p90). *(lincolnchildrensmuseum.org; adult/child $13/16)*

Strategic Air Command & Aerospace Museum: Massive hangars contain an example of every significant US bomber, from the B-17 to the B-52. Between Lincoln and Omaha on I-80. *(sacmuseum.org; adult/child $12/6)*

EATING & DRINKING IN LINCOLN: OUR PICKS

Dish: Lincoln's top restaurant presents inventive New American seasonal plates with locally sourced ingredients. *5-8:30pm or later Tue-Sat* $$

Hub Cafe: This creative cafe is a brunch-time favorite, best enjoyed from the sunny, park-facing seats. *7:30am-9pm Tue-Sat, to 2:30pm Sun* $

Other Room: Perhaps the best cocktail bar in the state hides behind a heavy metal door in the historic Haymarket district. *5pm-1am*

Boiler Brewing Co: A highly awarded former homebrewer now pours pints, often high-ABV, for the thirsty public. *3-10pm Mon-Thu, noon-midnight Fri & Sat, to 8pm Sun*

RUNZA

Nebraska's most iconic food is the runza, a rectangle of yeast-dough bread filled with ground beef and onions. This meaty sandwich was brought to the US by 19th-century Volga German immigrants who settled in Nebraska and Kansas (where the dish is called bierock).

The ubiquitous fast-food chain called Runza is the easiest place to try one. The first Runza opened in Lincoln in 1949, and though the original restaurant no longer exists, more than 80 other locations have popped up around the state, as well as a handful in Colorado, Iowa, Kansas and South Dakota. The classic flavor is still on the menu, but you can also order versions with mushroom and Swiss cheese, barbecue and bacon, or Southwest ranch and taco seasoning.

Pioneers on the prairie

The Homestead Act of 1862 forever altered the landscape and demographics of the western US territories, converting public land (which was Native land before the Indian Removal Act of 1830) to private ownership. Immigrants, formerly enslaved people, women and anyone else who could farm 160 acres for five years got the land cheap in exchange for back-breaking work.

The first plot of land claimed through the Homestead Act is now encompassed by **Homestead National Historical Park** *(nps.gov/home; free)*, 45 miles south of Lincoln. Start at the **Heritage Center**, which puts the Homestead Act into context, and then head outside to visit the **gravesite of Daniel Freeman**, said to have filed his homestead claim 10 minutes after midnight on the day the Act went into effect. None of the Freeman family's buildings still exist, but the 1867 **Palmer-Epard Cabin** behind the Heritage Center is from the era, originally constructed about 14 miles away. The Heritage Center closes at 5pm daily, but the trails around it through the tallgrass prairie are open until dusk.

Grand Island & Kearney

The changing face of the West

For an engaging look at the lives of the homesteaders, head to the **Stuhr Museum** *(stuhrmuseum.org; adult/child $14/12)* in Grand Island. More than 60 buildings from the 1800s were moved to this huge outdoor living-history museum, where reenactors in period dress feed the farm goats, work in the blacksmith shop and roam the wooden boardwalks. The museum gives a nod to the land's original inhabitants with a Pawnee Earth Lodge and a small bison enclosure.

Witness the sandhill crane migration

During their spring migration (mid-February to early April), more than 500,000 sandhill cranes – 80% of the world population – touch down along 80 miles of the Platte River in central Nebraska in one of the country's most spectacular wildlife events. Just off I-80 southwest of Grand Island, the **Crane Trust Nature and Visitor Center** *(cranetrust.org; closed Sun)* runs migration season tours on foot and by bus. East of Kearney, the **Iain Nicolson Audubon Center at Rowe Sanctuary** *(rowe.audubon.org; closed Sun and Mon)* also puts on guided tours. Reserve tours in advance; bookings open in January.

EATING & DRINKING IN GRAND ISLAND & KEARNEY: OUR PICKS

Coney Island Lunch Room: Old-school diner in downtown Grand Island offering hot dogs, burgers and malts. *8:30am-5pm Mon-Fri, to 3pm Sat* $

Archives: 2024-opened speakeasy below the tourism office in a historic building in Grand Island's adorable downtown. *4-11pm Thu, 6pm-1am Fri, from 1pm Sat*

Cunningham's Journal: Laid-back spot in downtown Kearney with a lengthy menu of pub grub and local beer. *11am-1am Mon-Sat, to midnight Sun* $$

Platte Valley Taphouse: The place to go for good IPAs and pizza in Kearney. Eat, drink and play cornhole in the beer garden. *3-11pm Mon-Wed, 1pm-1am Thu-Sat*

ZACK FRANK/SHUTTERSTOCK

Agate Fossil Beds National Monument

Outside migration season, both free-to-see visitor centers welcome travelers with informational displays and riverfront hiking trails to spot other waterfowl.

Converging trails around Kearney

The first outpost established to protect travelers on the California and Oregon Trails, the 1848 **Fort Kearny** *(outdoornebraska.gov/fortkearny; per vehicle $14, visitor center adult/child $5/1)* still sits among lonesome prairie about 9 miles southeast of Kearney. Today's two 1960s reconstructions are a little disappointing, but if you're here during the sandhill crane migration season, the park is a good place to see the birds.

To get a bigger-picture view of the trails under your feet, visit the **Archway** *(archway.org; adult/child $15/7)*, a museum that bends over the top of I-80 east of Kearney. An audio device leads you through hand-painted exhibits that you might think would border on hokey given the location of this attraction, but they actually do a decent job of telling colorful tales about the people who've passed this way, from pioneers in covered wagon trains to drivers zipping down the interstate.

Connect with Nebraska art

For a cultural stop in Kearney, check out the small but mighty **Museum of Nebraska Art** *(mona.unk.edu; free; closed Mon)*, the state's official art gallery. It's half set in modern premises that reopened in May 2025 after a four-year, $36.5-million expansion, and half in a neoclassical 1911 post office. Nearly two centuries of artwork, predating statehood, trace Nebraska's visual history through the creations of artists who were born, lived or worked in the state.

ROAD TRIP STOPS IN WESTERN NEBRASKA

Pony Express Station: Original log-built 1860 Pony Express stop in Gothenburg. *(ponyexpressstation.org; free)*

Buffalo Bill Ranch State Historical Park: Tour the home of Bill Cody, the father of rodeo and the famed Buffalo Bill's Wild West Show that ran for 30 years from 1883. *(park pass per vehicle $14, plus mansion tour adult/child $5/1)*

Carhenge: A faithful Stonehenge replica made of 39 wrecked cars. Kooky roadside art at its finest, 3 miles north of Alliance. *(carhenge.com; free)*

Agate Fossil Beds National Monument: Some 20 million years ago, this part of Nebraska was like the Serengeti in Africa today: a gathering place for a rich variety of creatures, now fossilized. *(nps.gov/agfo; free)*

HISTORIC TRAILS THROUGH NEBRASKA

Oregon Trail (1846–69): Nearly half a million settlers traveled this 2170-mile route in the largest voluntary mass migrations in human history.

California Trail (1841–69): Few settlers took to this 1600-mile trail until 1848, when gold was discovered near Sacramento, California.

Mormon Trail (1846–69): Fleeing religious persecution, members of the Church of Jesus Christ of Latter-day Saints packed up their lives in Illinois and made the journey to Utah, then not part of the United States.

Pony Express (1860–61): Express mail on horseback cut down the time to receive a message to 10 days. Operational for only 18 months before the telegraph took over.

Nebraska Panhandle

See iconic rock formations on the prairie

The remote and little-visited Nebraska Panhandle is perhaps the most evocative part of the state. Stark vistas stretch to the horizon in lands little changed in millennia, and rocky bluffs that can be seen from miles around rise out of the prairie.

At **Chimney Rock National Historic Site** *(history.nebraska.gov/rock)*, a 300ft-tall stone spire was so striking to travelers on the Oregon, California and Mormon Trails that it's estimated that 97% of pioneers mentioned it in their journals. The small **Chimney Rock Museum** *(adult/child $8/4; 9am-4pm)* has updated displays but isn't worth the admission fee. Instead, set off on the easy 2-mile loop trail *(free; dawn-dusk)* that gets closer to the base of the formation.

About 25 miles northwest, **Scotts Bluff National Monument** *(nps.gov/scbl; free)* was another important waypoint on the pioneer trails. The **visitor center** *(8am-6pm mid-May–Aug, to 4:30pm Sep–mid-May)* contains exhibits and the largest collection of original paintings and photos by William Henry Jackson, a Civil War veteran famous for his scenes of the American West. Walk in the footsteps of history on the mile-long **trail** *(dawn-dusk)* west of the visitor center, which follows the original path of the Oregon Trail and even has some swales – deep indentations in the dirt compressed by hundreds of thousands of wooden wagon wheels. Drive the **Summit Road** *(9am-5pm mid-May–Aug, to 4pm Sep–mid-May)* or hike the 3.2-mile **Saddle Rock Trail** to the top of the bluff for sweeping views.

War and peace at Fort Robinson State Park

The turbulent past of **Fort Robinson** *(outdoornebraska.gov/location/fort-robinson; per vehicle $14)* belies its peaceful atmosphere today. Guards killed Lakota chief Crazy Horse (Tȟašúŋke Witkó) here in 1877 when it served as the Red Cloud Indian Agency, brigades of Black troops known as Buffalo Soldiers were formed for the Civil War and it was a POW camp for Germans in WWII. Understand the complex history at the **Fort Robinson Museum** *(adult/child $5/3)*. Several of the old buildings are open to wander around, and you can even stay overnight in former officers' and soldiers' quarters from 1909. Bugle wake-up call not included.

EATING & DRINKING IN THE NEBRASKA PANHANDLE: OUR PICKS

Mixing Bowl: This Gering cafe's specials tap into the area's German immigrant history. *6am-3pm Wed-Fri, from 7am Sat & Sun* $

Gering Bakery: Fuel a day of hiking with doughnuts from this neon-signed spot in Gering, open since 1950. *5:30am-5:30pm Mon-Fri, to 1pm Sat* $

Flyover Brewing Company: Everyone in this attractive Scottsbluff brewery is enjoying a better brew (and view) than those at 40,000ft. *11am-11pm Tue-Sun*

Mark Ferrari Specialty Coffees: Find an unexpected taste of aloha in tiny Oshkosh, population 884. *8:30am-2pm Mon-Fri, to 12:30pm Sat*

ROBERT WALTMAN/SHUTTERSTOCK

Scotts Bluff National Monument

Valentine

Raft the Niobrara National Scenic River

Kayaking, canoeing or inner-tubing down the Niobrara (pronounced nigh-oh-BRAH-rah) draws scores of people to north-central Nebraska in summer. Sheer limestone bluffs, lush forests and more than 200 spring-fed waterfalls along the banks shatter any 'flat Nebraska' stereotypes.

Most float tours start from the town of Valentine. **Brewers Canoers and Tubers** *(brewerscanoers.com)* is one of the original outfitters in the area and was the first to introduce tubing on the Niobrara River. You can rent canoes, kayaks or tubes with them or arrange shuttles to and from launch and landing sites.

Monowi

Eat in Nebraska's smallest town

If you don't think a ghost town can have a strong sense of community, you haven't been to Monowi. Its lone resident is nonagenarian Elsie Eiler, who runs **Monowi Tavern** *(closed Mon)*. The bar and grill is a one-woman show, where Elsie cooks burgers, fries and steaks for a surprising number of customers. Her family has operated the tavern since 1971, and in addition to working as the cook and bartender, she's also Monowi's mayor. Farmers and people from all over the county sit down to catch up and share gossip, and travelers are welcomed just as warmly.

BEST NEBRASKA FESTIVALS

NCAA College World Series: The top Division I baseball teams head to Omaha's **Charles Schwab Field** every June. *(cwsomaha.com)*

Star City Pride: Lincoln turns rainbow with pride at this LGBTIQ+ parade in June. *(starcityprideevents.org)*

Kool-Aid Days: The sugary drink was invented in Hastings in 1927, and it's celebrated with boat races and a Kool-Aid drinking contest in August. *(kool-aiddays.com)*

Oregon Trail Days: In Gering, the state's oldest festival includes a street dance party and a chili cook-off. *(oregontraildays.com)*

Nebraska Star Party: Spy on the night sky in July at Merritt Reservoir, the state's only Dark Sky Park. *(nebraskastarparty.org)*

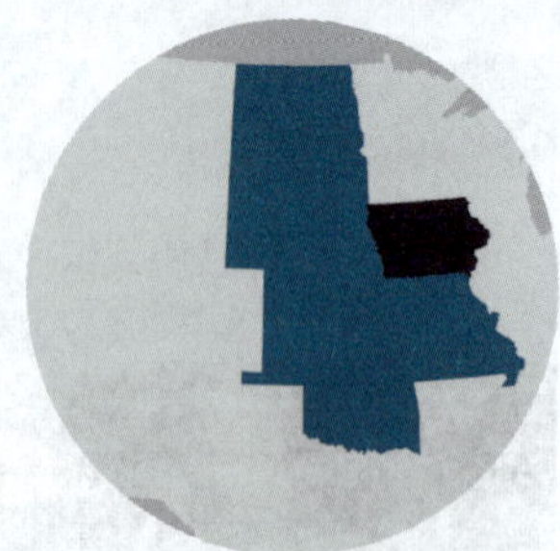

Iowa

HEARTLAND BEAUTY | FANTASTIC CYCLING | INNOVATIVE ARCHITECTURE

Places

TOP TIP

Get off the interstates and spend time on Iowa's backroads, which pass the farms and fields that comprise America's heartland. The state is home to 14 national and state scenic byways *(iowadot.gov)*, and you'll find at least one in every region. Slow down and soak up the pastoral beauty!

You'll come to appreciate the rumble strips that keep you alert while driving across Iowa's rural backroads, where miles and miles of fields and farmhouses cast a hypnotic spell – and stop signs pop up unexpectedly at lonely crossroads. Stretching east from the soaring Loess Hills across swaths of rolling farmland, the Hawkeye State packs in the pastoral beauty before bumping into bluffs along the Mississippi River. In the middle? The writers' town of Iowa City, the tradition-loving Amana Colonies, art-minded Des Moines and architecturally impressive Mason City. A network of biking trails link the state's picture-perfect towns.

Iowa emerges from slumber every four years as the make-or-break state for presidential hopefuls. The Iowa Caucus opens the national election battle, and wins by George W Bush in 2000 and Barack Obama in 2008 stunned many pundits and launched their victorious campaigns. Another statewide highlight is RAGBRAI, an annual multi-day bike ride that draws thousands of cyclists.

GETTING AROUND

You'll need a car to explore greater Iowa. I-80 runs east-west across the state, linking Des Moines with Chicago to the east and Omaha, NE, to the west. I-35 travels north–south, connecting Des Moines with Minneapolis to the north and Kansas City to the south. Iowa has a fantastic network of cycling trails, and they are a pretty option for exploring urban areas and beyond.

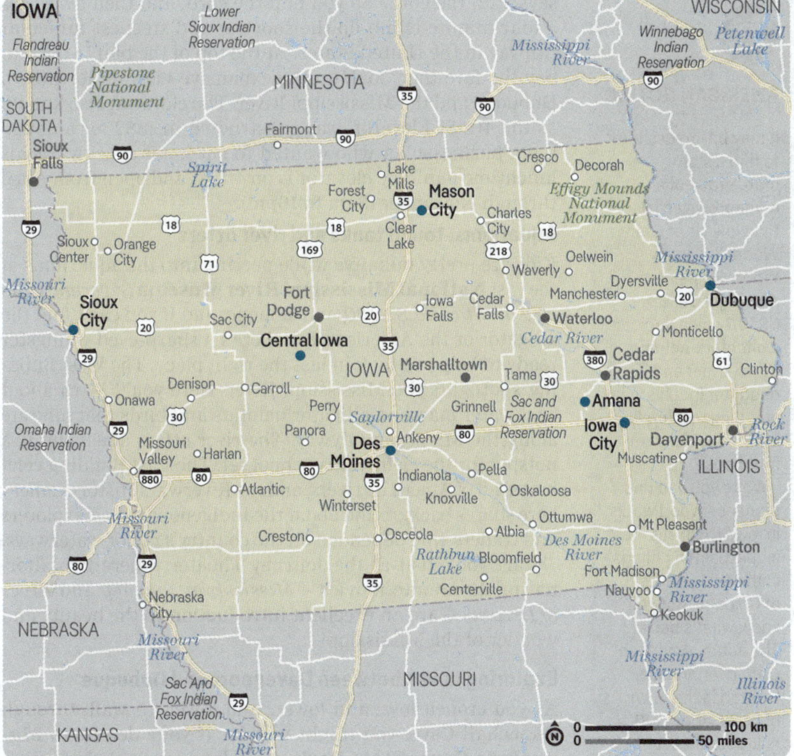

Dubuque & Around

Strolling the river cities

The historic city of **Dubuque**, with its 19th-century Victorian homes lining narrow streets between the Mississippi River and seven steep limestone hills, is a fine base for Great River Road explorations. Stroll the 9-mile path along the waterfront and explore neighborhoods in the midst of an urban revitalization that's drawing national acclaim. Don't miss the redeveloped Millwork District immediately north of downtown past 6th St. Its old wood-working factories are now home to great restaurants and nightlife. Red-brick walls are splashed with spectacular **murals** *(voicesproductions.org)* across downtown.

Davenport is the largest and most appealing of the Quad Cities about 70 miles south of Dubuque (the other three are Bettendorf in Iowa and Moline and Rock Island in Illinois). It has a grand riverfront setting with a vast network of walking and biking trails.

Ride the Fenelon Place Elevator

Stepping into Dubuque's tiny **Fenelon Place Elevator** *(fenelonplaceelevator.com; adult/child $2/1 roundtrip)* at 8:30am, especially if traveling solo, is a leap of faith. The sign

AMERICAN GOTHIC

It may be impossible to find a state more proud of a homegrown artist than Iowa is of Grant Wood. You know Wood. He painted *American Gothic* (1930), which depicts a pitchfork-holding Iowa farmer and his daughter (not his wife) standing resolutely before their tiny farmhouse.

While you can find plenty of Wood works in Iowa (p98), his most iconic painting hangs in the Art Institute of Chicago. But you know what's better? The actual *American Gothic* farmhouse, located in the town of Eldon about 100 miles southeast of Des Moines. The house sits beside the **American Gothic House Center** *(americangothic house.net; $5)*, which interprets the painting that sparked a million parodies. It even has loaner costumes so you can make your own parody selfie (for no fee) in front of the house.

says 'Pull the cord.' So you pull the cord, and then *whee!* It's a four-minute climb up the shortest and steepest funicular railway in the United States. At the top of the bluff, step out, pay the fare then soak up the expansive view of downtown Dubuque and the Mississippi River. The elevator, also known as the 4th St Elevator, was constructed in 1882 for a downtown businessman who wanted to get home quickly for his lunchtime nap! The elevator is on 4th St and open from April through November (8am to 10pm).

Aquariums, touch tanks and river otters

Kids are pretty talkative while peering into the aquariums at the vast **National Mississippi River Museum** *(rivermuseum.org; adult/child $26/20)* in Dubuque, and if you can't find the alligator or the American eel, there's a sharp-eyed youngster ready to help you look in just the right place. The West Building spotlights the Mississippi River. Here you'll learn about backwater marshes, alligator habitats and birds that migrate along the Mississippi flyway. The river otters aquarium is a hotspot for the elementary school set. The East Building celebrates all of America's rivers, and the Riverways History Gallery here shares background about the Indigenous tribes, explorers and traders who depended on the country's major waterways.

Start your visit at the Journey Theater, where two alternating 20-minute movies – *Mississippi Journey* and *River of Dreams* – are an excellent introduction to the beauty and wonder of the Mississippi.

Exploring caves between Davenport and Dubuque

As you crouch low...and lower...and lower, to walk through Dancehall Cave, you might wonder if your detour to **Maquoketa Caves State Park** *(iowadnr.gov; free)* was such a great idea. Don't worry, it was, especially if you're traveling with kids. And the ten-minute walk through the multi-room Dancehall is a highlight of a visit to this fun state park, where excited kids don headlamps before wiggling into small, marked caves. Two short loop trails, which pass 13 designated caves, link up at the vast Dancehall – where locals did indeed hold dance parties back in the day. The park is just off US 61 between Davenport and Dubuque, about 35 miles west of the Mississippi River.

Have a catch at the Field of Dreams

Several nights each week in summer the 'ghosts' of legendary baseball players step onto the **Field of Dreams** *(fieldofdreams moviesite.com; $20 donation)* baseball diamond from the

EATING & DRINKING AROUND DUBUQUE: OUR PICKS

Brazen Open Kitchen: Heavenly seasonal New American cuisine, plus inventive cocktails and a sizable wine list in the Millwork District. *4:30-9pm Mon-Sat* $$

L May Eatery: The creative thin crust pizzas are delicious at this chic downtown cafe. Works well for solos and celebratory couples alike. *hours vary* $$

Monk's: Every town needs a joint like Monk's: friendly folks in a creaky old house serving coffee in the morning and local beer at night. *7am-11pm most days*

Textile Brewing Co: Occupies an old sewing factory in Dyersville 30 miles west of Dubuque. Giant pretzels, fantastic flatbreads and tasty beer. *11am-9pm most days*

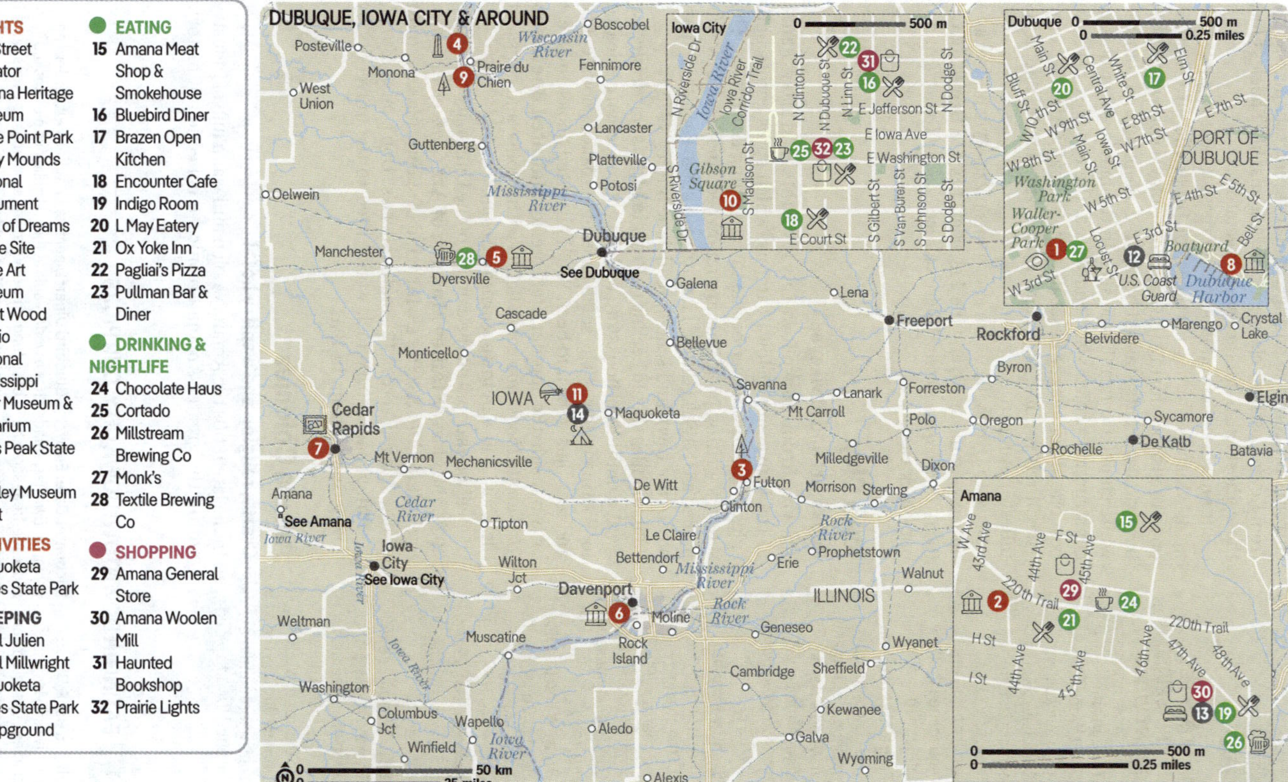

● **SIGHTS**
1 4th Street Elevator
2 Amana Heritage Museum
3 Eagle Point Park
4 Effigy Mounds National Monument
5 Field of Dreams Movie Site
6 Figge Art Museum
7 Grant Wood Studio
8 National Mississippi River Museum & Aquarium
9 Pikes Peak State Park
10 Stanley Museum of Art

● **ACTIVITIES**
11 Maquoketa Caves State Park

● **SLEEPING**
12 Hotel Julien
13 Hotel Millwright
14 Maquoketa Caves State Park Campground

● **EATING**
15 Amana Meat Shop & Smokehouse
16 Bluebird Diner
17 Brazen Open Kitchen
18 Encounter Cafe
19 Indigo Room
20 L May Eatery
21 Ox Yoke Inn
22 Pagliai's Pizza
23 Pullman Bar & Diner

● **DRINKING & NIGHTLIFE**
24 Chocolate Haus
25 Cortado
26 Millstream Brewing Co
27 Monk's
28 Textile Brewing Co

● **SHOPPING**
29 Amana General Store
30 Amana Woolen Mill
31 Haunted Bookshop
32 Prairie Lights

LANDSCAPES THAT INSPIRED GRANT WOOD

You can admire Grant Wood's (p96) Midwestern Regionalist works across eastern Iowa, as well as experiencing the landscapes that influenced him.

Figge Art Museum: This Davenport museum holds many of Wood's works. *(figgeartmuseum.org; adult/teen/child $14/10/8)*

Stanley Museum of Art: Look out for the strangely mesmerizing *Plaid Sweater* (1931) in Iowa City. *(stanleymuseum.org; free)*

Grant Wood Studio: Head to Cedar Rapids to see the spot where Wood painted *American Gothic* and other works. *(crma.org; free)*

Grant Wood Scenic Byway: If you're not a fan of museums, simply take a drive on this road, which ribbons through the rolling farmland that inspired Wood's work.

surrounding cornfield during a game or event, echoing a scene from Kevin Costner's classic movie. And just like Shoeless Joe, these ghosts also interact with spectators.

But no worries if you miss one of these 'Ghost Nights.' The field, which is 4 miles northeast of Dyersville off US 20, is open to visitors during the day. Come play catch with mitts, baseballs and bats stashed beside the diamond and tour the white clapboard farmhouse seen in the movie. After on-site construction projects are completed, the complex plans to host one Major League Baseball game annually. And the corn? They'll tell you it's 'knee-high by the 4th of July,' and at its tallest in August.

Drive to Dyersville for an enormous pizza-style pretzel and an easy-drinking Dyersville Lager at **Textile Brewing Co** (p61) *(textilebrews.com)*. There's a nice *Field of Dreams* mural one block east.

Iowa City

Books, art and hawkeyes

The vibe in downtown Iowa City is youthful and artsy thanks to the University of Iowa campus, which spills across both sides of the Iowa River beside the charming downtown. The school's writing programs are renowned, and Iowa City was named a UNESCO City of Literature in 2008. For a sharp parody of the town and school, read Jane Smiley's *Moo*.

Bibliophiles should beeline to **Prairie Lights** *(prairielights.com)*, a multi-level bookstore with an entire section dedicated to 'Writing in Iowa.' The small cafe serves baked goods, coffee and teas plus wine and beer. You'll find used books and a cat or two inside the appropriately creaky **Haunted Bookshop** *(thehauntedbookshop.com)*. Refuel with a coffee and croissant (delicious!) at **Cortado** *(cortadoic.com)*.

Opening its doors on the campus of the University of Iowa in 2022, the glossy **Stanley Museum of Art** *(stanleymuseum.org; adult/child $8/3)* is a whirlwind of spectacular art, most of it displayed across 12 small galleries. Don't miss *Mural*, a seminal Jackson Pollock work gifted to the university by Peggy Guggenheim in 1951.

Amana Colonies

Crafts, religion and a spiffy hotel

In the late 1800s the Amana woolen mill was a hub of industry within the greater Amana Colonies, a collection of historic

EATING IN DOWNTOWN IOWA CITY: OUR PICKS

Pullman Bar & Diner: Attentive service and decadent, upscale diner fare beside Prairie Lights. *8am-10pm Mon-Thu, to 10:30pm Fri & Sat, to 9pm Sun* $$

Encounter Cafe: Enjoy panini sandwiches, salads and made-from-scratch pastries. *7am-2:30pm* $

Bluebird Diner: Diner fare has a worldly spin at this busy, long-time downtown joint. *7am-9pm Mon-Sat to 8pm Sun* $

Pagliai's Pizza: Serving delicious pies cooked in stone-hearth ovens since 1957. *4-10pm* $$

SANDRA FOYT/SHUTTERSTOCK

Prairie Lights

German religious villages located 25 miles northwest of Iowa City. In 2020 the old mill welcomed its first guests under a brand new name and identity: the **Hotel Millwright**. An adaptive re-use project, this 66-room boutique hotel celebrates the stories and craftsmanship of the mill workers. It has also revitalized the villages, which have been a shopping and dining destination long known for its craft stores and family-style German restaurants.

If you're driving across Iowa on I-80, the colonies are a convenient stop just north of the interstate. Most attractions are located in the village of Amana, which is home to the **Amana Heritage Museum** *(amanaheritage.org; adult/child $10/5)*. The museum shares a good overview of the history of the colonies. Don't skip the short introductory film.

For books, toys, gifts and a variety of preserves, stop by the **Amana General Store** *(amanaheritage.com)*. Buy locally produced cheeses and smoked meats around the corner at the **Amana Meat Shop & Smokehouse** *(amanameatshop.com)*. Amana-made blankets, throws and scarves catch the eye at

HISTORY OF THE AMANA COLONIES

Seven villages are stretched along a 17-mile loop just north of I-80 west of Iowa City. All were established as German religious communes between 1855 and 1861 by Inspirationists who lived a utopian life with no wages paid and all assets communally owned. Communal kitchens served daily meals to all. During the Great Depression the community voted to end the communal way of living, although the Amana Church continues. Unlike the Amish and Mennonite religions, Inspirationists embrace modern technology (and tourism).

Today the well-preserved (and discreetly tasteful) villages offer a glimpse of this unique culture, and there are lots of arts, crafts, cheeses, baked goods and wines to buy.

EATING & DRINKING IN THE AMANA COLONIES

Ox Yoke Inn: Bratwurst, schnitzels and fried chicken. Family-style meals have refillable entrees and sides for all. *11am-7pm Mon-Thu, to 8pm Fri & Sat, 9am-6pm Sun* $

Indigo Room: Bustling restaurant with a cocktail bar inside Hotel Millwright. Enjoy elevated small plates and a few mains. *4-8pm Mom, to 9pm Tue-Sun* $$

Chocolate Haus: Sells delicious artisanal truffles and fudge as well as chocolate-y coffee drinks. Wonderful frappuccinos. *10am-5pm Mon-Sun, 11am-5pm Sun*

Millstream Brewing Co: Listen to German oom-pah-pah while sipping innovative craft beer beside the mill race near Hotel Millwright. *11am-7pm most days*

the **Amana Woolen Mill** *(amanawoolenmill.com)*, which is located in the original weaving building beside the hotel.

Des Moines

Butter cows and fried Twinkies on a stick

Much more than just country music and butter sculpture, the **Iowa State Fair** *(iowastatefair.org; adult/child $16/10)* draws more than one million visitors over its 11-day run in early August. Fairgoers can admire award-winning farm animals, and they have their pick of more than 50 food items, from deep-fried Twinkies to bacon-cheddar pretzel dogs, that are shoved on a stick. It's the setting for the Rodgers and Hammerstein musical *State Fair* and the 1945 film version. The fairgrounds are 3.5 miles east of downtown Des Moines.

If you're not in Iowa for the fair, try instead **Des Moines' Downtown Farmers Market** *(facebook.com/downtownfarmersmarket)*. Held Saturday mornings from May though October, this popular market – which began in 1975 – hosts hundreds of vendors selling produce, prepared foods, baked goods, meals, snacks and crafts.

A gold dome and top-drawer digs

You're looking pretty impressive there, **Iowa State Capitol** *(iowa.gov; free)*. Perched on a hill overlooking an enormous green lawn, this is one state capitol that is worth a closer look. Topped by a sparkling gold dome, the building soars 275ft. The bling-heavy interior is also a wonder, from the stained glass in the library to the spiral staircases. While exploring the 1st floor, be sure to look up to see the interior artistry of the dome. On the first floor you'll also find an intricate model of the USS *Iowa*. The enormous *Westward* mural, completed in 1905, draws you in for a closer look – are those angels protecting a wagon train? – while climbing from the 1st to the 2nd floor.

Parking is free in front of the building, and there's a public entrance under the front steps. After you're screened by security, walk straight ahead to the information desk for a self-guided tour pamphlet, or ask when the next guided tour departs. Tours last 90 minutes, but it's okay to spin off early.

Art and architecture in Des Moines

From its nondescript name to its ho-hum entry sign, the **Des Moines Art Center** *(desmoinesartcenter.org; free)* doesn't knock it out of the park when it comes to first impressions. But don't skip it. Three of the greatest architects of the modern era – Eliel Saarinen, IM Pei and Richard Meier – designed separate buildings within the complex. For visitors, it's easy to walk between them, and the varied architectural styles complement the collection's different artistic genres in striking ways. Matisse, Hopper, Rodin, Warhol and Basquiat are a few of the names represented.

From most points downtown it's an easy walk to the museum's satellite location, the **Pappajohn Sculpture Park**, where Jaume Plensa's enormous *Nomade* is particularly compelling. Grab a coffee near the park at eco-minded **Horizon Line**, where your to-go drink is served in a recyclable jar.

TOP SIGHTS ALONG IOWA'S GREAT RIVER ROAD

Iowa's Great River Road mostly hugs the Mississippi River along the state's eastern edge. It links with numerous country byways and passes through beautiful riverfront towns.

Effigy Mounds National Monument: Hundreds of Native American burial mounds sit in the bluffs above the Mississippi in northeast Iowa.

Pikes Peak State Park: A nature reserve at the confluence of the Wisconsin and Mississippi Rivers.

National Mississippi River Museum & Aquarium: Learn about life along the length of the Mississippi in Dubuque.

Eagle Point Park: Beautiful bluff-top park in Clinton with river views and elaborate 1930s stonework.

Figge Art Museum: This glass-walled museum in Davenport sparkles above the River Road, and is now illuminated at night.

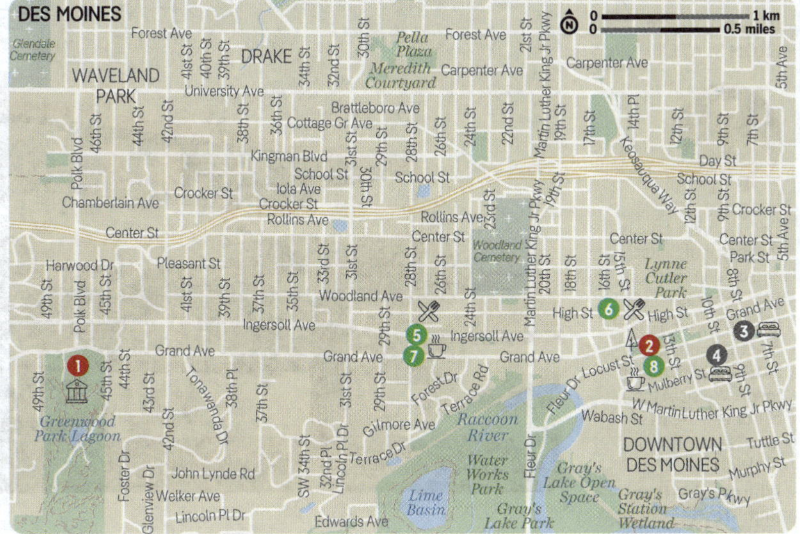

- **SIGHTS**
  - 1 Des Moines Art Center
  - 2 Pappajohn Sculpture Park
- **SLEEPING**
  - 3 Des Lux Hotel
  - 4 Hotel Fort Des Moines
- **EATING**
  - see 5 Harbinger
  - 5 Lachele's Fine Foods
  - 6 Lua Brewing
- **DRINKING & NIGHTLIFE**
  - 7 Chain & Spoke
  - 8 Horizon Line Coffee

Indie shops in West Des Moines

There's not a chain store in sight in **Valley Junction** *(valleyjunction.com)*, a former village that has been swallowed up by West Des Moines. This five-block commercial corner unfurls along Fifth St, which is lined with locally owned shops, cafes and antique stores housed in attractive old brick buildings.

Don't miss **Bozz Prints** *(bozzprints.com)*, a print shop selling a colorful array of Iowa-promoting stickers, magnets, shirts and postcards. Prints also celebrate the Midwest and national parks. You'll find Iowa-made products a few doors down at **Heart of Iowa Marketplace** *(heartofiowamarketplace.com)*. Writers won't leave **Quill & Nib** *(valleyjunction.com)* empty-handed – it's pens and journals galore.

Central Iowa

Silos, biker bars and black dirt

It's hard to miss the **High Trestle Bridge** *(inhf.org)* at night. Forty-one steel frames, illuminated by colorful LED lights, form a tunnel over the span, which soars 13 stories above the Des Moines River Valley. With its overlooks, interpretive signage and great birdwatching, the bridge is nearly

EATING & DRINKING IN DES MOINES: OUR PICKS

Lachele's Fine Foods: Construction workers and ladies who lunch converge at this tiny joint for delicious smash burgers. *11am-9pm Tue-Sat, 10am-3pm Sun* $

Harbinger: James Beard nominee Joe Tripp elevates Asian street food at this chic number. Many veggie options. *4-8pm Sun-Thu, to 9pm Fri & Sat* $

Lua Brewing: Nationally acclaimed brewpub has excellent beers, welcoming staff and delicious gourmet pub fare. *11am-10pm most days* $$

Chain & Spoke: What? A friendly bike shop? Yep, drop by for local cycling advice and fine coffee. *8am-5pm Mon-Fri, to 3pm Sat & Sun*

BICYCLE RIDES FROM SLATER

Taylor Christensen is the mayor of Slater and cofounder of Local Spokes.

Why is Slater a good starting point for a half-day bike ride in Iowa? We sit at the T of both the Heart of Iowa Nature Trail and the High Trestle Trail.

Who can ride the High Trestle Trail? It is perfect for novices or experienced cyclists. It's very clear and has a level grade – less than 2%. About every 7 miles there's a town. We will get families, with kids five to seven, to some very serious bikers.

What are some recommended stops for food and good cheer? In Madrid we have the **Flat Tire**, right on the trail. In Woodward they have the **Whistlin' Donkey**. All the bars do a great job of hosting, with live music and entertainment.

JIM PACKETT/SHUTTERSTOCK

as compelling in the daylight. It's also a fantastic final stop for cyclists pedaling the High Trestle Trail, a paved 25-mile walking and cycling path that links five small towns in central Iowa just north of Des Moines.

If you decide to take a half-day ride, you'll pass silos, fields and a few convivial trailside restaurants and bars. You'll likely see chipmunks, squirrels and rabbits, with frogs croaking songs of love (or is it hunger?) along the way. The trail, which links Ankeny and Woodward, is paved, mostly level and well marked. It's popular with families, and it links up with other long biking trails. For an e-bike rental, try **Local Spokes** *(thelocalspokes.com; half-day rental $50)* in Slater.

To see the illuminated bridge at night, you can park and hike a short distance to the span west of Madrid (*traveliowa .com/trails*).

Mason City

Frank Lloyd Wright and The Music Man

There's a lot going on in Mason City, and though it's not on the way to anywhere, this quirky place in north-central Iowa is a highly recommended stop if you are interested in

EATING & DRINKING IN MASON CITY: OUR PICKS

Three on the Tree Coffee & Cafe: Wake up with a pastry and coffee downtown before checking out the architecture. *7am-3pm* $

Birdsall's Ice Cream Co: Pause beneath the red-and-strip awning for a scoop, a sundae or a malt. Around since 1931. *noon-9pm* $

LD's Filling Station: All-American breakfast and lunch fare fueling the heartland, with decor embracing classic cars. *7am-8pm Wed-Fri, to 1pm Sat & Sun* $

Northwestern Steakhouse: Renowned statewide for its Greek-style broiled steaks. Order the spaghetti as your side. *4:30-9pm Mon-Sat* $$$

Stockman House

Prairie School architecture and, well, musicals. Architectural bona fides? The only remaining hotel designed by Frank Lloyd Wright, the **Historic Park Inn Hotel** *(historicparkinn.com)*, is downtown. The hotel is open for overnight guests and for those who just want to poke around and admire his vision. Don't miss the wonderful gift shop. You can also tour the **Stockman House** *(stockmanhouse.org; tour adult/child $15/5)*, a Prairie-style home also designed by Wright.

A self-guided walking tour passes a slew of nearby Prairie School, Usonian and Arts & Crafts–style homes designed by prominent architects in the early 1900s. Pick up a free walking tour map at the downtown **visitor center** *(visitmasoncityiowa.com)*.

Mason City was also the boyhood home of Meredith Willson, who wrote the Broadway musical *The Music Man*. The play was later turned into a Warner Brothers movie of the same name. The entire **Music Man Square** *(themusicmansquare.org)*, as seen in the movie, was recreated in Mason City and often hosts music events. Theater kids, join me now... *You got trouble, right here in River City...*

And take note: Mason City's cute downtown is anchored by a festive town square. If you're not careful with your planning, you might find yourself bumping elbows with the musical masses during the **North Iowa Band Festival**, the largest free marching-band competition in the Midwest.

Bil Baird and the Sound of Music puppets

Known globally in the mid-1900s for his modernist puppets and marionettes, puppeteer Bil Baird was a native of Mason City. His puppets made numerous appearances in Broadway productions and on television variety shows. His most famous creations are probably the Lonely Goatherd puppets, which made a memorable appearance in the movie *The Sound of*

CYCLING IOWA

With more than 2500 miles of paved cycling trails, Iowa is a top destination for cyclists. Trails cater to a variety of ages and skill levels, and they are often dotted with public art, festive bars and welcoming towns. The state is known internationally for its RAGBRAI ride (p104) in July.

Recommended trails include the Cedar Valley Trails, which link Cedar Falls with Waterloo in eastern Iowa; the High Trestle Trail in Central Iowa; and the Raccoon River Valley Trail, which connects small towns with the suburbs of Des Moines. A 9-mile extension to the High Trestle Trail in 2024 linked it to the Raccoon River route, forming a 120-mile loop.

WHAT THE HECK IS RAGBRAI?

Cyclists the world over are familiar with **RAGBRAI** *(ragbrai.com)*, a one-week bike ride across the state of Iowa every July. The ride, which always starts on the western side of the state, is non-competitive, and cyclists camp at eight host communities along the way. The total distance is around 470 miles.

The event attracts about 20,000 registered riders and is the best-attended cycling tour in the world. The name is an acronym for *Register*'s Annual Great Bicycle Ride Across Iowa; two reporters for the *Des Moines Register* took the first ride for a newspaper story in 1973.

SAXTON STUDIO/SHUTTERSTOCK

RAGBRAI riders

Music. Today, you can see the goat, one little girl in a pale pink coat, her gloating mama and the dancing couple at the **MacNider Art Museum** *(macniderart.org)* in Mason City. We're not sure where the goatherd went off to. Oh ho lay-dee odl lee o!

Sioux City

On the trail of Lewis and Clark

As they journeyed west along the Missouri River toward the Pacific Northwest, the Lewis and Clark expedition stopped near present day Sioux City. It was during this stop, on August 20, 1804, that Sgt Charles Floyd, a member of the corps, became ill and died, probably from appendicitis. He was the only person to die during the entire trek. You can learn much more about this event and other aspects of the journey at the **Lewis & Clark Interpretive Center**, which is beside the Missouri River. Inside, animatronic characters tell the story of the expedition. The information is geared toward younger visitors, but most everyone will learn something new from the exhibits, which can be fully explored in under an hour. Take exit 49 off I-29.

A bluff-top **obelisk** marks the final resting spot of Sgt Floyd, the first United States soldier to die west of the Mississippi River. A short drive from the interpretive center, his memorial is a tranquil spot to view the Missouri River and reflect on the bravery of the corps.

The iconic **Tastee Inn & Out** *(tasteeinnandout.com)* was not around when Lewis and Clark came through, but this retro drive-thru on the way to the Sergeant Floyd Monument has been around since 1955. There are two specials here: the Tastee, an Iowa loosemeat sandwich (a regional specialty that combines loose ground beef, onions and orange cheese), and onion chips, which are battered and fried.

North Dakota

BADLANDS BEAUTY | DINOSAUR FOSSILS | FARGO FUN

North Dakotans have a 'We're all in this together' charm that is pleasantly disarming after miles and miles of lonely driving. And oh, those drives. Fields of grain stretch beyond every horizon. Except for the rugged 'badlands' of the far west, geographic relief is subtle; often it's just a pond – known as a prairie pothole – creeping up against the interstate or a ruined homestead that break up the vista.

This is one of the least-visited states in the US. The lack of visitors, however, doesn't mean the state is sleepy. The Bakken oil boom (named for geologic formations beneath the surface) transformed the northwest quadrant into one vast drilling site. At night, fires burning off waste gas give the landscape hellish views. Though the boom has leveled off, once-quiet towns like Williston and Watford City have become industrial warrens.

Near the Montana border you'll find natural beauty that justifies a trip while the Missouri River is dotted with sights tied to the Lewis and Clark Expedition.

Places

GETTING AROUND

You'll need your own vehicle to explore the state. The only interstate is I-94, which runs east–west. North Dakota's main airports are in Bismarck, Fargo and Minot. Cities served by Amtrak's *Empire Builder* train include Fargo, Grand Forks, Minot and Williston. Jefferson Lines *(jeffersonlines.com)* runs limited bus services to Bismarck, Dickinson, Fargo and Grand Forks.

TOP TIP

The southwest quarter of North Dakota, including Medora, uses Mountain Time, which is one hour earlier than the rest of the state's Central Time.

Fargo

Pose by the Woodchipper

Visitor centers can be a little ho-hum. But that's amusingly not the case in Fargo. At the engaging **Fargo-Moorhead Visitors Center** you'll find the actual **woodchipper** from the 1996 movie *Fargo*. It was used in the scene where Gaear feeds the last of Carl's body into its maw and is discovered by Marge. You can reenact the scene – although not the results – while wearing Fargo-style hats and jamming in a fake leg (both provided). There's a reproduction out front. You'll find the visitor center off exit 348 on I-94 southwest of downtown.

Celebrate like nice Vikings

Step into the enormous **Brewhalla** *(brewhalla.com)* – an indoor/outdoor beer hall and market with loads of personality. Here you'll walk past bars slinging craft beer, families

TOP EXPERIENCE

Theodore Roosevelt National Park

Future president Theodore Roosevelt retreated from New York to this remote spot in his early 20s after losing both his wife and mother in a matter of hours. It's said that his time in the Dakota badlands inspired him to become an avid conservationist, and he set aside 230 million acres of federal land while in office. His North Dakota legacy is this beautiful 110-sq-mile national park.

ZAKZEINERT/SHUTTERSTOCK

TOP TIPS

- If escape is your goal, visit the remote, low-key Elkhorn Unit, where Roosevelt lived.
- Short on time? A quick stop at the free Painted Canyon Visitor Center off I-94 at exit 32 is recommended. View scenic badlands, hike trails and, possibly, see buffalo.

Scenic Drives

Green prairie grasses frame rock formations streaked with red, yellow, brown, black and silver minerals in two units of the park. The colors of these badlands change with the moods of nature and time of day. The bison, elk, pronghorn and prairie dogs strutting about are clearly living their best lives. To maximize sightseeing, many visitors drive the 36-mile scenic loop (U-shaped due to construction when we visited) in the South Unit. Make the short hike up **Buck Hill** and soak up the spectacular stillness. It's also well worth the journey to the North Unit for the 14-mile one-way drive to the **Oxbow Overlook** and its wide views into the vast and colorfully striated river canyon.

Hiking & Camping

In the South Unit, the 0.4-mile **Wind Canyon Trail** leads to a dramatic viewpoint over the Little Missouri River, especially scenic at sunset. In the North Unit, the 1.5-mile **Buckhorn Trail** passes a lively Prairie Dog Town. The **Caprock-Coulee Loop** is a 4.1-mile hike across a grassy butte into the badlands. Camp at **Cottonwood Campground** in the South Unit or **Juniper Campground** in the North Unit. For a good adventure, hike or cycle the 96-mile Maah Daah Hey Trail between the two units.

PRACTICALITIES

- nps.gov/thro
- admission $30/25 vehicle/motorcycle 7-day pass
- the park has three units: North, South and remote Elkhorn

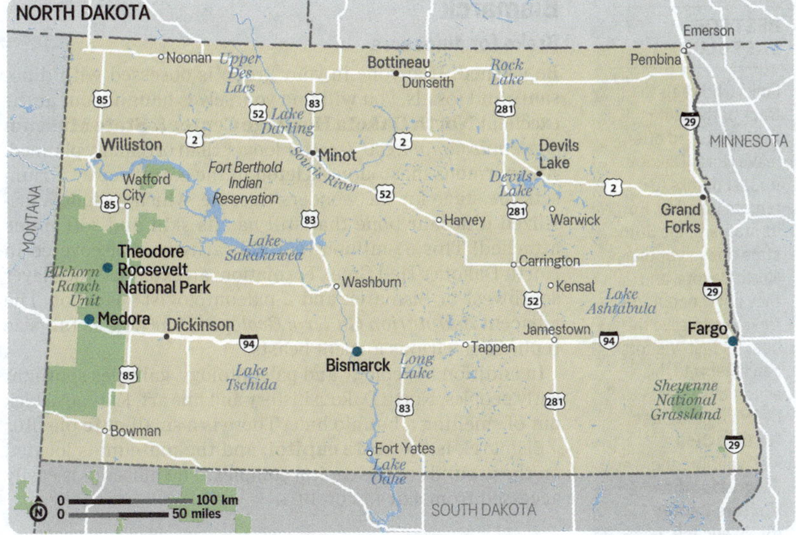

chilling by fire pits and communal areas buzzing with groups playing board games. You might even muscle past a cluster of conventioneers attending the Hel's Fury Tattoo Fest. This industrially hip space is anchored by **Drekker Brewing Co**, which has a slew of innovative draft beers on tap across the market, where you'll also find food stalls selling woodfired pizzas, noodle dishes and smashburgers. Small retail shops here stay local. The vibe is welcoming and friendly – if this is the future of third places in America, we like it.

Take an art break downtown

If you're staying downtown, stroll over to the ambitious **Plains Art Museum** *(plainsart.org; free)*. Exhibits are housed in a renovated International Harvester warehouse. The permanent collection includes contemporary works by Native American and African artists. Temporary exhibits spotlight 20th- and 21st-century art.

The skybridge linking the museum with the adjacent Burgum Center for Creativity is a piece of art in its own right. Along the length of the span, a pretty screen print captures the delicate beauty of the tallgrass prairie. Look for big and little bluestems, a Harvester mouse and gray wolf tracks as you walk.

BIG SCULPTURES, QUIET PLAINS

Between Fargo and Theodore Roosevelt National Park on I-94, you can break up the drive by veering off the highway at exit 72. The exit marks the northern start of the **Enchanted Highway**, a 32-mile stretch that passes a series of enormous whimsical sculptures by local artist Gary Greff. The 75-ton **Geese in Flight** soars above exit 72.

EATING & DRINKING IN FARGO: OUR PICKS

Wurst Bier Hall: German-style beer hall downtown ups the stakes with inventive sausage sandwiches, exotic meats and more than 35 beers on tap. *hours vary* **$**

Shack: A beloved local diner known for its pancakes and – queue *Fargo* accent – eggs. *6am-2pm Sat-Tue, to 8pm Wed-Fri* **$**

Rosewild: Elevated American fare for breakfast, lunch and dinner inside the new Hotel Jasper. Cocktails too. *7am-10pm* **$$**

Sky Prairie: Seasonal cocktail bar *(May-Sep)* atop Hotel Donaldson (p123) with views of downtown. *4-9pm Sat & Sun*

BEST FOR LAST CLUB

Folks who keep track of the states they've visited often leave North Dakota for last thanks to it remote location. But its status as the 50th state doesn't bother North Dakota, and they now encourage travelers to save the best for last. Visitors can celebrate this accomplishment by joining the **Best for Last Club** – just walk into the **Fargo-Moorhead Visitors Center** (p105) and tell them you've hit 50. After you sign a form, they'll take your photo in front of the Best for Last banner and hand you a certificate. There are currently 7,300 members. Does induction include North Dakota swag? You betcha.

Bismarck

Brake for dinosaurs

Be warned. If anyone in your group is obsessed with dinosaurs and fossils, you will find yourselves hanging out at the excellent **North Dakota Heritage Center & State Museum** *(statemuseum.nd.gov; free)* far longer than originally planned. An enormous mastodon skeleton in the entranceway atrium sets the stage for the wonders to come, which include a fossilized dinosaur bone that still has its skin and soft tissue attached! This 67-million-year-old rarity was discovered in North Dakota's Hell Creek Formation, an extended rock layer southwest of Bismarck and a paleontologist's jackpot. The adjacent *Adaptation Gallery: Geologic Time* houses full-size replicas of various ancient beasts.

In addition to geology and paleontology, galleries spotlight early peoples, North Dakota history and fine art. Kids get a kick out of smelling a buffalo hide. There is a small **cafe** on-site.

Bismarck is the **state capitol**, and the museum is located on the grounds of the capitol complex. The museum is easily accessed from exit 159 on I-94.

Medora

Say 'howdy!' near the national park

As you mosey past the old wooden buildings in tiny Medora, which lounges beside the entrance to Theodore Roosevelt National Park (p106), look for the jaunty statue of the park's namesake. Roosevelt spent time in Medora and this pocket of North Dakota in the late 1800s. As the plaque here notes, Roosevelt once claimed, 'It was here that the romance of my life began.'

Today, this gateway community treads a fine line between real cowboy town and hokey modern interpretation. We'll give a nod to the former thanks to the dusty cowboy we saw who strolled into the Farmhouse Cafe with boots clomping and spurs a jingling.

For travelers, comfortable lodgings are available across all budgets and there are a handful of places to eat. Check *medora.com* for details about historic sites and family-focused activities. The much-anticipated **Theodore Roosevelt National Library** is set to open in Medora in July 2026. Note that many businesses close from October through May.

EATING & DRINKING IN MEDORA: OUR PICKS

Medora Convenience & Liquor Store: The fresh breakfast biscuits are regional legends at this friendly gas station and store. They start selling 'em early. *5:30am-9pm* $

Farmhouse Cafe: Pancakes, omelets, chicken-fried steaks and endless coffee. Nice staff. Lunch offerings too. *7am-11am* $

Theodore's Dining Room: Don your cleanest shirt for bison *osso bucco* and pan-seared walleye at the fanciest joint in town. Excellent pork-belly cobb salad. *hours vary* $

Little Missouri Saloon: This old-timey saloon will whip you back to the Wild West. Live music in summer. Open year-round. *11am-1am*

South Dakota

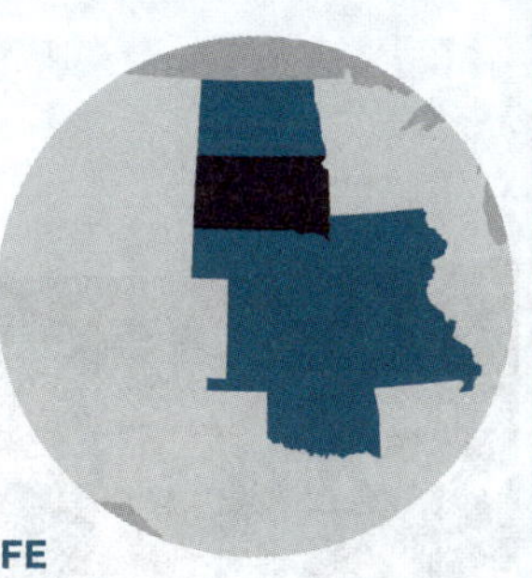

BLACK HILLS | SCENIC BYWAYS | ROAMING WILDLIFE

More than two million visitors walk the Avenue of Flags each year, squinting upward as they approach the iconic Mt Rushmore and its four presidential visages. And these attendance numbers are justified – it's a remarkable sight. But it's the unbound beauty of South Dakota that will likely stick with you. From the pine forests of the Black Hills to the ephemeral colors of the badlands to the windswept bluffs of the Missouri River, the natural beauty is rich and varied. And no one will forget their first sighting of a buffalo roaming prairie grasslands. The state's many scenic byways ribbon past these gorgeous landscapes as well as a crackerjack collection of old-school roadside attractions.

Historic and educational sites are abundant too, with mastodon fossils, old mining towns and abandoned missile silos all jostling for attention. The state is also the home of nine Native American tribes, and their stories and traditions are increasingly shared statewide.

Places

GETTING AROUND

Driving is the most efficient way to explore the state. I-90 links Sioux Falls in the east with Rapid City in the west. These cities have South Dakota's two main airports. Each has services to major American hubs. I-29 runs north–south and links Sioux Falls with Fargo, ND, to the north and Sioux City, IA, to the south. Jefferson Lines *(jeffersonlines.com)* buses stop in Rapid City, Wall, Mitchell and Sioux Falls along I-90.

Sioux Falls

Relax at Falls Park

It's hard to take a bad photo of the rambling waterfall that anchors **Falls Park** and the city of Sioux Falls. Paved trails frame the rocky cascades, and overlooks perch on the prettiest points. Our favorite spot? The footbridge over the Big Sioux River. The park has a perfectly placed cafe, and picnic tables are scattered about. You can also climb the five-story observation tower for high-elevation views of the action. Between mid-November and mid-January the park becomes a winter wonderland with 338,000 twinkling lights.

Continued on p113

TOP TIP

Roughly the western third of South Dakota – including the Black Hills and everything west of I-90 exit 177 and west of the Missouri River north of Pierre – uses Mountain Time, which is one hour earlier than Central Time in the rest of the state.

ABSTRACT ARTIST USA/SHUTTERSTOCK

TOP EXPERIENCE

Badlands National Park

The scenic wonders begin almost immediately along the Badlands Loop Rd, where the corrugated walls and crumbly spikes of an ancient floodplain shimmer ethereally in the afternoon light. It was understandably named *mako sica* (badland) by Native Americans, but the landscape is more secretive than bad – those geologic formations protect a motherlode of fossils. Above ground, buffalo roam the park's mixed-grass prairie.

DON'T MISS

- Ben Reifel Visitor Center
- Badlands Loop Rd
- Big Badlands Overlook
- Notch Trail
- Hay Butte Overlook
- Sheep Mountain Table

Park Overview

For those in a rush, the North Unit of the park is easily viewed on a one-hour drive along the **Badlands Loop Rd (Hwy 240)**. If you have an extra hour, however, several short hiking trails along the route will sling you right into the earthen wonderland here.

The park sprawls across grasslands south of I-90. The Pinnacles Entrance can be reached from exit 110, which is also the Wall Drug exit. You can access the Northeast Entrance from

PRACTICALITIES

● nps.gov/badl ● admission $15–30 for 7-day pass ● park open 24hrs ● visitor center hours vary

exit 131. The park's less accessible South Unit, also known as the Stronghold Unit, is on the Pine Ridge Indian Reservation and sees fewer visitors.

The **Ben Reifel Visitor Center** *(8am-5pm May-Aug, 9am-4pm Sep-Apr)* is located just south of the Northeast Entrance and is open year-round. Spend time here to check out the good exhibits. Don't miss the on-site **paleontology lab** *(mid-Jun–mid-Sep)* where you can watch staff prepare fossils. The **White River Visitor Center** is a small summer-only information outlet in the Stronghold Unit.

Badlands Loop Rd (Hwy 240)

The 39-mile Badlands Loop Rd stretches from the town of Cactus Flat west to the town of Wall, curving into the North Unit along a narrow ridge of rock formations known as the Badlands Wall. Carved by the White River, the wall separates the upper (to the north) and lower prairie. There are 12 overlooks and picnic areas along the way. For the best lighting and the most vibrant colors along the wall, make the drive before sunrise or sunset. The **Big Badlands Overlook** just south of the northeast entrance is particularly pretty at dawn.

Sage Creek Rim Road

This gravel road extends west from the Badlands Loop Rd, passing scenic overlooks and prairie-dog towns. Seeing buffalo is also a possibility. This drive is less traveled than the Badlands Loop Rd, and it is where most backcountry hikers and campers go to escape the crowds. There is almost no water or shade here, so don't strike out into the wilderness unprepared. For a quick introduction to scenery along the road, pull off at **Hay Butte Overlook** just west of the Badlands Loop Rd.

Hiking

Several short trails shoot into the badlands north of the Ben Reifel Visitor Center. The surreal **Door Trail** and its boardwalk lead to a scenic gap in the Badlands Wall. Take sunrise photos here. The **Notch Trail** twists through a canyon, scampers up a wooden ladder then curves along a crumbly ridge line to an expansive view of grasslands and more serrated walls. Both trailheads are accessed from the same parking lot.

Lodging & Camping

The cosy cabins at **Cedar Pass Lodge** *(mid-Apr–mid-Oct)* have air-conditioning, heat, microwaves and mini-fridges. The onsite restaurant serves breakfast, lunch and dinner. **Cedar Pass RV & Campground** *(late Mar–mid-Oct; campsites $37-47)* is the most popular place to pitch a tent in the park. Open year-round, **Sage Creek Campground** is primitive but also popular. Campsites are free.

SHEEP MOUNTAIN TABLE

For solitude and spectacular views of sweeping badlands, drive to **Sheep Mountain Table**, a plateau on the border of the North and South Units. The unpaved road to the overlook here is ideally tackled in a 4WD vehicle, but it shouldn't be too bad if the weather has been clear. The road beyond the overlook, however, is appropriate for 4WD and high-clearance vehicles only, but you can walk along the table from the overlook and soak up the otherworldly views.

TOP TIPS

- Hwy 44, which bisects the North and South Units, is a scenic route linking the Badlands and Rapid City. If you have extra time, take it to soak up the views and to avoid I-90.
- Keep at least 100ft from wildlife in the park. The animals may look approachable, but if they notice you, you are definitely too close.
- The park recommends two quarts of water per person for a two-hour hike.
- Do not collect fossils, plants, rocks or artifacts while exploring the park.

TOP EXPERIENCE

Wind Cave National Park

Home to the sixth-largest cave system in the world, Wind Cave is a sprawling treasure. But its wonders are not confined to its subterranean passages. It is also a haven for wildlife in the grasslands and forests south of Custer State Park. The namesake cave is laced with 167 miles of mapped passages. Cave tours, hikes and scenic drives are the primary activities.

CHERI ALGUIRE/SHUTTERSTOCK

TOP TIPS

- Reserve your tour before your visit. Tours are extremely popular and do sell out. You can book 30 days ahead.
- If you wing it, plan to arrive before the visitor center opens to join the line waiting to nab a ticket, particularly from March through October.

PRACTICALITIES

- nps.gov/wica
- open 24hr, tour times vary
- free admission
- tours $7-$17 at recreation.gov

Boxwork Formations

The cave's foremost feature is its collection of 'boxwork' calcite formations – 95% of all that are known to exist are here. The boxwork looks like honeycomb and dates back 60 to 100 million years.

Cave Tours

Three tours are offered year round: the easy Garden of Eden Tour, the family-friendly Natural Entrance Tour, and the strenuous Fairgrounds Tour. The unique boxwork formations can be seen on all three. The Candlelight Tour and the Wild Cave Tour are available from June through early August. Expect a lot of crawling on the Wild Cave Tour, and be aware that you will have to wriggle through a space that is 10 inches high and 3ft wide! The 30-minute Accessibility Tour is open to visitors in wheelchairs.

Hiking & Camping

More than 30 miles of trails navigate the grasslands and ponderosa pines that blanket the park. Keep watch for bison, elk, pronghorns and prairie dogs as you walk. The southern end of the 111-mile **Centennial Trail**, which links to Bear Butte State Park, begins on Hwy 87 north of the visitor center. Tucked in the pines beside the prairie, **Elk Mountain Campground** has 62 reservable spaces *($12–24 per site)*; backcountry camping *(free with permit)* is allowed in limited areas.

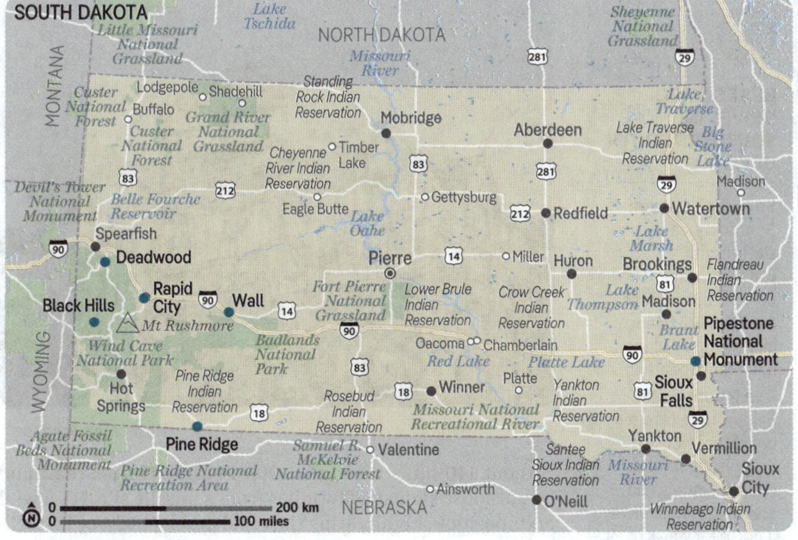

Continued from p109

For a fantastic meal, drive south from the park into downtown and take a seat at **MB Haskett Delicatessen** *(mbhaskett.com; hours vary)*. This retro cafe serves brilliant food throughout the day.

Scramble over quartzite at Palisades State Park

Ancient quartzite formations soar above Split Rock Creek at **Palisades State Park** (*gfp.sd.gov, vehicle $10-15*), a compact state park on the prairie about 20 miles northeast of Sioux Falls. As your kids clamber at the base of the quartzite, you might see experienced climbers rappeling down the face of a nearby cliff. And geologists take note: the quartzite here is 1.2 billion years old! Swimming is allowed, but no jumping from the rocks.

Roadside attractions between Sioux Falls and Wall Drug

Roadside attractions along I-90 keep boredom at bay as you cruise west across South Dakota.

First up is the cavernous **Corn Palace** (*cornpalace.com; free*) in Mitchell. Close to 300,000 ears of corn are used annually to create new murals on the outside of the building. Head inside to learn how the facade has evolved since its creation in 1892. And please, don't eat the murals – fresh popcorn is for sale inside if you're hungry.

Continue 70 miles to the bluff-top **Lewis & Clark Interpretive Center** and rest area near exit 263 south of Chamberlain. There are worthwhile exhibits here about the intrepid duo and their voyages on the Missouri River below, but the highlight is the staggering **Dignity: of Earth & Sky** statue. Framed by sky and prairie, this 50ft-tall rendering of a Sioux woman – her magnificent quilt held against the wind – honors the Lakota and Dakota tribes. The diamond-shaped LED lights in her quilt sparkle at night.

HELLO SIOUX FALLS!

Parked in the southeastern corner of South Dakota, the state's largest city lives up to its name at **Falls Park** (p109), where the Big Sioux River plunges through a long series of rock faces. Just south lies a buzzing downtown district with a burgeoning foodie scene and some of the best eats in the region. You'll find more than 80 outdoor sculptures along downtown's **SculptureWalk**. Park on S Phillips Ave to start your explorations. Several hotel chains cluster downtown near the river while a slightly cheaper collection of accommodations line I-29 and I-229.

BEST SCENIC DRIVES IN SOUTHERN SOUTH DAKOTA

Spearfish Canyon Scenic Byway: Dotted with waterfalls, this curvaceous 20-mile road (US 14A) cleaves into the heart of the hills from Spearfish.

Iron Mountain Rd: Enjoy a 16-mile roller coaster of wooden bridges, tight turns, narrow tunnels and stunning vistas. Drive it north for views of Mt Rushmore.

Needles Hwy: This 14-mile drive twists past granite spires, pine trees, aspens and beautiful Sylvan Lake.

Wildlife Loop Rd: You might see bison, prairie dogs and pronghorn on this 18-mile drive in Custer State Park.

Native American National and State Scenic Byway: Drive along the Missouri River, passing through tribal lands and prairies with a dramatic pause beside *Dignity: of Earth & Sky* (p113).

CHERI ALGUIRE/SHUTTERSTOCK

Hotel Alex Johnson

About 140 miles west, the 1909 **Prairie Homestead** and its outhouse sit just a few miles from a missile silo. It's a wild juxtaposition, highlighting the rapid development of US technology in the span of 60 years. The **Minuteman Missile National Historic Site** *(nps.gov/mimi)* holds one of 1000 Minutemen II intercontinental ballistic missiles housed across the Great Plains during the Cold War (and now retired). The sod house and the Minuteman Missile site's visitor center are reached from exit 131. Tours of the Delta-01 Minuteman Missile Launch Facility *(tours adult/child $12/8)* begin off exit 127.

Shimmering mineral deposits await at Badlands National Park (p110) at exit 131. And then, at exit 110, there it is, after miles of signs: Wall Drug.

Wall

Get lost at South Dakota's wackiest roadside attraction

Only a curmudgeon could ignore all the signs along I-90 encouraging drivers to stop at **Wall Drug** *(walldrug.com)*. Fortunately this warren of kitsch, which opened in 1931, does have a few worthwhile charms behind its Old West facade: 5¢ coffee, free ice water, good doughnuts, public restrooms and loads of diversions. Amid the fudge and knickknackery is a superb bookstore with great regional titles. There's also a store selling quality cowboy boots. Out back, ride the mythical jackalope and check out the historical photos. And yes, you can still buy aspirin in the drugstore.

Pine Ridge Reservation

Exploring Lakota history and culture

Home to the Oglala Lakota Sioux, the Pine Ridge Reservation sits within beautiful prairies and badlands south of Badlands National Park. Residents face systemic hardships, from crime to unemployment, and more than half the population lives below the poverty line.

Despite being at times a jarring dose of reality, it is also a place welcoming to visitors. Tune in to KILI (90.1FM), which often plays traditional music. For an introduction to the reservation, stop by the **Red Cloud Heritage Center** *(mahpiyaluta.org; free)*. This well-curated art museum has traditional and contemporary works, and a craft shop with locally made artisan goods. The center hosts the **Red Cloud Indian Art Show** from June to early August. It's 4 miles north of the town of Pine Ridge on Hwy 18.

It helps to read up on the history before you visit the **Wounded Knee Massacre Site**, 16 miles northeast of Pine Ridge town. The mass grave sits atop the hill near a church above the massacre site. Small memorials appear daily amid the stones listing dozens of names. You can park below the hill and walk up, or tackle the rutted road to the top in your car. It's a desolate place, with sweeping views. You may encounter locals selling jewelry as well as locals looking for donations. For more details about Wounded Knee, visit nearby **Oglala Lakota College Historical Center** *(olc.edu/about-olc/historical-center; 9am-5pm Mon-Fri; free)* or the **White River Visitor Center** (p111) at Badlands National Park.

WHAT ARE THE BLACK HILLS?

They call the Black Hills an evergreen island in a sea of high-prairie grassland. This stunning region on the Wyoming–South Dakota border lures scores of visitors with its winding canyons and wildly eroded 7000ft peaks. The region's name – the 'Black' comes from the dark ponderosa pine-covered slopes – was conferred by the Lakota Sioux. In the 1868 Fort Laramie Treaty, they were assured that the hills would be theirs for eternity, but the discovery of gold changed that and the Sioux were shoved out to low-value flatlands six years later. The 1990 film *Dances with Wolves* covers some of this period. You'll need several days to explore the byways, caves, bison herds, forests, Deadwood, and Mt Rushmore and Crazy Horse monuments.

Black Hills

Presidents, artwork and shopping in downtown

An appealing capital for the Black Hills region, **Rapid City** has a cosmopolitan air best appreciated in the lively downtown where well-preserved brick buildings, filled with quality shopping and dining, make 'Rapid' a good urban base. From a shifty-eyed Nixon to a triumphant Harry Truman, lifelike **statues of America's presidents** dot street corners throughout downtown. According to lore, they are 9/10s the size of their counterparts – so they all seem just a little too small. The info center on Main St is the current home of the Trump statue.

Out back, ponder the difference between graffiti and art on a stroll through colorful **Art Alley**. For more art, step into **Prairie Edge Trading Co & Galleries**, a three-story shop with a truly mesmerizing collection of art, furniture and home goods made by members of the Northern Plains tribes. You'll find books and art supplies here too. Just across the street is **Main Street Sq**, a pleasant place to relax amid sculptures and fountains. Pop into the grand lobby at the **Hotel Alex Johnson** for its hunt-lodge vibes. Pause by the wall of photos of former celebrity guests – we see you Jerry Seinfeld!

EATING & DRINKING IN DOWNTOWN RAPID CITY: OUR PICKS

Sour: Nationally acclaimed, this slick bakery serves delicious breads and pastries, with a few daily sandwiches. *7am-2pm Wed-Sun* $

Harriet & Oak: Top-notch bakery, cafe and coffee bar with fun boho vibe. Creative sandwiches too and good draft microbrews. *7am-4pm Tue-Sat, 8am-2pm Sun* $

Tally's Silver Spoon: Savor upscale diner fare at this chic cafe and bar. Breakfasts are good; creative regional fare served nightly. *7am-2pm, 4-9pm* $$

Independent Ale House: Changing lineup of the best microbrews from the region served at the 'Indie' and its vintage-style bar. *11am-9pm most nights*

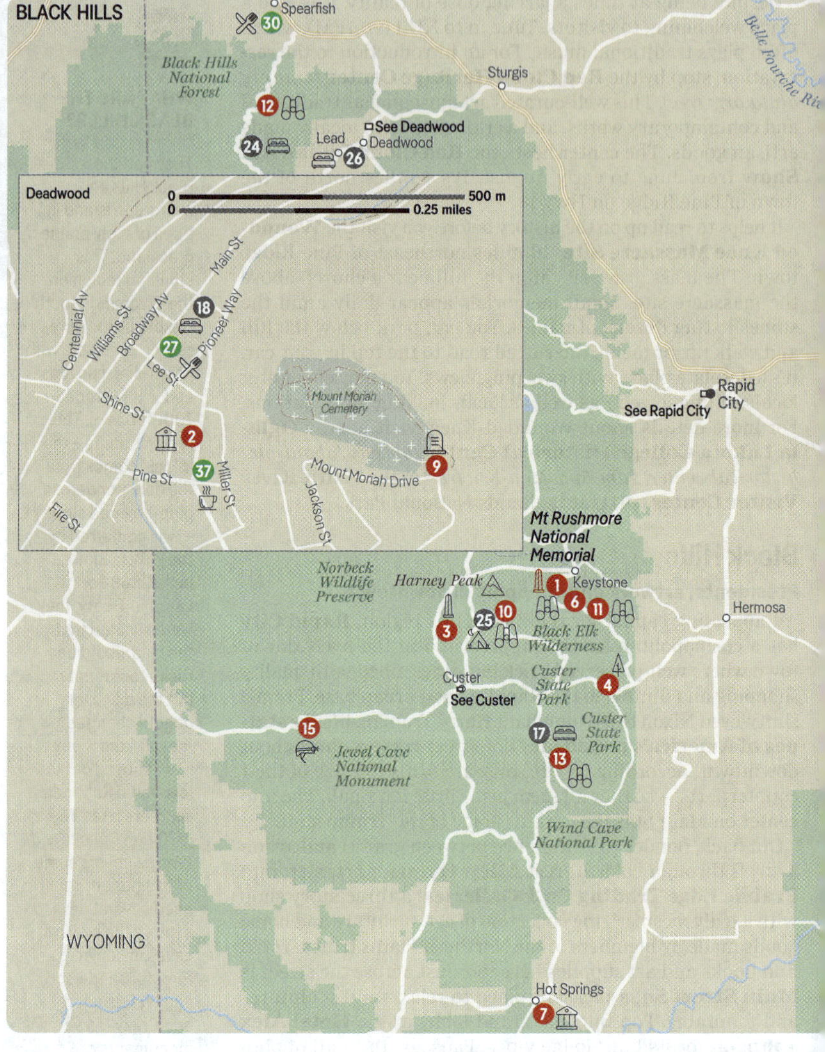

HIGHLIGHTS
1 Mt Rushmore National Memorial

SIGHTS
2 Adams Museum
3 Crazy Horse Memorial
4 Custer State Park
5 Hay Butte Overlook
6 Iron Mountain Rd
7 Mammoth Site
8 Minuteman Missile National Historic Site
9 Mount Moriah Cemetery
10 Needles Hwy
11 Peter Norbeck Scenic Byway
12 Spearfish Canyon Scenic Byway
13 Wildlife Loop Rd

ACTIVITIES
14 Door Trail
15 Jewel Cave National Monument
16 Notch Trail

SLEEPING
17 Blue Bell Lodge
18 Bullock Hotel
19 Cedar Pass Campground
20 Cedar Pass Lodge
21 Hotel Alex Johnson
22 Rocket Motel
23 Sage Creek Campground
24 Spearfish Canyon Lodge
25 Sylvan Lake Campground
26 Town Hall Inn

EATING
27 Deadwood Social Club
28 Harriet & Oak
29 Hjem AM
30 Killian's
31 Skogen Kitchen
32 Sour
33 Tally's Silver Spoon
34 Wild Spruce Market

DRINKING & NIGHTLIFE
35 Independent Ale House
36 Mt Rushmore Brewing Co
37 Pump House
see 27 Saloon No 10

SHOPPING
38 Prairie Edge
39 Wall Drug

INFORMATION
40 Ben Reifel Visitor Center
41 White River Visitor Center

TRANSPORT
42 Hwy 240 Badlands Loop Rd
43 Sheep Mountain Table

THE STORY OF WOUNDED KNEE

In 1890 the new Ghost Dance religion became popular and Lakota followers believed it would both bring back their ancestors and eliminate the white man. This struck fear into the area's soldiers and settlers, and the frenetic circle dances were outlawed. The 7th US Cavalry rounded up a band of Lakota people under Chief Big Foot and brought them to the small village of Wounded Knee.

On December 29, as the soldiers began to search for weapons, a shot was fired (nobody knows by whom), leading to the massacre of more than 250 men, women and children, most of them unarmed. It's one of the most infamous atrocities in US history. Twenty-five soldiers also died.

Admire presidential rockstars at Mt Rushmore

Glimpses of Washington's nose from the roads leading to this popular **monument** *(nps.gov/moru, parking $10)* never cease to surprise, and they are but harbingers of the full impact of this mountainside sculpture once you're up close (and past the dreary parking area). George Washington, Thomas Jefferson, Abraham Lincoln and Theodore Roosevelt each iconically stare into the distance in 60ft-tall granite glory.

Despite the crowds, there is something inspirational about the **Avenue of Flags**. Lined with the flags of all 50 states plus six districts and territories, this corridor of patriotism frames the presidents quite photogenically. If crowds are too thick, you can escape the hoopla on the 0.6-mile **Presidential Trail**. On this loop you can pause between the pines, in relative peace, to marvel at the artistry of sculptor Gutzon Borglum and the immense labor of the workers who created the memorial between 1927 and 1941. The trail also accesses the worthwhile **Sculptor's Studio**, which conveys the drama of how the monument came to be.

The official Park Service information centers have excellent bookstores. The main museum shares the story of the creation of the monument.

Mt Rushmore is a half-hour drive southwest of Rapid City via US 16. For rock-framed views of the presidents, approach via Iron Mountain Rd . The Crazy Horse Memorial is 16 miles south via Hwy 244 and US 365.

See the Crazy Horse Memorial

The world's largest **monument** *(crazyhorsememorial.org; $15-35 admission)* is this 563ft-tall work-in-progress (with a lot of work to go). When finished it will depict the Sioux leader astride his horse, pointing to the horizon saying, 'My lands are where my dead lie buried.' No one is predicting when the sculpture will be complete (the face was dedicated in 1998). Although you can see the mountain in the distance, you need to pay another $5 for a van ride to get close.

The memorial is a huge tourist draw, attracting more than one million visitors annually, but a trip here can feel underwhelming. Exhibits about Native Americans can seem haphazard and are often poorly contextualized. The focus of the place seems to be more on its Polish-American sculptor Korczak Ziolkowski and his family than the Lakota. For these reasons and others, the sculpture has drawn controversy (p120).

A scenic drive through the Black Hills

Driving the **Peter Norbeck Scenic Byway** is like flirting with a brand new crush: always exhilarating, occasionally challenging and sometimes you get a few butterflies. Named for the South Dakota senator who pushed for its creation in 1919, the oval-shaped byway is broken into four roads linking memorable destinations in the Black Hills.

Iron Mountain Rd (Hwy 16A) is the most diverse of the four, beloved for its pig-tailing loops, Mt Rushmore–framing tunnels and one gorgeous glide through sun-dappled pines. Tackle it early to avoid caravans of cars. The 14-mile **Needles**

MARYGAVANPHOTOS/SHUTTERSTOCK

Bison, Custer State Park

Hwy (Hwy 87) swoops below majestic granite spires, careens past rocky overlooks and slings through a super-narrow tunnel. The other two roads within the byway are Hwys 244 and 89.

And remember, there's no right way to drive the Black Hills, and the beauty of the place is evident no matter the byway. But there can be lots of traffic, and it can be confusing figuring out where you are when driving between sites – mostly on twisty two-lane roads with intermittent cell service. Plot out your route the night before, and note that splitting your time over two or three days is better than cramming everything into one frenzied day.

Driving times are often much longer than expected due to slow-moving traffic. RV drivers: visit *custerresorts.com* for tunnel measurements.

Wildlife-watching in Custer State Park

Your first animal sighting in **Custer State Park** *(gfp.sd.gov/parks; 7-day vehicle pass $25)* will likely be a white-tailed deer loping through the ponderosa pines that blanket the surrounding Black Hills. But soon after you turn onto the 18-mile **Wildlife Loop Rd** (p114), which swoops over untouched grasslands, the animal sightings grow thrillingly diverse. Watch bison lumber beside the road. Squint at pronghorns in the misty distance. And listen for the 'chirps' of prairie dogs

SOUTH DAKOTA'S TRIBAL NATIONS

There are nine Native American tribes in South Dakota. Their members constitute 15% of the state's population, and their tribal lands, or reservations, are scattered across tallgrass prairie, rolling grasslands, pine-dotted hills and remote badlands. The US government named the Lakota tribe the Sioux in 1825, and this term has come to apply to the Lakota, Dakota and Nakota peoples and their various bands.

Learn more at the engaging **Akta Lakota Museum & Cultural Center** at St Joseph's Indian School in Chamberlain. Visitors are welcome on reservations but should always ask for permission before taking photos, sketching or making audio and video recordings. Do not remove artifacts or disturb devotional sites.

EATING & DRINKING IN CUSTER: OUR PICKS

Skogen Kitchen: A James Beard nominee; a delicious global menu with luxury toppings like morels, caviar and sprinkles of pretension. *5-8:30pm Tue-Sat* **$$$**

Wild Spruce Market: Gourmet market with dips, specialty cheeses, produce and local bison beef. Buy drinks at the coffee and beer bar. *8:30am-6pm most days* **$**

HJEM AM: From the folks behind Skogen, HJEM serves decadent gourmet breakfasts. Reservations recommended. *8am-11am Wed-Fri, to noon Sat & Sun* **$$**

Mt Rushmore Brewing Co: The Rail Splitter Porter and other flagship beers give a nod to American history at this complex with two fine-dining restaurants. *11am-9pm*

CRAZY HORSE MEMORIAL REVISITED

Never photographed or persuaded to sign a meaningless treaty, Crazy Horse was chosen for a monument (p118) that Lakota Sioux elders hoped would balance the presidential focus of Mt Rushmore 16 miles north. In 1948 a Boston-born sculptor, Korczak Ziolkowski, started blasting granite. His family has continued the work since his death in 1982, and the monument has indeed become a counterpoint to Mt Rushmore.

On the flip side, some Lakota oppose the monument as a desecration of sacred land. Other concerns include the introductory film at the visitor center, which spotlights the Ziolkowski family with seemingly less emphasis on the stories of the Lakota. Native American exhibits and artifacts in the museums may be in need of better organization.

as they scamper between burrows.

To put it succinctly, this place is wonderful. The only reason this 111-sq-mile state park isn't a national park is that the state grabbed it first. What's here? One of the largest free-roaming bison herds in the world (about 1450) as well as elk, bighorn sheep, the famous 'begging burros' (donkeys seeking handouts) and more than 200 bird species.

Pick up the free Tatanka visitor guide at the entrance station for details about hiking, fishing and camping. It also includes a list of the park's daily programs. Don't miss the new **Bison Center**, where large video screens envelope you in the sights and sounds of a buffalo stampede. The corrals for the annual **buffalo round-up** are steps away. Another highlight is boulder-flanked **Sylvan Lake**; admire it from the Sylvan Lakeshore Trail.

Lodging options rival those of national parks. We're fond of the cabins and modern-rustic style of **Blue Bell Lodge**. For more information about buffalo, also known as bison, see p520.

Admire rare underground crystals

If you visit only one Black Hills cave, **Jewel Cave** *(nps.gov/jeca; tours $6-45)* would be a good choice. It's 13 miles west of Custer and is so named because colorful calcite crystals line many of its walls. More than 200 miles have been surveyed (about 3% of the passageway), making it the third-longest known cave in the world.

You can only enter the cave on guided tours. One unique option is the **Historic Lantern Tour**; your path is illuminated by handheld lanterns. Tours can be reserved 30 days in advance at *recreation.gov*. To avoid disappointment, advance reservations are highly recommended.

Mammoth-bone bonanza

Kids who love fossils – and anyone who thinks paleontology is cool – will 'dig' the **Mammoth Site** *(mammothsite.com; adult/child $15/12)* in the town of Hot Springs. About 26,000 years ago, hundreds of animals perished in a sinkhole here. Today you can walk around their exposed tusks and bones, which were discovered during a construction project in 1974. So far 61 mammoths – two woolly, 59 Columbian – have been found. The site is the largest left-as-found mammoth fossil display in the country and an active dig.

The self-guided tour around the bone bed pauses by a lab where assistants are happy to answer your questions. Bones of a dire wolf and giant sloth are displayed in the adjacent Great Hall.

Hot Springs is about 60 miles south of Rapid City.

Relaxing in hot springs

Empty your water bottles before heading into Hot Springs, an unhurried town south of the main Black Hills circuit. The big natural attraction here is the warm mineral springs feeding the Fall River. You can relax weary muscles in one of six outdoor pools at the stylish **Moccasin Springs Natural Mineral Spa** *(moccasinsprings.com; 2hr soak pass $31.80)*, where the water temperature ranges from 80 to 105 degrees. The onsite **Dragonfly** restaurant serves salads, sandwiches and shareable nibbles.

The best water you'll drink in the Black Hills flows freely from Kidney Springs, just down the road from Moccasin Springs. It's not cold, but it's also not so hot you'll regret it on a sultry day. An old gazebo marks the spot along the pretty Hot Springs River Walk, across the narrow Fall River from the heart of town. Fill up your water bottles at the faucet. And you might want to stick around – downtown is home to ornate 1890s red sandstone buildings that glow at sunset.

Deadwood

Step into the past

Settled illegally by gold rushers in the 1870s, Deadwood is now a National Historic Landmark. Its atmospheric streets are lined with gold-rush-era buildings lavishly restored with gambling dollars. The lyrically foul-mouthed *Deadwood* HBO series and subsequent 2019 movie brought celebrity status.

You'll likely be greeted by a docent when stepping into the refreshingly quirky **Adams Museum** *(deadwoodhistory.com; suggested donation adult/child $5/3)*, home to artifacts including a two-headed calf and a big lumpy gold nugget. These exhibits are part of a larger cabinet of curiosities originally curated by pioneer businessman WE Adams in the 1930s.

For more Wild West history, stroll casino-lined Historic Main Street. Don't miss **Saloon No 10** (p82) *(saloon10.com)*, where stuffed game and old photographs recall rowdier days. Wild Bill Hickok was shot and killed while playing cards at the bar's original location across the street. Fans of *Deadwood* will recall the conflicted but upstanding sheriff Seth Bullock. He opened the **Bullock Hotel** *(historicbullock.com)* in 1895, and this creaky place still welcomes guests – and maybe a few ghosts.

A short but steep drive climbs from downtown to **Mount Moriah Cemetery** *(cityofdeadwood.com; admission $2; cash only)*, where Calamity Jane, Wild Bill and Potato Creek Johnny, a colorful prospector, rest side by side.

WIND CAVE OR JEWEL CAVE?

Um, excuse me. A cave is not just a cave, and if you've seen one, you certainly have not seen them all. One problem for travelers in the Black Hills is that two extended cave systems, both managed by the federal park service, are open for tours. How to pick?

It's win-win. Jewel Cave is a 'wet' limestone cave filled with classic formations like stalactites and stalagmites. It also has sparkling calcite crystals clustered into unusual shapes. Wind Cave (p112) is a 'dry' cave with fewer of these classic favorites. Wind Cave does, however, hold 95% of the world's known boxwork, which is a rare, honeycomb patterned calcite. Wind Cave also has outdoor hiking trails.

EATING & DRINKING AROUND DEADWOOD: OUR PICKS

Deadwood Social Club: In the historic Saloon No 10 in Deadwood, this busy restaurant offers crowd-pleasing Italian fare plus steaks. *hours vary Mon-Sat* $$

Saloon No 10: Legendary bar in Deadwood with dark walls, sawdust floors and knickknackery galore. *9am-2am*

Pump House: Drink a cup of locally roasted coffee or craft beer in this old Texaco gas station in Deadwood. Good sandwiches too. *7am-5pm*

Killian's: Enjoy a gouda jalapeño burger or ahi club in Spearfish before driving the Spearfish Canyon Scenic Byway. Vegan options. *11am-10pm Sun-Wed, to 11pm Fri & Sat* $$

Places We Love to Stay

$ Budget $$ Midrange $$$ Top End

St Louis p54

Angad Arts Hotel $$ The art-filled rooms are eye candy, as are the expansive views from the rooftop bar.

St Louis Union Station Hotel $$ The hotel lobby bar is tops, set in the 1894 barrel-vaulted train station. Good downtown location, but rooms could use a refresh.

21c Museum Hotel $$$ Our favorite hotel in St Louis has taken over a 1920s YMCA, filling it with plush rooms and an art gallery partly in the old basketball court.

Kansas City p61

Crossroads Hotel $$ Hip hotel with comfy rooms, excellent rooftop and lobby bars, a walkable location and an inventive Italian restaurant on the ground floor.

Hotel Kansas City $$ This downtown Gothic Revival stunner feels just as sleek as when it opened as a private members' club in the 1920s.

Truitt $$ Feel right at home at one of KC's few locally owned accommodation options. This stately 1916 converted mansion has just eight uniquely decorated rooms near the Nelson-Atkins (p61).

Branson p66

Ozarker Lodge $$ This reinvented roadside motel has mid-mod touches, cedar soaking tubs overlooking a creek and firepits for s'more roasting.

Tulsa p74

Campbell Hotel $ Restored to its 1927-era Route 66 splendor, this historic hotel east of downtown has 26 rooms with hardwood floors and oversized furniture.

Mayo Hotel $$ When this hotel, once Oklahoma's tallest building, opened in 1925, it was the height of luxury, and it's still one of Tulsa's top stays. Excellent choice for art deco architecture admirers.

Oklahoma City p80

Classen Inn $ Well-priced mid-century motel near downtown that's had a mod makeover.

Bradford House $$ Built in 1912 as a luxury apartment house, it's now a boutique hotel with eccentric interior design and modern, comfortable rooms.

The National $$$ Our favorite historic stay in the region is in this 1930s bank. Have a drink in the gasp-worthy lobby bar in the former banking hall with marble floors, columns and huge murals.

Omaha p86

Kimpton Cottonwood Hotel $$ Built as a hotel in 1915 and reimagined for modern travelers. Fantastic pool area and a knock-out **steakhouse** (p88).

Hotel Deco $$ Alice in Wonderland meets art deco detailing in this 14-story 1930s building within walking distance of the Old Market. Once you've settled into your room, track down the Wicked Rabbit, the hotel's speakeasy.

Hotel Indigo $$$ The bold accents and mismatched prints hint at the quirky personality of this modern hotel in a beautiful historic brick building downtown.

Lincoln p88

Kindler Hotel $$ The capital city's first indie boutique hotel is this downtown gem within walking distance of the historic Haymarket district.

Graduate by Hilton $$ Your college years never go out of fashion at this retro kitsch hotel that caters to the permanent student in every grad. It has a tiki bar, old-school pinball machines in the lobby and eclectic room decor that's part luxe, part rumpus room.

Dubuque & Around p95

Maquoketa Caves State Park Campground $ Camp beneath the pines near caves and trails at this family friendly spot between Dubuque and Davenport.

Hotel Julien $$ Built in 1915, this spiffy eight-story hotel in Dubuque was once a refuge for Al Capone. Some rooms have Mississippi River views.

Amana Colonies p98

Hotel Millwright (p99) **$$** Decor inside this historic woolen mill gives a nod to the textile industry. Rooms have smart, contemporary appeal.

Des Moines p100

Hotel Fort Des Moines $$ A storied haunt for 20th-century powerbrokers and celebrities, this revamped number celebrates its roots with modern style.

Des Lux Hotel **$$$** Luxurious downtown hotel with 51 rooms and loads of eclectic modern touches. A lavish hot breakfast is included.

Mason City p102

Historic Park Inn Hotel (p103) **$$** Sleep inside a work of art at the only remaining hotel designed by Frank Lloyd Wright. Beside a lovely downtown square.

North Dakota p104

Juniper Campground (p106) **$** Sites are first come, first served at this pleasant campground set beneath junipers in Theodore Roosevelt National Park's wildlife-filled North Unit.

Rough Riders Hotel **$$** Old West meets New West at this upscale lodge in Medora, near the South Unit of Theodore Roosevelt National Park. Each room comes with a Teddy bear.

Hotel Donaldson **$$** Well-appointed rooms are each decorated by a regional artist. In Fargo; don't miss the rooftop Sky Prairie for cocktails with a city view.

Sioux Falls & Around p109

King Campground (p69) **$** Northeast of Sioux Falls, this new campground in Palisades State Park sprawls across a scenic plain close to trails, a creek and cool quartzite formations.

Black Hills p115

Sylvan Lake Campground **$** All of the campgrounds in Custer State Park are recommended, but this one is set in the forest a short walk from a uniquely gorgeous rock-fringed lake.

Rocket Motel **$** The neon sign is a jaunty welcome to this old-style motor court – a 'blast' from the past! – in Custer. Located in the center of town and well maintained.

Town Hall Inn **$** Near Deadwood in Lead, this 12-room inn occupies the 1912 Town Hall and has spacious suites named and themed for their former governmental purpose.

Spearfish Canyon Lodge **$$** Along a scenic byway, this Black Hills retreat sits near trails, streams and waterfalls in a gorgeous setting. Modern pine-y rooms are cozy.

Hotel Alex Johnson (p115) **$$$** The design of this 1927 classic in Rapid City magically blends Germanic Tudor architecture with traditional Lakota Sioux symbols.

Blue Bell Lodge (p120) **$$$** Chic cabins, ponderosa pines and buffalo stomping grounds in Custer State Park. Restaurant on-site and horseback trail rides nearby.

Rough Riders Hotel

MICHAEL GORDON/SHUTTERSTOCK

Researched and curated by Regis St Louis

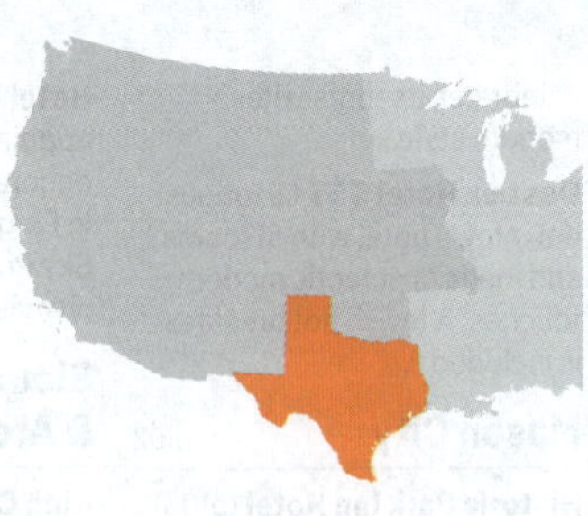

Texas

BIG SKIES AND OPEN ROADS

Dust off your boots and grab that cowboy hat: wide-ranging adventures in cities, mountains, deserts and beaches await in the Lone Star state.

Larger than many countries, Texas occupies a mammoth-sized footprint, both in terms of geography and the national psyche. Five of the country's 15 biggest cities are here in Texas. The state is home to the most valuable sports franchise in the world (Dallas Cowboys) and its cuisine (Tex-Mex) is known around the globe. Texas also has an astonishing diversity. Sure, there are sunny fields where the longhorn cattle roam, but this is also the land of craggy mountains and sunbaked deserts in the West, oasis-like springs in the Hill Country, and hundreds of miles of enticing Gulf Coast beaches.

Scenery aside, Texan cities and small towns alike offer a seemingly infinite array of attractions. You can explore cutting-edge art and culture, nightlife and cuisines from around the globe in Dallas, Fort Worth, Austin, San Antonio and Houston. There are atmospheric old music halls in tiny Hill Country settlements, and walkable neighborhoods bursting with creativity all across the state.

The Texas experience is about many things, from road trips across the windswept prairies to otherworldly art installations hidden on the edge of the wilderness. It's a place to create your own adventure, whether you're interested in hiking, rafting, stargazing, beach-hopping, birding, watching pro sports games or just immersing yourself in a place that's like nowhere else. Just don't try to pack in too much. You'd need a lifetime to experience it all.

ZORYANCHIK/SHUTTERSTOCK

THE MAIN AREAS

AUSTIN
Free-spirited city of green spaces and live music. p130

SAN ANTONIO & THE HILL COUNTRY
Historic missions, charming towns and wild beauty. p140

DALLAS & FORT WORTH
Cosmopolitan neighbors of culture and Western lore. p150

HOUSTON & THE GULF COAST
Multicultural epicenter and glorious beaches. p157

WEST TEXAS & BIG BEND
Where the mountains meet the desert. p166

For places to stay in Texas, see p172

BILL KENNEDY/SHUTTERSTOCK

Big Bend National Park (p168)

Find Your Way

The bigger cities in Texas are found mostly on the eastern half of the state. Beaches and seaside towns stretch down the Gulf Coast, while deserts and mountains lie in the far west.

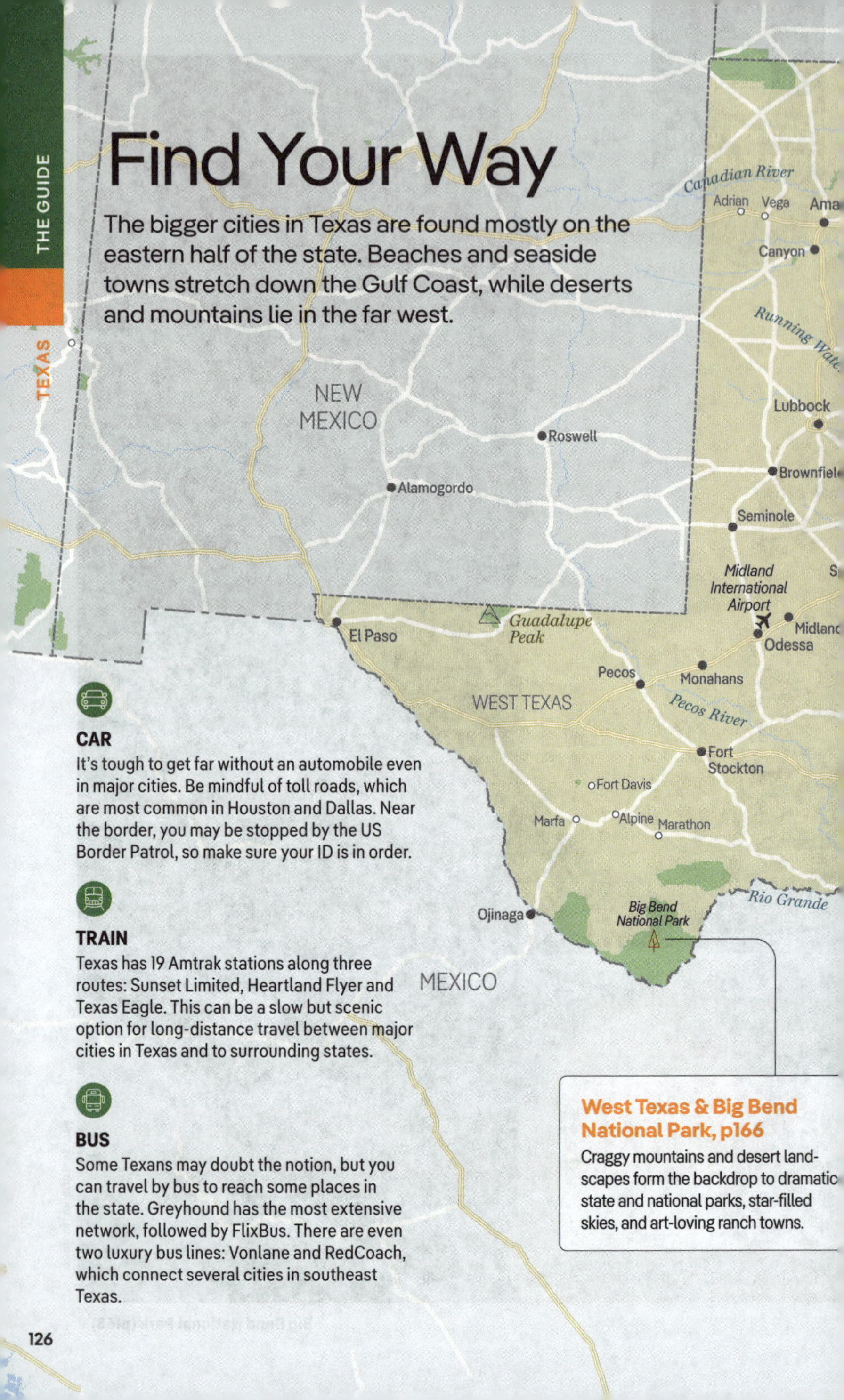

CAR

It's tough to get far without an automobile even in major cities. Be mindful of toll roads, which are most common in Houston and Dallas. Near the border, you may be stopped by the US Border Patrol, so make sure your ID is in order.

TRAIN

Texas has 19 Amtrak stations along three routes: Sunset Limited, Heartland Flyer and Texas Eagle. This can be a slow but scenic option for long-distance travel between major cities in Texas and to surrounding states.

BUS

Some Texans may doubt the notion, but you can travel by bus to reach some places in the state. Greyhound has the most extensive network, followed by FlixBus. There are even two luxury bus lines: Vonlane and RedCoach, which connect several cities in southeast Texas.

West Texas & Big Bend National Park, p166

Craggy mountains and desert landscapes form the backdrop to dramatic state and national parks, star-filled skies, and art-loving ranch towns.

Dallas & Fort Worth, p150
Two vibrant gateways to Texas pack a wealth of attractions, from cutting-edge art galleries to longhorn cattle drives.
Austin, p130
Texas' ever-changing capital city has long been a bastion of diversity, creative talent and progressive ideals that stands out from the rest of the state.
Houston & the Gulf Coast, p157
From top-class museums to space shuttle tours, H-Town is a cultural dynamo – and launchpad to wild beaches and seaside towns.
San Antonio & the Hill Country, p140
The birthplace of the republic, San Antonio is at the heart of Texas' story. Outdoor adventures and picturesque small towns await in the nearby Hill Country.
0 200 km
0 100 miles
OKLAHOMA
Red River
Brazos River
Trinity River
Wichita Falls
Sherman
Paris
Denton
Fort Worth Historic Stockyards
Grapevine
Dallas
Jefferson
Fort Worth
Arlington
Canton
Marshall
Abilene
Fort Worth Botanic Garden
Waxahachie
Tyler
Corsicana
Nacogdoches
San Angelo
Waco
Crockett
Temple
Bryan
Sonora
Washington-on-the-Brazos
Barton Springs Pool
Austin
Fredericksburg
Luckenbach
South Congress
Beaumont
Orange
Lady Bird Johnson Wildflower Center
Lockhart
Museum of Fine Arts
Houston
Port Arthur
Boerne
San Antonio
Schulenburg
Seguin
Gonzales
The Alamo
River Walk
Space Center Houston
West Columbia
Goliad
Victoria
Three Rivers
Rockport
Fulton
Corpus Christi
Port Aransas
Kingsville
Laredo
Rio Grande City
Harlingen
McAllen
Weslaco
Port Isabel
Brownsville

Plan Your Time

The Texas experience is about many things: big-city culture in Dallas and Houston, small towns and swimming holes in Hill Country, beaches on the Gulf Coast, and desert and mountain wilderness in the west.

EMMA_GRIFFITHS/SHUTTERSTOCK

Barton Springs Pool (p135)

A Full Day in Austin

● Wake up with a refreshing dip in **Barton Springs Pool** (p135), where the water stays cool year-round. Mosey over to **South Congress** (p131) to shop before pausing for a pick-me-up at **Jo's Coffee** (p133) and a selfie at the **I Love You So Much mural**. Later get a dose of Lone Star culture at the **Bullock Texas State History Museum** (p130), with its eye-catching, interactive exhibits. Get in line for lunch at **Franklin Barbecue** or **La Barbecue** (p138) before heading out for a flower-filled stroll at the **Zilker Botanical Garden** (p133).

● In the evening, grab a bite off a **food truck** (p132), then join the party people on **6th St** (p138). Alternatively, focus on Austin's fabled music scene at the **Continental Club** (p137).

SEASONAL HIGHLIGHTS

With festivals and pleasant weather, spring (late March to May) and fall (September to early November) are ideal times to visit. Summer swelters (cool off at the beach or an inland swimming spot).

MARCH

Creative and tech types congregate in Austin for **South by Southwest** (p137) , which takes over downtown for nine days. Key components include film screenings, a comedy festival, art exhibitions and big concerts.

APRIL

Fiesta San Antonio (p144) is an 11-day celebration of the city's heritage and culture that dates back to 1891, and features loads of concerts, parades with costumes and marching bands, riverside events, feasting and merrymaking.

JUNE

Hurricane season starts in the Gulf of Mexico (and runs through November), with the worst storms typically arriving in August or September. Be weather aware if traveling to Houston or the Gulf Coast during these months.

Weekend in San Antonio & the Hill Country

Start your day in San Antonio with breakfast at ultra-festive **Mi Tierra** (p144) then explore **Historic Market Square** (p144), where Mexican craft stores transport you south. Head to the **Alamo** (p140) to learn about Texas' most visited monument.

Head up to the open-air restaurants at the **Pearl** (p144), a former brewery turned entertainment complex. Afterwards, stroll along the lovely **River Walk** (p143) and visit the impressive Latin American collections inside the **San Antonio Museum of Art** (p144).

On your second day, hit the road for a scenic drive into Hill Country. Visit the charming town of **Boerne** (p147), followed by a hike and river swim in **Guadalupe River State Park** (p146).

Ten-Day Road Trip

Start in Dallas at the **Sixth Floor Museum** (p150) to learn about Dallas' darkest day, then head over to **Bishop Arts District** (p152) for shopping, strolling and cafe-hopping. In neighboring Fort Worth, see cowboys in action during the daily cattle drive at **Fort Worth Stockyards** (p154), followed by boot-scootin' at **Billy Bob's Texas** (p154).

Drive south to Houston, taking in the **Museum District** (p157) and exploring **Montrose** (p162). Admire NASA's **Space Center Houston** (p163), then head to the Gulf for beach time in **Port Aransas** (p164).

Go northwest to San Antonio, stopping at the **missions** (p145) south of town, then veer west for experimental art in **Marfa** (p168), stargazing at the **McDonald Observatory** (p167) and exhilarating hikes in **Big Bend National Park** (p168).

SEPTEMBER

In Dallas, the **State Fair of Texas** (p154) brings ample amusement over 24 consecutive days. Carnival rides, livestock shows, concerts, fireworks and wondrous food stalls are a few draws for the 2 million-plus visitors each year.

OCTOBER

Make the journey to Marfa in West Texas to experience three days of creativity during the **Chinati Weekend** (p168). There's live music, artist talks and special exhibitions. Most events are free and open to the public.

NOVEMBER

Along the Gulf Coast, the colder months bring migrating birds passing through in huge flocks. November is a great month to see some of Texas' avian stars – endangered whooping cranes – at the **Aransas National Wildlife Reserve** (p164).

DECEMBER

Football season runs from September to January, but December is particularly exciting with NFL playoffs underway. You can also catch pro basketball. Houston is a great spot for seeing games live.

Austin

LIVE MUSIC | GREEN SPACES | BARBECUE

GETTING AROUND

The best way to get around Austin is to rent a car or use rideshare apps. Parking is expensive downtown.

Downtown Austin is laid out on a grid and best explored on foot. Bird, Lime and CapMetro rent scooters and bikes all over town, starting at $1. Download the apps to search pickup locations and to rent and return them.

It's fine to take the bus between the airport and downtown, but other routes can sometimes feel unsafe. CapMetro Rail has good service, but covers just nine stations between downtown and north Austin. Download the CapMetro app to purchase tickets.

Only a few decades ago, Austin was mostly known as a laid-back town full of slackers and no real industry besides the live music scene. Locals hopped about town in their flip-flops, cooling off at creeks under the blazing sun before emptying their pockets in dingy dive bars come dusk. Later, Austin became a safe space in the south for the queer community and for creatives honing their craft. Next came the Silicon Valley folk, lured in by tax incentives and a budding tech scene. The result has been an economic explosion and a city reimagined, which is usually what happens when a juicy secret gets out. Experience Austin's delights gastronomically through the city's blossoming food scene, during one of the capital's huge festivals like SXSW and Austin City Limits, or through the natural outdoor wonders that stretch from the outskirts right into the heart of downtown.

Capital Culture

Austin's top museums

Austin's museums might not have nationwide name recognition, but they'll surprise you. The mainstays clustered around Congress Ave satisfy an appetite for art, history and culture. The exterior walls at **The Contemporary Austin** routinely moonlight as canvases for national artists like Jenny Holzer – and outside means free viewing. Across the street, explore works by Mexican and Latino artists at the **Mexic-Arte Museum**, which also has a thoughtful gift shop. The **Bullock Texas State History Museum** takes visitors through

TOP TIP

From March until late October, the best free show in town happens beneath the Congress Avenue Bridge. Just after sunset, vast swarms of Mexican free-tailed bats emerge into the night in a feeding frenzy. Grab a spot on the sidewalk along the bridge or on the southeast corner, close to the Austin American-Statesman building.

the state's history by way of interactive exhibits and a 4D special-effects IMAX theater.

For retro discovery, the **Museum of the Weird** carries a collection of curiosities and oddities displayed in the tradition of PT Barnum. Speaking of weird, the **Cathedral of Junk** may not qualify as a museum, but the towering sculpture fills artist Vince Hannemann's backyard with everything from dolls and car bumpers to toilets and lawn-mower tires. Just call Hannemann *(512-299-7413)* ahead of time to make an appointment.

Get to Know South Congress

Austin's trendiest street

South Congress, or SoCo as it's often abbreviated, is equal parts authentic charm and commercialized cool, with plenty of food, shopping and entertainment options. Austin-born favorites like **Home Slice Pizza**, **Hopdoddy Burger Bar** and **Amy's Ice Cream** whet the appetites of a daytime crowd fresh from a dip in Lady Bird Lake, while sought-after reservations at **Otoko** and **June's** give people a good reason to change into fresh clothes.

Boutiques range from vintage to contemporary and keep all tastes satisfied for hours on end, including shops to pick

HIGHLIGHTS
1 Franklin Barbecue

SIGHTS
2 Bullock Texas State History Museum
3 Cathedral of Junk
4 Red Bud Isle

SLEEPING
5 ARRIVE Austin

EATING
6 Cuantos Tacos
7 La Barbecue
8 Leroy & Lewis Barbecue
9 Micklethwait Barbecue
10 The Vegan Nom

ENTERTAINMENT
11 AFS Cinema
12 Bullock Museum IMAX Theater

SOUTH AUSTIN

South Congress Avenue

EATING IN AUSTIN: FOOD TRUCKS

Gordough's: Take their word for it when they say these are big, fat doughnuts. One is more than enough here. *10am-midnight Mon-Fri, from 8am Sat & Sun* $

The Vegan Nom: Vegan food truck serving up delicious tacos, nachos and burritos on the east side of town. *8am-2pm & 5-10pm Mon-Fri, 8am-10pm Sat & Sun* $

Kiin Di: Fantastic Thai food along South Lamar. The Killer Noodles are a must-try. *4:30-9pm Wed-Sun* $

Cuantos Tacos: Austin's must-visit yellow truck for Mexican-style street tacos. Make sure to try the suadero. *11am-10pm Tue-Sat* $

HIGHLIGHTS
1 Barton Springs Pool
2 South Congress
3 Zilker Park

SIGHTS
4 Broken Spoke
5 I Love You So Much Mural
6 Open Room Austin
7 Pfluger Pedestrian Bridge
8 Sand Beach Park
9 Willie Nelson Mural
10 Zilker Botanical Garden

SLEEPING
11 Austin Motel
12 Carpenter Hotel
13 Hotel San José
14 South Congress Hotel

EATING
15 Amy's Ice Creams
16 Better Half Coffee & Cocktails
17 Clark's Oyster Bar
18 Dovetail Pizza
19 El Alma
20 Fresa's
21 Gordough's
22 Home Slice Pizza
23 Hopdoddy Burger Bar
24 Jo's Coffee
25 June's
26 Kiin Di
27 Loro
28 Otoko
29 Perla's
30 Polvos
31 Terry Black's BBQ
32 Uchi

DRINKING & NIGHTLIFE
33 ABGB
34 Bouldin Acres
35 Continental Club
36 Courtyard Lounge at Hotel San José
37 Donn's Depot
38 Nightcap
39 Saxon Pub
40 Tiki Tatsu-Ya

ENTERTAINMENT
41 Alamo Drafthouse Cinema
42 Austin City Limits Music Festival
43 Austin Trail of Lights
44 Eeyore's Birthday Party
45 Food & Wine Festival
46 Reggae Festival

up some cowboy boots. Cafes are well staggered along the strip, with highlights like **Jo's Coffee** and its famous **I Love You So Much mural**. Another must see/photograph is the **Willie Nelson For President mural** on Elizabeth St a few blocks away.

Zilker Park & Barton Springs Pool

Bask under the Texan sun

The beloved 358-acre **Zilker Park** is a year-round haven for humans and dogs alike in Austin. Spring is when the flowers bloom at **Zilker Botanical Garden** and when the sky is colorfully decorated by the **ABC Kite Fest**. Summer brings sunbathers and revelers armed with giant coolers, as well as the free **Blues on the Green** concert series across multiple evenings in June and July. Fall provides cooler weather for Zilker's most famous event, the **Austin City Limits Music Festival** *(aclfestival.com)*. December's lack of white powder doesn't deter the park's festive efforts, as Zilker becomes the **Austin Trail of Lights** with 2 million bulbs, 90 Christmas trees, twinkling light tunnels and a merry sleigh of displays.

OTHER FAVORITE OUTDOOR SPOTS

Ky Harkey, founder of The Visitor Experience and former director of interpretation at Texas Parks & Wildlife, highlights his favorite outdoor spots in Austin. *Insta: @kyharkey*

Parking is really challenging at **Red Bud Isle**, but you can also access it by paddleboard or kayak for a super-unique experience. **McKinney Falls** is the only state park within Austin's city limits. People can camp and see live music on the same day. The **Pfluger Pedestrian Bridge** (p136) is one of my favorite spots in Austin at sunrise or sunset. **Sand Beach Park** has an art installation called **Open Room Austin** (p136). It's this grand, colorful picnic table that's 24ft long. You can't reserve it – it's meant to bring different groups of people together.

EATING IN DOWNTOWN AUSTIN: OUR PICKS

Better Half Coffee & Cocktails: A great spot for breakfast, brunch, lunch or dinner. *8am-3pm Mon, to 10pm Tue-Thu & Sun, to 11pm Fri & Sat* $$

Taqueria 10 de 10: A taco speakeasy. Enter through ReyRey bar in the alleyway between 2nd and 3rd Sts. *11:30am-10pm Sun-Wed, to 1am Thu-Sat* $

Clark's Oyster Bar: Oysters on the half shell and other seafood options inside a beautiful space in Old West Austin. *11am-10pm Sun-Thu, to 11pm Fri & Sat* $$

Arlo Grey: Fine-dining menu from Top Chef host (and winner) Kristen Kish and a prime spot to watch the South Congress bats. *5-10pm Wed-Sun* $$$

DOWNTOWN AUSTIN

0 — 400 m
0 — 0.2 miles

House Park
Duncan Park
Shoal Creek Greenbelt
Wooldridge Square
Republic Square
Texas State Capitol
Waterloo Park
Waller Creek
DOWNTOWN
WAREHOUSE DISTRICT
Brush Park
Palm Park
Red River Cultural District
6th Street
Shoal Creek
Lady Bird Lake
Vic Mathias Shores
Downtown
Ann & Roy Butler Hike-and-Bike Trail
Ann & Roy Butler Hike-and-Bike Trail & Boardwalk
Congress Ave Bridge

W 15th St, W 14th St, W 13th St, W 12th St, W 11th St, W 10th St, W 9th St, W 8th St, W 7th St, W 6th St, W 5th St, W 4th St, W 3rd St, W 2nd St, W 11th St, E 15th St, E 14th St, E 13th St, E 12th St, E 11th St, E 10th St, E 9th St, E 8th St, E 7th St, E 6th St, E 5th St, E 4th St, E 3rd St, E 2nd St, E Cesar Chavez St (E 1st St), Driskill St, Willow St, Spence St, Shoal Creek Blvd, Henderson St, Wood St, West Ave, Rio Grande St, Nueces St, San Antonio St, Guadalupe St, Lavaca St, Colorado St, Congress Ave, S Congress Ave, Brazos St, San Jacinto Blvd, Trinity St, Neches St, Red River St, Sabine St, N IH 35 Frontage Rd, S IH 35 Frontage Rd

Bullock Texas State History Museum (0.2mi);
Bullock Museum IMAX Theater (0.2mi)
Cuantos Tacos (0.4mi)
Franklin Barbecue (0.2mi)
ARRIVE Austin (0.8mi)
The Vegan Nom (1mi);
La Barbecue (1.1mi)
Open Room Austin (0.25mi);
Pfluger Pedestrian Bridge (0.25mi);
Sand Beach Park (0.25mi)
See Warehouse District

Warehouse District
WAREHOUSE DISTRICT
Lavaca St
Colorado St
W 4th St
0 — 100 m
0 — 0.05 miles

DRINKING IN DOWNTOWN AUSTIN: OUR PICKS

Donn's Depot: A former train depot turned dive bar and go-to hang-out for many in Austin. Live music most nights. *2pm-2am Mon-Fri, 6pm-2am Sat*

Elephant Room: An underground jazz bar that's exactly what you'd want in an underground jazz bar. *5pm-2am Mon-Fri, 8pm-2am Sat, 7pm-1am Sun*

Roosevelt Room: One of Austin's top cocktail bars with a jaw-dropping menu of drinks that spans different eras. *3pm-midnight Sun-Wed, to 2am Thu-Sat*

Nightcap: Old bungalow house turned bar-restaurant with a great outdoor view of the hustle and bustle along W 6th. *5-10pm Tue & Wed, to midnight Thu-Sat*

HIGHLIGHTS
1 6th Street
2 Red River Cultural District
3 Texas State Capitol

SIGHTS
4 Austin Public Library
5 Butterfly Bridge
6 Deep Roots Community Garden
7 Mexic-Arte Museum
8 Museum of the Weird
9 Shoal Creek Greenbelt
10 Tau Ceti
11 The Contemporary Austin
12 Waterloo Park
13 Willie Nelson Statue

ACTIVITIES
14 9th St BMX Park
15 Ann and Roy Butler Hike-and-Bike Trail

SLEEPING
16 Firehouse Hostel
17 Hotel Van Zandt
18 The Driskill

EATING
19 Arlo Grey
20 Stubb's Bar-B-Q
21 Taqueria 10 de 10
22 Walton's Fancy & Staple

DRINKING & NIGHTLIFE
23 Barbarella's
24 Blind Pig Pub
25 Cheer Up Charlies
26 Clive Bar
27 Coconut Club
28 Elephant Room
29 Highland Lounge
30 Iron Bear
31 Jackalope
32 Kung Fu Saloon
33 Lucille
34 Neon Grotto
35 Oilcan Harry's
36 Pete's Dueling Piano Bar
37 Rain
38 Rainey Street
39 Roosevelt Room
40 Rustic Tap
41 Star Bar

ENTERTAINMENT
42 Blue Starlite Urban Drive-In
43 Creek & The Cave
44 Esther's Follies
45 Mohawk
46 Paramount Theatre
47 Pecan Street Festival
48 South By Southwest
49 Violet Crown Cinema

Don't miss Zilker's summer savior, **Barton Springs Pool**, a 3-acre outdoor swimming spot fed by cold-water natural springs from deep underground. The water temperature averages between 68°F and 70°F (20-21°C) all year, particularly wonderful on those brutally hot summer days when the thermostat frequently hits triple digits. In the winter, admission fees are waived for those interested in a complimentary dose of cryotherapy.

A Hike-&-Bike Trail

Skip the gym

The **Ann and Roy Butler Hike-and-Bike Trail** is Austin's outdoor gym. Whether it's a walk, run, bike ride or quality time with your pup, this is where Austin congregates to get outside and burn calories – all while taking in stunning views of downtown. The 10-mile trail loops around Lady Bird Lake, using the Roberta Crenshaw Bridge under MoPac (to the west) and Longhorn Shores (to the east) to form a circle, and features public art exhibits and a live music series in the fall.

BEST AUSTIN FESTIVALS & EVENTS

Austin knows how to party and is much more than just SXSW and ACL.

Reggae Festival: Two days of reggae for a cause every April, raising more than $1 million for the Central Texas Food Bank in 30-plus years.

Pecan Street Festival: A free downtown music and arts festival held twice a year.

Eeyore's Birthday Party: A day-long party in late April to raise money for nonprofits in honor of Eeyore, Winnie-the-Pooh's habitually sad buddy.

Trail of Lights: Annual celebration in Zilker Park each December to ring in the holiday season.

Food & Wine Festival: The absolute best of Austin's culinary scene gets together in Zilker Park each November.

EATING IN SOUTH AUSTIN: OUR PICKS

Polvos: Delicious interior Mexican food. Now three locations, but visit the original on S 1st St for the atmosphere. *9:30am-10pm Sun-Thu, to 11pm Fri & Sat* $$

Fresa's: Another S 1st St favorite. The specialty here is wood-grilled chicken, but top it with the jalapeño crema. *11am-10pm Mon-Fri, 10am-10pm Sat & Sun* $

Dovetail Pizza: A little fancier than a normal, neighborhood pizza joint. Also located on S 1st. *11am-10pm Sun-Thu, to 11pm Fri & Sat* $$

Terry Black's BBQ: A long line on weekends, but it moves quickly. You might spend longer finding a place to park. *10:30am-9:30pm Sun-Thu, to 10pm Fri & Sat* $$

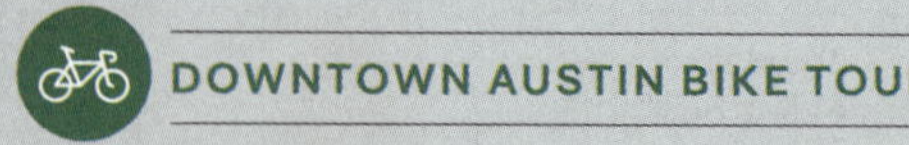

DOWNTOWN AUSTIN BIKE TOUR

Witness the best of downtown Austin on two wheels. An e-bike can be rented using the CapMetro Bikeshare app at Riverside/South Lamar Station.

START	END	LENGTH
Pfluger Pedestrian Bridge	Central Public Library	Roughly 5 miles; 50-60 minutes

Cross over the ❶ **Pfluger Pedestrian Bridge**, and circle back through Sand Beach Park to turn left on the Lance Armstrong Bikeway. Ride past ❷ **Open Room Austin**, a large picnic table slash public art installation. Turn left on West Ave and then right on 2nd St to go over the ❸ **Butterfly Bridge**. At the corner of 2nd and Lavaca, stop at the ❹ **Willie Nelson statue** at Austin City Limits Live. Keep heading east and pause for more pictures at the ❺ **Tau Ceti rainbow mural** at 2nd and Brazos. In two more blocks, turn left on Trinity St, then right on the bike path on 4th St before turning left on Red River St. Two blocks down, cross ❻ **6th Street** (p138), one of the country's most famous stretches of bars and clubs. Continue north through the ❼ **Red River Cultural District** (p139), a hub for live music. At 12th and Red River, ride through ❽ **Waterloo Park**, a new green space in downtown. Head back to 12th St and take a right up the hill toward the ❾ **State Capitol**. Ride through the grounds and exit the west gate along 12th St. At 12th and Shoal Creek Boulevard, turn left to enter the ❿ **Shoal Creek Greenbelt**. While approaching Duncan Neighborhood Park, take a slight left to avoid stairs before finding the ⓫ **9th St BMX Park**. Turn right on the trail and then a sharp left to cross the creek and pass the ⓬ **Deep Roots Community Garden**. Continue on Shoal Creek Trail until it hits the Lance Armstrong Bikeway at the ⓭ **Central Public Library**. There are stations nearby to dock your bike.

South by Southwest

Downtown Austin's March transformation

For Austin at its liveliest, visit in March during **SXSW**. Founded in 1987, the annual 10-day event features a celebration of technology, film, music, education and culture. Stop by for film premieres at the **Paramount Theatre** (p139), see hotshot new artists perform at **Mohawk** (p139), watch big-name comedians at **Esther's Follies**, and check out exhibits, panels and keynotes galore at the **Austin Convention Center**. Badge prices range from $700 to $1700, but there are also free shows for those without company budgets.

South Austin Entertainment

Where to let loose

South Austin continues to pull its weight in helping the city maintain its reputation as the Live Music Capital of the World. No visit is complete without a ticket to the **Continental Club**. Since 1955, the Continental has evolved from supper club to burlesque club to a legendary live-music stage.

Two of Austin's other most legendary live-music joints exist along a stretch of South Lamar. **Saxon Pub** is a cozy spot for happy hour or shows, and Austin mainstays like Bob Schneider and the Resentments still play regular gigs there. **Broken Spoke** is a dance hall famed for its country music and two-step lessons.

Lady Bird Johnson Wildflower Center

Bluebonnet heaven

The 284-acre **Lady Bird Johnson Wildflower Center** has been delighting generations since 1982. Every type of Texan native wildflower is represented on its grounds, with nearly 900 species of plants from the different regions of the state, which includes bluebonnets in the spring, of course. The center also offers bird-watching on the wildflower-rimmed trails, an interactive kids garden, a 1-mile tree arboretum and a quaint cafe with patio seating to rest your stems and refuel.

AUSTIN'S BEST MOVIE VENUES

Austin's film scene was born from Richard Linklater's 1990 flick *Slacker*, which acutely detailed the city's culture and vibe. Austin is now home to several film festivals and some of the best theaters in the country.

Alamo Drafthouse Cinema: Iconic Austin chain with beer and food delivery to your seat. Just don't talk or text during the movie.

Violet Crown Cinema: Small theater downtown with only a couple of rows for each screen.

AFS Cinema: Home theater of the Austin Film Society, founded by Linklater, on the city's north side.

Blue Starlite Urban Drive-In: Watch movies from your car on a downtown rooftop.

Bullock Museum IMAX Theater: The biggest screen inside the city's biggest history museum.

EATING IN SOUTH AUSTIN: DATE NIGHT SPOTS

Uchi: One of Austin's most popular high-end restaurants. Named one of the 20 most important restaurants in the country. *4-10pm Sun-Thu, to 11pm Fri & Sat* $$$

Loro: Asian-BBQ fusion from chefs Tyson Cole of Uchi and Aaron Franklin of Franklin Barbecue. *11am-10pm Sun-Thu, to 11pm Fri & Sat* $$

El Alma: Authentic Mexican food in a beautiful space at the Barton Springs location. *11am-10pm Mon-Thu, 11am-11pm Fri, 10am-11pm Sat, 10am-10pm Sun* $$

Perla's: Seafood and oysters while sitting underneath the trees on a massive patio along South Congress. *11:30am-10pm Sun-Thu, to 11pm Fri, 10:30am-11pm Sat* $$

TIPS FOR THE FRANKLIN LINE

Standing in line for Franklin Barbecue on a Saturday morning is a rite of passage for many Texans. **Aaron Franklin**, the pit master himself, helps you navigate the wait. *Insta: @franklinbbq)*

Show up early. I would probably get here at about 8:30am. You won't be right up front, but you won't be out in full sun.

Wear comfortable shoes. You're going to be on your feet for a while. We do have a ton of chairs as loaners, though.

Stay hydrated. You're probably gonna drink some beers later.

Make new friends. People come from all over the world to hang out, and everybody's got a reason.

Be hungry. We'll crush you. It's gonna be a great nap afterwards, though.

ERIC LAUDONIEN/SHUTTERSTOCK

Neon Grotto

Austin's Barbecue Showdown

Top-notch smokers

Award-winning **Franklin Barbecue** *(franklinbbq.com)* has long been touted as the best barbecue in Austin and turned pit master Aaron Franklin into a national celebrity on the food scene. Spending a Saturday morning waiting for hours on a fold-out chair in front of the restaurant for a taste of that fatty brisket is as much an experience as the eating part.

But Franklin has plenty of legit competition for the barbecue crown these days. **La Barbecue** *(labarbecue.com)* has become one of Austin's favorite smokehouses since its opening in 2011.

Once known only for its famed food truck **Micklethwait Barbecue** *(craftmeatsaustin.com)* opened its first bricks-and-mortar location in Austin inside an old church in late 2024.

Further out, **Leroy & Lewis Barbecue** *(leroyandlewis bbq.com)* is a new-school barbecue joint that has gone from a small truck to its own, frequently sold-out store on Austin's south side.

Going Out on 6th Street

As wild or tame as you want

Any discussion of a night out in Austin likely starts with its famed **6th Street**. Locals call the portion from I-35 to roughly Congress Ave 'Dirty 6th,' and it's lined with bars and clubs that get rowdy after the sun goes down. Dirty 6th is primarily occupied by college students on the hunt for cheap-ish drinks, or bachelorette parties looking to let loose. This stretch has some fabled dive spots, including **The Jackalope**, **Blind Pig Pub** and **Pete's Dueling Piano Bar**.

The vibe changes somewhat dramatically as the party moves up to 'West 6th,' from San Antonio St to Lamar. Here, there's a slightly older crowd and establishments like **Star Bar**, **The Rustic Tap** and **Kung Fu Saloon**. Some of the city's trendiest restaurants can also be found on W 6th, such as **Walton's Fancy & Staple**, owned by Austin adoptee Sandra Bullock.

Another popular option for a night on the town is **Rainey Street**, a several-block stretch of old bungalow homes turned into bars like **Clive Bar** and **Lucille**. This area is under constant renovation with a new high-rise condo building seemingly going up every time someone turns around.

If you're looking for live performances, head to the **Red River Cultural District** along Red River St, which is home to **Mohawk**, a long-time favorite venue for smaller shows, and **The Creek & The Cave**, a stand-up comedy club. By day, **Stubb's** is a barbecue restaurant, but at night it becomes one of Austin's bigger outdoor concert stages. Street parking is easier to find here along the Red River side streets, and there are plenty of food trucks to keep your belly full.

LGBTIQ+ Nightlife

Party with a rainbow crew

The thriving queer community is what distinguishes Austin from the rest of Texas. Celebrate love and acceptance on and around the 4th St Warehouse District, where colorful gay bars stand loud and proud. **Rain**, **Coconut Club**, **Neon Grotto** and **Oilcan Harry's**, the oldest of them all, are must-visits near the rainbow pedestrian crossing.

In the Red River Cultural District, **Cheer Up Charlies** has a killer dance floor, a ton of live music and a vegan food truck out back. Also on Red River, **Barbarella's** hosts the TuezGayz dance parties.

After the bars close, keep going after hours at **Highland Lounge** – and make sure to do drag brunch the next morning at **The Iron Bear**.

Paramount Theatre

Glamorous entertainment

For more than 100 years, the **Paramount Theatre** on Congress Ave in the heart of downtown Austin has entertained people within its majestic, art deco walls. The likes of Miles Davis, Katharine Hepburn, Maya Angelou and Burt Bacharach have all taken to its prestigious stage. Today the restored auditorium continues to treat crowds with music, comedy and movies.

LGBTIQ+ AUSTIN

Colton Ashabranner is the marketing and communications manager at the Austin LGBT Chamber of Commerce. *Insta: @coltonashh*

Austin is very unique in that we don't actually have a gayborhood. We have 4th St, which is the unofficial LGBTIQ+ district, but we're everywhere – and I would say Austin is very welcoming to our community. There are so many LGBTIQ-owned and ally businesses in Austin. Check out the Chamber events calendar *(membership.austinlgbtchamber.com/events)* or **Gay Do 512** *(gay.do512.com)*. The *Austin Chronicle* also has a section called Qmmunity *(austinchronicle.com/events/qmmunity)* where they share upcoming events. There are so many options, and there's always something to do.

DRINKING IN SOUTH AUSTIN: MUST-TRY SPOTS

Courtyard Lounge at Hotel San Jose: Gorgeous outdoor bar at one of the premier boutique hotels in the city. *noon-10pm Mon-Thu, to midnight Fri & Sat*

ABGB: Award-winning local brewery with plenty of outdoor seating, great pizza and live music. *11:30am-11pm Tue-Fri, noon-midnight Sat, noon-10pm Sun*

Bouldin Acres: Outdoor playground for adults (and your canine companion) with pickleball courts and other games. *11am-midnight*

Tiki Tatsu-Ya: Tiki bar with a wild aesthetic inside meant to take you on an immersive journey to paradise. *4pm-midnight Mon-Fri, 1pm-midnight Sat, 4-10pm Sun*

San Antonio & the Hill Country

RIVERSIDE EXPLORING | SPANISH ARCHITECTURE | OUTDOOR ADVENTURES

GETTING AROUND

Around downtown, it's easy to walk, ride a bike or take the bus. Avoid the hassle and cost of parking and leave your car at the free lot at P+R Ellis Alley; it's a short bus ride from there to downtown (take No 25 or No 100).

Buses operated by VIA *(viainfo.net)* provide service around town. You can pay in cash ($1.30) or with the VIA goMobile+ app.

Various B-Cycle bike-share stations are scattered around downtown – as well as at the southern Missions.

You'll need a car when you're ready to head to the Hill Country.

One of Texas' most attractive major cities, San Antonio has long captivated visitors. The legendary Alamo, that iconic symbol of Texan independence, stands at the heart of the city, while the River Walk, a glorious network of waterside pathways that's tucked below street level and lined with bars and restaurants, offers leisurely strolling through downtown and beyond.

The San Antonio River has long been an integral part of life here. The headwaters were sacred to Indigenous tribes, and today the river flows past many of the city's must-see neighborhoods, including the trendy Pearl and historic King William, and reaches the edge of the historic missions south of town – part of a UNESCO World Heritage site.

San Antonio puts you in close proximity to the Hill Country, a beautiful region known for its charming small towns, refreshing swimming holes and rugged state parks. The wildflower-lined back roads are gateways to memorable scenic drives.

Exploring the Alamo

The famous battle site

The much-fabled **Alamo** *(thealamo.org)* is where Davy Crockett, James Bowie and 200 other revolutionaries died in 1836 during a battle against Mexican troops. There's much to see beyond the old church: reconstructed parts of the mission turned fort, various films that shed light on the past, and an impressive collection (admission $14) donated by Alamo enthusiast and '80s pop star Phil Collins. Admission to the church is free.

Continued on p144

TOP TIP

Don't leave San Antonio without trying a puffy taco, which is a corn tortilla fired up into a puffy, crispy form that's then filled with the usual taco accouterments. It originated in San Antonio in the 1950s. **Tito's Mexican Restaurant** serves some of the best near downtown.

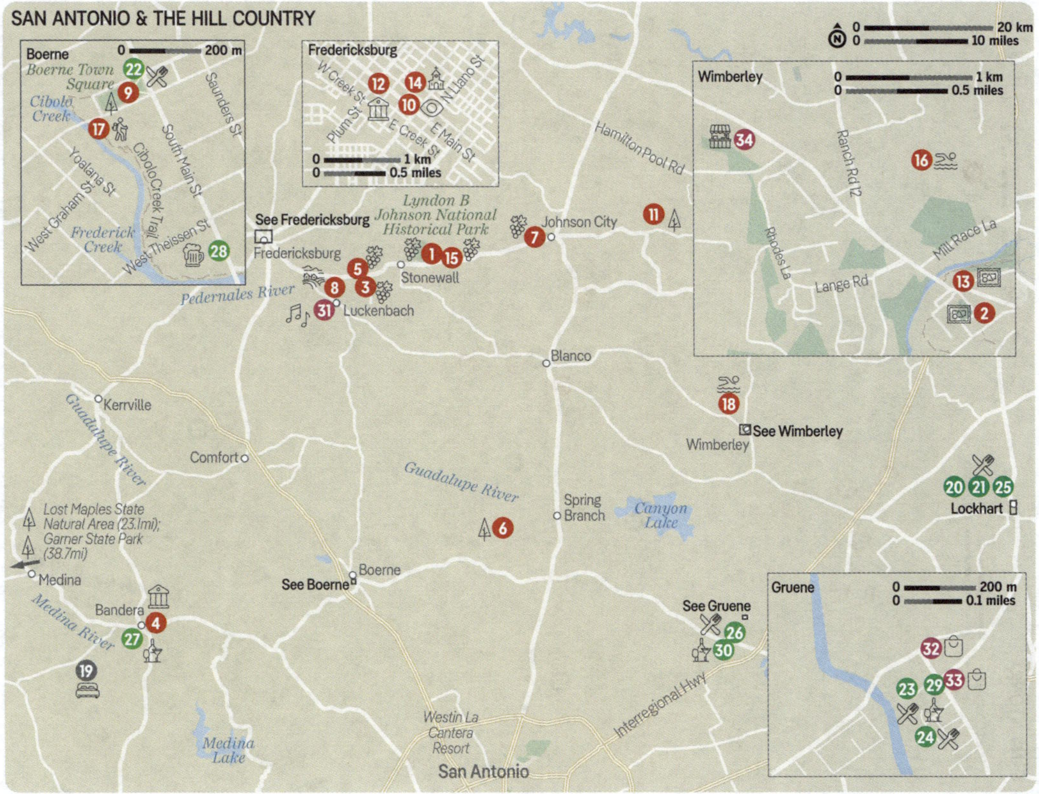

SAN ANTONIO & THE HILL COUNTRY

SIGHTS
1 Ab Astris
2 Art on 12
3 Becker Vineyards
4 Frontier Times Museum
5 Grape Creek
6 Guadalupe River State Park
7 Lost Draw Cellars
8 Luckenbach
9 Main Plaza Park
10 Marktplatz
11 Pedernales Falls State Park
12 Pioneer Museum
13 Pitzer's Fine Arts
14 Vereins Kirche
15 William Chris Vineyards

ACTIVITIES
16 Blue Hole Regional Park
17 Cibolo Creek Trail
18 Jacob's Well Natural Area

SLEEPING
19 Dixie Dude Ranch

EATING
20 Barb's BQ
21 Black's Barbecue
22 Dienger Trading Co
23 Gristmill River Restaurant
24 Gruene River Grill
25 Kreuz Market
26 Naegelin's German Bakery

DRINKING & NIGHTLIFE
27 11th Street Cowboy Bar
28 Cibolo Creek Brewing Co
29 Gruene Hall
30 Pour Haus

ENTERTAINMENT
31 Luckenbach Dance Hall

SHOPPING
32 Barn
33 Gruene General Store
34 Wimberley Market Days

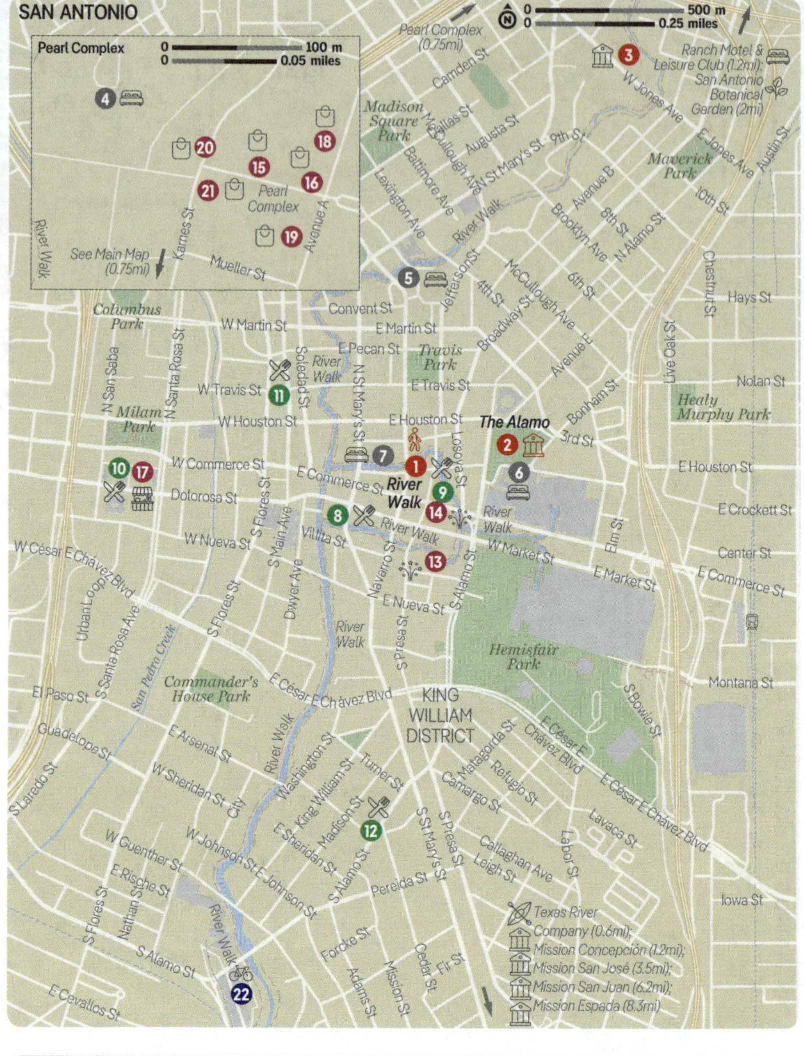

HIGHLIGHTS
1 River Walk
2 The Alamo

SIGHTS
3 San Antonio Museum of Art

SLEEPING
4 Hotel Emma
5 Hotel Havana
6 Menger Hotel
7 Omni La Mansión del Rio

EATING
8 Biga
9 Boudro's
10 Mi Tierra Cafe & Bakery
11 Pinkerton's Barbecue
12 Tito's Mexican Restaurant

ENTERTAINMENT
13 Fiesta Noche del Rio
14 Fiesta San Antonio

SHOPPING
15 Adelante
16 Dos Carolinas
17 Historic Market Square
18 King Ranch Saddle Shop
19 Niche at Pearl
20 The Pearl
21 The Twig Book Shop

TRANSPORT
22 Blue Star Bike Shop

TOP EXPERIENCE

The River Walk

A little slice of Europe in the heart of downtown, the 15-mile River Walk is an essential part of the San Antonio experience. Wandering this charming network of canals and pedestrian walkways, set just below the downtown streets, you can pass landscaped gardens and riverfront cafes, and linger on stone footbridges that arch gracefully across the water.

Dining & People Watching

The river makes a loop around one section of downtown, and this is the most commercial part of the River Walk. Here you'll find numerous restaurants and bars overlooking the water. It's lively day and night, with twinkling lights in the trees and music spilling out onto open terraces.

Peaceful Strolls

For a more peaceful experience, follow the river north or south of downtown. It's a memorable 1.7-mile walk from Houston St up to the Pearl District. Along the way, signposts point out unique river features – like the remains of the dam built by the visionary River Walk architect Robert Hugman in 1941. Look out for mosaics and other public artwork. Beneath the I-35 overpass, a school of larger-than-life fish floats overhead – an art installation by Donald Lipski. There's also an artificial grotto, complete with waterfall, near Newell Ave.

Boat Trips

On a fleet of of ecofriendly electric boats, **Go Rio** *(goriocruises.com)* operates narrated cruises ($16) that touch on San Antonio's history and culture. Boats depart from three different locations, including a dock below Commerce St near the Shops at Rivercenter mall. If you want to hop on and off, Go Rio runs a shuttle between downtown and the Museum Reach (north of downtown), with 15 different stops. Departures run roughly hourly between noon and 7pm (one-day pass $22).

TOP TIPS

- Rent kayaks from Texas River Company *(txrivercompany.com)*, which launches from Roosevelt Park, about 2 miles south of downtown.
- The southern River Walk is great for cycling. You can hire from Blue Star Bike Shop *(bluestarbikeshop.com)* and ride down to the missions (9 miles to the furthest).

PRACTICALITIES

- Check out *thesanantonioriverwalk.com* for info on exhibits and upcoming events.

SAN ANTONIO'S BIGGEST EVENTS

Fiesta San Antonio: Over 11 days in late April, this citywide party features river and flower-filled street parades, mariachi concerts and 100 other events.

Day of the Dead: In October, San Antonio hosts one of the biggest Day of the Day celebrations with traditional altars and parades.

Battle of the Alamo: History comes to life during the commemoration of the 13-day siege, held from late February to early March.

Holiday River Parade: Gear up for the holidays with a festive parade and dazzling lights along the River Walk. It happens in late November.

Fiesta Noche del Rio: On Friday and Saturday nights in June and July catch Latin music and dancing at the Arneson River Theater.

Continued from p140

Guided tours are available throughout the day for $45 (reserve ahead). For in-depth exploration at your own pace, book a self-guided audio tour for $20.

Little Mexico

Shops, food and entertainment

About half a mile west of the River Walk, **Historic Market Square** *(marketsquaresa.com)* is a little piece of Mexico in downtown San Antonio. It's a fair approximation of a trip south of the border, with Mexican food, mariachi bands and more than 100 locally owned shops filled with Mexican folk art, handmade goods and clothes. A big chunk of the square is taken up by **El Mercado**, the largest Mexican marketplace outside of Mexico.

Treasures from Latin America & Beyond

5000 years of art

The **San Antonio Museum of Art** *(samuseum.org; adult/child $22/free)* houses an impressive trove of Latin American art, including Spanish Colonial, Mexican and pre-Columbian – one of the most comprehensive collections in the US. Beyond Latin American works, the museum holds a little of everything, from Egyptian antiquities to contemporary abstracts, as well as an impressive Asian wing with a collection of Chinese ceramics, paintings and decorative items.

Fun at the Pearl

Shopping, dining and concerts

A former brewery turned urban playground, **The Pearl** *(atpearl.com)* is a large complex with restaurants, shops, a boutique hotel, green spaces, a splash pad for kids and a branch of the CIA – as in Culinary Institute of America. It sits near the River Walk, and there's even a shaded amphitheater overlooking the water. The best time to visit the Pearl is on weekend mornings, when you can catch one of its captivating markets *(atpearl.com/weekend-market)*.

Botanical Bounty

Flora from Texas and beyond

The **San Antonio Botanical Garden** *(sabot.org; adult/child $22/15)* is an immaculately tended, 38-acre complex with a variety of diverse environments. One area not to miss is the

EATING IN SAN ANTONIO: OUR PICKS

Boudro's: Ideal waterfront spot for indulging in blue crab tostadas, prickly pear margaritas and other creative temptations. *11am-10:30pm* $$$

Mi Tierra Cafe y Panaderia: This festive Mexican eatery and bakery in Market Sq is a San Antonio landmark, opened in 1941. *8am-10pm* $$

Biga: A welcoming outdoor patio on the River Walk and an acclaimed menu of New American cuisine. *5-9:30pm* $$$

Pinkerton's Barbecue: Fires up some of San Antonio's best barbecue, which you can enjoy at picnic tables overlooking a small park. *11am-9pm* $$

TOP EXPERIENCE

The Mission Trail

Spain's missionary presence can best be felt at the ruins of the four missions south of town, all overseen by the National Park Service as part of the San Antonio Missions National Historical Park. The San Antonio missions were constructed in the 18th century, and Catholic services are still held in the churches, which are supported by vibrant communities.

Mission Concepción

Mission Concepción

Heading south from San Antonio, **Mission Concepción** is first mission along the Mission Trail and the oldest unrestored stone church in the country.

Mission San José

Known in its time as the Queen of the Missions, **San José** is the largest and arguably the most beautiful of the four. Because it's a little more remote and pastoral, surrounded by thick stone walls, you can really get a sense of what life was like here in the 18th and 19th centuries.

Mission San Juan

Founded in 1731, this **mission** was once self-sustaining with orchards and gardens just outside the walls and farm fields further off. Take the **Yanaguana Trail** behind the church down to the river to see some of a natural ecosystem that was common before the arrival of the Spanish.

Mission Espada

The southernmost stop on the Mission Trail is also the oldest, dating from 1690. The **church** was built between 1745 and 1756. It's the best place to check out the historic *acequias,* which were dug by the mission inhabitants in the 1700s and used to water the farm fields.

TOP TIPS

- Mission San José is home to the main park visitor center, with free tours (10am and 11am).
- You can get here by cycling an extension of the River Walk.
- Mission San José's mariachi mass at noon on Sunday (in Spanish) is a San Antonio tradition.

PRACTICALITIES

- See *nps.gov/saan* for maps, opening hours and background information.

BEST STATE PARKS & SWIMMING SPOTS IN THE HILL COUNTRY

Garner State Park *(adult/child $8/free)* Float in a tube ($10) beneath limestone cliffs and rolling green hills.

Guadalupe River State Park (p146) *(adult/child $7/free)* Straddles a 4-mile stretch of the sparkling, bald-cypress-tree-lined Guadalupe River, and it's great for water activities and hiking.

Pedernales Falls State Park *(adult/child $6/free)* Trails wind through forests, atop ridges and along the churning riverside.

Lost Maples State Natural Area *(adult/child $6/free)* Summertime swimming, hiking amid limestone canyons and grasslands, and colorful leaves in autumn.

Jacob's Well Natural Area *(adult/child $9/5; jwna.checkfront.com/reserve)* A glorious setting for a swim, though you'll need to reserve ahead.

Blue Hole Regional Park *(adult/child $12/8; wimberleyparksandrec.com/blue-hole-swimming)* Leap into the spring-fed waters of Cypress Creek. Reserve ahead.

Black's Barbecue

Texas Native Trail with three separate sections devoted to South Texas, the Hill Country and the eastern Pineywoods – which has a small lake ringed with bald cypress trees.

Historic Gruene's Fabled Dance Hall

Local crafts and live music

Settled by German farmers in the mid-1800s, the welcoming and historic town of Gruene (pronounced 'green') is the musical heart of the region. Pick up a cowboy hat from the **Gruene General Store** *(gruenegeneralstore.com)* and browse ceramics made by local artists at **The Barn** *(thebarningruene.com)*. Later, head to **Gruene Hall** *(gruenehall.com)*, an 1878 dance hall with free live music every night of the week.

Tubing in New Braunfels & Gruene

Waterside adventures

During the summer, nothing beats floating on the cool and easy-flowing waters of the Guadalupe and Comal rivers. When the sun gets to be too much, you can cool off with a swim, then hop back in the tube and continue along. Dozens of local outfitters rent tubes, and at the end of your trip, you'll be bused back to your starting point. **Texas Tubes** *(texastubes.com; $25)* is a recommended outfitter in New Braunfels, while **Rockin' R River Rides** *(rockinr.com; $25)* is the best choice in Gruene.

Eating Barbecue in Lockhart

Famous food spots

Back in 2003 the Texas Legislature officially named Lockhart the 'Barbecue Capital of Texas.' You can eat well at any of its barbecue restaurants. A good place to start is **Kreuz Market** (*kreuzmarket.com*). A local landmark since 1900, this barn-like eatery is famed for its dry rub meats – no sauce needed. Another stalwart is **Black's Barbecue** (*blacksbbq.com*), open since 1932 – and a favorite of President LBJ. This classic barbecue spot serves up buttery rich ribs and juicy sausage.

At **Barb's BQ** (*barbsbq.com*), the young pitmaster has turned the barbecue world on its head with her tender, delicately spiced brisket, ribs and lamb. It's open Saturday and Sunday only (11am to 3pm). Go early as they always sell out.

Strolling Boerne

Shops, restaurants and parks

Settled by German immigrants in 1849, the attractive town of Boerne (pronounced 'Bernie') has more than 140 restored historical structures.

The half-mile stretch of Main St between River Rd and Blanco St makes for some rewarding exploring. Start off the ramble at the **Main Plaza Park**. On its northeastern corner, stop in the **Dienger Trading Co** (*thediengertradingco.com*), a bistro, bakery and boutique in an 1884 grocery-store building. A few blocks south of there, the kid-friendly **Cibolo Creek Brewing Co** (*cibolocreekbrewing.com*) is a pleasant indoor-outdoor spot for craft beers and satisfying cooking.

A pleasant add-on to Main St exploring is a walk along the **Cibolo Creek Trail**, which follows a pretty creekside some 1.7 miles all the way to City Park. Once there, you can experience more fine scenery at the **Cibolo Center for Conservation**, which has short trails through native Texan woods, marshland and along Cibolo Creek.

Cowboy Culture in Bandera

Western lore

Bandera brands itself the Cowboy Capital of the World. While touristy, with staged gunfights (Saturdays at 10am and noon) and shops selling cowboy attire, Bandera still has an air of authenticity, particularly among the cowboy bars and honky-tonks. Near town, the 725-acre **Dixie Dude Ranch** (*dixiedude ranch.com*) offers horseback riding, campfire sing-alongs and other activities.

For a little perspective on bygone days in Bandera, stop by the **Frontier Times Museum** (*frontiertimesmuseum.org; adult/child $8/4*), which has displays of Western art and cowboy tchotchkes such as guns and branding irons.

BEST VINEYARDS OF HILL COUNTRY

Hill Country's wine destination is **Hwy 290** (*wineroad290.com*) which has over 50 wineries, many open to tastings and tours. Leave the driving to **290 Wine Shuttle** (*290wineshuttle.com; per person $50*).

Lost Draw Cellars Produces top-quality wines that showcase the terroir of the Texas High Plains.

Becker Vineyards One of the oldest and best wineries in the region, with a tasting room that's modeled on a German barn.

Grape Creek Resembles Tuscany with its spread of vineyards and stone buildings.

Ab Astris A boutique winery that produces handcrafted vintages, with a focus on lesser-known grape varieties.

William Chris Vineyards Hill Country's most famous winery with great views and premium wines.

EATING & DRINKING IN NEW BRAUNFELS & GRUENE: OUR PICKS

Gristmill River Restaurant: Get a deckside table and enjoy ribs, steak and catfish in an 1800s cotton gin behind Gruene Hall. *11am-9pm* $$

Gruene River Grill: The rustic dining room in Gruene makes a relaxed setting for American and Tex-Mex comfort food. *11am-9pm* $$

Naegelin's German Bakery: Pick up strudels and kolaches from this legendary New Braunfels bakery – the oldest in Texas. *6:30am-5pm Mon-Sat, 8am-2pm Sun* $

Pour Haus: Take a seat in the yard, and enjoy craft brews and delicious street tacos while catching live music in New Braunfels. *4pm-midnight Mon-Fri, 1pm-midnight Sat & Sun*

THE PERILOUS JOURNEY FROM GERMANY

In 1845 in Germany, overpopulation, low wages and widespread poverty inspired some to seek a better life abroad. Those that came to Texas faced a daunting journey that began with a two-month trip aboard a cramped, unsanitary ship to reach Indianola on the Gulf. Once there, the travelers discovered that war had broken out between Mexico and the US, and onward transportation was not available. This left 4000 people languishing on the beach with little shelter, impure water, contaminated food and soon-to-be-rampant disease. Over 1400 died that summer. As weeks passed, those who were able set out on foot, leaving behind many of their possessions as they trudged 200 miles through rugged lands to newly christened settlements where they would begin a new life.

Afterwards, sip a Shiner at the **11th Street Cowboy Bar** *(11thstcowboybar.com)*, billed as the 'Biggest Little Honky Tonk in Texas.'

Gallery Hopping in Wimberley

Galleries, markets and swimming spots

Small, charming Wimberley is famed as an artists' community. **Art on 12** *(arton12.com)* features works by dozens of local and regional artists. Nearby, check out the paintings and sculpture of **Pitzer's Fine Arts** *(pitzersart.com)*, another well-respected gallery. Afterwards, treat yourself to a meal at one of Wimberley's charming creekside restaurants like **The Leaning Pear**, with its elevated comfort fare, or the **Creekhouse Kitchen & Bar** with creative fare and a lovely forested backdrop.

From March to December, the first Saturday of the month is **Wimberley Market Day** *(wimberleymarketday.com)*, featuring live music, food stalls and more than 400 vendors selling arts, crafts and more.

German Roots in Fredericksburg

Pioneer architecture and schnitzel

One of the Hill Country's most vibrant towns, Fredericksburg is a former 19th-century German settlement with its history woven into the landscape. Its street signs proclaim 'Willkommen,' and you'll be welcome indeed along its main street, lined with historic buildings that house German restaurants, beer gardens, antique stores and wine-tasting rooms.

For insight into what life was like for Fredericksburg's first settlers, visit the **Pioneer Museum** *(pioneermuseum.org; adult/child $12/5)*, with its collection of restored historic buildings that you can wander through.

Music, dancing and schnitzel are on the menu every October, when Fredericksburg celebrates its German heritage with Texas' largest **Oktoberfest** *(oktoberfestinfbg.com)*. Families crowd around for oompah bands, kegs of German beer and schnitzels galore. On Saturday, join hands for the Chicken Dance!

Legendary Luckenbach

Music-loving enclave

Made up of a handful of Old West structures, tiny **Luckenbach** *(luckenbachtexas.com)* is big on Texas charm. By day, the main activity is sitting at a picnic table under an old oak tree with a cold bottle of Shiner Bock beer and listening to guitar pickers. On Friday nights, two-stepping couples whirl around the dance floor of **Luckenbach Dance Hall**.

STROLL FREDERICKSBURG'S PAST

Peer past the souvenir shops to discover Fredericksburg's immigrant past amid striking buildings from the late 19th century and early 1900s.

START	END	LENGTH
Nimitz Hotel	St Mary's Catholic Church	1 mile; 1½ hours

Start at the former 1 **Nimitz Hotel**, an 1860 building with a curious facade (meant to emulate a steamboat) that once hosted stagecoach travelers. Today it houses one big section of the National Museum of the Pacific War. Cross the street (carefully) and continue to 2 **249 E Main St**. The typical home, built in 1866, is the birthplace of Chester Nimitz, who would go on to command the US Naval fleet in WWII (and sign the Japanese surrender documents in Tokyo Bay). The hometown hero is the reason the museum resides in Fredericksburg.

The heart of town is 3 **Marktplatz**, a green space and centuries-old hub of the community. The octagonal building in the square's center is a 1935 reconstruction (and 2020 remodeling) of the 4 **Vereins Kirche**, which served as the town church, meeting hall and school.

Continue along Main St and turn down Milam. You'll soon spot one of Texas' original tiny homes. Known as a Sunday house, the 5 **Weber House** was used by early Fredericksburgers for their stay on weekends when driving in from the country to do their shopping, attend social gatherings and go to church. Around the corner, 6 **St Mary's Catholic Church** is one of the so-called 'painted churches' of Texas, its 1908 Gothic design replete with stained glass, artwork and stenciling.

Behind Vereins Kirche, **statues** of Fredericksburg founder John O Meusebach and Comanche Chief Santa Anna seal their treaty (never broken) over the peace pipe.

The picturesque **Old Gillespie County Courthouse**, which functioned from 1882 to 1939, today houses the public library. A few vintage photos are inside.

The easy-to-spot pachyderm indicated you'd reached the **White Elephant Saloon**, which opened in 1888. Nowadays, it's once again a bar.

North Milam St
West Main St
South Milam St
N Orange St
W Austin St
N Crocker St
W San Antonio St
S Orange St
W Creek St
S Crockett St
S Nimitz Pkwy
North Adams St
Gillespie County Park
South State Hwy 16
North Llano St
Town Creek
S Llano St
N Lincoln St
E Austin St
N Washington St
East Main St
START
END
0 200 m
0 0.1 miles

Dallas & Fort Worth

ARTS & CULTURE | CATTLE DRIVES | NIGHTLIFE

GETTING AROUND

Trinity Railway Express (TRE) makes the one-hour journey between EBJ Union Station in Dallas and Fort Worth Central Station every 30 to 60 minutes. Within Dallas, you can also take light rail lines operated by DART (Dallas Area Rapid Transit; *dart.org*), with the handy green line serving the Arts District, Deep Ellum and Fair Park.

In Fort Worth, buses operated by Trinity Metro connect areas of interest to most travelers. Travel between the Fort Worth Stockyards and Downtown is easy with the Orange Line. There are also myriad buses in Dallas operated by DART, plus a streetcar between Downtown Dallas and Bishop Arts.

Dallas, the 'Big D,' is Texas' most mythologized city, rich in the stuff of which American legends are woven – including oil barons, cowboys and cheerleaders. Excellent museums in the massive, recently developed Arts District downtown offer world-class displays of art and sculpture, while unmissable sites commemorate the city's rendezvous with history in 1963, as the site of President John F Kennedy's assassination. For the quintessential Dallas experience, explore its distinctive neighborhoods, like down-and-dirty Deep Ellum, pivotal in the stories of blues and jazz, or contemporary hipster hang-outs like the Bishop Arts District.

Famous as being 'Where the West Begins,' Fort Worth hasn't lost touch with its cowboy roots. It first rose to prominence during the great open-range cattle drives of the late 19th century. These days, the legendary Stockyards are the prime visitor destination, hosting cattle drives, rodeos and Billy Bob's, the world's biggest honky-tonk. Downtown Fort Worth, 3 miles south, is bursting with restaurants and bars.

A Dark Day in Dallas

The assassination of JFK

A good place to dive into one of America's most disturbing days is at the **Sixth Floor Museum** *(jfk.org; adult/child $25/21)*. Set in the former Book Depository where Lee Harvey Oswald fired those fateful shots, the museum gives a riveting account of the events that transpired on November 22, 1963.

TOP TIP

Plan your downtown Dallas visit around lunchtime, when you can enjoy wide-ranging global flavors at the Exchange Food Hall. There's also a festive happy hour buzz at the bars in the area in the early evening during the week – weekends are fairly dead downtown, but lively in Deep Ellum.

Dallas Farmers Market

Photographs, audio clips, news footage and eyewitness accounts make you feel almost as if you're experiencing it live.

Dealey Plaza, across the street from the museum, is where JFK was assassinated. The whole area is now a National Historic Landmark, with several signs detailing the day's events.

The Heart of Urban Life

Explore AT&T Discovery District

See the downtown renaissance of Dallas at the **AT&T Discovery District** *(discoverydistrictdallas.com)*, which features multimedia installations, concerts and an open-air plaza that has free movie screenings and big games shown on a 104ft video wall. By day, the best reason to come here is to munch your way around the **Exchange Food Hall**, with vendors serving tacos, pizzas, sliders, Indian curries, creative salads and Mediterranean fare.

The Best Food Hall in Dallas

Food stalls and shops

Since 1941, the **Dallas Farmers Market** *(dallasfarmersmarket.org)* has been a top spot for fresh provisions. These days,

BEST SHOPPING IN DEEP ELLUM

Dated Faded Worn: A pricey but well-curated vintage shop with T-shirts, denim and shoes.

Deep Vellum: One of Dallas' best indie bookshops (and small-press publishers).

Rocket Fizz: A kaleidoscopic selection of vintage and contemporary candies and sodas.

Jade & Clover: You'll find jewelry, candles and alpaca socks, along with a much-loved plant bar.

EATING & DRINKING IN DEEP ELLUM: OUR PICKS

Pecan Lodge: Dallas' best barbecue spot fires up mouthwatering brisket and smoky ribs, plus collard greens, okra and peach cobbler. *11am-8pm Tue-Sun, to 3pm Mon* **$$**

Velvet Taco: The taco is elevated to high art with fillings like beer-battered cauliflower and sweet chile shrimp. *11am-midnight Sun-Thu, to 4am Fri & Sat* **$**

AllGood Cafe: Art-filled street-corner diner with hearty breakfasts and Tex-Mex, plus a stage for live music Thursday to Saturday. *8am-3pm Sun-Wed, to 9pm Thu-Sat* **$**

Dot's Hop House & Courtyard: Has a charming courtyard, big beer menu and delicious comfort fare (like duck-fat fries). *4pm-1am Mon-Wed, noon-1am Thu-Sun* **$$**

the market has a capacious food hall where you can enjoy lattes, tacos, banh mi, sushi, thali platters, barbecue and juices.

On weekends, head to the nearby open-sided **Shed** for farm-fresh produce as well as handmade soaps, cutting boards, jewelry, and lots of other crafts and seasonal items.

Creative Deep Ellum

Music and art

Embodying the neighborhood's most creative aspect, **Deep Ellum Art Co** *(deepellumart.co)* is a spacious 5000-sq-ft multi-use venue that features an art gallery, concert stage and a backyard of art installations, murals, food trucks and yard games.

Trees *(treesdallas.com; admission from $15)* has been a mainstay in Deep Ellum since its opening back in 1990. The wide-ranging lineup leans toward indie rock, hip-hop and EDM, with concerts four or five nights a week.

Uptown's Scenic Trail

Walking, running and cycling

To enjoy some see-and-be-seen walking, running or cycling, hit the tree-lined **Katy Trail** *(katytraildallas.org)*. The former railroad line stretches for 3.5 miles from N Houston St (just above the American Airlines Center) in the south to Airline Rd in the north. Post walk or run, stop in the Katy Trail Ice House, a scenic spot with outdoor tables for barbecue and craft beers.

Exploring Bishop Arts District

Crafts, records and books

One-of-a-kind boutiques, eye-catching galleries and an array of creative eating and drinking spaces line the streets of Bishop Arts District, Dallas' most walkable neighborhood.

Start your wander along Bishop Ave at **Mosaic Makers Collective** *(mosaicmakers.co)*, featuring beautifully made jewelry, clothing, stationery and housewares, all created by female artisans and designers. Across the street, **Spinster Records** *(spinsterrecords.com)* has a brilliant selection of new and used vinyl (plus a few CDs and old-school cassettes).

Continue along N Bishop Ave to **Dolly on Bishop** *(dollypythonvintage.com)*,which is crammed full of vintage apparel and curiosities dating from the 1940s to 1980s. Book lovers should definitely make the slight detour to W 8th St for **The**

BEST OF DALLAS' ARTS DISTRICT

The country's largest arts district stretches across some 118 acres just north of Downtown Dallas.

Perot Museum of Nature & Science *(adult/child $25/15)* A kid pleaser with five floors of interactive exhibits, plus massive dinosaur skeletons.

Dallas Museum of Art *(free)* One of Texas' best collections, with treasures that span centuries (and continents).

Klyde Warren Park Take a break between museum-hopping at this green space and community hub for outdoor yoga, movie screenings and markets. There are also food trucks and several restaurants.

Nasher Sculpture Center *(adult/child $10/free)* An impressive array of works by renowned sculptors past and present.

Crow Museum of Asian Art *(free)* Beautiful works in artfully designed exhibition halls.

EATING IN BISHOP ARTS: OUR PICKS

Tribal All Day Cafe: An inviting vegan-friendly spot with smoothies, seasonal vegetable bowls and breakfast burritos. *8am-5:30pm Mon-Sat, to 4pm Sun* $

Taco y Vino: A delightful mashup of creative Mexican fare, tacos and good wines with a lively ambience and a spacious backyard. *11am-10pm Mon-Sat, to 3pm Sun* $$

The Mayor's House by Selda: Excellent Turkish cooking in a historic building with multiple dining rooms and a breezy front porch. *noon-11pm* $$

Lucia: Reserve well ahead for a table at this award-winning restaurant serving up top-notch creative Italian fare. *5-10pm Tue-Sat* $$$

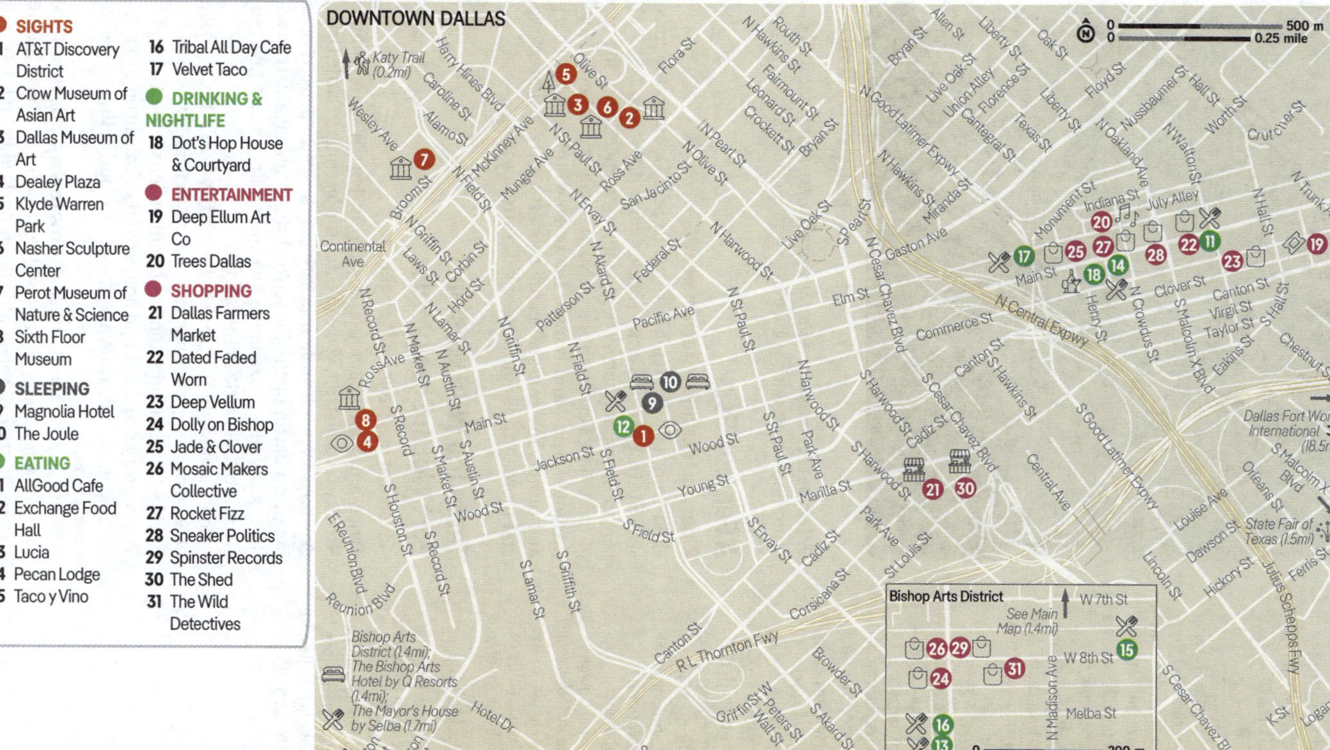

SIGHTS

1 AT&T Discovery District
2 Crow Museum of Asian Art
3 Dallas Museum of Art
4 Dealey Plaza
5 Klyde Warren Park
6 Nasher Sculpture Center
7 Perot Museum of Nature & Science
8 Sixth Floor Museum

SLEEPING

9 Magnolia Hotel
10 The Joule

EATING

11 AllGood Cafe
12 Exchange Food Hall
13 Lucia
14 Pecan Lodge
15 Taco y Vino
16 Tribal All Day Cafe
17 Velvet Taco

DRINKING & NIGHTLIFE

18 Dot's Hop House & Courtyard

ENTERTAINMENT

19 Deep Ellum Art Co
20 Trees Dallas

SHOPPING

21 Dallas Farmers Market
22 Dated Faded Worn
23 Deep Vellum
24 Dolly on Bishop
25 Jade & Clover
26 Mosaic Makers Collective
27 Rocket Fizz
28 Sneaker Politics
29 Spinster Records
30 The Shed
31 The Wild Detectives

BEST MUSEUMS IN FORT WORTH CULTURAL DISTRICT

Amon Carter Museum of American Art *(free)* Showcases works by some of the nation's most famous painters and sculptors.

Kimbell Art Museum *(free)* Has a small but surprising collection that allows you to hone in on single masterpieces like Caravaggio's *The Cardsharps* or El Greco's *Portrait of Dr Francisco de Pisa.*

The Modern *(adult/child $16/free)* Inside a building that appears to float above the surrounding reflecting pools, the Modern hosts groundbreaking contemporary exhibitions.

National Cowgirl Museum *(adult/child $12/6)* Explores the myth and reality of cowgirls in American culture, with interactive exhibits.

Fort Worth Museum of Science & History *(adult/child $16/12)* Kid-friendly galleries brimming with fossils, astronomy thrills and fun things to do.

MD GLOBAL/SHUTTERSTOCK

Ferris wheel, State Fair of Texas

Wild Detectives *(thewilddetectives.com)*, a tiny but well curated bookstore with good coffee and a small bar.

A Famous Fair

Rides, snacks and entertainment

Held from late September through mid-October, the massive **State Fair of Texas** *(bigtex.com; adult/child $25/18)* is a showcase for carnivalesque amusement. Come ride one of the tallest Ferris wheels in North America, eat corn dogs (invented here), and browse the prize-winning cows, sheep and quilts. You can also enjoy concerts, parades, fireworks and more. Admission varies by day (from $15).

Taste the Wild West in Fort Worth Stockyards

A world of cowboys and longhorns

Twice a day (at 11:30am and 4pm) in Fort Worth's famous **Stockyards** district, you can catch the legendary Cattle Drive. Cowboys wearing authentic 19th-century garb drive 17 or so longhorn cattle of the Fort Worth herd up the dusty road. Spectators line E Exchange Ave and an announcer gives insight into the cattle drives of old.

Come sundown, the place to be is **Billy Bob's Texas** *(billybobstexas.com)*, a former cattle barn that today houses the world's largest honky-tonk (stretching across 100,000 sq ft). Top country stars, DJs and house bands perform on two stages. Friday and Saturday nights see live bull riding in the indoor arena.

Alternatively, the 3400-seat **Cowtown Coliseum** *(cowtowncoliseum.com)*, built in 1908 to host the first-ever indoor rodeos, hosts live rodeo at 7:30pm on Friday and Saturday nights year-round.

WANDER THE HISTORIC STOCKYARDS

See why Fort Worth was the gateway to the West as you explore the hidden attractions of the Historic Stockyards.

START	END	LENGTH
Exchange Ave	Exchange Ave	3/4 mile; 1½ hours

Follow the sidewalk along brick-lined Exchange Ave past the 1 **Fort Worth Stock Yards sign** that dates from 1910. Set back from the road is the 2 **Cowtown Coliseum**, setting for weekend rodeos and other events. If the doors are open, wander inside for a look at photos and memorabilia from legendary rodeo performers of the past. Next door, the 3 **Livestock Exchange** once served as the offices for cattle traders and occasional longhorn auctions are still held (nowadays via video-satellite feed). You can freely wander the old building; a small museum in back gives insight into the people and events that shaped the Stockyards. Head over to the 4 **viewing deck** above the corral for a look at the Fort Worth herd. A signpost has pictures and descriptions of each animal. Across Exchange Ave, the 5 **Stockyards Station**, which opened in 1876, was used to ship cattle by rail to markets in Kansas City. Though it's now a mall, peek down the corridors to see old photos from the past.

Continue to shop-lined 6 **Mule Alley** and take the small lane down to 7 **Marine Creek**, a trickling waterway where you can sometimes spot herons and other wading birds. Follow the peaceful 8 **waterside path** under Exchange Ave before returning once again to the bustle of the Stockyards, with its myriad shopping and dining options.

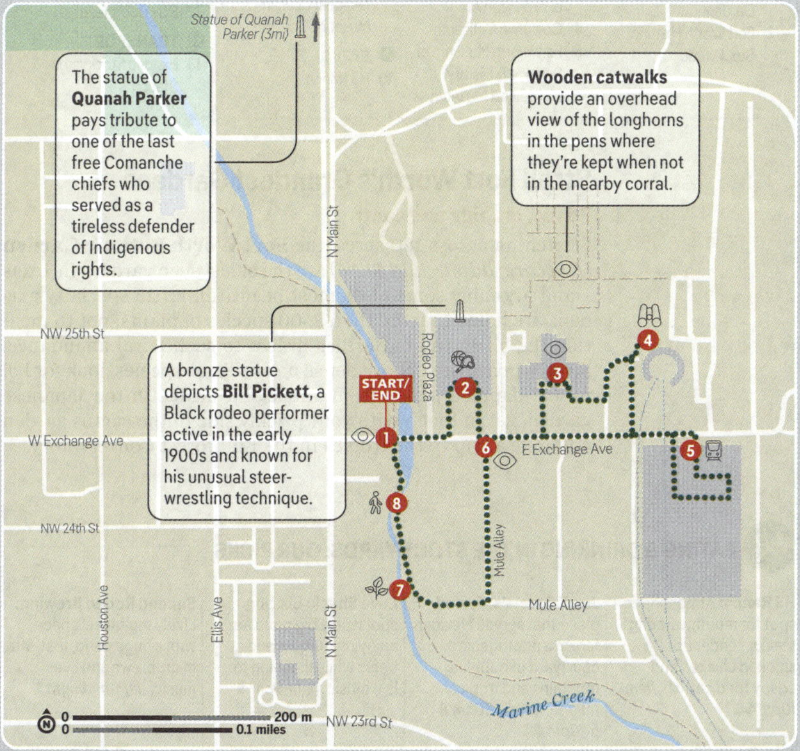

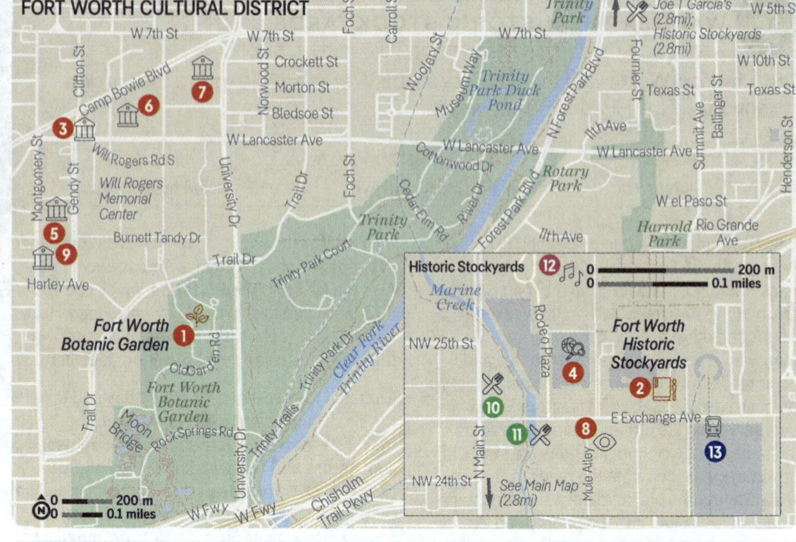

HIGHLIGHTS
1 Fort Worth Botanic Garden
2 Fort Worth Historic Stockyards

SIGHTS
3 Amon Carter Museum of American Art
4 Cowtown Coliseum
5 Fort Worth Museum of Science & History
6 Kimbell Art Museum
7 Modern
8 Mule Alley
9 National Cowgirl Museum

EATING
10 H3 Ranch
11 Love Shack

ENTERTAINMENT
12 Billy Bob's Texas

TRANSPORT
13 Historic Stockyards Station

Stroll Fort Worth's Grandest Gardens

Roses, orchids and cacti

Stretching across 120 acres, the **Fort Worth Botanic Garden** *(fwbg.org; adult/child $12/6)* are the oldest such gardens in Texas – and arguably some of its most beautiful. Its 23 specialty gardens are home to more than 2500 species of plants, not to mention the birds and butterflies drawn to such floral abundance. Stroll a boardwalk above dense native Texas species, look for koi in leaf-dappled ponds from an elegant bridge in the Japanese garden, get in touch with your prickly side in the cactus garden and take a trip to the tropics in the Rainforest Conservatory.

EATING & DRINKING IN THE STOCKYARDS: OUR PICKS

H3 Ranch: Atmospheric spot for mouthwatering steaks, tender ribs, smoked chicken and crispy fried catfish. *11am-10pm* $$

Joe T Garcia's: Famed place that serves Mexican fare in a photogenic courtyard of bubbling fountains and tropical foliage. *11am-2:30pm & 5-10pm* $$

Love Shack: Buzzing spot with a big patio for enjoying burgers and beers while listening to live music. *11am-9pm* $

Second Rodeo Brewing: Lively multilevel space with a huge patio, first-rate microbrews and live music. *11am-midnight* $

Houston & the Gulf Coast

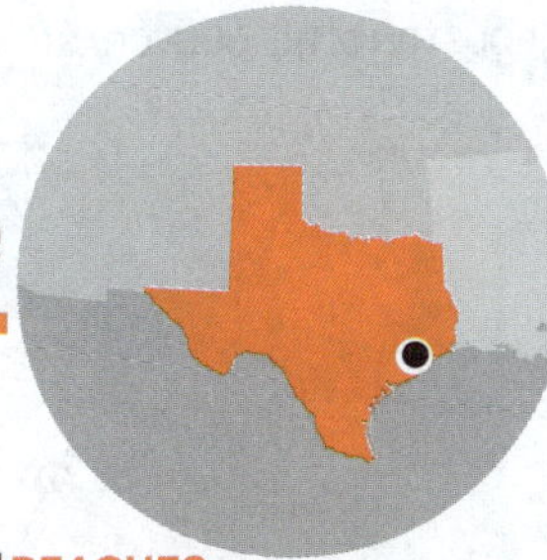

ARTS & ENTERTAINMENT | CUISINE & COCKTAILS | BEACHES

Houston's massive size places it among the top 10 US cities in both area and population, encompassing a fair bit of everything that makes Texas great. Big Oil brings in major investment in fine arts and public spaces, though you can still find cowboy boots and Texas swagger even here in the big city.

The city would take a lifetime to explore completely, but with just a few days it's easy to enjoy the highlights: downtown's revitalized Main St of bars and restaurants, the Museum District's excellent art and cultural centers, plus the indie shops and nightlife of Montrose. It's also worth setting aside a day to see NASA's Space Center Houston.

Houston makes a great starting point for a road trip down the Gulf Coast, which has hundreds of miles of beaches, historic settlements like Galveston and plenty of outdoor adventures – both on and off the water.

GETTING AROUND

Downtown is quite compact and walkable. To travel elsewhere within the city, Houston's three METRORail train lines converge downtown around the square formed by Main, Rusk, Capitol and Fannin streets. Regular services connecting the Theater District and downtown to the Museum District, Hermann Park and NRG Stadium are convenient for travel across the limited route network. Heading down the Gulf Coast, you'll want a car. It's about a six-hour drive (370 miles) if making a straight shot from Houston to South Padre Island, though you could easily spend a few days stopping at coastal enclaves along the way.

Modern Arts in the Museum District

Cutting-edge art and artists

The Museum District is home to a number of top-notch modern-art exhibition spaces.

If time is limited, focus on the fantastic **Museum of Fine Arts** *(mfah.org; adult/child $24/free)*, with thousands of works of art spread across three main buildings connected by underground tunnels (each a work of art itself). You could easily spend a day exploring the museum's permanent collections and special exhibitions.

TOP TIP

Travelers exploring the Museum District in depth will benefit from the **CityPass** *(citypass.com/houston; adult/child $76/63)*, which includes entry to the Space Center Houston complex and the choice of four from the Museum of Fine Arts, Museum of Natural Science, Houston Zoo, Downtown Aquarium, Children's Museum and Kemah Boardwalk.

HOUSTON & THE GULF COAST
Galveston
0 1 km
0 0.5 miles
Harborside Dr (Ave A)
Postoffice St (Ave E)
Rosenberg Ave (25th St)
20th St
Broadway Ave (Ave J)
37th St
Ave K
Seawall Blvd
27
3
9
5
Western Houston
0 5 km
0 2.5 miles
21
22
6
Market Square Park
Live Oak Park
Mary Elliott Park
Hermann Square
Baldwin Park
Levy Park
Dunlavy Park
Peggy Park
Rice University
Riverside Park
Hermann Park
19
10
San Antonio
Pleasanton
Pearsall
Kenedy
Campbellton
Goliad
Dilley
Frio River
San Antonio River
Three Rivers
Cotulla
Tilden
Beeville
Nueces River
Goose Island State Park
Copano Bay
Mathis
Sinton
Encinal
Freer
San Diego
Alice
Robstown
See Port Aransas
Corpus Christi
Port Aransas
Webb
MEXICO
Laredo
Nuevo Laredo
Benavides
Kingsville
Mustang Island
Riviera
Baffin Bay
83
Hebbronville
Falfurrias
Laguna Madre Intracoastal Waterway
Río Grande
Zapata
Port Aransas
0 1 km
0 0.5 miles
11
14
13
15
8
Mustang Island
Raymondville
Harlingen
See South Padre Island
Port Isabel
Boca Chica
Brownsville

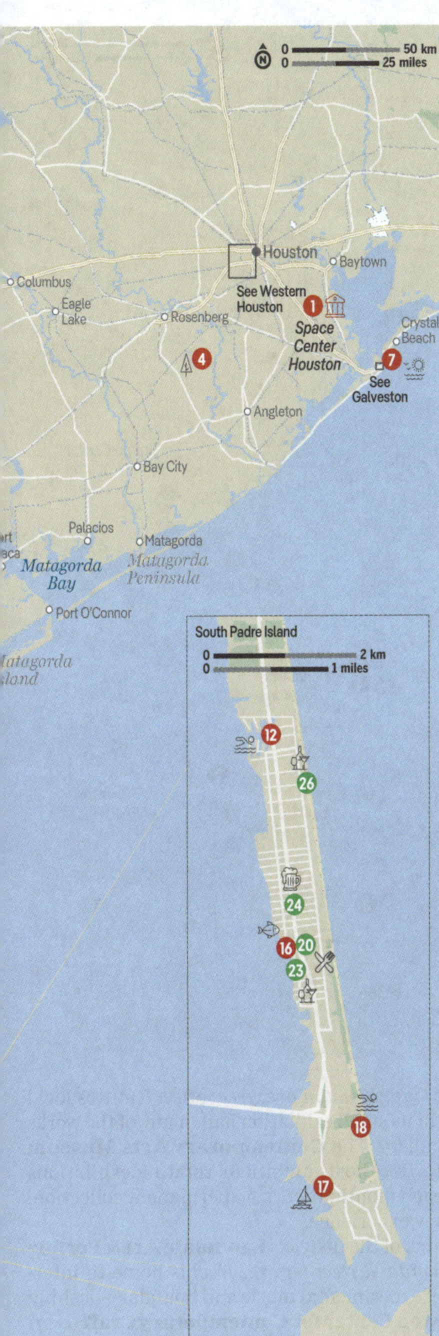

HIGHLIGHTS
1 Space Center Houston

SIGHTS
2 Aransas National Wildlife Refuge
3 Bishop's Palace
4 Brazos Bend State Park
5 Bryan Museum
6 Buffalo Bayou Park
7 East Beach
8 IB Magee Beach Park
9 Moody Mansion
10 NRG Stadium
11 San José Island

ACTIVITIES
12 Air Padre Kiteboarding
13 Deep Sea Headquarters
14 Fisherman's Wharf
15 Horace Caldwell Fishing Pier
16 Jim's Pier
17 The Original Dolphin Watch
18 Sonny's Beach Service

EATING
19 Blood Bros BBQ
20 Grapevine Cafe
21 Pinkerton's Barbecue
22 Truth BBQ

DRINKING & NIGHTLIFE
23 Louie's Backyard
24 Padre Island Brewing Company
25 Saint Arnold Brewing Company
26 Wanna Wanna Beach Bar & Grill

ENTERTAINMENT
27 Grand 1894 Opera House

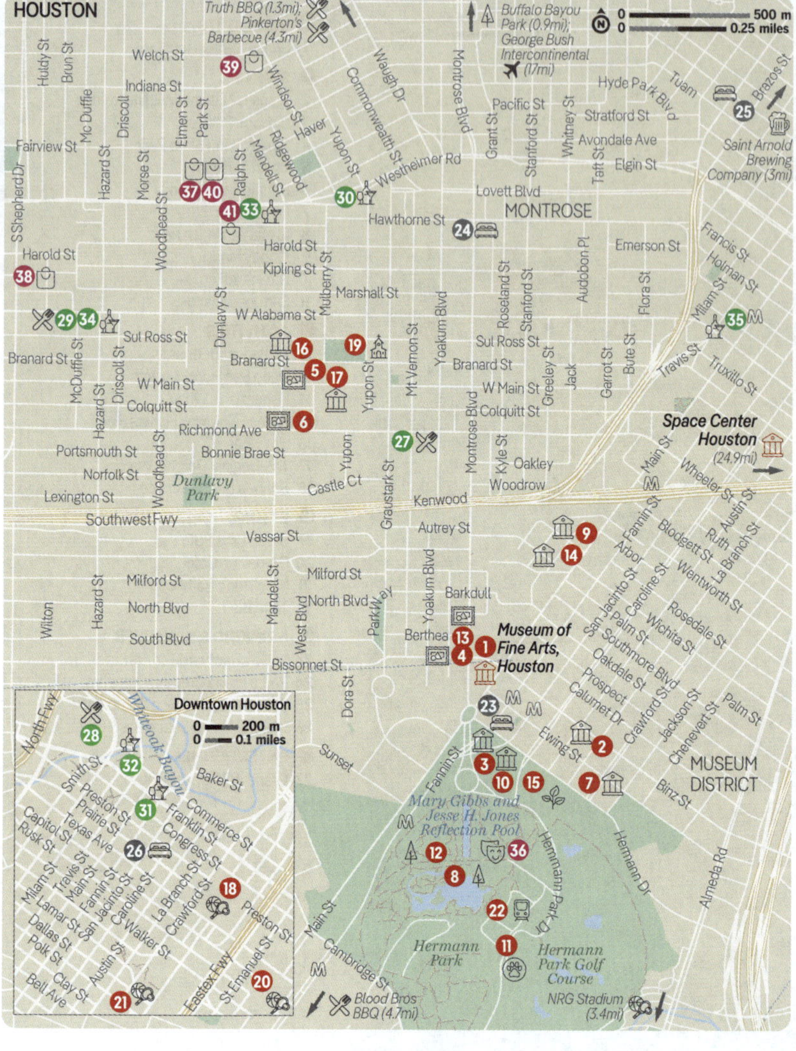

The **Jung Center** *(junghouston.org; free)* often features local and regional artists in its small exhibition hall; many of the works are for sale in the gallery. The **Contemporary Arts Museum Houston** *(camh.org; free)* hosts ambitious rotating exhibitions and several events each month; there's no permanent collection, so every visit is a new experience.

On the northern edge of the district, **Lawndale Art & Performance Center** *(lawndaleartcenter.org; free)* is home to interdisciplinary works of experimental music and boundary-pushing art. Next door, **Houston Center for Contemporary Craft** *(crafthouston.org; free)* is dedicated exclusively to crafts – the workers spaces here remain open in between rotating exhibits.

HIGHLIGHTS
1 Museum of Fine Arts, Houston

SIGHTS
2 Children's Museum Houston
3 Cockrell Butterfly Center
4 Contemporary Arts Museum Houston
5 Cy Twombly Gallery
6 Dan Flavin Installation at Richmond Hall
7 Health Museum
8 Hermann Park
9 Houston Center for Contemporary Craft
10 Houston Museum of Natural Science
11 Houston Zoo
12 Japanese Garden
13 Jung Center
14 Lawndale Art & Performance Center
15 McGovern Centennial Gardens
16 Menil Collection
17 Menil Drawing Institute
18 Minute Maid Park
19 Rothko Chapel
20 Shell Energy Stadium
21 Toyota Center

ACTIVITIES
22 Hermann Park Railroad

SLEEPING
23 Hotel ZaZa
24 La Colombe d'Or Hotel
25 La Maison in Midtown
26 Magnolia Hotel

EATING
27 Pit Room
28 POST Houston
29 Tacos Tierra Caliente

DRINKING & NIGHTLIFE
30 Anvil Bar & Refuge
31 Captain Foxheart's Bad News Bar & Spirit Lodge
32 Houston Watch Company
33 Poison Girl
34 West Alabama Ice House
35 Winnie's

ENTERTAINMENT
36 Miller Outdoor Theatre

SHOPPING
37 BJ Oldies
38 Buffalo Exchange
39 Guild Shop
40 Old Blue House
41 Pavement

Explore Buffalo Bayou

Art-lined trails and skyscraper views

Just northwest of downtown, the 2.3-mile-long **Buffalo Bayou Park** is dotted throughout with public art, dog parks, sporting grounds, and even 250,000 Mexican free-tailed bats that depart en masse at sunset from their roosts under the Waugh Drive bridge. The most interesting section for visitors stretches along the south shore from the Sabine Street Water Works to Waugh Dr, an easy one-hour stroll that takes in the bulk of the permanent art installations and nice views of the bayou.

Dine & Dance at POST

Renovated food and events venue

On the edge of downtown, **POST Houston** *(posthtx.com; 11am-9pm)* is home to over 30 restaurants ranging from West African **ChòpnBlok** to a branch of beloved Austin-based Japanese street food **Eastside King** as well as tacos, fancy grilled cheese and others. Atop the building the 5-acre **Skylawn** offers superb views of the downtown skyline, and POST hosts markets, DJ nights, film screenings and other events.

A Walk in Hermann Park

Outdoor art and natural surroundings

The lawns of **Hermann Park** *(hermannpark.org)* make an excellent sunny-day outing. Squirrels and ducks wander freely through the 445-acre expanse, much of which is encircled by the small-gauge **Hermann Park Railroad** *(full day $6)* that makes a loop every 25 minutes. Stop at the meticulously planned **Japanese Garden** and the sculpture-filled spaces of the **McGovern Centennial Gardens** before checking the schedule at the **Miller Outdoor Theatre** *(milleroutdoortheatre.com)* for open-air performances.

BEST FESTIVALS IN HOUSTON

Houston Livestock Show & Rodeo: Join 2 million locals for rodeos, carnival rides and live music each February/March at NRG Stadium.

Art Car Parade: April's biggest bash features hundreds of mobile masterworks cruising downtown.

Art Bike Parade: A newish take on the Art Car concept now for human-powered locomotion, each May.

Pride Houston: The Pride Parade left its historic Montrose roots in 2015 for the wider streets of downtown each June.

Freedom Over Texas: Houston's biggest July 4th celebrations take place in Eleanor Tinsley Park.

Bayou City Art Festival: Enjoy October's lower temperatures at the outdoor art fest in Memorial Park.

TOP HOUSTON ATTRACTIONS FOR FAMILIES

Children's Museum Houston: Activity-filled museum, where little ones can learn how stuff works, create inventions, play games or draw in an open-air art studio.

Health Museum: More play space than museum with an oversized crawl-through colon, a 12ft-tall beating heart and brain displays.

Houston Museum of Natural Science: (HMNS) Covers archaeology to zoology and plenty in between.

Cockrell Butterfly Center: Watch winged species all around you, inside this separate-admission space in the HMNS.

Houston Zoo: Zookeeper talks, a large children's zoo with playgrounds and petting zoos, and highlights like the World of Primates (buy tickets ahead; *houstonzoo.org)* with raised wooden walkways through the animals' habitats.

Wandering Montrose

The best way to explore

A mashup of trendy and countercultural, Montrose mixes fancy cocktail bars with Texas icehouses (open-air taverns that sell cheap beer), and is one of Houston's most walkable districts. Hit the pavement for a stroll amid antique shops and colorful consignment stores, refreshing over cold drinks along the way.

The intersection of Dunlavy St and Westheimer Rd is a good starting point, where both **Old Blue House** and **BJ Oldies** are reliable sources of antiques and oddities. Surrounding here are numerous small stores of varying quality – **The Guild Shop** *(theguildshop.org)* is large enough to appeal to all sorts, while **Pavement** *(pavement.store)* and national chain **Buffalo Exchange** *(buffaloexchange.com)* focus exclusively on clothing at somewhat higher standards and corresponding prices.

After shopping, stop at local classic **Poison Girl** *(poisongirlbar.com)* for an excellent whiskey selection and generous happy hour, or **Anvil** *(anvilhouston.com)* for one of the city's best selections of cocktails – don't miss poorly hidden 'speakeasy' Refuge around back. Expect pure Texas vibes at **West Alabama Ice House** *(westalabamaicehouse.net),* where outdoor seating and good cheap beer attracts a cross-section of Montrose and Houston locals – as does excellent taco truck **Tierra Caliente** *(tacostierracalientemx.com)* across the street.

Arts in Montrose

Building on the Menils' vision

Spread across 30 acres on the southern side of Montrose, the **Menil Collection** *(menil.org)* galleries and installations are curated from the private holdings of Houston-based French philanthropists Dominique and John de Menil, who relocated here in the early 1940s. The main building – designed by Italian architect Renzo Piano – houses an eclectic collection spanning cubism and surrealism, African and Pacific tribal cultures, and far more.

Nearby, the **Dan Flavin Installation** and **Cy Twombly Gallery** both house permanent single-artist exhibitions – the latter building was custom-built for the purpose. The smaller galleries inside **Menil Drawing Institute** display regularly changing drawing exhibits. Between gallery visits, look for large-scale sculptural installations throughout the shady campus.

DRINKING IN HOUSTON: COCKTAIL BARS

Houston Watch Company: Dimly lit favorite off Main St with engaging bartenders and a generous happy hour. *4pm-2am Tue-Sat*

Captain Foxheart's Bad News Bar: Speakeasy with a budget-friendly happy hour and even better list of handcrafted cocktails. *5pm-2am*

Winnie's: Craft cocktails just barely edge out the excellent oysters and lunch menu for top spot here. *11am-10pm Mon-Thu, to 11pm Fri-Sun*

Saint Arnold Brewing Company: The big name in Houston brewing, straight from the source at its Fifth Ward brewpub and beer garden. *11am-10pm Sun-Thu, to 11pm Fri & Sat*

Alongside the Menil collections, **Rothko Chapel** *(rothkochapel.org)* is a nondenominational sacred space hung with 14 large-scale monotonal paintings by abstract expressionist Mark Rothko. The quiet, meditative chamber evokes strong feelings among Houstonians, particularly within the art community. In early 2024 an expansion to the site was announced to include an event plaza, meditation garden and program center to be completed in 2026.

All these galleries are free to the public; note that they're all closed Monday and Tuesday.

Journey into Outer Space

Exploring NASA's Space Center

A 30-minute drive southeast of downtown, Johnson Space Center has served as mission control for all NASA space flights to the present day starting with the Gemini 4 mission in 1965. The **Space Center Houston** *(spacecenter.org/visitor-information; adult/child $45/40)* complex showcases interactive exhibits and short films on the history of space flight, and artifacts from the US space program, including moon rocks and numerous vehicles used by NASA astronauts.

The most popular aspect for many visitors – and the only way the public can access the actual Johnson Space Center campus – are the NASA tram tours. Three separate itineraries travel to Rocket Park, Historic Mission Control tours (additional $15 surcharge) and the Astronaut Training Facility (available on a first-come, first-served basis, with reservations made at Guest Services).

You can save a few dollars (and time spent in line) by buying tickets in advance.

Gators in the Grasslands

Walking trails and wildlife in Brazos Bend

Alligators lie along the lake shores, wading birds and waterfowl calls echo through the live oak, and bird-watchers hunker behind waterfront blinds trying to capture it all at **Brazos Bend State Park** *(adult/child $7/free)*, just 45 miles south of Houston. Here 37 miles of walking trails make this a popular weekend getaway. Reserve ahead for fall and spring weekends, when the park fills to capacity.

CATCHING THE BIG GAME

During home games (baseball, basketball, football) fans flood into downtown stadiums as well as bars and restaurants in surrounding neighborhoods.

Houston Astros *(mlb.com/astros)* See baseball games at **Daikin Park**, on the edge of historic downtown, late March to early October.

Houston Rockets *(nba.com/rockets)* From October to April, basketball games take over the **Toyota Center** on the southeast edge of downtown.

Houston Dynamo *(houstondynamofc.com)* Soccer fans can get their fix at **Shell Energy Stadium** in East Downtown (EaDo) from February to October.

Houston Texans *(houstondynamofc.com)* Biggest of all are the football games happening at **NRG Stadium** from September to January. Though far from downtown, the stadium is easily reached on the Red Line METRORail.

EATING IN HOUSTON: BARBECUE

Truth BBQ: Top-rated Texas barbecue joint. Expect a wait, but enjoy the views and smell of the smokers in the meantime. *hours vary* $$$

Pinkerton's Barbecue: Slow-smoked meat eaten at shared tables; a classic barbecue experience in the city. *11am-9pm Sun & Tue-Thu, to 10pm Fri & Sat* $$$

Blood Bros BBQ: Houston loves fusion; great meats here incorporate East Asian-inspired techniques and ingredients. *11am-3pm Wed-Sun, plus 6-9pm Thu-Sat* $$

The Pit Room: Neighborhood joint in Montrose equally popular for a lunch special or an after-hours cold one on the patio. *11am-9pm* $$

THE 1900 STORM

Once Texas' largest city and the nation's third-largest seaport, Galveston was dealt a devastating blow by a hurricane in 1900. Estimates show as many as one-fifth of the island's population died in the storm – making it the deadliest disaster in US history at the time – and around a quarter of the city's residents were left homeless.

In response, the city undertook massive public-works projects – raising the entire city by up to 11ft and constructing a 17ft seawall that would eventually extend 10 miles along the Gulf Coast. Galveston's economy never fully recovered, as ship traffic moved to nearby Houston and with it much of the income that made Galveston prosper.

DANITA DELIMONT/SHUTTERSTOCK

Spoonbills, Aransas National Wildlife Refuge

Coastal Charm in Galveston

Architecture and beach-hopping

Part historic Southern town, part sunburned beach resort, Galveston Island is Houston's favorite seaside bolthole.

Self-guided tours of the **Grand 1894 Opera House** *(thegrand.com; $5)* offer visitors a peek behind the curtains of Texas' official opera house, though not backstage access.

The former Galveston Orphans' Home is now the **Bryan Museum** *(thebryanmuseum.org; adult/child $15/free)*, with excellent exhibitions on Galveston and Texan history as well as an audio tour featuring residents' recollections of life in the Home.

Self-guided tours of both **Bishop's Palace** *(galvestonhistory.org; adult/youth $15/12)* and **Moody Mansion** *(moodymansion.org; adult/youth $15/7)* showcase the lifestyles of late-1800s Galveston elites, the latter boasting an excellent audioguide that adds familial context to the site.

After exploring the historic center, enjoy some downtime on the seaside. **East Beach** on the (eastern) tip of the island is party central in summer, but go west, and you'll pass miles of appealing beaches.

Hang out in Port Aransas

Texas' favorite coastal escape

On the northern tip of Mustang Island, Port Aransas is, for many lifelong Texans, the most appealing beach destination on this state's coast. The pace is relaxed, and daily life is dominated by beachgoing and sunset drinks. Connected to the mainland by a free ferry service, Port A feels like leaving real life behind.

IB Magee Beach Park and the **Horace Caldwell Fishing Pier** are great spots for swimming and fishing. Alternatively get in touch with outfitters like Texas Surf Camps *(texassurfcamps.com)* and Island Surf Rentals *(islandsurfrentals.com)* to add a bit of water-sports action to your trip. The latter has kayaks, beach bikes and paddle boards, in addition to surf gear, for rent.

Deep Sea Headquarters *(deepseaheadquarters.com)* arranges everything from half-day to offshore or overnight fishing trips. In addition, chartered trips of all sizes leave most days from **Fisherman's Wharf**, which is also home to dolphin tours, sunset cruises and the jetty boat that carries visitors across to the undeveloped **San José Island**.

Go Birding in Aransas NWR

A coastal driving tour

For bird-watchers, **Aransas National Wildlife Refuge** is a premier site on the Texas coast. More than 400 species have been documented here, and even people who don't carry binoculars and bird checklists get caught up in the frenzy. The scenery at Aransas NWR alone is spectacular. The blue Aransas Bay waters are speckled with green islets ringed with white sand. Native dune grasses blow gently in the breeze while songbirds provide background music. The easiest way to experience the refuge is by driving the 16-mile auto tour (starting on the road just past the visitor center), which features plenty of opportunities to stop and fish along piers, hike on nature trails or bird-watch from the observation tower.

Off-Shore Adventures in South Padre Island

Fun on the water

Near the southern tip of the Gulf Coast, the small resort town of South Padre Island is famed for its sparkling shoreline and clear waters. While the long beaches running through the city are built up and generally busy, miles and miles of undeveloped sand run to the Mansfield Cut channel at the north of the island.

The Laguna Madre is renowned for wind-powered water sports. You can take lessons or rent gear from **Air Padre Kiteboarding** *(airpadrekiteboarding.com)* or fly high with **Sonny's Beach Service** *(sonnysbeachservice.com),* which offers parasailing.

For those looking for a more low-key adventure, there's kayaking and paddleboarding, along with a variety of boat trips. The **Original Dolphin Watch** *(theoriginaldolphinwatch.com)* heads out multiple times a day to get a glimpse at the pods of dolphins that call this area home.

FISHING ON SOUTH PADRE

No matter which chartered fishing guide you go with, there's a good chance you'll start and end your trip at **Jim's Pier** on the bay side of South Padre Island. This is the main dock at SPI for getting on and off boats, and it's also a fully stocked bait and tackle shop. In addition, if you need advice or help finding a guide to match what you want to do, the staff at Jim's Pier has a list of guides they can get you in contact with. They also offer fish-cleaning services after your trip. Prices vary depending on the type of fish you catch, but it's usually a couple of dollars per fish to have them fileted right there for you.

EATING & DRINKING AT SOUTH PADRE ISLAND: OUR PICKS

Padre Island Brewing Company: Burgers, pizza and seafood with freshly brewed beer on tap. *11:30am-10pm Mon-Sat, to 9pm Sun* **$$**

Grapevine Cafe: Great choice for breakfast and lunch with coffee beans roasted in-house. *7:30am-3pm* **$$**

Louie's Backyard: Iconic SPI hang-out on the bayside with fireworks every Friday during summer (June to August). *11:30am-2am*

Wanna Wanna Beach Bar & Grill: Longtime favorite tiki bar steps from the sand that's known for its turbo piña coladas. *11:30am-10pm*

West Texas & Big Bend National Park

OUTDOOR ADVENTURES | DESERT LANDSCAPES | ART-LOVING TOWNS

GETTING AROUND

Public transit is limited and inconvenient beyond El Paso, and it won't get you to Big Bend National Park. Amtrak trains stop in El Paso and Alpine, while Greyhound buses connect El Paso to Fort Stockton for buses to Marfa and Alpine.

You'll need a car to experience West Texas fully. Rent a vehicle at the airport in El Paso or pick up a Jeep rental in Alpine. You'll want a high-clearance 4WD vehicle if backcountry driving is on your itinerary. Fly into El Paso International Airport to minimize your drive time to Big Bend National Park.

West Texas is home to the tallest mountains in the state, some of the darkest skies in the world, two national parks and a vast canyon that's second in size to the Grand Canyon. The only major city in the area is El Paso, which is closer to San Diego, California, than it is to Houston or Dallas.

The region's biggest attraction is Big Bend National Park, where mountain peaks soar above a vast unforgiving desert, while the Rio Grande winds its ways past steep canyons carved out of limestone. Amid this 1252-square-mile wilderness, there are ample opportunities for hiking, camping, backcountry driving, stargazing and even paddling along the Rio Grande River.

Quirky small towns fill the gaps between large swaths of unspoiled nature and sprawling ranches. Visit art galleries, shop independent boutiques, listen to small-town jam sessions or dive deep into Texas history.

The Artistry of Alpine

Mural-filled town

Set at the foot of the Davis Mountains, the railroad and ranching town of Alpine might be West Texas' best-kept secret. Independent boutiques, antique stores and lively coffee shops line streets that feel like a movie set. Murals are everywhere – even in the alleys. And when the light hits the mountains around golden hour, it's easy to see why artists are drawn to this place.

TOP TIP

Big Bend is a hot desert park, and heat advisories are common, even in the fall. Avoid long hikes during the middle of the day, drink lots of water, use sunscreen and wear protective clothing, and carry extra water with you in case of an emergency.

Checkout the **Welcome to Alpine** mural down the street from the historic **Holland Hotel** and the **Cattle Drive** mural across the street. Pop into the **Big Bend Gallery** *(facebook.com/bigbendartscouncil.org)* to shop for pieces from local artists that are more affordable than you might expect. Then go to the **Museum of the Big Bend** *(museumofthebigbend.com; adult/child $10/free)* for a hefty dose of West Texas–inspired fine art.

From the Springs to the Stars

Stellar highlights near Fort Davis

The **Fort Davis National Historic Site** *(nps.gov/foda; per vehicle $20)* protects a beautifully sited frontier fort established in 1854, at the northeast edge of modern Fort Davis (town). Staffed exclusively by Black soldiers between 1867 and 1881, it was abandoned in 1891, but today you can explore five of the remaining buildings set amid scores of ruins.

Thirty-three miles north of Fort Davis, **Balmorhea State Park** *(tpwd.texas.gov/state-parks/balmorhea; adult/child $7/free)* is a literal oasis in the West Texas desert. This state park is home to the world's largest spring-fed swimming pool (maximum depth 25ft), offering snorkelers and divers a chance to swim with turtles, catfish, minnows and endangered fish like the Pecos gambusia and Comanche Springs pupfish. If you're traveling during the summer, purchase day passes in advance online.

One of the best parties in West Texas starts after sunset high in the Fort Davis mountains. Here at the **McDonald Observatory** *(mcdonaldobservatory.org; adult/child $25/20)*, astronomers lead visitors on a guided tour of the constellations in the night sky. Guests at these Star Parties can peek

STARGAZING IN BIG BEND

Big Bend National Park is home to some of the darkest skies in the world, and it's one of best places in North America for stargazing. National park rangers offer regular night sky programs, including moonlight walks and star parties.

For the best views of the starry skies here, give your eyes a chance to adjust to the dark. It typically take about a half-hour for eyes to acclimate to total darkness, but once they do, you'll be able to see many more stars than perhaps you thought possible. Using a phone can disrupt your night vision, so keep it in your pocket and opt for a red LED light if needed.

BEST SHOPPING IN MARFA

Marfa Mood Mercantile: A tiny boutique selling gourmet pet treats, artisan jewelry and local gifts.

Raba Marfa: A stylish vintage store where the clothes and accessories will make you feel ready to grace a magazine cover.

Wrong Store: An impeccably curated indie shop that feels more like a gallery of unique treasures.

Cactus Liquors: Obscure spirits, unique beers, fine wines and a walk-up window.

Cobra Rock: Pick up a pair of custom-made handcrafted leather boots.

Texas Rose: Shop for West Texas–inspired art, clothing and accessories.

Garza Marfa: A chic furniture and textiles store.

at the Milky Way through powerful telescopes, check out exhibits in the visitors center, or just relax under a blanket of stars. Reserve ahead.

Marfa's Modern Art & Mystery Lights

Offbeat adventures in a desert town

Plonked down on the edge of the desert, the small town of Marfa is a wild mash-up of cowboy culture and cutting-edge art. Start off the Marfa experience at **The Chinati Foundation** *(chinati.org; adult/child $37/free),* an abandoned army base that now houses one of the world's largest permanent installations of minimalist art. Visits are by one of three guided tours, costing $15 to $35 (free for kids) depending on how much art you want to see. Reservations are essential. One of the best times to experience it is in mid-October, when **Chinati Weekend** *(chinati.org/chinati-weekend)* takes place. For two days there are gallery open houses with free-flowing wine, plus special exhibitions and events.

No matter when you visit, stop at **Ballroom Marfa** *(ballroommarfa.org),* a gallery that hosts rotating exhibitions in a former military dance hall. Across the street, **RULE Gallery** *(rulegallery.com)* shows contemporary abstract and conceptual photography, sculpture and paintings in a space that's also the curator's home. For the latest information on events and exhibits, check out the Marfa Gallery Guide *(marfagalleryguide.com).*

After sundown, keep an eye out of the **Marfa Mystery Lights**. For more than a century, people have watched unexplained glowing orbs appear on the horizon. Stop at the **Marfa Lights Viewing Area** (on Highway 90) east of Marfa and see if you can spot them for yourself.

Adventures in Big Bend National Park

Where the mountains meet the desert

Big Bend National Park *(nps.gov/bibe; per vehicle $30)* boasts more than 150 miles of hiking trails. An excellent introduction to the park's varied landscapes is the 4.8-mile round-trip Lost Mine Trail. The gently sloping switchbacks climb over 1000ft through a cool, shaded forest of juniper, oak and pine trees. Take in views of Juniper Canyon and Casa Grande Peak as you approach the main viewpoint, from where cliffs, craggy peaks and lush canyons are everywhere you look.

WHERE TO EAT & DRINK IN MARFA: OUR PICKS

Para Llevar: Wood-fired sourdough pizzas, sandwiches and salads in an upscale bodega and wine shop. *11am-8pm* $$

Angel's Restaurant: A casual spot for authentic Mexican food. Try the smothered burrito, chili relleno or enchiladas. *7am-8pm Mon-Sat, 8am-2pm Sun* $

Planet Marfa: A quirky beer garden with free peanuts and a surprisingly good menu. *1-10pm, to midnight Fri & Sat* $

Marfa Spirit Co: A distillery and tasting room that feels like a favorite neighborhood bar. *3-11pm Thu-Sat, 11am-7pm Sun*

After a day on the trail, head to **Boquillas Hot Springs**, a secluded 105°F pool overlooking the Rio Grande. Be prepared: it's a half-mile (round-trip) hike to the springs, and there are no changing facilities (bathing suits required).

River trips can range from a few hours to a few days. **Angell Expeditions** *(angellexpeditions.com)* offers guided raft, canoe and kayaking trips as does **Big Bend River Tours** *(bigbendrivertours.com)*.

Climb the Highest Peak in Texas

Trails of the Guadalupe Mountains

In a remote desert setting near the border of Texas and New Mexico, **Guadalupe Mountains National Park** *(nps.gov/gumo/index; adult/child $10/free)* has jagged peaks, spires and canyons. There are more than 80 miles of trails here, though most people have their sights set on climbing Guadalupe Peak, the state's highest point at 8751ft. Spectacular views await on the strenuous ascent (3000ft elevation gain) on the 8.5-mile round-trip hike.

SIGHTS
1 Ballroom Marfa
2 Chinati Foundation

EATING
3 Angel's Restaurant
4 Para Llevar

DRINKING & NIGHTLIFE
5 Marfa Spirit Co
6 Planet Marfa

SHOPPING
7 Cactus Liquors
8 Cobra Rock
9 Garza Marfa
10 Marfa Mood Mercantile
11 Raba Marfa
12 Texas Rose
13 Wrong Store

PALO DURO ESSENTIALS

Hiking Ample water is crucial. The park recommends one quart per person per hour. Start early. You'll beat the crowds and have a better chance to see wildlife by heading out around dawn.

Food The **Trading Post** (about 2.5 miles past the visitor center) has breakfast sandwiches, burgers, fries, ice cream and other snacks. Open 9:30am to 6pm.

Camping The park has four different camping areas ($16 to $26 per site), including one spot (**Fortress Cliff** area) for tent campers only. Several first-come, first-served permits for hike-in primitive camping ($12) are also available.

Cabins and glamping Cabins range from rustic to well equipped ($50 to $160). Several have stunning views. There's also luxury glamping tents ($300).

REGIS ST LOUIS; COURTESY OF THE CITY OF LUBBOCK, BUDDY HOLLY CENTER

Buddy Holly Center

The Canyons & High Plains of the Panhandle

Scenic drive through Texas' northwest

Home to wildlife-rich canyons, shortgrass prairies and empty highways stretching beneath big open skies, the Texas Panhandle makes a memorable setting for a road trip.

Start off in the sizable town of **Lubbock**. Learn about an early rock-and-roll legend on a visit to the **Buddy Holly Center** *(ci.lubbock.tx.us/departments/buddy-holly-center; adult/child $10/5)*. Afterwards, take a journey into the past at the **Museum of Texas Tech University** *(depts.ttu.edu/museumttu; admission free)*, which also displays textiles and pottery from some 20 different Southwest Native American tribes. Next door the **National Ranching Heritage Center** *(ranchingheritage.org; free)*, follow a 1.5-mile path around a historical park containing 19th- and early-20th-century buildings, including an old schoolhouse, a rural church and vintage windmills.

From Lubbock, get behind the wheel for the 100-mile drive up to **Caprock Canyons State Park** *(adult/child $5/free)*, home to 26 miles of rugged trails, plus prairie-dog towns and freely roaming bison.

Back in the car, drive 90 miles northwest to reach **Palo Duro Canyon State Park** *(adult/child $8/free)*, home to the second-largest canyon in the United States. You'll find some impressive hiking trails including the famous 2.8-mile (one way) Lighthouse Trail, which takes you to a 312ft monolith.

End your journey in the city of **Amarillo** (25 miles northwest of the canyon). Here you can refuel at the **Big Texan** *(bigtexan.com)*, a huge kitschy steakhouse. Nearby, you can explore some of the curious sites sprinkled along old Route 66, like the **Cadillac Ranch**, which features a row of Cadillacs, buried hood first, near a wheat field 10 miles west of Amarillo.

DISCOVER DOWNTOWN EL PASO

Visit free museums and a beautifully restored theater from the 1930, take in public art and shop for bargains in the heart of the city.

START	END	LENGTH
El Paso Museum of History	Plaza Hotel Pioneer Park	1.2 miles; 2-3 hours

Start at the 1 **El Paso Museum of History**, in the heart of the downtown museum district, to learn how city evolved from a railroad stop into a vibrant multicultural destination. Continue along N Santa Fe St to browse the Southwestern art at the 2 **El Paso Museum of Art** (admission free), founded in 1959 and housed in a former Greyhound station.

Next head to the nearby 3 **Plaza Theatre**. The 1930s single-screen movie theater is an impressive example of Spanish Colonial Revival architecture and was almost demolished in the 1980s. Schedule your visit around one of the theater's free tours.

Across the street, pop into the 4 **Hotel Paso del Norte** to admire the Tiffany Glass dome above the bar.

Check out the public art work 5 **Bienvenido**, a giant yellow door installed in 2021; it's one of many works you'll find in downtown. While here make a detour down 6 **El Paso St**.

Finish at the 7 **Plaza Hotel Pioneer Park**, where you can admire the Texas decor before heading up to its La Perla rooftop bar for a drink.

Elizabeth Taylor once lived in the penthouse at **Plaza Hotel**; the bar – which offers some of the best mountain views in the city – was once her terrace.

El Paso Museum of Art has a small space that also pays homage to the late musical icon Selena.

Pop into **Dave's A Pawn Shop** while on El Paso St; it's one of the oddest retail experiences in the city. Shop for bargains while admiring well-preserved architecture.

Places We Love to Stay

$ Budget $$ Midrange $$$ Top End

Austin

p130

Firehouse Hostel $ Hostel with shared dorms and private suites. Find the speakeasy behind the reception's bookshelf.

The Driskill $$ Legendary hotel on 6th Street that's been in business since 1886. The site of LBJ and Lady Bird's first date – and supposedly haunted, as well.

Hotel Van Zandt $$ Enjoy in-suite record players, live music in the restaurant and a rooftop pool, with quick access to Rainey St.

ARRIVE Austin $$ This chic 2019 build along the bars, restaurants and music venues of E 6th is a local landmark thanks to its unique exterior architecture.

Austin Motel $$ This historic 1938 spot has a riot of rainbow colors in its quirky rooms – and one of the most famous neon signs in town.

Hotel San José $$ Bungalow-style hotel with roots dating back to the 1930s. Rooms surround the courtyard lounge that's a favorite hang-out spot for locals.

Carpenter Hotel $$ Prime location that's a short walk away from Zilker Park, Barton Springs and Lady Bird Lake.

South Congress Hotel $$$ A hip boutique hotel with a sexy rooftop pool and the home of Café No Sé, one of the best dessert spots in all of Austin.

San Antonio

p140

Hotel Havana $$ Quiet location set apart from other River Walk hotels by Cuba-inspired, boho-chic rooms from Texas design guru and hotelier Liz Lambert.

Menger Hotel $$ You can't get closer to the Alamo than this historic hotel, built next door just 23 years after the famous battle.

Ranch Motel & Leisure Club $$ On the edge of Brackenridge Park, this 1940s motel was given a contemporary makeover without losing its vintage charm.

Omni La Mansión Del Rio $$$ Luxe property in the middle of the River Walk born out of 19th-century religious-school buildings in the Spanish-Mexican hacienda style.

Hotel Emma $$$ The epicenter of the Pearl District blends Victorian-era decor with post-industrial edge, while guest rooms evoke a stylish but understated Texas ranch.

Hill Country

p146

Peach Tree Inn & Suites $ Less than a 10-minute walk to Fredericksburg's Main St, this homey place offers good value for its quiet rooms and spacious suites.

The Vaquero Motel $ The rooms at this well-maintained Bandera motel have a rustic, Western design with chunky wood furnishings. It's an easy walk to bars and restaurants.

The Kendall $$ This charming Southern Colonial-style inn on Cibolo Creek in Boerne has one-of-a-kind rooms, including one set in a converted chapel.

Gruene Mansion Inn $$$ This cluster of buildings in Gruene is practically its own village, with atmospheric rooms in the mansion, a former carriage house and the old barns.

Dallas

p150

Magnolia Hotel $$ In a 29-story 1922 building, the Magnolia is an old classic with good prices for the no-nonsense rooms and a great location.

Canvas Hotel $$ Rooms have exposed-brick walls and big windows in this former industrial space turned boutique hotel. Rooftop pool and other inviting common areas.

The Bishop Arts Hotel by Q Resorts $$ About a half-mile north of Bishop Arts, this good-value but unstaffed place has sunny rooms and a small dip pool.

The Joule $$$ Aside from well-equipped rooms with rain showers and spa amenities, this neo-Gothic beauty has an art-filled lobby, stylish eateries and cantilevered rooftop pool.

Fort Worth

p154

Stockyards Hotel $$ This 1907 gem has Western-themed art, handsome cowboy-inspired rooms and a grand Old West lobby.

Miss Molly's $$ The former boarding house turned bordello currently enjoys a third act as an eight-room, possibly haunted guesthouse with antique Western-style decor.

The Ashton Hotel $$ Wide range of comfy rooms (including spa suites) in a six-story building dating back to 1915 with a great location off Sundance Sq.

Hotel Drover $$$ Fort Worth's best hotel has rustic-chic rooms, beautiful outdoor spaces, and atmospheric eating and drinking options.

Houston p157

Magnolia Hotel $$ Stylish velvet- and damask-layered rooms in this 1926 downtown favorite, once home to the *Houston Post & Dispatch* printers.

La Maison in Midtown $$ One of very few excellent B&Bs in Houston, surrounded by appealing dining and nightlife.

Hotel ZaZa $$$ Hip and flamboyant, from bordello-esque colors to zebra-accent chairs, ZaZa is good fun.

La Colombe d'Or $$$ A museum-like interior and refined French dining in the heart of Montrose keep this luxury suites popular.

Gulf Coast p164

Manor on 17th $$ Beautifully-renovated 1890 mansion in Galveston's East End with complimentary 4pm happy hour each day and nightcaps every evening.

The Tarpon Inn $$ Rebuilt after several hurricanes, this Port Aransas island mainstay has been operating in some form since 1900.

Dancing Dunes $$ Five funky beach cabins in Port Aransas around a connecting porch have a fun, ramshackle atmosphere.

Isla Grand Beach Resort $$ Longtime South Padre Island favorite on the beach with two great pools if you don't want to get super sandy.

Big Bend & West Texas p166

Ocotillos Village $ A collection of handsomely designed A-frame cabins in Terlingua, with outdoor showers and shared indoor bathroom facilities a few steps away.

Holland Hotel (p167) $ This historic property in the heart of Alpine has a gorgeous courtyard, freshly renovated lobby and rooms full of character.

Maverick Inn $ This southwestern-style property in Alpine looks like it came out of an old Western. It has 21 guest rooms, a pool and is pet friendly.

El Cosmico $$ Designed by famed hotelier Liz Lambert, this camp-style bohemian property in Marfa rents teepees, trailers and safari tents with outdoor showers.

Hotel Limpia $$ This charming historic hotel in Fort Davis is the ideal place to lay your head after a Star Party at McDonald Observatory. Take your pick from Victorian-style rooms, 1920s-era guest suites or budget-friendly rooms.

Gage Hotel $$$ This luxurious southwestern-style hotel in Marathon is true Texas treasure and the closest hotel to Big Bend National Park.

JOSHUA RAINEY PHOTOGRAPHY/SHUTTERSTOCK

Hotel Emma

Researched and curated by Liza Prado

Rocky Mountains

EPIC BEAUTY MEETS OUTDOOR ADVENTURE

A four-state wonderland of mountains, rivers and alpine forests, renowned for outdoor adventuring and rich in history, arts, small-town life and urban centers.

Welcome to the Rocky Mountains, where the Great Plains meet the rugged backbone of the continent. It's a vast region, rife with towering peaks and glacial lakes, dense forests and rushing rivers. Also red-rock canyons and sand dunes, volcano-scapes and hot springs. It's a veritable playground for outdoors enthusiasts, with eight national parks and over 100 million acres of public land. World-class skiing? Check. Epic rafting and fly-fishing? Check. Hiking, climbing and mountain biking? Check, check, check. The ways and places to get an adrenaline rush are nearly endless.

But there's more to the Rockies than the outdoors. History is visible everywhere – cliff dwellings, battlefields, ghost towns and trading posts turned forts...even some of the world's best dinosaur sites. Collectively, they tell the multilayered history of the West: one of survival and conflict, fortune-seeking and possibility.

And the Rocky Mountain region continues to evolve. Today, it has a wealth of terrific cities, from Denver to Boulder, Missoula to Boise, each with engaging museums and performing arts, plus nightlife, craft breweries and culinary excellence (hello Michelin stars). Prefer something smaller? Check out historic towns turned glitzy destinations like Aspen, Jackson and Ketchum.

To visit the Rocky Mountains is to have at your fingertips spectacular landscapes, rich history, and thriving urban and small town life – the hard part is deciding where to go.

HARRY HAYASHI/SHUTTERSTOCK

THE MAIN AREAS

For places to stay in the Rocky Mountains, see p248

YEGOROV/SHUTTERSTOCK

Bison, Yellowstone National Park (p218)

Find Your Way

The Rocky Mountain states cover a vast and varied region, extending 1100 miles from the towering sand dunes of southern Colorado to the stunning glacial-carved peaks of northern Montana. The Rocky Mountains themselves are the backbone of it all.

Idaho, p237
A secret stash of stunning landscapes, with evocative names like Sawtooth Mountains and Craters of the Moon, plus charming towns like Boise and Ketchum.

Wyoming, p209
A place of contrasts, from the captivating beauty of Yellowstone and Grand Tetons to stark high plains, windblown towns and compelling Indigenous sites.

CAR

To fully explore the region, you'll need a car. It'll give you freedom to stop in small towns, explore national parks and forests, tour archaeological zones, and access trailheads and ski resorts, all at your own pace. In winter, consider a 4WD vehicle.

BUS

Bus service is limited. Greyhound travels between the bigger cities in the Rocky Mountain region (and beyond), while smaller companies like Bustang, Jefferson Lines and Salt Lake Express provide service to a handful of small towns in each state.

PLANE

Flying within the region cuts down your travel time tremendously – a plus if you're short on time or hate long-haul drives. Denver has the only major international airport in the Rocky Mountain region, but there are several small airports scattered around each state.

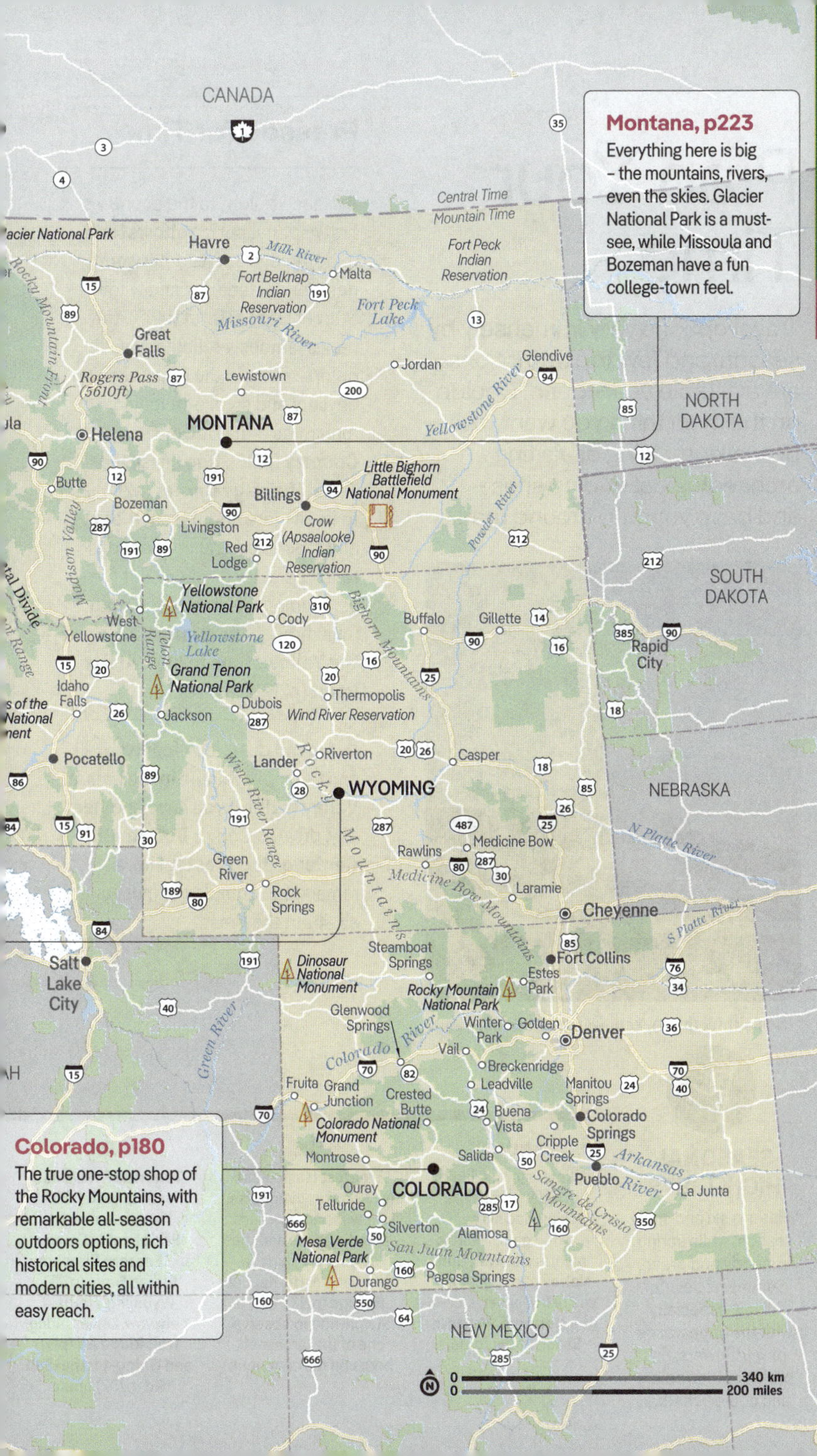

Montana, p223

Everything here is big – the mountains, rivers, even the skies. Glacier National Park is a must-see, while Missoula and Bozeman have a fun college-town feel.

Colorado, p180

The true one-stop shop of the Rocky Mountains, with remarkable all-season outdoors options, rich historical sites and modern cities, all within easy reach.

Plan Your Time

Travel options vary immensely by season, and few top attractions are available year-round. Decide on the main thing you want to do – hiking, skiing or visiting archaeological or dino sites – and base your trip around that.

VOLKV/SHUTTERSTOCK

Old Faithful (p218), Yellowstone National Park

Pressed for Time

- Head straight to the country's first national park: **Yellowstone** (p218), known for its otherworldly geothermal features and wildlife. Start at **Old Faithful** (p218), the park's famously reliable geyser, before taking in the other gushing geysers and smoke-belching fumaroles that dot **Geyser Country** (p218). Don't miss the **Tribal Heritage Center** (p219) to learn more about local tribes and their ancestral connections to the park. Later, check out the astounding views of thundering falls through the **Grand Canyon of the Yellowstone** (p219) – **Artist Point** (p219) is a must see.

- Around dusk, look for bison, elk and other big wildlife in the **Lamar Valley** (p219). If you have another day, drive to Cody's **Buffalo Bill Center of the West** (p216), a remarkable complex of museums all about the West.

SEASONAL HIGHLIGHTS

Winter is ski and snow season, while spring is muddy and green. Summer is best for hiking, especially with the appearance of wildflowers. Fall brings golden colors and cooler weather.

JANUARY

Winter storms dump powder across the Rockies, and ski season is in full gear. Head to resorts like **Vail**, **Sun Valley** and **Big Sky**. If you're in Denver, stop in the **National Western Stock Show** (p186).

MARCH

Treefort Music Fest (p239) takes over Boise, showcasing hundreds of indie bands and the city's artsy spirit. In Jackson's **National Elk Refuge** (p217), take a sleigh-ride to observe one of the largest elk herds on the continent.

JUNE

Telluride Bluegrass Festival (p203) kicks off summer along with **PrideFest** in Denver and **Eastern Shoshone Indian Days** (p213), Wyoming's largest powwow. Drives along **Trail Ridge Rd** (p191) and **Going-to-the-Sun Rd** (p232) open.

A Weeklong Road Trip

- With some room to breathe, start in **Mesa Verde National Park** (p200), known for its impressive cliff dwellings, and take a ranger-led tour – prepare to climb ladders and crawl through tunnels. Next drive to **Telluride** (p203), a charming mountain town tucked into a box canyon, and hike to Colorado's tallest waterfall, **Bridal Veil Falls** (p203).

- Bright and early, straight-shot it to **Black Canyon of the Gunnison National Park** (p204) for the spectacular canyon vistas along South Rim Rd. From there, drive to **Dinosaur National Monument** (p205), making sure to see the Quarry Wall, with some 1500 dino bones embedded in it. Next, spend time in **Grand Teton National Park** (p222), taking in its jagged peaks and shimmering lakes before ending your trip in **Yellowstone** (p218).

Two Weeks to Travel Around

- Begin your Rocky Mountain odyssey in **Denver** (p184), soaking in its urban energy. From there, head to **Rocky Mountain National Park** (p190) for epic hiking on alpine trails and wildflower-filled meadows. Take **Trail Ridge Rd** (p191) through the park before crossing into Wyoming.

- Continue to cowboy chic **Jackson**, making time to visit **National Museum of Wildlife Art** (p217) before exploring the majestic **Grand Teton National Park** (p222). Drive into Idaho though the gorgeous **Teton Valley** to the volcanic landscapes of **Craters of the Moon** (p246). From there, cross into Montana – big sky country – stopping at the vibrant **Missoula People's Market** (p231) before exploring **Glacier National Park** (p232) on foot, wheels or boat. Wrap up your trip at iconic **Yellowstone** (p218).

JULY

Crested Butte's **Wildflower Festival** (p198), Cheyenne's **Frontier Days** (p211) and **Sun Valley Music Festival** (p244). The mountains fill with hikers and campers, and paddlers take on the rivers.

SEPTEMBER

Cooler days begin and crowds disperse – a good time to visit national parks like **Yellowstone** (p218), **Glacier** (p232) and **Mesa Verde**. Listen for the bugling elks in **Rocky Mountain National Park** (p190).

OCTOBER

Aspen paints the region in brilliant yellows; **Grand Teton National Park** (p222) and **Million Dollar Hwy** are beautiful. **Colorado National Monument** (p206) and **Craters of the Moon** (p246) cool off, optimal for outdoor adventure.

DECEMBER

Powder hounds hit the slopes, though the snow can be hit or miss (discounted lift tickets make up for it). Hot springs like **Strawberry Park** (p193) and **Ouray** (p202) provide an easy way to warm up.

Colorado

EPIC LANDSCAPES | URBAN ENERGY | SPORTS

Colorado is a place of striking contrasts and seemingly endless adventure. Towering peaks, red-rock canyons, dense forests and surreal sand dunes make for a landscape that's as diverse as it is beautiful. In winter, world-renowned ski resorts like Aspen and Vail draw powder hounds from near and far, while summer brings hikers and mountain bikers to alpine trails and meadows awash in wildflowers. Off trail, you can unwind in natural hot springs or explore ancient cliff dwellings at Mesa Verde National Park. Add to all that the creative energy of cities like Denver and Boulder – with their vibrant food and craft-beer scenes, street art and museums – and the mountain chic of historic mining towns, and you've got a destination that blends outdoor adventure, layered history, cultural depth and laid-back urban cool. All that under big, bluebird skies.

TOP TIP

Altitude sickness is a real thing in Colorado. Stay hydrated, take it easy and allow a few days to acclimatize. A little light-headedness, slight headaches and sluggishness are normal. But if you experience severe and continued nausea, headache and dizziness, consult a doctor and/or get to lower altitudes.

GETTING AROUND

Most visitors arrive through **Denver International Airport** (DIA) though regional airports dot Colorado. **Bustang** *(ridebustang.com)* provides bus service to towns along the I-70 and I-25 corridors, as well as harder-to-reach destinations like Telluride and Crested Butte. To explore further, a car is essential. City roads and highways are paved and generally well maintained; smaller mountain towns often have dirt or gravel roads. A 4WD vehicle is helpful in winter, especially on icy roads. Some mountain passes close seasonally or when driving conditions are hazardous. Before heading out, check **Colorado Department of Transportation** *(codot.gov/travel)* for road closures and weather warnings.

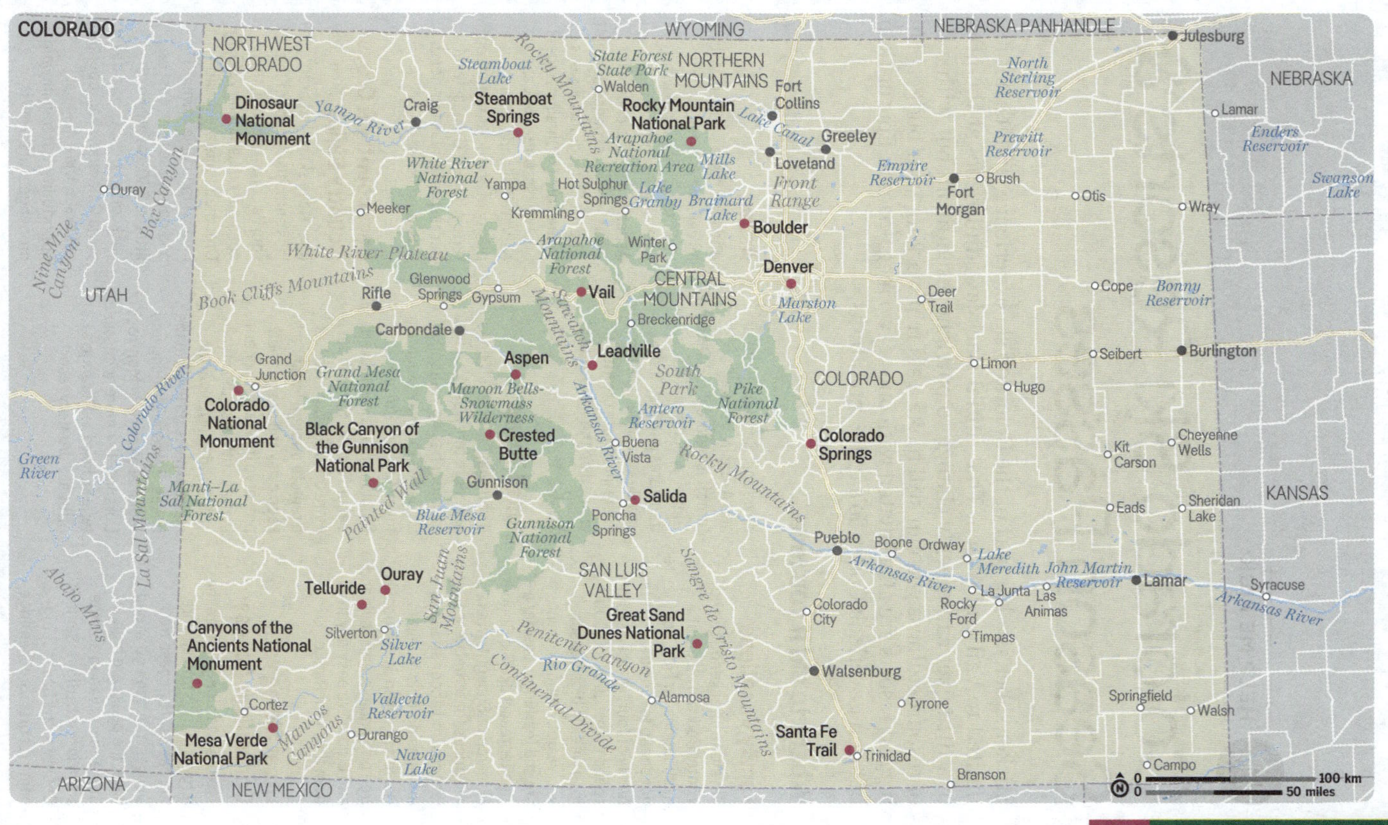
COLORADO
WYOMING
NEBRASKA PANHANDLE
NEBRASKA
KANSAS
UTAH
ARIZONA
NEW MEXICO
NORTHWEST COLORADO
NORTHERN MOUNTAINS
CENTRAL MOUNTAINS
COLORADO
SAN LUIS VALLEY
Dinosaur National Monument
Yampa River
Craig
Steamboat Lake
Steamboat Springs
Rocky Mountains
State Forest State Park
Walden
Rocky Mountain National Park
Arapahoe National Recreation Area
Fort Collins
Lake Canal
Greeley
Loveland
Mills Lake
Front Range
Lake Granby
Brainard Lake
Boulder
Julesburg
North Sterling Reservoir
Prewitt Reservoir
Empire Reservoir
Fort Morgan
Brush
Otis
Wray
Lamar
Enders Reservoir
Swanson Lake
Ouray
Box Canyon
Nine Mile Canyon
White River National Forest
Yampa
Meeker
Hot Sulphur Springs
Kremmling
White River Plateau
Arapahoe National Forest
Winter Park
Denver
Book Cliffs Mountains
Rifle
Glenwood Springs
Gypsum
Vail
Sawatch Mountains
Breckenridge
Marston Lake
Deer Trail
Cope
Bonny Reservoir
Carbondale
Leadville
Aspen
Grand Junction
Grand Mesa National Forest
Colorado River
South Park
Pike National Forest
Limon
Seibert
Burlington
Hugo
Colorado National Monument
Maroon Bells-Snowmass Wilderness
Antero Reservoir
Arkansas River
Black Canyon of the Gunnison National Park
Crested Butte
Buena Vista
Colorado Springs
Kit Carson
Cheyenne Wells
Green River
Manti–La Sal National Forest
La Sal Mountains
Painted Wall
Gunnison
Salida
Eads
Sheridan Lake
Blue Mesa Reservoir
Gunnison National Forest
Poncha Springs
Pueblo
Boone
Ordway
Lake Meredith
John Martin Reservoir
Lamar
Syracuse
Arkansas River
La Junta
Las Animas
Rocky Ford
Timpas
Abajo Mtns
San Juan Mountains
Ouray
Telluride
Silverton
Silver Lake
Great Sand Dunes National Park
Sangre de Cristo Mountains
Colorado City
Canyons of the Ancients National Monument
Penitente Canyon
Rio Grande
Continental Divide
Walsenburg
Alamosa
Tyrone
Springfield
Walsh
Cortez
Vallecito Reservoir
Mancos Canyons
Durango
Mesa Verde National Park
Navajo Lake
Santa Fe Trail
Trinidad
Branson
Campo
0 100 km
0 50 miles

Colorado Ski Resorts & Season Passes

Sticker shock is a big part of the Colorado ski experience, and it's not just limited to Vail and Aspen. That initial slack-jawed disbelief at the price of a lift ticket can quickly change to outright resentment, but with a bit of resourcefulness you can still make a ski trip work for your budget. The biggest resorts are all affiliated with one of two mega-passes, Epic or Ikon, but don't overlook Colorado's indie mountains.

Where to ski if you love...

Family Vacations

Keystone, Breckenridge and Winter Park are all great destinations for kids, but they're not cheap for an out-of-state family of four: you can easily spend upwards of $10,000 for a week in high season. If you've got young kids who are still learning, consider a smaller resort like Ski Cooper, Monarch or Sunlight, where the prices for rental gear, lessons and accommodation are considerably cheaper. Howelsen Hill in Steamboat is free on Sundays, and Loveland and Eldora are easy day trips from the Front Range.

Great Skiing with Convenient Access

The resorts along I-70 are the largest in the state and are the easiest to access from Denver. You can't go wrong here: the peaks are high, the terrain is varied and the snow is featherlight. Summit County alone has four big-name resorts: Breckenridge, Keystone, Copper Mountain and A-Basin. Winter Park's turnoff is before the Eisenhower Tunnel, which sometimes translates into less traffic. Vail and Beaver Creek are the jewels in the interstate crown, but are located on the other side of Vail Pass.

Small Towns

If you want shorter lift lines and more throwback charm, consider basing yourself in an out-of-the-way mountain town. Crested Butte is a fabulous hideaway tucked behind Aspen. Steamboat is more upscale, but also has a remote enough location to keep away the crowds and preserve its Western charm. In the southwest, the steeps at Telluride and Silverton make experts go weak in the knees, but require flying into regional airports in Montrose or Durango. For more accessible terrain, head to Durango's offbeat Purgatory resort.

Aspen

And then there's Aspen. With its celebrity glitter, historic downtown and some of the best scenery in the state, Aspen is a terrific choice for those with an expense account. One lift ticket grants access to the Four Mountains: Aspen, Snowmass, Buttermilk and Aspen Highlands. There's plenty of upside-down-steep terrain here, X Games–level terrain parks, plus top-notch kids' amenities.

Backcountry & Cross-Country Skiing

If you love skiing but are less enthusiastic about the sport's corporate turn, then consider cross-country skiing. Groomed trails are found in most mountain towns, and day passes can cost as little as $30. Going into the backcountry, either on a day trip or via Colorado's backcountry hut system, is a magical opportunity, but training and proper gear are a must.

Vail (p193)

HOW TO

Don't overlook independent resorts like Telluride, Silverton, Wolf Creek, Monarch and Loveland, which also offer incredible skiing and deep powder.

Save money by packing a picnic. It sounds obvious, but the number of people who pay outrageous prices for cafeteria food is astounding.

Want first tracks in backcountry glades after a big storm? Go snowcat skiing at Purgatory, Steamboat, Shrine Pass, Jones Pass, Aspen, Monarch or Loveland.

Got the itch for steep lines and an 'I can't believe this is real' backdrop? Fork out for heli skiing in Silverton or Telluride.

Ikon Pass Versus Epic Pass

There has been a tremendous amount of corporate consolidation in the US ski industry, and the biggest names are now all affiliated with one of two season passes: Ikon or Epic. Don't get confused by the word 'season' – these passes are fully customizable, from one day to unlimited, and from a handful of local hills to the whole hog, including destinations scattered around the world. If you're headed to a big resort, getting a pass in advance – the best deals are offered in spring for the following year – will save you money and allow you the luxury of skiing in more than one place. Passes also come with perks, like discounted tickets for friends and family.

Ikon *(ikonpass.com; four-day/base/full $479/969/1359)* offers access to Winter Park, Copper, Steamboat, Eldora, A-Basin and Aspen in Colorado. Other destinations range from Big Sky (Montana) to Alta and Snowbird (Utah), and Jackson Hole (Wyoming) to Chamonix (France). The Winter Park local passes *(midweek/full $559/749)* are a cheaper option.

Epic *(epicpass.com; four-day/local/full $423/762/1025)* offers access to Vail, Breckenridge, Keystone, Beaver Creek and Crested Butte in Colorado. Other destinations include Whistler (Canada), Park City (Utah), and Heavenly, Northstar and Kirkwood at Lake Tahoe. If you're looking for a more targeted pass, consider the Summit Value Pass *(Breckenridge and Keystone $615)* or Keystone Plus *(Keystone plus five days at Crested Butte $408)*.

THE MARADE

Denver's **Marade** – part march, part parade – is a huge, joyous, serious, welcoming, historic, and thoroughly Denver event. It's the largest Martin Luther King Jr Day celebration in the country, bringing together tens of thousands of Denverites to celebrate the life of Dr King and continue his fight for social justice. It's a massive outpouring of local people – students, elders, politicians, artists, workers, families with strollers, and activists with bullhorns – joining and chanting to manifest a better world. (Even when it's snowing, which it often does in January.) Marchers gather at the Dr King statue in City Park (p186) and march down Colfax Ave to **Civic Center Park** for rousing speeches.

Denver

Tony venues and train tickets

An iconic landmark, the Beaux-Art style **Union Station** *(denverunionstation.com; free)* opened its doors in 1914 and has served as Denver's transportation hub ever since. But it's way more than that. Wander through the Great Hall, with soaring ceilings, chandeliers and cozy leather couches; lively bars and cocktail lounges line the walls alongside ice-cream shops and bookstores. Or indulge yourself at one of the swanky restaurants – including **Mercantile** *(mercantiledenver.com)* and **Ultreia** *(ultreiadenver.com)*, brainchildren of James Beard Award–winning chefs. Or stay overnight at one of Denver's best hotels, **The Crawford** *(thecrawfordhotel.com)*. In summer, come for its outdoor plaza, where you can peruse its popular **Saturday farmers market**, while its **pop-up fountain** entices kids (and kids at heart) to play in the urban sprinklers.

World-class performances

Come to the **Denver Performing Arts Complex** *(artscomplex.com; prices vary)*, where you can score tickets almost nightly. Across four city blocks, you'll find 10 venues connected by a sky-high glass canopy, among them the historic **Ellie Caulkins Opera House** (aka 'the Ellie'), a luxe 2200-seat theater where Opera Colorado and Colorado Ballet perform. Or head to the magnificent **Boettcher Concert Hall**, the nation's first concert-hall-in-the-round, where the **Colorado Symphony** plays classics as well as modern-day crowd-pleasers. The Arts Complex's theater wing, the similarly named **Denver Center for the Performing Arts** (called 'The DCPA'), has eight venues staging everything from experimental productions to Broadway musicals. If you're a theater junkie, take a **behind-the-scenes theater tour** *(per person $12)* with stops in dressing rooms, design studios and costume shops. Purchase tickets online for big discounts, sometimes starting at just $10 per ticket for kids, students and seniors.

Have fun in Confluence Park

Named for the meeting of the South Platte River and Cherry Creek, **Confluence Park** is a pocket of outdoorsy activity in downtown Denver. Picnic on its terraced lawns, jog along the waterfront, or just sun and splash on the park's small sandy beach. In the summer, rent inner tubes and kayaks to ride on a fun human-made stretch of white water. Rentals available at **Confluence Kayaks** *(confluencekayaks.com; per day from $55)*.

Catch a ball (game)

Coors Field *(mlb.com/rockies/ballpark)* is one of the MLB's most home-run-friendly ballparks (apparently, it's the thin air), and catching a **Rockies** game *(mlb.com/rockies; adult/child from $4/1)* is easy with 80 home games and tickets starting at just $1 in the Rockpile (aka centerfield). Theme nights include freebies like trucker hats and commemorative cups; come decked out in your purple, black and silver best to fit right in. Die-hard fan? **Stadium tours** *(adult/child $27/10)* run 70 to 80 minutes and include the field, clubhouses and mile-high seats.

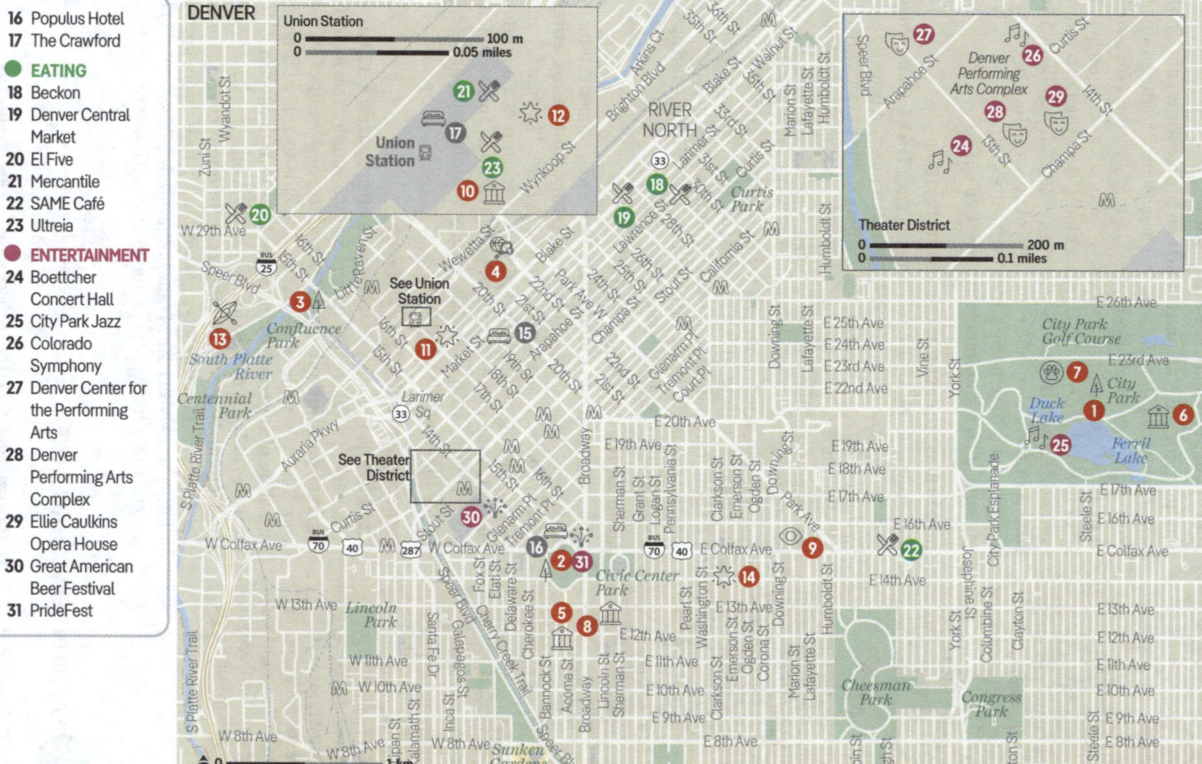

● **SIGHTS**
1 City Park
2 Civic Center Park
see 4 Colorado Rockies
3 Confluence Park
4 Coors Field
5 Denver Art Museum
6 Denver Museum of Nature & Science
7 Denver Zoo
8 History Colorado Center
9 The Center on Colfax
10 Union Station

● **ACTIVITIES**
11 Aspire Tours
12 Colorado Cannabis Tours
13 Confluence Kayaks
14 Historic Denver

● **SLEEPING**
15 Hostel Fish
16 Populus Hotel
17 The Crawford

● **EATING**
18 Beckon
19 Denver Central Market
20 El Five
21 Mercantile
22 SAME Café
23 Ultreia

● **ENTERTAINMENT**
24 Boettcher Concert Hall
25 City Park Jazz
26 Colorado Symphony
27 Denver Center for the Performing Arts
28 Denver Performing Arts Complex
29 Ellie Caulkins Opera House
30 Great American Beer Festival
31 PrideFest

THE CENTER

Established in 1976, **The Center on Colfax** *(lgbtqcolorado.org)*, called simply 'the Center,' is the largest LGBTIQ+ community center in the Rocky Mountain region. A vital hub for support, advocacy and education, its support services span from youth (Rainbow Alley) to elder (Sage of the Rockies) and transgender programming. It's a good resource for LGBTIQ+ travelers too. Health services (including HIV testing and prevention), counseling and legal referrals are freely given. Or come for a drop-in event – watch parties, cooking classes and yoga are regularly offered. The Center also hosts the must-experience Denver's annual **PrideFest** *(denverpride.org)*, one of the largest and most festive LGBTIQ+ pride events in the US.

Sport your stetson at the Stock Show

Saddle up for the **National Western Stock Show** *(nationalwestern.com; adult/child from $17/4)*, a Denver tradition since 1906. A 16-day event held every January in the **National Western Center** *(nationalwesterncenter.com)*, it includes 20 or more rodeos, 15,000 farm animals, dancing horses and even dog shows. Don't miss the iconic kick-off parade, when dozens of Longhorn cattle are herded down 17th St in downtown Denver, high heels and power suits giving way to cowboy hats, chaps and impressive belt buckles.

Take in masterpieces at Denver Art Museum

The crown jewel of Denver's art scene, **DAM** *(denverartmuseum.org; adult/child $27-30/free)* houses an eclectic collection of art, from Old Master painters to the modern greats. It's also home to a stunningly rich collection of Native American art, one of the world's largest. Special exhibitions keep the museum buzzing year-round and interactive art stations keep kids engaged. Choose a few exhibits to see and wander the rest of the time – it's a massive museum spread between the Hamilton Building, a work of modern angular art, and the Martin Building, a fortress-like structure glittering in over a million reflective tiles.

All about the Centennial State

Learn all about the Centennial State, from ancient to modern times, at the state-of-the-art **History Colorado Center** *(historycolorado.org; adult/child $15/free)*. Thoughtful and ever-changing exhibits present the spectrum of Coloradan voices. If time permits, fold some of the museum's excellent programming into your visit – a city walking tour, archaeological dig, a lecture and more.

Cornucopia of activity at City Park

City Park is the largest of Denver's open spaces, a 320-acre megapark just east of downtown. Stretch your legs on its leafy **trails** or **paddleboat** *(wheelfunrentals.com; adult/child per hour $12/7)* on its lakes. Or bring the kids to run wild on its sprawling **playgrounds** and **splash pads** or to check out the creatures at **Denver Zoo** *(denverzoo.org; adult/child $25/19)*. The **Denver Museum of Nature & Science** *(DMNS, dmns.org; adult/child $26/21)* is another family fave. From spring to fall, a weekly **farmers market** *(cityparkfarmersmarket.com)* brings a festival-like atmosphere, with live music, food

EATING IN DENVER: OUR PICKS

SAME Café: Pay-what-you-can, fair-exchange cafe serving ever-changing menu of healthy dishes, including vegetarian options. Walk-in volunteers welcome. *11am-2:30pm Mon-Fri* $

Denver Central Market: Warehouse turned gourmet marketplace, this food hall wows with its style and meal options. *8am-9pm Sun-Thu, to 11pm Fri & Sat* $-$$

El Five: Mediterranean-style tapas and floor-to-ceiling city views. Summer nights bring patio seating. *5-10pm Sun-Thu, to 11pm Fri & Sat* $$

Beckon: Intimate Michelin-starred restaurant with sumptuous, ever-changing Scandinavian-inspired menu. Prepayment required. *5-10pm Wed-Sat* $$$

JAY YUAN/SHUTTERSTOCK

Red Rocks Amphitheater

trucks and all manner of picnic fixin's. Summer nights also brings thousands for free **jazz concerts** *(cityparkjazz.org)*. And, that view! Skyscrapers with snowcapped mountains in the background...the icing on City Park's multilayered cake.

Experience a giant beer fest

Colorado takes its beer seriously, and with over 150 breweries in metro Denver, you certainly won't go thirsty. If you're visiting in late September/early October, try scoring tickets to the **Great American Beer Festival** *(greatamericanbeer festival.com; from $85)*, the largest beer festival in the US. It draws over 2000 master brewers, with over 9000 beers vying for Best of Show medals in 263 categories. General admission includes unlimited 1oz tastings; pairings – small dishes created by lauded chefs – with a menu of beers are also offered. Best of all is the comradery of you and 40,000 beer buddies, all tasting outstanding brews one ounce at a time.

Be wowed by RiNo's murals

Unexpected and totally fabulous, the trendy RiNo neighborhood is draped in hundreds of murals. Bright, opinionated and ever-changing, the artwork stops you in your tracks, speaking to Denver's diversity, history and day-to-day musings. Wander the neighborhood to take them in, using **RiNo's website** *(rinoartdistrict.org/art/murals)* to find local faves. Or take a guided tour with **Denver Graffiti Tour** *(denvergraffititour.com; adult/child $30/15)*, known for its small groups and custom tours.

Catch a concert at Red Rocks Amphitheater

There's something almost primal about attending a concert at **Red Rocks Amphitheater** *(redrocksonline.com)* – the sounds of instruments enveloping you, the sight of people dancing under an umbrella of stars and the iconic 300ft-high red sandstone monoliths standing guard on either side. For many, it's reason enough for a trip to Colorado. Renowned for its natural acoustics and stunning beauty, Red Rocks is

BEST TOURS: DENVER & AROUND

Historic Denver: Denver's preservation society offers 90-minute docent-led tours *(historicdenver.org)* of the city's oldest neighborhoods.

Denver Microbrew Tours: Knowledgeable guides lead 2½-hour tours *(denvermicro brewtour.com)* of award-winning breweries in LoDo and RiNo, tasting at least 10 brews.

Local Table Tours: Guided walking tours *(localtable tours.com)* cover some of Denver's top restaurants, integrating drink pairings and neighborhood history.

Colorado Cannabis Tours: Party-bus tours *(colorado cannabistours. com)* from two to 3½ hours, including grow operations and dispensaries.

Aspire Tours: Half- and full-day driving tours *(aspire-tours. com)* of Denver and surrounding areas, including sightseeing and hiking stops.

OPEN SPACE IS NO ACCIDENT

Boulder's unique and vast swathe of undeveloped land started back in 1898 when the city helped purchase the plot that became Chautauqua Park. In 1907 the government floated a public bond to buy Flagstaff Mountain, and in 1912 purchased 1200 more pristine mountain acres. Then, in 1967, Boulder voters legislated their love of the land by approving a sales tax specifically to buy, manage and maintain open space. This was historic. No other US city had ever voted to tax themselves specifically for open space and Boulder's Open Space and Mountain Parks *(osmp.org)* office was launched. In 1989 76% of voters increased the tax by nearly 100%; today the OSMP protects over 46,000 acres of land, criss-crossed with 155 miles of hiking trails.

synonymous with big-ticket concerts of all genres, even symphony orchestras. If a show isn't in the cards, the venue and its surrounding 816 acres are free to visit during the day. The amphitheater also regularly hosts events like early morning **yoga** *(per person $20)* and **movie nights** *(per person $20).*

The footprints of giants

The discovery site of the first stegosaur, **Dinosaur Ridge** *(dinoridge.org; free)* also has some of the world's best preserved dinosaur tracks and fossils. Sandwiched between Hwy 470 and Red Rocks Amphitheater, the exposed rock surfaces here reveal over 250 dinosaur footprints and sandstone-encased fossils dating to the Jurassic and Cretaceous periods. A steep, paved **interpretive trail** (2.2-mile round trip) leads through the site, signage providing insight into the behavior, movement and tropical environment of the dinosaurs that once roamed here. A **self-guided audio tour** *($8)* can be downloaded at the Visitors Center. Or take a 45-minute **bus tour** *(adult/child $20/14),* which includes three stops and a cheery guide.

Boulder

Shopping around Pearl St

Pearl Street Mall is the heart of downtown Boulder, a tree-shaded pedestrian zone filled with kids' climbing boulders and splash fountains, and lined with shops and galleries. People-watching aside, shopping is Pearl's raison d'être. Outdoor wear figures large with everybody from Italy's **La Sportiva** and Japan's **Montbell** to North American brands like **Patagonia**, **North Face** and **Black Diamond**. But it's not all ultralight puffies. Vintage shops like **Apocalypse** and **Heady Bauer** have a definite disco-hippie Boulder vibe, while trendy boutiques like **Bliss** and **Jones + Company** are a fun browse. Whatever you do, don't miss **Piece, Love & Chocolate** at the west end of Pearl St, a perfect place to relax with a decadent chocolate truffle.

Culture at Dairy Arts Center

The top cultural hub in town is the **Dairy Arts Center** *(thedairy.org),* a historic milk-processing factory turned arts center. It's a state-of-the-art facility with three stages, four gallery spaces and a 60-seat cinema. There's always something going on, from film screenings and plays to modern dance and art exhibits. The exhibits are always free.

EATING IN BOULDER: OUR PICKS

Mountain Sun: The town's favorite brewery is as Boulder as it gets. Great burgers, chili and brews, like Annapurna Amber. *noon-11pm Wed-Sun* $

Rosetta Hall: A sophisticated food hall, serving everything from falafel to green papaya salad to empanadas. Rooftop bar too. *8am-11pm* $$

Leaf: An ethical and elegant kitchen that serves meat-free gems, using ingredients grown at the restaurant's organic farm in nearby Lafayette. *11:30am-9pm* $$

Frasca: James Beard, Michelin and others have all named the northern Italian cuisine here as Boulder's finest. Prix-fixe menus only; reserve well ahead. *5-9pm* $$$

SIGHTS
1 Pearl Street Mall

SLEEPING
2 St Julien Hotel & Spa

EATING
3 Boulder County Farmers Market
4 Frasca
5 Leaf
6 Mountain Sun
7 Rosetta Hall

SHOPPING
8 Apocalypse
9 Black Diamond
10 Bliss
11 Heady Bauer
12 Jones + Company
13 La Sportiva
14 Montbell
15 North Face
16 Patagonia
17 Piece, Love & Chocolate

Lake of Glass

TOP EXPERIENCE

Rocky Mountain National Park

Colorado's crown jewel, Rocky Mountain National Park (RMNP) encompasses 415 sq miles of granite mountain top, alpine lake, wildflower-filled meadow, star-filled nights, and adventures large and small. Summer brings big-time crowds, but leave the main trailheads behind and you'll quickly find your own patch of solitude, so long as you're willing to share it with the wildlife that calls this place home.

DON'T MISS

- Trail Ridge Rd
- Kawuneeche Valley
- Lake of Glass hike
- Wild Basin Trailhead
- Moraine Park Discovery Center

Bear Lake Hiking

The **Bear Lake** and **Glacier Gorge Junction** trailheads are the most popular destinations in the park, and for good reason. From here you'll have a front-row vantage point of the dramatic glacial valleys and hulking granite summits that make Rocky Mountain such a singular landscape.

Hikes range from easy jaunts to **Alberta Falls** (1.6 miles) or **Dream Lake** (2.2 miles) and **Emerald Lake** (3.6 miles)

PRACTICALITIES

● nps.gov/romo ● per vehicle $30 ● 24hr

to more challenging excursions that follow the glacial valleys up to their origins. **Mills Lake** (5.6 miles) is a good choice, as is the **Loch** (6.2 miles), which can be extended to the exquisite **Lake of Glass** and **Sky Pond** (9.8 miles). And while **Flattop Mountain** (12,324ft, 8.8 miles) may not be the park's best summit, there's no denying its magnetic pull from down below. Note: in summer, the Bear Lake Corridor requires a special entry reservation between 5am and 6pm – buy early.

Wildlife Watching

RMNP is home to some 800 elk, 350 bighorn sheep, 60 moose, 20 to 30 bears, an unknown number of mountain lions and countless mule deer – and those are just the big guys. Smaller critters include beavers, marmots, pikas, porcupines, otters, foxes, coyotes and some 270 species of birds. While you probably won't spot the more elusive animals, if you pay attention, you'll likely see or hear traces of their passage. Good places to look for wildlife include **Moraine Park** (start with its excellent **Discovery Center**), **Beaver Meadows**, **Sheep Lakes**, **Trail Ridge Rd** and the marshy areas in the **Kawuneeche Valley**.

Driving Trail Ridge Road

The highest continuous paved highway in North America, Trail Ridge Rd is a remarkable 4000ft climb, offering visitors the chance to experience the Rockies' high-alpine tundra, complete with bighorn sheep, whistling marmots and eye-squinting panoramas in all directions. You can start in the east or west entrances of the park, make it a through trip or an out-and-back adventure, use it as a springboard for high-altitude hikes, or simply content yourself with a dozen superlative-worthy view points. In July, the lichen-covered boulders also light up with wildflowers. Among the can't-miss sights are the **Alpine Visitor Center** (11,796ft), which looks out over a hazy expanse of 400 sq miles, and the info-packed **Tundra Communities Trail**. Further west is the Continental Divide. Expect to spend a half-day exploring. Note: Trail Ridge Rd is only open from June through mid-October.

Rocky Mountain for Kids

The Park is an incredibly fun place for families to explore, though it may take some trial and error to find everyone's happy place. Budget time for special activities – horseback riding, a ropes course, ranger activities – to break up the monotony of driving around and posing for photos.

Don't miss the **Junior Ranger Headquarters** in Hidden Valley, which runs kids-themed programs throughout the day. A few family-friendly destinations in RMNP include Nymph and Dream Lakes (Bear Lake trailhead), Gem Lake (Lumpy Ridge Trailhead), MacGregor Ranch (adjacent to Lumpy Ridge), Eugenia Mine (Longs Peak Trailhead), Calypso Cascades (Wild Basin Trailhead), the Moraine Park Discovery Center (Bear Lake Rd), the Alpine Visitor Center (Trail Ridge Rd) and Lily Lake and Mountain (Hwy 7).

BEAR LAKE ALTERNATIVES

Couldn't score a coveted Bear Lake permit? Try these alternatives:

Fall River Area Hiking, bighorn-sheep spotting and a high-altitude drive.

Lumpy Ridge Trailhead Inspiring rambles among giant boulders and granite crags; Gem Lake (3.4 miles) is a favorite.

Wild Basin Trailhead Often overlooked, the southern corner of the park is chock-full of waterfalls.

Longs Peak Trailhead Variety of hikes from kid-friendly to the lung-busting peak.

TOP TIPS

- Timed entry tickets *(recreation.gov)* are required between late May and mid-October; buy your ticket on the first day of the month prior to your entry (ie May 1 for a June visit). Need a last-minute ticket? Reservations (40% of all available tickets) go on sale at 7pm for the following day.
- Most high-country trails are snowbound through late June; plan accordingly.
- Avoid encroaching on wildlife, for your safety and theirs. Stay at least 75ft away from elk and sheep, and 120ft away from moose and bears. And please, don't feed anything, no matter how cute it looks.

BOLDER BOULDER

Boulder's biggest party is, unsurprisingly, a 10km footrace held every Memorial Day, snow or shine. With more than 50,000 runners and pros mingling with costumed racers, live bands and sideline merrymakers, **Bolder Boulder** *(bolderboulder.com)* may be the most fun 10km run in the US. Course-side antics range from slip and slides and Elvis impersonators to red, white and blue paragliders spiraling down to the race's end at Folsom Field. Participants are divided into 100 waves, with wheelchairs going first, followed by the pros. Then come the walkers, elementary school kids and the costumed – eventually everyone makes it to the finish line. The latest addition to the race calendar is Colder Boulder, a 5km race in early December.

Hike in Chautauqua Park

Historic **Chautauqua Park** *(chautauqua.com)* is the gateway to Boulder's most magnificent swathe of open space: a wide-open prairie adjoining the iconic **Flatirons**, 1000ft red-rock slabs rising up out of the earth. It's a popular place for hikers, climbers and trail runners with 15 trails winding through the park.

No matter your destination, most people start on the **Chautauqua Trail** (1.5-mile loop), a relatively easy walk through a grassy meadow. If you're itching to go higher, the **Flatirons Loop Trail** (2.5 miles) leads you to the base of the First Flatiron, where climbers rope up for ascents; or do the full 700ft of elevation gain up to the top, following the trail as it zigzags up between the First and Second Flatirons. Want to go farther yet? The **Royal Arch Trail** (3.5 miles) has been a Boulder classic for over a century. This roughly 2½-hour trek leads you up to a natural arch past the Third Flatiron and has fantastic views. Expect to do some scrambling. The trails here connect to the rest of the city's open space via the long-distance **Mesa Trail**, giving you lots of options to customize your walk.

Founded in 1898 as part of the national Chautauqua Movement – an initiative aimed at adult education in rural settings – the park remains a cultural hub featuring historic cottages and dining hall as well as a 1300-seat auditorium that hosts world-class musicians, performers and speakers each summer. Plan ahead – events often sell out.

Parking is limited. On summer weekends and holidays, visitors are encouraged to take the free **Park-to-Park Shuttle** *(bouldercolorado.gov)*, which runs from downtown and satellite parking lots.

Farm fresh

The twice-weekly **Boulder County Farmers Market**, a block-long sprawl in front of the Dushanbe Teahouse, is a massive spring and summer bazaar of colorful, mostly organic 100% local food. Find flowers and herbs, as well as brain-sized mushrooms, delicate squash blossoms, crusty pretzels, vegan dips, grass-fed beef, raw granola and yogurt. Live music is as standard as the family picnics in the park along Boulder Creek. The Saturday market is a real community event, and it feels like the whole city comes out to socialize in the morning (8am-2pm). The Wednesday evening market (3:30-7:30pm) tends to be a little less busy, but it's still a notable midweek gathering place. In true Boulder style, all waste from the farmers market is recycled or composted. The market is closed in winter.

Steamboat Springs

Skiing Steamboat

Famous for its light and fluffy powder, **Steamboat Mountain Resort** *(steamboat.com; adult/child $285/230)* boasts stats that speak for themselves: 182 marked runs; 3668ft of vertical, and 3741 acres of terrain. While the summit tops out at 10,568ft, Steamboat makes up for its dearth of high-altitude steeps with super-fun tree slaloming runs. Serious skiers will also dig a number of mogul runs on the hill, and although

DAVID A LITMAN/SHUTTERSTOCK

Strawberry Park Hot Springs

these trails are a virtual factory of Olympic skiers and snowboarders, you don't have to be world class to enjoy them. Wide, well-groomed runs are ideal cruising for intermediate skiers, making this mountain among Colorado's best all-rounders, particularly for families. Throw in the cowboy-style charm and back-of-beyond location, and you have all the makings for a winter wonderland.

Steamboat's hot springs

Just 7 miles north of Steamboat, **Strawberry Park Hot Springs** *(strawberryhotsprings.com; $20)* is an idyllic spot: a handful of natural outdoor pools set beside a cool mountain stream and nothing but acres of wilderness surrounding you. Evening visits are particularly magical: whether you're treated to a meteor shower or a full moon rising through the pines, soaking in the steaming pools – with the occasional river plunge – is a marvelously restorative experience. Note that after dark, it's adults only. In winter, you'll need AWD and snow tires to get here; if your vehicle isn't equipped, or if it's a busy weekend, take the shuttle instead.

Vail

Ski the back bowls

Vail Mountain *(vail.com; adult/child lift ticket $319/220)* is hands-down one of the best ski resorts in the world, with 5317 skiable acres, 278 trails and, ahem, some of the highest

ANCIENT ASPENS

Come late September, Colorado's roads fill with leaf peepers, out in search of the glorious golden hues that wash across the mountainsides. Aspens, of course, are well known for their quaking leaves, but there's more to this tree than meets the eye. In fact, many aspen groves are not made up of individual trees, but are instead a single interconnected organism – the aspen's most common method of reproduction is cloning, where one plant sends out identical reproductions of itself via its root system. Because of this, aspens are not only considered the world's largest organism, but also the oldest: the Pando Grove in Utah (over 40,000 'stems' strong) is considered to be at least 10,000 years old.

EATING IN VAIL: OUR PICKS

Big Bear Bistro: An affordable fave in Vail Village, serving gourmet coffee, breakfast burritos and some damn good sandwiches at lunch. *8am-3pm* $

The Little Diner: The most popular place for a made-from-scratch breakfast is in Lionshead. No reservations. *7am-2pm* $$

Alpenrose: For the full alpine experience, get your pretzels, rösti and fondue at this Swiss German–themed restaurant. *11:30am-10pm* $$$

Sweet Basil: Vail's most celebrated restaurant: excellent seasonal, eclectic New American fare. *noon-3pm & 5-9pm Wed-Sun, 5-9pm Mon & Tue* $$$

THE VAIL DREAM

Tenth Mountain Division veteran Peter Seibert and his friend Earl Eaton climbed Vail Mountain in the winter of 1957. After one long look at those luscious back bowls, the pair knew they'd struck gold. At the time, the mountain was owned by the forest service and local ranchers. Seibert and Eaton recruited a series of investors and lawyers, eventually got a permit from the forest service and convinced nearly all of the local ranchers to sell. Much of the construction budget was raised by convincing investors to chip in $10,000 for a condo unit and a lifetime season pass. Finally, on December 15, 1962, the dream came alive. The cost of a lift ticket? $5 for nine runs.

lift-ticket prices on the continent. You can subdivide the mountain into three main zones: the front side (best for beginners and intermediate skiers), where most of the runs are groomed and the north-facing slopes offer good snow cover, even on sunny spring days; the back bowls (best for advanced skiers), with seven legendary bowls; and Blue Sky Basin (best for experts), with a more backcountry feel, including tree skiing, glades and cliffs. Distances are vast, and you'll spend a lot of time getting from one place to another, so if you have a specific destination in mind, plan carefully.

Summer adventures

All the usual suspects set up shop at Vail during the summer, from cycling to ziplining.

Bearcat Stables *(bearcatstables.com; from $80)* run one- to three-hour horseback rides, as well as longer trips like a four-day ride to Aspen. For wading and float-fishing trips, try **Gore Creek Fly Fishermen** *(gorecreekflyfisherman.com; from $345)*.

Zip Adventures *(zipadventures.com; $170)* runs six zipline tours over Alkali Canyon – followed by a cliff jump – with plenty of time to work on your primal scream.

Apex Mountain School *(apexmountainschool.com; $200-450)* offers guided climbing and mountaineering trips in both summer and winter, while **Bike Valet** *(bikevalet.com; rentals from $40)* rents cycles and runs a shuttle up to Vail Pass for the easy, scenic cruise back down.

Vail's summer amusement park, **Epic Discovery** *(vail.com; from $119)*, gets so-so reviews, though the **gondola ride** *(adult/child $59/39)* into the high country will always be impressive.

Leadville

Climb to the top of Colorado

Colorado's tallest peak and the second-highest in the continental US, **Mt Elbert** (14,433ft) is a relatively gentle giant. There are three established routes to the top, none of which are technical. The most common approach is via the northeast ridge; it's a 9-mile round trip hike with 4700ft of elevation gain, so expect to spend most of the day. The turnoff for the main trailhead is just south of Leadville on Rte 300. If you have 4WD, the South Mt Elbert Trailhead is accessed via Hwy 82, just east of Twin Lakes. It's a slightly shorter hike with only 4100ft of elevation gain.

Aspen

Skiing the four mountains

Aspen, for all its wealth, owes its current status to the surrounding slopes. Above all, this is a ski town and one of the best in America, with four mountains accessible from a **single lift ticket** *(aspensnowmass.com; adult/child lift ticket $244/164)* – each offering a different adventurous twist.

Aspen Mountain offers more than 3000ft of steep vertical right from the front door of the Little Nell. There's no

LANAG/SHUTTERSTOCK

Aspen

beginner terrain here, just 800 acres of bumps, trees and World Cup–worthy runs.

Snowmass is the biggest of the four, with over 3300 acres of ridable terrain and 150 miles of trails – this is the best all-around choice. At some point make your way to the Elk Camp chairlift, which has awesome views of the Maroon Bells from the top.

Buttermilk has lots of beginner-friendly cruisers, but it also has some gnarly terrain parks: this is where you can ride the same hits and 22ft superpipe as Chloe Kim and Shaun White.

Last but not least is **Aspen Highlands**. Although there are some beginner and intermediate runs, the Highlands is all about extreme skiing in the stunning hike-to Highland Bowl: expect chutes, vertiginous drop-offs, glades and super steep lines that plunge 3600 vertical feet.

Art galleries and museums

With a handful of outstanding art venues, Aspen is the state's most culturally happening spot west of Denver. Start with **Aspen Art Museum** *(aspenartmuseum.org; free)*, with three floors of gallery space enveloped in a striking exterior designed by Pritzker Prize–winner Shigeru Ban. Lesser known is Aspen Institute's **Resnick Center for Herbert Bayer Studies** *(the bayercenter.org; free)*, with rotating exhibits related to the Austrian artist and longtime Aspen resident – a Bauhaus treat. Smaller galleries, meanwhile, are everywhere – follow

BACKCOUNTRY HUT TRIPS

For some, backcountry skiing is what it's all about: pristine snow, all-pervading quiet and the magic of waking up in the wilderness on a winter's day. If you're keen, look into the **Summit Huts Association** *(summithuts.org)*, which operates five huts that are accessible by ski and snowshoe, and usually sleep around 20 people. All have amenities such as wood-burning stoves, full kitchens and solar-powered lights; in addition, three have wood-burning saunas. The most popular hut is Francie's Cabin, a great choice for first-timers (though all groups should have at least one experienced, avalanche-trained member). Note that you need to enter a lottery by February 15 to book a hut for the following year.

EATING IN ASPEN: OUR PICKS

Big Wrap: These vaguely healthy and definitely affordable wraps have won over legions of fans. Downstairs from the main sidewalk. *10am-6pm Mon-Sat* $

Spring Cafe: Vegetarian juice bar and cafe, with tofu scrambles, tempeh burgers, seitan fajitas and plenty of greens. *7am-5pm, from 8am Sat & Sun* $$

Bosq: Chef Barclay Dodge's playful, locally sourced menu (eg bison tartare) earned him Aspen's first Michelin star. Prix-fixe menu only. *5:30-10pm* $$$

Pine Creek Cookhouse: This log-cabin restaurant is past Ashcroft's ghost town and is accessible via sleigh, skis or horseback. *lunch & dinner Dec-Mar & mid-Jun-Sep* $$$

BEST ENTERTAINMENT IN ASPEN

Belly Up: The top nightspot in town, showcasing performers from John Legend to the Chainsmokers in intimate surrounds.

Silver City Aspen: This cowpoke-themed saloon in the basement of the historic Elks Building hosts live music performances as well as a weekly karaoke night.

Wheeler Opera House: A working theater since 1889, the Wheeler still stages opera, stand-up comedy, concerts and musicals.

Theatre Aspen: The gorgeous garden complex in Rio Grande Park is the summer home of the local theater, which puts on award-winning musicals and plays.

your curiosity, and you're sure to turn up something unique. Longstanding studios include **Galerie Maximillian**, **Christopher Martin Gallery** (a specialist in reverse glass painting) and **Baldwin Gallery**.

Hike the Maroon Bells

If you have but one day to enjoy a slice of pristine wilderness, spend it in the shadow of Colorado's most iconic mountains: the pyramid-shaped twins of **North Maroon Peak** (14,014ft) and **South Maroon Peak** (14,156ft). Eleven miles southwest of Aspen, it all starts at **Maroon Lake**, a stunning spot backed by the towering, striated summits. The surrounding wilderness area contains nine passes over 12,000ft and six fourteeners. Some jut into jagged granite towers, others are a more generous slope and curve. You can spend an hour here or several days: the choice is yours. **Crater Lake** is only 1.8 miles one-way, but if you're hungry for a little bit more, press on to **Buckskin Pass** (12,462ft; 4.8 miles one-way) – from the narrow ledge you can see mountains erupt in all directions. This is the start of the popular **Four Pass Loop** (28 miles), a stunning multiday backpacking trip that crosses three other 12,000ft passes. Parking is extremely limited at Maroon Bells. Instead, take a shuttle from **Aspen Highlands** (p195) *(aspenchamber.org; adult/child $16/10; late May-Oct)*; advanced purchase required.

Salida

Rafting the Arkansas

The headwaters of the Arkansas are Colorado's best-known stretch of white water, with everything from extreme rapids to mellow ripples. Although most rafting companies cover the river from Leadville to the Royal Gorge, the most popular trips descend through **Browns Canyon National Monument**, a 16-mile stretch that includes class-III to -IV rapids, running between Buena Vista and Salida.

If you're with young kids, Bighorn Sheep Canyon is a good bet. Those after more of an adrenaline rush can head upstream to the Numbers or downstream to the Royal Gorge (Cañon City), both of which are class IV to V. If you'd like to go solo, outfitters also rent duckies (inflatable kayaks).

Most companies are based just south of Buena Vista, close to where Hwys 24 and 285 diverge, and typically offer full-day adventure packages including zipline tours, via ferrata or horseback riding. Established outfitters include **Rocky Mountain Outdoor Center** *(rmoc.com)*, **Independent Whitewater** *(raftsalida.com)* and **River Runners** *(riverrunnersltd.com)*. Expect to spend from $100 to 160 for a half to a full day of rafting.

Biking Monarch Crest Trail

If you've mountain biked before, then you know: **Monarch Crest Trail** awaits. One of the most famous rides in Colorado, this is an extreme 35-mile adventure, with fabulous high-altitude views. It starts off at Monarch Pass (11,312ft), follows

Maroon Bells

the exposed ridge 12 miles to Marshall Pass and then either cuts down to Poncha Springs on an old railroad grade or hooks onto the Rainbow Trail. In Salida, rentals are available from **Sub-Culture Cyclery** *(subculturecyclery.com; half-day rental $70)*, and **Absolute Bikes** *(absolutebikes.com; $39)* runs shuttles to the trailhead on Fridays through Sundays at 8am. **High Valley Bike Shuttle** *(monarchcrest.com; $42)* also picks up cyclists in Poncha Springs and brings them up to the trailhead twice daily, at 8am and 10am.

Explore St Elmo ghost town

An old gold-mining ghost town tucked amid the Collegiate Peaks, **St Elmo** makes for a fun excursion. The drive is gorgeous, wending its way past stands of redolent ponderosa pine, a wildlife-viewing meadow and jagged peaks before petering out at what is Colorado's best-preserved ghost town. Over 40 buildings remain, most built around 1881: the schoolhouse, an old mercantile building and a miners' exchange are among the best kept, all providing a fascinating peek into Colorado's past, when gold and silver ruled these hills. St Elmo is located on County Rd 162, which becomes dirt about half-way up. It's no problem in summer, but in winter you'll want an AWD. Try to avoid weekends here, when ATV and snowmobile enthusiasts use St Elmo as a staging point – the revving of not-too-distant engines can take away some of the charm.

Crested Butte

Brave the Teocalli Bowls

One of Colorado's best, **Crested Butte Mountain Resort** *(skicb.com; adult/child lift ticket $195/127)* is known for its stomach-lurching steeps, with infamous runs like Rambo and Banana Chute bestowing bragging rights onto survivors. The Teocalli Bowls near the summit offer more extreme lines, including a backcountry-esque 20-minute hike out at the bottom. It's not all daredevil plunges, though – the town also has

RAFTING TIPS

Water flow varies by season, so time your visit for late May or early June for a wilder ride, when snowmelt has the river raging. If you've got young kids or are looking for a more relaxed experience, go in July or August when the water level is lower and warmer. Note that if you are rafting as a family, kids need to be at least six (sometimes older, depending on the trip) and weigh a minimum of 50lb. Early in the season, you'll need to wear a wetsuit (included) topped with a rain jacket, and whenever you go, take a wide-brimmed hat and sunglasses. Finally, bring a change of clothes for the end of the trip and don't forget to tip your guide.

FAT-TIRE REVOLUTIONARY

In April 1998, Neil Murdoch – local CB eccentric and the founder of mountain biking as the world knows it – slipped out town with just his clothes and a bike, hours before federal marshals closed in. Murdoch, aka Richard Barrister, had settled in little-known Crested Butte in 1974 after skipping bail on a cocaine-smuggling charge in New Mexico. A consummate tinkerer, Murdoch began outfitting old Schwinn bikes to be ridden off-road, including adding low gears and wide knobby tires – thus the 'Fat-Tire Revolution' was born. When he disappeared, Crested Butte rallied behind Murdoch in absentia, even establishing a fund for his legal defense. He was eventually caught in 2001 but is still revered as the godfather of mountain biking.

a terrific **Nordic Center** *(cbnordic.org; lift ticket $25)* with 50km of groomed trails and a special ski-in gourmet dinner at **Magic Meadows Yurt** (reserve). The **Adaptive Sports Center** *(adaptivesports.org)*, meanwhile, promotes mountain access for people of all abilities.

The birthplace of mountain biking

Crested Butte is one of the places that brought mountain biking to the world and it absolutely lives up to the hype. Take your pick between a fantastic **mountain bike park** *(skicb.com; lift tickets from $65)* or 450 miles of smooth-flowing singletrack crossing wildflower- and aspen-clad hills and meadows. The **Lupine Loop** is a great first trail, with outrageous views across the Slate River Valley. The 13-mile intermediate level ride has just enough climbing to keep you honest, interspersed with fun, flowing descents. **Big Al's Bicycle Heaven** *(bigalsbicycleheaven.com)* and **Alpineer** *(alpineer.com)* have rentals, maps and gear.

Wildflowers Everywhere

More than skiing, more than its mountain chic ethos, even more than mountain biking, Crested Butte is most famous for one thing: wildflowers. From vast hillsides of mule's ears to riverside pockets of elephant heads and shooting stars, and practically everywhere between, Crested Butte is saturated in wildflowers. Not surprisingly, the town hosts a popular **Wildflower Festival** *(crestedbuttewildflowerfestival.org)*, typically in the second week of July. The programming is almost as varied as the flowers, from guided hikes to painting and photography classes, and even guidance on how to identify medicinal and edible flowers. One unique option is a wildflower tour with the **Rocky Mountain Biological Laboratory**, a research and educational institute in the one-time ghost town Gothic, just north of town.

Canyon of the Ancients National Monument

Explore Ancestral Puebloan ruins

Visually stunning and imbued with ineffable spiritual energy, **Canyon of the Ancients National Monument** *(blm.gov/visit/canyons-ancient-national-monument; free)* is home to the largest known concentration of archaeological sites in the country – more than 6000 at last count. The ruins, accessible off rough roads and remote trails, are spread over 170,000 acres of public land and span 12,000 years of human

EATING IN CRESTED BUTTE: OUR PICKS

Frank's Deli: Local fave serving hearty sandwiches and breakfast burritos perfect for the trail. Ask about the specials. *9am-6pm Mon-Sat* $

Secret Stash: Award-winning pizzeria with a boho vibe, teahouse seating and tapestries included. Cocktails pack a serious punch. *11am-9pm* $$

Sunflower: Inventive, locally sourced dishes served in a homey cabin-like setting. Menu changes with seasonal ingredients. *6-10pm Wed-Sat* $$$

Breadery: Chewy sourdough flatbreads meet shared plates (pear ricotta ravioli), and soups and salads for a family style meal. Fresh bread to go. *5-9pm Wed-Sun* $$$

TRAVELLER70/SHUTTERSTOCK

Lowry Pueblo, Canyon of the Ancients National Monument

history. They range from singular hogans (traditional Navajo homes) to entire ancient pueblos – once-thriving population centers that persisted for thousands of years.

Canyon of the Ancients Visitor Center and Museum *(blm.gov/visit/canyons-ancients-national-monumentvisitor-center-and-museum; museum adult/child $6/free)* is an important first stop. A fascinating museum and research center, it has informative films and exhibits. Touch base with the rangers here; they can recommend specific sites and supply maps. A high-clearance vehicle is highly recommended. The **Southwest Colorado Canyons Alliance** *(swcocanyons.org; half/full day from $50/84)* also runs excellent tours.

The easiest ruin to visit is **Lowry Pueblo**, about 25 miles northwest of the visitors center on (mostly) paved roads. Dating to 1060 CE, the site has several stone structures and nine kivas (ceremonial enclosures), including the 47ft-wide Grand Kiva, believed to have been used for spiritual rites.

Alternatively, head to the southern entrance of Sand Canyon Trail, a relatively flat 6.5-mile (one way) trail through the breathtaking **McElmo Canyon**, with several cliff dwellings tucked into alcoves along the way. The largest, **Saddlehorn Pueblo**, is 1 mile from the trailhead.

Ouray & Around

Drive the Million Dollar Hwy

Deep in the San Juan Mountains, the **Million Dollar Hwy** connects the towns of Ouray and Silverton, and is a mind-blowingly scenic drive – one of Colorado's best. Twenty-five miles of hairpin turns and tight S-bends cut through the Uncompahgre Gorge, whose steep mountainsides loom large and close, rising into lofty, mist-shrouded peaks, while the valley floor lies far below, dotted with fir trees and wildflowers. Drive with caution – the road is formidable, even in good weather, and the lack of guardrails doesn't help. Be sure to take advantage of pullouts to see the dramatic **Bear Creek Falls** and 360-degree views from **Red Mountain Pass** (11,018ft).

WHY I LOVE CANYON OF THE ANCIENTS

Liza Prado, Lonely Planet writer.

Hiking solo through McElmo Canyon, the sky bright, the red earth dotted with yucca plants and sage brush, I can almost see them. The people who once called this red canyon home, carrying woven baskets filled with plants and berries, passing me on their way to their adobe brick homes that, remarkably, still stand in the alcoves. I can almost smell the smoke from their cooking fires and hear the sounds of their everyday life carried through the canyon – the chatter, the chopping of wood, the children playing. This place transports me, fills me with wonder and reminds me that, regardless of time or circumstance, we're all connected. For me, that's what travel is all about.

THOMAS TROMPETER/SHUTTERSTOCK

Cliff Palace

TOP EXPERIENCE

Mesa Verde National Park

Mesa Verde National Park spans 81 sq miles over two broad mesas, both rife with Ancestral Puebloan dwellings. Some are on the mesa tops, but the most compelling are built into high cliffs. While many are visible from overlooks, touring them means adventure at great heights, peering over edges, clambering up and down ladders and crawling through tunnels...all to experience these magnificent dwellings up close.

DON'T MISS

- Cliff Palace
- Balcony House
- Step House
- Petroglyph Point Trail
- Mesa Top Loop Rd
- Long House
- Cultural Performances

Ranger Tours

Taking a ranger-led tour is one of the most rewarding ways to experience Mesa Verde. You'll deep-dive into the history and lives of the Ancestral Puebloans and have access to otherwise restricted sites such as **Cliff Palace** and **Balcony House**, plus **Long House**, a sprawling dwelling in the park's rugged backcountry. They're not for the faint of heart! Most involve walking along cliff edges, climbing up and down wooden pole ladders and crawling through tight spaces. But they're so worth it. Plan on taking two tours if you have the time; buy tickets in advance – they sell out fast.

PRACTICALITIES

● nps.gov/meve ● per vehicle $20-30 ● 24hr

Cliff Palace

Cliff Palace is the largest known cliff dwelling in the American southwest, a grand engineering achievement with 151 rooms and 23 kivas (ceremonial enclosures) that once housed 25 families. It's remarkable for its fine construction and efficient design. Walk through it on a 45-minute tour, retracing the paths taken by the enclave's original inhabitants. If you can't join a tour, check out the site from afar from the Sun Temple overlook on Mesa Top Loop Rd.

Balcony House

The **Balcony House** tour requires you to descend a 100ft staircase, climb a 32ft ladder and crawl through a 12ft tunnel...and that's just to get there. There are more ladders and steps on the way out. It's well worth the effort: the 38-room village is built in a cliffside alcove with a long arching roof, and offers views of Soda Canyon, 600ft below.

Step House

Wetherill Mesa has the park's only self-guided cliff dwelling: **Step House**. A short but steep 0.8-mile trail leads to a two-in-one village, with 7th-century pit houses standing alongside 13th-century multistoried dwellings. Information booklets are available near the trailhead; a ranger is typically at the site to answer questions.

Mesa Top Loop Rd

A complement (or alternative) to scrambling through the cliff dwellings is a 6-mile driving tour along the **Mesa Top Loop Rd**. At various pull-offs, you can enjoy magnificent overlooks of Cliff Palace and other cliff dwellings, or take short paths to a dozen different surface sites (no teetering ladders on this route). A free **audio tour** *(nps.gov/podcasts/podcasts-mtl-audiotour.htm)* guides the way.

Petroglyph Point Trail

The 2.4-mile loop **Petroglyph Point Trail** follows a leafy footpath once used by the Ancestral Puebloans. Dropping below the canyon rim, it's occasionally steep and rocky before making a short scramble back to the top of the mesa. Look for the petroglyphs at the 1.4-mile mark – a 35ft-wide wall with almost three dozen human and animal figures, spirals and handprints. A gate at the trailhead is locked in the evenings. If you arrive in the early morning, begin the trail in reverse.

Dances & Demonstrations

In summer, the park hosts cultural dances and pottery demonstrations by Native peoples with ancestral connections to Mesa Verde. Fascinating and educational, the events are a way to learn about Mesa Verde's ancient inhabitants and their modern-day descendants. Events are in the Morefield Campground (p248) amphitheater or the main visitor center, typically in the evening.

STARGAZING IN MESA VERDE

An International Dark Sky Park, Mesa Verde's remote location, high elevation and arid climate make it one of the best places in the country to enjoy the night skies. Rangers offer regular nighttime programs, from lectures and star parties to astrophotography workshops, all for free. Alternatively, stop at an overlook (or step out of your tent) to take in the sky on your own.

TOP TIPS

- Visit mid-May to mid-October. Winter and spring bring closures to several areas and amenities, and tours are suspended.
- Tickets for ranger tours can only be purchased online *(recreation.gov)* or by phone, up to 14 days in advance. Tours often sell out, so reserve early.
- Information booklets are stocked in metal bins around the park.
- Fill your tank before you arrive – you'll be driving a lot. At a pinch, there's a gas station at Morefield Campground.
- Cellphone service is limited; download audio tours and maps ahead of time.
- Except for holiday weekends, Morefield Campground almost always has walk-up availability.

THE SUN DANCE

Ricky Hayes, Weeminuche Ute tribal member.

The Sun Dance is one of the most sacred ceremonies for my people, and one I've participated in several times over the course of my life. It's performed as a deep blessing for the tribe and the earth. It takes place the third week in June in a specially made lodge on Sleeping Ute Mountain, on the north side of the reservation. For four days, we pray, dance and fast – no food or water. The ceremony is sometimes called the Thirst Dance because of it. The fasting is especially difficult, given the physical effort and the heat. Many people collapse but eventually rise and continue.

KIT LEONG/SHUTTERSTOCK

Ouray Hot Springs

Hiking high above Ouray

Forming nearly a complete loop around Ouray, the 6-mile **Perimeter Trail** is one of the most scenic ways to experience the 'Switzerland of America.' Beginning across from the **visitor center** *(visitouray.com)*, the clockwise trail charts an up-and-down path through forests and aspen groves and across creeks and meadows. Highlights include the spectacular **Cascade Falls**, **Baby Bathtubs** (a series of smooth tub-like rock divots) plus the **Ouray Via Ferrata** *(ourayviaferrata.org)* and **Ice Park** *(ourayicepark.com)*, where you can spy people clambering along sheer rock faces or climbing frozen cascades. The pièce de résistance is **Box Cañon Falls** *(visitouray.com/box-canyon-falls; adult/child $7/5)*, a thundering 285ft waterfall that drops into a spectacular quartzite canyon.

Soak in historic springs

For a healing soak or kiddish fun, try **Ouray Hot Springs** *(visitouray.com/ourayhotspringspool; adult/child $26/16)*. The springs were used and considered sacred by the Ute people before they were pushed from the region; later, miners soaked in the same waters to help their tired bodies. Today, the springs are a year-round waterpark surrounded by 13,000ft peaks. Come for the eight-lane lap pool, waterslides, a climbing wall overhanging a splash pool and several adults-only soaking areas (74°F to 106°F; 23°C to 41°C). The geothermal water is crystal clear and free of sulfur smells – a major plus.

EATING IN OURAY: OUR PICKS

Maggie's Kitchen: Graffiti-bombed hole-in-the-wall known for deliciously sloppy burgers and onion rings. Seating on the deck. *11am-8pm Thu-Sat, to 6pm Sun* $

Kami's Samis: Bright, modern spot with decadent breakfasts, hearty burritos and gourmet sandwiches. Loads of vegan, gluten- and dairy-free options. *7am-2pm* $$

The Smokehouse: Finger-lickin' BBQ joint serving generous portions of goodness, smoked 'low and slow.' Perfect for a post-hike meal. *8am-2pm Mon-Wed, 8am-2pm & 5-9pm Thu-Sun* $$

Brickhouse 737: Cozy, upscale restaurant serving contemporary American cuisine with flair. Creative top-shelf cocktails. Reservations recommended. *5-9pm* $$$

Telluride

Telluride's past

A national historic landmark, Telluride is one of the country's most iconic Victorian-era towns, its streets lined with elegant buildings that once served as flophouses, saloons, schoolhouses and churches. Stop into the Smithsonian-affiliated **Telluride Historical Museum** *(telluridemuseum.org; adult/child $9/6)* to learn about Telluride's beginning as a Ute hunting ground, its mining past and its transformation into a world-class ski town. **Guided walking tours** *($15)* also offered on summer and fall afternoons.

Waterfalls, lakes and panoramic views

A network of trails branch out like arteries from the heart of Telluride, crisscrossing the town's box canyon, from easy strolls along the scenic **Telluride River Trail** (4.4 miles) to the strenuous, wildflower-filled **Sneffels Highline Trail** (12.5 miles). For something in between, hike to Colorado's tallest waterfall, the 365ft **Bridal Veil Falls** (2.5 miles to the bottom, 3.4 miles to the top), along rocky switchbacks through a thick aspen forest, passing two smaller waterfalls along the way. From there, extend your hike by continuing along a narrow mining road, passing through alpine meadows and forests to the otherworldly **Blue Lake** (5.7 miles, 12,400ft).

Ski and board in style

Known for plunging runs and deep powder, those gorgeous San Juan Mountain views and a certain high-society *je ne sais quoi*, **Telluride Ski Resort** *(tellurideskiresort.com; adult/child lift ticket $245/125)* is a special place. Decently sized in terms of lifts and acres – it has three distinct areas served by 19 lifts – Telluride has an outsize supply of advanced and expert terrain, from steeps to trees to wide open cirques, and even more if you are willing to hike for it, including iconic Palmyra Peak. There are also ample options for beginners and intermediate cruisers, including the playful, 4.6-mile Galloping Goose run.

Banjos, hula hoops and more

Telluride Bluegrass Festival *(bluegrass.com/telluride)* is the town's most famous fest, a summer solstice celebration of folk music and mountain life. It draws big-name bands and over 10,000 revelers daily – many donning hula hoops as dance partners. The main stage is set in the leafy town park

TELLURIDE TOURS

Telluride Offroad Adventures: Enjoy rugged passes and stunning scenery on a variety of deluxe 4WD tours, from two-hour jaunts to full-day adventures.

Telluride Wranglers: Authentic and adventurous trail rides of various lengths and skill levels, with small groups and expert guides.

Telluride Flyfishers: Memorable all-levels fly-fishing trips on the San Miguel and Dolores rivers, or hiking to alpine lakes and streams.

Telluride Outside: One-stop shop for excellent year-round adventuring, from snowmobiling to 4WD tours to stand-up paddleboarding.

Mountain Trip: Born out of an Alaska mountaineering school; trips include rock climbing, backcountry skiing and more.

EATING IN TELLURIDE: OUR PICKS

Brown Dog Pizza: Buzzing pizza joint known for its award-winning Detroit-style pizza. Come early or prepare to wait for a table. *11:30am-9pm* **$**

Butcher & Baker: Cute breakfast spot with generous to-go sandwiches and sides perfect for the trail. *7am-8pm Mon-Sat, 8am-2pm Sun* **$$**

Wood Ear: Ramen meets Texas smokehouse at this inventive underground spot. Creative cocktails available to go in reusable plastic flasks. *5-9pm* **$$$**

221 South Oak: New American cuisine by award-winning chef Eliza Gavin. Dine in the historic home or the leafy patio. *10am-1pm & 5-9:30pm Sun, from 5pm Mon-Sat* **$$$**

INTERNATIONAL DARK SKY PARK

Black Canyon of the Gunnison is an outstanding place for stargazing, thanks to its clear, dry weather and exceptionally dark skies. In 2015 the park became one of Colorado's first International Dark Sky Places (the state has 10), thanks to the park's work to limit light pollution and educate visitors on topics like astronomy and nocturnal ecosystems. Summer brings loads of **free astronomy programs** by park rangers and members of the Black Canyon Astronomical Society. In September, the park hosts **AstroFest**, with nightly telescope viewings, constellation tours, guest lectures by astronomers and info on the park's nocturnal animals.

with late-night concerts and free workshops held in smaller venues around town. Tickets sell out fast for the June event – buy early and consider a combo ticket-and-camping package for an all-in experience.

Telluride also hosts some two-dozen other festivals throughout the year. Faves include **Mountainfilm** *(mountainfilm.org)*, a documentary film festival held every Memorial Day Weekend (late May); **Telluride Mushroom Festival** *(tellurideinstitute.org/telluride-mushroom-festival)*, a celebration and education on all things fungi the third weekend in August (don't miss the parade); the internationally renowned **Telluride Film Festival** *(telluridefilmfestival.org)* over Labor Day Weekend (early September), and the season-ending **Blues & Brews Festival** *(tellurideblues.com)* in mid-September.

Black Canyon of the Gunnison National Park & Around

Views and climbing around a national park

With 2000ft-high canyon walls and colorful craggy spires, a drive along the spectacular south rim of the **Black Canyon of the Gunnison National Park** *(nps.gov/blca, per vehicle $30)* is the most popular way to experience it. For 7 miles, the flat, winding and paved **South Rim Rd** hugs the canyon's edge with a dozen overlooks offering heart-stopping views. Good pullouts include **Pulpit Rock Overlook**, a finger-like outcropping with expansive river views; **Chasm View**, the canyon's narrowest point, and **Painted Wall**, Colorado's tallest vertical cliff (2250ft), named after the magnificent pink pegmatite stripes that stretch half a mile across. Be aware there are few guardrails – keep small children close and watch your step, especially while taking selfies.

If you're an experienced climber, don't miss the lesser-traveled **North Rim**. An 80-mile drive from the South Rim (there's no bridge over the canyon), the area has 145 multipitch climbing routes rated between 5.9 and 5.13, including along the **North Chasm** and to the top of the **Painted Wall**. Wilderness permits are required, available for free at the **North Rim Ranger Station**. For guided climbing trips try **Mountain Trip** *(mountaintrip.com)* or **IRIS** *(irisalpine.com)*, an outdoors company catering to women, non-binary and trans people.

Note: in winter, South Rim Rd is only open to vehicles up to the visitor center; the remainder is open to cross-country skiers and snowshoers only. The North Rim roads are entirely closed.

Learn about the Ute

One of the few American museums dedicated to a single tribe, the **Ute Indian Museum** *(historycolorado.org/ute-indian-museum; adult/child $7/free)* in Montrose examines the many cultural and historical layers of Colorado's longest continuous residents. Artifacts, displays, videos and hands-on exhibits paint a powerful portrait of the Ute people, past and present. There are regular speaker series and film screenings, too. The museum sits on the homestead of legendary Ute Chief Ouray and his wife, Chipeta.

TOP EXPERIENCE

Dinosaur National Monument

At the end of desolate stretches of blacktop, Dinosaur National Monument is arguably Colorado's most remote destination. But for travelers fascinated by prehistoric life, it's worth every lonely mile. Spanning the Colorado–Utah border, it's one of the few places on earth where you can reach out and touch a dinosaur skeleton, snarling in its final pose, petrified eternally in rock and stone.

The Fossils

The park's indoor highlight is in Utah – the 150ft-long **Dinosaur Quarry Wall** with some 1500 dinosaur bones embedded in it. Part of an ancient riverbed where the remains of Jurassic-era dinosaurs were deposited and later fossilized, bones from allosaurus to stegosaurus can be seen.

Just outside, the **Fossil Discovery Trail** is one of the world's most spectacular open-air collections of fossils, with dinosaur bones, marine creatures and plants visible in the rocks. The moderate 1.2-mile trail has interpretive signs explaining the sights and distinct geological stages.

Panoramic Views

In Colorado, **Harpers Corner Trail** is a moderate 2-mile hike through juniper forests that eventually open to views of the park's winding canyons. At the trail's end, hikers are rewarded with spectacular views of the confluence of the Yampa and Green rivers at jutting **Steamboat Rock**. The trailhead is off Harpers Corner Rd, a scenic drive in itself.

Rafting

Rafting the Green and Yampa rivers is a popular way to experience the park. Expect class-III and -IV rapids, red-hued canyons, sandstone formations and petroglyphs. **Adrift** *(adrift.com; adult/child from $120/99)* and **OARS** *(oars.com; from $1049)* offer single and multiday trips, beginning in Utah.

TOP TIPS

- The Utah and Colorado entrances are 28 miles apart – about a 30-minute drive. Plan accordingly, especially to include a quarry visit.
- Services are few and far. Before heading out, fill your tank and be sure to carry drinks and snacks.

PRACTICALITIES

- nps.gov/dino
- per vehicle $25
- 24hr

TOP EXPERIENCE

Colorado National Monument

Colorado National Monument is a stunning natural area. Just 16 miles west of Grand Junction, it's a warren of canyons, their sheer walls painted a gorgeous cedar red and punctuated by long, rocky fins, dramatic sandstone spires and massive overhangs. It's an adventurer's (and photographer's) dream.

DON MAMMOSER/SHUTTERSTOCK

TOP TIPS

- Rim Rock Dr can close in winter or after storms – check the website for current conditions.
- Arrive in early morning for sightings of bighorn sheep, mule deer and golden eagles.
- Rim Rock Dr is popular with cyclists. Give them space on the narrow, curvy road.

PRACTICALITIES

- nps.gov/colm
- per vehicle $25
- 24hr

Driving Past Red Rocks

The most popular way to experience the park is driving the paved 23-mile **Rim Rock Dr**, which weaves along the cliff edges, with 19 pull-outs offering vertiginous vistas of the red sandstone cliffs, monoliths and formations carved by millions of years of erosion. Pull-outs have interpretive signage explaining the park's history, geology, flora and fauna.

Hiking Through the Park

Forty-six miles of trails make for outstanding and varied hikes, allowing visitors to appreciate the landscape close-up. Popular trails include **Devil's Kitchen** (1.9 miles round trip), a short hike and scramble to a large stone outcrop; and **Monument Canyon Trail** (11.6 miles round trip), which passes many of the park's most interesting natural features, including **Kissing Couple**, **Independence Monument** and **Coke Ovens**.

Climbing Sandstone

Colorado National Monument is a dream for experienced rock climbers, with towering sandstone spires of smooth rock interspersed with cracks, chimneys and ledges. Some favorites include **Otto's Route** on Independence Monument, the park's iconic 450ft sandstone monolith (5.9 rating); and **Sentinel Spire** with its beautiful crack routes such as West Face (5.11 rating), with steep, challenging terrain and breathtaking exposure. Head to **Gearhead Outfitters** *(gearheadoutfitters.com)* in Grand Junction for equipment, maps and route recommendations.

Colorado Springs

Olympic tour

The **Colorado Springs Olympic Training Center** *(usopc.org/training-centers; adult/child $16/12)* is one of just three such centers in the country. Tour the training facility (maybe spotting a few Olympic hopefuls in action), or check out the **US Olympic & Paralympic Museum** *(usopm.org; adult/child $30/17)* 2.5 miles away. The museum's spectacular and accessibly designed complex houses 12 galleries capturing Olympic history through memorabilia, athlete profiles and interactive training exhibits.

See the Garden of the Gods

This gorgeous vein of red sandstone (about 290 million years old) appears elsewhere along Colorado's Front Range, but the exquisitely thin cathedral spires and mountain backdrop of the **Garden of the Gods** *(gardenofgods.com; free)* are particularly striking. Gazing from the base of the highest rock formations on the **Perkins Central Garden Trail** inspires awe and humility. From there, numerous paved trails lead to central formations such as the **Kissing Camels**, **Three Graces** and **Montezuma's Tower**. Depending on your timing, you could easily spend an hour or two here. For more park information, stop in at the excellent visitors center. In summer, consider visiting **Rock Ledge Ranch** *(rockledgeranch.com; adult/child $8/4)*, a living history museum near the park entrance, that gives insight into the lives of the Utes and 19th-century homesteaders in the region.

Summit Pikes Peak

Pikes Peak *(coloradosprings.gov/drivepikespeak)* at 14,115ft may not be the tallest of Colorado's 54 fourteeners, but it's certainly the most popular – over 500,000 people summit it yearly. Called Mountain of the Sun by the Ute, it crowns the southern Front Range, majestically rising 7800ft from the plains. There are three ways to ascend it, all from Manitou Springs: Pikes Peak Hwy winding 19 miles to the top (three hours round trip; timed-entry reservations required late May to September); the 1891 cog railway (three hours round trip; reservations necessary), and **Barr Trail**, which most hikers split into a two-day trip due to the 7800ft elevation gain, camping at Barr Camp (10,200ft).

THE GREAT FRUITCAKE TOSS

Through the years it's been suggested that leftover fruitcakes (are there fruitcakes that are not leftover?) reincarnate as anything from doorstops to science experiments to an eco-friendly answer to street paving. Manitou has the answer: the **Great Fruitcake Toss** *(manitousprings.org)*, held each January in Memorial Park. Tosses are assessed for distance, balance, accuracy and aim, and fruitcakes are launched by mechanical devices. For staunch defenders of the edibility of fruitcakes, there's a bake-off for the best organic, non-GMO, natural fruitcake. The event supports the Manitou Springs Food Pantry and the tossed leftovers go to Jezebel the pig at Sun Mountain, so everyone is a winner.

EATING IN COLORADO SPRINGS: OUR PICKS

Birdtree Cafe: Fanciful and lively, with all-day breakfast and lunch. Veg/vegan options, rich coffee, gorgeous cocktails and a patio across from Acacia Park. *hours vary* $$

TAPAteria: Beautifully rendered, gluten-free Spanish tapas, with an extensive Spanish wine list. There's a 'secret' patio out back. *noon-10pm* $$

Uchenna: Expect homestyle cooking and a warm family atmosphere at chef Maya's Ethiopian restaurant, tucked in a shopping mall. *11:30am-2:30pm & 5-9pm Tue-Sat* $$

Westside Cantina: Vibrant and festive (the patio is lovely), offering cocktails and tacos with distinctive flavors and fresh ingredients. *hours vary* $$

THE SANTA FE TRAIL

The Santa Fe Trail linked Missouri with New Mexico (a Mexican province from 1821 to 1848), bringing manufactured goods west, and Mexican silver and Native American jewelry and blankets east. The 800-mile route took seven to eight weeks to cross in a covered wagon, and was defined by monotony and hardship. Near Dodge City in Kansas, the route divided: the southern road (Cimarron Route) cut down into New Mexico and was shorter but more dangerous, while the northern road (Mountain Route) continued through Bent's Fort and Trinidad, and was longer but safer. With the expansion of the railroad west, trade along the route eventually diminished, coming to a close in 1880.

SEAN XU/SHUTTERSTOCK

Great Sand Dunes National Park

Great Sand Dunes National Park

Experience a natural wonder

A standout even in a state with a tapestry of exceptional beauty, **Great Sand Dunes National Park** *(nps.gov/grsa; per vehicle $25)* appears like an undulating sea of sand bounded by jagged peaks and scrubby plains. Home to the tallest dunes in North America, including 750ft **Star Dune**, its hikes can be challenging on the shifting sand but the rewards are otherworldly views. For a thrill, try sandboarding down the sandy slopes on special wood planks; rentals are available at **Great Sand Dunes Oasis** *(greatdunes.com)* near the park entrance. If you time it right, you can even enjoy a beach day alongside the dunes – in late spring, **Medano Creek** is born from snowmelt that flows from the mountains, perfect for wading and water play, disappearing by mid-summer.

Santa Fe Trail

A drive through Colorado's complicated past

Drive Hwy 350 to experience the western reaches of the Great Plains and the Santa Fe Trail. Start at **Bent's Old Fort National Historic Site** *(nps.gov/beol)*. The beautifully restored adobe fort, used between 1833 and 1849, was once a cultural crossroads and the busiest settlement west of the Missouri.

Head northeast to Fort Lyon, where on November 29, 1864, US soldiers attacked a peaceful Cheyenne and Arapaho encampment. More than 150 people, mostly elders, women and children, were slaughtered, an event commemorated at nearby **Sand Creek Massacre National Historic Site** *(nps.gov/sand)*.

Drive through Granada to **Amache National Historic Site** *(nps.gov/amch)*. A WWII Japanese internment camp, it was the result of a racist response to the bombing of Pearl Harbor that forced the relocation and incarceration of people of Japanese descent, mostly US citizens. Amache once held 7567 prisoners, all brought from central California.

Wyoming

OTHERWORLDLY LANDSCAPES | COWBOY CULTURE | NATIVE HERITAGE

Wyoming is a land of extremes. Much of the state is a vast expanse of windswept plains and sagebrush hills, baking (or freezing) under brooding skies. Towns are infused with western grit and residents are content to keep this chunk of the West wild. But the country's least populated state (less than 600,000 inhabitants) is also home to one of the busiest and most recognizable natural destinations in the world, Yellowstone National Park, with its iconic geysers, unique geology and abundant wildlife. Add to that the glitzy ski destination of Jackson Hole and the truly grand Teton Range, and you'll forget Wyoming ever seemed so isolated. Wyoming also has a rich Native American history, including sites like Medicine Wheel and Devil's Tower National Monument. The Wind River Reservation hosts a remarkable regional powwow and is the final resting place of Sacajawea, the teenage mother who famously aided the Lewis and Clark expedition.

Places

TOP TIP

The weather can change quickly throughout the entire state. Be sure to wear layers and check out **Wyoming Road Conditions** *(wyoroad.info)* before setting off. If the weather gets rough, highway patrol will shut an entire interstate until it clears.

GETTING AROUND

Wyoming has several airports, **Jackson Hole Airport** being the biggest and **Laramie Regional Airport** typically the cheapest. Once here, the long distances between destinations make having your own car much preferred – the **Greyhound** *(greyhound.com)* bus is mostly limited to small towns in the south and east. While 4WD may not be essential, a high-clearance vehicle will make navigating dirt roads easier. Wyoming is notorious for its winds and fierce gusts; take special care if you are driving a recreational vehicle (RV) or pulling a trailer. Gas stations are rare, even on major highways – don't miss a chance to gas up.

WYOMING
MONTANA
0 100 km
0 50 miles
Cooke City
Yellowstone National Park
Absaroka Range
Shoshone National Forest
Powell
Lovell
Medicine Wheel National Historic Landmark
Sheridan
Devil's Tower National Monument
Black Hills National Forest
Yellowstone Lake
North Absaroka Wilderness
Cody
Greybull
Basin
Cloud Peak Wilderness
Buffalo
Devil's Tower National Monument
Sundance
Spearfish
SOUTH DAKOTA
John D Rockefeller Jr Memorial Parkway
Washakie Wilderness
Bighorn River
Bighorn National Forest
Gillette
Moorcroft
Black Hills
Black Hills National Forest
Rapid City
St Anthony
Teton Range
Teton Wilderness
Worland
Ten Sleep
Jedediah Smith Wilderness
Colter Bay Village
Snake River
Teton National Forest
Bighorn Mountains
Kaycee
Sussex
Newcastle
Badlands National Park
Jackson
Dubois
Wind River Reservation
Thermopolis
Thunder Basin National Grassland
Caribou National Forest
Gros Ventre Wilderness
Blackfoot
Fitzpatrick Wilderness
Midwest
Hot Springs
Big Wind River
Shoshoni
Buffalo Gap National Grassland
IDAHO
Bridger Wilderness
Fort Washakie
Riverton
WYOMING
Pinedale
Soda Springs
Lander
Casper
Chadron
Bridger National Forest
Sinks Canyon State Park
Douglas
NEBRASKA
Bear River
Wind River Range
Sweetwater River
Medicine Bow National Forest
Fort Laramie
NEBRASKA PANHANDLE
UTAH
Green River
Laramie Range
Wheatland
Fort Laramie National Historic Site
Torrington
Alliance
Yampa River
Great Divide Basin
Rawlins
Cache National Forest
Green River
Rock Springs
Rocky Mountains
Medicine Bow Mountains
N Platte River
Great Salt Lake
Flaming Gorge National Recreation Area
Encampment River Wilderness
Medicine Bow National Forest
Laramie
Flaming Gorge National Recreation Area
Savage Run Wilderness
Cheyenne
Sidney
Salt Lake City
High Uintas Wilderness
Green River
NORTHWEST COLORADO
NORTHERN MOUNTAINS
90
25
80

Cheyenne

Experience Cheyenne Frontier Days

Every late July since 1897, **Cheyenne Frontier Days** *(cfdrodeo.com; prices vary)* – the country's largest rodeo and celebration of all things Wyoming – has been taking over the capital city. A 10-day showcase of cowboy culture, the heart of the action is in Frontier Park, where rodeo events like bronco and bull riding, barrel racing and team roping bring top contenders and big prize money. If the events are sold out or are just too pricey, free tickets to qualifying rounds, or 'slack' rodeos, are offered too. Or check out the wildly popular Frontier Town, recreating 19th-century life with costumed characters, making sure to stop in the Indian Village, where modern-day Native dance and storytelling traditions are showcased. Evenings bring big-name music acts to Frontier Park's arena too. In town, check out the seemingly nonstop lineup of concerts, parades, air shows, carnivals and chili cook-offs that transform the typically sleepy town.

A walk through the Old West

For a deep dive into Cheyenne's pioneer past and rodeo present, visit the **Old West Museum** *(cfdrodeo.com/event/old-west-museum; adult/child $15/10)* on the Cheyenne Frontier Days rodeo grounds. It's chock-full of rodeo memorabilia, from saddles to trophies. It also displays cowboy art and photography, houses a fine collection of horse-drawn buggies, and dispenses nuggets of history – such as the story of Steamboat, the unrideable bronco who likely isn't the one depicted on Wyoming's license plates (though many will tell you he is).

All about Wyoming's history

While in Cheyenne, stop in the **Wyoming State Museum** *(wyomuseum.wyo.gov; free)* a thoughtfully curated attraction focused exclusively on the state's natural and cultural history. Spread across two floors, exhibits showcase Wyoming's dinosaur findings and modern-day wildlife, mining and national parks, plus Native American peoples and pioneers. Three to four temporary exhibits keep the museum current. If you're traveling with little ones, don't miss the hands-on area with dress-up clothes, a pint-size tipi and a recreated chuck wagon.

MARDI GRAS OF THE WEST

Sam Masoudi, Chief Investment Officer, Wyoming Retirement System.

Frontier Days in Cheyenne is a really big deal. The city gets taken over with it! People dress up for it, and there are a lot of hardcore cowboys and a decent number of bikers too. If you're going to watch rodeo, it's extraordinary, with some of the best bull riders in the country and lots of other events like women's barrel racing and cattle drives. It also has one of the biggest country-music concerts in the country. There are chuck-wagon cook-offs, too, where people prep dishes only using ingredients and tools available during pioneer days. Plus, there's a US Air Force Thunderbirds flyover. It's all really interesting, so fun. It's like the Mardi Gras of Western culture!

EATING IN CHEYENNE: OUR PICKS

Luxury Diner: Go-to breakfast spot, set in a turn-of-the-20th-century trolley car. If in doubt, order anything with green chili. *7am-2pm Mon-Sat, to 1pm Sun* $

2 Doors Down: Popular burger joint specializing in offbeat toppings, from teriyaki to mac 'n' cheese. Bottomless fries too. *11am-9pm Mon-Sat* $

Napoli's: Upscale dinner spot with an art-deco ambiance. Expect mouthwatering Italian fare and attentive service. Don't miss the tiramisu. *4-9pm Tue-Sat* $$

Bunkhouse Bar & Grill: Honky-tonk serving steaks and Rocky Mountain oyster sandwiches. Live music on weekends. *11am-8pm Wed-Thu & Sun, 11am-11pm Fri & Sat* $$

SACAJAWEA

Sacajawea, the famed Shoshone interpreter on the Lewis and Clark expedition, has all but disappeared into popular myth. But this remarkable teenager embodied profound intelligence and resourcefulness. Born near Salmon, Idaho in 1788, she was kidnapped and enslaved by Hidatsa tribesmen at age 12. Two years later, a pregnant Sacajawea joined the expedition with her proclaimed husband, a French-Canadian fur trader who 'won' her gambling. Her presence proved invaluable; beyond her linguistic abilities, she helped secure horses and safe passage from the Shoshone. Though the details of her death are debated, Shoshone oral tradition holds she lived on the Wind River Reservation, dying in 1884. Her gravestone and statue sit on a quiet hillside cemetery in Fort Washakie.

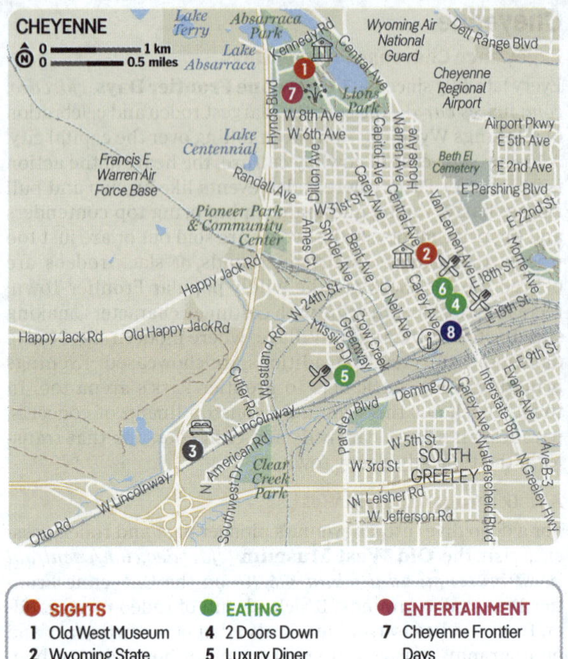

SIGHTS
1 Old West Museum
2 Wyoming State Museum

SLEEPING
3 Cheyenne Guest Inn

EATING
4 2 Doors Down
5 Luxury Diner
6 Napoli's

ENTERTAINMENT
7 Cheyenne Frontier Days

INFORMATION
8 Cheyenne Visitor Center

Touring Cheyenne's public art

Cowboy boots are about as Wyoming as Buffalo Bill, and sculptures of colorful, larger-than-life boots add quirky charm to downtown Cheyenne. Even better, these boots can talk. Stop by the **Cheyenne Visitor Center** *(cheyenne.org)* for the brochure *These Boots are made for Talking* (or download it from the website). With the brochure in hand, follow the map to any of the 35 boot-sculptures, dial 307-316-0067, then enter the number of the boot as shown on the brochure – you'll hear the story of the boot from the artist and, in the process, learn a whole new side to the city's history.

Laramie

Spend time in prison

Stop at the impressively restored **Wyoming Territorial Prison State Historic Site** *(wyoparks.wyo.gov; adult/child $9/4.50)* to learn all about the reality of prison life in the Wild West. It is also the only prison to have held Butch Cassidy, who was in for grand larceny from 1894 to '96, only to emerge a well-connected criminal who fast became one of history's greatest robbers. His life story is told in thrilling detail in a back room, while the faces of other 'malicious and desperate outlaws' – including several women – stare hauntingly at you as you explore the main cellblocks. Outside, tour the factory where convicts produced more than 700 brooms a day – one of the prison's short-lived revenue-generating schemes. Staff members are posted throughout the site, happily answering questions; free guided tours offered May to September.

Marvel at prehistoric finds

The Morrison Formation – a vast Jurassic-era sedimentary rock layer – stretches from New Mexico to Montana, with its fossil-rich center in Wyoming. This 150-million-year-old formation has produced some of the world's most significant dinosaur discoveries in paleontology, many of which are housed in the University of Wyoming's tiny, but well-worth-a-stop, **Geological Museum** *(uwyo.edu/geomuseum; free)*. Inside, marvel at a towering 75ft apatosaurus skeleton (formerly known as the brontosaurus) as well as a rare *Diatryma gigantea*, a 7ft-tall, flightless carnivorous bird that once roamed the region's prehistoric swamps. Be sure to linger at the 'Prep Lab' observation window, where researchers liberate brittle fossils from solid rock.

Sinks Canyon State Park

See a geological phenomenon

Six miles southwest of Lander lies **Sinks Canyon State Park** *(sinkscanyonstatepark.org; free)*, a beautiful forested park nestled deep in a glacial canyon. Popular for day hikes, it's best known for a geological phenomenon involving the Middle Fork of the Popo Agie River. Here, the fast-flowing river suddenly turns into a large limestone cavern, disappearing into cracks and fissures at its back wall, known as the Sinks. The river is not seen again for nearly a quarter-mile, until it reemerges in a tranquil pool called the Rise, which is filled with enormous trout. Despite the short distance between the two, dye tests indicate that in addition to taking over two hours for the river to make the subterranean journey, it also reemerges warmer and more voluminous. The reason continues to intrigue scientists. A paved trail between the two areas makes for a scenic walk, with interpretive signs along the way explaining more about the geology, ecology and history of the park.

Fort Washakie

Wyoming's largest powwow

In late June, head to Fort Washakie on the Wind River Reservation – home of the Eastern Shoshone and Northern Arapaho peoples – where **Eastern Shoshone Indian Days** *(windriver.org; free)* is hosted. The largest and longest-running powwow in Wyoming, the three-day event is a spectacular intertribal celebration of Native identity; expect all manner of competitive dancing, drumming groups and Grand Entry ceremonies, participants of all ages decked out in magnificent regalia. Beyond the arena, artisans and food vendors line the grounds, selling

MATTHEW SHEPARD

In October 1998, Matthew Shepard, a student at University of Wyoming in Laramie, was attacked and brutally beaten, tied to a roadside fence, and left to die – all because he was gay. Shepard's murder drew national attention to hate crimes against LGBTIQ+ people and spurred an outpouring of grief, outrage, activism and urgent creativity, including the critically acclaimed play *The Laramie Project*. Shepard's parents founded the **Matthew Shepard Foundation** *(matthewshepard.org)*, dedicated to promoting LGBTIQ+ rights, which helped to expand federal hate-crime legislation to include sexual orientation and gender identity. A memorial bench for Shephard now sits at University of Wyoming; it bears the quiet inscription 'He continues to make a difference.'

GREEN RIVER RENDEZVOUS

In mid-July, the town of Pinedale hosts the **Green River Rendezvous Festival** *(green riverrendezvous.com)*, a four-day celebration of the region's mountain man heritage. The event commemorates the annual summer 'Rendezvous' of the early 1800s where fur trappers, Native Americans and traders would gather to buy supplies, trade goods and generally party. Today, the event includes a lively parade down Main Street, historical reenactments, shooting demonstrations, craft fairs and cultural performances by Shoshone and Arapaho people. Presentations by historians are also offered at the Museum of the Mountain Man, for those looking for a deeper dive into Wyoming's frontier history.

TERI VIRBICKIS/SHUTTERSTOCK

Devil's Tower National Monument

Native goods, art and eats. While the powwow is open to the public, be mindful when taking photographs – the arena is considered a sacred place. Keep an ear out for announcements limiting photography; if in doubt, ask before snapping a pic.

Visit the Shoshone Tribal Cultural Center

Inside Fort Washakie School, learn all about the history of Wind River Reservation and its people at the **Shoshone Tribal Cultural Center** *(easternshoshone.org/cultural-center; free)*. Exhibits highlight Eastern Shoshone history and contemporary tribal life as well as the legacy of Chief Washakie, renowned for his ability to navigate the changing physical and political landscapes of the West during the 1800s. There's also a display on the life of Sacajawea, Lewis and Clark's now-famous guide and interpreter. For a deeper dive in the Eastern Shoshone, ask about **guided tours of the reservation** *(by donation)*; led by staff member Robyn Rofkar, tours last a few hours to multiple days, providing unique insights into the tribe's history and enduring culture.

Pinesdale

Learn about the early pioneers

Make a pitstop in Pinedale for **Museum of the Mountain Man** *(museumofthemountainman.com, adult/child $10, free)*, a fascinating museum that deep-dives into the history of the

EATING NEAR FORT WASHAKIE & LANDER: OUR PICKS

Middle Fork: Welcoming breakfast place with local ingredients and homemade baked goods. The eggs Benedict with cottage bacon is tops. *7am-2pm* $

Lander Bake Shop: Family-owned from-scratch bakery and cafe. Sit down for brekkie and order a sandwich for the trail. *7am-4pm Mon-Fri, 8am-2pm Sat & Sun* $

Gannett Grill: Casual spot known for its local grass-fed beef burgers and stone-oven pizzas. In summer, nab a seat on the leafy patio. *11am-10pm* $

Cowfish: Upscale restaurant with surf-and-turf menu, perfect for date night. Order a flight of craft beer, delivered from the attached brewery. *5-10pm* $$$

fur trappers who came to the West during the 1820s in search of beaver pelts. An essential part of the region's development, exhibits cover everything from their food and clothing to trapping methods and marriage to Native American women.

Fort Laramie

Imagine life in a fort

In Wyoming's eastern plains, **Fort Laramie National Historic Site** *(nps.gov/fola; free)* is one of the most historically important sites in the state. Established as a fur trading post in 1834, it quickly became a place of rest and restocking for emigrants traveling on the Oregon, Mormon Pioneer and California Trails. By 1849, with surging numbers of Gold Rush fortune seekers – and increasing conflicts with Plains tribespeople – it transformed into one of the largest military forts in the West. Today, you can visit 22 original structures, including enlisted barracks, officers' quarters, a bakery and the post trader's store. Many are furnished with period artifacts. Interpretive signs provide historical context, while the visitor center has exhibits on the fort's complex role in westward expansion and the Indian Wars (don't miss the excellent film). During summer, you also can interact with staff in period dress, who talk about life in the fort and provide demonstrations in things like blacksmithing and military drills. Guided tours available from late May to early September.

Devil's Tower National Monument

Visit a sacred place

Devil's Tower National Monument *(nps.gov/deto; per car $25),* in northeastern Wyoming, is a dramatic, nearly vertical monolith, rising 1267ft above the Belle Fourche River. Designated the first US national monument in 1906, the tower consists of striking hexagonal columns, some 20ft wide, formed over 50 million years ago. For 20 Native American tribes, the tower – often called Bear Lodge or Bear's Tipi – is a deeply spiritual site. For rock climbers, it is considered one of the best crack climbing spots in the world. Except in June, when tribes request a voluntary climbing moratorium to hold sacred ceremonies, you'll see climbers tackling the tower on over 140 routes. If you'd like to join the crowd, **Sylvan Rocks** *(sylvanrocks.com)* and **Devils Tower Climbing Guides** *(devilstowerlodge.com/Climb)* are highly recommended guides, especially for newbies. Or keep both feet on the ground, and hike the 1.3-mile **Tower Trail** circling the base, with close-up views of the tower. Keep your eyes peeled for prairie dogs.

Medicine Wheel National Historic Landmark

An ancient place of prayer

Medicine Wheel National Historic Landmark *(fs.usda.gov; free)* sits atop Medicine Mountain in Wyoming's Bighorn Range at nearly 10,000ft. A remarkable 80-ft-wide limestone circle with 28 spokes radiating from its central cairn, it is a

INFINITE OUTDOORS ACCESS GRANTED

Accessing public lands in the West is often far more difficult than maps suggest. Though these lands are publicly owned, nearly 16 million acres across the West are considered 'landlocked' – surrounded by private property, with fences and 'No Trespassing' signs blocking entry. In Wyoming alone, over 4.25 million acres of Bureau of Land Management (BLM), state and national forest lands fall into this category. To address this problem, **Infinite Outdoors Access Granted** *(infiniteoutdoorsusa.com/access-granted)* launched an app in 2025 to help outdoor enthusiasts find free entry points to private lands bordering public lands. With an increasing demand for access to public land, this seems to be a viable solution. Time will tell.

sacred site for several Plains tribes. For centuries, it has been used for countless ceremonies, prayers and vision quests. Today, the wheel remains an active sacred site, where cloth bundles, eagle feathers and other offerings are tied to nearby fences. Visitors are welcome to visit from mid-June through September – a well-maintained 1.5-mile trail leads there. Be aware access is occasionally restricted for ceremonies; if one takes place while you're on-site, do not take photographs. And be sure not to touch the offerings.

Cody

A dark episode in US history

Following the Japanese bombing of Pearl Harbor, more than 110,000 Japanese Americans were sent to 10 detention camps across the US. **Heart Mountain Relocation Center** *(heartmountain.org; adult/child $14/10)* in northern Wyoming was among them. Approximately 14,000 Japanese Americans were forcibly relocated from their West Coast homes to live in the 450 flimsy tar-paper barracks that once stood here. Nevertheless, they made the best of their three years of confinement, setting up a newspaper, two theaters and a high school in what quickly became Wyoming's third-largest town. Though few original structures remain – a residential barrack, hospital and root cellar – a free app allows you to point your cellphone at 16 designated stops to see real-time scenes from the internment camp, making it easier to imagine what life was once like here. Be sure to set aside plenty of time to see the powerful exhibits in the interpretive center.

GROWING FOOD IN CAPTIVITY

The first year was particularly difficult for the Japanese-American prisoners at Heart Mountain. Torn from their homes hundreds of miles away, they suffered amid the challenging climate and isolation of remote Wyoming. The bland canned food and poor-quality meat only made things worse. James Ito, who grew up on a farm in southern California and graduated from the Berkeley College of Agriculture, organized the Japanese-American farmers among the camp and set to work. Within a year, the camp was growing most of its own food, and by 1945, they were producing a surplus – a remarkable achievement given the growing conditions of the high Wyoming desert. Ito later held a position with the US Department of Agriculture.

Explore everything Western

Do not miss Wyoming's most impressive human-made attraction: **Buffalo Bill Center of the West** *(centerofthewest.org; adult/child $23/16)*. This sprawling complex of museums showcases everything Western, from the spectacle of Buffalo Bill's world-famous Wild West shows and galleries featuring powerful frontier-oriented artwork in **Buffalo Bill Museum** to the **Cody Firearms Museum**, with over 7000 pieces. Meanwhile, the **Draper Museum of Natural History** brilliantly explores the Yellowstone region's ecosystem; look for Teddy Roosevelt's saddle and one of the world's last buffalo tipis. Be sure to spend time in the visually absorbing **Plains Indian Museum**, an exploration of the past and present of several tribes, as well as the **Whitney Western Art Museum**, home to a world-class collection of Western art plus the recreated

EATING IN CODY: OUR PICKS

Beta Coffeehouse: Locals' favorite boho coffee shop serving baked goods, breakfast fare, and all manner of coffee drinks. *7am-2pm Tue-Fri, 8am-1pm Sat* $

Fat Racks BBQ: Food truck turned diner serving smoky Texas-style BBQ with all the fixings. Eat at outdoor picnic tables or take to go. *11am-7pm Mon-Sat* $$

Pat's Brew House: Woman-owned and -operated brewery with an eclectic menu – steamed mussels to cheeseburgers – plus craft beers on tap. *11am-9pm Wed-Sun* $$

Cody Cattle Company: Popular Western-style buffet – grilled meats, beans, cornbread and more – paired with live country music. *5-7:30pm, summer only* $$$

studio of renowned artist Frederic Remington. Entry is valid for two consecutive days – and you'll need 'em.

Jackson

See elk herds up close

If you're here in winter, head to the **National Elk Refuge & Greater Yellowstone Visitor Center** *(fws.gov/refuge/national-elk; free)*, headquarters for the 24,700-acre reserve on the northeast edge of town. Established in 1912 to protect diminishing numbers of elk herds, it's home to one of North America's largest elk populations, with numbers reaching over 7000 in the colder months. (In summer, the herds migrate into the mountains.) From mid-December to early April, **guided tours on horse-drawn sleighs** *(nersleighrides.com; adult/child $40/25)* take you into the heart of the herd for close-up views, with the snow-covered peaks of the Grand Tetons in the distance. Alternatively, take a free **audio driving tour** through 3.5 miles of the reserve, available on the website; free binoculars, as well as educational exhibits, available at the visitor center.

Mushing in the backcountry

Experience Wyoming's wintry backcountry from a dog's point of view with five-time Iditarod veteran Billy Snodgrass' **Continental Divide Dogsled Adventures** *(dogsledadventures.com; from $190)*. Excursions leave from the Togwotee Mountain Lodge in the Bridger-Teton National Forest, with one or two passengers per sled and a guide driving the team. You'll learn dogsled lore and the sport's history while teams of eight to 14 Alaskan huskies whisk you through the wilderness. Want to mush? Most guides will teach you on a safe stretch of the trail. Round-trip transportation from Jackson available too.

Admire the wild indoors

Set aside a morning in Jackson to visit the nation's only museum dedicated exclusively to wildlife art: **National Museum of Wildlife Art** *(wildlifeart.org, adult/child $18/10)*, a two-story building housing over 5000 works by traditional wildlife masters like Carl Rungius and John Audubon, and modern icons like Pablo Picasso and Andy Warhol. Wander through the collection or take a tour using the museum's excellent app, available in Spanish and English. Kid-geared activities throughout the galleries keep little ones engaged too.

Continued on p220

JACKSON'S BEST OUTDOOR OUTFITTERS

Hole Hiking Experience: Excellent hiking and snowshoeing excursions with naturalists, from two hours to overnight.

Grand Fishing Adventures: Guided fly-fishing on the Snake, Green and Salt rivers, plus exclusive access to Fish Creek.

Dave Hansen Whitewater: Reputable outfit for white-water trips on the Snake River with class II and III rapids.

Jackson Hole EcoTour Operators: Wildlife-watching tours (in vehicles) plus half-day snowshoe and cross-country ski excursions.

Teton Backcountry Guides: Backcountry ski trips including a day of climbing followed by long (3000ft) descents.

Hoback Sports: Rent mountain bikes, road bikes, e-bikes, skis and snowboards.

EATING IN JACKSON: OUR PICKS

Persephone Café Jackson: French bakery-cafe featuring artisanal breads, pastries and breakfast masterpieces. In summer, patio seating is tops. *7am-6pm Mon-Sat, 7am-3pm Sun* $$

Café Genevieve: Log-cabin cafe serving homestyle breakfast and hearty salads and sandwiches. Breakfast s'mores are good anytime. *8am-2pm Mon-Fri, to 2:30pm Sat & Sun* $$

Gather in Jackson Hole: Upscale yet laid-back restaurant featuring modern American fare with Asian and Mediterranean twists. Elk, trout and bison feature prominently. *5-9pm* $$$

Gun Barrel Steak and Game House: Jackson's best steakhouse, offering all manner of game. Set in a one-time wildlife museum; taxidermy still features large. *5-9pm* $$$

BERZINA/SHUTTERSTOCK

Grand Prismatic Spring

TOP EXPERIENCE

Yellowstone National Park

Teeming with wildlife, America's first national park also contains some of its wildest lands. Yellowstone is home to over 60% of the world's geysers – hot springs that periodically erupt in towering explosions of water. And while these astounding phenomena, and their neighboring Technicolor hot springs and bubbling mud pots draw in over 4.5 million visitors yearly, the surrounding canyons, mountains and forests are no less impressive.

DON'T MISS

- Old Faithful
- Grand Prismatic Spring
- Artist Point
- Yellowstone Lake
- Tribal Heritage Center

Geyser Country

Yellowstone's **Geyser Country** holds the park's most spectacular geothermal features (over half the world's total) within the world's densest concentration of geysers (over 200 spouters in 1.5 sq miles). Many have boardwalks circling them, making it easy (and safe) to observe them up close. Don't miss **Old Faithful**, the park's poster child, spouting some 8000 gallons of water 180ft into the air every 90-ish minutes; **Black Sand Geyser Canyon** with its steaming vents and bubbling pools contrasted against rugged cliffs; and **Grand Prismatic Spring**, a 330-ft-wide shimmering hot spring, the largest in

PRACTICALITIES

● nps.gov/yell ● per vehicle $35 ● 24hr

the country. Most of Yellowstone's geysers line the Firehole River, whose tributaries feed 21 of the park's 110 waterfalls.

Mammoth Country

Mammoth Country is renowned for its geothermal terraces and the towering Gallatin Range to the northwest. **Mammoth Hot Springs** is the area's main attraction, a graceful collection of travertine terraces and cascading hot pools. Some terraces are bone dry; others sparkle with hundreds of minuscule pools, coral-like formations and a fabulous palette of colors. An hour's worth of boardwalks wind their way through a landscape so otherworldly it provided the backdrop for the planet Vulcan in *Star Trek* (1979).

Tower-Roosevelt Country

Ancient petrified forests, the wildlife-rich **Lamar Valley**, its tributary trout streams of Slough and Pebble Creeks, and the dramatic and craggy peaks of the Absaroka Range are the highlights in this remote, scenic and undeveloped region. Come to see one of the largest herds of bison and elk in North America.

Canyon Country

A series of scenic overlooks linked by hiking trails punctuate the cliffs, precipices and waterfalls of the **Grand Canyon of the Yellowstone**. Here the Yellowstone River continues to gouge out a fault line through an ancient geyser basin, most impressively at **Lower Falls**. South Rim Dr leads to the canyon's most spectacular overlook, at **Artist Point**, while North Rim Dr accesses the daring precipices of the Upper and Lower Falls.

Lake Country

Yellowstone Lake (7733ft) is Lake Country's shimmering centerpiece – one of the world's largest alpine lakes, with the biggest inland population of cutthroat trout in the US. Yellowstone River emerges from the north end of the lake and flows through Hayden Valley into the Grand Canyon of the Yellowstone. The lake's southern and eastern borders flank the steep Absaroka Range and the pristine Thorofare region, some of the wildest and remotest lands in the lower 48. This watery wilderness is best explored by boat; rentals available at **Bridge Bay Marina** *(yellowstonenationalparklodges.com; rowboat/motor boat from $53/76)*.

Tribal Heritage Center

Located near **Old Faithful Visitor Education Center**, the **Tribal Heritage Center** pays homage to the region's 27 associated tribal nations. From mid-May through mid-October, Indigenous artists, historians and craft makers give presentations and demonstrations in everything from beadwork and moccasin-making to storytelling and dancing. It's a great place to learn from people with a deep connection to Yellowstone.

BISON PROWESS

Despite their docile, hulking appearance, bison are surprisingly agile. They become increasingly uneasy when approached. A raised tail indicates one of two possibilities: a charge or discharge. Statistically, bison are much more dangerous than bears. Every year visitors are gored and seriously injured, sometimes even killed, by bison. Keep your distance to avoid becoming an unwilling rodeo clown, especially in August when it's rutting season.

TOP TIPS

- Visit in May or October. Services may be limited, but there will be far fewer people.
- Hit the trail. Most (95%) of visitors never set foot on a backcountry trail; only 1% camp at a backcountry site (permit required).
- Bike the park. Most campgrounds have underutilized hiker/cyclist sites, and youcan slip through any traffic jam.
- Mimic the wildlife. Be active during the golden hours after dawn and before dusk.
- Pack a lunch. Eat at one of the park's many overlooked and often lovely scenic picnic areas.
- Wintertime means you'll likely have Old Faithful to yourself. Just bundle up.

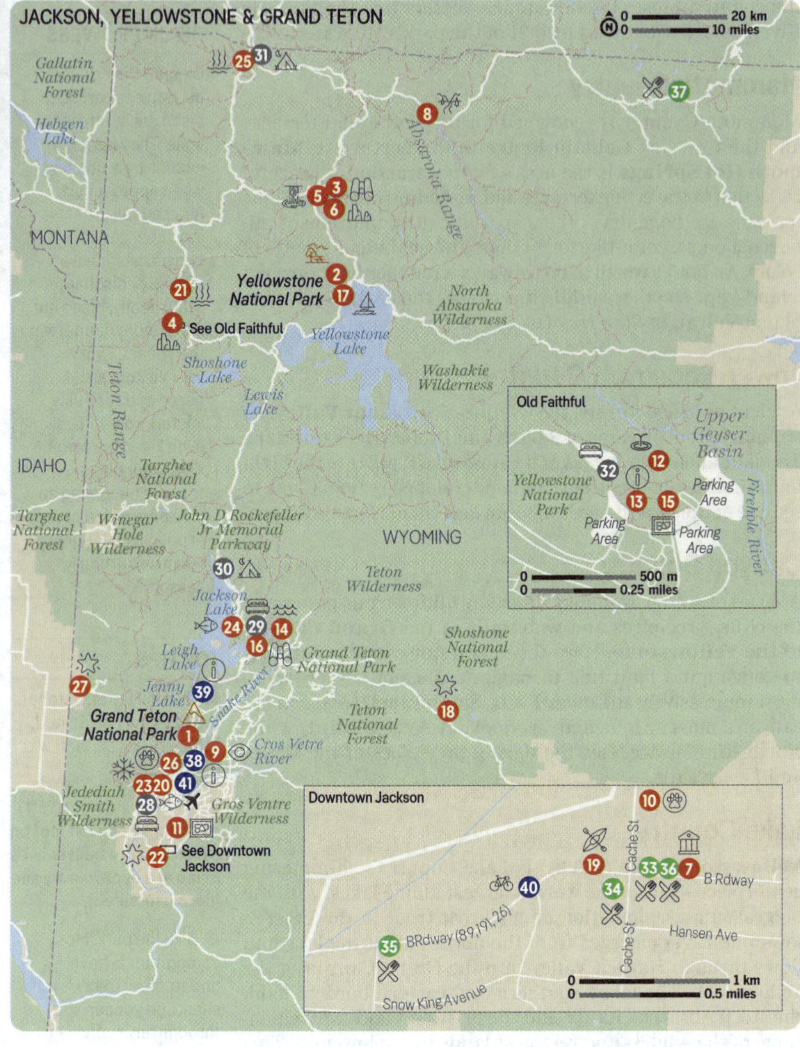

Continued from p217
Even if the museum is closed, the mile-long sculpture trail is worth visiting with works of art set into the rugged hillside, all with spectacular views over the National Elk Refuge (p217).

Examine Jackson's past

Stop at **History Jackson Hole** *(jacksonholehistory.org; adult/child $12/free)*, a state-of-the-art museum chronicling over 11,000 years of regional history through interactive displays and storytelling. Open artifact drawers and watch documentaries, peruse digital photo libraries, and step inside two preserved

HIGHLIGHTS
1 Grand Teton National Park
2 Yellowstone National Park

SIGHTS
3 Artist Point
4 Black Sand Geyser Canyon
5 Brink of the Lower Falls
6 Grand Canyon of the Yellowstone
7 History Jackson Hole
8 Lamar Valley
9 Mormon Row
10 National Elk Refuge & Greater Yellowstone Visitor Center
11 National Museum of Wildlife Art
12 Old Faithful
13 Old Faithful Visitor Education Center
14 Oxbow Bend
15 Tribal Heritage Center
16 Willow Flats Turnout

ACTIVITIES
17 Bridge Bay Marina
18 Continental Divide Dogsled Adventures
19 Dave Hansen Whitewater
20 Grand Fishing Adventures
21 Grand Prismatic Spring
22 Jackson Hole EcoTour Operators
23 Jackson Hole Mountain Resort
24 Jackson Lake
see 39 Jenny Lake Boating
25 Mammoth Hot Springs
26 Moose-Wilson Road
27 Teton Backcountry Guides

SLEEPING
28 Hostel
29 Jackson Lake Lodge
30 Lizard Creek Campground
31 Mammoth Campground
32 Old Faithful Inn

EATING
33 Cafe Genevieve
34 Gather in Jackson Hole
35 Gun Barrel Steak and Game House
36 Persephone Café Jackson
37 Top of the World Resort

INFORMATION
38 Craig Thomas Discovery & Visitor Center
39 Jenny Lake Visitor Center

TRANSPORT
40 Hoback Sports
41 Jackson Hole Airport

frontier-era cabins. Biographies dot the space in a loose timeline, introducing notable Native Americans, homesteaders, ranchers and skiers. Head upstairs to check out the community-curated gallery, which explores ever-changing themes.

Skiing a winter wonderland

Nestled in the Tetons just 12 miles from downtown Jackson, **Jackson Hole Mountain Resort** *(jacksonhole.com; lift tickets from $218)* is one of the country's top mountain destinations. Spread across two mountains – **Après Vous** and **Rendezvous** – the resort is renowned for its steep, dramatic terrain, stunning alpine views and deep, consistent snowfall (over 450in annually). It also has the steepest continuous vertical drop in North America – 4139ft – offering a challenge for intermediate and expert skiers and snowboarders. While there's no doubt the resort is world-class, Jackson Hole also provides rare open access to expansive wilderness skiing. If you have avalanche training, consider venturing into the 3000 acres of unpatrolled, backcountry terrain of the Bridger-Teton National Forest. Alternatively, hire one of the **resort's backcountry guides** *(jacksonhole.com/mountain-sports-school/backcountry; per person $393-1330)* to help navigate the rugged landscape, ensuring a safer powder adventure beyond the resort boundaries.

JACKON'S ANTLERS

Jackson's Town Square is famous for its four iconic arches made entirely of elk antlers. The arches weigh several tons, each made up of 2000 to 3000 antlers collected from the National Elk Refuge (p217) by local Boy Scouts, an annual spring tradition since the mid-1960s. No animals are harmed during the collecting – the antlers are naturally dropped by elk before being gathered. The arches attract thousands of visitors yearly, each posing next to and under the antlers, hoping for a classic Jackson photo op.

TOP EXPERIENCE

Grand Teton National Park

Awe-inspiring in their grandeur, the Tetons have captivated the imagination from the moment humans laid eyes on them: 12 glacier-carved summits framing the singular Grand Teton (13,775ft). While the view is breathtaking from the valley floor, it only gets more impressive on the trail or on the water. In winter, the Tetons make a magical setting for snowshoeing and cross-country skiing.

Hidden Falls

TOP TIPS

- Stop in the **Craig Thomas Discovery & Visitor Center** for excellent exhibits and films as well as ranger help desks.
- Don't approach wildlife. Maintain at least 100yd from bears and wolves, 25yd from all others.
- Wear layers. The weather can change rapidly year-round.

PRACTICALITIES

- nps.gov/grte
- per vehicle $35
- 24hr

Scenic Drives

Cruise along **Hwy 191** and **Teton Park Rd**, stopping at staggeringly beautiful viewpoints, many with signage with interesting facts about the park. Make a slight detour to **Mormon Row**, home to the iconic Moulton Barns with the Tetons rising dramatically behind – possibly the most photographed site in the park. Or drive up **Signal Mountain Summit Rd** for sweeping mountain views.

Wildlife Watching

Head to **Oxbow Bend**, **Willow Flats** and **Moose–Wilson Rd** at dawn or dusk for your best chances of spotting moose, elk, grizzlies and bald eagles. Bring binoculars and be patient.

Hiking

Jenny Lake has a variety of breathtaking trail options. Consider hopping on a **shuttle boat** *(adult/child round trip $20/12)* to hike to **Hidden Falls** and **Inspiration Point** – a short hike with big-time views. For longer treks, head from there into **Forks of Cascade Canyon** (9.2-mile round trip) with alpine lakes and terrain.

On the Water

Rent **kayaks** *(from $35)* on **Jackson Lake** or **Jenny Lake** to experience the park from the water. Or take a **scenic rafting trip** *(adult/child from $126/74)* on the Snake River from **Jackson Lake Lodge** (p249).

Montana

MOUNTAIN ADVENTURE | COLLEGE VIBE | INDIGENOUS PRESENCE

Welcome to Big Sky Country, where the Great Plains hit the Rockies and just about anything seems possible. At Glacier National Park, known for its towering sculpted mountains and abundant grizzly bears, visitors can enjoy terrific vistas and guided boat rides in long finger-lakes formed by ancient glaciers. Montana's numerous rivers, including the Blackfoot and the Clark Fork, are famous for their rugged beauty and outstanding fishing (and for nearly stymying explorers Lewis and Clark near present-day Great Falls). Nearby, Missoula and Bozeman are lively college towns with urban energy and plenty to do, from fascinating museums to world-class skiing. And Montana's many Native American sites include a bison reserve near Flathead Lake and the Little Bighorn Battlefield National Monument, where Cheyenne, Sioux and Arapahoe warriors quashed an ill-fated attack by Lt Col George Custer. Come, explore and take in one of the most dramatically beautiful corners of the continent.

Places

GETTING AROUND

Montana's busiest airport is **Bozeman Yellowstone International Airport**, a good starting point both for trips deeper into the state and into Yellowstone National Park. Missoula and Billings also have well-connected airports.

Greyhound *(greyhound.com)* and **Jefferson Lines** *(jeffersonlines.com)* bus passengers around the state, while **Amtrak's Empire Builder** train *(amtrak.com/empire-builder-train)* can be an attractive option for accessing Glacier National Park and other parts of northern Montana.

A private car provides much more flexibility. Just remember it's a gigantic state, with deceptively long drives between popular sites; gas up when you can to avoid getting stranded.

TOP TIP

Snow can fall in Montana well into June, particularly at higher elevations and in northern regions like Glacier National Park (p232). Be sure to check forecasts and road conditions year-round. And pack layers.

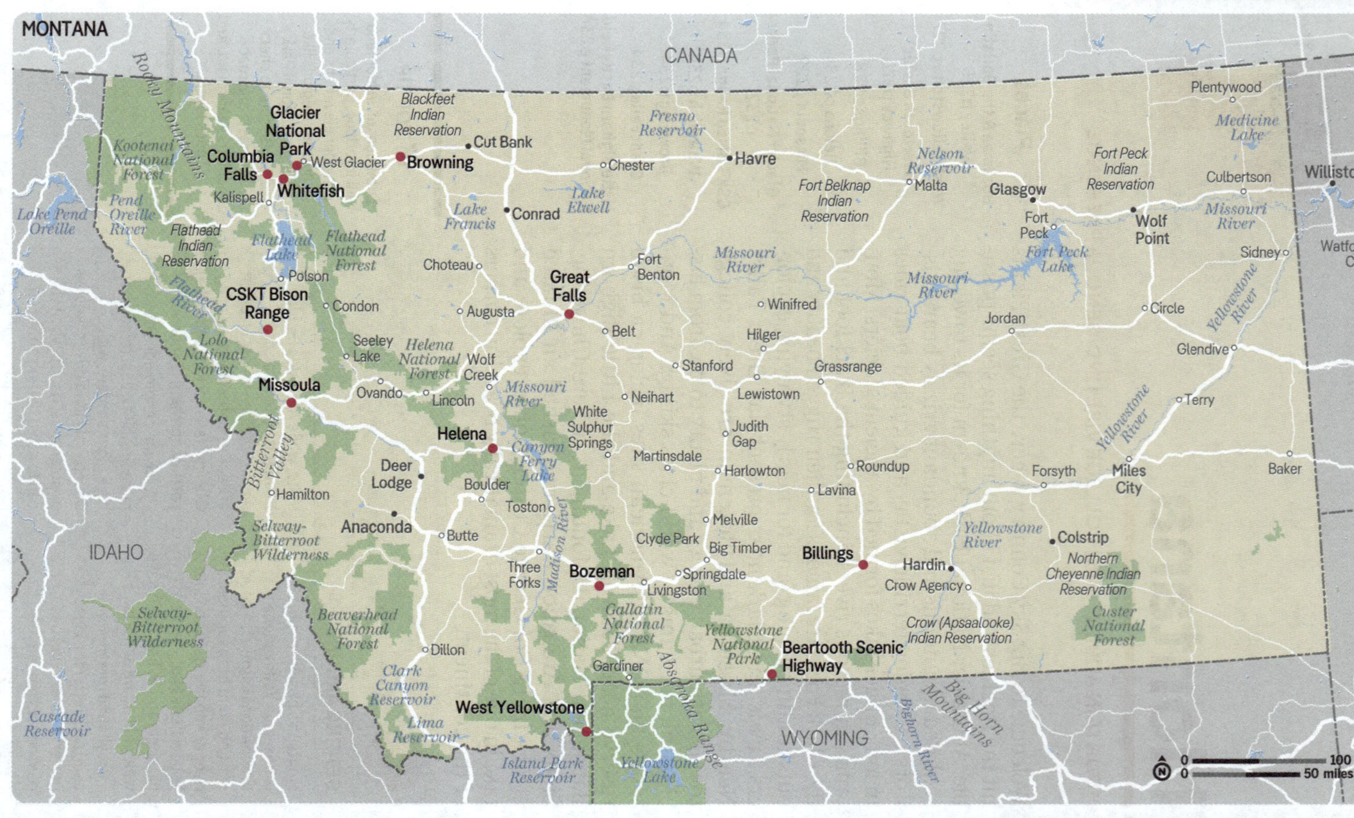
MONTANA
CANADA
IDAHO
WYOMING
Rocky Mountains
Kootenai National Forest
Lake Pend Oreille
Pend Oreille River
Glacier National Park
Columbia Falls
West Glacier
Whitefish
Kalispell
Blackfeet Indian Reservation
Cut Bank
Browning
Chester
Havre
Fresno Reservoir
Flathead Indian Reservation
Flathead Lake
Flathead National Forest
Polson
Lake Francis
Conrad
Lake Elwell
CSKT Bison Range
Flathead River
Condon
Choteau
Augusta
Great Falls
Fort Benton
Belt
Lolo National Forest
Seeley Lake
Helena National Forest
Wolf Creek
Missoula
Ovando
Lincoln
Missouri River
Bitterroot Valley
Hamilton
Helena
Canyon Ferry Lake
White Sulphur Springs
Neihart
Stanford
Deer Lodge
Boulder
Toston
Anaconda
Butte
Selway-Bitterroot Wilderness
Three Forks
Madison River
Bozeman
Livingston
Springdale
Clyde Park
Big Timber
Melville
Martinsdale
Harlowton
Judith Gap
Lewistown
Hilger
Winifred
Grassrange
Roundup
Lavina
Billings
Hardin
Crow Agency
Crow (Apsaalooke) Indian Reservation
Beartooth Scenic Highway
Yellowstone National Park
Gallatin National Forest
Gardiner
Absaroka Range
Beaverhead National Forest
Dillon
Clark Canyon Reservoir
Lima Reservoir
West Yellowstone
Island Park Reservoir
Yellowstone Lake
Cascade Reservoir
Big Horn Mountains
Bighorn River
Fort Belknap Indian Reservation
Nelson Reservoir
Malta
Glasgow
Fort Peck
Fort Peck Lake
Fort Peck Indian Reservation
Wolf Point
Jordan
Circle
Glendive
Terry
Yellowstone River
Forsyth
Miles City
Colstrip
Northern Cheyenne Indian Reservation
Custer National Forest
Baker
Sidney
Plentywood
Medicine Lake
Culbertson
Williston
Watford City
0 100 km
0 50 miles

Bozeman & the Gallatin Valley

Montana's dinosaurs and peoples

One of Bozeman's most engaging museums, **Museum of the Rockies** *(museumoftherockies.org; adult/child $20/13)* focuses on the paleontological history of Montana with spectacular dinosaur exhibits that include an edmontosaurus jaw with its battery of teeth and the largest T-rex skull ever discovered. Multimedia displays include life-size dinosaur recreations that remind you that many dinosaurs were in fact clad in feathers and that sharks once swam the tropical seas covering current-day Montana. Once you've had your paleontological fill, a set of galleries focus on the cultural history of the state, including its Native American tribes, while **planetarium shows** ($5 extra) offer insight into the cosmos. In summer, don't miss the outdoor **Living History Farm**, an original 1889 homestead worked by staff in period clothing who happily engage with you, offering a glimpse into Montana's pioneer days.

The artsy side of Bozeman

A bulwark of the creative scene in Bozeman, the **Emerson Center for the Arts & Culture** *(theemerson.org; free)* is a nonprofit set in a 1918 public school building. Located a couple of blocks from Main St, here you can see – and buy – works by regional artists in the galleries and boutiques lining the 1st floor; come in the evening to take in the occasional indie film, musical performance, and open-mic night in the refurbished auditorium, the **Crawford Theater** *(prices vary)*. If you're visiting in summer, be sure to join locals for a taste of Bozeman at the free, ever-popular **Lunch on the Lawn** from 11am to 1pm on Wednesdays, with food trucks, live music and a general sense of revelry.

Hitting the trails

When it comes to hiking around Bozeman, the Gallatin Valley has a treasure trove of trails covering almost 2300 miles, much of it within **Custer Gallatin National Forest** *(fs.usda.gov/custergallatin)*. One standout is **Cinnamon Mountain Trail**, a moderately challenging 8.2-mile out-and-back trail that leads to the summit (9350ft), with spectacular 360-degree views of the surrounding peaks and valleys. For a slightly less demanding option, try **Lava Lake Trail** instead. A local favorite, the 6-mile round-trip trail winds through a

A GIANT OF PALEONTOLOGY

The former curator of the Museum of the Rockies is larger than life. Paleontologist Jack Horner is widely believed to have been the model for the character Dr Alan Grant in the book *Jurassic Park* and served as technical adviser to all the films. And yes, they did extract soft tissue from a Tyrannosaurus thigh bone, right here in Bozeman. Among scientists, Horner is perhaps best known for his discoveries related to the large herbivorous maiasaura, offering clear evidence that some dinosaurs cared for their young. Horner published over 100 research papers as well as a handful of books, including three titles about dinosaurs for children.

EATING IN BOZEMAN: OUR PICKS

Bozeman Coop Downtown: Community-owned grocery store with an array of prepared foods plus organic salad bar. *9am-8pm Mon-Sat, 11am-5pm Sun* $

Jam!: Breakfast fave, serving American classics plus offbeat international dishes. Puerco verde crêpe, anyone? Call ahead to get on the waitlist. *7am-3pm* $$

Montana Ale Works: Industrial-chic warehouse with award-winning craft brews and elevated pub grub, including wagyu, elk and bison burgers. *4-9:30pm* $$

Shan: James Beard finalist serving Chinese- and Thai-inspired dishes integrating locally sourced meats; set in a cozy *izakaya*-style dining room. *4:30-9pm Tue-Sat* $$

FLY-FISHING KNOW-HOW

Most of fly-fishing's etiquette boils down to not crowding other anglers or spooking the fish they're targeting. A few pointers:

Anglers working upstream (which will be most of them) generally have the right of way.

Avoid 'high holing' (stepping into the water directly upstream of an angler) or standing on the bank opposite someone – this can spook rising fish.

If someone is at a nice spot but not fishing, they may be 'resting the hole.' Ask if they plan to keep fishing there; if so, move on. By the same token, don't monopolize good spots. And be kind to folks who are still learning, especially kids – we've all been there once.

GOODLUZ/SHUTTERSTOCK

Fly fishing, Montana

forested canyon ending at a stunning alpine lake. Both hikes are especially beautiful in summer and early fall, when wildflowers are in bloom.

A river runs through It

Ever since Robert Redford and Brad Pitt made it look sexy in the 1992 classic *A River Runs Through It*, Montana has been closely tied to fly-fishing cool. Whether you are just learning or you're a world-class trout wrangler, the wide, fast rivers are always spectacularly beautiful and filled with fish. For DIY trout fishing, the **Gallatin River**, 8 miles southwest of Bozeman along Hwy 191, has the most accessible, consistent

DRINKING IN BOZEMAN: OUR PICKS

Bozeman Taproom: Popular sports bar with breezy rooftop seating. Order a flight from over 50 craft brews on tap. *11am-midnight Sun-Thu, to 1am Fri & Sat*

Plonk Bozeman: Stylish wine bar with an impressive selection of international bottles. Pair with a charcuterie board. *3pm-midnight Sun-Thu, to 1am Fri & Sat*

Treeline Coffee Roasters: Sit under shade trees sipping the best coffee in town, or head inside to the heady aroma of the roasting room. *6:30am-4pm*

Bridger Brewing: Friendly brewery offering a rotating selection of craft beers and mountain views. If in doubt, order the Lee Metcalfe Pale Ale. *11:30am-8:30pm*

angling spots, closely followed by the beautiful **Yellowstone River**, 25 miles east of Bozeman in Paradise Valley. If you'd like a hand, **Montana Angler** *(montanaangler.com)* and **Gallatin River Guides** *(montanaflyfishing.com)* offer guided fly-fishing trips and equipment rentals.

Year-round in Big Sky Resort

Big Sky *(bigskyresort.com; adult/child lift ticket $198/119)* is big skiing. Located between Bozeman and Yellowstone National Park, it's the fourth-largest ski hill in North America, covering 5800 acres of skiable terrain across four mountains. It's known for its steepness (4350ft vertical drop) and its surplus of advanced and expert trails; take the tram to **Lone Peak** (elevation 11,167ft) for 360-degree views and expert-only runs. Or come after the snow melts, when the resort transforms into a mountain-biking and hiking hub. You'll find over 40 miles of trails, accessible by two **scenic lifts** *(per person $25, with bicycle $40)*. Expect wildflower-filled meadows and high alpine ridges crisscrossed with all-level trails. Bike rentals available on site.

All about soul turns

Located just 16 miles north of Bozeman, **Bridger Bowl** *(bridgerbowl.com; adult/child lift ticket $84/39)* is the US' leading nonprofit ski resort. The 2000-acre, community-owned gem has a fiercely loyal following and is a true skier's mountain, with serious terrain and unpretentious mood (and affordable lift tickets to boot). Known for its 'cold smoke' – light, dry powder that blankets the slopes all winter – Bridger offers surprisingly good skiing and boarding for all levels. But its claim to fame is surely the Ridge – a massive ridgeline overlooking the entire resort, accessible only by hiking, with no official trails, and plenty of unmarked cliffs and chutes. Avalanche gear and training required.

West Yellowstone

Close encounters with apex predators

Near Yellowstone's west entrance, **Grizzly & Wolf Discovery Center** *(grizzlydiscoveryctr.org; adult/child $16.50/11.50)* is worth a stop to learn more about the region's creatures. A well-regarded refuge, it's home to grizzly bears and wolves – most removed from the wild after becoming habituated to humans and becoming a 'nuisance.' Several observation programs are offered. Among the most popular is watching one or two bears serve as 'product testers' while staffers share their backstories. Typically, they grapple with a cooler or trash can filled with treats; if they can't break in after an hour, the item earns a 'bear-proof' label. In the Naturalist Cabin, you can observe wolf packs – and even stare into the golden eyes of a wolf – through oversized windows. Staff is on hand to teach about their behavior and personality traits. If you have time, check out the sections dedicated to otters, reptiles, raptors and fish. The small on-site museum also provides fascinating and sometimes surprising insights.

BACKCOUNTRY IN BRIDGER

Wendy Bianchini, Montana State University, Instructor, Department of Health Development & Community Health.

Nothing feels better than doing a handful of Ridge hikes at Bridger Bowl. In a way, it feels more like ski mountaineering: traversing or boot packing with your skis on your back, and wearing an avalanche beacon. Hiking at Bridger opens access to some pretty spectacular mountain terrain – steep chutes, big bowls and rocky cliffs. The skiing is really fun and challenging! It's not necessarily something I'd recommend to somebody who doesn't know their way around, though. If people are passing through and want to check it out, they should talk to ski patrol and locals to get information so they can ski the Ridge...and do it safely.

POWWOW ETIQUETTE

Listen to the master of ceremonies for announcements related to protocol such as when to sit or stand, and when to refrain from taking photos or recording an event.

Do not call a Native person's outfit a 'costume'. Traditional clothing and adornments are called 'regalia,' and are often beloved family heirlooms and sources of deep pride.

Avoid touching anyone's clothing or headdress. If you're tempted, ask permission. (Prepare to be denied.)

Ask before taking photos. While it's typically acceptable to take photos of intertribal competitions, ask before taking candid photos of individuals.

Do not record drumming. Ask permission from the Head Singer if you want to record a song.

Beartooth Scenic Highway

Driving the Beartooth Scenic Hwy

Take a drive along the breathtaking **Beartooth Scenic Hwy**, one of the most beautiful routes in the country and a destination in its own right. Connecting the town of Red Lodge to Yellowstone's northeast entrance, the 68-mile-long road passes through Wyoming along a twisting, turning alpine route back into Montana. It's known for its vistas: alpine lakes and dramatic canyons plus sky-high peaks like the jagged **Bear's Tooth**, **Index Peak** and **Pilot Peak**. You'll even see skiers at **Beartooth Basin** *(beartoothbasin.com; half/full-day lift ticket $40/50)*, a high-altitude summer ski area. The road crests at **Beartooth Pass West Summit**, where **Top of the World Resort** *(topoftheworldresort.com)* makes a good pit stop for coffee before descending past **Beartooth Butte** to **Clarks Fork Trailhead**, a popular hiking area. The road is open May to October, taking around three hours to complete.

Billings

Crow Fair

Started as a harvest festival in 1904, **Crow Fair** *(crow-nsn.gov/crow-fair.html)* is a spectacular weeklong gathering of Plains tribes held every August in the town of Crow Agency. One of the largest Native American gatherings in the country, it draws tens of thousands to the banks of the Little Bighorn River, where attendees set up hundreds of tipis. Each day begins with a parade of families filing past tipis on horseback, in traditional regalia; afternoons bring powwows with competitive dancers in beaded dress and feathers, all-Native rodeos and death-defying relay races. Plenty of food vendors make it easy to fill up on classic Native treats (fry bread with powdered sugar, anyone?), while nearby artisans showcase handcrafted jewelry and goods. At heart a social event, the Crow Fair is a powerful expression of community, where all are welcome. Consider staying overnight in your own tipi, falling asleep to the sound of drums; **rentals available on site** *(ndnbattletours@gmail.com)*.

Helena

A walk through historic Helena

Helena's historic heart beats along **Last Chance Gulch**, a winding pedestrian mall that traces the path of a gold strike made by four down-and-out prospectors in 1864. That lucky

EATING IN HELENA: OUR PICKS

No Sweat Café: Wildly popular brunch spot with vegan and gluten-free options. Lunch menu integrates global flavors. *7am-2pm Tue-Fri, from 8am Sat & Sun* $

Bad Betty's BBQ: Simple spot serving award-winning Southern-style BBQ, from brisket and ribs to pulled pork. *11am-3pm & 4-8pm Wed-Fri, 11am-3pm Tue & Sat* $

Windbag Saloon & Grill: One-time brothel turned pub, serving hearty burgers and sandwiches. Twice-daily happy hour. *11am-midnight Mon-Fri, from 10am Sat & Sun* $$

Ristorante Bella Roma: Upscale restaurant with authentic Italian flavors, homemade pastas and local ingredients. Prix-fix menu and wine pairings. *5-10pm Tue-Sun* $$$

Pilot and Index Peaks

find – millions in placer gold – sparked a boom that transformed the gulch into Montana's lovely state capitol. Spend a morning on the mall strolling past the grand 19th-century buildings, many of them home to boutiques and cafes; interpretive signs and public art along the way bring the town's Wild West past to life. For more historic spots, head to nearby **Reeder's Alley**, Helena's oldest surviving neighborhood. Built in the 1870s, the narrow brick road is lined with log cabins and early city dwellings; while most are filled with small businesses, informational placards offer insight into the structures and people who first inhabited them. Want more info? Take a **guided walking tour** of Helena with **The Foundation for Montana History** *(mthistory.org; adult/child from $10/8)*.

BRENNAN'S WAVE

Brennan's Wave is an artificial white-water feature on the Clark Fork River in downtown Missoula. On warm summer nights, crowds gather at Caras Park to watch surfers and kayakers shred and paddle in the surf, a treat in this mountain town. But the wave is more than just a playground. It's a living memorial to Brennan Guth, a Missoulian and world-class kayaker, who died while kayaking Chile's Río Palguín in 2001. It was his vision to transform the river's irrigation diversion into a training ground for white-water athletes. After his death, the community rallied around that vision, raising over $300,000 to transform the river. In 2006, Brennan's Wave debuted; it later hosted the 2010 US Freestyle Kayaking Championships. Brennan would be proud.

Missoula

Wander into the past

Deep in the Garnet Range forest, **Garnet Ghost Town** *(garnetghosttown.org; adult/child $10/free)* is one of Montana's best-preserved mining towns. Over two dozen buildings in a state of 'arrested decay' are scattered along the mountainside – weathered cabins, saloons, general stores, a hotel from the

EATING IN MISSOULA: OUR PICKS

Bernice's Bakery: Beloved from-scratch bakery-cafe with delicious pastries and an ever-changing menu of sandwiches, soups and salads. *6am-6pm Mon-Sat, 8am-4pm Sun* $

Dinosaur Café: No-frills place with extraordinary Cajun food from jambalaya to po' boys. Located in Charley's Bar, a Missoula institution. *11am-9pm Mon-Fri, from noon Sat* $

Iron Horse Bar & Grill: Casual restaurant with an extensive international menu, from ahi tuna to BBQ. Set in a repurposed train depot. *11am-10pm* $$

Boxcar Bistro: Elegant European-style bistro – evocative of the dining cars of yesteryear – with a French-inspired menu. Perfect for a date night. *4-9pm Tue-Sat* $$$

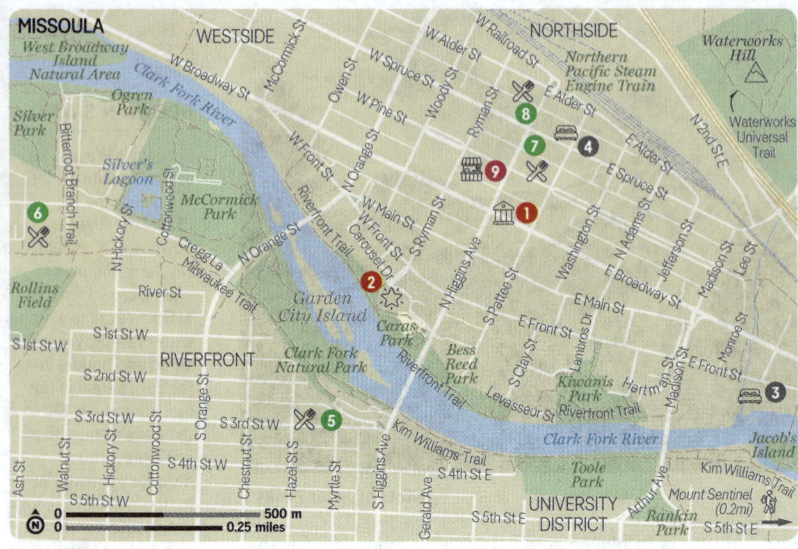

SIGHTS
1 Missoula Art Museum

ACTIVITIES
2 A Carousel for Missoula

SLEEPING
3 Goldsmith's Riverfront Inn
4 Shady Spruce Hostel

EATING
5 Bernice's Bakery
6 Boxcar Bistro
7 Dinosaur Café
8 Iron Horse Bar & Grill

SHOPPING
9 Missoula People's Market

late 1800s – transporting you to gold-rush days, when mining towns were built overnight and vanished almost as quickly. It's an evocative place, where you can wander around buildings that once bustled with over 1000 people, imagining what life was once like here. Informational placards lend more info and friendly forest rangers are often present and happy to answer questions. Several hiking and biking trails make it easy to spend the day here. Or stay overnight; in winter, two **primitive cabins** with no electricity or running water are available by lottery *(per night $50)*. The rub? From January to April, the site is only accessible by snowmobile or skis/snowshoe. Located about 40 miles east of Missoula, at the end of a 6-mile-long dirt road.

Take in regional art

All hail a city that encourages free-thinking art and then displays it free of charge! Set in a renovated public library, the sleek **Missoula Art Museum** *(artsmissoula.org; free)* is a small but powerful space, showcasing works by regional and local artists, with a focus on Native American works. Head to the top floor for special exhibits.

All about smokejumpers

When you're in town, don't miss the fascinating **Missoula Smokejumper Visitor Center** *(fs.usda.gov; by donation)*. Part of an active base for the heroic men and women who parachute into forests to combat wildfires, it's the starting point for an hour-long **tour** by a smokejumper, who guides you through the facilities to see where the crew lives and trains, including areas where they painstakingly sew, inspect and test their own parachuting gear. It's a humbling tour, offering a rare glimpse into the dangerous profession. Afterwards, check out the visitor center exhibits, which explore

KIRK FISHER/SHUTTERSTOCK

A Carousel for Missoula

the evolving nature of wildfire management in the face of warming climates. For deeper insight into the courage and cost of the job, pick up Norman Maclean's *Young Men and Fire* (1992), a tribute to Montana's Mann Gulch fire that took the lives of 12 smokejumpers.

Enjoy an artisanal fair

The highlight of summertime in Missoula is **Missoula People's Market** *(missoulapeoplesmarket.org; free)*, an artisanal fair held every Saturday morning from May through September. A popular community affair, the market transforms West Pine Street into a vibrant pedestrian zone filled with more than 80 stalls showcasing handmade goods by local artisans. Live music fills the air as you peruse stands filled with everything from pottery, jewelry and photography to leatherwork, wood carvings and organic skincare products. Food vendors make it that much easier to make a day of it.

Kiddie fun

If you're traveling with little ones, take a spin on **A Carousel for Missoula** *(carouselformissoula.com; adult/child $2/1)*, a beloved carousel with 40 hand-carved and individually painted horses and chariots. It was created by an army of volunteer artists who rallied around a local cabinet-maker's dream to restore a bit of whimsy to downtown. Afterwards, pop into **Dragon Hallow**, a fantastical playground next door, the product of another volunteer town effort.

Take on Mt Sentinel

The steep **Mt Sentinel** switchback trail (1.5-mile round trip) behind the University of Montana football stadium leads up to a concrete whitewashed 'M' (visible for miles around) on the 5158ft Mt Sentinel. Tackle it on a warm summer evening for glistening views of the city and its spectacular environs, including the Clark Fork River and mountains beyond. The trailhead is at Phyllis Washington Park on the eastern edge of campus.

FORT MISSOULA: ALIEN DETENTION CENTER

During WWII, Fort Missoula, originally an army post, was repurposed into an Alien Detention Center where around 1000 Japanese men were held. These lawful US residents, community leaders and successful professionals in West Coast towns were deemed 'enemy aliens' for no other reason than their Japanese heritage. Detainees lived in barracks behind barbed wire and under guard, undergoing hearings to determine whether they posed a threat to the US. None were charged with any crime. Eventually, they were transferred to Japanese internment camps like Amache (p208), Heart Mountain (p216) and Minidoka (p245). They remained unlawfully detained for the rest of the war, casualties of wartime hysteria and racial discrimination.

VACLAV SEBEK/SHUTTERSTOCK

TOP EXPERIENCE

Glacier National Park

Few places on earth are as magnificent and pristine as Glacier National Park. Protected in 1910, the glacially carved remnants of an ancient thrust fault left behind a brilliant landscape of snowcapped pinnacles, plunging waterfalls and glassy turquoise lakes. Its dense forests are home to an abundance of bears, while smart park management has kept the place accessible and authentically wild.

DON'T MISS

- Driving Going-to-the-Sun Rd
- Hiking Grinnell Glacier
- Wildlife-watching
- Paddling on Swiftcurrent Lake
- Blackfeet Nation exhibits and programming

Drive Going-to-the-Sun Road

Cutting through the center of Glacier National Park, **Going-to-the-Sun Rd** connects **West Glacier** with **St Mary** in the east. This epic rollercoaster ride over the Continental Divide, an engineering marvel chiseled out of raw mountainside, is considered one of the most spectacular roads in the US. Spanning 50 miles, it climbs up to Logan Pass (6646ft) and is bursting with soaring vistas, hiking opportunities, glacial melt spewing down the rocks and rushing waterfalls. Don't miss pullouts like **Bird Woman Falls Overlook**, with views

PRACTICALITIES

● nps.gov/glac ● summer/winter per vehicle $35/25 ● 24hr

of the highest waterfall (492ft) on the drive; and **Jackson Glacier Overlook**, to spy one of the remaining 25 glaciers in the park on the side of Mt Jackson (10,052ft). The entire road is usually open from late June to early October.

Hike Hidden Gems

Glacier is a hiker's paradise, with over 700 miles of trails. Near **Logan Pass**, the **Highline Trail** (11.6-mile round trip) hugs cliffs and wildflower meadows with sweeping mountain views, while the **Hidden Lake Overlook** (3-mile round trip) offers a shorter, family-friendly option. In **Many Glacier**, don't miss the hike to **Grinnell Glacier** (10.6-mile round trip), one of the most dramatic treks in the park, offering up-close views of a rapidly receding glacier (or shorten the hike to 7.6 miles by taking a boat shuttle across Swiftcurrent Lake). Other must-hikes include **Avalanche Lake** (4-mile round trip) via the **Trail of the Cedars** (0.9-mile round trip), an accessible raised-boardwalk loop through a cedar forest, and the moderate loop around **Iceberg Lake** (9.6-mile round trip), where floating ice dots a turquoise basin well into summer.

Wildlife Watching

Glacier is home to an incredible variety of wildlife. Head out early or stay out late for the best chances to see animals in motion. Search the rugged **Rising Wolf Mountain** slopes for sure-footed creatures like bighorn sheep and mountain goats. Meanwhile, moose are often seen at sunset along the road into **Two Medicine**. Look out for bear tracks in prairie environments and flower fields, plus **Dawson Pass** and **Scenic Point Trail**. Be sure to carry bear spray and follow park guidelines for a safe experience.

Experience the Water

Six **historic boats** *(glacierparkboats.com; adult/child $27/13.50)* – some dating back to the 1920s – ply four of Glacier's attractive mountain lakes, and some of them combine the float with a short **guided hike** led by interpretive, often witty, guides. For more solitude (and a bit of a workout), you also can rent **rowboats** ($32.50 per hour), **kayaks** ($32.50 per hour) and **paddleboards** ($24.20 per hour) at Lake McDonald, Swiftcurrent Lake and Two Medicine Lake.

Take a Century-Old Sightseeing Tour

Glacier's vintage buses, known as the 'Rubies of the Rockies,' are emblems of the park. Introduced in 1914, the elongated Model 706s have open tops for unobstructed views, but can be covered when it rains. A dozen **Red Bus Tours** *(glacier nationalparklodges.com; adult/child from $60/30)* whizz visitors around the park, hitting the big attractions and views – they range from a few hours to nine hours and run from mid-May to late September. Tours depart from several locations on both sides of the park.

BEAR ENCOUNTERS

Running Bad idea. Bears are faster, and running may elicit an attack from a non-aggressive bear.

Bear spray If a bear charges, spray a one- to two-second blast when the bear is 30ft away.

If the bear makes contact Drop, lie flat on your stomach and cover your neck with your hands. Don't move until the bear has left.

TOP TIPS

- Visit St Mary Visitor Center to learn about the Blackfeet Nation and its deep connections to the park land, from carefully curated exhibits and ranger talks to cultural programs.
- Park rangers will give tutorials on how to properly use bear spray – be sure to ask.
- Snow can fall year-round in the park; check weather conditions before heading out.
- A free hop-on, hop-off shuttle runs along Going-to-the-Sun Rd between Apgar and St Mary visitor centers. Buses leave every 15 to 30 minutes from Apgar (every 30 to 45 minutes from St Mary). The last trips down from Logan Pass leave at 7pm.

WARRIORS OF THE FOREST

The 3000-sq-mile **Blackfeet Indian Reservation** sits east of Glacier National Park and borders Canada, spanning an area twice the size of the park. It's home to 9500 tribal members, including those from the Northern Piegan (Blackfeet), Southern Piegan and Blood tribes, who lived in the Alberta area north of the border in the 1700s. The Blackfeet were best known for their horse and gun skills and had a reputation as exceptionally formidable warriors.

This spirit continues today, exemplified by the Chief Mountain Hotshots, an elite Blackfeet firefighting crew based in Browning. Known as the 'Warriors of the Forest,' this crew works in large-scale wildland firefighting, typically working 15 to 20 large fires and traveling between 10,000 and 20,000 miles each year.

CSKT Bison Range

Meet a living legacy

Home to over 350 bison, the **CSKT Bison Range** *(bisonrange.org; per vehicle $20)* spans 18,500 acres of grasslands, forests and rolling hills on the Flathead Indian Reservation. The bison are direct descendants of a small herd protected in the 1800s by tribal members at a time when bison were nearly extinct, making the herd biologically and culturally significant. Two dirt roads traverse the range: the 14-mile **Prairie Dr** and 19-mile **Red Sleep Mountain Dr** (open summer only), which climbs 2000ft for sweeping views of the Mission Mountains and surrounding valleys. Along the way, keep your eyes peeled for bison grazing, calves nursing and bulls wallowing in dust. You might also see elk, bighorn sheep, pronghorn and even black bears.

Whitefish

Family-friendly winter sports

Big mountain skiing at **Whitefish Mountain Resort** *(skiwhitefish.com; lift ticket adult/child $110/55)* is a laid-back affair, great for families as well as expert skiers and snowboarders willing to hike up in order to rip up off-piste double-black-diamond glades. The mountain is known for its fog, but on bluebird days, views from the summit are unsurpassed. When there's fresh powder, join locals who ditch work to make fresh tracks.

Browning

Learn all about the Plains Indians

Don't be fooled by the drab exterior of the **Museum of the Plains Indians** *(doi.gov/iacb/ourmuseums; adult/child $7/3)* on the Blackfeet Reservation – inside, you'll find rich and meticulously curated exhibits on the history and cultures of the Northern Plains tribes, including the Crow, Cree, Sioux, Cheyenne and Blackfeet. Themes range from the arts and religion to hunting and warfare; expect detailed signage alongside all manner of ceremonial regalia, art, tools, toys and more. In summer, stop into the adjacent studio to watch local Native American artists at work, giving demonstrations and selling their works, too.

Great Falls

Step into the Lewis and Clark Expedition

As you're driving through Montana, make a pit stop in Great Falls to visit **Lewis and Clark National Historic Trail Interpretive Center** *(fs.usda.gov; adult/child $8/free)*. A labyrinthine museum, it tells the fascinating story of the 2½-year, 8000-mile trek of Meriwether Lewis and William Clark, American explorers commissioned by President Jefferson to map the newly acquired lands of the Louisiana Purchase,

Whitefish Mountain Resort

establish trade with Native American tribes and find a water route to the Pacific. The exhibits deep-dive into the journey with hands-on displays, films and even a two-story diorama depicting Lewis and Clark's men hauling canoes around the waterfalls of modern-day Great Falls. Keep your eyes peeled for Seaman, a volunteer therapy dog representing Lewis' beloved Newfoundland dog, the only four-legged member of the expedition.

Marvel at C.M. Russell's Art

Another excellent stop in Great Falls is the **C.M. Russell Museum** *(cmrussell.org; adult/child $20/7)*, a sprawling complex of buildings dedicated to the art and life of Charles M Russell (1864–1926), the iconic 'cowboy artist' of the American West. Begin in the museum, home to one of the largest Russell collections in the world – over 2000 oil paintings, watercolors, sculptures and illustrated letters – which rotates through its 16 different galleries and a sculpture garden. Afterwards, head next door to Russell's log studio, built of cedar telephone poles, and his Victorian-era home, both outfitted with period furnishings and Russell's personal effects; signage provides context on his life, family and friendships.

CASINOS EVERYWHERE

As you drive through Montana, one thing stands out: casinos – over 1300 of them. Their proliferation stems from a 1972 change to the state constitution granting the legislature authority to legalize gambling on a case-by-case basis. This paved the way for small-scale gaming across the state.

Most 'casinos' are tucked into in the corners of bars, restaurants, bowling alleys or gas stations. You won't find roulette wheels or blackjack dealers – just rows of video gambling machines offering poker, keno and line games. These machines are common in rural towns and larger cities, providing convenient entertainment for passersby. For business owners, they're a financial lifeline: a single machine can generate $28,000 annually.

TOP EXPERIENCE

Little Bighorn Battlefield National Monument

The Little Bighorn Battlefield National Monument, on the Crow (Apsáalooke) Reservation, 65 miles southeast of Billings, marks General George Custer's famous 'last stand.' Here, in 1876, Lakota Sioux and Cheyenne warriors led by Crazy Horse and Sitting Bull won a major victory – briefly boosting Native American resistance before US forces crushed it, forcing most Plains tribes onto reservations within five years.

TOP TIPS

- Battlefield Tour Rd closes 30 to 45 minutes before the official park closure; arrive early enough to assure you have time to drive through the site.
- In summer, visit in the early morning for cooler temperatures and fewer people.

PRACTICALITIES

- nps.gov/libi
- per vehicle $25
- 8am-6pm Fri-Sun Jun-Sep, to 4pm Oct-May

Self-Guided Tour

Battlefield Tour Rd runs through the site, a 4.5-mile road with frequent turnouts featuring free cellphone audio guides and informative panels that bring the conflict alive. Across the fields and valleys, and within sight of the road, white tombstones indicate where US soldiers are buried, while red granite markers symbolize where Native American warriors died. Crowning the battlefield is **Last Stand Hill**, where Custer fell, and nearby **Indian Memorial** is a fascinating tribute to the Sioux and Cheyenne stories.

Apsáalooke Tours

Learn more about the battle with **Apsáalooke Tours** *(adult/child $17/10)*. Led by Crow guides, these excellent one-hour bus tours give deeper insight into the conflict from a Plains tribespeople's perspective, from precognitive dreams to war traditions. Tours run every 1½ hours from 9am to 3pm Memorial Day to Labor Day, leaving from the parking lot.

Visitor Center

The visitor center offers deeper insight on the 1876 battle with well-conceived exhibits, a 20-minute film and artifacts including Native ledger art, weapons and uniforms – plus original soldiers' grave markers made from cartridges and handwritten name slips.

Idaho

OUTDOORSY | RUGGED BEAUTY | INDEPENDENT SPIRIT

Wedged between Montana and Oregon, Idaho is one of the most underrated destinations in the western US. The oddly shaped state has nearly 4 million acres of wilderness and some of the most scenic landscapes of the lower 48. The Sawtooth National Recreation Area and remote Bitterroot Mountains offer outstanding mountain escapes, from hiking trails and alpine lakes, to thrilling mountain biking. The Salmon River, aka the River of No Return, is arguably the country's premier white-water rafting destination. On the opposite extreme, Craters of the Moon National Monument has a dramatic (and vaguely apocalyptic) char-black volcanic landscape, nearly devoid of vegetation. Meanwhile, Boise, the state capital, is an appealing place to linger, whether museum hopping or strolling along the Boise River Greenbelt, which winds through town. And of course there's Sun Valley, ski resort of the stars, home of the world's first chairlift, and still swanky after all these years.

Places

TOP TIP

Plan ahead when traveling through mountainous and rural areas: cell service can be spotty, so download offline maps. Keep your gas tank full and add cushion time between destinations - winding roads, mountain passes and unexpected gravel stretches can slow things down.

GETTING AROUND

Small but busy **Boise Airport** is well connected, with nonstop flights to several domestic cities. Interstate bus lines like **Greyhound** *(greyhound.com)* and **Salt Lake Express** *(saltlakeexpress.com)* will get you to and from Boise, and a handful of other cities, but service within the state is fairly limited. For that, a private vehicle is essential. You won't need 4WD to get to Craters of the Moon National Monument (p246) and other major destinations, especially in the summer. But many remote areas are only reachable by dirt road, and having a high-clearance vehicle will make travel there easier and safer.

IDAHO
CANADA
Colville National Forest
Kootenai National Forest
Rocky Mountains
Glacier National Park
Blackfeet Indian Reservation
Cut Bank
Two Medicine Valley
Bonners Ferry
Idaho Panhandle
Libby
Whitefish
Sandpoint
MONTANA
Kalispell
Hungry Horse Reservoir
Flathead National Forest
Rocky Mountain Front
Lake Pend Oreille
Kaniksu National Forest
Flathead Lake
Bob Marshall Wilderness
Missouri River
Post Falls
Coeur d'Alene National Forest
Flathead Indian Reservation
Polson
Great Falls
Coeur d'Alene
Thompson Falls
Wallace
Mission Valley
Seeley-Swan Valley
Cœur d'Alene Lake
Saint Joe National Forest
Saint Joe National Forest
Helena National Forest
Lewis and Clark National Forest
Lolo National Forest
Missoula
Missouri River
Lolo
Helena
Canyon Ferry Lake
IDAHO
Moscow
Bitterroot Range
Clearwater National Forest
Deerlodge National Forest
Lewiston
Clarkston
Nez Percé Indian Reservation
Rocky Mountains
Hamilton
Anaconda
Selway-Bitterroot Wilderness
Bitterroot National Forest
Beaverhead National Forest
Butte
Salmon River Scenic Byway
Gallatin National Forest
Nez Perce National Forest
Pioneer Mountains
Spanish Peaks
Wallowa Mountains
Salmon National Forest
Dillon
Madison Valley
Payette National Forest
Salmon
Yellowstone National Park
Payette Lake
West Yellowstone
Challis National Forest
McCall
Snake River
Cascade Reservoir
Selway-Bitterroot Wilderness
Bitterroot Range
Challis
Targhee National Forest
Teton Range
Deadwood Reservoir
Salmon River Scenic Byway
Weiser
Stanley
Payette
Ontario
Boise National Forest
Mud Lake
Rexburg
Driggs
Idaho City
Craters of the Moon National Monument & Reserve
Teton National Forest
Caldwell
Sawtooth National Forest
Sun Valley
Ketchum
Idaho Falls
Nampa
Boise
Caribou National Forest
Blackfoot
Fort Hall Indian Reservation
Palisades Reservoir
Mahogany Mtns
Snake River Plain
Mountain Home
Pocatello
Snake River
American Falls Reservoir
Blackfoot Reservoir
Minidoka National Historic Site
Lake Walcott
Bannock Range
Bridger National Forest
Twin Falls
Wellsville Mountains
Raft River Mountains
Preston
Riddle
Bear Lake
Jackpot
Owyhee
Humboldt National Forest
Tremonton
Cache National Forest
Pilot Range
Great Salt Lake
Brigham City
NEVADA
Newfoundland Evaporation Basin
UTAH
0 50 km
0 25 miles
Wells

Boise

Museum-hopping in the park

In the heart of downtown Boise, the leafy **Julia Davis Park** is home to several museums, making it an easy place to spend a day – and to learn about the state – rain or shine. Start at the **Idaho State Museum** *(history.idaho.gov/museum; adult/child $10/5)*, a state-of-the-art building that uses Idaho's spectacularly diverse landscapes as the backdrop to its development, both in people and place. Exhibits are well conceived, integrating multimedia elements as well as kid-friendly installations. The Origins Gallery, with its Native American voices, is especially rewarding. Next door, the **Idaho Black History Museum** *(ibhm.org; free)* is housed in the historic St Paul Baptist Church building, the first Black church in Idaho. Simple exhibits line the one-room museum, outlining Black presence and achievement in the state. Nearby, don't be fooled by the nondescript building that houses **Boise Art Museum** *(boiseartmuseum.org; adult/child $9/5)*. Inside, the permanent collection includes masterpieces by heavy hitters like Ansel Adams and Deborah Butterfield while ever-changing temporary exhibits keep the space feeling current. Be sure to use the free cellphone audio and ASL guides.

Meandering on Boise River Greenbelt

Snaking its way through town, the **Boise River Greenbelt** is a lovely 29-mile-long riverside path with bridges, benches and shaded spots connecting a series of parks, many named after prominent Boise women. It originated as a plan in the 1960s to prevent development in the Boise River's floodplain in order to provide open space in the rapidly growing city. Today, the Greenbelt is just that: a path popular for its easy access to nature, especially known for the 150 types of birds seen year-round, from blue herons to bald eagles. Take an afternoon stroll along the river or explore further on an e-bike rental from **Sunrise Electric Bikes** *(sunrise-ebikes.com; from $40)*. To make a day of it, stop in at one of Julia Davis Park's museums, watch surfers at Boise Whitewater Park (p241) or enjoy a riverfront tasting at Telaya Wine Co (p241) or **Payette Brewing Co** *(payettebrewing.com)*.

Urban water play

There is no better way to spend a sunny summer day in Boise than floating down the river. Put in at **Barber Park**, where **Boise River Raft & Tube** *(boiseriverraftandtube.com)* rents

TREEFORT MUSIC FESTIVAL

One of Idaho's most popular events, **Treefort Music Fest** *(treefortmusicfest.com)* is a five-day indie music festival held every March in downtown Boise. Over 400 bands are featured at over 60 venues, from outdoor stages in Julia Davis Park to pop-ups in cafes, breweries and even shuttle buses. The fest draws tens of thousands of people showcasing Boise's vibrant, artsy spirit. Beyond music, the festival also features themed spaces or 'forts' around town like Foodfort, Filmfort, Comedyfort, Yogafort, Hackfort and Dragfort, which offer immersive experiences like food tastings, stand-up acts, wellness sessions, drag shows and more. Be sure to buy festival passes in advance – they often sell out.

EATING IN BOISE: OUR PICKS

The Warehouse: Cavernous food hall with 13 independent kitchens serving everything from burgers to fusion Vietnamese-Basque eats. *hours vary* $

Goldy's Breakfast Bistro: No-frills breakfast fave with hearty portions, scratch pancakes and hollandaise sauce. Arrive early or expect a wait. *7am-2pm* $$

Fork: Restaurant Row go-to serving a wide range of locally sourced dishes. Don't miss the asparagus fries. *hours vary* $$$

STIL: Small-batch ice-cream shop scooping creative flavors, which are paired with local beers and wines. *hours vary* $

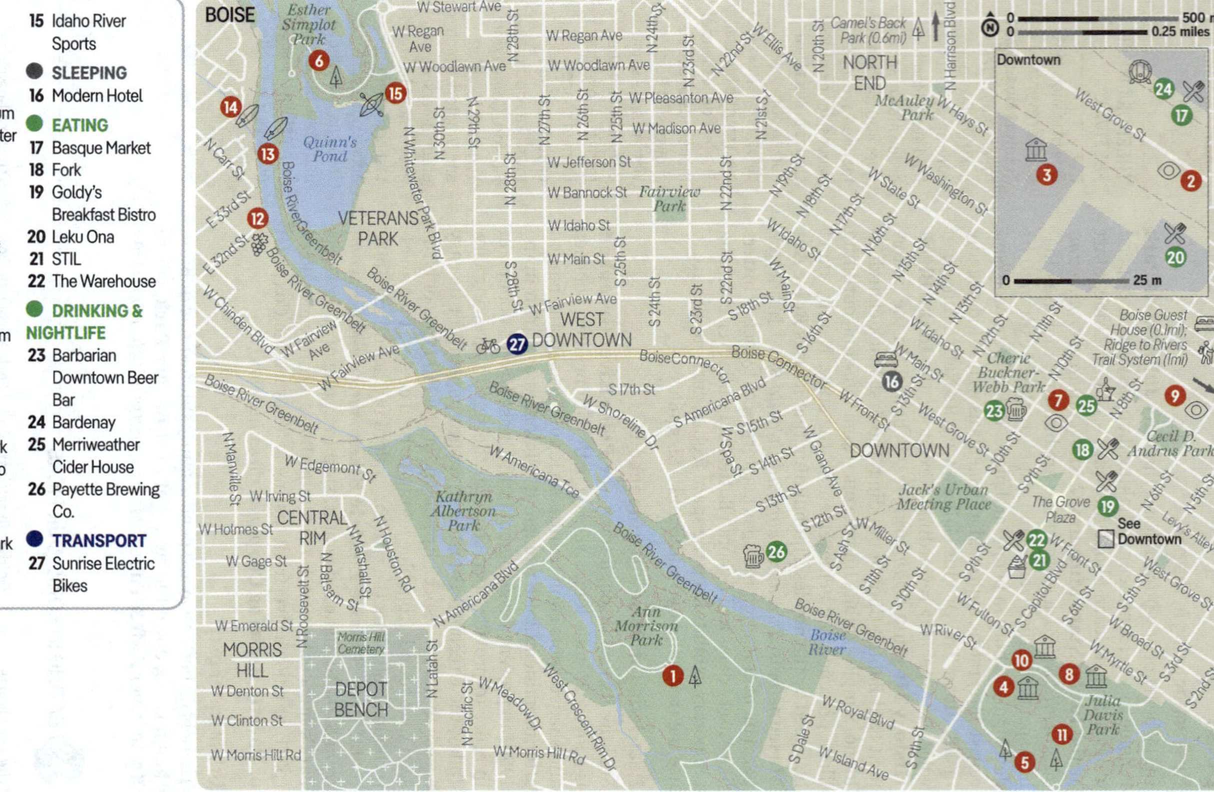

SIGHTS

1 Ann Morrison Park
2 Basque Block
3 Basque Museum & Cultural Center
4 Boise Art Museum
5 Boise River Greenbelt
6 Esther Simplot Park
7 Freak Alley
8 Idaho Black History Museum
9 Idaho State Capitol
10 Idaho State Museum
11 Julia Davis Park
12 Telaya Wine Co

ACTIVITIES

13 Boise Whitewater Park
14 Corridor
15 Idaho River Sports

SLEEPING

16 Modern Hotel

EATING

17 Basque Market
18 Fork
19 Goldy's Breakfast Bistro
20 Leku Ona
21 STIL
22 The Warehouse

DRINKING & NIGHTLIFE

23 Barbarian Downtown Beer Bar
24 Bardenay
25 Merriweather Cider House
26 Payette Brewing Co.

TRANSPORT

27 Sunrise Electric Bikes

tubes *(single/double $18/40)*, **rafts** *(four/six-person $75/85)* and **kayaks** *($50)* for self-guided 6-mile, 1½- to three-hour floats downstream to **Ann Morrison Park**. Return your watercraft there or take a shuttle bus back to Barber. Available June through August depending on river flows.

Or if you prefer a little more action, beeline to **Boise Whitewater Park**, where hydraulically controlled waves change daily, beckoning surfers, paddleboarders and kayakers year-round. There are no lifeguards, so know your limits – the rides can be rough! For rentals, steps away **Corridor** *(surfboise.com)* rents **surfboards** *(from $20)* and **wetsuits** *(from $15)* while in adjacent **Esther Simplot Park**, **Idaho River Sports** *(idahoriversports.com)* offers **kayak** and **paddleboards** *(from $25)*.

Take in street art

You don't have to wander far in Downtown Boise to stumble upon **Freak Alley** *(freakalleyboise.com)*, one of the largest open-air public art spaces in the West. Tucked between office buildings and trendy restaurants near Bannock and 9th streets, the gallery started in 2002 with just one painted door and has grown to become a two-block-long alley draped in vibrant murals created by over 200 artists. Every summer, more are added and existing works refreshed, providing a window into Boise's independent-minded artist community. Selfies encouraged.

A window into Basque Country

Boise is home to one of the largest Basque populations outside Spain, with approximately 16,000 residing here. The original émigrés arrived in the 1910s to work as shepherds when sheep outnumbered people seven to one. Few continue that work today, but many extended families have remained, and the rich elements of their distinct culture can be seen on a small stretch of Grove Street in downtown Boise known as **Basque Block** *(thebasqueblock.com)*. A leafy block, it's anchored by the **Basque Museum & Cultural Center** *(basquemuseum.eus; adult/child $7/5)*, a well-conceived space outlining the history of the Basque in Boise through detailed multimedia exhibits; the historic **Cyrus Jacobs-Uberuaga House**, a one-time Basque boardinghouse, also sits on-site. If the museum is closed, murals, sculptures, sidewalk etchings and interpretive signs provide insight into the Boise Basque community; the street itself incorporates the symbols and colors of the Basque flag. If hunger strikes, small businesses like

ARBORGLYPHS

The trees of the Wood River Valley and Boise National Forest bear a unique and picturesque record of alpine life about a century ago. Sheepherders, mostly Basque, carved pictures and messages into soft aspen and birch trunks as they drove their flocks between grazing lands.

Known today as 'arborglyphs,' the carvings date to the early and mid-1900s – the older ones are long gone as these smooth-barked trees are relatively short-lived (even more so with climate change).

Some of the pictures are remarkably detailed – boardinghouses, horses, birds, even the occasional naked woman – while poems about missing home capture the solitary lives of Idaho's early sheepherders.

DRINKING IN BOISE: OUR PICKS

Barbarian Downtown Beer Bar: Artisanal taproom known for its wide-ranging suds, from IPAs and sours to barrel-aged beers. *hours vary*

Merriweather Cider House: Family-owned cidery incorporating all manner of fruits. If in doubt, order the award-winning Plum Dandy. *hours vary*

Telaya Wine Co: Industrial-chic tasting room serving wines from Idaho and Washington. *noon-7:30pm Mon-Wed, to 8:30pm Thu-Sat, to 6:30pm Sun*

Bardenay: The country's first distillery-pub, pouring rum and whiskey made in-house. Located on Basque Block. *hours vary*

IDAHO'S SHAPE

Idaho owes its unusual shape to the warping effects of greed and politics. Originally, the Idaho Territory was massive (and roughly square), including most of today's Montana and Wyoming. When the Montana Territory was proposed in 1864, the border was to be set along the Continental Divide. But behind the scenes Idaho Supreme Court Justice Sidney Edgerton quietly convinced Congress to move the border west to the Bitterroot Mountains, lopping an extra 27,500 sq miles from Idaho, leaving just that narrow panhandle. It turns out Edgerton had been paid by Montana miners to lobby for the change. He went on to lay claim to the rich Bitterroot and Deer Lodge valleys and was named Montana's first governor.

ROBERT CROW/SHUTTERSTOCK

World Center for Birds of Prey

the **Basque Market** *(thebasquemarket.com)* and **Leku Ona** *(boisebasquefood.com)* offer traditional foods like braised chorizo or *croquetas*. In warmer months, their street-front patios are perfect for taking in the lineup of cultural events that are hosted outdoors, most integrating folk dancing and accordion beats.

Visiting the World Center for Birds of Prey

On Boise's south side, the **World Center for Birds of Prey** *(peregrinefund.org; adult/child $14/9)* is the headquarters of the Peregrine Fund, a nonprofit that has single-handedly brought back several species of raptors from the brink of extinction since the 1970s – from the peregrine falcon, the world's fastest bird, to the iconic California condor. Their method? A combination of captive breeding, habitat protection, local education and scientific research. Today, the center has several areas open to the public, including bird habitats, exhibit halls describing their work plus livestreams of on-site nesting areas. Knowledgeable staff members are ever-present and happy to talk raptors. Be sure to set aside time for a live raptor presentation – they are excellent!

Hiking Boise's Ridge to Rivers Trails

Easy access to some 210 miles of trails – hiking, mountain biking and horseback riding – is one of the best parts of visiting Boise. The **Ridge to Rivers** *(ridgetorivers.org)* trails meander across the city's foothills, eventually crossing grasslands, scrub slopes and tree-lined creeks on their way to the mountainous terrain of **Boise National Forest**. The options are almost endless: from short, leisurely strolls with skyscraper views to steep, challenging trails up mountainsides. For the most convenient access to the wilderness head to **Cottonwood Creek Trailhead** just east of the **capitol building**, or **Camel's Back Park** to the north. Check the Ridge to Rivers' website for detailed information about the trails, including interactive maps and current conditions.

Idaho Panhandle

Ride an epic trail

Take a ride through the spectacularly scenic Bitterroot Mountains on the **Route of the Hiawatha** *(ridethehiawatha.com; trail pass adult/child $20/16, shuttle adult/child $20/16)*. A 15-mile gravel trail near the Idaho-Montana border, the family-friendly route follows an old rail line, starting with the 1.66-mile St Paul Pass Tunnel - damp and completely dark - requiring a headlamp, a hoodie and some nerve. From there, the trail descends gradually through thick verdant forest, passing through eight rocky tunnels and crossing seven high trestle bridges, the highest 230-ft above the valley floor. Interpretative signs explain the route's railroad history, providing places to catch your breath and take some photos too. Shuttle buses save riders the uphill ride back. Bike rentals, including lamps, are available at the trailhead by reservation only. Book early. You also can save a few bucks by booking your trail passes and shuttle tickets online. Open late May to mid-September, weather-permitting.

Ketchum & Sun Valley

Hit historic slopes

Set in the stunning Sawtooth Mountains, **Sun Valley Resort** *(sunvalley.com; adult/child lift ticket $123/242)* began as the first purpose-built ski resort in the US, a venture by the Union Pacific Railroad to boost ridership. It opened in 1936 to much fanfare, thanks to both its luxury lodge and the world's first chairlift; the resort continued to gain cachet with the presence of celebrities like Ernest Hemingway, Ingrid Bergman and Gary Cooper, who received free trips as part of a marketing plan. It worked. Sun Valley and nearby Ketchum have been synonymous with luxury skiing and swanky Hollywood clientele ever since.

Today, join snow-sports lovers who flock here for the powder (and celebrity-spotting) on its two distinct mountains: **Dollar Mountain**, a treeless hill with mellow runs and extensive terrain parks; and **Bald Mountain** (aka Baldy), a favorite for its long cruisers, steep pitches and bowls. Both sit on opposite sides of Hwy 75; free shuttles from the resort village and Ketchum get you to either.

THE GEM STATE

Although long-running nickname, 'the Gem State,' was originally a reference to the state's rugged beauty. But miners searching for gold in Idaho's rivers would regularly stumble upon sparkling garnets, agates and jaspers in their pans. Gem mining began in earnest in the late 1800s, growing alongside Idaho's gold and silver booms, and expanding to include other stones. By 1967, over 70 different precious and semiprecious stones had been found in the state. The same year, the star garnet – a deep-red gemstone showing a four- or six-pointed star – was designated the state gem. Found only in India and Idaho, these garnets cemented Idaho's unique place in the gem world, as well as the appropriateness of its nickname.

DRINKING IN KETCHUM: OUR PICKS

TNT Taproom: Historic dynamite shed turned tap room with a rotating selection of local craft beers plus biodynamic wines. *2-9pm Mon-Thu, to 10pm Fri & Sat*

Warfield Distillery and Brewer:: Classy, laid-back gastropub with a rooftop bar and creative cocktails featuring award-winning organic spirits. *11:30am-9pm*

Grumpy's: Longtime local fave, this dive bar is known for its 32oz schooners of beer, chilled-out vibe, and beer-can wall décor. *11am-9pm*

Whiskey's on Main: Upscale sports bar with live music and dancing on weekends. *11am-10pm Sun-Tue, to midnight Wed-Thu, to 1am Sat & Sun*

THE ROUNDHOUSE

Kristine Bretall, Community Engagement Manager, Wood River Museum.

I love hiking in Sun Valley! And the smell when you're outdoors. In summertime, there's this scent of sage; it's this very lovely thing. In wintertime, it's this cold-snow, wood-smoke sort of a thing. And I love getting somewhere, anywhere, I can get up high. Like the **Roundhouse** on Bald Mountain. It's this octagonal structure built by Union Pacific Railroad engineers for skiers to stop and warm up. (It resembles one of those buildings used to turn around train engines.) It's an incredibly beautiful spot where you can really get a perspective on the landscape and see what it looks like all around.

Enjoy Sun Valley Music Festival

On summer evenings from late July to early August, join the crowd at the **Sun Valley Music Festival** *(svmusicfestival.org; free)*, the country's largest privately funded classical music event. For this free series, locals and visitors alike fill the open-air **Sun Valley Pavilion** (first-come-first-served seating) or spread blankets across its lawn to hear orchestral performances by some of the world's top musicians; expect everything from major symphonic works to modern pop. The atmosphere is informal – people come in hiking clothes, picnics are laid out and kids play nearby while the sound of the orchestra floats through mountain air. Come early for pre-concert talks.

Summer nights on ice

A summer showcase featured since 1937, **Sun Valley on Ice** *(sunvalley.com; grandstand adult/child from $104/58)* blends elite figure skating with panoramic mountain views. Held at the outdoor rink next to the **Sun Valley Lodge**, the Saturday night performances run from July through early September. Each show features Olympic and world-class skaters delivering solos, duets and ensemble pieces. Seating is up-close in the grandstands – a treat – or on the terrace, with buffet dinner included. Stay afterwards for autographs or meet-and-greets with the skaters.

Deep dive into the past

Learn all about the fascinating history of Sun Valley and Ketchum at the **Wood River Museum of History and Culture** *(comlib.org/museum; free)*. An arm of the Community Library, the engaging little museum traces the region's evolution from Shoshone and Bannock homelands to glitterati ski resort and town. Interactive exhibits include displays on sheep ranching, ski heritage and local oral histories though in true Sun Valley style, the exhibit on celebrity writer Ernest Hemingway kinda steals the show.

Stanley

Out in the Sawtooths

You'll find rivers to boat, mountains to climb, more than 300 lakes to fish, and over 700 miles of trails to hike or mountain bike in the dramatic **Sawtooth National Recreation Area** *(fs.usda.gov/sawtooth)*. It protects 1170 sq miles of public lands stretching between Ketchum and Stanley, offering almost endless opportunities for exploration and recreation.

EATING IN KETCHUM: OUR PICKS

Johnny G's Subshack: Sandwich shop serving up excellent 6in to 12in hoagies. Choose a specialty sub or build your own. *11am-4pm Mon-Fri, to 3pm Sat* $

Kneadery: Breakfast fave with a log-cabin vibe, including taxidermied creatures. Expect hearty egg dishes, French toast and freshly made pancakes. *8am-2pm* $$

Rickshaw: Cozy spot specializing in mouthwatering Southeast Asian street food. In summer, ask for a table on the leafy patio. *hours vary* $$

Fiamma: Upscale Italian with open kitchen concept highlighting its live-fire cooking. Its seasonal menu is mostly locally sourced. *4:30-10pm Wed-Sat, 10am-2pm Sun* $$$

There are several access points to the Sawtooths; among the most popular is **Galena Lodge** *(galenalodge.com)*. A community-owned spot that works in partnership with the National Forest Service, it serves as a hub to over 45 miles of well-maintained trails that crisscross the gorgeous Boulder Mountains. In the summer come for the hiking, mountain biking and wildflower-filled landscapes. In winter, it's all about cross-country skiing and snowshoeing, with groomed trails that wind through the snowy forest and alpine meadows. Friendly staffers provide trail recommendations though **snowshoeing tours** *(groups of minimum 3 people, per person $70)* and **guided mountain bike rides** *(from $175)* are a popular way to explore the area. Bike, ski and snowshoe rentals also available on-site as are hearty meals that will keep you fueled for the day.

Rafting the River of No Return

Rafting the **Middle Fork of the Salmon River** (aka River of No Return) is considered one of the greatest white-water trips in North America: a 104-mile route that winds its way through the heart of the River of No Return Wilderness Area, one of the most remote landscapes in the Lower 48. It's a clear, cold, fast-moving river – boats pass through deep canyons, alpine forest and granite gorges, and over 100 rapids, many class III and IV. Off the water, rafters can hike to waterfalls and soak in natural hot springs, spotting ancient pictographs and abandoned mining cabins along the way (not to mention bighorn sheep, bald eagles and black bear). Nights are spent camped on sandy riverbanks, eating around a campfire and sleeping under a blanket of stars.

Permits are required to ride the Middle Fork year-round; they are awarded by **lottery** *(recreation.gov)* but the competition is stiff – only about 2% of applicants receive one. Instead, most use river outfitters to access the river and to take care of all the details, from permits and shuttle service to meal prep and camp setup. Most are based in or near the sleepy towns of Salmon and Stanley, which come to life during the brief summer months. Recommended outfitters include **Solitude River Trips** *(rivertrips.com; six-day trip per person from $3250)* and **Idaho River Journeys** *(idahoriverjourneys.com; six-day trip per person from $3395)*.

Minidoka National Historic Site

Contemplate wrongful imprisonment

Located near the farming community of Jerome, **Minidoka National Historic Site** *(nps.gov/miin; free)* memorializes the incarceration of over 13,000 Japanese Americans who were forced to leave their homes by the US government to be unjustly imprisoned here during WWII. The internment camp, one of 10 in the country, was established under Executive Order 9066 as a racist reaction to the bombing of Pearl Harbor. Today, visitors can walk a 1.6-mile-long gravel **trail** past original structures like barracks, a mess hall, fire station and guard tower. Interpretive panels share personal stories

ERNEST HEMINGWAY

Ernest Hemingway's connection to Idaho ran deep, rooted in the wild, open landscapes that echoed his passion for the outdoors. He first visited Sun Valley in 1939, lured by Union Pacific's campaign to bring celebrities to the new ski resort. Captivated by the location, Hemingway returned almost yearly, hunting in the Sawtooth Mountains, fishing Silver Creek and writing prolifically. He eventually purchased a home in Ketchum, where he took his own life in 1961. Today, visitors can pay their respects at the **Hemingway Memorial** beside **Trail Creek** as well as his gravesite in **Ketchum Cemetery**. His final home, the **Hemingway House and Preserve**, is used for writer-in-residence programs, a lasting legacy.

TOP EXPERIENCE

Craters of the Moon National Monument & Reserve

This is a spectacularly vast, otherworldly place. Beginning some 15,000 years ago, a series of volcanic eruptions laid waste to the Snake River Plain, leaving a blistered land of lunar-like craters, lava-tube caves and fissures. The last eruption took place a mere 2000 years ago. The result is now a 750,000-acre national monument that's well worth a visit.

TOP TIPS

- The nearest gas station is in Cary, 25 miles away – be sure to gas up before arriving.
- From November to April, Loop Rd is closed to vehicular traffic; it's reserved for cross-country skiers and snowshoers. Plan accordingly.

PRACTICALITIES

- nps.gov/crmo
- per vehicle $20
- 24hrs

Drive Loop Road

A scenic **7-mile road** winds its way through the reserve, each turn revealing dramatic volcanic landscapes. Stop at pullouts for the views and signage, which give in-depth insight into the geology, flora, fauna and human history of the place.

Hike Volcanic Landscapes

Eight trails crisscross the reserve, offering a striking variety of features. If you're short on time, opt for the **North Crater Flow Trail** (0.3 miles), a breathtaking boardwalk suspended over young lava fields with snowcapped mountains in the distance; or take a short, steep climb to the summit of the jet-black **Inferno Cone** (0.4 miles), with 360-degree views of the reserve. For a longer hike, head to **Tree Molds Trail** (2 miles), an out-and-back trail with ancient trees preserved in hardened lava – subtle but haunting.

Enter Lava Tubes

Over **700 caves** exist in the reserve, most created by underground rivers of lava. **Indian Tunnel** is the largest and most accessible – an 800ft-long cave with a partially collapsed roof. Expect to scramble over jagged rock and uneven floors. **Cave permits** are required to enter, available for free at the visitor center.

and photographs that illuminate the harshness of life here – barbed wire, armed guards, extreme weather, minimal privacy…a memorial to Japanese-American resilience but also a reminder of the fragility of civil rights. The visitor center, open on weekends only, has further exhibits and a 30-minute film; ask about the excellent ranger led tours.

Blackfoot

Idaho Potato Museum

Driving through Blackfoot, you can't miss it – a statue of a gigantic baked potato (complete with sour cream and a pat of butter). It sits in front of the **Idaho Potato Museum** *(idahopotatomuseum.com; adult/child $7/3.50)*, a surprisingly engaging museum taking on the potato, from its global history and cultivation to its importance in Idaho. The exhibits are multilayered, including everything from films about McDonalds' fries to hands-on science experiments. There's also a bit of kitsch – animatronic displays, Mr. Potato Head stations, even the world's largest potato chip (25in by 14in). Don't miss the gift shop for quirky merch; and if you need a snack, the on-site cafe serves all manner of potato treats.

Driggs

Fly high at a hot-air balloon festival

For four days surrounding the July 4 holiday, the town of Driggs hosts the annual **Teton Valley Balloon Fest** *(tetonvalleyballoonrally.org; per vehicle $20)*, a quintessential Rocky Mountain festival, with colorful hot-air balloons soaring high above the verdant valley, the jagged, snowcapped Teton peaks in the background. It's a photographer's dream. Come at sunrise for tethered rides and the mass launch – over four dozen balloons ascending into bluebird skies. And return in the evening for the 'Rally Up and Get Down' party with live music, food-truck fare and giant balloons illuminating the Teton Valley Fairgrounds.

PERRING BRIDGE BASE JUMPERS

Standing 486ft above the Snake River, the **Perrine Bridge** in Twin Falls is the only human-made structure in the US where BASE jumping is allowed year-round without a permit. The extreme sport involves parachuting from a fixed object like a building, bridge or cliff and landing below – an especially dangerous endeavor due to low altitudes and short freefall times. At Perrine Bridge, BASE jumpers launch from platforms on the traffic-congested bridge, free-falling before deploying their parachutes to land in the canyon bottom. Nearly every day, you can see specially trained athletes from around the world preparing their parachutes in the parking lot and under nearby trees while captivated spectators line the bridge and the canyon rim.

EATING IN DRIGGS: OUR PICKS

Provisions Local Kitchen: Popular spot serving heaping plates of breakfast faves, sandwiches, salads and Mexican specialties like *choriqueso. 7am-3pm* $

Captain Ron's Smokehouse: Tiny shack serving finger-licking BBQ with all the fixin's. Eat at parking-lot picnic tables. *11am-4pm Tue-Sat* $

Citizen 33: Industrial-farmhouse style taproom serving tasty craft brews and elevated pub grub. If in doubt, get the mashed potatoes. *4-9pm* $$

Forage Bistro: High-end restaurant with casual vibe; the seasonal menu focuses on locally farmed meat and veggies. Happy-hour charcuterie boards. *noon-8pm* $$$

Places We Love to Stay

$ Budget $$ Midrange $$$ Top End

Denver p184

Hostel Fish $ Swanky hostel with plush dorms and cozy common areas. On-site bar plus neighborhood pub crawls bring a party feel.

Populus Hotel $$$ Luxurious carbon-forward hotel with nature-inspired features inside and out. Stunning city views. Rooms are a study in understated elegance.

Boulder p188

St Julien Hotel & Spa $$$ In the heart of downtown, Boulder's finest hotel is modern and refined with Flatiron views and a spa.

Rocky Mountain National Park p190

Glacier Basin Campground $ Ideally located in the Bear Lake corridor and surrounded by evergreens; 73 sites.

Murphy's Resort $$ Overlooking Lake Estes, this motor lodge has plenty of family-friendly activities. Six miles from the park.

Northern Colorado p192

Echo Park Campground (Dinosaur National Monument) $ Gorgeous, primitive Colorado-side campground at the confluence of the Yampa and Green rivers; 4WD highly recommended. First come, first served.

Vista Verde Guest Ranch (Steamboat Springs) $$$ The most luxurious of Colorado's top-end guest ranches. If you have the means, this is it.

Central Colorado p193

Crested Butte Hostel (Crested Butte) $ Luxurious hostel with restaurant-grade kitchen, crackling fireplace and a mix of dorms and private rooms.

Amigo Motor Lodge (Salida) $$ This cool motel is not only Southwestern stylish, it's got five retro trailers to sleep in.

Sebastian Hotel (Vail) $$$ Sophisticated hotel showcasing contemporary art and an impressive list of amenities, including a mountainside ski valet and luxury spa.

Mollie Aspen (Aspen) $$$ Make like Rihanna and book a room at Aspen's coolest new digs, with understated minimalist design and rooftop pool.

Western Colorado p198

Morefield Campground (Mesa Verde National Park) $ Full-service campground in a grassy canyon, 5 miles from the visitor center. General store sells basics.

South Rim Campground (Black Canyon of the Gunnison National Park) $ Large campground in a high-altitude scrub forest. Running water available summer only.

Saddlehorn Campground (Colorado National Monument) $ The park's only drive-up campground; potable water and flush toilets available. Open year-round.

Box Canyon Lodge & Hot Springs (Ouray) $$ Geothermically heated motel with modern pine-board rooms and 24/7 access to spring-fed hot tubs.

Telluride p203

Telluride Town Park Campground $ Creekside campground in the heart of Telluride, with showers, wi-fi, a pool and tennis.

Camel's Garden $$$ Ski-in, ski-out condo-hotel at the base of the gondola. Hit the 25ft hot tub at sunset.

Southeast Colorado p207

Pinyon Flats Campground (Great Sand Dunes National Park) $ Official park campground, with great location near the dune field. Reserve months ahead.

Cheyenne Mountain Resort (Colorado Springs) $$$ Overlooking Cheyenne Mountain, this woodsy resort has an air of indulgence with golf, a spa and lake activities.

Southeast Wyoming p211

Cheyenne Guest Inn (Cheyenne) $ Older, well-maintained inn with spick-and-span rooms and a tiny indoor pool. Continental breakfast included.

Mad Carpenter Inn (Laramie) $ Charming guesthouse with cozy, wood-trimmed rooms, a fully equipped cottage and a serious game room. Hot breakfast included.

Lander (Fort Washakie) p213

Mill House $$ Boutique hotel set in a beautifully renovated flour mill in downtown Lander; suites are modern with artful touches.

Northern Wyoming p215

The Cody (Cody) $$ New Western chic with green credentials; there's an indoor pool and hot tub, plus free breakfast.

Devil's Tower Lodge (Devil's Tower HS) $$ Unparalleled views and warm hospitality make this an excellent base, especially for climbers. Full breakfast included.

Yellowstone National Park p218

Mammoth Campground $ Yellowstone's only campground open year-round has 85 sites set amid scattered junipers and Douglas firs.

Old Faithful Inn $$$ Variety of rooms in a historic log-walled inn with a frenetic lobby that quietens by night.

Grand Teton National Park & Around p222

Lizard Creek Campground (Grand Teton NP) $ Small campground with pleasantly shaded sites set amid spruce-and-fir forest on the shores of Jackson Lake.

The Hostel (Jackson Hole) $$ Skiers' favorite for budget accommodations, including four-bed rooms, plus spacious lounge with pool table.

Jackson Lake Lodge (Grand Teton NP) $$$ Attractive hotel-style rooms and cottages, some with dramatic mountain views.

Bozeman & the Gallatin Valley p225

Howlers Inn (Bozeman) $$ Cozy log cabin-style B&B on a sanctuary for rescued captive-born wolves; profits support the cause.

RSVP Motel (Bozeman) $$$ Stylish upscale motel with colorful rooms and a great little on-site cafe and restaurant.

Rainbow Ranch Lodge (Big Sky) $$$ Rustic-chic lodge with stylish rooms, most with stone fireplaces and balconies. Located 5 miles from Big Sky turnoff.

Helena p228

Lamplighter Cabins & Suites $$ Cute, uniquely decorated cabins and contemporary suites, some with kitchenettes. Located steps from downtown.

Missoula p229

Shady Spruce Hostel $ Centrally located hostel in a renovated Victorian home; private rooms and dorms are clean, bright and spacious. Modern guest kitchen too.

Goldsmith's Riverfront Inn $$ Charming riverfront home converted into six cheery suites and fully equipped apartments.

Glacier National Park p232

Bowman Lake Campground $ Spacious sites in forested grounds, and beautiful Bowman Lake is only steps away.

Many Glacier Hotel $$$ A massive, Swiss-chalet-inspired lodge in a wondrous lakefront setting in the park.

Great Falls p234

Hotel Arvon $$ Boutique hotel set in a beautifully renovated historic building. Rooms are modern and spacious. Breakfast and parking included.

Boise p239

Modern Hotel $ Urban-chic motel with midcentury-modern rooms. A trendy on-site bar means creative cocktails by the firepit.

Boise Guest House $$ Historic home beautifully transformed into six tasteful suites with kitchenettes. There's a verdant backyard plus cruiser bikes.

Ketchum p243

Best Western Tyrolean Lodge $$ Chalet-themed motel with dated but comfortable rooms. Breakfast buffet included too. The best budget hotel in town.

Limelight Hotel $$$ Trendy downtown hotel with luxe rooms, many with mountain views. Outdoor pool, full breakfast and complimentary airport shuttle too.

Craters of the Moon National Park p246

Lava Flow Campground $ Small campsite set on volcanic landscape. Water and flush toilets available May to November only. First come, first served.

Driggs p247

Teton Valley Cabins $-$$ Pleasant log cabins on a forested lot, some with kitchenettes. In evenings, roast marshmallows around the communal fire pit.

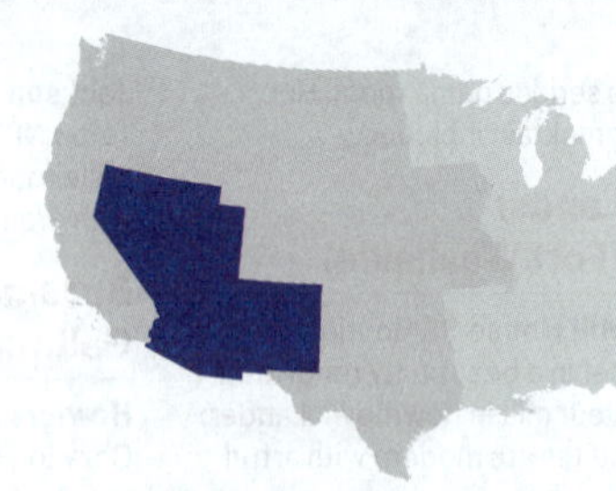

Curated by
Anthony Ham

Southwest USA

ONE OF AMERICA'S GRAND EPICS

Soulful deserts and weirdly wonderful mountains. Frenetic cities and ancient stories. Las Vegas and the Grand Canyon. Welcome to America's fabulous west.

The Southwest could only happen in America. Take an astonishing landscape, the kind of place that is both cinematic in scope and part of a deeply American tradition of starring on the silver screen. Overlay that with a fascinating roll-call of civilizations, from the Ancestral Puebloans and Native American cultures like the Hopi, Navajo and Apache to the gunslingers and bandits (like Butch Cassidy or Billy the Kid) of the Wild West. And then, carrying all of this with you as you go – perhaps along Route 66 – rush headlong into the future toward places like Las Vegas or the space race of Las Cruces. Then let your mind consider the supernatural at Roswell and Area 51. And as you contemplate this remarkable collage that is America writ large, tuck into a meal laced with the green chiles of New Mexico in all their fiery manifestations.

But it's the backdrop to all of this – the landscapes that bring such gravitas to this corner of the country – that is the real star of the show. Yes, the Grand Canyon has no rivals. But the Mojave and Sonoran Deserts, the deep canyons and hallucinatory rock formations of Utah's national parks, or Monument Valley and the Petrified Forest, also combine to make a compelling case for calling the Southwest America's mostly wildly beautiful corner.

LHBLLC/SHUTTERSTOCK

THE MAIN AREAS

LAS VEGAS
Nevada's brightly lit capital of glitz. p256

NEVADA
Desert landscapes and cities. p262

PHOENIX
Arizona's cultured gateway and capital. p268

GRAND CANYON NATIONAL PARK
A true wonder of the natural world. p272

For places to stay in Southwest USA, see p338

WIRESTOCK CREATORS/SHUTTERSTOCK

Skywalk (p279), Grand Canyon West

Find Your Way

Deserts, mountains and a very far horizon make for miraculous, big-sky road-making – no wonder Route 66 sends everyone a little crazy. Getting around is easy but requires careful map-plotting. Distances are huge. Plan accordingly.

Utah, p302
Explore Mormon culture in Salt Lake City, then head for five of America's best national parks: Arches, Canyonlands, Capitol Reef, Bryce Canyon and Zion.

Nevada, p262
Reno, the Mojave Desert, Hoover Dam, Area 51... It's amazing how much Nevada packs into an area that's almost entirely (and beautifully) desert.

Las Vegas, p256
The Strip (Las Vegas Blvd) is among the most famous streets in the world. Fremont St and the Arts District are just as exciting.

Phoenix, p268
Arizona's capital, Phoenix is the epicenter of culture and cuisine in the Sonoran Desert, and luxurious resorts abound. Alfresco dining and sunsets are highlights.

Grand Canyon National Park, p272
This geologic wonder is worth the hype, with billion-year-old rocks, luminous sunsets and hiking trails that immerse you in its vast beauty.

TRAIN & BUS

Amtrak (trains) and Greyhound (buses) cross the Southwest. They're more useful for reaching the Southwest (or crossing it from one side to the other) than they are for traveling within the region.

CAR

Having your own vehicle means there are few places you can't go; consider renting a 4WD for following enticing dirt side roads. Most roads are in excellent condition, but plan for long stretches of tarmac between gas stations.

PLANE

To make the most of your time, flying a couple of legs is worth considering. Phoenix, Las Vegas, Reno, Salt Lake City, Santa Fe and Albuquerque receive flights from across the US, but you can also fly between them and other towns of the Southwest.

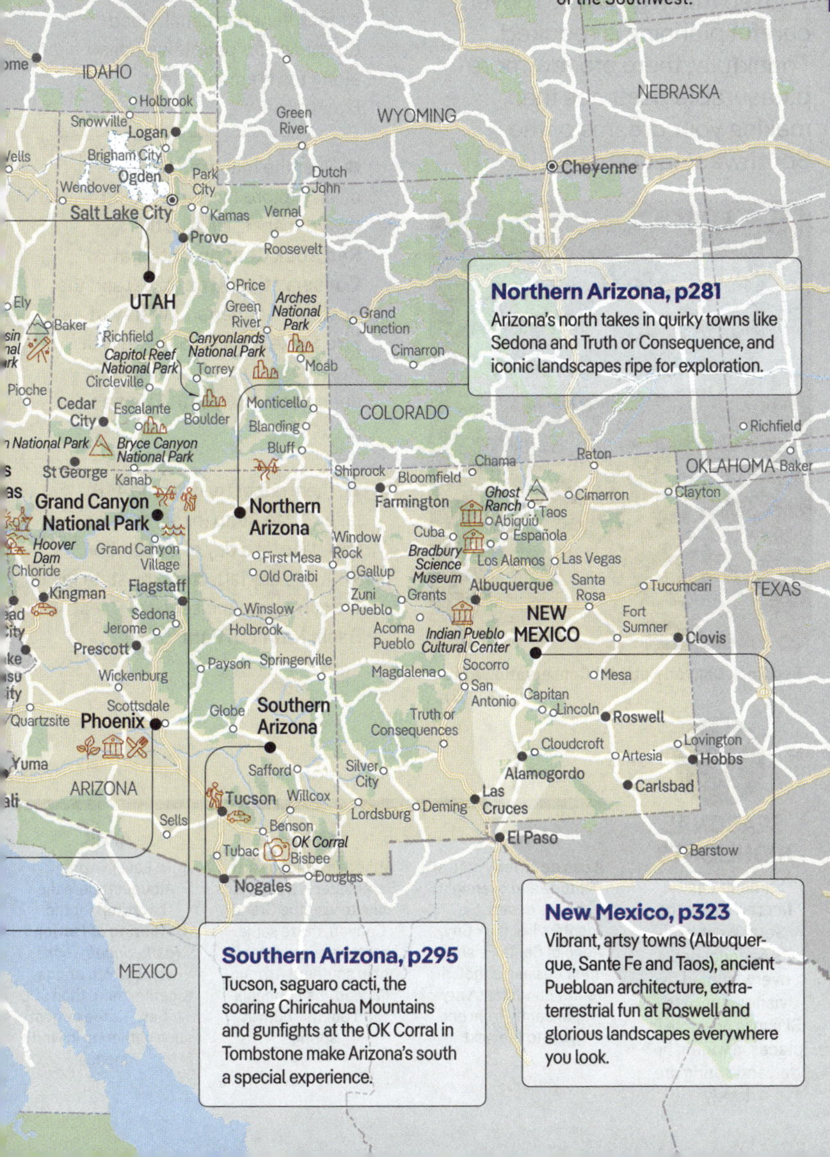

Northern Arizona, p281

Arizona's north takes in quirky towns like Sedona and Truth or Consequence, and iconic landscapes ripe for exploration.

Southern Arizona, p295

Tucson, saguaro cacti, the soaring Chiricahua Mountains and gunfights at the OK Corral in Tombstone make Arizona's south a special experience.

New Mexico, p323

Vibrant, artsy towns (Albuquerque, Sante Fe and Taos), ancient Puebloan architecture, extra-terrestrial fun at Roswell and glorious landscapes everywhere you look.

Plan Your Time

With so much ground to cover, careful planning is required. Thankfully, there are few more pleasurable pastimes than making your dreams of the Southwest take shape.

CAYCE CLIFFORD FOR LONELY PLANET

Red Rock Canyon National Conservation Area (p262)

Seven Nevada Days

- Begin two days in **Las Vegas** (p256) with a wander around the Strip, taking note of the Egyptian pyramid, summiting the Eiffel Tower and riding a gondola in a mock Venetian canal. Head downtown for people-watching along the Fremont Street Experience.

- Over the following two days, explore the surrounding desertscapes, such as the **Red Rock Canyon National Conservation Area** (p262) and the geologic wonderland **Valley of Fire State Park** (p263), and visit the **Hoover Dam** (p263) and the eerie ghost town of **St Thomas** (p264).

- Then, rather than driving 440 miles, fly to **Reno** (p264) and use it as a base for a day of exploration. With one day left, cross the state for the stirring magnificence of **Great Basin National Park** (p267).

SEASONAL HIGHLIGHTS

Summer can be fiercely hot in the Southwest, and its national parks overwhelmed by visitor numbers. Skiing is possible in places in winter, but fall and spring are lovely.

JANUARY

It can be bitterly cold at altitude and overnight in the desert. Ski centers like Park City, Reno or Santa Fe are at their busiest, although snow conditions vary significantly from one year to the next.

MARCH

Although June to early September is a popular time to visit the Grand Canyon, those same months are unbearably hot in southern Arizona. Instead, visit Phoenix and points south in spring.

APRIL

Late in April, Albuquerque is the backdrop for the **Gathering of Nations** *(gatheringofnations.com)*, which brings together more than 500 tribes; it's the largest such gathering in North America.

Ten Arizona Days

- Head to the South Rim of the **Grand Canyon** (p276) for two days of exploring this utterly magnificent natural wonder, with at least another day around the low-key **Grand Canyon North Rim** (p278). Concentrate on following a small number of trails and seeing a handful of overlooks well, rather than racing around and trying to see everything. Allow an extra couple of days for Grand Canyon hikes.

- Loop around the crimson buttes of **Monument Valley** (p289), then start your **Route 66** (p293) retro drive in Kingman. Sip microbrews in **Flagstaff** (p287) and follow gorgeous **Oak Creek Canyon** (p285) to **Sedona** (p281) where you can try and locate your chakra. Swing through **Jerome** (p286) and **Prescott** (p286) for art and history.

Two Weeks in Utah & New Mexico

- Begin with a day spent exploring the Mormon story in multi-dimensional **Salt Lake City** (p305), followed by a couple of days each in two of Utah's best national parks where you're spoiled for choice: **Zion** (p320), **Bryce Canyon** (p318), **Arches** (p314), **Canyonlands** or **Capitol Reef** (p313). If you have the time, visit them all.

- Fly from Salt Lake City to **Albuquerque** (p325), which is worth a couple of days for its museums and opportunities to feast on feisty New Mexican dishes. **Taos** (p330) is another fun place to catch the magic of New Mexico.

- Reserve your final day for **White Sands National Park** (p337) or the little green men of **Roswell** (p334).

JUNE

Warmer temperatures in northern New Mexico are perfect for wildflower-laden hikes and rafting around Taos. Further afield, summer has yet to set the Southwest fully ablaze and summer crowds have yet to arrive en masse.

JULY

July 24 is **Pioneer Day** in Utah, a state holiday remembering the arrival of the first Mormon pioneers in 1847. Reenactors march through Salt Lake City, while non-Mormons prefer to mark it as 'Pie and Beer Day.'

OCTOBER

Neon aspen leaves, mild temperatures and so many festivals, including Albuquerque's **International Balloon Fiesta**. Apart from anything else, it's a beautiful time to be anywhere in the Southwest.

DECEMBER

Don your cowboy hat and spurs as **National Finals Rodeo** returns Las Vegas to its Western roots. On New Year's Eve, the Strip becomes a huge party as thousands turn out for headliner bands and fireworks.

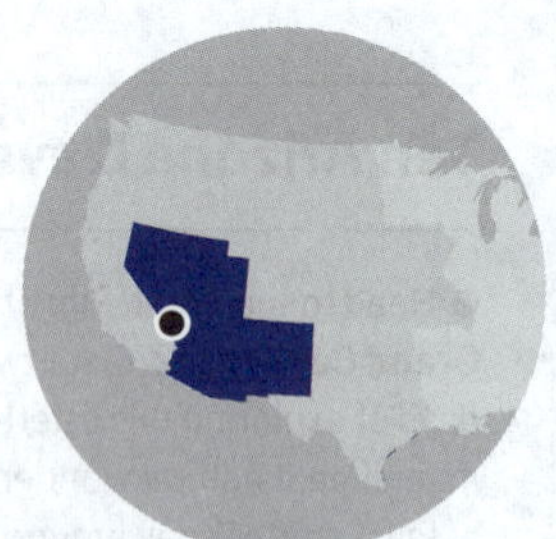

Las Vegas

NON-STOP ENTERTAINMENT | SPECTATOR SPORTS | GREAT DINING

TOP TIP

If you're new to gambling, or on a budget, it makes sense to try your luck Downtown rather than on the Strip. Downtown casinos offer games with slightly better odds, and minimum bets are significantly lower.

The story of Las Vegas begins in Downtown, where the city was founded in 1905. That's right: this historic core and its casinos were thriving long before the glitz of Las Vegas Blvd took the spotlight, and in recent years, Vegas' Downtown has staged a comeback. The five-block Fremont Street Experience, beneath a canopy of millions of LED lights, debuted in the mid-1990s. Then in 2012, Zappos' CEO Tony Hsieh infused $350 million into revitalizing the neighborhood.

But Las Vegas is also the Strip – a 4-mile eruption of color and possibility also known as Las Vegas Blvd. This is what happens when unchecked indulgence reigns. Love it or loathe it, this over-the-top 'playground for grown-ups' taps into the hopes and dreams of the masses. They no longer come for just the gambling, either, but for the dazzling performances, intriguing art installations, world-class restaurants and ever-popular sporting events that relentlessly infuse the Strip with new energy.

Fremont Street

The beating heart of Downtown

Streaking down the center of Vegas' historic district, the **Fremont Street Experience** *(vegasexperience.com)* is a

GETTING AROUND

Downtown is mostly walkable. Most of the action is at the Fremont Street Experience, where you'll be on foot. If you prefer exploring on two wheels, the RTC bike-share program has stations Downtown. Taxis are widely available in front of hotels, and rideshares are popular (just be sure you're at the right pick-up area). The free Downtown Loop bus stops at all the big attractions. Walking the Strip is an adventure, often involving sidewalk performances, escalators and pedestrian bridges over the highway.

SEAN PAVONE/SHUTTERSTOCK

'Welcome to Fabulous Las Vegas' sign

five-block pedestrian mall lined with old-school casinos and topped by an arched steel canopy. Hourly from dusk until midnight, the 1400ft-long canopy turns on a six-minute light-and-sound show. The shows are cheesy, but mesmerizing if you're drunk. It's even more exhilarating if you happen to be zooming by on the zipline cables attached to the 12-story **SlotZilla** *(vegasexperience.com/slotzilla-zip-line; from $49)*, a slot-machine-themed platform at the mall's eastern end.

WEDDING CHAPELS

Driving along Las Vegas Blvd, it's impossible to miss the abundance of wedding chapels – a testament to how easy it is to get married here.

Near the iconic 'Welcome to Fabulous Las Vegas' sign, the **Little Church of the West** is one of the oldest of the dozens of wedding chapels in Las Vegas. Since 1941 this one has hosted the weddings of celebrities including Judy Garland and Mark Herron, Richard Gere and Cindy Crawford, and Billy Bob Thornton and Angelina Jolie. Hang around outdoors for a few minutes and you'll probably see some newlyweds posing for pictures.

Welcome to Fabulous Las Vegas

Arriving on the Strip

The **'Welcome to Fabulous Las Vegas' sign**, in the center of bustling Las Vegas Blvd, makes for a great place to start your explorations. In a city famous for neon signs, this one reigns supreme, and is the unofficial beginning of the Strip.

Designed by Betty Willis at the end of the 1950s, this sign is a classic photo op and a reminder of Vegas' past. Get here by midmorning to avoid long lines of jovial, selfie-seeking tourists.

EATING ON THE STRIP: BEST RESTAURANTS

Golden Steer: The Rat Pack, Marilyn Monroe and Elvis all dined at this fabulously retro steakhouse with steer's head out front. *4:30-9:45pm* **$$$**

Joël Robuchon: In the famous chef's art deco-inspired dining room, seasonal tasting menus deliver the meal of a lifetime. *5-9:30pm* **$$$**

Peppermill: This Vegas institution is famous for its campy atmosphere, firepit-fountains and massive portions. *hours vary* **$$**

Delilah: See and be seen in this modern supper club that drips with style and regularly attracts A-list celebs. No photos. *hours vary* **$$$**

HIGHLIGHTS
1 Fremont Street Experience
2 Strat
3 Welcome to Las Vegas Sign

SIGHTS
4 Eiffel Tower Experience
5 Graceland Wedding Chapel
6 High Roller
7 Little Church of the West
8 Mob Museum
9 Neon Museum

ACTIVITIES
10 SlotZilla

SLEEPING
11 Cosmopolitan
12 El Cortez
13 Luxor
14 Skylofts

EATING
15 Barry's Downtown Prime
16 Carson Kitchen
17 Delilah
18 Eiffel Tower Restaurant
19 Esther's Kitchen
20 Golden Steer
21 Joël Robuchon
22 Main St Provisions
23 Peppermill
24 Top of the World

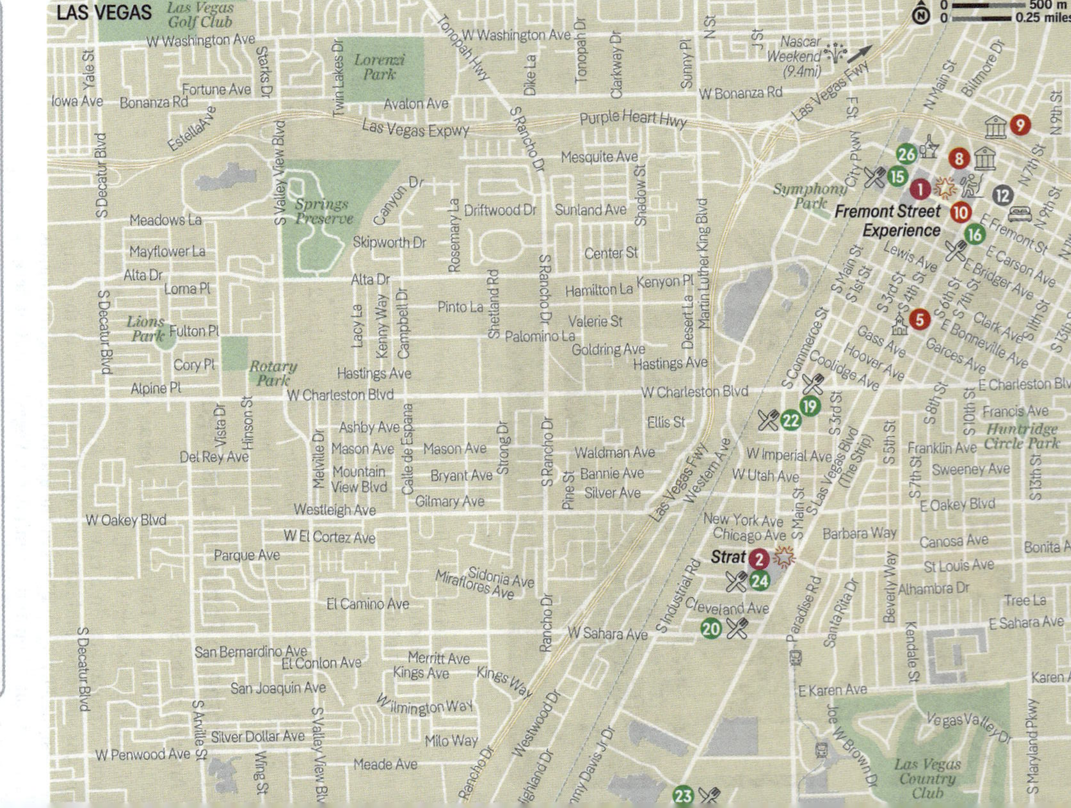

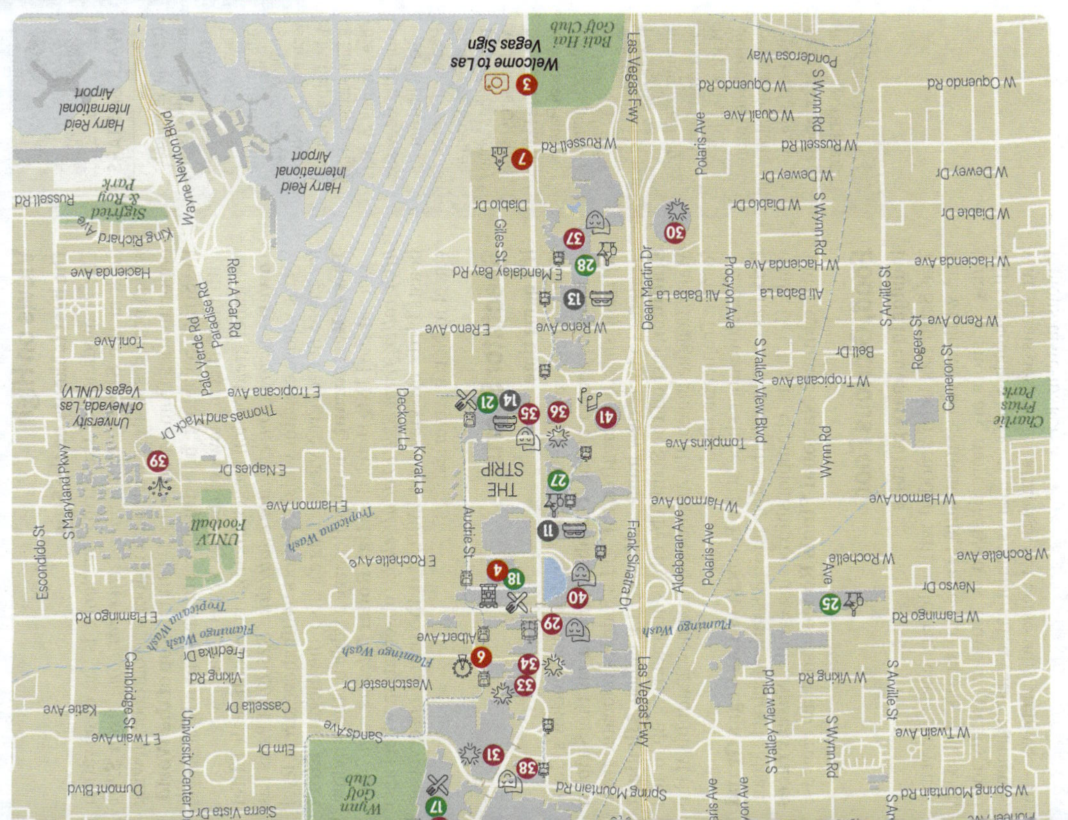

DRINKING & NIGHTLIFE
- **25** Ghostbar
- **26** Legacy Club
- **27** Skybar
- **28** Skyfall Lounge

ENTERTAINMENT
- **29** Absinthe
- **30** Allegiant Stadium
- **31** Atomic Saloon Show
- **32** Awakening
- **33** Big Elvis
- **34** DiscoShow
- **35** Kà
- **36** Mad Apple
- **37** Michael Jackson ONE
- **38** Mystère
- **39** National Finals Rodeo
- **40** O
- **41** T-Mobile Arena

WALK OF STARS

It's nowhere near as extensive as the Hollywood Walk of Fame, but the Strip has gotten into the game of recognizing some of the folks who helped to make it famous by putting their names in stars along the sidewalks.

You'll find Rat Packers Dean Martin and Frank Sinatra, plus siblings Donny and Marie Osmond, outside the Flamingo. In front of Paris, look for legendary performers Wayne Newton and Elvis Presley, as well as longtime drag performer Frank Marino. The full list includes more performers along with other notable folks such as composers, humanitarians and producers.

Views on High

The best lookouts on the Strip

The granddaddy of the Strip's overlooks is the observation deck at the **Strat** *(Stratosphere; thestrat.com; from $20)*, which provides visitors with both indoor and outdoor viewing opportunities from a whopping 1149ft up. **Top of the World**, the Strat's revolving, fine-dining restaurant, provides guests with magnificent views of the Las Vegas Valley.

Another great option for getting high is the half-scale **Eiffel Tower** *(caesars.com; elevator adult/child $25/19)* at Paris Las Vegas, whose elevator whisks visitors 540ft above street level for great 360-degree views. There's also the elegant **Eiffel Tower Restaurant**, 110ft up. Reserve a table by the window.

Over at the LINQ Hotel, the **High Roller** *(caesars.com/linq/high-roller; from $29/10 adult/child)* observation wheel also boasts bird's-eye views. At 550ft, it is the tallest observation wheel in North America.

Spectator Sports

It's game time

Want to catch a game in Vegas? Professional hockey's Golden Knights set up at the **T-Mobile Arena** on the Strip in 2017, and shortly thereafter, the NFL's Raiders relocated from Oakland to their new home at Vegas' $1.9 billion **Allegiant Stadium**, just off the Strip. The city is also gearing up to add Major League Baseball's Athletics with a new stadium at the former Tropicana site.

Each November since 2023, Formula 1's **Las Vegas Grand Prix** has transformed the Strip into a 3.8-mile racetrack. Meanwhile, UFC fights, championship boxing events, **Nascar races** and the annual **National Finals Rodeo** also draw crowds.

Food, Glorious Food

Indulge in culinary pursuits

The Strip has been studded with celebrity chefs for years. And while all-you-can-eat buffets and $10 steaks still exist, today's visitors are more likely to be found in trendy food halls or seeking out ever more sophisticated establishments, with meals designed – although not personally prepared – by famous taste-makers.

If food is your *raison d'être,* look no further than **Lip Smacking Foodie Tours** *(lipsmackingfoodietours.com)*.

DRINKING ON THE STRIP: BEST ROOFTOP BARS WITH STRIP VIEWS

GhostBar: Off the Strip at Palms, this 55th-floor club with outdoor deck is reached by a private lift. Fun vibe, great DJs. *7pm-2am Wed-Sat*

Skybar: Floor-to-ceiling windows enhance the vistas from this classy 23rd-floor bar at Waldorf Astoria. Great cocktails, too. *hours vary*

Skyfall Lounge: Sophistication, creative seasonal cocktails and killer views align on the 64th floor of Delano. *5pm-midnight*

Legacy Club: Downtown penthouse lounge on Circa's 60th floor with panoramic Strip views and killer weekend parties. *4pm-2am*

Showtime on the Strip

Are you not entertained?

Las Vegas is a hub for the world's top entertainers, and the nightly performances up and down the Strip reflect this remarkable consolidation of talent.

Cirque du Soleil captivates with its five productions: **O** at the Bellagio is a mesmerizing water-based show, featuring high-flying acrobatics and surreal aquatic stunts; **Kà** at MGM Grand tells a tale of familial love and conflict on a rotating, oftentimes vertical stage; **Michael Jackson ONE** at Mandalay Bay pays tribute to the King of Pop; **Mad Apple** is a homage to New York City in (where else) New York–New York; and **Mystère** at Treasure Island combines classic circus artistry with vibrant costumes and high-energy stunts.

Absinthe at Caesars Palace blends incredible acrobatic feats with edgy humor in an intimate setting beneath a Big Top. Meanwhile, **Atomic Saloon Show** at the Venetian is a mix of burlesque, comedy and acrobatics in a rowdy, Wild West–themed saloon. **DiscoShow**, in the LINQ Hotel, is a thrilling love letter to disco that invites the audience into the dance party.

The Wynn adds its own magic with **Awakening**, an extraordinary spectacle combining innovative stage design, elaborate costumes and mind-blowing special effects in a mythical adventure story.

Then there are, of course, the residencies. Superstars perform in resort theaters seating thousands for weeks, months and even years on end. And pop icons, comedians and magicians regularly perform at the Strip's many venues. Plan ahead and look into who you might be able to catch in residence.

The Mob & Neon Lights

Learn about gangsters and see vintage signs

The highly respected **Mob Museum** *(National Museum of Organized Crime & Law Enforcement; themobmuseum.org; from $34.95)* chronicles the era when gangsters controlled Las Vegas and got rich stealing casino profits. The museum shares gangster stories alongside those of the law enforcement officers whose job it was to nail the bad guys.

While not old itself, **Neon Museum** *(neonmuseum.org; adult/child $25/12.50 day, $35/17.50 evening)* is chock-full of vintage signs that once hung on long-gone properties such as Binion's Horseshoe, the Moulin Rouge and Stardust.

FINDING ELVIS

Elvis has definitely left the building. In 1976 he ended a run of 636 shows at the International (later the Las Vegas Hilton). Now the Westgate, the hotel honors the King with a bronze statue in the lobby. Its International Theater remains, still attracting top-tier headliners.

Downtown's **Graceland Wedding Chapel** offers couples a package that includes an Elvis impersonator. And although Elvis-themed shows come and go, **Big Elvis** has been a hit in Strip lounges since 2002. Pete Vallee's voice is as rich as his jumpsuit is big. He once weighed an incredible 945lb but has since shed hundreds. He performs for free four afternoons a week at Harrah's.

EATING DOWNTOWN: BEST BITES

Carson Kitchen: Tiny eatery with an industrial vibe, a rooftop patio and excellent shared plates of creative American classics. *hours vary* $$

Barry's Downtown Prime: Classy steakhouse; cuts are mouthwatering and lobster mac explodes from the shell. *hours vary* $$$

Esther's Kitchen: A cozy, popular restaurant with excellent Italian cuisine at commendable prices. *hours vary* $$

Main St Provisions: Delicious modern American place, it feels like a neighborhood staple while still offering foie gras add-ons. *hours vary* $$

Nevada

SCENIC LANDSCAPES | OUTDOOR ADVENTURE | URBAN CULTURE

Places

TOP TIP

The Mojave Desert is the driest desert in North America, and visitors often don't realize that just because they don't feel sweaty, they're still perspiring; it instantly evaporates in the hot and dry conditions. Dehydration can be deadly, so carry and consume lots of water.

Nevada has soul to go with the glitz and glamor of Las Vegas. Much of that comes from the Mojave Desert, which is a destination in itself, perhaps even the necessary counterpoint to the bright lights of Vegas. All across the Mojave, stunning natural wonders – the wind- and water-carved landscapes of Red Rock Canyon and the Valley of Fire, for example – rise from the desert floor. Even the human footprint can be seen on a grand scale, such as at the Hoover Dam, while the haunting ruins of St Thomas are a reminder of how fragile the human presence can be out here.

Ranging further afield, Reno, with its echoes of the Burning Man Festival, is like a more manageable Vegas but with history and art instead of nonstop show business. It's also an emerging adventure hub. In other words, there are good reasons why Nevada draws tens of millions of visitors each year.

Mojave Desert

Exploring the unspoiled desert

Drive just about any direction from Las Vegas and before long you'll be at one of Southern Nevada's wonderful natural resources that are light-years away from the neon of the Strip. Just 20 miles from the resorts, **Red Rock Canyon National Conservation Area** *(redrockcanyonlv.org; vehicle/bicycle $20/10; reservations required 8am-5pm Oct-May)* welcomes

GETTING AROUND

If you're short on time, tours out of Vegas can get you to highlights such as Hoover Dam, Red Rock Canyon and Valley of Fire, and coaches travel as far as the Grand Canyon. But given the state's great distances and the remoteness of popular destinations, to fully soak in the delights, a car – or better yet, a high-clearance SUV – is required. It's the only way you can reach off-the-beaten-path places. Rental cars are available at airports and some hotels. If you're sticking to the cities, several airlines (including Southwest and Spirit) connect Las Vegas and Reno.

more than two million visitors each year. There's a visitor center and a 13-mile paved road that winds through multicolored formations of sandstone. Visitors can hike or bike the paved road.

For a much less crowded desert park with great trails and petroglyphs, head south from Las Vegas to **Sloan Canyon National Conservation Area** *(blm.gov)*.

Travelers willing to venture further afield will relish their drive or hike through spectacular **Valley of Fire State Park** *(parks.nv.gov/parks/valley-of-fire; Nevada/non-Nevada vehicles $10/15)*. About an hour from Las Vegas, the park is home to mile after mile of awe-inspiring, otherworldly geologic curiosities, some with pastel hues and others rust-colored.

Hoover Dam

Hoover Dam and a Lake Mead ghost town

About 35 miles east of Las Vegas, Hoover Dam is an engineering marvel built in the 1930s to harness the Colorado River while providing a dependable water supply to Southern California and generating hydroelectric power. Although the dam's hydroelectric output has been significantly reduced due to drought in recent years, the towering 726ft structure still controls the

A CITY WITHOUT CASINOS

In all Nevada, there are only two communities where gambling remains illegal. The small Lincoln County town of Panaca is one and Boulder City is the other.

Built during the Great Depression to house dam builders, **Boulder City** was under control of the federal government, which saw gambling as a costly vice that should be discouraged. In 1931, after gambling had been legalized elsewhere in Nevada, the highway between Boulder City and Las Vegas became a busy thoroughfare as workers flocked to Downtown gambling halls in search of fortune – or at least an escape from the drudgery of their jobs. Now, there are casinos a few miles to the east and west of Boulder City.

RENO'S BEST EVENTS

Reno River Festival: The world's top freestyle kayakers compete in a mad paddling dash through Whitewater Park in mid-May.

Hot August Nights: Celebration of hot rods and rock 'n' roll in early August in various locations around Reno and beyond.

Great Reno Balloon Race: In one of Reno's most inspiring spectacles, more than 100 hot-air balloons race across the desert over three days every September.

Artown: Throughout July, this Riverwalk District celebration centers on art and culture, with hundreds of events, workshops and performances.

Reno Rodeo: Each June, roping and bull-riding action takes place at the Livestock Events Center, with a five-day cattle drive across the high desert.

flooding of the Colorado River, helps to irrigate more than 1.5 million acres of land and provides water to 25 million people.

Visit to learn about how 21,000 men built the dam during the height of the Great Depression – and how climate change threatens to diminish its functionality. First, though, you'll want to drive across the top of the dam into Arizona for the best views of the hulking construction. Another remarkable view can be found back in Nevada, where an accessible, albeit uphill, walkway leads to the sidewalk along the Mike O'Callaghan–Pat Tillman Memorial Bridge. Hold the railing when it's windy – this isn't for anyone with a fear of heights.

History buffs can delve deeper on a guided tour. They begin at the **Hoover Dam Parking Garage & Visitor Center** (which got a fancy new exhibition center in 2025). The one-hour dam tour ($30) explores historic tunnels, takes in the Colorado River through a ventilation shaft and rides an elevator to the top.

Hoover Dam created the enormous **Lake Mead**, which is actually a reservoir, in the 1930s. The lake is bisected by the Nevada–Arizona state line. The highlight of visiting Lake Mead is **St Thomas Ghost Town**. Navigate the deeply rutted road for roughly 3 miles to the end. From the history-filled kiosks, there's a 2.5-mile desert trail leading to the remains of the town flooded by the creation of Lake Mead following the construction of Hoover Dam. Submerged under 60ft of water for nearly eight decades, the foundations and walls of some of St Thomas' buildings have eerily re-emerged during the drought.

Reno

Learn Reno's historical story

Driving in beneath the downtown arch that proclaims Reno 'the Biggest Little City in the World,' and eyeballing its gaudy casinos and mid-century modern architecture, you may be tempted to label it a smaller Las Vegas. But once you've strolled through the Riverwalk District along the alpine-fed Truckee River, grabbed brunch and cocktails at a hip bistro in Midtown and been intrigued by public art at every turn, the truth becomes clear: Reno has a fascinating story and has come into its own.

The **Nevada Museum of Art** *(nevadaart.org; adult/child $15/3)* building was inspired by the geological formations of the Black Rock Desert to the north, and inside, a floating staircase leads to galleries showcasing its temporary exhibits and eclectic collection. Visitors are free to explore the Sky Room on the 4th floor, essentially a rooftop penthouse and patio with killer views, and a 50,000-sq-ft wing that opened in 2025.

EATING IN RENO: OUR PICKS

Beline Carniceria & Deli: Reno's best Mexican at this market counter and restaurant north of town. Don't miss the tortas. *9am-7pm* $

Perenn: Locals are obsessed with the boules and baguettes at this hip bakery. *7am-noon Midtown, to 2:30pm Village at Rancharrah* $

Brasserie Saint James: Eclectic menu, plus beers made using water from an aquifer underneath it. Great patio. *11am-9pm Tue-Sun* $$

Atlantis Steakhouse: Highly rated place serving premium Allen Brothers and Wagyu beef. Special-occasion vibes. *5-10pm Wed-Sun* $$$

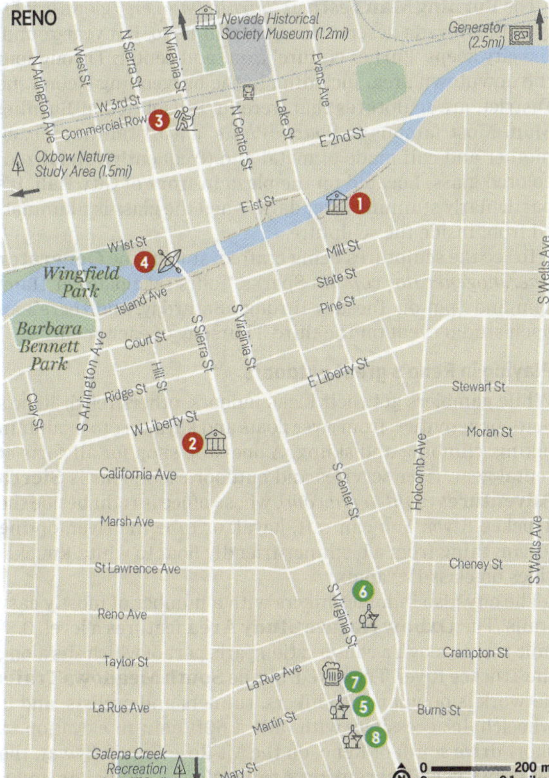

SIGHTS

1 National Automobile Museum
2 Nevada Museum of Art

ACTIVITIES

3 BaseCamp
4 Sierra Adventures

DRINKING & NIGHTLIFE

5 Craft Wine & Beer
6 Death & Taxes
7 Local Beer Works
8 Rum Sugar Lime

Get an understanding of the region's vibrant past with a visit to the **Nevada Historical Society Museum** *(nvculture .org/historicalsociety; adult/child $6/free)*. Opened in 1904, it's the state's oldest museum. Just beyond the entrance is its pride and joy: a collection of priceless, 19th-century baskets woven by Dat-So-La-Lee, a Washoe woman who lived in the area. Another exhibit explores the rich history of mining, and there's also a section devoted specifically to Reno's history.

The **National Automobile Museum** *(automuseum.org; adult/child $15/10)* has casino pioneer Bill Harrah to thank for its existence. While building resorts across the state, Harrah also amassed a mind-boggling collection of 1400 vintage cars, many of which used to be kept in warehouses in neighboring Sparks. The museum's gems include a 1907 Thomas Flyer 35, a 1937 Cord 812 and an original Batmobile from the 1960s.

Burning brightly year-round

Each August, 'Burners' from around the world descend on the Black Rock Desert to build Black Rock City, tear it down, and set fire to an effigy of 'the man,' with plenty of peace, love, music, art, nakedness, drugs, sex and frivolity thrown in.

RENO'S QUICKIE DIVORCES

Long before Las Vegas developed the moniker of 'Wedding Capital,' Reno's reputation focused on 'quickie' divorces. The process, also known as 'migratory divorce,' took six weeks, but that was quick compared to the long, drawn-out procedures elsewhere, which typically assigned marital property to husbands. In Reno, owners of everything from private homes to dude ranches to luxury hotels got in on the act of offering short-term rentals to women who, once they had lived in Nevada for six weeks, could get a divorce decree citing just about any circumstance. Thousands flocked to Reno from the 1930s to the '60s, but when divorce laws were relaxed in other states, the 'quickie divorce' industry fell into a steady decline.

AREA 51

After years of refusing to acknowledge that Area 51 existed, in 2013 the US government admitted that the desert site was used to develop specialized aircraft. Skeptics, however, believe that aliens from a UFO crash site near Roswell (p334), New Mexico, were brought to Area 51 in 1947. The unconfirmed legends continue to lure believers to the nearby Extraterrestrial Highway (NV375) and its alien-themed attractions.

From Ash Springs, it's a five-minute drive north on US 93 to the turnoff for NV 375, the road that runs tantalizingly close to Area 51. The junction is marked by the **ET Fresh Jerky** shop, which sells alien-themed merchandise and a wide variety of jerky flavors supposedly made from cows surrounding Area 51.

The **Burning Man Festival** *(burningman.org)* glows brightly in the Nevada desert 115 miles from Reno. But year-round, the city keeps 'Burner culture' front and center. Throughout the downtown area, including in the burgeoning Neon Line District, are sculptures that were first displayed at Burning Man. Most famous is *Space Whale,* a 40ft-tall humpback mother and calf made of metal and (frequently vandalized) colored glass. Located on the plaza in front of City Hall, it's particularly stunning after dark, when the glass is illuminated from inside the sculpture.

To see the sculptures being crafted, stop by the **Generator** *(therenogenerator.com)* in Sparks. Tours take place at 11am, 1pm and 5pm on Tuesday through Saturday, and there's an open studio event on the third Thursday of each month.

Playing in Reno's great outdoors

While gamblers get their kicks indoors, others relish Reno's outdoor activities, from river floats and kayaking to mountain biking, climbing and skiing. A one-stop shop for all sorts of rental gear, river services and outdoor excursions is **Sierra Adventures** *(wildsierra.com),* whose office is right beside the Truckee River. You can raft, kayak or tube the river, opting for anything from a beginner-friendly float to white-knuckle rides on class IV rapids.

The city also indulges hikers with a number of mostly easy trails. The **Oxbow Nature Study Area** features a level, 0.8-mile trail through a conservation park, part of which sits along the Truckee River. The paved, 5-mile **South Meadows Trails** network is popular with hikers, runners and cyclists, and is wheelchair-accessible, with only a 60ft gain in elevation. A short drive south of Reno, on the Mt Rose Scenic Byway, the **Galena Creek Recreation Area** *(galenacreekvisitorcenter.org)* has a great visitor center and a paved interpretive trail out back, plus a few longer trails. Two other recommended hikes just outside the city include **Hunter Creek Trail** (to a 30ft waterfall) and **Tom Cooke Trail** (along a scenic river).

A non-gaming property downtown, the Whitney Peak Hotel is known for **BaseCamp** *(basecampreno.com)*. Along with a state-of-the-art indoor bouldering gym, BaseCamp includes outdoor climbing challenges on the hotel's east wall. The Big Wall, which holds a Guinness World Record as the planet's largest outdoor climbing wall, sends thrill-seekers on a 164ft ascent to the roof. BaseCamp also offers climbs and climbing classes for every skill level, from beginner to world-class professional athlete.

DRINKING IN RENO: OUR PICKS

Local Beer Works: Solid craft beers and fun seasonal specials. Don't miss the Irish Stout aged in Frey Ranch bourbon bottles. *hours vary*

Craft Wine & Beer: A bottle shop with products from small local brewers and growers, a cute little bar, a good crowd and tastings. *hours vary*

Death & Taxes: Perch on a Victorian barstool and sip delicious cocktails like works of art at this all-black, death-themed tavern. *hours vary*

Rum Sugar Lime: A bright and chic tropical cocktail bar in Midtown; killer rum drinks, strong list of non-alcoholic libations. *4pm-midnight Tue-Sun*

TOP EXPERIENCE

Great Basin National Park

One of the least-visited national parks, Great Basin National Park is a must for people in search of solitude and natural beauty. The free-to-visit park is lorded over by Wheeler Peak, a 13,063ft ice-sculpted horn, which shelters a shrinking but still-visible glacier. Hiking and camping opportunities abound, and the park is a designated International Dark Sky Park.

Wheeler Peak

Wheeler Peak Scenic Drive

Ascending 3000ft over 12 miles, this out-and-back scenic drive rises steeply through several distinct eco-regions. It winds first through low-lying sagebrush, then up past pinyon pines, a mountain mahogany wilderness, a mixed-conifer forest peppered with aspens and, finally, a zone of subalpine forest, at which point astonishing views of Wheeler come into sight.

Hitting the Trails

Great Basin is a hiker's wonderland, with over 60 miles of trails. The 26 trails traverse mountains studded with ancient forests and meander around glacier-fed lakes, and one even leads to Nevada's only glacier. Hikers of all levels will find plenty of options.

The **Glacier Trail** is one of the park's best. It culminates at the rock glacier ensconced beneath Wheeler Peak, and the 8.4-mile round trip also brings you to a grove of ancient bristlecone pines, the world's oldest non-cloned organisms.

Lehman Caves

A colossal marble cavern, Lehman Caves has a staggering collection of formations including stalactites, stalagmites, helictites, flowstone, popcorn and rare shields. They are a fragile resource, accessible only by guided tour.

TOP TIPS

- Baker (population 36), less than 5 miles from the park, has lodgings and food.
- The park has five developed campgrounds ($20 per night).
- Book your Lehman Caves tour two weeks in advance; spots fill quickly.
- Don't miss the evening astronomy ranger program - it's excellent.

PRACTICALITIES

- nps.gov/grba

Phoenix

ENDLESS SUNSHINE | SOUTHWEST CULTURE | OUTDOOR ADVENTURES

TOP TIP
Consider the weather before booking. From January to March, warm desert temps make Phoenix a popular winter retreat for snowbirds. June to August is scorching hot, but you can score incredible deals on upscale resorts. Temps are nearly perfect in October and November, before winter's peak rates arrive.

A thriving desert metropolis, Phoenix is the cultural and economic heart of Arizona. The city is also a convenient base for desert and red-rock wanderings. Southwestern and Mexican restaurants abound and swanky resorts stand ready to pamper. With more than 300 days of sunshine a year, exploring, eating and relaxing should be on your agenda – except in the searing heat from June to August.

The city offers an opera, ballet, several theaters and three of the state's finest museums – the Heard, Phoenix Art and Musical Instrument museums – while the Desert Botanical Garden is a stunning introduction to the region's ecology. There are plenty of options to hike, mountain bike and climb in the regional parks, all easily accessible. Golf may as well be the official sport of the area, with nearly 200 courses covering Greater Phoenix. So slather on the sunscreen and get outside.

Visit the Heard Museum

Native American art and culture

A 30ft-long fence of blown-glass cactus ribs and small sculptures of desert animals is an evocative portal into the Home

GETTING AROUND

To hop around Greater Phoenix, a car is a must in this colossal urban sprawl. Rent one on arrival at Sky Harbor International, Phoenix's major airport. The much smaller Phoenix-Mesa Gateway Airport on the easternmost edge of the Valley of the Sun only serves Allegiant Air and Sun Country Airlines. Phoenix public transportation is not as expansive as other major US cities, but the reliable Valley Metro light rail covers Phoenix proper, Tempe and Mesa. If you stay in one general part of town, Uber and Lyft rideshare will be sufficient for your stay.

HIGHLIGHTS

1 Desert Botanical Garden
2 Heard Museum

SIGHTS

3 Phoenix Art Museum

ACTIVITIES

4 Phoenix Mountains Preserve
5 Piestewa Peak

EATING

6 Churchill
7 Culinary Dropout at the Yard
8 Durant's
9 Fry Bread House
10 Green New American Vegetarian
11 LON's at the Hermosa Inn
12 Pa'la
13 Pizzeria Bianco
14 Steak 44
15 Taco Chelo
16 The Henry
17 théa

DRINKING & NIGHTLIFE

18 Arizona Wilderness DTPHX
19 Bar Bianco
20 Bitter & Twisted
21 Century Grand
22 Greenwood Brewing
23 monOrchid
24 Wandering Tortoise

SHOPPING

25 Garden Shop at the Desert Botanical Garden
26 Heard Museum Shop & Bookstore
27 MADE Art Boutique
28 Phoenix General
29 Soleri Studios at Cosanti

Gallery, the heart of the **Heard Museum** *(heard.org; adult/child $26/10)* and a showcase for the art and culture of the 22 sovereign tribes in Arizona. Poems, quotes and videos supplement the baskets, ceramics, jewelry, textiles and Hopi kachinas (spirit dolls) on display.

The Heard is one of the best museums of its kind in the US. Annual events enliven the grounds, including competitions of mesmerizing hoop dancing in February and the Indian Fair & Market in March.

HIKING IN PHOENIX

It's actually pretty easy to escape the urban jungle and immerse yourself in the unique beauty of the Sonoran Desert. When the weather's right, enthusiastic hikers flood the trails on **Camelback Mountain, Piestewa Peak** and **South Mountain Park** for the sweeping views of the Valley, while Pinnacle Peak and Tom's Thumb in the McDowell Sonoran Preserve are challenging but can't-miss climbs in Scottsdale.

Find maps and trail descriptions for the above from *@arizonahikers guide* on Instagram or at *phoenix.gov*. Remember to carry lots of water as you'll be hiking in the harsh Arizona sun. If you want a more remote experience, try the East Valley's Superstition Mountains.

CHRIS CURTIS/SHUTTERSTOCK

Desert Botanical Garden

Desert Plant Life

Saguaros, wildflowers and butterflies

Reconnect with nature and learn about desert plant life at the 55-acre **Desert Botanical Garden** *(dbg.org; adult/child $32.95/14.95)*. There are 2 miles' worth of looping trails arranged by theme, including a Sonoran Desert nature loop and an edible desert garden. The showstopping Desert Wildflower Loop trail showcases bluebells and Mexican gold poppies blooming from March to May. It's stunning year-round, but busiest and most colorful in the flowering spring season.

Ramble Down Roosevelt Row

Downtown arts and beer gardens

The *Welcome to Roosevelt Row* mural on the corner of Roosevelt and N 7th Sts is a launchpad for downtown's most vibrant neighborhood.

First, for a good craft beer, pop into the stylish indoor-outdoor digs at **Greenwood Brewing** *(greenwoodbrews.com)* or snag a table in the beer garden at the welcoming **Arizona Wilderness DTPHX** (p272; *azwbeer.com)*. Snack on the tacos, duck-fat fries and churro bites. Dinner options range from tacos and tortas at trendy **Taco Chelo** *(instagram.com/tacochelo)* to elite burgers and pizza at the **Churchill** *(thechurchillphx.com)*, a shaded courtyard housing multiple food stands, bars and locally owned shops. The **monOrchid** *(monorchid.com)* is a coffee shop, gallery, gift shop, brewery and event space rolled into one. On the first Friday of the month, 70 or so galleries open for mingling and art viewing (6pm to 10pm).

Sample Native American Tastes

Award-winning indigenous menus

For a rewarding culinary tour through locally sourced native dishes, drive to **Kai Restaurant** *(kairestaurant.com)*. Here, Native American cuisine – based on traditional crops grown along the Gila River – includes creations such as grilled buffalo tenderloin with smoked corn puree and cholla buds, or wild scallops with beef tongue pastrami and tepary-bean crackling. Kai is located at the **Sheraton Grand at Wild Horse Pass** *(wildhorsepass.com)* on the Gila River Indian Reservation in Chandler. Book ahead and dress nicely.

Back in Phoenix, try the **Fry Bread House** *(frybreadhouse az.com)*. Known as an elephant ear or Navajo taco, frybread is a flat piece of fried dough topped with meat, beans and veggies, or, for dessert, smeared with honey.

Hiking Piestewa Peak & Phoenix Mountains Preserve

Steep hike to city views

Covered in saguaros, ocotillos and teddy-bear cholla, the picturesque summit of **Piestewa Peak** *(phoenix.gov/parks)* was previously known as Squaw Peak. It was renamed for a local soldier, Lori Piestewa, who was killed in Iraq in 2003. Be warned: the 1.2-mile trek to the 2608ft peak is difficult but hugely popular for the south-facing views of downtown Phoenix. The surrounding **Phoenix Mountains Preserve** *(phoenix.gov/parks)* has nearly 70 trails and typically gets jammed on winter weekends.

For an easier hike, follow the Freedom Trail around the base of the peak. Look for parking lots along Piestewa Peak Dr within the park.

ORIENTATION

The Valley of the Sun is ringed by mountains that encompass a hot pancake, otherwise known as Greater Phoenix. A few important east–west roads cut across town: beginning in the south, these are Washington St, Van Buren St, Roosevelt St, McDowell Rd, Indian School Rd and Camelback Rd.

Phoenix is Arizona's largest city and houses the state capitol, the oldest buildings, several important museums and pro sports facilities. Scottsdale starts at around 56th St, east of Phoenix. The main drag, Scottsdale Rd, is technically 72nd St. Southeast of Phoenix is Tempe ('tem-*pee*'), home of Arizona State University, which is anchored around Mill Ave and University Rd.

EATING IN PHOENIX: OUR PICKS

théa: Order pasta, seafood and skewers for the table at the Global Ambassador hotel rooftop. *4-10pm Mon-Fri, from noon Sat & Sun* **$$$**

Steak 44: Top-tier steaks and seafood in a stunning setting. Check online for the dress code. *4-10pm Sun-Thu, to 11pm Fri & Sat* **$$$**

Pa'la: Seasonal veg and sustainably sourced seafood served hot off the grill. Two locations. *5-10pm Tue-Sat, to 9pm Sun* **$$**

The Henry: A cozy, elegant stop. Short rib, seafood and salad options and a deep wine list. *7am-9pm Sun-Thu, to 10pm Fri & Sat* **$$$**

Durant's: A gloriously old-school steakhouse with cozy red-velvet booths, juicy steaks and effortless cool. *4-8:30pm Wed-Sun* **$$$**

Culinary Dropout at the Yard: Next-level pub food between games of cornhole and ping-pong in this open-air space. *hours vary* **$$**

Green New American Vegetarian: Mock meats as good as, if not better than, their carnivorous counterparts. *11am-9pm Mon-Sat* **$**

LON's at the Hermosa Inn: Quaint hacienda where Phoenicians bring guests for fine dining and glorious sunsets. *7am-9pm* **$$$**

BEST PLACES TO SHOP IN PHOENIX

Soleri Studios at Cosanti: Studio of Frank Lloyd Wright student Paolo Soleri, whose signature bronze and ceramic bells are crafted and sold here.

MADE Art Boutique: Jewelry, ceramics, art prints, candles and more from mostly local artists. On Roosevelt Row in downtown Phoenix.

Garden Shop at the Desert Botanical Garden: Plant your own desert garden with a starter cactus kit, plus Southwestern cards and cactus jellies.

Phoenix General: Bring the smell of desert rain to your shower with one of the sustainably harvested creosote bundles.

Heard Museum Shop & Bookstore: Top-notch collection of American Indian original arts and crafts.

Chris Bianco: 35+ Years of Pizza Wizardry

Wood-fired pizzas and gourmet sandwiches

Awarded the Outstanding Restaurateur award by the James Beard Foundation in 2022, Chris Bianco has been crafting thin-crusted wood-fired pizzas in Phoenix since 1988. In the process, he pioneered an 'artisanal pizza revolution' nationwide and expanded from his downtown mothership to a half-dozen successful ventures. The tiny **Pizzeria Bianco** *(pizzeriabianco.com)* is the original restaurant – a convenient stop for travelers exploring Heritage Square. Pro tip: there is almost always a wait, so put your name on the list before exploring the square, or pop next door to **Bar Bianco** for a glass of waiting wine.

Get Inspired at the Phoenix Art Museum

Western, contemporary and totally immersive art

Make a beeline for the **Phoenix Art Museum** *(phxart.org; adult/child $28/18)* to see how the Arizona landscape has inspired everyone from early pioneers to modernists. From here, Arizona's premier repository of fine art only gets more interesting, with works by Claude Monet, Frida Kahlo, Georgia O'Keeffe and Kehinde Wiley. Navigate to the far-back reaches of the museum for a trippy moment inside Yayoi Kusama's infinity mirror room, *You Who Are Getting Obliterated in the Dancing Swarm of Fireflies*.

Explore South Mountain Park

Morning hikes and petroglyphs

Pima Canyon is just one of many hiking destinations at the enormous **South Mountain Park** *(phoenix.gov/parks)*, where a 51-mile network of trails (leashed dogs allowed) dips through canyons, over cacti-studded hills and past granite walls. Hike or drive to **Dobbins Lookout** for valley views at sunset.

The main entrance is at 10211 S Central Ave; the Pima Canyon entrance is at 4771 E Pima Canyon Rd.

DRINKING IN PHOENIX: OUR PICKS

Wandering Tortoise: Unpretentious hangout with 20+ draft beers and a fridge full of cans. Food truck on-site, with outside food welcome. Dog-friendly. *hours vary*

Arizona Wilderness DTPHX: Environmentally conscious beers with some of the best brewery food around. Duck-fat fries are a must. *11am-11pm Mon-Thu, to midnight Fri & Sat, to 10pm Sun*

Century Grand: With three different bar concepts under one roof, this place consistently lands on lists for the best cocktail bars in the US. *4pm-midnight Tue-Thu, from 2:30pm Fri-Sun*

Bitter & Twisted: Sip a playful Bear Witness out of a honey bear bottle, or let the expert bar staff surprise you. *4pm-midnight Tue-Thu, to 1am Fri & Sat*

Grand Canyon National Park

SPECTACULAR SCENERY I MEMORABLE TRAILS I FASCINATING GEOLOGY

The Grand Canyon lives up to the hype: its immensity, its grandeur, its beauty and its very age all scream for superlatives. At about two billion years old, the layer of Vishnu schist at the bottom of the canyon is some of the oldest exposed rock on the planet. It was exposed by the Colorado River, which continues to carve its way 277 miles through the canyon – as it has for the past six million years.

At Grand Canyon National Park, you can descend into the canyon depths, stroll the rim or relax at an outcrop at either the North or South Rims. Though views from both rims are equally stunning, the South Rim boasts many more official and dramatic overlooks. One of the most beautiful, however, was the view that whispered from the Grand Canyon Lodge's patio on the canyon's quieter north side; the lodge burned to the ground in mid-2025, but there are other views nearby.

A 215-mile drive, or a strenuous day hike, connects the two rims.

GETTING AROUND

The South Rim is an easy 60-mile drive north of I-40 at Williams. Hwy 67 is the only road to the North Rim, closed December 1 to mid-May. Although the North Rim is only 11 miles from the South as the crow flies, it's a 215-mile, four- to five-hour drive.

Grand Canyon Village is congested March to September. Park at one of the four visitor center lots and catch a free shuttle bus. There are smaller lots at Shrine of the Ages, Market Plaza, Yavapai Geology Museum and Backcountry Information Center.

Rock Out at the Geology Museum

Rock layers and the Trail of Time

Take a moment to find the Colorado River while gazing through the large windows that overlook the canyon from the small **Yavapai Geology Museum** *(nps.gov/grca; free)*, where interpretive panels explain the formations below. Behind you, a topographic relief map highlights the canyon's multilayered geologic history. From here, walk west along the Trail of Time about 1.5 miles to the **Grand Canyon Village Historic District**. The trail traces the history of the canyon's formation – each meter equals one million years of geologic history. Stop by for a ranger geology talk at the museum at 11am daily.

TOP TIP

The park is an International Dark Sky Park, so evening light pollution is minimal and stargazing is superb. Bring a flashlight to dinner at the North Rim – the walk to your room is dark!

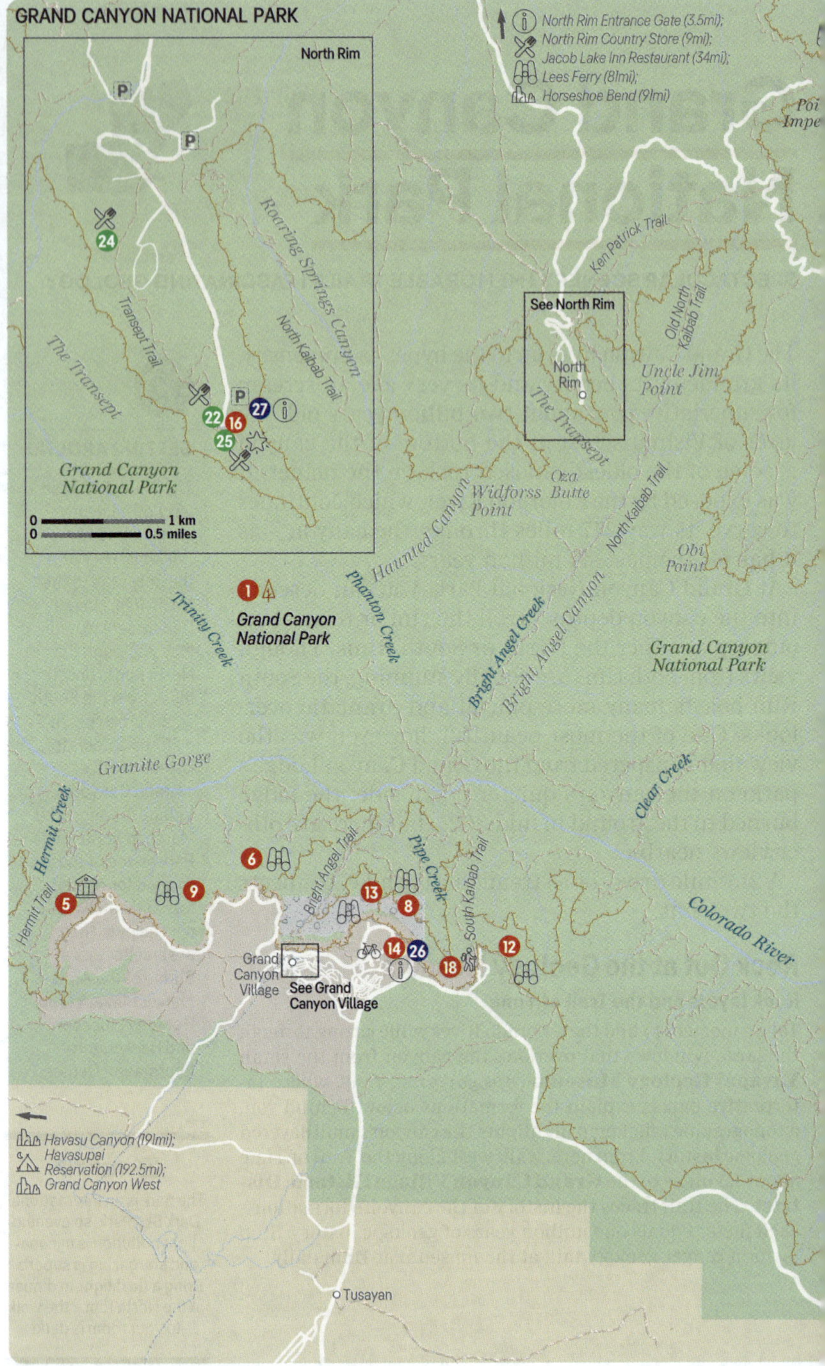
GRAND CANYON NATIONAL PARK
North Rim Entrance Gate (3.5mi);
North Rim Country Store (9mi);
Jacob Lake Inn Restaurant (34mi);
Lees Ferry (81mi);
Horseshoe Bend (91mi)
North Rim
P
Roaring Springs Canyon
Transept Trail
North Kaibab Trail
The Transept
24
22
16
27
25
Grand Canyon National Park
0 1 km
0 0.5 miles
Ken Patrick Trail
See North Rim
North Rim
The Transept
Old North Kaibab Trail
Uncle Jim Point
Oza Butte
Widforss Point
Haunted Canyon
North Kaibab Trail
Obi Point
1
Grand Canyon National Park
Trinity Creek
Phantom Creek
Bright Angel Creek
Bright Angel Canyon
Grand Canyon National Park
Granite Gorge
Clear Creek
Hermit Creek
Hermit Trail
5
9
6
Bright Angel Trail
13
8
Pipe Creek
South Kaibab Trail
12
Colorado River
14
26
18
Grand Canyon Village
See Grand Canyon Village
Havasu Canyon (191mi);
Havasupai Reservation (192.5mi);
Grand Canyon West
Tusayan

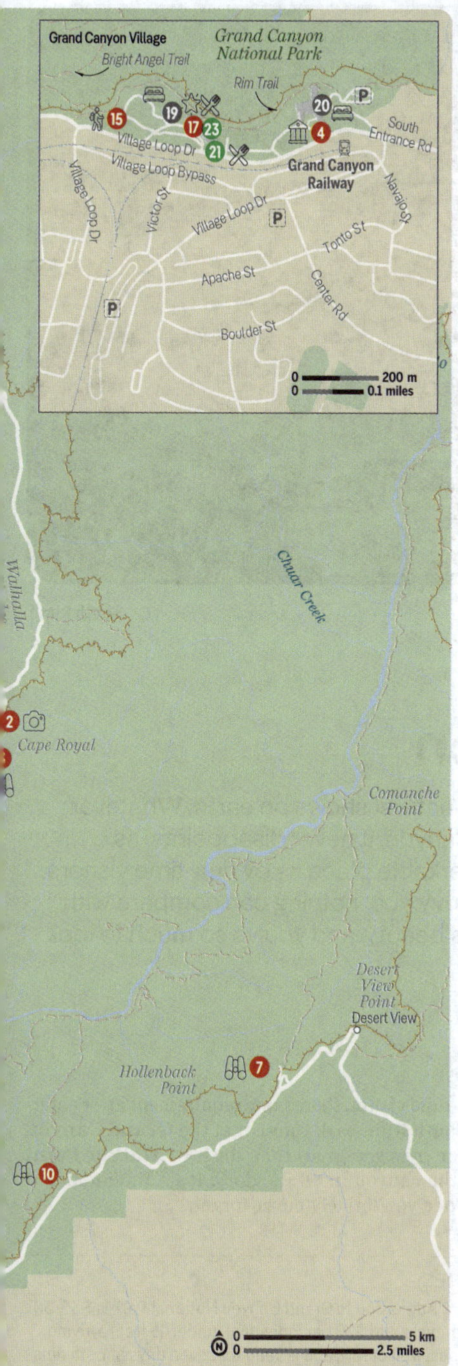

HIGHLIGHTS
1 Grand Canyon National Park

SIGHTS
2 Angels Window
3 Cape Royal Point
4 Grand Canyon Village Historic District
5 Hermits Rest
6 Hopi Point
7 Lipan Point
8 Mather Point
9 Mohave Point
10 Moran Point
11 Point Imperial
12 Yaki Point
13 Yavapai Geology Museum

ACTIVITIES
14 Bright Angel Bicycles
15 Bright Angel Trail
16 Canyon Trail Rides
17 Grand Canyon Mule Rides
18 South Kaibab Trail

SLEEPING
19 Bright Angel Lodge
20 El Tovar

EATING
21 Arizona Steakhouse
22 Deli in the Pines
see 20 El Tovar Dining Room
23 Harvey House Cafe
24 North Rim General Store
25 Rough Rider Saloon

INFORMATION
26 Grand Canyon Visitor Center
27 Old North Rim Visitor Center site

FELA SANU/SHUTTERSTOCK

South Rim

TOP EXPERIENCE

Grand Canyon

Welcome to one of the greatest natural shows on earth. Whatever you've heard about the Grand Canyon, it never disappoints, as beloved by veterans of this remarkable place as by first-time visitors. If you are among the latter, we envy you: nothing can compare with the first time you lay eyes on this beauty, and you've so much to look forward to.

DON'T MISS

- Mather Point
- Grand Canyon Visitor Center
- Bright Angel Trail
- South Kaibab Trail
- Rafting the Colorado River

Big View

If you're a first-time visitor, there's one requirement after entering from the South Rim: park your car at the **Grand Canyon Visitor Center** *(nps.gov/grca)* then dash to **Mather Point** to gaze upon the canyon in all its glory. It's a time-honored tradition and one you'll likely never forget.

PRACTICALITIES

● nps.gov/grca ● Admission to Grand Canyon National Park is $35/30 per vehicle/motorcycle and $20 per individual (under-15 free) arriving by foot, bicycle, bus, trail or raft, and is valid for seven days at both rims.

After that first mad glimpse, however, it's worth spending time at the visitor center itself. On the visitor-center plaza, bulletin boards and kiosks display information about ranger programs, the weather and tours. You'll also find helpful trail summaries. Inside is a ranger-staffed information desk, a lecture hall and a theater screening *Grand Canyon: A Journey of Wonder* – an introduction to the park's geology, history, and plant and animal life – and *We Are Grand Canyon,* a welcome from the 11 regional tribal communities. Each film is 24 minutes. The visitor center is also a stop on several shuttle routes.

Hike into the Canyon

As you'll quickly discover, the **Bright Angel Trail** is spectacularly scenic as it makes a 7.8-mile descent to the Colorado River. Though steep, long stretches near the start of this trail are not overly precarious, making this an excellent choice for families. Day hikers should turn around at one of the two rest houses (3- or 6-mile round trip) or hit the trail at dawn for longer hikes to Indian Garden and Plateau Point (9.2- and 12.2-mile round trip).

The **South Kaibab Trail** combines stunning scenery and unobstructed 360-degree views. Steep, rough and wholly exposed, this ridgeline descent plummets 4470ft along 6.4 miles to the Colorado River. You'll twist down tight switchbacks – flanked by a wall of Kaibab Limestone – before reaching Ooh Aah Point, a popular marked turnaround, at 0.9 miles. If you have more time, continue to Cedar Ridge at 1.4 miles. In addition to expansive views of the canyon, you'll find pit toilets here and a large, red-dirt overlook – mostly without shade – for a picnic.

Rafting the Grand Canyon

As you push off from **Lees Ferry** and float toward the soaring red walls of Marble Canyon, the sense of anticipation is something you won't soon forget. To come? More than 160 sets of rapids, camping under the stars, a float down the turquoise waters of the Little Colorado, hikes into mysterious slot canyons and a sense of camaraderie born from shared adventure – and no outside communications. Yep, a weeklong rafting trip on the Colorado River is a worthy bucket-list adventure, and one that is totally doable by the average traveler.

Consider the following before booking a trip: the number of days you want to be on the river, where you want to begin and end, and the type of boat – dory, oar-powered raft, paddle-steered raft or a motorized pontoon raft. The latter are the only ones that can travel the canyon's 277-mile course in a week. The national park *(nps.gov/grca)* has approved 15 commercial outfitters, listed on its website.

GAS & GARAGES AT THE GRAND CANYON

The **Desert View Chevron Service Station** is the only gas station on the South Rim, but gas stations in Tusayan are about 7 miles south of Grand Canyon Village. There is one gas station in the park on the North Rim, near the campground. You can also fill up in Jacob Lake or on Rte 67 at the **North Rim Country Store**.

TOP TIPS

- No cash is accepted at either the South or North entrance gates – credit/debit cards only.
- From the South Entrance it's 5 miles to the Grand Canyon Visitor Center, the primary informational hub.
- Transportation desks at Bright Angel, Maswik and Yavapai Lodges book bus tours.
- The Bright Angel desk also assists with Phantom Ranch and mule-ride reservations.
- The Backcountry Information Center supplies maps and backcountry permits.
- Cars are not allowed on the road to the South Kaibab Trailhead and Yaki Point nor, from March through November, on Hermit Rd.

BEST OVERLOOKS

Mohave Point: For a look at the river and three rapids. With multiple viewing spots, Mohave is particularly good for sunrise and sunset in high season.

Hopi Point: Magnificent east-west views, making it an excellent choice for dawn and dusk.

Lipan Point: Geology buffs: you can clearly see the tilting layered rocks of the Grand Canyon Supergroup here.

Moran Point: River views and excellent panorama of the canyon's geologic history. Named after Thomas Moran, the landscape painter who spent many winters at the canyon from 1899 to 1920.

Yaki Point: A favorite spot to watch the sunrise warm the canyon's features.

DUSTY ROADS/SHUTTERSTOCK

Angels Window

Shake the Crowds along Hermit Road

Hike, bike or ride the shuttle

Dotted with nine incredible canyon overlooks and roughly paralleling the rim, the 7-mile Hermit Rd stretches west from Grand Canyon Village Historic District to **Hermits Rest**. Designed by Mary Colter in 1913, the low-slung stone building at Hermits Rest is the South Rim's westernmost scenic overlook. The road is accessible year-round by bike, bus tour and by hiking the Rim Trail. Private vehicles can drive it December through February only. From March 1 through November 30, a park shuttle services all overlooks.

One of the best ways to experience Hermit Rd is by bike; rent one at **Bright Angel Bicycles**. You can also hike between shuttle stops via the Rim Trail.

Ride a Mule on the North or South Rim

Epic views and private cabins

If you take a mule ride, you're going to be sore – even if the ride lasts just an hour or two. But weary muscles have not scared away riders – they've been clip-clopping to the bottom

EATING ON THE SOUTH RIM: OUR PICKS

Harvey House Cafe: Savor a double-bacon cheeseburger and other American fare with canyon views. *6:30-10:30am, 11am-3pm & 4-9:30pm* $$

Arizona Steakhouse: Not just steaks – salads, sandwiches and burgers are on the menu, steps from South Rim. *11:30am-3pm & 4:30-9pm* $$

El Tovar Dining Room: Park dining at its best; windows frame the Rim Trail and canyon. Reserve. *6-10am, 11am-2:30pm & 4:30-9:30pm* $$$

of the Grand Canyon for more than 100 years. On the South Rim, **mule rides** *(grandcanyonlodges.com; from $1231)* follow the Bright Angel Trail – a bumpy, 10-mile trip with big views – to Phantom Ranch, which sits just north of the Colorado River. After one or two nights, they saddle up for an 8-mile ascent on the South Kaibab Trail. All meals are included in the ticket price. Make your reservation 15 months in advance.

Family-run **Canyon Trail Rides** *(canyonriders.com; 1/3hr $60/120)* offers one- and three-hour trips on the North Rim from mid-May through mid-October.

Drive the Scenic Cape Royal Road

North Rim ponderosas and canyon views

Cape Royal Rd is a scenic must-do for any North Rim visitor. And your payoff after driving it is the chance to stand upon **Angels Window**, a natural arch that juts into the canyon, dropping dramatically on three sides. A place for awe and plenty of photos.

Descending gradually from the trailhead at 8200ft to 7865ft at Cape Royal, Cape Royal Rd ribbons scenically for 15 miles through evergreens and ponderosas. Along the way you can take the spur road to 8803ft-tall **Point Imperial**, the highest viewpoint in the park, for a look at Marble Canyon.

At the end of the drive, a 0.6-mile paved path, lined with pinyon, cliffrose and interpretive signs, leads to the arch and to **Cape Royal Point**, arguably the best view from this side of the canyon.

Peer Through a Glass Skywalk

A transparent overlook

The glass-bottomed **Skywalk**, perched 4000ft above the floor of the Grand Canyon, is not for the faint of heart. But it is pretty darn cool. The Skywalk is one of several attractions at **Grand Canyon West** *(grandcanyonwest.com; general admission & Skywalk $68)*, a commercial venture managed by the Hualapai Nation.

Also be aware that Grand Canyon West is not part of the Grand Canyon National Park, which is 240 miles east. But it is a convenient, if pricey, place to see the canyon if you're staying in Las Vegas.

TIPS FOR THE GRAND CANYON

Avoid the temptation to run from overlook to overlook, snapping photos, looking for that perfect view and determined to see them all. A few hours sitting on a rock, the sun on your face and miles of layered canyon expanding in panorama around you, may just be the perfect canyon experience.

The canyon is best appreciated slowly, with patience, humility and respect.

Never hike to the river and back in one day.

Bring a cooler and snacks. Park food is notoriously bad and expensive.

Stay hydrated; dehydration and altitude sickness can ruin a canyon visit.

Spend at least three nights in the park, and let the park reveal itself slowly.

EATING ON THE NORTH RIM: OUR PICKS

North Rim General Store: Beside the campground, this market sells basic grocery items, plus snacks and ice cream. *7am-9pm* $

Deli in the Pines: Takeaway salads and sandwiches for a picnic, plus pizza, soft-serve ice cream. Elk chili is the winner. *10am-8pm* $

Rough Rider Saloon: Grab morning pastries and breakfast burritos at the counter; slices of pizza in the evening. *11am-11pm* $

Jacob Lake Inn Restaurant: Welcoming spot for breakfast, lunch or dinner 45 miles north of the North Rim. Great cookies! *7am-9pm* $$

GETTING STARTED AT THE NORTH RIM

The **North Rim Entrance Gate**, 31 miles south of Jacob Lake, does not accept cash; only credit and debit cards. The entrance is open 24 hours; a pass is valid for seven days.

From here, it's another 13 miles to where the visitor center and **Grand Canyon Lodge** were located, until a fire in 2025 destroyed them. Check the National Park Service website *(nps.gov)* for updates. Without the Grand Canyon Lodge, which was the only lodging inside the park on the North Rim, the nearest accommodations are in Jacobs Lake.

Full services are available on the North Rim from mid-May through mid-October. From December 1 to May 14, North Rim roads are closed to all vehicles.

RONNYBAS/SHUTTERSTOCK

Havasu Falls

Swimming Holes & Blue-Green Waterfalls

Get in the water

The blue-green waterfalls of **Havasu Canyon** are among the Grand Canyon region's greatest treasures. Tucked away in a hidden valley, the five stunning, spring-fed waterfalls – and their inviting azure swimming holes – sit in the heart of the 185,000-acre **Havasupai Reservation** *(havasupai reservations.com)*, which can only be accessed by trail.

The Havasupai Reservation is located south of the Colorado River and four hours west of Grand Canyon National Park's South Rim, off Route 66.

Hike or Paddle at Horseshoe Bend

Views and kayaks

Calling the view dramatic at **Horseshoe Bend** *(horseshoe bend.co; car/motorcycle parking $10/5)* is a wild understatement. The scenic overlook here sits on sheer cliffs that drop 1000ft to the river below, which carves a perfect horseshoe through the Navajo sandstone. And guardrails are few.

The trailhead is south of Page off Hwy 89, just past Mile 545. It's a 1.2-mile round-trip walk from the parking lot.

You can also **kayak** *(kayakhorsehoebend.com or kayakthe colorado.com; from $115)* the Colorado River through Horseshoe Bend and admire its soaring grandeur from below. **Horseshoe Bend Slot Canyon Tours** takes you to views from the south.

Northern Arizona

ANCIENT CULTURES | SPIRITUAL JOURNEYS | DESERT LANDSCAPES

If you broaden your horizons beyond Phoenix and the Grand Canyon, you'll move through the heartland of the American West. This is a world where crimson buttes, saguaros and ponderosa pines are the backdrop for outdoor adventures. Elsewhere, mountain towns and cliff dwellings offer introductions to a fascinating past.

Grand Canyon National Park may be Arizona's biggest draw, but it's also a launchpad for visits to nearby sites that delve into the culture and history of 11 tribal nations. Much of the area in the north and center of the state lies on, or just below, the Colorado Plateau, a high-desert playground that is cool, wooded and mountainous. Anchored by Flagstaff, this region is blessed with the state's most diverse and scenic sites. As a starting point, you can explore a vortex in Sedona, camp beside Oak Creek Canyon, or admire the 1000-year-old dwellings of the Ancestral Puebloans. Stargazing is amazing everywhere.

Places

TOP TIP

A Red Rock Pass ($5/15 day/week) covers everything from parking to spending time exploring National Forest land around Sedona, Oak Creek Canyon, Flagstaff and surrounds. It's available at ranger stations, visitor centers, most trailheads and *recreation.gov*.

Sedona & Around

Good vibes and vortexes

It's hard to have a bad day in Sedona. Red rock buttes, forested canyons and lush creek sides – it's a spectacular backdrop that has long attracted spiritual seekers, artists and healers. Over

GETTING AROUND

The sixth-largest state in the US, Arizona rewards those who explore by car; rentals are available from airports, but you'll find a better deal closer to your hotel. The main airports are at Phoenix, Flagstaff and, in the south, Tucson, with regular flights between the three. And if you prefer to ride the rails, Amtrak connects Los Angeles with Kingman, Flagstaff and Winslow on the daily *Southwest Chief*, which continues east to Albuquerque, NM. The daily scenic Grand Canyon Railway runs between Williams and Grand Canyon Village.

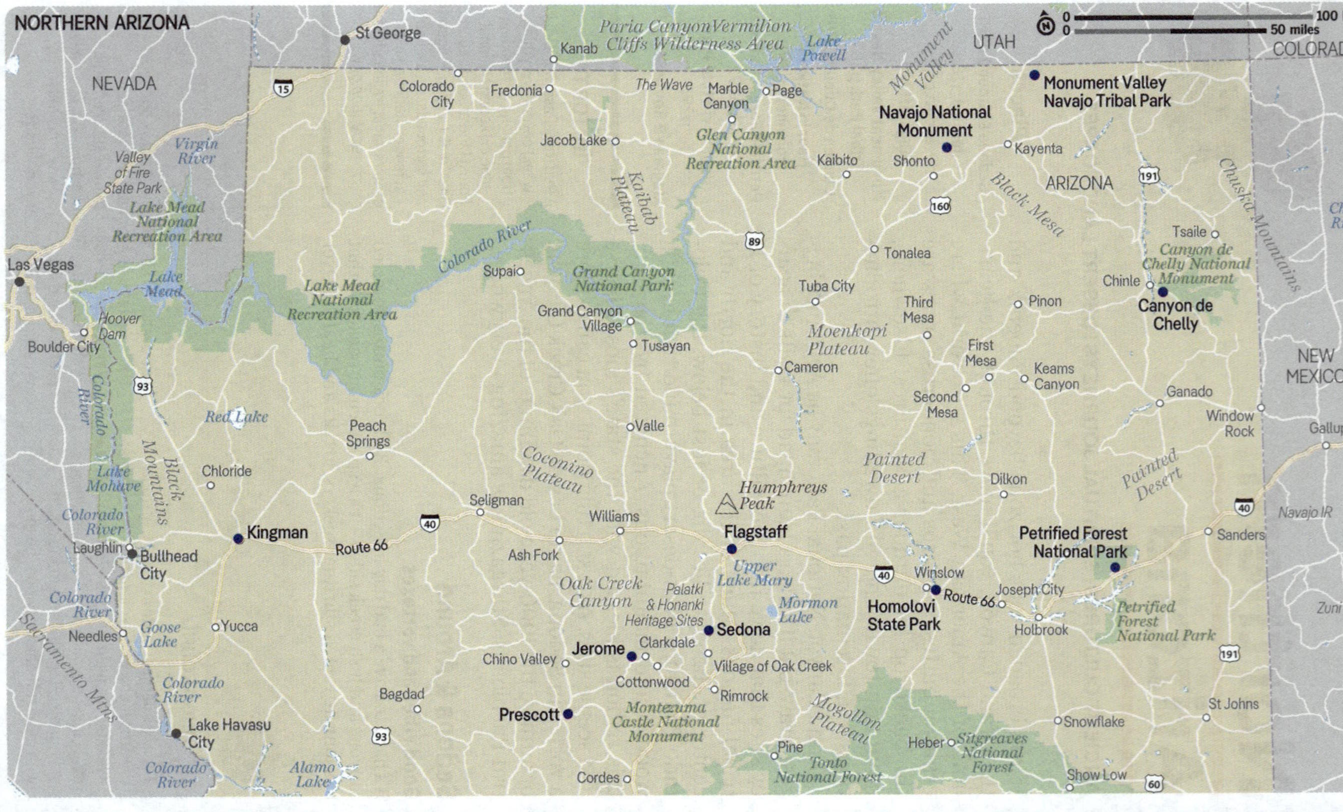
NORTHERN ARIZONA
0 100 km
0 50 miles
N
NEVADA
UTAH
COLORADO
ARIZONA
NEW MEXICO
St George
Kanab
Paria Canyon Vermilion Cliffs Wilderness Area
Lake Powell
Monument Valley
Monument Valley Navajo Tribal Park
Navajo National Monument
Colorado City
Fredonia
The Wave
Marble Canyon
Page
Jacob Lake
Glen Canyon National Recreation Area
Kaibito
Shonto
Kayenta
Black Mesa
Valley of Fire State Park
Virgin River
Lake Mead National Recreation Area
Kaibab Plateau
Chuska Mountains
Chaco River
Tsaile
Canyon de Chelly National Monument
Chinle
Canyon de Chelly
Las Vegas
Lake Mead
Hoover Dam
Boulder City
Colorado River
Supai
Grand Canyon National Park
Grand Canyon Village
Tusayan
Tonalea
Tuba City
Third Mesa
Pinon
Moenkopi Plateau
First Mesa
Keams Canyon
Second Mesa
Cameron
Ganado
Window Rock
Gallup
Red Lake
Peach Springs
Valle
Coconino Plateau
Painted Desert
Dilkon
Chloride
Black Mountains
Lake Mohave
Humphreys Peak
Seligman
Williams
Kingman
Route 66
Flagstaff
Petrified Forest National Park
Navajo IR
Sanders
Laughlin
Bullhead City
Ash Fork
Upper Lake Mary
Winslow
Joseph City
Oak Creek Canyon
Palatki & Honanki Heritage Sites
Mormon Lake
Homolovi State Park
Holbrook
Zuni IR
Needles
Goose Lake
Yucca
Sedona
Jerome
Clarkdale
Chino Valley
Village of Oak Creek
Cottonwood
Rimrock
Sacramento Mtns
Bagdad
Prescott
Montezuma Castle National Monument
Mogollon Plateau
St Johns
Snowflake
Lake Havasu City
Pine
Heber
Sitgreaves National Forest
Tonto National Forest
Alamo Lake
Cordes
Show Low
15
93
40
89
160
191
60

the years Sedona has developed into an extremely popular New Age destination. The reason? Spiritual-minded folks believe that the sandstone formations here hold vortexes, which vibrate to the frequencies of the deepest earth energies. Many believe this energy encourages healing and spiritual well-being.

To learn more, step inside the **Center for the New Age** *(sedonanewagestore.com)*, the big purple building on Hwy 179 south of Uptown. Shelves of this metaphysical superstore are crammed with crystals, spirituality books and vortex guides. Similar shops are scattered across town. The best-known vortexes are **Bell Rock** (near the Village of Oak Creek), **Cathedral Rock** (near Red Rock Crossing), **Airport Mesa** (Airport Rd) and **Boynton Canyon**.

Airport Mesa is the closest to town, and the drive up Airport Rd opens up to panoramic views of the valley. It's a half-mile walk from the mesa-top parking lot ($3) to the best viewpoint: a red rock hilltop with astounding 360-degree views.

Red rocks encourage deep thoughts at two beloved spots in Sedona. The better known of the two is the **Chapel of the Holy Cross** *(chapeloftheholycross.com; free)*, a small 1956 Roman Catholic chapel that soars from the surrounding rock like a slice of the majestic land itself.

A consecrated Buddhist shrine is set quite stunningly amid pinyon and juniper pine and the ubiquitous rocks at the low-key **Amitabha Stupa & Peace Park** *(tara.org/amitabha-stupa; free)* in West Sedona. Trails meander past colorful prayer flags, leading to a labyrinth and more red rock views.

Petroglyphs and cliff dwellings

The more than 1000 images (deer, turtles, birds, an embracing couple) carved into the sandstone panels at **Crane Petroglyph Heritage Site** *(fs.usda.gov; 9:30am-3pm Fri-Mon)* were created by the Sinagua people between 1150 and 1400 CE.

Seven miles of dirt road in northwestern Sedona lead to 1000-year-old Sinaguan cliff dwellings and rock art at the **Palatki Heritage Site** *(fs.usda.gov; reservations required)*, which is perched enchantingly on the edge of the wilderness. You can view more Sinaguan ruins 3 miles north at sister site **Honanki**. Both are open from 9:30am to 3pm Thursday to Tuesday and to noon Wednesday.

Red Rock ($5 per vehicle) and National Park passes (price varies) grant admission to all three sites, which are located in the Coconino National Forest.

BEST HIKES IN SEDONA & OAK CREEK CANYON

Bell Rock & Courthouse Butte: Easy 4-mile loop; follows multiuse Bell Rock Pathway around the immense Bell Rock then circles Courthouse Butte.

Boynton Canyon: Pretty 6-mile round-trip hike with shaded stretches, petroglyphs and Sinaguan ruins. Look for the side trail to Kachina Woman rock formation.

Devil's Bridge: Crowded, but the namesake arch is a photogenic prize on this 4-mile round-trip hike from Mescal Trailhead.

West Fork Trail: A 6½-mile round-trip Oak Creek Canyon hike with 13 creek crossings; red rock walls soar more than 200ft in some places. Gorgeous October foliage.

EATING IN SEDONA & AROUND: OUR PICKS

Sedonuts: Apple fritter is the top seller, but we dig the Red Rock Oreo at this decadent West Sedona doughnut shop. *6am-noon* $

Indian Gardens Cafe & Market: The breakfast sandwich is a delicious mess of eggs, chimichurri, cheddar; in Oak Creek Canyon. *8am-4pm Sat-Thu, to 8pm Fri* $$

Hudson: Prickly pear ribs, smoked-salmon bruschetta and fireball chicken wings infuse Sedona with urban cool. Great red-rock views. *11:30am-9pm* $$$

Mariposa: Stunning red-rock views and divine Latin-inspired food from the grill are the hallmarks of this upmarket option. *11am-2pm & 4-9pm* $$$

SIGHTS
1 Airport Mesa
2 Amitabha Stupa & Peace Park
3 Arizona Stronghold
4 Caduceus Cellars
5 Chapel of the Holy Cross
6 Honanki Heritage Site
7 Javelina Leap Vineyard
8 Merkin Vineyards Hilltop Winery & Trattoria
9 Oak Creek Vineyards
10 Oak Creek Vista
11 Page Springs Cellars
12 Palatki Heritage Site
13 Red Rock Crossing/ Crescent Moon Picnic Site

ACTIVITIES
14 Bell Rock
15 Boynton Canyon
16 Cathedral Rock
17 Devil's Bridge
18 Slide Rock State Park
19 West Fork Trail

EATING
20 Hudson
21 Indian Gardens Cafe & Market
22 Mariposa
23 Sedonuts

SHOPPING
24 Center for the New Age

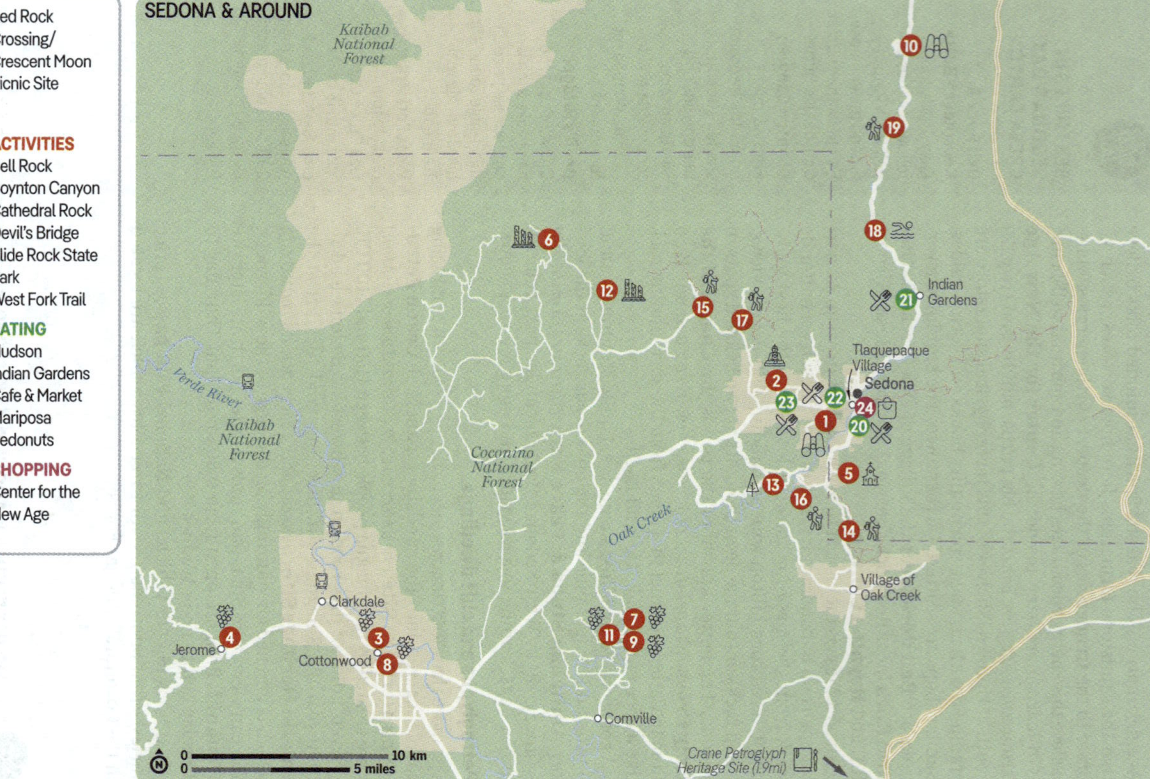

Hike Oak Creek Canyon

From the soaring overlook at **Oak Creek Vista**, 14 miles south of Flagstaff, the pine-draped glory of Oak Creek Canyon swoops south to the horizon like an unruly child just released from Nature's time-out. From the overlook, you'll corkscrew down Hwy 89A into the 13-mile canyon, where russet and vermilion cliffs soar above the creek and the highway. Giant cottonwoods clump along the waterway, providing a scenic, shady backdrop for trout fishing and swimming. If hiking is on your agenda, pull over for the popular **West Fork Trail**, which crosses Oak Creek 13 times as it winds through the canyon. Its imposing walls can soar more than 200ft.

A few miles south, an 80ft sandstone chute whisks swimmers through Oak Creek at **Slide Rock State Park** *(azstateparks.com; $10-30 per vehicle)*. The chute and the rock slides here are a blast but they can get oppressively crowded in summer, particularly between 10am and 3pm.

Drive the Red Rock scenic routes

The easiest scenic drive is also one of the best: the **Red Rock Scenic Byway** *(redrockscenicbyway.org)*. This National Scenic Byway and All-American Road tracks Hwy 179 from I-17 (exit 298) north of Phoenix for 7.5 miles, passing red hills and the Red Rock Ranger District Visitor Center before ending just north of the Village of Oak Creek in a pull-over, grab-your-camera explosion of red-rock impressiveness that includes Bell Rock and Courthouse Butte.

Any time is a good time to drive the winding 7-mile **Red Rock Loop Road**, which can be accessed via Upper Red Rock Loop Rd off Hwy 89A, 4 miles west of the Y intersection in Sedona. First up is the **Crescent Moon Picnic Site** *(vehicle/pedestrian $12/3)*, where a small army of photographers usually gathers at sunset at Red Rock Crossing to record the dramatic light show unfolding on iconic **Cathedral Rock**, a vortex.

Taste Verde Valley wines

The **Merkin Vineyards Hilltop Winery & Trattoria** *(merkintrattoria.com)* in Old Town Cottonwood – a 25-minute drive from Sedona – has a grand patio with sweeping views of the Verde Valley, where you can sip some darn good wines while nibbling on bruschetta and lasagna 'cupcakes.'

Merkin is one of two dozen or so vineyards, wineries and tasting rooms in the well-watered valley of the Verde River. Bringing star power to the **wine trail** *(vvwinetrail.com)* is Maynard James Keenan, lead singer of the band Tool and owner of Merkin Vineyards and **Caduceus Cellars** *(caduceus.org)*. His 2010 documentary *Blood into Vine* takes a no-holds-barred look at the northern Arizona wine industry.

Another good stop in Old Town Cottonwood is the tasting room at **Arizona Stronghold** *(azstronghold.com)*. Three wineries with tasting rooms hug a scrubby stretch of Page Springs Rd between Sedona and Cottonwood, near Cornville: bistro-housing **Page Springs Cellars** *(pagespringscelllars.com)*, the welcoming **Oak Creek Vineyards** *(oakcreekvineyards,net)* and the mellow-rock-playing **Javelina Leap Vineyard & Winery** *(javelinaleapwinery.com)*.

SEDONA SHUTTLES

Several helpful **shuttles** *(sedonashuttle.com)* crisscross the city.

Free **hiker shuttles** run to the most popular trailheads Thursday to Sunday, 7am to 5:30pm, with extra days when it's busy. These shuttles pick up passengers from three park-and-ride lots and run to Cathedral Rock/Little Horse, Dry Creek Vista/Mescal and Soldier Pass. Be aware that the Cathedral Rock and Soldier Pass Trailhead lots are closed to cars on the days the shuttle is running.

The new **Sedona Shuttle Connect** *(6:30am-6pm Thu-Sun; one way $2)* is an on-demand, app-driven service with stops in a defined area. **Verde Shuttle** *(6am-10pm; one way $2)* connects Sedona with Cottonwood, with stops along the way.

ARIZONA TIME ZONES

Arizona is on Mountain Time (seven hours behind GMT). It is the only Western state not to observe daylight saving time from spring to fall. The exception is the Navajo Reservation, which – in keeping with those parts of the reservation located in Utah and New Mexico – does observe daylight saving time. Confusingly, the small Hopi Reservation, which it surrounds, follows Arizona. The varying time zones come into play in Page and Monument Valley, which straddle the Arizona/Utah state line, during daylight saving time. Many hotels have two clocks on the wall, so you'll know what the times are. Keep the discrepancy in mind when scheduling tours in the region or your hotel check-in.

Jerome

Galleries, saloons and old hotels

Jerome can really mess with your mind: it can be hard to tell whether the buildings are winning or losing their battle with gravity. The **Sliding Jail**, lodged in the dirt southeast of the **Chamber of Commerce** visitor center, has moved 225ft from its original 1927 location. It isn't surprising, considering that there are 88 miles of tunnels, many of which were frequently dynamited and cut into steep hills, under your feet.

Main St is home to the engaging **Mine Museum** *(jerome historicalsociety.com; $2),* which spotlights local characters and stories. Just north, the allegedly haunted 1898 **Connor Hotel** (p338; *connorhotel.com)* was the town's first solid-stone lodging – don't miss the **Spirit Room**, the fun in-house saloon with murals sporting bordello scenes. From here, a climb leads to **Jerome Grand Hotel** (p338; *jeromegrand hotel.com),* the one-time home of the United Verde Hospital. Known for its ghosts and the venerable **Asylum Restaurant** *(asylumrestaurant.com),* it's a cool place to enjoy expansive views of the crimson-gold rocks of Sedona and the Verde Valley.

Prescott

Have a beer on Whiskey Row

Montezuma St, west of the plaza, was the infamous **Whiskey Row**, where 40 drinking establishments supplied suds to rough-hewn cowboys and miners. In 1900 a devastating fire destroyed 25 saloons, five hotels and the red-light district, although several early buildings remain. Many are still bars to this day, mixed with boutiques, galleries and restaurants.

Push through the swinging doors to enter the historic **Palace Saloon** *(whiskeyrowpalace.com).* It can be hard to tell if the men in cowboy hats are costumed waiters or actual cowboys. But no mind. This bar was once frequented by Wyatt Earp and Doc Holliday, so Old West duds come with the territory. Rebuilt in 1901 after the fire, it displays a museum's worth of Old West photos and artifacts. A scene from the 1972 Steve McQueen movie *Junior Bonner* was filmed here, and a mural honoring the film covers an inside wall.

Art, history, booze and good eats collide in the saloon and other century-old buildings surrounding **Yavapai County Courthouse**, which anchors an elm-shaded plaza in the heart of Prescott. Pause for breakfast or lunch at the cafe inside historic Hotel St Michael (p338).

EATING IN JEROME & PRESCOTT: OUR PICKS

Haunted Hamburger: Perched high on a Jerome hill, this beloved hamburger joint also serves big views and tasty margaritas. *11am-9pm* $

Clinkscale: Hot new kid in Jerome serving New American fare in stylish digs. *8:30am-8:30pm* $$

Farm Provisions: Farm-to-table Prescott favorite with gourmet options like deep-fried deviled eggs or kicky tacos with cilantro aioli. *11am-9pm Wed-Sun* $$

El Gato Azul: Creative Southwest and Spanish dishes that all sound good, including green-chile mac and cheese in Prescott. *11am-8pm most days* $$

Mt Elden

Buildings east and south of the plaza escaped the fire. The three-story Burmister Building houses a snazzy gift shop as well as **Superstition Meadery** *(superstitionmeadery.com)* and the **County Seat** *(countyseataz.com)* restaurant.

The **Chamber of Commerce Visitor Center** leads free guided walking tours (10am, Friday to Sunday from May to October).

Flagstaff

Flagstaff at all hours

Begin your Flagstaff day with chilaquiles and banana-split French toast at the now-legendary downtown **MartAnne's bistro** *(martannes.com)*. Come hungry for this one. Red walls, black booths and a bevy of oil paintings convey a unique, salon-like feel, and this Day of the Dead vibe is part of the quirky charm. And it ultimately plays well with the wonderfully messy creations on the menu. Of these, the Jerry el Mujeriego (Jerry the Womanizer; a green-chile pork enchilada topped with cheese, sour cream and two eggs) takes the top honors. Just don't plan on doing anything too strenuous immediately afterward. It's open 8:30am to 8pm most days.

Once you've recovered, it's time for a museum. Housed in an arts-and-crafts-style stone building, the small but excellent **Museum of Northern Arizona** *(musnaz.org; adult/Native American/child $15/10/10)* spotlights regional Native American archaeology, history and culture, as well as geology, biology and the arts. Representatives from 10 regional tribes worked with museum curators to select items displayed in the 'Native Peoples of the Colorado Plateau' ethnological exhibit, where you'll see baskets, pottery, jewelry and even a skateboard. Video messages from tribal members enhance the experience. On the way to the Grand Canyon, the museum makes a wonderful introduction to the human and natural history of the region.

TOP HIKES IN FLAGSTAFF

Fatman's Loop: Moderate 2-mile loop with volcanic rock formations, city views, varied trees and one tight squeeze. Begins 5 miles northeast of downtown.

Elden Lookout: Six-mile round-trip hike with a steep 2300ft climb to the summit of Mt Elden, a lava dome. End at a historic fire tower with views of Flagstaff, Sunset Crater and the San Francisco Peaks.

Aspen Nature Loop Trail: On the slopes of Mt Humphreys, this 2.5-mile trail loops past wildflowers, meadows and a forest thick with aspen, spruce and pine.

Kachina Trail: Aspens glow a luminous yellow in fall on this moderate forest-and-meadows trail on Mt Humphreys. It's a 10-mile round trip.

DISCOVER ROUTE 66 & HISTORIC HOTELS

Enjoy a mix of culture and history on this easy downtown walk that takes in public art, a gallery and Old West hotels.

START	END	LENGTH
Flagstaff Visitor Center	Flagstaff Visitor Center	0.5 miles; 30 minutes

Exploring downtown Flagstaff is an agreeable experience – just don't get hit by a passing train. Daily, more than 100 of them whizz past the 1 **Flagstaff Visitor Center**, which shares space with Amtrak inside a Tudor Revival station house. For details about the city's 40 murals, pick up the Flagstaff Public Art Map. Across San Francisco St, the bronze 2 **Gandy Dancer** statue depicts a hardworking railroad man. Cross Route 66 and stroll into downtown, where Old West heritage looms large. Pop into the 3 **Artists' Gallery** for locally made art, jewelry and ceramics. A neon sign towers over the 4 **Hotel Monte Vista**, which opened in 1927. Past guests include John Wayne, Clark Gable and Humphrey Bogart.

Built in 1888 by the Babbitt family on the northwest corner of Aspen Ave and San Francisco St, the sandstone 5 **Babbitt Building** was the first two-story structure in town. A long-running department store, it now houses an outdoor gear and apparel shop. In summer, 6 **Heritage Square** is a hub for festivals, movies and live music. Home to three separate bars, the 1900 7 **Weatherford Hotel** (p338) is the coolest building in town. Two icons of the west, artist Thomas Moran and author Zane Grey, are former guests. Open since 1917, the 8 **Orpheum** hosts live music, films and community events. Cross Route 66 again and return to the visitor center.

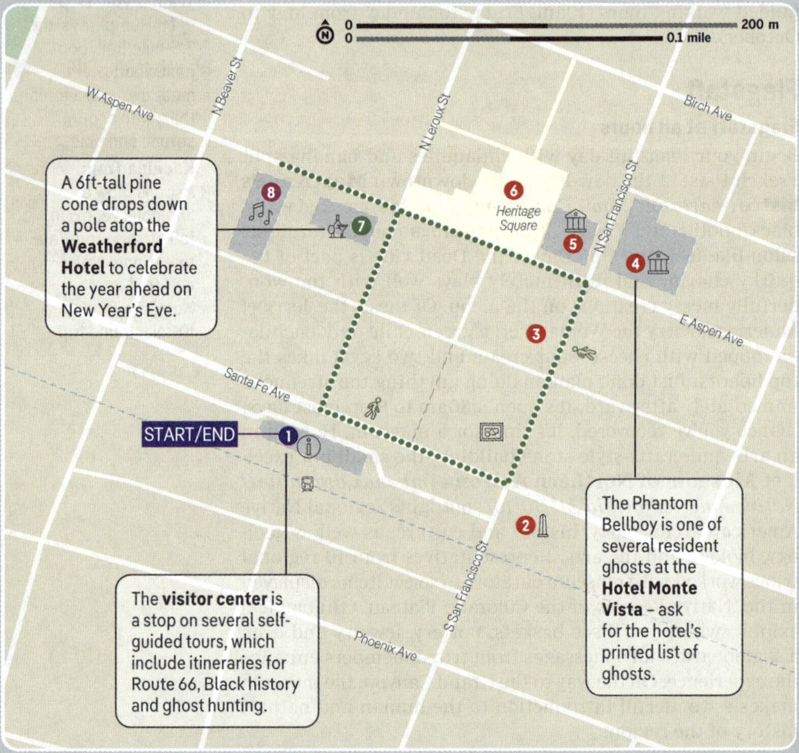

A 6ft-tall pine cone drops down a pole atop the **Weatherford Hotel** to celebrate the year ahead on New Year's Eve.

START/END

The **visitor center** is a stop on several self-guided tours, which include itineraries for Route 66, Black history and ghost hunting.

The Phantom Bellboy is one of several resident ghosts at the **Hotel Monte Vista** – ask for the hotel's printed list of ghosts.

As darkness falls, the **Museum Club** *(museumclub.net)*, an enormous log cabin perched right beside Route 66, comes into its own. To appreciate fully the kitschy appeal of this country-music roadhouse, sometimes called the Zoo, step inside to the large wooden dance floor, animal mounts and a sumptuous elixir-filled mahogany bar. Stick around for the band to fully immerse in the fun. Check its website for the live-music schedule and free line-dancing lessons.

Then when it's *really* dark, it's time for some stargazing. Flagstaff became an official Dark Sky City in 2001 – the very first community in the world to earn this designation from the International Dark-Sky Association. Cherished by astronomers for its dark and cloud-free night skies, Flagstaff is home to **Lowell Observatory** *(lowell.edu; adult/child/senior $35/20/30)* where you can check the marquee for details about daily talks and tours. At night, the Giovale building slides back to expose its telescopes – and budding astronomers – to a jaw-dropping view of the night sky. Evening constellation tours start nearby. For information about star parties and celebrations visit flagstaffdarkskies.org.

Monument Valley Navajo Tribal Park

Explore Monument Valley and Navajo history

If you drive south from Utah on Hwy 163, the rugged sandstone formations of **Monument Valley Navajo Tribal Park** *(navajonationparks.org; $8 per person)* initially rise into view like the ramparts of a prehistoric fortress, a huddled collection of red and gold defenses protecting ancient secrets.

Up close they're hypnotic, an alluring mix of familiar and elusive. Yes, we've seen them in the John Ford Westerns, but the big screen doesn't capture the changing patterns of light, the imposing height, or the strangeness of the angles and forms. You'll see the most striking formations from the rough **17-mile dirt road** *(7am-7pm; shorter hours in winter)* that loops through the park.

The **Wildcat Trail** is a 3.8-mile loop trail around the West Mitten formation that begins at the entrance to the 17-mile drive.

Rounding out your experience (and understanding) of these Navajo lands, it's time to listen to revisit the past. The Navajo Nation became the new owners of **Goulding's Lodge** *(gouldings.com)*, a storied trading post and hotel near the tribal park, in 2023. Harry Goulding and his wife Leone (better known as 'Mike') established the trading post in 1925. In

GUIDED TOURS

Tour guides at Monument Valley shower you with details about the reservation, movie trivia and whatever else comes to mind. They can also take you into the backcountry.

Navajo guides set up kiosks in the parking lot at the visitor center. They are pretty easygoing, so don't worry about high-pressure sales. Tours leave frequently in summer, less so in winter.

Outfits in Kayenta and at Goulding's Lodge also offer tours. To reserve in advance, check out the list of guides on the tribal park's website *(navajo nationparks.org)*. Rates start at about $70 for a 2½-hour motorized trip, and may require a two-person minimum. You do not need a guide to hike the Wildcat Trail.

EATING IN FLAGSTAFF: OUR PICKS

Karma Sushi Bar: Delicious sushi, but the tonkotsu ramen is legendary. On Route 66. *11am-9pm Sun-Thu, to 10pm Fri & Sat* $

Pizzicletta: Come here for gourmet toppings heaped on wood-fired pizzas. *noon-9pm Fri-Mon, 5-9pm Tue-Thu* $$

Josephine's: New American fare in a 1911 arts-and-crafts bungalow. Good for Saturday breakfast. *5-8:30pm Mon-Sat, 9am-2pm Sat* $$

Tinderbox Kitchen: Casual sophistication, chef-driven fare. Annex Cocktail Lounge for drinks. *3-10pm Mon-Thu, to midnight Fri & Sat* $$$

GHOST TOWNS

The discovery of gold, silver and copper brought fortune seekers to Arizona from the 1860s. New towns mushroomed overnight near the richest mines, and they were notoriously wild and dangerous places. Abandoned mining towns are scattered across the state's scrub-covered mountains and deserts. Typically there is not much to see at these sites unless you're into rusty equipment and weathered wooden shacks, but they can be cool for photos and for understanding the harshness of mining-town life.

For a list of sites across Arizona and the Southwest, visit americansouthwest.net/ghost-towns.html. For an atmospheric introduction, visit **Vulture City & Mine** *(vulturecityghosttown.com; adult/child $18/10)*, 12 miles west of Wickenburg.

KOJIHIRANO/ISTOCKPHOTO/GETTY IMAGES

the ensuing years, Goulding convinced director John Ford to film his Westerns in the butte-dotted valley. Today Goulding's is home to the lodge as well as a restaurant, a campground and a free museum inside the old trading post. Step inside the museum to see a replica of the store, a room dedicated to the movies shot here, the couple's upstairs living quarters and a collection of black-and-white photos of Navajos and the surrounding landscape.

Canyon de Chelly

Embrace the silence at Spider Rock

If you drive to the **Spider Rock Overlook** at Canyon de Chelly in the late afternoon, you might just have the place to yourself. And the empty silence is strangely invigorating as you gaze down at **Spider Rock**, a 800ft bifurcated sandstone spire guarding the place where **Canyon de Chelly National Monument** *(nps.gov/cach; free)* meets Monument Canyon. The overlook is the fifth and final stop on the 16-mile **South Rim Drive**, which runs along the main canyon and shares dramatic vistas.

EATING IN MONUMENT VALLEY & KAYENTA: OUR PICKS

Blue Coffee Pot: So this is where everybody is. This busy spot in Kayenta serves Navajo tacos and diner fare. *7am-9pm Mon-Fri* $

Amigo Cafe & Coffee Bar: Huevos rancheros, burgers with chipotle aioli, mutton tostadas on this tasty menu in Kayenta. *8am-8pm Tue-Sat* $

Stagecoach Restaurant: Impressive views in Goulding's Lodge. So-so American and Navajo fare and can swarm with tourists. *7am-9pm* $$

View Restaurant: The Navajo food doesn't always shine, but whoa, that view of the monuments is sublime. *7-11am & 5-9:30pm* $$

Spider Rock, Canyon de Chelly

For the most part, **North Rim Drive** follows a side canyon called Canyon del Muerto, which has four overlooks. At the first, **Antelope House Overlook**, a short walk ends at stunning cliff-top views of a natural rock fortress and cliff dwellings. To see the latter, walk to your right from the walled **Navajo Fortress Viewpoint** to a second walled overlook.

If you have a 4WD, you could go a little further. Past the mouth of Canyon de Chelly, heading deeper into the valley, the canyon's sandstone walls soar ever higher, narrowing your views of the sky. But the view ahead? It grows lush, filling with crops, livestock and cottonwood trees, all hugging a growing stream. Petroglyphs and cliff dwellings here are portals to the past, while hogans (homes) and fences give a nod to the vibrant present.

Check the **Navajo Nation Parks & Recreation** website *(navajonationsparks.org)* or stop by the national monument visitor center for a list of tour guides. Guided trips with **Beauty Way Jeep Tours** *(beautywaytours.com; 3hr tour $95.40)* travel all the way to White House Ruin deep in the canyon.

Navajo Code Talkers

WWII prompted the first large exodus of Native Americans from the reservations, when they joined the US war effort. The most famous were the Navajo code talkers – 420 US marines who used a code based on their language for vital messages in the Pacific Theater. Navajo is a notoriously complex Athabascan language, and Japan never broke the code. Code talkers were considered essential to US victory. You'll find code-talker exhibits at the Burger King in Kayenta and the **Explore Navajo Interactive Museum** in Tuba City. The work of the code talkers was kept classified until 1968, and they were granted Congressional Gold Medals in 2001.

STANDING ON THE CORNER IN WINSLOW

Thanks to the lyrics of the Eagles' catchy '70s tune 'Take It Easy,' tiny Winslow is now a popular roadside spot. At the small **Standin' on the Corner Park** on Route 66 you can pose with a life-size bronze statue of a hitchhiker backed by a charmingly hokey trompe l'oeil mural of that famous girl – my Lord! – in the song's famous flatbed Ford. Above, a painted eagle keeps an eye on the action.

For information about Winslow and historic exhibits, stop by the town **visitor center**, which is tucked inside the renovated Lorenzo Hubbell Trading Post five blocks west of the park.

WHAT IS A PETRIFIED LOG?

The Painted Desert at Petrified Forest National Park is strewn with fossilized logs predating the dinosaurs. The 'trees' are fragmented, fossilized 225-million-year-old logs scattered over a vast area of semidesert grassland. Many are huge – up to 6ft in diameter – and at least one spans a ravine to form a natural bridge. The trees arrived via major floods, only to be buried beneath silica-rich volcanic ash before they could decompose. Groundwater dissolved the silica, carried it through the logs and crystallized it into solid, sparkly quartz mashed up with iron, carbon, manganese and other minerals. Uplift and erosion eventually exposed the logs.

Navajo National Monument

Solitude and cliff dwellings

Hikers who love history, beauty and a bit of a challenge should detour to the serene **Navajo National Monument** *(nps.gov/nava; free)*, which is anchored by two sublimely well-preserved cliff dwellings. But plan ahead. The monument sits in a remote corner of the Navajo Reservation between Monument Valley and Tuba City, and the guided cliff-dwelling hikes are only offered on certain days.

You'll reach **Betatakin**, which translates as 'ledge house,' on a strenuous, ranger-led, 5-mile round-trip hike (late May to early September) that leaves the visitor center early on Saturdays and Sundays. This hike is first come, first served. For a distant glimpse of Betatakin, follow the easy **Sandal Trail** about half a mile from the visitor center.

The trail to the astonishingly beautiful **Keet Seel**, the largest Ancestral Puebloan structure in Arizona, is a challenging two-day guided hike (17 miles round trip; May to September) with one night of backcountry camping – and possibly quicksand! This trip is capped at 20 people. Register and confirm dates in March.

Petrified Forest National Park

Crystallized logs, petroglyphs and badlands

The 28-mile scenic drive through the **Petrified Forest National Park** *(nps.gov/pefo; car/motorcycle/bicycle/pedestrian $25/20/15/15)* has more than a dozen pullouts with interpretive signs and short trails. Several trails near the southern entrance provide the best access for close-ups of the petrified logs: the 0.4-mile **Giant Logs Trail** (with the park's largest log behind the Rainbow Forest Museum), the 1.6-mile **Long Logs Trail**, the 0.75-mile **Crystal Forest Loop** and the **Jasper Forest lookout**.

A highlight in the center section is a 3-mile loop drive to **Blue Mesa**, where you'll be treated to 360-degree views of spectacular badlands, log falls and logs balancing atop hills with the leathery texture of elephant skin. The 0.9-mile **Blue Mesa Trail** drops scenically into the badlands. Nearby, at the bottom of a ravine, hundreds of petroglyphs are splashed across **Newspaper Rock** like some prehistoric bulletin board. You'll find more petroglyphs and Ancestral Puebloan ruins at **Puerco Pueblo**.

North of I-40 lies a Route 66 interpretive marker and an especially brilliant section of the **Painted Desert**. Nature puts on a kaleidoscopic show here at sunset: the most mesmerizing views are from **Kachina Point** behind the historic **Painted Desert Inn**. The Painted Desert is a beautiful place to camp. A free permit is required. Pick one up at the **Painted Desert Visitor Center** at the north entrance before 4:30pm.

Videos describing how the logs were fossilized run regularly at Painted Desert Visitor Center and the visitor center at **Rainbow Forest Museum** near the south entrance. Both visitor centers have park exhibits, maps and gift shops.

STEVEN GROUP/SHUTTERSTOCK

Petrified Forest National Park

Homolovi State Park

Petroglyphs and ancient pueblos

A grasslands park beside the Little Colorado River, **Homolovi State Park** *(azstateparks.com; vehicle/pedestrian/bicycle $7/3/3)* protects artifacts and archaeological sites within the sacred Hopi homeland. Short hikes lead to petroglyphs and partly excavated pueblos, most likely built by the Ancestral Hopi. The trail to the **Homolovi II ruins** is paved and wheelchair accessible. Before the area was converted into a park in 1993, bold thieves used backhoes to remove artifacts.

There's a **campground** with electric hookups, water and showers near the excavated pueblos. The park is 3 miles northeast of Winslow via Hwy 87.

Kingman & Route 66

Celebrate Route 66 – and some new stuff!

The best attractions along Route 66 are eye-catching and enormous, and the drive-thru Route 66 sign at the **Kingman Visitor Center** *(explorekingman.com)* is no exception. Park your ride beneath the sign, then, if you're alone, ask a kind-hearted stranger to take your photo. The visitor center, tucked inside the 1907 Powerhouse, stocks the requisite free brochures, but the big draw is the engaging **Route 66 Museum** *(mohavemusuem.org; adult/child $10/free)*, which shares an informative historical overview of travel along the Mother Road.

From here, it's a short drive to Beale St, the axis of the historic downtown. After sunset, cruise Route 66 and immerse yourself in its neon glory. The next morning, breakfast is served with a side of kitsch at **Mr D'z Route 66 Diner**, a roadside vision in turquoise and 1950s nostalgia.

PETRIFIED FOREST ORIENTATION

Straddling I-40, Petrified Forest National Park has an entrance at exit 311 off I-40 in the north, and another off Hwy 180 in the south. These are the only two entrances, and a 28-mile paved scenic road within the park links them. Note that the south entrance has the highest concentration of petrified wood and so is the most interesting part of this park.

To reach the south entrance from I-40, without following the park scenic road, you will need to leave the interstate at exit 285 and follow signs to Hwy 180 and the national park. The south entrance is 18 miles from I-40, so you can't simply pull over for a quick look if you're on I-40.

ROUTE 66, UNINTERRUPTED

North of Kingman, Route 66 arcs north away from I-40 for 115 dusty miles through the high desert. It merges with I-40 near Seligman then reappears briefly as Main St in Williams. Cell service is unreliable and gas stations are rare, so make sure you have enough fuel. The road is not heavily traveled, and you'll likely find that your car is the only vehicle on the road for miles at a time. The total distance to Williams is 130 miles.

Nicknamed the 'Mother Road' by novelist John Steinbeck and completed in 1926, Route 66 travels through eight states, linking a series of small towns between Chicago and Los Angeles.

MAGIC ALBERTO/SHUTTERSTOCK

Kingman (p293)

Leaving Kingman, 9 miles east of Peach Springs, a plaster dinosaur marks your arrival at **Grand Canyon Caverns** *(gccaverns.com; per person $69.95)*. Tours of this fascinating cave complex deep underground run regularly. Above ground, you'll find a campground, motel and restaurant. The complex is now owned by the Havasupai Tribe, and the motel doubles as the check-in point for tours.

Further along, look for red-and-white Burma Shave signs on the 23 miles of road slicing through the rolling hills to **Seligman**, the inspiration for Radiator Springs in Pixar's *Cars*. Angel Delgadillo retired from **Angel's Barbershop** *(route66giftshop.com; 9am-5pm)* in roadside Seligman in 2022 at age 95 – but his barber's chair is still there. Today the barbershop is a museum and souvenir store. Angel's madcap brother Juan, who died in 2004, ruled prankishly supreme over the nearby **Delgadillo's Snow Cap** – a Route 66 institution still serving burgers and ice cream. Beware the fake mustard bottle! For a full-service meal, try the German and American dishes at **Westside Lilo's Cafe** *(westsidelilos.com)*.

From Seligman, one of the last sets of **Burma Shave signs** reads: 'Passing cars… When you can't see… May get you a glimpse… Of eternity.'

DRINKING IN KINGMAN: OUR PICKS

Cellar Door: Downtown wine bar with more than 120 wines and dozens of beers, live music and trivia nights. *varies 3-9pm Wed-Sat*

Rickety Cricket: Creative beer selections – we're looking at you Snoszberry – plus pizza, nachos and tiramisu. *varies 11am-9pm*

Liquid Bistro & Coffee Shop: Low-key coffee shop with mid-century cool, but no kitsch. Distinctive turquoise-and-white digs. *7am-3pm*

Desert Diamond Distillery: Sample whiskey and rum at this small distillery near Kingman airport. *10am-5pm Sun-Thu, to 6pm Fri & Sat*

Southern Arizona

VIBRANT CITY | OLD WEST | SCENIC DRIVES

Arizona's deep south concentrates some of the state's most rewarding attractions. Tucson is one of the most engaging towns in the entire West, a cultural powerhouse, not to mention an emerging culinary superstar. It has so much to offer, both as an underrated destination in its own right and as gateway to a region that can seem like a stereotype of the Old West. You barely need to leave Tucson before Saguaro National Park and the Sonoran Desert offer up classic landscapes and the world's most recognizable cactus. A little further afield, it's the old mining town of Bisbee and gunfights at the OK Corral in Tombstone; the latter is one of the must-see places if you're eager to immerse yourself in the legends of the storied West. Crowning this beautiful region are the Santa Catalina Mountains, which are the perfect place to explore on a series of scenic drives.

Places

TOP TIP

Don't be fooled by how close the attractions of southern Arizona can appear: it's only by comparison to the rest of the state. Plan to spend longer than you expect, and add a day or two to your plans to allow you to follow curiosity down quiet back roads.

Tucson

Explore an Arizona desert city

Set in a flat valley hemmed in by snaggle-toothed mountains and swaths of saguaro, Arizona's second-largest city smoothly blends Native American, Spanish, Mexican and Anglo traditions. Distinct neighborhoods and 19th-century buildings

GETTING AROUND

As ever out here in the West, having your own vehicle will greatly enhance your experience: many attractions in these parts can only be reached in your own SUV or 4WD. Rental is easy (book ahead to ensure the best rates) at Tucson airport or downtown. Tucson International Airport serves southern Arizona, with regular flights around the Southwest. Part of the mix for getting to Tucson from beyond the region includes train: Amtrak's thrice-weekly *Sunset Limited* links Tucson with LA, Houston and New Orleans.

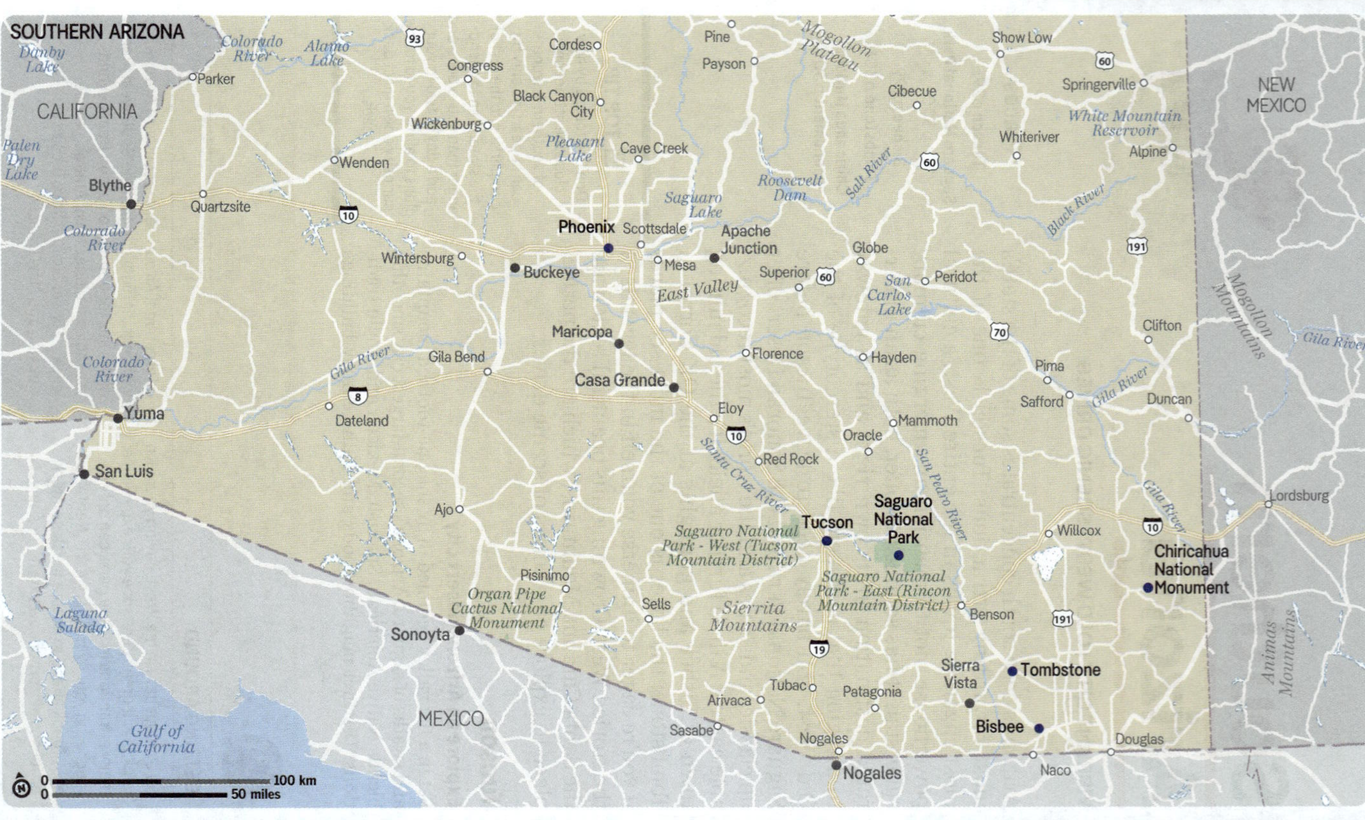
SOUTHERN ARIZONA
CALIFORNIA
NEW MEXICO
MEXICO
Danby Lake
Colorado River
Alamo Lake
Parker
Palen Dry Lake
Blythe
Quartzsite
Wenden
Wickenburg
Congress
Cordes
Black Canyon City
Pleasant Lake
Cave Creek
Pine
Payson
Mogollon Plateau
Show Low
Springerville
Cibecue
Whiteriver
White Mountain Reservoir
Alpine
Roosevelt Dam
Salt River
Black River
Saguaro Lake
Phoenix
Scottsdale
Apache Junction
Mesa
Globe
Superior
Peridot
San Carlos Lake
East Valley
Wintersburg
Buckeye
Maricopa
Casa Grande
Florence
Hayden
Clifton
Mogollon Mountains
Gila River
Pima
Safford
Duncan
Gila Bend
Dateland
Yuma
San Luis
Eloy
Mammoth
Oracle
Red Rock
Santa Cruz River
San Pedro River
Ajo
Tucson
Saguaro National Park
Saguaro National Park - West (Tucson Mountain District)
Saguaro National Park - East (Rincon Mountain District)
Willcox
Lordsburg
Chiricahua National Monument
Pisinimo
Organ Pipe Cactus National Monument
Sells
Sierrita Mountains
Benson
Sonoyta
Laguna Salada
Tubac
Arivaca
Patagonia
Sierra Vista
Tombstone
Bisbee
Animas Mountains
Sasabe
Nogales
Douglas
Naco
Gulf of California
0 100 km
0 50 miles

give a rich sense of community and history not found in more modern, sprawling Phoenix. The eclectic shopping, affordable restaurants, whimsical murals and fun-loving dive bars don't let you forget Tucson is a college town at heart, home turf to the 50,000-strong University of Arizona (U of A).

The **Tucson Museum of Art** *(tucsonmuseumofart.org; adult/child $15/free)* is part of the low-key **Presidio Historic District** and embraces the site of the community's original Spanish fort and upmarket 'Snob Hollow.' This is one of the oldest continually inhabited places in North America: the **Spanish Presidio de San Augustín del Tucson** *(tucsonpresidio.com; adult/child $9/6)* dates back to 1775, but the fort itself was built over a Hohokam site that has been dated to between 700 and 900 CE. The district teems with adobe townhouses and restored 19th-century mansions. **Old Town Artisans** *(oldtownartisanstucson.com)* is the place for Mexican and Southwestern art and crafts.

When it's time to eat, tucked in a rambling downtown hacienda, the buzzing **El Charro Café** (p299; *elcharrocafe.com)* celebrated its centennial in 2022. Overseen by chef-owner Carlotta Flores, it's famous for its *carne seca,* sundried lean beef that's been reconstituted, shredded and grilled with green chile and onions. The fabulous margaritas also pack a serious punch. The restaurant's original matriarch, Monica Flin, is said to have invented the chimichanga after accidentally dropping a burrito into a deep fryer.

Elsewhere, Tucson's signature dish is the Sonoran dog, a bacon-wrapped hot dog layered with tomatillo salsa, pinto beans, shredded cheese, mayo ketchup, mustard, chopped tomatoes and onions. Dig into one at one of two **BK Carne Asada & Hot Dogs** *(bktacos.com)* locations.

And as the day draws to a close, you have a couple of great options for watching the sunset in west Tucson. The **Brown Mountain Trail** *(pima.gov)* climbs past saguaros, cholla and other desert vegetation to sweeping ridgeline views of the Tucson Mountains, the Tohono O'odham Reservation, the Santa Rosa Mountains and the Aguirre Valley. This view is awash in luminous color at sunset. If you don't want to hike, drive to the **Gates Pass Scenic Lookout** *(nps.gov)* on West Gates Pass Rd for a splendid, expansive sunset view of the saguaro-dotted mountain pass.

Drive the Mt Lemmon Scenic Byway

Generations of Tucsonans have escaped the summer heat by driving up Mt Lemmon in the Santa Catalina Mountains. You

BEST UNIQUE TUCSON MUSEUMS

Ignite Sign Art Museum: More than 900 old neon signs, primarily from Tucson, light up the museum. Watch a neon bending demo or take a class.

Mini Time Machine Museum of Miniatures: Delightful museum with intriguing dioramas that are fantastical and historical.

Pima Air & Space Museum: An SR-71 Blackbird spy plane and B-52 bomber are among the stars of this extraordinary private aircraft museum.

Center for Creative Photography: Ever-changing, high-caliber exhibits. Administers the archives of Ansel Adams.

Coit Museum (formerly the History of Pharmacy Museum): Old-timey tinctures and a full-size pharmacy replica once found on Disneyland's Main Street, USA.

EATING IN TUCSON: OUR PICKS

Charro Steak & Del Rey: Scrumptious steaks, seafood and libations in a modern rustic space. *3-9pm* $$$

Beyond Bread: Daily breads and a mouthwatering array of sandwiches. Several locations. *7am-7pm* $

HUB Restaurant & Ice Creamery: Upscale comfort food in exposed-brick digs on Congress St. Save room for ice cream. *11am-9pm Sun-Thu, to 11pm Fri & Sat* $$

Maynards: Regionally sourced and seasonal American fare in the Historic Depot downtown. *5-9pm Wed-Sun* $$

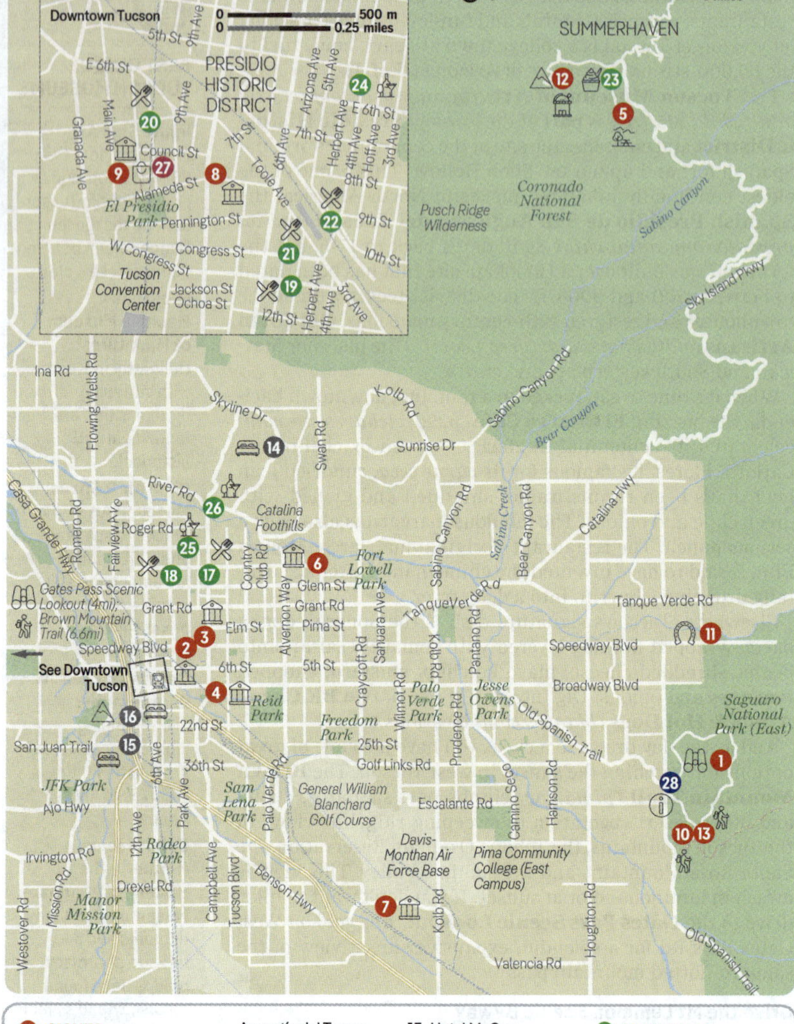

SIGHTS
1 Cactus Forest Loop Drive
2 Center for Creative Photography
3 Coit Museum
4 Ignite Sign Art Museum
5 Marshall Gulch Picnic Area
6 Mini Time Machine Museum of Miniatures
7 Pima Air & Space Museum
8 Spanish Presidio de San Augustín del Tucson
9 Tucson Museum of Art

ACTIVITIES
10 Freeman Homestead Trailhead
11 Houston's Horseback Riding
12 Mt Lemmon SkyCenter Observatory
13 Tanque Verde Ridge

SLEEPING
14 Hacienda del Sol Guest Ranch Resort
15 Hotel McCoy
16 Tuxon

EATING
17 Beyond Bread
18 BK Carne Asada & Hot Dogs
19 Charro Steak & Del Rey
20 El Charro Café
21 HUB Restaurant & Ice Creamery
22 Maynards
23 Mt Lemmon Cookie Cabin

DRINKING & NIGHTLIFE
24 BOCA by Chef Maria Mazon
25 Guadalajara Original Grill
26 Reforma Modern Mexican

SHOPPING
27 Old Town Artisans

INFORMATION
28 Rincon Mountain Visitor Center

can follow their tracks on the very picturesque **Mt Lemmon Scenic Byway** (also called the Catalina Hwy Scenic Drive), which meanders 27 miles from saguaro-dappled desert to pine-covered forest near the summit (9157ft). Allow at least three hours for the round trip and watch for cyclists.

Of the vista points, Babad Do'ag, Windy Point and Aspen are the most rewarding. In lofty Summerhaven, everybody stops for ice cream and cookies the size of your face at the **Mt Lemmon Cookie Cabin** *(thecookiecabin.org)*. Nearby, the loop connecting the **Marshall Gulch Trail & Aspen Trail** *(fs.usda.gov; day pass per vehicle $8)* is a recommended 4-mile hike through ponderosas, aspens and firs.

You can attend an evening SkyNights StarGazing Program at the **Mt Lemmon SkyCenter Observatory** *(skycenter.arizona.edu; adult/child $85/60)*. Reserve a spot at least one week in advance.

MT LEMMON: NEED TO KNOW

There is no cost for the drive or for stopping at the vista points, but to explore the forest you must get the **Coronado Recreation Pass** *(fs.usda.gov; per day/week $8/10)*. Buy it online, at trailside kiosks or at the Palisades Visitor Center (Mile 19.6).

For an audio tour explaining the science behind the sights you'll see along the 27-mile drive, download the free Mt Lemmon Audio Tour app on your smartphone (see visittucson.org).

Several campsites line the drive, with overnight rates ranging from $20 to $28. Call the Pima County Sheriff's Road Conditions hotline at 520-547-7510 for road conditions.

Bisbee

Mining museum and mine tour

Bisbee built its fortune on ore discovered in the surrounding Mule Mountains. In their 19th- and 20th-century heyday, the underground and open-pit mines here coughed up copper worth more than $6 billion.

Start your day with huevos rancheros at the **Bisbee Breakfast Club**, followed by a stroll along adjacent Erie St. Lined with vintage cars and pickup trucks, as well as storefronts from an earlier era, the street is an eerily accurate model of a mid-century downtown.

Now it's time to go underground. You'll don a hard hat and a safety vest during the pre-trip orientation at the **Queen Mine** *(copperqueenmine.com; adult/child $16/8)* south of downtown. Today, visitors ride 1500ft into the mountain on a subterranean mine train, often guided by the mountain's last miners or their offspring.

In the 1897 former headquarters of the Copper Queen Consolidated Mining Company, the **Bisbee Mining & Historical Museum** *(bisbeemuseum.org; adult/child $10/free)* traces the town's past.

Echoes of Bisbee ripple out across the surrounding countryside. A former mining community southeast of Bisbee, Lowell was mostly consumed by the adjacent Lavender Pit mine. Today, this short strip of Americana – mostly abandoned

DRINKING IN TUCSON: WHERE TO GET A MARGARITA

El Charro Café: There are 18 delicious margaritas on the menu, and all of them pack a punch. *11am-9pm Wed-Sat, to 8pm Sun*

Guadalajara Original Grill: The frozen Bandera margarita is stacked with three colorful layers – green, white and red – to resemble the Mexican flag. *11am-10pm Sun-Thu, to 11pm Fri & Sat*

BOCA by Chef Maria Mazon: They serve them by the carafe, and at happy hour the house margaritas are $8. *noon-9pm Mon & Tue, to 10pm Fri & Sat, to 8pm Sun*

Reforma Modern Mexican: Mango habanero, blueberry basil, blood orange, prickly pear are among Reforma's elevated options. Kick back and sip away on its beautiful patio. *hours vary*

TOP EXPERIENCE

Saguaro National Park

Saguaros are icons of the American Southwest, and an entire cactus army of these majestic, ribbed sentinels is protected in Saguaro National Park. Exploring these strange life forms - they can really mess with your mind on a moonlit night - is the main reason to visit this beautiful park.

HIGH FLIERS/SHUTTERSTOCK

Go for a Drive or Ride

The 8-mile **Cactus Forest Loop Drive** *(nps.gov/sagu)* in the Rincon Mountain District is special, and its beauty is open to drivers and cyclists alike. The scrubby desert scenery here also evokes the Old West. To embrace the John Wayne vibe, saddle up for a horseback ride with family-run **Houston's Horseback Riding** *(tucsonhorsebackriding.com)*.

Hike Saguaro Trails

Hikers pressed for time can follow the 1-mile round-trip **Freeman Homestead Trail** *(nps.gov/sagu)* to a grove of massive saguaros. For a full-fledged desert adventure with high-elevation views, head out on the steep and rocky **Tanque Verde Ridge Trail** *(nps.gov/sagu)*, which climbs to the summit of Tanque Verde Peak and back in 18 miles. An $8 backcountry camping permit is required for overnight use. The **Rincon Mountain Visitor Center** *(nps.gov/sagu)* has information about day hikes, horseback riding and backcountry camping. Seven-day passes per vehicle/motorcycle/bicycle cost $25/20/15. Cash is not accepted.

Learn about Saguaros

Saguaros (suh-*wah*-ros) only grow in the Sonoran Desert and they do so slowly, taking about 15 years to reach a foot in height, 50 years to reach 7ft and almost a century before they begin to take on their typical many-armed appearance. In April each year, the cacti begin blossoming with lovely white blooms – Arizona's state flower. By June and July the flowers give way to ripe red fruit that local Native Americans use for food. It is illegal to damage or remove saguaros.

TOP TIPS

- The national park is divided into east and west, separated by 30 miles and Tucson itself.
- Each section distributes its own hiking guide with maps and trail summaries.
- The busy season runs November through March; temperatures range from the high 50°Fs to mid-70°Fs (around 14°C to 24°C).

– gives a nostalgic nod to the 1950s. Just north on Hwy 80, look for the not-so-truthful 'Scenic View' sign. It's pointing toward the Lavender Pit, an immense stair-stepped gash in the ground that produced about 600,000 tons of copper between 1950 and 1974.

Tombstone

OK Corral and Old West museums

If you were to visit one town to capture the essence of the Wild West, we'd make it Tombstone.

Like death and taxes, the daily reenactment of the gunfight at the **OK Corral** *(ok-corral.com)* is a sure thing. Before the show, you'll see Doc Holliday and the Earp brothers silently stroll down dusty Allen St. The thrice-daily performance ($10) takes place inside the corral, which is the heart of both historic and touristic Tombstone.

From here, plank sidewalks and dirt roads are portals to the Old West, with wooden storefronts and a horse-drawn stagecoach setting the scene. It's hokey, but also fun, and it's easy to imagine cowboys, gunslingers and miners roaming the streets.

The **Bird Cage Theatre** *(tombstonebirdcage.com)* was a one-stop sin-o-rama, with onstage shows as well as a saloon, dance hall, gambling parlor and a home for 'negotiable affections.' Today, with its dusty knickknacks, illicit history and ghost tours, it's ground zero for kitschy deliciousness – a place for which road trips are made.

And the epitaphs at **Boothill Graveyard** *(discoverboothill.com; $6)* tell you everything you need to know about living – and dying – in Tombstone in the late 1800s. 'Murdered.' 'Shot.' 'Suicide.' They spotlight the violence of the place, where life was hard and often short. The graves of Billy Clanton and Tom and Frank McLaury, all killed at the shoot-out at the OK Corral, are in Row 2. Some headstones are twistedly poetic: the oft-quoted epitaph for Lester Moore, a Wells Fargo agent, may be the most famous: 'Here lies Lester Moore, Four slugs from a .44, No Les, no More.'

GUNFIGHT AT THE OK CORRAL

Tombstone is the location of the infamous 1881 gunfight at the OK Corral, when Wyatt Earp, his brothers Virgil and Morgan, and their friend Doc Holliday gunned down outlaws Billy Clanton and Tom and Frank McLaury, who belonged to a loose association of rustlers and thieves called the Cowboys. On the day of the shoot-out, the Cowboys had come to Tombstone and were in apparent violation of the law, requiring them to check their weapons. The ensuing gunfight only lasted about 30 seconds but so caught people's imaginations that it not only made it into the history books, but also onto the silver screen – many times – including the 1993 flick *Tombstone*, starring Kurt Russell and Val Kilmer.

Chiricahua National Monument

Volcanic rocks and Apache history

From the viewing area at Massai Point, the rhyolite rock pinnacles at the remote **Chiricahua National Monument** *(nps.gov/chir)* resemble a goblin army, a vast force ready to march down the mountain and do battle for their goblin king. This rugged yet whimsical wonderland, covering nearly 19 sq miles across a desert sky island in the Chiricahua Mountains, is one of Arizona's most evocative landscapes, a wind-chiseled volcanic landscape of fluted pinnacles, natural bridges, balancing boulders and soaring spires. The remoteness made Chiricahua (cheery-*cow*-wha) a favorite hiding place of Apache warrior Cochise and his men in the 1800s. The park is a two-hour drive from Tucson.

APACHE CONFLICTS

For decades, US forces pushed west across the continent, killing or forcibly moving tribes of Native Americans who were in their way. The last serious conflicts were between US troops and the Apache, partly because raiding was the essential path to manhood for the tribe. US forces and settlers moving into Apache land became obvious targets for the raids that were part of the Apache way of life. This continued under the leadership of Mangas Coloradas, Cochise, Victorio and Geronimo.

Geronimo surrendered in 1886 after being promised that he and the Apache would be imprisoned for two years, then allowed to return to their homeland. As with many promises made during those years, this one was broken.

AZCAT/SHUTTERSTOCK

Chiricahua National Monument (p301)

Past the entrance, the paved **Bonita Canyon Scenic Drive** climbs 8 miles to **Massai Point** at 6870ft, passing several scenic pullouts and trailheads. If you're short on time, hit the **Massai Point Nature Trail** (0.5 miles round trip), the most common stop for photos, or hike the **Echo Canyon Trail** at least half a mile to the **Grottoes**, an amazing 'cathedral' of giant boulders where you can lie still and enjoy the wind-brushed silence. The most striking formations cluster in the **Heart of Rocks**, reached via several linking trails on a 7.3-mile round-trip hike. A free hiker shuttle runs from Faraway Ranch and Bonita Campground to the Echo Canyon and Massai Point trailheads from September to May. Reserve ahead.

Chiricahua is one of 127 designated Dark Sky Parks worldwide, making it an increasingly popular destination for astrophotography. Depending on the time of year, you'll have clear views of the Milky Way, Orion, Big Dipper and comets at night. There is no cell-phone service in the park and very limited service in the surrounding area. Water is available only at the visitor center. The closest gas station is 27 miles away in Sunizona. The nearest community, Willcox, is 37 miles away.

Utah

STIRRING LANDSCAPES | NATIONAL PARKS | MORMON HEARTLAND

Before Native people and Mormon pioneers, dinosaurs once roamed this land, and remnants of all three collide in the 45th state. Utah's incredible diversity of geological formations were shaped by millions of years of erosion, despite there being so little water in sight. Utah boasts five national parks – the densest concentration of any state, with Arches, Canyonlands, Capitol Reef, Bryce Canyon and Zion – that rank among the big hitters of the American wild. And with dozens more national monuments, recreation areas and state parks, everything in this state feels ready-made for big adventures. Towns like Moab and Park City can seem like they're set up for getting you out and into nature on a mountain bike, skis or a white-water raft. In the midst of it all, Salt Lake City, the heartbeat of Mormon belief and governance, is one of the most intriguing urban experiences anywhere in the US.

Places

TOP TIP

Distances in Utah are longer than they look and each national park is worth exploring in depth. You'd need *at least* a couple of weeks to do them all well. If you're here for a shorter period, plan to see one or two parks well, rather than trying to do too much.

GETTING AROUND

As is so often true out in the West, unless your itinerary is limited to a few locations, having your own set of wheels is essential for getting around Utah. Rent a car in Salt Lake City or even Las Vegas, Nevada. If you're staying in a town like Salt Lake City, Moab or Park City, shuttle and other buses sometimes connect you with nearby ski stations or hiking trailheads. Amtrak has five stations in Utah on the *California Zephyr* line, but the daily departures mean the train is not a viable option for most travelers.

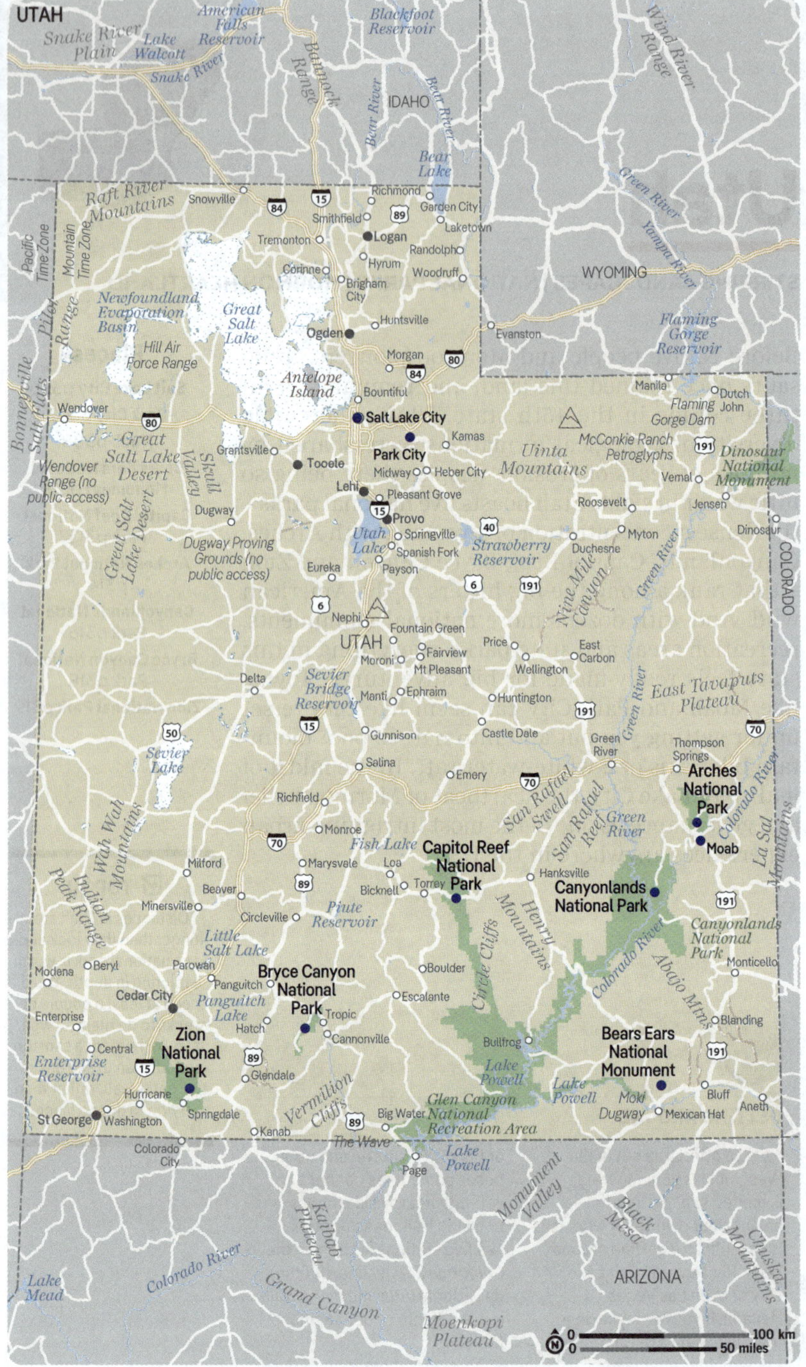
UTAH
Snake River Plain
Lake Walcott
American Falls Reservoir
Snake River
Bannock Range
Blackfoot Reservoir
Bear River
IDAHO
Bear Lake
Wind River Range
Green River
Yampa River
WYOMING
Flaming Gorge Reservoir
Raft River Mountains
Snowville
Richmond
Garden City
Smithfield
Laketown
Tremonton
Logan
Randolph
Hyrum
Corinne
Brigham City
Woodruff
Pacific Time Zone
Mountain Time Zone
Pilot Range
Newfoundland Evaporation Basin
Great Salt Lake
Huntsville
Ogden
Evanston
Hill Air Force Range
Morgan
Antelope Island
Bountiful
Manila
Dutch John
Flaming Gorge Dam
Bonneville Salt Flats
Wendover
Salt Lake City
Kamas
McConkie Ranch Petroglyphs
Great Salt Lake Desert
Grantsville
Park City
Uinta Mountains
Dinosaur National Monument
Wendover Range (no public access)
Skull Valley
Tooele
Midway
Heber City
Vernal
Lehi
Pleasant Grove
Roosevelt
Jensen
Dugway
Provo
Springville
Myton
Dinosaur
Utah Lake
Spanish Fork
Strawberry Reservoir
Duchesne
Dugway Proving Grounds (no public access)
Payson
Eureka
Nine Mile Canyon
Green River
COLORADO
Nephi
Fountain Green
UTAH
Price
East Carbon
Fairview
Moroni
Wellington
Mt Pleasant
Delta
Sevier Bridge Reservoir
Manti
Ephraim
Huntington
East Tavaputs Plateau
Gunnison
Castle Dale
Sevier Lake
Green River
Thompson Springs
Salina
Emery
Arches National Park
San Rafael Swell
San Rafael Reef
Richfield
Colorado River
Wah Wah Mountains
Monroe
Fish Lake
Capitol Reef National Park
Moab
La Sal Mountains
Milford
Marysvale
Loa
Hanksville
Indian Peak Range
Beaver
Bicknell
Torrey
Canyonlands National Park
Minersville
Piute Reservoir
Circleville
Henry Mountains
Little Salt Lake
Circle Cliffs
Abajo Mtns
Modena
Beryl
Parowan
Boulder
Monticello
Panguitch
Bryce Canyon National Park
Cedar City
Panguitch Lake
Escalante
Tropic
Enterprise
Hatch
Blanding
Cannonville
Bears Ears National Monument
Zion National Park
Central
Bullfrog
Enterprise Reservoir
Glendale
Lake Powell
Hurricane
Vermilion Cliffs
Glen Canyon National Recreation Area
Moki Dugway
Bluff
Mexican Hat
Aneth
St George
Washington
Springdale
Kanab
Big Water
The Wave
Colorado City
Page
Monument Valley
Black Mesa
Kaibab Plateau
Chuska Mountains
ARIZONA
Lake Mead
Colorado River
Grand Canyon
Moenkopi Plateau
0 100 km
0 50 miles

Salt Lake City

Explore Mormon SLC

Founded in 1847 by Mormon pioneers in what was then Mexican territory outside the boundaries of the US, Salt Lake City (SLC) remains the headquarters of the Church of Jesus Christ of Latter-day Saints; it's the Mormon equivalent of Vatican City for Catholics.

The epicenter of the Church of Jesus Christ of Latter-day Saints (LDS) is **Temple Square** *(churchofjesuschrist.org; free)* in the heart of downtown Salt Lake City. Members of the church, wearing name badges and modest clothing, happily assist with questions and directions. (Don't worry, they won't try to convert you unless you express interest.)

Start your visit at the **Conference Center**, which is serving as a visitor center during ongoing renovations. Join a tour or poke around the grand 21,000-seat auditorium yourself. Don't miss the rooftop garden with expansive views of the Salt Lake Valley.

Lording over Temple Square is the impressive **Salt Lake Temple**, the largest LDS temple in the world, completed in 1893 after more than 40 years of construction. The interior is open only to church members in good standing. Six spires, the tallest measuring 210ft, reach into the heavens. Home to the world-famous Tabernacle Choir, the **Salt Lake Tabernacle** is a domed 1867 auditorium with an 11,623-pipe organ and incredible acoustics – wait for the demonstration of a pin being dropped, which can be heard almost 200ft away.

Time your visit for noon Monday to Saturday or 2pm Sunday for a free organ recital (without the choir). The choir rehearses on Thursday evenings (7:30pm to 9:30pm) and Sunday mornings (8:15am to 9:30am) but is sometimes on tour elsewhere; check *thetabernaclechoir.org/upcoming-events*.

West of Temple Square, the **Church History Museum** gets into the nitty-gritty of the church's foundations. About a 5-mile drive east of Temple Square, the 450-acre **This Is The Place Heritage Park** *(thisistheplace.org; adult/child $18.95/14.95)* is dedicated to the 1847 arrival of the Mormons in Utah. Buy tickets at the Pioneer Center and then head into the living history village, which has several streets of original and replica pioneer buildings. Inside, costumed docents recount mid-19th-century life.

HIP 'HOODS

Get under the skin of Salt Lake by exploring the neighborhoods beyond downtown.

9th & 9th (900 South & 900 East): Several spots fly Pride flags in this mini 'gayborhood.' In 2016, 900 South was renamed Harvey Milk Blvd in honor of the gay-rights activist.

Sugar House: Walkable neighborhood with restaurants, coffee shops, breweries and a beloved urban park.

15th & 15th (1500 South & 1500 East): Enclave of excellent international restaurants and an indie bookstore.

Marmalade: This historic district west of the capitol is ideal for architecture lovers, so called because it was an orchard for early Mormon settlers.

EATING IN SALT LAKE CITY: OUR PICKS

Copper Onion: Elevated American food served brasserie style: think ricotta dumplings and Wagyu stroganoff. *11:30am-10pm or later Mon-Fri, from 10:30am Sat & Sun* $$

Lucky 13: Divey bar with the best burgers in the capital. The Nutter Butter Burger with peanut butter is a divine, delicious mess. *10am-2am* $

Red Iguana: Mexican food that's worth the inevitable wait. Get the mole sampler to try all its famous sauces. *11am-9pm or later* $$

Pago: Beautifully plated farm-to-table New American dishes pair perfectly with the acclaimed wine list. *5-9pm* $$$

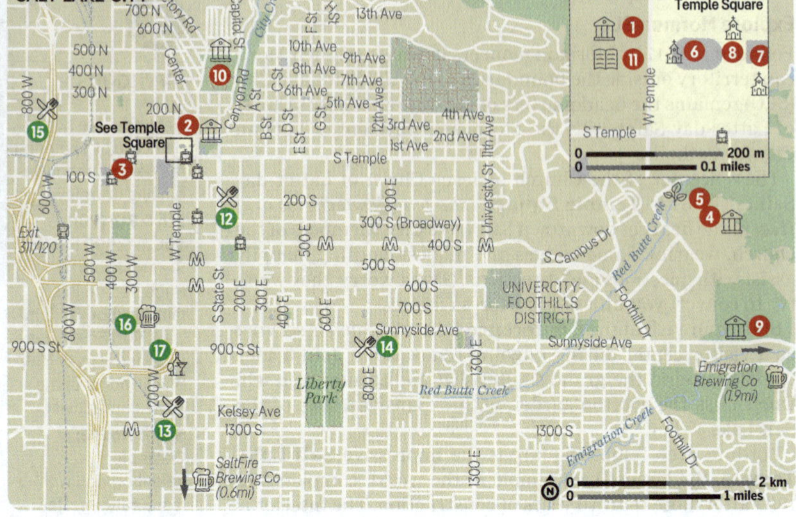

SIGHTS
1 Church History Museum
2 Conference Center
3 Delta Center
4 Natural History Museum of Utah
5 Red Butte Garden
6 Salt Lake Tabernacle
7 Salt Lake Temple
8 Temple Square
9 This Is the Place Heritage Park
10 Utah State Capitol

ACTIVITIES
11 FamilySearch Library

EATING
12 Copper Onion
13 Lucky 13
14 Pago
15 Red Iguana

DRINKING & NIGHTLIFE
16 Fisher Brewing Company
17 Water Witch

Trace your family tree

Mormons believe that families can be united in heaven for eternity, and since 1894 the church has collected genealogical records. Open to all, the church-sponsored **FamilySearch Library** *(familysearch.org/en/library; free)* houses the largest repository of family history on the planet, with information on more than three billion deceased people from around the world.

Friendly researchers can help you track down records of your family and will even print out a free 3ft-by-2ft full-color poster of the lineage documented during your visit for you to take home.

Tour the Utah State Capitol

Completed in 1916, the neoclassical-style **Utah State Capitol** *(utahstatecapitol.utah.gov; free)* is where state laws have been made for more than a century. You're free to wander around

DRINKING IN SALT LAKE CITY: OUR PICKS

Fisher Brewing Company: Known for its experimental brews made in a former auto shop. *11am-10pm or later*

Emigration Brewing Co: 'Mountain minimalist' brewery in a scenic canyon setting. *5-9pm Mon-Fri, from 10am Sat, 10am-2pm Sun*

SaltFire Brewing Co: Sociable taproom with friendly bartenders. Don't miss the chai stout. *3-9pm Mon-Thu, to 11pm Fri, noon-11pm Sat, to 8pm Sun*

Water Witch: Go 'roulette' and allow the mixologists to pour perfection from the cocktail shaker. *3pm-1am Mon-Wed, from noon Thu-Sun*

the five floors yourself or join a guided tour, which run on the hour between 10am and 3pm Monday to Friday. Guided tours give access to the basement, where you can see the base isolators that can move up to 2ft to protect the building from earthquakes. The capitol's interior dome, which reaches 165ft above the rotunda floor, steals the show.

Culture on campus

Established in 1850, the University of Utah, often shortened to 'the U,' provides lessons in history, botany and art for all, no matter your enrollment status.

The **Natural History Museum of Utah** *(nhmu.utah.edu; adult/child $22.95/17.95)* is housed in the sleek, modern Rio Tinto Center in the foothills of the Wasatch Mountains. The five-floor building showcases a dozen permanent exhibits, including displays on Utah's Native tribes, the Great Salt Lake and dinosaurs. Put on your hiking shoes before you head next door to **Red Butte Garden** *(redbuttegarden.org; adult/child $16/8)*, which has 5 miles of trails in addition to 21 acres of beautifully tended display gardens, originally cultivated by a botany professor.

Park City

Activities for all seasons

From boarder dudes to families with tots, everyone is on the slopes at **Park City Mountain Resort** *(parkcitymountain.com; day lift ticket adult/child from $140/73)*. The awesome terrain – 7300 acres of skiable slopes rising above the Old Town – couldn't be more family friendly or more accessible, with ski-in-ski-out access to Park City's Main St via the **Town Lift**. This area offers 344 runs (8% beginner, 44% intermediate, 48% advanced) and is a particular favorite for snowboarders – it hosted snowboarding and skiing half-pipe events in the 2002 Winter Games and is putting them on again in 2034. The first ski area you reach when visiting Park City from Salt Lake City, **Canyons Village** is part of Park City Mountain Resort and is known for having the first heated-seat chairlift in North America, the Orange Bubble Express.

On Park City's southern side, **Deer Valley** *(deervalley.com; day lift ticket adult/child from $229/142)* is a skiers-only resort of superlatives: superb dining, a complimentary ski valet so you can drop them off like a coat check and even tissue boxes at the base of the slopes. Deer Valley has 123 runs (25% beginner, 43% intermediate, 32% advanced) and a vertical

SALT LAKE CITY PRACTICALITIES

SLC is a car-centric city, but TRAX, the light-rail system, is a great way to get around. Buy tickets (one way/24hr $2.50/5) from machines at station platforms or on the **Transit app** *(transitapp.com)*. Cycle lanes abound. Grab a set of wheels from **Greenbike** *(greenbikeutah.org)*, SLC's bike-share system. For parking, download the **Park SLC app** *(parkslc.com)*. Spaces are often limited to two hours on weekdays ($2.25 per hour).

Attraction costs add up quickly, so check whether buying the **Salt Lake Connect Pass** *(visitsaltlake.com)* makes sense. It's valid for one, two or 365 days and also includes places in Park City and Snowbird.

EATING IN PARK CITY: OUR PICKS

Davanza's: Crowd into the small space to carb load for another day on the slopes with burgers, sandwiches and pizzas. *11am-9pm* **$**

Farm: Slope-side bistro-style dining room in Park City that uses seasonal local ingredients. *11:30am-10pm Dec-Apr* **$$$**

Five5eeds: Australian cafe serving strong coffee and all-day breakfasts of smashed avo toast and pulled pork Benedict. *7:30am-3pm* **$$**

Top of Main Brew Pub: Utah's first craft brewery still serves pints and pub grub. *11:30am-9pm Mon-Fri, from 10:30am Sat & Sun* **$$**

BEST MOAB BIKE SHOPS

Moab Cyclery: High-performance bike shop offering tours and rentals. Offers shuttles and good half-day, full-day, multiday and multisport tours.

Bike Fiend: Specialists in desert bikepacking, with everything you need for your overnight trip, including bags.

Poison Spider Bicycles: Shuttles to Bar M, Whole Enchilada and more, allowing you to have more riding time and fun.

Chile Pepper Bike Shop: Rent, service or buy a bike to explore the nearby desert at this friendly shop.

E-Bike Moab: The place to pick up bikes to cover longer distances quickly.

Rim Cyclery: Moab's longest-running family-owned bike shop offers tours, rentals and repairs.

drop of 3000ft. Its East Village expansion will nearly triple Deer Valley in size.

Fun in Park City doesn't stop when the snow melts. More than 300 miles of hiking and mountain-biking trails crisscross the mountains, and you'll feel on top of the world in the peaks over the town. Pick up summer trail maps at the resorts or the **Park City Visitors Center** *(visitparkcity.com)*. The ski resorts and outdoor outfitters around town rent mountain bikes.

Watch Olympians

Built for the 2002 Winter Games, **Utah Olympic Park** *(utaholympiclegacy.org)* was the site of the Games' ski jumping, bobsleigh, skeleton and luge events, and it will host many events again for the 2034 Games. The US Ski Team practices here year-round, and when there's no snow on the slopes, you can watch freestyle jumpers land in a bubble-filled jetted pool.

Not content to sit on the sidelines? Pretend to be an Olympian for the day by taking a 60mph **bobsleigh ride** *(per person winter/summer $225/100)* with up to 5Gs of centrifugal force. **Guided tours of the park** *(adult/child $20/15)* are available at 11am, 1pm and 3pm daily – even just peering over the edge of the ski jump is an adrenaline rush.

Moab

Scenic off-road drives

Moab's hundreds of miles of primitive back roads are coveted by 4WD enthusiasts. **Hell's Revenge** *(blm.gov/visit/hells-revenge-trailhead)* is the best-known 4WD road in Moab, but the extreme terrain mandates solid driving experience. It's in the BLM-administered area east of town and follows an 8.2-mile route up and down shockingly steep slickrock.

The 33-mile **Hurrah Pass** offers jaw-dropping vistas of the Colorado River, Dead Horse Point and **Grand View Point** in Canyonlands National Park, while on the other side of the Colorado River, the 15-mile scenic desert drive on **Potash Road** passes mining remnants on the way into dry country with soaring rock walls and solitude.

Outfitters such as **Cliffhanger Jeep Rental** *(cliffhangerjeeprental.com)* and **Twisted Jeeps** *(twistedjeeps.com)* rent Rubicons and Wranglers. If you'd rather someone else does the driving, join a group 4WD tour, dubbed 'land safaris,' in modified six- to eight-person Humvee-like vehicles. **Dan Mick's Jeep Tours** *(danmick.com)* is a highly regarded local operation that visits some 25 trails, including Hell's Revenge.

DRINKING IN MOAB: OUR PICKS

Proper Burger & Brewing Co: Southerly outpost of the SLC brewery; heaven for hopheads. *11:30am-9pm or later Wed-Mon*

Moab Brewery: The hometown brewery makes nearly a dozen beers in the vats just behind the bar area. *11:30am-8pm*

Woody's Tavern: 'World famous' neighborhood bar open for 60-plus years; live music on Fridays and Saturdays. *2pm-1am*

Moab Coffee Roasters: Low-key downtown spot to kick back with coffee, gelato and affogato. *7am-7pm Mar-Oct, to 5pm Nov-Feb*

JAKUB ZAJIC/SHUTTERSTOCK

Utah Olympic Park

The country's mountain-biking capital

Moab's mountain biking is world famous. Challenging trails ascend steep slickrock and wind through woods and up 4WD roads outside of town in every direction. Bike-shop websites and **Discover Moab** *(discovermoab.com/mountainbiking)* are good trail resources.

East of town in the Sand Flats Recreation Area, Moab's legendary **Slickrock Trail** *(blm.gov/visit/slickrock-national-recreation-trail; 1-/7-/365-day pass $5/10/20)* will kick your butt. The physically and technically difficult 12-mile round-trip route is for experts only, as is the practice loop. Plan on half a day.

Beat the heat on the **Moonlight Meadow Trail**, a 10.8-mile loop among aspens and pines that reaches a 10,500ft altitude in the La Sal Mountains south of Moab. The nearby **Whole Enchilada** trail system combines six routes that offer everything from high-mountain descents to slickrock. It's a full-day affair for advanced riders, with 7500ft of vertical drop and 34 miles of trails.

White waters of the Colorado and canyons

Rafting might be the highlight of your visit to Moab. Choose from full-day floats, white-water trips, multiday excursions and jet-boat trips.

Half- and full-day trips stick to the Colorado River, northeast of Moab. With class I to II rapids, the most popular stretch of

MOAB'S MOVIE HISTORY

Even if you haven't been to the countryside around Moab before, you've almost certainly seen it. This stunning scenery has starred as the background of major movies for nearly a century. The **Moab Museum of Film & Western Heritage** (*redcliffslodge.com/the-lodge/moab-museum-of-film-and-western-heritage; free*), based at Red Cliffs Lodge on Hwy 128, has memorabilia from locally shot movies, and the ranch itself was the filming location for many of the first films set around Moab, such as *Wagon Master* and *Rio Grande*.

Movies as diverse as *Austin Powers*, *Thelma & Louise* and *Mission Impossible II* have been filmed here. Actor and director Kevin Costner premiered his locally shot passion project *Horizon: An American Saga* in 2024.

EATING IN MOAB: OUR PICKS

Desert Bistro: Southeastern Utah's top restaurant, serving perfectly plated game and seafood in an 1892 dance hall. *5-9pm* **$$$**

Moab Food Truck Park: A dozen-plus trucks dishing up crowd-pleasing Chinese dishes, pizza, hot dogs, sushi and more. *11am-9pm* **$**

Milt's Stop & Eat: Moab's oldest restaurant (established 1954), with classic diner grub: burgers, fries and milkshakes. *11am-8pm* **$**

Birdy's Finer Diner: Elevated comfort food in an Insta-worthy former Denny's covered in bold wallpaper and mod furnishings. *5:30-9:30pm Wed-Sun* **$$$**

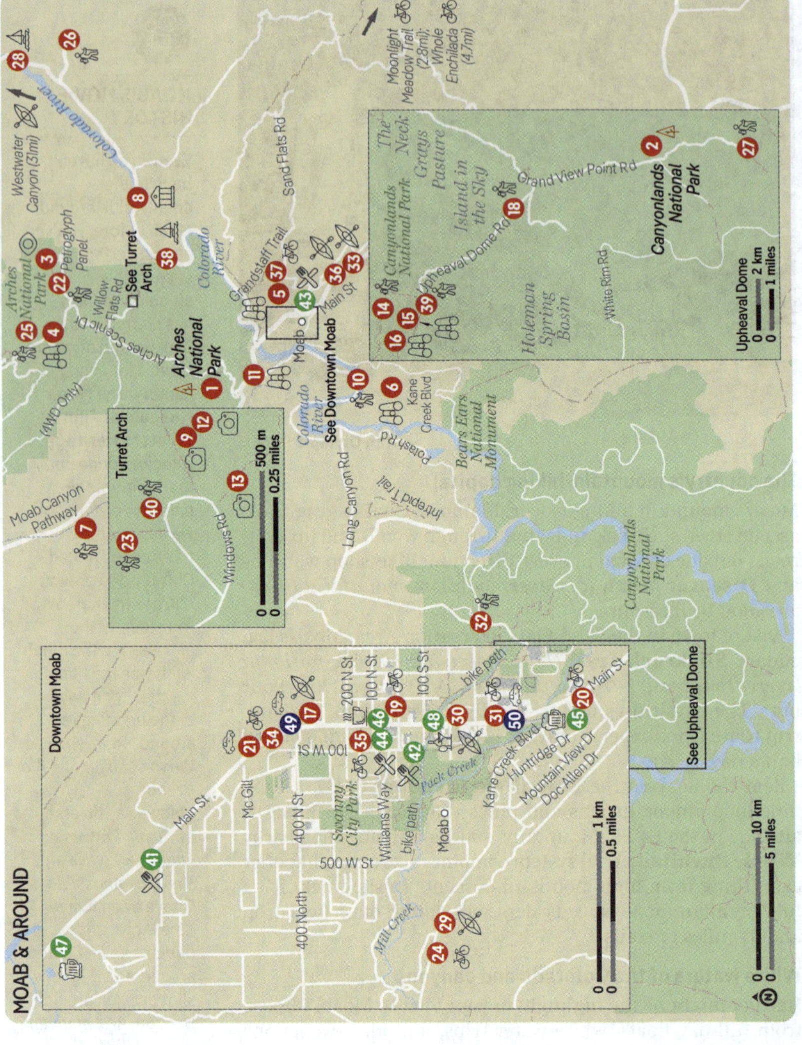

river near Moab is from **Hittle Bottom** to **Takeout Beach**, perfect for first-timers.

Longer multiday expeditions head to Cataract Canyon, Westwater Canyon and Desolation Canyon. The legendary class V rapids of **Cataract Canyon** are Utah's most intense stretch of white water. Outfitters run excursions lasting two to six days.

Find serious white water at **Westwater Canyon**, which boasts class III and IV rapids squeezed by 1200ft rock walls. Over on the Green River, **Desolation Canyon** is an epic four- to six-day adventure that starts with a scenic flight from Moab to the launch point.

HIGHLIGHTS
1 Arches National Park
2 Canyonlands National Park

SIGHTS
3 Delicate Arch
4 Fiery Furnace Viewpoint
5 Hell's Revenge
6 Hurrah Pass
7 Mill Canyon Dinosaur Tracksite
8 Moab Museum of Film & Western Heritage
9 North Window
10 Poison Spider Trailhead
11 Potash Road
12 South Window
13 Turret Arch
14 Upheaval Dome
15 Upheaval Dome First Overlook
16 Upheaval Dome Second Overlook

ACTIVITIES
17 Adrift Adventures
18 Aztec Butte Trail
19 Bike Fiend
20 Chile Pepper Bike Shop
21 Dan Mick's Jeep Tours
22 Delicate Arch Trailhead
23 Double Arch Trail
24 E-Bike Moab
25 Fiery Furnace
26 Fisher Towers Trail
27 Grand View Point Trail
28 Hittle Bottom
29 Mild to Wild
30 Moab Adventure Center
31 Moab Cyclery
32 Neck Spring Trail
33 OARS
34 Poison Spider Bicycles
35 Rim Cyclery
36 Sheri Griffith River Expeditions
37 Slickrock Trail
38 Takeout Beach
39 Upheaval Dome Trailhead
40 Windows Trailhead

EATING
41 Birdy's Finer Diner
42 Desert Bistro
43 Milt's Stop & Eat
44 Moab Food Truck Park

DRINKING & NIGHTLIFE
45 Moab Brewery
46 Moab Coffee Roasters
47 Proper Burger & Brewing Co
48 Woody's Tavern

TRANSPORT
49 Cliffhanger Jeep Rental
50 Twisted Jeeps

Rafting season runs from April to September; the jet-boating season lasts longer. Water levels crest in May and June.

Discover dinosaur tracks near Moab

The first fossils found in the western US were discovered near Moab in 1859. Just off Potash Rd (Hwy 279), the **Poison Spider Dinosaur Tracksite** *(free)* has prints from at least 10 three-toed meat-eating theropods walking along the edge of a lake.

At the **Mill Canyon Dinosaur Tracksite** *(blm.gov/visit/mill-canyon-dinosaur-trailhead-interpretive-site; free)* north of Moab, a raised boardwalk leads travelers above prints from at least 10 species of dinosaur. They include sickle-clawed raptors and long-necked herbivores as well as crocodile ancestors, giving it the most diversity of any site in North America, with 200 individual tracks.

Copper Ridge Dinosaur Tracksite *(blm.gov/visit/copper-ridge-dinosaur-tracks-interpretive-site; free)* is the first place in Utah where the prints of a Jurassic-period sauropod (a herbivore with a long neck) were discovered.

Bears Ears National Monument

Hike through ancient landscapes and cultures

The first national monument created at the request of Native tribes, **Bears Ears** *(blm.gov/visit/bears-ears-national-monument)* covers more than 2100 sq miles and is named for a pair of reddish, nearly symmetrical buttes. The huge area protects sites of cultural significance to Native people, with ancient rock art, cliff dwellings, ceremonial sites and granaries. Bears Ears has been the focus of political ping-pong

BEST RAFTING COMPANIES

Mild to Wild: Excellent rafting trips for any amount of time, including half-day sessions. *(mild2wildrafting.com)*

Adrift Adventures: Combine a trip on the river with a Jeep tour. *(adrift.net)*

OARS: Has a permit for Canyonlands and runs epic weeklong expeditions that raft and hike to tough-to-reach parts of the national park. *(oars.com)*

Sheri Griffith River Expeditions: Operating since 1971, this rafting specialist offers a great selection of activities, from family floats to rapids. *(griffithexp.com)*

Moab Adventure Center: Tons of boat tours for every level of adrenaline, including thrilling jet boats. *(moabadventurecenter.com)*

VISIT WITH RESPECT

Bears Ears is a delicate environment, in terms of both the environment and archaeology. Keep the impact of your visit to a minimum by following these guidelines.

Leave fossils and cultural artifacts undisturbed: This includes pieces of pottery, corn cobs, animal tracks and bones.

Steer clear of ancient structures: Do not touch, climb or stand on historic buildings or lean on their walls.

Stay on established trails and roads: Protect cryptobiotic soil by walking and driving on durable surfaces.

Use rubber-tipped hiking poles: Sharp tips scratch the rocks.

Pay your fees: This money ensures that sites are monitored and facilities are maintained.

for several years. In one of his final acts as president, Barack Obama designated the land as a national monument in 2016, but when Donald Trump took over the White House, he cut the monument's size by 85%. Biden later issued a proclamation that restored Bears Ears to its original size.

Given its recent establishment and back-and-forth status, Bears Ears can be confusing to visit. The monument doesn't have clear entrances, and signage on the ground is minimal, so you might not even know when you're in it. Start your visit at the **Kane Gulch Ranger Station** *(blm.gov/visit/kane-gulch-ranger-station; open spring & fall only)* on Hwy 261 or the **Bears Ears Education Center** *(bearsearspartnership.org/education-center)* in Bluff, a community-run information center with interpretative displays. At either spot, pick up maps and ask for advice on exploring the area.

Bears Ears is divided into three sections: Indian Creek, Cedar Mesa and the San Juan River. Cedar Mesa is the most easily accessible area, mostly along Hwy 95. Some sites, such as the 700-year-old **Mule Canyon Kiva**, are short and easy roadside stops. The 1-mile round-trip **Butler Wash Trail** crosses slickrock to reach a viewpoint looking toward a cliff dwelling across the chasm. An easy 2-mile hike along the South Fork creek of Mule Canyon leads to small Ancestral Puebloan granaries known as **House on Fire**, so named because one of the small dwellings appears to be engulfed in flames due to an unusual gold-orange sandstone overhang.

One of the largest and most evocative archaeological sites is **Moon House**, which has 49 rooms across three well-preserved dwellings. Its name comes from pictographs that show the lunar phases. Access to Moon House is limited to 20 people per day, doled out by permit on recreation.gov for $5 per person, plus a $6 reservation fee. Permits often sell out several days in advance, and in spring and fall they must be validated in person at the Kane Gulch Ranger Station or the **BLM Monticello Field Office** *(blm.gov/office/monticello-field-office)*, a 1½-hour drive from the trail. The road to the trailhead requires a high-clearance 4WD vehicle.

Hiking in the canyons of Cedar Mesa, including to House on Fire, requires day-use permits (per person per day/week $5/10), which you can purchase on recreation.gov (cell signal is poor, so do this in advance) or by using the fee envelopes at trailheads. Backpackers also need permits to camp overnight.

The land protected by Bears Ears National Monument remains sacred to five Native tribes – the Hopi, Navajo, Ute Mountain Ute, Zuni and Ute – who formed a coalition in 2015 to appeal for its preservation. Louis Williams, a member of Diné Bikéyah (the Navajo Nation), founded tour company **Ancient Wayves** *(tourancientwayves.com)* to enrich visitors' experience of hiking in Shash Jaa' (Bears Ears in Diné) with a Native perspective. Hikes head to trailheads around Cedar Mesa, Butler Wash and other locations for half-day, full-day and multiday excursions.

In addition to hikes, Williams, a longtime river runner, also operates rafting trips on the San Juan, the northern boundary of Diné Bikéyah.

TOP EXPERIENCE

Capitol Reef National Park

In a forgotten fold of the Colorado Plateau, slot canyons appear as cathedrals cut from the earth, and giant cream-colored domes arc into perfectly blue skies. Capitol Reef National Park doesn't always make it onto travelers' itineraries. Discover petroglyphs and early Mormon settlements, sandstone streaks and hidden arches, as you hike a labyrinth of canyons stretching back millions of years.

Cassidy Arch

Grand Wash

Grand Wash, Capitol Reef's most captivating canyon off Scenic Dr, is worth visiting just to walk between the Narrows' sheer walls. This flat, easy hike with just 200ft of elevation change is sandwiched between the sides of a Navajo sandstone canyon that at one point tower 80 stories high but are only 15ft apart.

Cassidy Arch

A 3.3-mile round-trip side trail from Grand Wash leads to Cassidy Arch, a natural red-rock formation. With 670ft of elevation change, this hike is more difficult than Grand Wash, switchbacking up the cliffside and traversing some sheer drops, but the views en route are worth it. The arch is named after Utah-born Butch Cassidy, who, according to legend, hid from the law high on these cliffs.

Hickman Bridge Trail

Hickman Bridge Trail, Capitol Reef's most popular trail, is diverse, offering a canyon and desert-wash walk to a natural bridge, plus big-sky views and spring wildflowers. This hike is easy enough for anyone to enjoy. Because the route is largely exposed, it's best to hike in the early morning.

TOP TIPS

- Capitol Reef's gateway town is tiny Torrey, population 257, 11 miles west, where you'll find restaurants, gas stations and accommodations.
- Torrey doesn't have a full-sized grocery store; if you need specific items, Loa lies 17 miles west.

PRACTICALITIES

- nps.gov/care
- 7-day pass per vehicle $20
- national parks pass accepted

Delicate Arch

TOP EXPERIENCE

Arches National Park

Giant sandstone arcs frame snowy peaks and desert landscapes at Arches National Park, home to 2000 rock arches, the highest density of them anywhere on earth. You'll lose all perspective on size at some, and a scenic drive through the park makes the spectacular arches accessible to all. Arches has many short trails, with most of the main sights close to paved roads.

DON'T MISS

- Windows Trail
- Turret Arch
- Double Arch Trail
- Delicate Arch
- Fiery Furnace
- Fiery Furnace Viewpoint
- Baby Arch

The Windows Trail

The Windows Trail is an easy 1-mile loop trail that gently climbs to three massive photogenic arches: North Window, South Window and Turret Arch. It's hard to grasp the immensity of these gigantic marvels until you're beside them. This hike is one of the busiest in the park, but you can leave some of the crowds behind by returning on the longer **Windows Primitive Loop**, with a beautiful back view of the two

PRACTICALITIES

● nps.gov/arch ● 7-day pass per vehicle $30
● national parks pass accepted

windows. The primitive trail is less obvious and doesn't have as many trail markers.

The trail forks about 500ft from the parking lot. Take the left fork and head to the **North Window**, which measures 51ft high and 93ft wide and frames the distant desert. A spur trail (part of the Windows Primitive Loop) heads to the **South Window**, sitting higher from the ground than the North Window. The main Windows Loop trail then circles to the castle-like **Turret Arch**.

For a bonus arch, head back to the parking lot and set off on the 0.6-mile **Double Arch Trail**. Double Arch is the tallest in the park at 112ft, and you're allowed to walk and scramble underneath it (but not on the arch itself).

Delicate Arch

You've seen Delicate Arch before: it's the unofficial state symbol, stamping nearly every Utah tourist brochure and gracing license plates. While two viewpoints provide perspective (and an easier hike) from below, the best way to experience the arch is close up.

The trail to Delicate Arch may seem interminable on the way up, but the rewards are so great that you'll quickly forget the toil, provided you wear rubber-soled hiking shoes and drink a quart of water along the way – there is zero shade. This hike is best tackled early in the day when you'll feel less like an ant under a magnifying glass.

Fiery Furnace

So named because of its spectacular rock formations that glow red and orange in the sunset, the narrow sandstone maze of Fiery Furnace has no marked trails and provides an extra level of adventure for hikers. Because of the extreme nature of wayfinding here (online maps and GPS do not work well because of the high canyon walls), as well as sections that require jumping across ledges and shimmying through crevices, permits are required – the only hike in Arches where they are mandatory.

Permits come in two flavors: ranger-led ($16 per person) or self-guided ($10 per person). Purchase them on recreation.gov a week in advance.

The National Park Service recommends that people hiking Fiery Furnace for the first time go on a ranger-guided tour. Permits must be picked up the day before or the day of the hike at the Arches National Park Visitor Center, which opens at 7:30am.

If you don't manage to snag a hiking permit, still survey the scene from the **Fiery Furnace viewpoint**.

OUTSTANDING ARCHES

Karen Henker has worked at the national park for more than a decade.

Double Arch
More than 100ft high, this arch in the Windows section is the park's tallest.

Baby Arch
Not marked on the park map, this one near the Courthouse Towers is a hidden treasure.

Delicate Arch
I recommend the easy Lower Viewpoint walk; the long hike up is like climbing 50 flights of stairs.

TOP TIPS

- If you're planning to visit between 7am and 4pm from April through October, you must reserve an hour-long entry window on recreation.gov, which costs $2 and doesn't include the park entry fee.
- Driving is the best way to get around. There's no shuttle or public transportation. Some companies in Moab run bus tours through the park.
- Cyclists beware: it's a steep climb right after the visitor center and about 17 miles one way to the end of the scenic drive.
- The park has no non-camping accommodations or anywhere to buy food.
- Usually no cell-phone service. Download maps and apps before you arrive.

Aztec Butte

TOP EXPERIENCE

Canyonlands National Park

A 527-sq-mile vision of ancient earth, Canyonlands National Park is Utah's largest – and least-visited – national park. Vast serpentine canyons tipped with white cliffs loom 1000ft over the Colorado and Green Rivers. Skyward-reaching needles and spires, deep craters, swirling tie-dye mesas and majestic buttes dot the landscape. The 6000ft-high Island in the Sky promises some of the most enthralling vistas in Utah.

DON'T MISS

- Island in the Sky
- Neck Spring
- Aztec Butte
- Upheaval Dome Trail
- Needles District
- Slickrock Trail
- Chesler Park Loop

Neck Spring

One of Canyonlands' few loop trails, Neck Spring (5.6 miles, moderately challenging) is good for solitude seekers. Despite its proximity to the visitor center, this trail attracts few hikers, perhaps because it doesn't take in the panoramic vistas that are the signature of **Island in the Sky**, but this stream canyon is a magnet for wildlife and fills with wildflowers in springtime as one of the plateau's rare water sources.

PRACTICALITIES

- nps.gov/cany
- 7-day pass per vehicle $30
- national parks pass accepted

Aztec Butte

Shortly after the turnoff on Upheaval Dome Rd, the moderately challenging 1.4-mile round-trip Aztec Butte Trail climbs to the only archaeological site at Island in the Sky. The short ascent of a Navajo sandstone dome yields stellar views; it's a steep hike over slickrock to the top.

A little more than a quarter mile from the parking area, a spur trail leads to a granary built around 1200 to 1300 CE, tucked below an overhang on the butte's northern side. (Despite the name, the structure was built by Ancestral Puebloans, not the Aztecs.) Use the cairns and switchbacks to follow the route up to the butte, which levels off at the top, revealing panoramic views and endless sky.

Upheaval Dome

Was Upheaval Dome created by salt or something from outer space? Scientists disagree over how the feature formed. Some suggest it's a collapsed salt dome, while more recent research posits that it was the site of a meteorite strike some 60 million years ago. Scope out the geological drama on the moderately challenging **Upheaval Dome Trail**, which leads to two overlooks that gaze out at the 3-mile-wide crater.

It's an easy 0.3 miles one way to the **first overlook**. To reach the **second overlook**, return to the fork in the trail and bear right, descending over slickrock before clambering to a final steep ascent. From here, you have a broader panorama of the surrounding landscape. The afternoon light is magnificent, and this viewpoint adds only 1 mile to the trip.

Slickrock Trail

Over in the Canyonlands' Needles District, the ridgeline Slickrock Trail (2.4 miles, easy) is high above the canyons with views below, almost entirely on its namesake type of stone. Keep an eye out during your hike – bighorn sheep are occasionally seen here.

If you're short on time, at least visit **Viewpoint 1** for a panorama where giant red cliffs hang like curtains below high buttes and mesas, the district's namesake needles touch the sky, and the La Sal and Abajo Mountains lord over the whole scene.

Chesler Park Loop

Get among the namesake 'needles' formations on the Chesler Park Loop, an awesome 11-mile route across desert grasslands, past towering red-and-white-striped pinnacles, and between deep, narrow slot canyons, some only 2ft across. Elevation changes are mild, but the distance makes it a challenging day hike. Make sure you plan your route and download maps in advance, as this area has a number of intersecting circular trails.

WHO WERE THE ANCESTRAL PUEBLOANS?

The Ancestral Puebloans were a Native people who lived across the Four Corners region (modern-day Utah, Colorado, New Mexico and Arizona) from as far back as the 12th century BCE. Prime examples of their impressive architecture can be found at Mesa Verde National Park (p200) in southwestern Colorado. Their modern descendants include the Pueblo, Hopi and Zuni.

TOP TIPS

- The park's two rivers form a Y that divides the park into four separate districts, inaccessible to one another from within the park.
- Cradled atop the Y, Island in the Sky is the most developed and visited district because of its proximity to Moab and Arches National Park's entrance, both about 30 miles from the visitor center.
- The easiest way to visit Canyonlands' Island in the Sky district is by car. There is no shuttle system or public transportation.
- Some companies in Moab run bus tours through the park.
- From Island in the Sky, it's a two-hour drive south to the Needles.

RICHARD WESTLUND/SHUTTERSTOCK

Fairyland Loop

TOP EXPERIENCE

Bryce Canyon National Park

You never forget your first sight of otherworldly Bryce Canyon National Park. Yes, you're still in the desert, but it's the wonderful power of water that sculpted this soft sandstone and limestone into alien formations that tickle the imagination. Though it's the smallest of Utah's national parks, Bryce Canyon stands among the most prized. In Utah, that's quite a claim.

DON'T MISS

- Rim Trail
- Silent City
- Thor's Hammer
- Fairyland Loop
- Tower Bridge
- Peekaboo Loop Trail

Rim Trail

The easiest hike in the national park, the 0.5- to 5.5-mile (one-way) Rim Trail outlines Bryce Amphitheater from Fairyland Point to Bryce Point, promising a journey of incredible views. From Bryce Point to **Inspiration Point**, the trail skirts the canyon rim atop white cliffs, revealing gorgeous formations, including the Wall of Windows. After passing briefly through trees, it continues along the ridge top to the uppermost level of Inspiration Point, 1.3 miles from Bryce Point. The leg to

PRACTICALITIES

- nps.gov/brca
- 7-day pass per vehicle $35
- national parks pass accepted

Sunset Point drops 200ft in 0.75 miles, winding its way along limestone-capped cliffs. Below the rim, **Silent City** rises in all its hoodoo glory.

Stay the course and look for **Thor's Hammer** as you continue the 0.5-mile stroll along a paved path to **Sunrise Point**, the most crowded stretch of trail in the entire park. The views are worth it. Past Sunrise Point the crowds thin as the trail climbs 150ft toward North Campground. Topping out near North Campground, the path ambles across gently rolling hills on the forested plateau before rejoining the canyon rim at Fairyland Point, 2.5 miles from Sunrise Point.

Fairyland Loop

Fairyland Loop is a great 8-mile day hike and a good workout, with 1900ft of elevation gain. Unlike Bryce Amphitheater, Fairyland is spared the crowds. This trail is difficult primarily because it meanders in and out of the hoodoos, down into washes, and up and over saddles.

This trail begins at **Fairyland Point** and circles the majestic cliffs of flat-topped, 8076ft Boat Mesa, emerging on the rim near Sunrise Point. The last 2.5 miles of the loop follow the Rim Trail back to the trailhead.

From Fairyland Point, the trail dips gradually below the rim. At Fairyland Canyon, 600ft below your starting point, towers of deep-orange stone stand like giant totem poles. Zigzagging up and down, the trail eventually reaches a seasonal wash on the floor of Campbell Canyon. Keep an eye out for **Tower Bridge**, which connects three spires to two windows. To reach the base of the formation, take the clearly marked dead-end spur from the wash. From Tower Bridge it's a 950ft climb over 1.5 miles to the Rim Trail.

Peekaboo Loop Trail

An ideal half-day hike, the Peekaboo Loop Trail sees the most variety of terrain and scenery in Bryce, with 1560ft of elevation change.

From Bryce Point, follow signs to the Peekaboo Connecting Trail east of the parking area. Just over a mile down the trail, past where hoodoo columns take on a bright orange hue, work your way down the switchbacks, watching for the **Wall of Windows**, which juts above the hoodoos atop a sheer vertical cliff face perpendicular to the canyon rim.

As you continue, you'll pass ancient bristlecone pines, some of whose roots are over 1000 years old; an inch of these trees' trunks represents a century of growth. Other highlights include the cluster of delicate red spires at Fairy Castle, spectacular views of Silent City, and the Cathedral, a majestic wall of buttress-like hoodoos.

SEEING STARS IN BRYCE CANYON

Amateur astronomers are in for a treat at Bryce Canyon. The National Park Service puts on some 100 astronomy programs a year, including an **Astronomy Festival** in June, full-moon hikes and regular ranger talks. Check the park's calendar online (nps.gov/brca/planyourvisit/calendar.htm) and stop by the visitor center when you arrive to see what's happening while you're here.

TOP TIPS

- When the free park shuttle is running, you can take it to any one point and return from another, instead of backtracking to your car.
- You can join the Rim Trail anywhere along its 5.5-mile route. Note that shuttle buses don't stop at Fairyland.
- If you time your visit for the new moon, when the skies are darkest, watch as the Milky Way shimmers all the way to the horizon.
- At full moon, see the hoodoos take on spooky personalities when rangers lead 1- to 2-mile walks (taking about two hours) among the formations in the moonlight. Reserve a spot ($1) on *recreation.gov.*

GALYNA ANDRUSHKO/SHUTTERSTOCK

The Narrows

TOP EXPERIENCE

Zion National Park

Visiting heavenly Zion National Park can feel like a religious experience. The park's soaring red and white cliffs, one of Utah's most dramatic natural wonders, rise high over the Virgin River. From the canyon floor to Zion's highest peak there is nearly 5000ft of elevation change, resulting in a fabulous range of ecozones and experiences.

DON'T MISS

- Riverside Walk
- The Narrows
- Emerald Pools Trails
- Canyon Overlook Trail
- Observation Point

Riverside Walk

The easy 2-mile out-and-back Riverside Walk is the dry and paved part of the experience, for those who like an easy adventure. Shadowed from the sun by lofty canyon walls, this fun path parallels the Virgin River's slippery cobblestones and rambles by seeps, hanging gardens and wading spots. Points along the way give access to the riverbank and water, making it a family favorite.

The Narrows: Zion's Classic Hike

At the end of the Riverside Walk, stairs descend to the water and the adventure begins. Hiking through a rocky river in

PRACTICALITIES

- nps.gov/zion
- 7-day pass per vehicle $35
- national parks pass accepted

ankle- to chest-deep water as the canyon walls rise up to 1000ft tall and press in to just 20ft wide: the Narrows is quintessential Zion.

The best part about hiking the Narrows is that you can walk for as little or as long as you'd like and still have a great time; the further you go, the smaller the crowds. This out-and-back route is not about reaching a specific spot, but simply soaking up the scene. Day hikers are allowed to go as far as **Big Spring**. Don't underestimate the difficulty or distance (9.4 miles return, about eight hours).

You'll want a sturdy hiking stick to avoid falling in the water, plus quick-drying fabrics, layers and proper footwear. In cooler months, bring waterproof bags and warm, waterproof gear, which you can rent from outfitters near the park entrance like **Zion Outfitter** *(zionoutfitter.com/narrows-rentals)*.

Emerald Pools

Short and sweet, the Emerald Pools trails are a superb introduction to Zion's unique ecology and microhabitats. The paved **Lower Emerald Pool Trail**, the easiest of the three, gradually rises and falls for 0.6 miles before reaching the first pool. Waterfalls cascade down a multicolored, mineral-stained overhang, misting the trail (and you) as you pass beneath. A dirt trail ascends 150ft to the less dramatic **Middle Emerald Pool** feeding the waterfalls below. From here a steep 0.5-mile spur leads to the **Upper Emerald Pool**. It's the loveliest grotto of all, surrounded by Lady Mountain's sheer-walled skirts.

Canyon Overlook Trail

A convenient stop off Hwy 9, the 1-mile out-and-back Canyon Overlook Trail is a relatively quick hike with a much photographed panoramic vista. Although it's not a particularly strenuous hike, the slickrock terrain is somewhat rugged. The final sweeping Canyon Overlook has lower Zion Canyon views. The hike's most challenging part might be finding somewhere to park. If the small lot near the trailhead is full or if you're coming from Mt Carmel, park in the overflow lots 300ft east of the **Zion–Mt Carmel Tunnel**.

Observation Point

It feels deliciously like cheating to wander along a mostly flat woodland path and then descend to Observation Point, which towers more than 700ft above **Angels Landing** – you get all of the rewards with hardly any of the work. If you're planning to hike Angels Landing, know that you can't just show up and hike it; you have to apply for a permit.

The **trailhead** is at the end of a small parking area off a 4WD road in East Zion. The parking lot fills early, and the road is often too rough for standard sedans. Instead, book a spot on a shuttle run by **East Zion Adventures** *(eastzionadventures.com; round trip per person $7)*, which leaves from nearby Zion Ponderosa Ranch Resort (p339).

CAUTION

Preparation and timing are the keys to a successful Narrows adventure. *Always* check conditions and the flash-flood forecast with rangers before setting off. A sudden rainstorm miles away can send down a surge of rock- and log-filled water that sweeps away everything in its path. Some years there's little change in water levels, but the Narrows could be closed in April, May or June.

TOP TIPS

- Avoid visiting in summer if you can: this is the third most-visited national park in the country and summers can feel claustrophobic.
- For most of the year, private vehicles are not allowed on Zion Canyon Scenic Drive. Instead, you must ride the Zion Park Shuttle, which makes nine stops between the visitor center and the Temple of Sinawava.
- Limited free parking is available inside the park; arrive as early as possible.

DRIVING THE COLORADO RIVER SCENIC BYWAY

The curvy Colorado River Scenic Byway (Hwy 128) follows the winding waters through gorgeous red-rock country of high cliffs, alfalfa fields and sagebrush.

START	END	LENGTH
Matrimony Spring	Dewey Bridge	30 miles; 1½ hours

The Colorado River forms Arches National Park's southern boundary for the first 15 miles of this journey. Near the start of the 'river road' just east of Hwy 191, 1 **Matrimony Spring** is said to have magical properties, and couples who drink from it might soon hear wedding bells. After the first major bend is the 2 **Grandstaff Canyon Trailhead**, which leads to a beautiful arch.

At the head of the next bend (6 miles from Hwy 191), spot boulderers on the rocks at 3 **Big Bend Recreation Site**, where you can picnic by the river. As you round the mesa near Red Cliffs Lodge, look on the right for 4 **Castleton Tower**, a narrow 400ft sandstone spire that rises above Castle Valley and is one of the area's most iconic rock climbs. In the 1960s and '70s, Chevrolet filmed TV commercials here, helicoptering a car to the summit. Carry on to the turnoff for 5 **Fisher Towers**. The 900ft-high Titan, standing solemnly at the end of the formation, is the country's tallest freestanding natural tower.

The road finally crosses the river at 6 **Dewey Bridge**, where you might spot rafters drifting by. The scenic byway soon ends at a three-way intersection. Return to Moab or double back to the La Sal Mountain Loop Rd. You're also less than 10 miles from I-70.

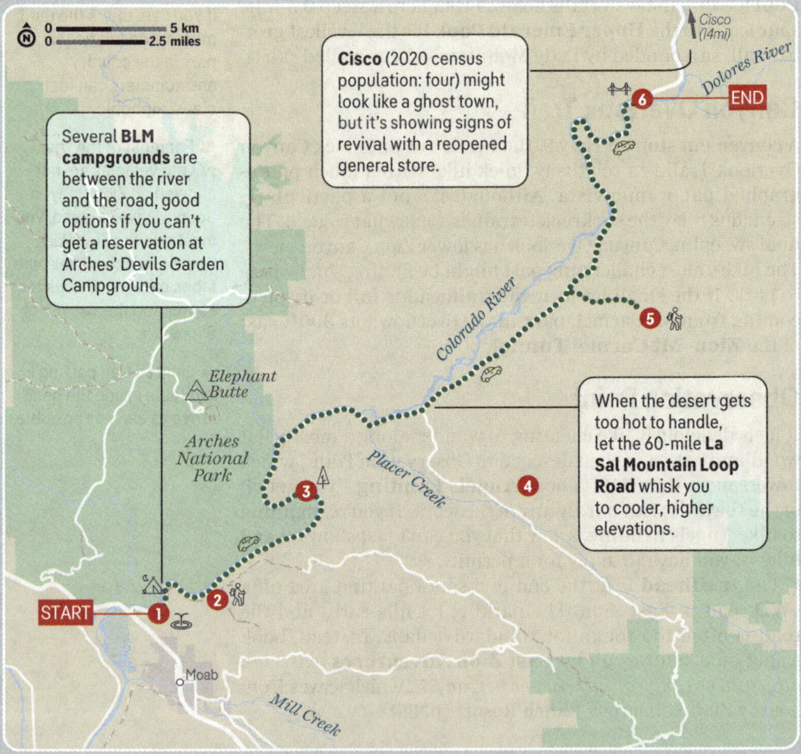

New Mexico

FASCINATING HISTORY | UFO MYSTERIES | SPACE RACE

Traveling in New Mexico is a journey through time and space. It's one big living museum, home to 1000-year-old Indigenous dwellings and some of the longest continuously inhabited communities in the US. It's also the setting for the most famous alleged UFO sighting, it's where the Space Race began, and the state now has the first airport serving trips beyond earth's orbit.

New Mexico doesn't have a single standout city or site – Santa Fe, Taos, Albuquerque and its phenomenal national parks all top the list. The best way to visit is with a road trip along one of many scenic byways or retro Route 66, where neon signs and dry shrubs transform into ghost towns and high-mountain forests.

The best way to fuel any New Mexico adventure? With chili (or chile, as it's spelled here) – practically everything is smothered with the delicious spicy fruit and the chance to explore New Mexico's unique culinary culture is yet another very good reason to visit.

Places

TOP TIP

Don't make too many UFO jokes around New Mexicans. There's a good chance they've seen something in the sky that they can't explain. Despite its small population, New Mexico often ranks near the top when it comes to UFO sightings compared to other states.

GETTING AROUND

Renting a car is your best bet if you want to travel beyond Albuquerque and Santa Fe. Both cities have plenty of rental offices. A 4WD drive is desirable, especially in the Four Corners Region, but most cars with high clearance should do. Between cities, you can take the Rail Runner Express commuter train from Albuquerque to Santa Fe. Albuquerque and Santa Fe have internal bus services. Greyhound serves some cities and towns, though they're usually best for getting to and from New Mexico rather than around the state.

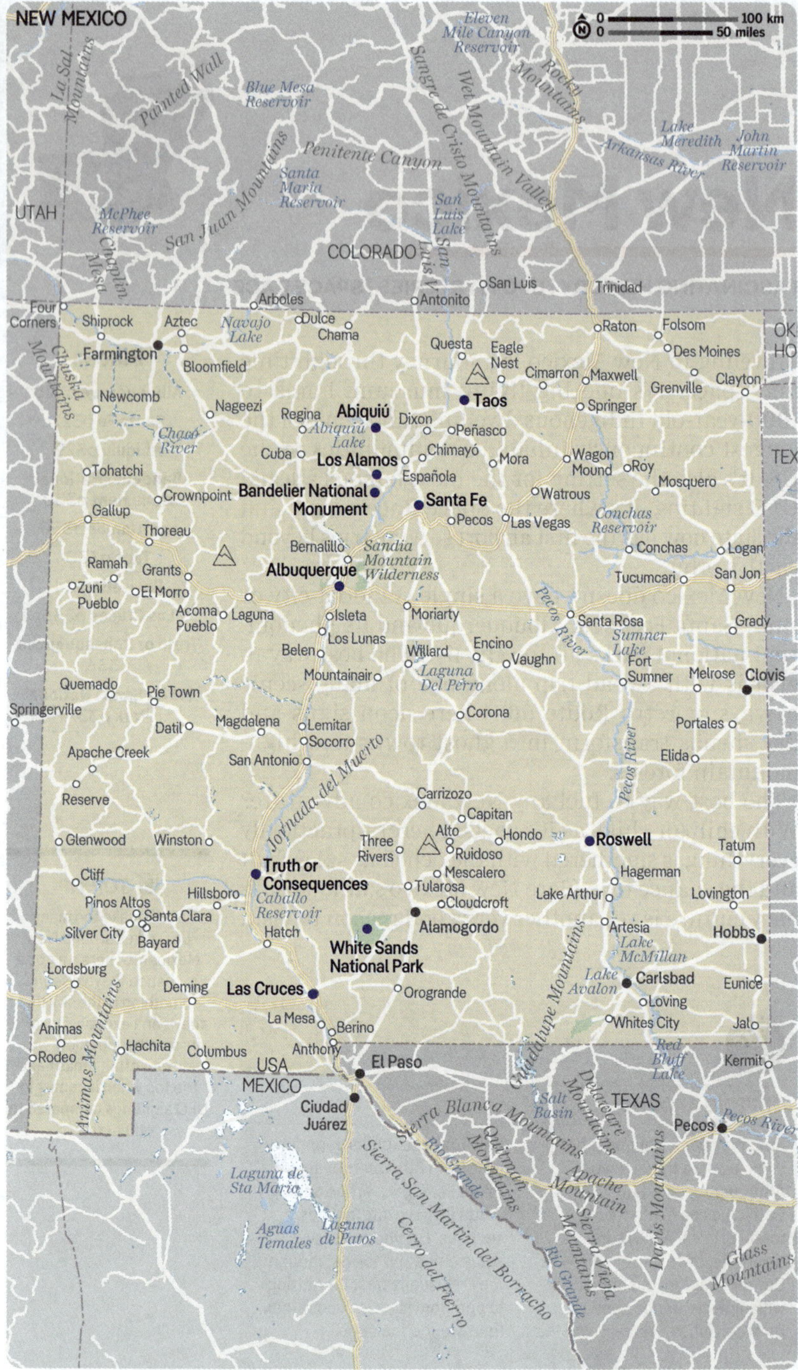
NEW MEXICO
0 100 km
0 50 miles
UTAH
COLORADO
USA
MEXICO
TEXAS
Farmington
Abiquiú
Taos
Los Alamos
Bandelier National Monument
Santa Fe
Albuquerque
Truth or Consequences
Roswell
Clovis
Alamogordo
White Sands National Park
Las Cruces
Hobbs
Carlsbad
El Paso
Ciudad Juárez
Pecos
Four Corners
Shiprock
Aztec
Bloomfield
Arboles
Navajo Lake
Dulce
Chama
Antonito
San Luis
Trinidad
Raton
Folsom
Des Moines
Questa
Eagle Nest
Cimarron
Maxwell
Clayton
Grenville
Springer
Newcomb
Nageezi
Regina
Abiquiú Lake
Dixon
Peñasco
Chaco River
Cuba
Chimayó
Mora
Wagon Mound
Roy
Mosquero
Española
Watrous
Tohatchi
Crownpoint
Gallup
Thoreau
Pecos
Las Vegas
Conchas Reservoir
Conchas
Logan
Bernalillo
Sandia Mountain Wilderness
Ramah
Grants
Zuni Pueblo
El Morro
Acoma Pueblo
Laguna
Isleta
Moriarty
Tucumcari
San Jon
Santa Rosa
Pecos River
Sumner Lake
Grady
Los Lunas
Belen
Willard
Encino
Vaughn
Fort Sumner
Melrose
Mountainair
Laguna Del Perro
Quemado
Pie Town
Springerville
Datil
Magdalena
Lemitar
Socorro
Corona
Portales
Apache Creek
San Antonio
Elida
Jornada del Muerto
Reserve
Carrizozo
Capitan
Alto
Hondo
Glenwood
Winston
Three Rivers
Ruidoso
Tatum
Cliff
Mescalero
Hagerman
Tularosa
Hillsboro
Caballo Reservoir
Cloudcroft
Lake Arthur
Lovington
Pinos Altos
Santa Clara
Silver City
Bayard
Hatch
Artesia
Lake McMillan
Lordsburg
Lake Avalon
Eunice
Deming
Orogrande
Loving
La Mesa
Berino
Whites City
Jal
Animas
Hachita
Anthony
Rodeo
Columbus
Red Bluff Lake
Kermit
Guadalupe Mountains
Animas Mountains
Chuska Mountains
La Sal Mountains
Painted Wall
Blue Mesa Reservoir
Eleven Mile Canyon Reservoir
Sangre de Cristo Mountains
Wet Mountain Valley
Rocky Mountains
Lake Meredith
John Martin Reservoir
Arkansas River
Penitente Canyon
Santa Maria Reservoir
San Juan Mountains
McPhee Reservoir
Chaplin Mesa
San Luis Lake
San Luis V
Salt Basin
Delaware Mountains
Sierra Blanca Mountains
Quitman Mountains
Apache Mountain
Sierra Vieja Mountains
Davis Mountains
Glass Mountains
Rio Grande
Sierra San Martin del Borracho
Cerro del Fierro
Laguna de Sta Maria
Aguas Temales
Laguna de Patos
Pecos River

Albuquerque

Wander the century-old adobe houses

Once a homeland for the Tiwa people, starting around 1250, 'Alburquerque' was taken over by Spain in the 1680 Pueblo Revolt, and in 1706, 15 Spanish families settled here in Old Town. The neighborhood's plaza and **San Felipe de Neri Church** *(sanfelipedeneri.org; free entry)* – look out for the Virgen de Guadalupe carved inside a tree trunk outside the church – were the hub of daily life and a major rest stop for those passing through. Outlaw Billy the Kid allegedly frequented a brothel or two here in the 1870s.

The plaza graciously remains, and Old Town is starting to evolve, especially since the COVID-19 pandemic, with quality shops and galleries promoting New Mexican artisans hoping to revamp the historic core.

When your feet get tired, have a Southwestern lunch at **Church Street Cafe** *(churchstreetcafe.com),* before tasting chile wine at **Noisy Water Winery** *(noisywaterwinery.com)* and pondering the cool art in the adjacent **Lapis Room** *(lapisroom.com).*

The world's largest balloon festival

What started at a shopping mall in 1972 has ballooned, quite literally, into one of America's largest festivals, attracting nearly one million people every year to **Balloon Fiesta Park** *(balloonfiesta.com; free park entry; Balloon Fiesta tickets $15)* on the northern edge of Albuquerque city limits for nine days in early October. Standing beneath so many balloons is a surreal experience; the 2022 fest reported a record 648.

You arrive at the grounds before sunrise and are ushered into parking lots (shuttles can get you to the grounds and an app tracks where you parked). Then you're greeted by dozens of vendors offering everything from loaded ribbon fries to hot coffee and, of course, breakfast burritos. At dawn, referees in striped uniforms clear the hordes as balloons are laid out flat before being launched one by one. Besides sunrise flights, events throughout the day include drone shows, chainsaw exhibitions, a sunset flight and fireworks.

Riding in a balloon is typically reserved for local crews, though **Rainbow Ryders** *(rainbowryders.com; prices vary)* offers a handful of visitor spots. You'll have a better chance of booking sunrise flights throughout the year.

Balloon Fiesta Park is also home to the **Anderson-Abruzzo Albuquerque International Balloon Museum**

GREEN OR RED CHILE?

New Mexico is not the same as south of the border or even Texas. It has its own distinct flavors, influenced by Pueblo and other Indigenous groups, Spain, Mexico and Hispanic or Mexican Americans.

The dominant ingredient in New Mexican food is chile (spelled like the country, not the meat stew), a spicy bell pepper infused into everything from chocolate to wine, though you'll find it most often as a sauce. Red or green? That's a question you'll hear in New Mexico, asking you to choose your type of chile sauce. Green chiles ripen first and tend to be spicier. Undecided? Ask for Christmas, which means half and half.

Vegetarians beware that chile sauces are usually made with pork.

EATING IN ALBUQUERQUE: BEST NEW MEXICAN FOOD

Sadie's: Gigantic portions of New Mexican food. Seriously, do not tackle the large nachos alone. *10:30am-10pm* $

El Pinto: Delicious plates in a Southwestern-themed dining room in an old hacienda. Try red-chile ribs. *11am-9pm Sun-Thu, to 10pm Fri & Sat* $

Los Cuates: Our favorite branch on Lomas Blvd has a low-key retro dining room and good red- or green-chile rellenos. Try the cucumber jalapeño margaritas. *11am-9pm* $

Los Compadres: Route 66 spot with a huge menu (and lineup) and classics like saucy carne adovada. *9am-8pm Tue-Sat, to 2pm Sun* $

SIGHTS
1 Anderson-Abruzzo Albuquerque International Balloon Museum
2 Indian Pueblo Cultural Center
3 Lapis Room
4 San Felipe de Neri Church

ACTIVITIES
5 Rainbow Ryders

SLEEPING
6 Hotel Chaco
7 Monterey Motel
8 Painted Lady

EATING
9 Church Street Cafe
10 El Pinto
11 Indian Pueblo Kitchen
12 Los Compadres
13 Los Cuates
14 Sadie's

DRINKING & NIGHTLIFE
15 High Noon Saloon
16 Noisy Water Winery

ENTERTAINMENT
17 Gathering of Nations Powwow
18 International Balloon Fiesta

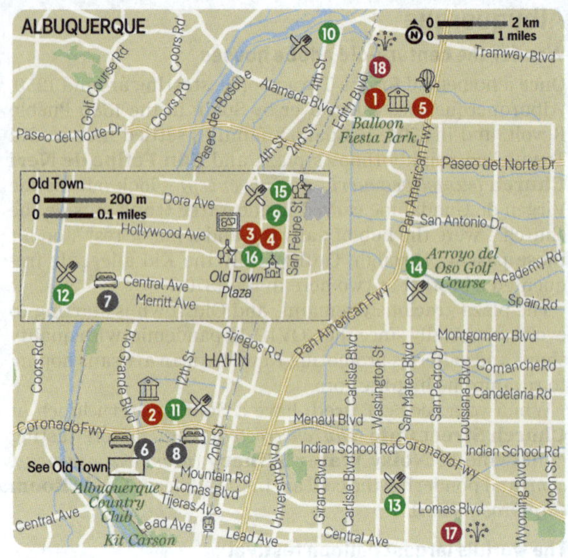

(balloonmuseum.com; adult/child/under 5 $6/3/free), which details the history of hot-air balloon flights dating to 1783 with interactive exhibits and games for kids.

Find out about Pueblo culture

North of I-40 on 12th St was the site of one of America's first 'Indian' schools, where Indigenous children were forcibly assimilated and punished for speaking their language or practicing their culture. The land has since been reclaimed by 19 of New Mexico's Pueblo tribes and transformed into the fascinating **Indian Pueblo Cultural Center** *(indianpueblo.org; adult/child/under 5 $12/8/free)*. Learn about the knowledge of agriculture and the stars that allowed thousands of Indigenous groups to thrive in the Southwest through artifacts, interactive videos and exhibits. Guided tours are offered at noon on Thursdays and Fridays.

The center is also home to one of Albuquerque's best places to try New Mexican cuisine, **Indian Pueblo Kitchen** *(indianpueblokitchen.org)*, which serves fry-bread tacos, housemade stews served with Pueblo oven bread and red- or green-chile-smothered enchiladas alongside the Three Sisters (corn, beans and squash).

At the end of April, Albuquerque hosts North America's biggest powwow, **Gathering of Nations** *(gatheringofnations.*

EATING IN SANTA FE: BEST NEW MEXICAN FOOD

Tia Sophia's: The first to put breakfast burritos on a menu and to offer Christmas sauces. *7am-2pm Mon-Sat, 8am-1pm Sun* **$**

La Choza: Local favorite, often with a line; blue-corn versions of the specialties and cocktails. *11am-2:30pm & 4:30-9pm Mon-Sat* **$$**

Cafe Pasqual's: Cozy space with New Mexico classics and dishes that lean south of the border. *8am-9:30pm Wed-Mon* **$$**

Coyote Cafe: Credited with putting upscale Southwest cuisine on the culinary map. *11:30am-9pm Sun-Thu, to 9:30pm Fri & Sat* **$$$**

com; entry from $25 per person), which attracts more than 500 tribes from across the Americas and beyond.

Santa Fe

Roam the historic city center

New Mexico's state capital feels culturally, aesthetically and geographically different to others in the US. There are many reasons for this. One of the biggest reasons is that, founded in 1607, it's the oldest capital in the nation and was one of the earliest European settlements – this is reflected in Santa Fe's distinctive architecture. Pueblo Revival style dominates the landscape with low-slung, earth-colored adobe houses inspired by pueblos – built with mud, earth and straw – plus striking old churches, chapels and missions.

Santa Fe is easily walkable and peppered with memorable sites. Start from the **Plaza**, which has stood as the heart of the city for 400 years. The close-by **St Francis Cathedral** *(cbsfa.org; free)* with its dramatic facade in Romanesque Revival style looks more suited to Europe than the Wild West, but inside it's New Mexican in appearance with a Hispanic altarpiece and folk art.

Two minutes by foot south is the **Loretto Chapel** *(loretto chapel.com; adult/child/under 5 $5/3/free)*, the first Gothic-style building west of the Mississippi. The chapel was built by French and Italian architects in 1878, but its unsupported wooden staircase, St Joseph's Miraculous Staircase, is what draws the crowds, spiraling upward without center or side supports.

Up Old Santa Fe Trail, **San Miguel Mission** *(sanmiguel chapel.org; free)* is considered the oldest Catholic Church in the US. Next to the mission, the blue-doored **Casa Vieja** (1646) is considered the oldest house in the US.

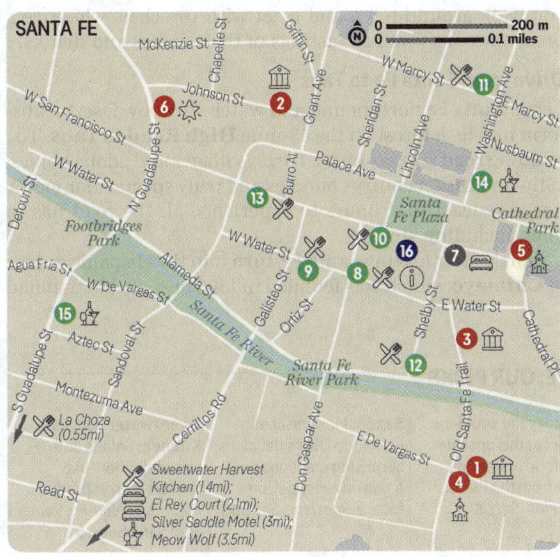

SIGHTS
1 Casa Vieja
2 Georgia O'Keeffe Museum
3 Loretto Chapel
4 San Miguel Mission
5 St Francis Cathedral

ACTIVITIES
6 Santa Fe School of Cooking

SLEEPING
7 La Fonda

EATING
8 Cafe Pasqual's
9 Coyote Cafe
10 Five & Dime
11 Horno
12 Sazón
13 Tia Sophia's

DRINKING & NIGHTLIFE
14 Anasazi
15 Cowgirl

INFORMATION
16 Santa Fe Plaza Visitor Center

NEW MEXICO CULTURAL FESTIVALS

San Ildefenso Feast Day: Traditional dances and Taos Pueblo's famous pottery; January 23.

Taos Fall Arts Festival: Celebrating the creativity of the area; October.

1680 Pueblo Revolt Anniversary: Picuris Pueblo, 20 miles south of Taos, celebrates with a ceremonial foot race, pole climb, dances; August 10.

Fiestas de Taos: Dance and music pours onto the streets in this celebration of Spanish culture; July.

MARGARITA TRAIL

Get a Margarita Trail booklet at the **Santa Fe Visitor Center** or download the app ($2.99) for the ultimate Santa Fe booze crawl. More than 50 restaurants and bars offer jazzed-up margaritas that are $1 off with the booklet or app. Drinks include the **Meow Wolf** Meowgarita (reposado tequila, Cointreau, agave, fresh lime juice, butterfly-pea-flower tea topped with a puffy colorful cloud); the **Cowgirl** Cadillac Margarita (Dulce Vida tequila, Grand Marnier, sweet and sour mix, lime and orange juice); and the **Anasazi** Sandia y Pepino Margarita (Mi Campo tequila, agave, watermelon and cucumber juice, tajin-lime salt rim). Get a stamp at each bar to win prizes, including a T-shirt. You can only earn two stamps per 12 hours.

Ski, hike and bike

Sitting at more than 7000ft above sea level, Santa Fe is the USA's highest state capital, bordered by the imposing Sangre de Cristo Mountains (part of the Rocky Mountains). It never feels claustrophobic, thanks to easy access to nature and outdoor pursuits like hikes and skiing.

Just 16 miles from town, **Ski Santa Fe** *(skisantafe.com; ski passes $48-90 depending on ability)* in the Sangre de Cristo Mountains offers dry powder like its more famous cousin, Taos Ski Valley, with a higher base elevation (10,350ft). It includes seven lifts and 86 runs. **North Central Regional District** *(ncrtd.org/ski-bus)* offers free buses to the top, stopping along trailheads on the way up the mountain.

Trails here range from all-day adventures to short strolls. From the ski basin parking lot, the challenging 10.8-mile **Raven's Ridge** loop cuts east along the **Upper Winsor Trail** after the first steep mile of switchbacks to follow the Pecos Wilderness boundary high above the tree line to the top of **Lake Peak** (12,409ft).

Aspen Vista, the premier path for immersing yourself in the magical bright-yellow fall foliage, lives up to its name. The first mile of the 11.5-mile full-day trail is easy, gaining little elevation and following an old dirt road.

Learn to cook like a New Mexican

Once you've eaten plenty of breakfast burritos, enchiladas and gallons of green chile, you can learn how to make New Mexican food at home with a specialty cooking class. Family-run **Santa Fe School of Cooking** *(santafeschoolofcooking.com; 3hr class from $100)* has been teaching New Mexican cuisine for more than three decades and offers a number of different kinds of classes in a beautiful space west of the Plaza.

On Fridays, the cooking school leads restaurant tours where you walk around town and meet with top chefs who give a presentation as well as tastings of their dishes and drinks.

Drive from Santa Fe to Taos

Leave Santa Fe northbound and watch shrubby desert transform into lush forest on the 58-mile **High Road to Taos**. The winding road zigzags up past artsy villages and adobe homes, 18th- and 19th- century churches and truly spectacular views. Leave at least four hours to experience all the road has to offer, including stops.

Shortly after leaving Santa Fe, turn into the Hispanic village of **Chimayó**, which was founded in 1598 on a pueblo that had

EATING IN SANTA FE: OUR PICKS

Five & Dime General Store: Try a Frito Pie – chile, beans, beef, onions and cheese in a bag of Fritos. *9am-9pm* $

Horno: Try the squid-ink capellini at this upscale street-food restaurant a block from the Plaza. *5-9pm Mon-Sat* $$

Sazón: Mexican chef Fernando Olea's delicious, surprising creations put a grin on every patron's face. *5-9pm Mon-Sat* $$$

Sweetwater Harvest Kitchen: Salads and smoothies here use farmers market produce. *10am-3pm Mon-Fri, 9am-3pm Sat & Sun* $$

AMBER WALKER/SHUTTERSTOCK

El Santuario de Chimayó

been abandoned 200 years prior and holds major significance for Catholics. **El Santuario de Chimayó** *(holychimayo.us; free)* was built in 1816 atop a spot of 'holy dirt' said to be miraculous and to hold curative powers. During Holy Week (mid-April) some 30,000 pilgrims walk to Chimayó from Santa Fe in the largest Catholic pilgrimage in the US.

Up the road, turn off into **Truchas**, an 18th-century Spanish town with century-old adobe buildings and a couple of galleries. In **Peñasco**, the **Peñasco Theatre** *(facebook.com/penascotheatre; prices vary)* bills itself as the area's only solar-powered hand-built adobe theatre. Continue northbound by making a U-turn at Hwy 518 to the most forested part of the road to Taos (p330).

Abiquiú

Hike in Georgia O'Keeffe's footsteps

Iconic artist Georgia O'Keeffe spent summers on mesmerizing **Ghost Ranch** *(ghostranch.org; adult/child $10/free)* with its multicolored bluffs, gorgeous canyons, plains and grasslands filled with spectacular trails. O'Keeffe painted more than 100 paintings on these grounds.

Many visit to do the 3-mile climb up to **Chimney Rock**, an enormous pillar that breaks off from the mesa top with breathtaking views.

O'Keeffe's main **home** and studio, where she lived from 1949 to 1984, sits 12 miles south of Ghost Ranch in Abiquiú. It has Native American and Spanish Colonial building styles, and some rooms date to 1744. It was given National Historic Landmark status in 1998 and is now part of Santa Fe's **Georgia O'Keeffe Museum** *(okeeffemuseum.org; adult/child/under 5 $22/12/free)*. There's also a nearby **O'Keeffe Welcome Center** next to the Abiquiu Inn, with a gift shop and some of her personal effects.

CONTINENTAL DIVIDE TRAIL

Hundreds of thru-hikers brave the 3100-mile Continental Divide Trail each year, which crosses into New Mexico's **San Pedro Parks Wilderness** northwest of Santa Fe. The trail is less popular but no less extraordinary than some of the US' 11 other National Scenic Trails, including the Appalachian and Pacific Crest trails. Many begin the trail on the US border with Chihuahua in Mexico and wind all the way to Alberta, Canada. It takes six months if you hike 17 miles a day.

In New Mexico, the trail stretches 820 miles from the Southwestern desert through Silver City and Gila National Forest to Grants, Jemez Mountains and the Chama Wilderness before hitting the Colorado Rockies. It can also be hiked in shorter segments.

OPPENHEIMER'S DOWNFALL

J Robert Oppenheimer was born in New York in 1904, visited New Mexico as a teen, then studied at Harvard, Cambridge and Göttingen in Germany before being selected as the physicist in charge of the Manhattan Project. After the bombs were dropped on Japan in 1945, Oppenheimer opposed continued development of nuclear weapons. FBI Director J Edgar Hoover began to investigate Oppenheimer for Communist Party links and while none were found, he was stripped of his security clearance in 1954 during the Red Scare, and dismissed for opposing the arms race.

The US went on to do more than 1000 nuclear tests until 1992. *Oppenheimer,* a film directed by Christopher Nolan, was released in 2023.

Bandelier National Monument

Ancient Indigenous caves and petroglyphs

Ancestors of Navajo and current Pueblo people lived in this 33,000-acre area now run by the National Park Service. Some 3000 settlements have been discovered in **Bandelier National Monument** *(nps.gov/band; $25 per vehicle).*

You can visit some of the cave dwellings, just 400yd from the visitor center, by climbing ladders on the 1.4-mile **Pueblo Loop Trail**. There are also remains of adobe-brick buildings and petroglyphs on the cliff face. If you're up for a bigger day of hiking, Bandelier is 70% wilderness with 70 miles of backcountry trails. Get a backcountry permit at the visitor center.

Los Alamos

Where the atomic bomb was born

Los Alamos occupies a special place in US history as one of the creation places of the atomic bomb, and its excellent **Bradbury Science Museum** *(lanl.gov/engage/bradbury; free)* is worth making a trip for. Learn about the history and people behind the Manhattan Project, see a replica of the bomb dropped on Nagasaki and learn about the government research that continues today, including nanoscience, sustainable technology and preventing infectious diseases.

The story here doesn't flinch from the truth. It was here, in 1942 at the height of WWII, that Franklin D Roosevelt called on Lieutenant General Leslie Richard Groves Jr and physicist J Robert Oppenheimer to assemble a secret lab to develop a weapon unlike anything the world had ever seen. The result was the world's first atomic bomb detonation, on July 16, 1945, at the Trinity Site in southern New Mexico. The nuclear bombs designed by the Manhattan Project killed an estimated 135,000 to 215,000 people.

Taos

See where Pueblo culture thrives

A magical spot even by the standards of this Land of Enchantment, Taos is a beautiful town in northern New Mexico surrounded by 12,300ft snowcapped peaks that hit a sage-speckled plateau before plummeting 800ft into the Rio Grande Gorge.

One of the oldest continuously inhabited communities in the US and both a UNESCO World Heritage Site and US National Historic Landmark, **Taos Pueblo** *(taospueblo.com; adult/child under 10 $25/free)* is an extraordinary place to

EATING IN TAOS: OUR PICKS

La Cueva Cafe: Probably Taos' most popular restaurant. New Mexican classics from breakfast to close. *10am-8pm Mon-Fri, to 5pm Sat* $

ACEQ: Pronounced 'ah-sec,' this popular Arroyo Seco spot has great food and is Guy Fieri-approved. *5-10pm* $$

Love Apple: Romantic candlelit restaurant in a 19th-century chapel serving seasonal fare and funky wines. Cash only. *5-9pm Wed-Sun* $$

Chokola: Fair-trade and organic bean-to-bar chocolate tasting room in the Plaza for six kinds of mousse, ice cream, cakes and bars. *11am-6pm* $

HIGHLIGHTS
1 Bradbury Science Museum
2 Ghost Ranch

SIGHTS
3 Bandelier National Monument
4 DH Lawrence Ranch & Memorial
5 El Santuario de Chimayó
6 Georgia O'Keeffe Home
7 O'Keeffe Welcome Center
8 Parsons Gallery of the West
9 Plaza
10 Robert L Parsons Fine Art Gallery
11 San Geronimo Church
12 San Pedro Parks Wilderness
13 Taos Pueblo
14 Wilder Nightingale Fine Art

ACTIVITIES
15 Devisadero Loop Trail
16 Far Flung Adventures
17 New Mexico River Adventures
18 Rift Valley
19 Ski Santa Fe
see 15 South Boundary
20 Taos Ski Valley
21 West Rim

SLEEPING
22 Doña Luz Inn
23 Historic Taos Inn

EATING
24 ACEQ
25 Chokola
26 La Cueva Cafe
27 Los Ojos Restaurant & Saloon
28 Love Apple

ENTERTAINMENT
29 Peñasco Theatre

SHOPPING
30 El Rincón Trading Post

ENCHANTED CIRCLE SCENIC DRIVE

One of the prettiest drives in this Land of Enchantment, along the aptly named Enchanted Circle Scenic Byway, circling Wheeler Peak.

START	END	LENGTH
Taos	Taos	90 miles; 3–6 hours

This drive along Hwys 522, 38 and 64 passes crystalline lakes, pine forests draped with feldspar, alpine highlands, windswept meadows and old-timey ski towns. From ❶ **Taos** head north to Hispanic town ❷ **Questa**, whose name is a typo – it was originally called 'cuesta,' Spanish for cliff or large hill. Questa's adobe St Anthony's Church was built in 1842 but collapsed in 2008. Fortunately, locals volunteered 49,000 hours to revive it, and it was reconsecrated in 2016. Northeast of town, ❸ **Latir Peak Wilderness** has sweet but intense multiday backpacking trails that ascend 12,708ft up the mountain.

A gold-mining boomtown in the 19th and 20th centuries with saloons and brothels, ❹ **Red River** is now a family-friendly ski town. The main drag is lined with shops, with German-style wooden lodges mixed with an Old West theme. On summer Saturdays at 4pm outside ❺ **Frye's Trading Post**, catch the cowboy shoot-out reenactment, a Red River tradition since 1950.

The western part of the trail flattens out and mountain runoff accumulates in 2400-acre ❻ **Eagle Nest Lake State Park**, filled with pike and motorboats in summer. ❼ **Angel Fire** looks like time-share condo land, but it's a popular ski hill with mostly blue and green runs and plenty of lodges. Loop around the remainder of Rte 64 for 18 miles through farmland and Carson forest, then back to Taos.

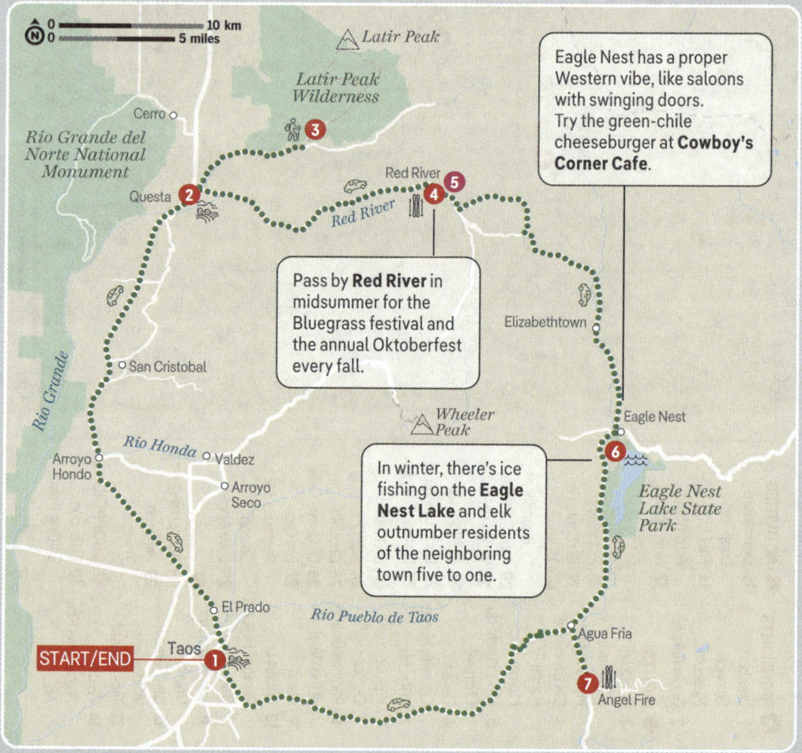

Eagle Nest has a proper Western vibe, like saloons with swinging doors. Try the green-chile cheeseburger at **Cowboy's Corner Cafe**.

Pass by **Red River** in midsummer for the Bluegrass festival and the annual Oktoberfest every fall.

In winter, there's ice fishing on the **Eagle Nest Lake** and elk outnumber residents of the neighboring town five to one.

0 10 km
0 5 miles
Latir Peak
Latir Peak Wilderness
Cerro
Rio Grande del Norte National Monument
Questa
Red River
Red River
Elizabethtown
San Cristobal
Rio Grande
Wheeler Peak
Eagle Nest
Rio Honda
Valdez
Arroyo Hondo
Arroyo Seco
Eagle Nest Lake State Park
El Prado
Rio Pueblo de Taos
Agua Fria
START/END
Taos
Angel Fire

KWAN TSE/SHUTTERSTOCK

Eagle Nest Lake State Park

see New Mexican Pueblo culture thriving in the present day. Three miles northeast of Taos Plaza, the Pueblo's multistory mud-and-straw adobe apartments stand tall and proud under the backdrop of the Sangre de Cristo Mountains, as they've done for 1000 years.

Taos Pueblo welcomes visitors for guided tours. Visitors are taught about Pueblo ways of life, adobe architecture and history, including the 1680 Pueblo Revolt that tossed out the Spanish. You can also visit Taos Pueblo's unique **San Geronimo Church** *(ologtaos.com; free)*, which highlights Mary rather than Jesus at the pulpit.

Taos Pueblo is closed from late winter (usually end of January) to the third week of March.

The art of Taos

Taos went on to become a trading post on the Santa Fe Trail and later an attraction for early-20th-century artist transplants from New York and California, who came to visit and couldn't leave after witnessing the sapphire-blue skies and paint-stroke sunsets.

Taos centers on its atmospheric **Plaza**, with a green park and benches in the middle of a square of adobe homes, the old courthouse and Taos jail on the north side of the Plaza, and buildings dating to 1796. The nearby **Robert L Parsons Fine Art Gallery** *(parsonsart.com)* on Bent St sells works from Taos Society of Artists painters. Its sister, **Parsons Gallery of the West** *(parsonsart.com/parsonswest)* on Kit Carson Rd, features 20 different artists, mostly from Taos, in a beautiful hacienda built in 1803. Across the road, **Wilder Nightingale Fine Art** *(wnightingale.com)* has been selling an eclectic collection of contemporary Taos art for more than 30 years from its huge gallery. For Indigenous art and jewelry, pop into the dusty museum-like **El Rincón Trading Post** *(instagram.com/elrincontradingpost)*, which has been open since 1909 and hasn't changed much.

BEST MOUNTAIN-BIKING TRAILS AROUND TAOS

Taos Ski Valley & Angel Fire: Ride the lifts and zoom down the mountain.

Rift Valley: Mostly flat, winding single-track trail suitable for intermediate cyclists and fun for advanced riders.

South Boundary: Twenty-eight-mile ride considered one of the nation's best mountain-bike trails. Experienced cyclists only.

West Rim: Easy 9-mile trail in Rio Grande del Norte with great views of the Rio Grande Gorge.

Devisadero: Steep and difficult trail with plenty of rocks. Watch out for rattlesnakes.

BEST SALOONS IN NEW MEXICO

Melody Groves, author of *Hoist a Cold One! Historic Bars of the Southwest*, shares New Mexico's best Old West saloons.

No Scum Allowed: Funky White Oaks bar in an 1884 building – the best part is the name.

Double Eagle: During the Civil War, Confederate officers used the back room of this Mesilla bar as a ballroom.

High Noon Saloon: Albuquerque Old Town saloon bar dating to 1785. It's now a steakhouse and apparently haunted.

Buckhorn Saloon: This Pinos Altos saloon north of Silver City is old, as is the bar itself.

Los Ojos: This Jemez Springs place is 100 years old and cool, too. Stop for beer or food.

Tackle the rivers

From April through October, sections of the Rio Grande near Taos are the best places in New Mexico to go white-water rafting. Guides lead trips into the turbulent **Taos Box** north of town, which has lots of class IV and sometimes class V rapids. Boats do tend to flip, and the remoteness of this area makes it extra scary – and thrilling. If Taos Box intimidates you, the **Racecourse** and **Lower Gorge** downriver near Pilar are popular family-friendly spots with gentler waves.

You can book half-, full- or multiday rafting trips with the reputable and knowledgeable **New Mexico River Adventures** *(newmexicoriveradventures.com; rafting $40-450)* and **Far Flung Adventures** *(farflung.com; rafting $54-400)*, which has been in the business since 1976 and has permits from the Forest Service and local tribes. Rock climbing, horseback riding and fly-fishing tours are also available.

Taos and DH Lawrence

British poet and novelist David Herbert Lawrence might have only spent two years (1924–26) on the 160-acre ranch he owned here with his wife Frieda, but it was enough to declare that New Mexico 'changed me forever.' Fans of the author who wrote such classics as *Lady Chatterley's Lover* can visit **DH Lawrence Ranch** *(dhlawrenceranch.unm.edu; free but donations welcome; 9:30am-3:30pm Tue-Thu)*, 20 miles north of Taos, now administered by the University of New Mexico. If you manage to make the narrow opening window, you can visit the famous Lawrence Tree painted by Georgia O'Keeffe, the cabin Dorothy Brett stayed in when Lawrence invited her to start a utopian society and the 19th-century homesteader's cabin where the writer worked on *St Mawr, David* and *The Plumed Serpent*.

Roswell

Put on your tinfoil hat

In July 1947, two years after the first atomic bomb test in Trinity, 350 people say they witnessed an unidentified flying object crash in the desert outside Roswell. More than 75 years later, questions remain about the crash. Was it a flying saucer, as UFO fanatics believe? Or was it a weather balloon as the US government argued? Or was it something else?

Put on a tinfoil hat and investigate the answer at Roswell's **International UFO Museum & Research Center** *(roswellufomuseum.com; adult/child $7/4)*. The museum

EATING IN ROSWELL: OUR PICKS

El Coco Pirata: Probably your best meal in southeast New Mexico. All about seafood, with fresh ceviche and shrimp platters. *10am-9pm* $

Cowboy Cafe: Beloved of locals, this breakfast joint serves hearty New Mexican specialties and burgers. *6am-2pm* $

Martin's Capitol Cafe: Adobe building with Moorish arches. New Mexico classics like burritos, stuffed sopaipillas. *6am-8:30pm Mon-Sat* $

Antigua Cocina: Mexican specialties like *cochinita pibil, chile en nogada* and steak with a big tequila list. *11am-10pm Mon-Thu* $$

STEVE LAGRECA/SHUTTERSTOCK

International UFO Museum & Research Center

details accounts of the Roswell incident and what happened in the aftermath.

Continue your investigation around the corner at **Spaceport Roswell** *(spaceportroswellnm.com; adult/child $14.40/9.50)*, where you can put on VR glasses to experience what it might've been like to be on board the flying saucer that crashed outside Roswell, or join Neil Armstrong on the *Apollo 11* mission to the Moon. Across the street, walk beside aliens and try not to get abducted at **Roswell UFO Spacewalk** *(roswellspacewalk.com; $6)*, an immersive room filled with creepy dayglow decor and lights.

Las Cruces

Feel the downtown vibe

Las Cruces and its older and smaller sister city Mesilla sit in a broad desert basin beneath the striking eastern peaks of the Organ Mountains. There's something special about the combination of bright, white sunlight, glassy blue skies, flowering cacti, rippling red mountains and desert lowland landscape found here. It's worth stopping by to experience New Mexico's most Hispanic/Latinx-influenced city (60% identify as such), and explore Mesilla's cute adobe homes.

Start by walking along Main St in downtown Las Cruces on a Saturday morning and you'll see this sleepy city come to life. From 8:30am to 1pm, vendors at the **Farmers & Crafts**

CONFEDERATE CAPITAL

In July 1861, a small Confederate force from Texas humiliated a force of Union soldiers more than three times its size, between Fort Fillmore (near Mesilla) and San Augustin Pass. Mesilla went on to briefly become the capital of the Confederate Territory of Arizona, but Confederate control only lasted five weeks before soldiers fled the city and then the state.

The Civil War–era **Fort Selden Historic Site** *(museumfoundation.org; adult/child $5/free)*, 20 minutes from downtown Las Cruces, had about 1800 soldiers at its prime, including more than 400 African Americans. Inside is a detailed one-room exhibit, and outside are the fort ruins, including its jail, bakery and barracks. Entry is free with a **New Mexico Culture Pass**.

EATING IN LAS CRUCES: OUR PICKS

!Andele!: Mesilla New Mexican place with a salsa bar, homemade nachos, loaded hot dogs. *8am-9pm Tue-Sun, to 2:30pm Mon* $

La Nueva Casita: Bargain Mexican and New Mexican food, primarily for breakfast. Try the *machaca* scrambled eggs. *9am-3pm Wed-Mon* $

Chala's Wood-Fired Grill: New Mexican done right in Mesilla. Try house-smoked pulled pork. *8am-9pm Mon-Thu, to 9:30pm Fri & Sat, to 2pm Sun* $

Spotted Dog Brewery: Green-chile pesto wings, burgers, cheese, craft beer. *11:30am-10:30pm Mon-Thu, to midnight Fri & Sat, noon-8:30pm Sun* $$

BORDER PATROL

Along I-25, some 22 or so miles north of Las Cruces, signs will tell you to slow down to pass through a US border checkpoint. These types of government checkpoints are common in the southern part of the state, being so close to the border, and you're nearly guaranteed to see one if you're driving. If waved over, you'll have to answer a few questions, or you might not have to do anything at all as a green light flashes you through. Always carry ID, including a valid tourist visa if you're a foreign citizen, as well as car registration or the rental agreement. Be polite and allow them to search inside the trunk if they ask.

Market *(farmersandcraftsmarketoflascruces.com; free)* show off their hauls of local pecans and Hatch chiles, while food trucks sling tacos and churros. Local artisans are here, too, selling pottery, jewelry, fun shirts and the like. Someone might be jamming at **Downtown Blues Coffee** *(downtownbluescoffee.com)*, a cafe, record store and hub of cultural life.

Range a little further and **Mesilla**, technically its own distinct town 4 miles south of downtown, is Las Cruces' most historic neighborhood, and walking around here feels like being in 19th-century Mexico; the trial of outlaw Billy the Kid happened here in 1881. Today Mesilla is a beautifully preserved slice of history with cute adobe houses and a beautiful historic plaza with its 1855 **Basilica of San Albino** *(sanalbino.org; free)*.

The birthplace of the Space Race

Being a high-elevation desert, southern New Mexico is a great place to see the stars – and to launch spaceships.

In Alamogordo, a dusty town at the base of Lincoln National Forest's mountains an hour east of Las Cruces, is the **New Mexico Museum of Space History** *(nmspacemuseum.org; adult/child $8/6)*. Built like a space shuttle, this four-floor museum has interesting exhibits that take you from the history of Indigenous awareness of the stars to Robert H Goddard's liquid fuel rocket test in 1926 to the atomic bomb and modern space tourism.

The tradition continues at Virgin Galactic's **Spaceport America** *(spaceportamerica.com)*, the world's first commercial spaceport and an active rocket test facility, one hour north of Las Cruces. While not open for pop-ins, you can visit by booking a private tour with **Final Frontier Tours** *(spaceportamerica.com/visit; adult/child $49.99/29.99)*. Inside the facility, you'll visit mission control, speak with firefighters about potential crashes, ride the runway and test out the Multi-Axis Trainer (MAT), which prepares astronauts for zero gravity.

Truth or Consequences

Hippies and hot springs

Vying for the title of New Mexico's quirkiest town (the competition is admittedly stiff) is Truth or Consequences (also called T or C), 75 miles north of Las Cruces. Formerly known as Hot Springs, the municipality changed its name in 1950 when the then-host of a radio show called Truth or Consequences promised to air the 10th-anniversary program in the town that changed its name to the title of the show.

Today, Truth or Consequences has an artsy, transient, end-of-the-world vibe, like Joshua Tree 30 years ago. Its small downtown is packed with art galleries and eclectic gift shops. But the main reason to come to Truth or Consequences is to soak in its hot springs. Most hotels and private dwellings have them – all they need to do is dig – but the best are at **Riverbend Hot Springs** *(riverbendhotsprings.com; common pools from $25, private from $35 per 50min)*.

TOP EXPERIENCE

White Sands National Park

Fifty miles east of Las Cruces, ethereal snow-white sand dunes roll on as far as the eye can see like something out of a dream. The phenomenal 275-sq-mile White Sands National Park is nowhere near the ocean; the dunes are actually made from powdered gypsum crystals that blew from an ancient sea over the San Andres and Sacramento Mountains 4000 to 7000 years ago.

Drive

From the visitor center, drive the 16-mile scenic sandy loop (fine for cars and RVs) and stop along the way to sink your toes in the dunes. The temperature can change by 50°F in a day. Bring lots of water (1 gallon per day per person). Picnic areas along the drive offer shaded benches for lunch.

Walk (or Slide)

Walking in the silence and solitude of the dunes is almost a spiritual experience, especially at sunrise or sunset when the sea of sand sparkles. Escape the crowds on the **Alkali Flat**, a 5-mile round-trip backcountry trail through the heart of White Sands (follow the markers as it's easy to get lost). It's really a winter trail but possible to hike if you come early before it's hot. Or try the simple 1-mile loop **Dune Life Nature Trail**, which climbs two steep dunes rich with desert plant life.

Tumble down the dune or slide down on a sled or sandbar of your choice. You can buy/rent a plastic saucer ($24.99/15) at the visitor-center gift shop. You can rent a board for $25 to surf the dunes. Buy wax to make it a faster experience.

Camp

You can camp in the vast desert on the 2-mile round-trip **Backcountry Camping Loop Trail** (no water, shade or toilets). When darkness falls, the dunes mirror the night sky for ultimate blackness – the Milky Way is visible on a moonless night. At the time of research, camping was unavailable due to maintenance – check before a visit.

TOP TIPS

- Map GPS points on your trail, including where your car is. It's easy to get lost.
- The dunes get more impressive further into the park, so go to the furthest point first.
- Bring sunglasses and sunscreen – reflection can cause sunburn under your chin.
- Note that the park can close during nearby missile tests.

PRACTICALITIES

- nps.gov/whsa
- $25 per vehicle

Places We Love to Stay

$** Budget **$$** Midrange **$$$ Top End

Las Vegas p256

Luxor $ A pyramid-shaped, Egyptian-themed resort with cutting-edge entertainment and comfy rooms.

El Cortez $ A Fremont St icon since 1941, when the mob ran the joint. Recently revamped and adults only.

Cosmopolitan $$ These digs are the hippest on the Strip, with rooms featuring balconies, Japanese tubs and plush furnishings.

Skylofts $$$ Inside the MGM Grand, these glamorous two-story apartments have every indulgence, from spa tubs to gourmet kitchens. Butler included.

Southern Nevada p262

Baker Creek Campground $ Unfurl your tent next to an alpine stream under a canopy of aspens in Great Basin National Park.

Atlatl Rock Campground $ Gorgeous sites among sandstone formations at the heart of jaw-dropping Valley of Fire State Park.

Hidden Canyon Retreat $$ A breathtaking and historic resort tucked into a vast canyon and stretching over 375 acres near Great Basin National Park.

Grand Canyon National Park p273

Bright Angel Lodge $ Simple lodge rooms and rustic cabins on the canyon edge are excellent budget accommodations.

El Tovar $$$ Public spaces in this wooden lodge ooze old-world national-park glamor, but room aesthetics vary in appeal.

Sedona & Around p281

Wigwam Motel $ Each room at this 1937 motel on Route 66 in Holbrook is a self-contained concrete tipi.

La Posada $$ An impressively restored 1930s hacienda in Winslow with artistic, period-styled rooms named for illustrious former guests.

Jerome p286

Connor Hotel $ Twelve restored rooms capture the Victorian period, with pedestal sinks, flower wallpaper and pressed-tin ceilings.

Jerome Grand $$$ Built in 1926 as a hospital, the sturdy fortress plays up its unusual history with halls filled with relics of the past.

Prescott p286

Hotel St Michael $$ Gargoyles, ghosts and a 1925 elevator keep things offbeat at this Victorian-era hotel on Whiskey Row.

Hotel Vendome $$ This dapper inn, dating from 1917, blends up-to-date style with period touches. Ask about the ghost (Abby) in room 16.

Flagstaff p287

Americana Motor Hotel $ Revamped rooms celebrate the '70s with disco balls and space-age decor. Fun vibe and two free drinks at check-in.

Weatherford Hotel $ It's not for everyone – and potentially loud – but this historic hotel in the thick of the action downtown maintains turn-of-the-20th-century authenticity.

Canyon de Chelly p290

Thunderbird Lodge $ This ranch-style hotel with modern rooms is the only lodging in the park. Offers canyon tours.

Spider Rock Campground $ Peaceful Navajo-run campground surrounded by pinyon and juniper trees.

Tucson p295

Tuxon $ Former Motel 6 converted into a minimalist-chic dream. Immediately west of downtown off I-10.

Hotel McCoy $$ Welcoming guests with genuine friendliness and emblazoned with murals, this is our local favorite. Enjoy local craft beer at night and an oatmeal bar in the morning.

Hacienda del Sol Guest Ranch Resort $$$ This relaxing refuge has artist-designed Southwest-style rooms and teems with unique touches.

Bisbee p299

Shady Dell $ Vintage Airstreams feature mid-century decor at this retro-minded trailer park in Bisbee.

Copper Queen Hotel $$ Older than the state of Arizona itself, Copper Queen Hotel opened in 1902 and was John Wayne's Bisbee hotel of choice. Most of the original decor remains.

Torrey p313

Torrey Schoolhouse B&B $$ Sleep in the now-cozy former classrooms of this 1917 schoolhouse.

Skyview $$$ Reach the rooms, some with private hot tubs, through a 'slot canyon' art installation, or spend a starry night in a geodesic dome.

Bryce Canyon National Park & City p318

Lodge at Bryce Canyon $$ Charmingly rustic 1920s lodge; the cabins are a better pick than the generic motel-style rooms.

Bryce Canyon Grand Hotel $$ The large, clean rooms here are a step up from other hotels clustered outside the park entrance.

East Zion p320

Zion Ponderosa Ranch Resort $$ Families love this activity-rich ranch on 6.25 sq miles with swimming pools, climbing walls and mini-golf.

Zion Mountain Ranch $$$ A luxury ranch with six types of cabins, larger lodges and its own herd of roaming bison.

Albuquerque p325

Monterey Motel $ Revived Route 66 motel near Old Town with Tempur-Pedic mattresses, color-changing pool and bar.

Painted Lady $$ Former 19th-century brothel transformed into a bed and brew (beer) and backyard trolley taproom.

Hotel Chaco $$$ Modern Pueblo-style boutique hotel beautifully decorated with precious art; great rooftop bar.

Santa Fe p327

Silver Saddle Motel $ A 1958 Route 66 motel revived in 2022 with a hip California vibe and sleek modern bathrooms.

El Rey Court $$ Revived 1936 auto court with 85 stylish rooms, saltwater pool and bar with live music every Wednesday.

La Fonda $$$ Former end to Santa Fe Trail, then a Harvey House designed by John Gaw Meem and now a luxury hotel on the Plaza.

Taos p330

Doña Luz Inn $$ Each of the eight rooms in this joyful B&B is a work of Southwestern art.

Historic Taos Inn $$ Old inn with wooden furnishings, adobe fireplaces, lots of Southwest charm and a good restaurant.

Roswell Area p334

Roswell Inn $ Rare independent motel updated in 2015 with bargain prices and continental breakfast.

Home2 Suites by Hilton $$ Fresh four-floor Hilton with a pool, gym and buffet breakfast. Roswell's nicest option.

Las Cruces p335

Best Western Mission Inn $ Prettier than your typical chain hotel. Adobe walls and Hispanic art at reception.

Lundeen Inn of the Arts $ Cozy, seven-room family-run alternative to chains. Also hosts a gallery with Southwestern art.

Chandelier Bar, Cosmopolitan

ANTARES NS/SHUTTERSTOCK

Researched and curated by Helena Smith

California

THE LEISURELY LEFT COAST

Epic national parks, wild coastlines, spectacular cities and a progressive vibe. What's not to like, California?

From misty Northern California redwood forests to sun-kissed Southern California beaches, the enchanted Golden State makes Disneyland seem normal. Combining bohemian spirit and high-tech savvy, California embraces contrast and contradictions. It is home to both vibrant metropolises and rugged wilderness, snowy mountains and desert expanses, and miles and miles of spectacular coastline.

It was here that the hurly-burly Gold Rush kicked off in the mid-19th century, where poet and naturalist John Muir rhapsodized about the Sierra Nevada's 'range of light,' where Jack Kerouac and the Beat Generation defined what it meant to hit the road, and where the twin dream factories of tech and entertainment flourished.

Above all, this is a state that celebrates the good life – whether that means cracking open a bottle of old-vine zinfandel, climbing a 14,000ft peak or surfing the Pacific. The Golden State has surged ahead of France to become the world's sixth-largest economy. But like a kid that's grown too fast, California still hasn't figured out how to handle the hassles that come along with such rapid growth, including housing shortages, traffic gridlock and rising costs of living.

Escapism is always an option here, thanks to Hollywood blockbusters and legalized marijuana dispensaries. But California is coming to grips with its international status and taking leading roles in such global issues as environmental standards, online privacy, marriage equality and immigrant rights.

MICHAEL RUNKEL/GETTY IMAGES

THE MAIN AREAS

SAN FRANCISCO & THE BAY AREA
Vertiginous streetscapes and a beautiful bay. p346

NORTHERN CALIFORNIA: REDWOODS & WINE COUNTRY
Giant trees and tasty vintages. p371

YOSEMITE, LAKE TAHOE & GOLD COUNTRY
Towering rock faces and historic towns. p385

For places to stay in California, see p437

ANASTASIA_PHOTOGRAPHY/SHUTTERSTOCK

Hiker, Joshua Tree National Park (p423)

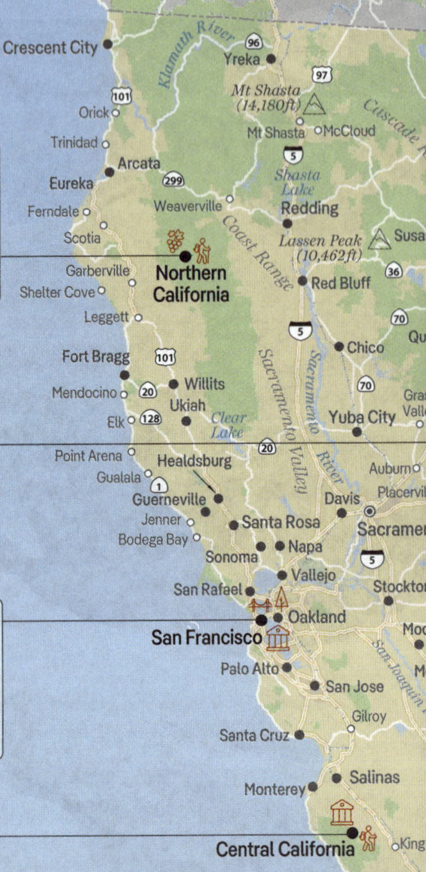

Northern California: Redwoods & Wine Country, p371

California's redwoods will stop you in your tracks. Or possibly send you to the nearest vineyard for fine local vintages.

Yosemite, Lake Tahoe & Gold Country, p385

Yosemite's improbable sheer rocks are nature at its most imposing, Lake Tahoe lures hikers and skiers, and the Gold Country's pretty cities entice.

San Francisco & the Bay Area, p346

Grab your coat and a handful of glitter, and enter a wonderland of fog and fabulousness. So long, inhibitions; hello, San Francisco!

Central California: The Coast & Sacramento, p397

Cali's capital features a wealth of historic buildings, its streets overarched with trees, while coastal California is romantically windswept.

Los Angeles & the Deserts, p409

LA's life-affirming moments: a cracked-ice cocktail, a hike into Griffith Park, a pink-washed sunset over Venice Beach, the perfect taco...

Southern California: Disneyland to San Diego, p427

Sunny San Diego is a collection of villages tied into a laid-back city with 60 beaches. Disneyland represents the ultimate escape from reality.

0 200 km
0 100 miles

Find Your Way

California crams incredible geographic diversity into 163,696 sq miles: the mighty Sierras, the fertile Central Valley, a craggy coastline and arid deserts. From lofty Mt Whitney to the depths of Death Valley, there's a lot of ground to cover.

TRAIN

The California coast provides superb scenery for the north-south *Coast Starlight* and *Pacific Surfliner* trains; the Capitol Corridor route cuts east-west across the north of the state; while the *San Joaquins* trains cross the Central Valley and Sacramento, with connections to Yosemite.

CAR

Between LA, San Francisco and Northern California, the fastest route is I-5 through the San Joaquin Valley. Hwy 101 is slower but more picturesque. The most scenic – and slowest – route is Hwy 1 (Pacific Coast Hwy), but check first to see if there are closures.

BUS

Greyhound and Amtrak Thruway buses connect destinations across the state, providing an affordable alternative to car travel. You can speed up your trip by combining rail travel with bus trips to more out-of-the way places.

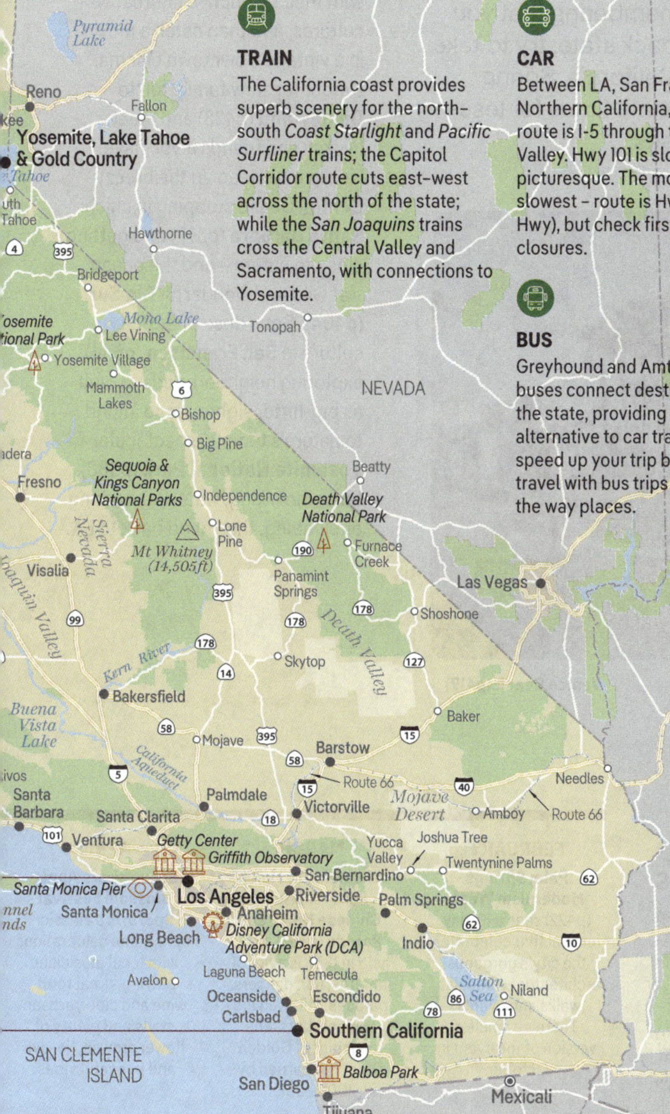

Plan Your Time

It's worth remembering that you are in a laid-back state: try to take your time in California. Spring and fall are prime times for less-pressured visits.

PANDORA PICTURES/SHUTTERSTOCK

Venice Beach (p419)

One Week to Explore

- Trying to capture California in a nutshell you can start with the superlative galleries and sweeping beaches of **Los Angeles** (p409), with their distinctive alternative cultures, and then catch a movie in a vintage Downtown cinema. Detour for zany family fun to **Disneyland** (p428) and meet Mickey and friends if you have kids in tow. Head up the breezy Central Coast, stopping in chichi **Santa Barbara** (p397) and getting close to nature – and the ocean – at wild and wonderful **Big Sur** (p404). Get a dose of big-city culture in **San Francisco** (p346), exploring neighborhoods as well as big-hitter sights. Head inland to nature's temple, spectacular **Yosemite National Park** (p388), for some hiking, waterfall-bathing or climbing, then head back to LA.

SEASONAL HIGHLIGHTS

Californians know how to have fun, and you'll never be far from a festival or event. In a food-loving state, many of these are focused on celebrating fine seasonal produce.

FEBRUARY

Palm Springs Modernism Week (p422) sees a 10-day festival that celebrates the city's gorgeous architecture with talks, walks and events. There's a smaller version of the event in October.

MARCH

In February or March, San Francisco's **Chinese New Year Parade** (p357), first held in 1851, is a riot of lanterns, lion dancers, parades, stilt walkers and acrobats. The magnificent Golden Dragon is carried by 100 people.

APRIL

Sebastapol's **Apple Blossom Festival** (p375) is a classic springtime celebration, with local musicians playing, great food, wine and cider, artisan stalls and plenty of flower crowns, tie-dye and peaceful vibes.

Two Weeks in the Golden State

- Follow the earlier one-week itinerary, but at a less frenetic pace, taking time for more ocean stops at destinations such as **Carmel-by-the-Sea** (p403). Add side trips to NorCal's **Wine Country** (p371) for leisurely vineyard visits and farm-to-fork eating, with excursions to see some big trees, or head to magnificent **Lake Tahoe** (p385), perched high up in the Sierra Nevada, which draws hikers and water-sports fans as well as skiers and snowboarders in the winter months.

- In Southern California, laid-back **San Diego** (p433) takes you off the usual city trail and offers a multitude of beaches for dipping and dreaming, while **Joshua Tree National Park** (p423), near the chic desert resort of **Palm Springs** (p422), features some truly arresting plant life and vistas.

California for a Month

- Do everything described in the earlier itineraries, and then some. From San Francisco, head up the foggy north coast, starting in Marin County at **Point Reyes** (p367). Stroll Victorian-era **Mendocino** (p376) and **Eureka** (p380), find yourself on the **Lost Coast** (p379) and ramble through fern-filled **Redwood National & State Parks** (p381), whose lofty trees will keep you gazing upwards.

- Inland, snap a perfect photo of **Mt Shasta** (p382), drive through **Lassen Volcanic National Park** (p384) with its sulfur ponds and bubbling mud pools, and visit California's historic and enchanting **Gold Country** (p385), with time to absorb alternative culture and pine-cloaked hills in picturesque **Nevada City** (p395). Trace the backbone of the Eastern Sierra before winding down into **Death Valley** (p424).

JUNE

Art at the Source (p375) in Sonoma sees artist studios opening around town and across the area, with printmaking, painting, sculpture, jewelry-making and more. It's a great time to buy unique local gifts.

JULY

July 4th celebrations usher in **high summer** in California. While temperatures and visitor numbers are often high, it is nonetheless an action-packed time to visit. Be sure to book accommodations in advance.

SEPTEMBER

The ultimate small town event and celebration of seasonal fare, the **Kelseyville Pear Festival** (p379) sees three stages crammed with musicians and dancers, plus over 100 craft and food vendors.

OCTOBER

In late October and early November, the **Paderewski Festival** (p402) in Paso Robles comprises concerts showcasing the work of Polish musician turned rancher Ignacy Paderewski.

San Francisco & the Bay Area

RADICAL THINKING | ARCHITECTURAL GLORY | WILD BAY

GETTING AROUND

Muni buses connect the Wharf, Marina and Presidio with points beyond; Golden Gate Transit crosses the bridge; and Presidio GO shuttles cover Presidio parks. Download maps and schedules – especially if you're headed to the Presidio, where cell signal is variable. The best way to see Fisherman's Wharf and Presidio nature trails is at your own pace, with frequent stops for entertainment and photos. Cover the waterfront on rental bikes with pickups at the Presidio and/or Wharf, but book ahead on weekends.

Adventurous food, wild entertainment, trippy tech: a weekend in San Francisco can seem like a quick trip into the future, except that you're surrounded by bedazzling Victorian architecture. Gold found in nearby Sierra Nevada foothills turned a sleepy 800-person village into a port city of 100,000 freewheeling prospectors, opera divas, con artists and laborers from across the globe. The psychedelic '60s took off here, and the Summer of Love brought free food, love and music to the Haight. As in San Francisco's early days, new ideas keep arriving here. So come on in: you're just in time for its next act. In the Bay Area, visit wizened ancient redwoods body-blocking the sun, and herds of elephant seals on the sands of Point Reyes. Oakland is the diverse, radically proud place San Francisco once was, while Berkeley, with its long-standing university, continues at the forefront of left-leaning political causes.

R&R in the Presidio

Play in an ex-army outpost

'Presidio' means fort in Spanish – but in San Francisco, it's a playground for the people. It started in 1776 as a Spanish military post built by conscripted Ohlone people, and was officially retired from its military duties in 1996. To the obvious delight of shorebirds, puppies, locals and visitors, the **Presidio of San Francisco** is now a national park. To allow wildlife to thrive in the park, commuter traffic was rerouted underground – revealing glorious views clear across the bay from driftwood-shaped picnic benches at **Tunnel Tops** park, with the nature-themed **Outpost Playground** downhill. This is wildly popular for its nature-themed play structures, water features, nearby food trucks, picnic facilities and clean bathrooms.

On hot days, race the crowds to **Baker Beach**, the sandy Presidio cove with spectacular views of the Golden Gate framed by wind-sculpted pines – plus nude sunbathing behind the

SAN FRANCISCO & THE BAY AREA

rocks on the clothing-optional, gay-friendly, no-photography-allowed north end. Picnickers and sand-castle architects stick to the sandy south end, near the parking.

Other rest and recreation opportunities abound here. Civilians can now throw strikes at the post's **Presidio Bowl bowling alley** *(presidiobowl.com; per lane up to 6 people before 6pm weekdays/weekends $55/75, after 6pm weekdays/weekends $75/85, shoe rental $7.50)* or bounce off walls inside an ex-airplane hangar lined with trampolines called the **House of Air** *(houseofair.com; adult/child 1hr $20-28)*. The post's former PX (provisions warehouse) is now a **Sports Basement** *(sportsbasement.com)* that stocks bikes, wetsuits and other sporting equipment to rent, buy or trade.

TOP TIP

Plan outfits strategically, as coastal weather shifts suddenly. Dress in layers: windbreaker for Golden Gate Bridge hikes, cozy sweater for panoramic Presidio picnics and nice (but washable) shirt for seafood feasts at the Wharf or Marina.

EATING IN THE PRESIDIO: FOOD TRUCKS TO CHASE

Borsch Mobile: Ukrainian comfort food like borscht and potato dumplings warm the belly on a blustery day. *hours vary* $

Señor Sisig: Filipino-style saucy, succulent meats and adobo garlic rice folded into a burrito – lunch is a wrap. *hours vary* $

Fort Point Beer: Brews crafted just uphill go down even easier on sunny Presidio Parade Grounds with Dungeness crab rolls. *hours vary* $

Kabob Trolley: Get your pick of Afghani-spiced meats described as 'hella Halal' packed into sliders, wrapped into 'gyrritos,' or piled on fries to share... maybe. *hours vary* $

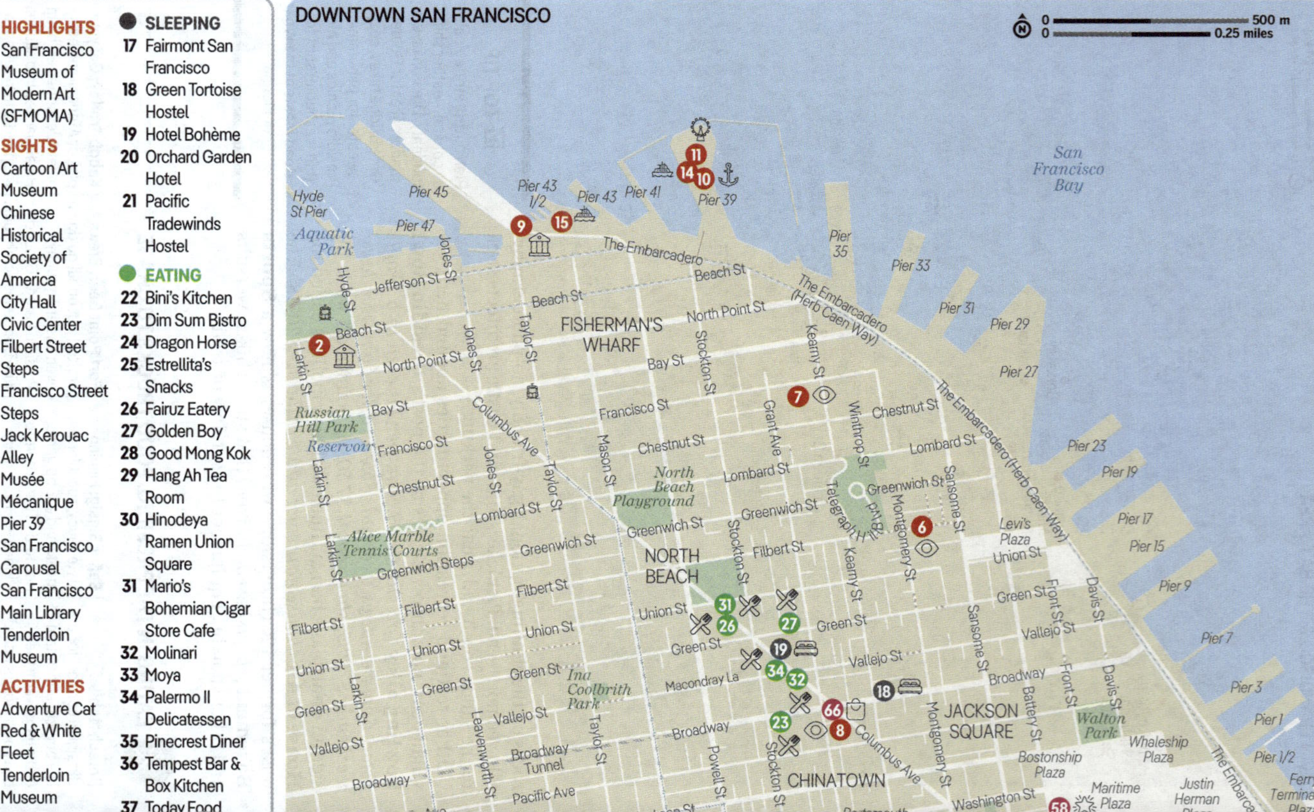

HIGHLIGHTS
1 San Francisco Museum of Modern Art (SFMOMA)

SIGHTS
2 Cartoon Art Museum
3 Chinese Historical Society of America
4 City Hall
5 Civic Center
6 Filbert Street Steps
7 Francisco Street Steps
8 Jack Kerouac Alley
9 Musée Mécanique
10 Pier 39
11 San Francisco Carousel
12 San Francisco Main Library
13 Tenderloin Museum

ACTIVITIES
14 Adventure Cat
15 Red & White Fleet
16 Tenderloin Museum

SLEEPING
17 Fairmont San Francisco
18 Green Tortoise Hostel
19 Hotel Bohème
20 Orchard Garden Hotel
21 Pacific Tradewinds Hostel

EATING
22 Bini's Kitchen
23 Dim Sum Bistro
24 Dragon Horse
25 Estrellita's Snacks
26 Fairuz Eatery
27 Golden Boy
28 Good Mong Kok
29 Hang Ah Tea Room
30 Hinodeya Ramen Union Square
31 Mario's Bohemian Cigar Store Cafe
32 Molinari
33 Moya
34 Palermo II Delicatessen
35 Pinecrest Diner
36 Tempest Bar & Box Kitchen
37 Today Food

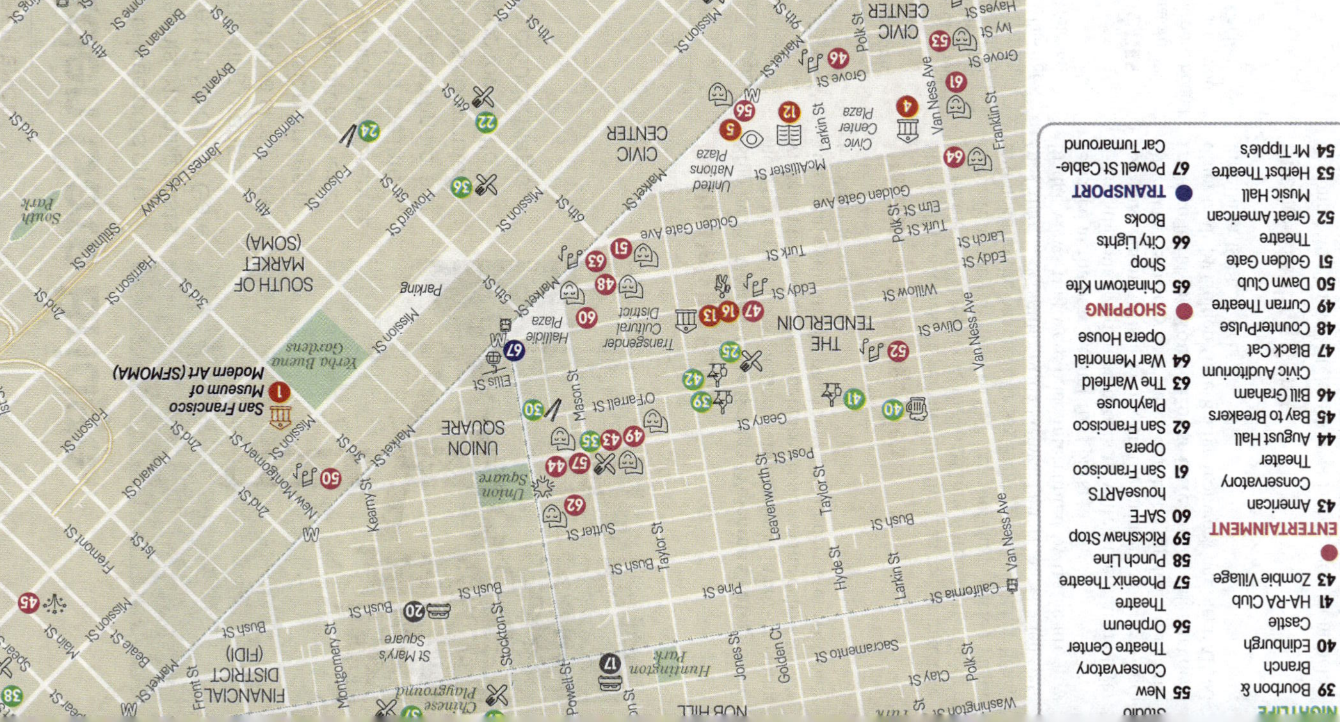
NIGHTLIFE
39 Bourbon & Branch
40 Edinburgh Castle
41 HA-RA Club
43 Zombie Village
ENTERTAINMENT
43 American Conservatory Theater
44 August Hall
45 Bay to Breakers
46 Bill Graham Civic Auditorium
47 Black Cat
48 CounterPulse
49 Curran Theatre
50 Dawn Club
51 Golden Gate Theatre
52 Great American Music Hall
53 Herbst Theatre
54 Mr Tipple's
Studio
55 New Conservatory Theatre Center
56 Orpheum Theatre
57 Phoenix Theatre
58 Punch Line
59 Rickshaw Stop
60 SAFE houseARTS
61 San Francisco Opera
62 San Francisco Playhouse
63 The Warfield
64 War Memorial Opera House
SHOPPING
65 Chinatown Kite Shop
66 City Lights Books
TRANSPORT
67 Powell St Cable-Car Turnaround
FINANCIAL DISTRICT (FIDI)
UNION SQUARE
SOUTH OF MARKET (SOMA)
THE TENDERLOIN
CIVIC CENTER
NOB HILL
San Francisco Museum of Modern Art (SFMOMA)
Yerba Buena Gardens
Union Square
South Park
St Mary's Square
Huntington Park
Chinese Playground
Hallidie Plaza
Transgender Cultural District
United Nations Plaza
Civic Center Plaza
Parking
Market St
Mission St
Howard St
Folsom St
Harrison St
Bryant St
Brannan St
Townsend St
King St
Van Ness Ave
Powell St
Stockton St
Geary St
O'Farrell St
Eddy St
Turk St
Golden Gate Ave

TOP EXPERIENCE

Golden Gate Bridge

No other bridge puts on a show like this. Morning mists lift to reveal the Golden Gate Bridge, glowing orange-red against blue skies: the sleek suspension bridge is painted a signature shade called International Orange. Stick around for the late-afternoon grand finale: as fog swallows commute traffic, deco towers float above the clouds. Magic.

CANADASTOCK/SHUTTERSTOCK ©

TOP TIPS

- Always wear a water-resistant outer layer.
- Bicycles and e-bikes are allowed on bridge sidewalks, but not skateboards, electric scooters or skates.
- Volunteer City Guides lead free bridge tours ($20 donation suggested) most Sundays and Thursdays at 11am, departing from outside the Welcome Center.

PRACTICALITIES

- goldengate.org
- vehicle toll: northbound free, southbound $9.50
- Welcome Center: 9am-6pm

Death-Defying Feats

Stop by the **Golden Gate Bridge Welcome Center** to witness precarious construction work captured in jaw-dropping vintage photos – riveters balance atop swaying cables 80 stories high, while divers plummet 110ft underwater with only a rubber hose for air.

Unbelievable Bridge Views

Sunny days are best to get the full effect, as red-orange towers pierce blue skies above the sparkling waters of the Golden Gate. To make the most of SF's rare hot days, pack a picnic and head to the beach at Crissy Field (p353) or Baker Beach (p346) for spectacular bridge views. Panoramic Golden Gate Bridge views that were once interrupted by traffic are now revealed at the new Tunnel Tops park.

Fog aficionados don raincoats to watch the marine layer roll past Marin's Vista Point, on the bridge's northern end. Or you can stay dry and watch acrobatic fog feats over fair-trade coffee at the **Round House Café**, the circular art deco diner built by Golden Gate Bridge ironwork engineer Alfred Finnila in 1938.

Scene-Stealing Cameos

Cinema buffs know Hitchcock was right: seen from below at Fort Point, the bridge induces a thrilling case of *Vertigo*.

TOP EXPERIENCE

Golden Gate Park

When San Franciscans refer to 'the park,' there's only one that gets the definite article: Golden Gate Park. Everything SF holds dear is here: free spirits and free music, butterfly domes and underground art, chatty penguins and hushed redwood groves, tenacious bonsai and massive, mellow bison. Landmark venues celebrating nature, music, art and science are dotted across the park's 1017 acres.

Japanese Tea Garden

Art in the Park

There's no denying the park's all-star art attraction: the **de Young Museum** *(famsf.org; adult/youth $20/free)*. The cross-cultural collection featuring Olmec stone heads and Turkish kilims alongside California crafts and avant-garde American art has been broadening artistic horizons for a century.

Park Music Events

Golden Gate Park has hosted epic festivals ever since the 1967 Human Be-In, when free spirits gathered to 'tune in, turn on, drop out.' Today, multistage festivals are held around Polo Fields – notably free **Hardly Strictly Bluegrass** *(hardlystrictly bluegrass.com)*, held in the first weekend in October.

Natural Wonders

At the east entrance to the park, you can't miss the grandly elegant **Conservatory of Flowers** *(gggp.org; adult/youth & senior/child $17/7/3)*. This gloriously restored 1878 Victorian greenhouse is home to freaky outer-space orchids and serene floating lilies. **San Francisco Botanical Garden** *(gggp.org; adult/youth & senior/child $17/7/3)* covers a world of vegetation, from South African savanna to New Zealand cloud forest.

Since 1894 the 5-acre **Japanese Tea Garden** *(gggp.org; adult/youth & senior/child $15/7/3; first hour free)* has blushed pink with cherry blossoms in spring and turned flaming red with maple leaves in fall.

TOP TIPS

- John F Kennedy Dr is pedestrian-only starting at 9th Ave – a weekend hot spot with roller disco and free Lindy Hop dance lessons.
- Volunteer docents lead free tours covering park history; for times, see sfcityguides.org.

PRACTICALITIES

- sfrecpark.org
- 24hr
- free

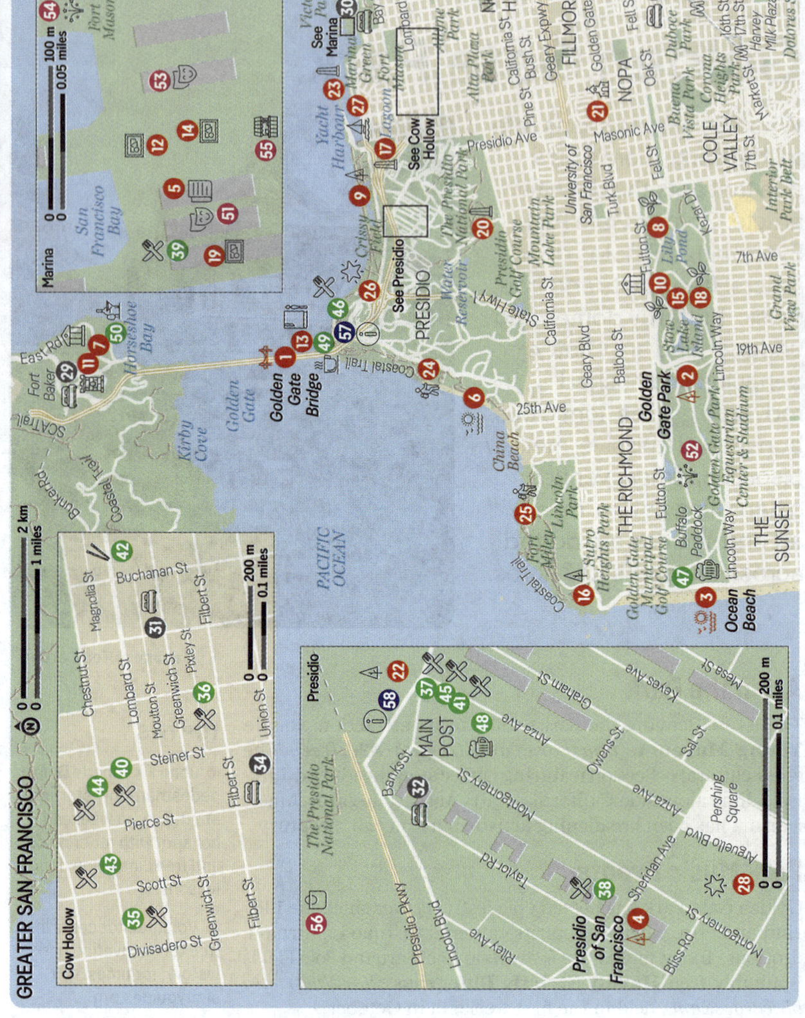

Happy Trails

Walk on San Fran's wild side

Hiking adventures begin at the **Presidio Visitors Center**, well-supplied with trail maps. For a moderately challenging, inspirational 1.4-mile hike, follow the **Ecology Trail** through redwood groves and spring wildflower meadows to **Inspiration Point** for bird's-eye bay views, then push onward to reach the Presidio's artistic pinnacle: Andy Goldsworthy's **Spire**, made from reclaimed cypress trees. Adventurous hikers take on the 2.7-mile **Batteries to Bluffs Trail**, heading uphill above Baker Beach (p346) to splendid Golden Gate Bridge vistas.

HIGHLIGHTS
1 Golden Gate Bridge
2 Golden Gate Park
3 Ocean Beach
4 Presidio of San Francisco

SIGHTS
5 Arion Press
6 Baker Beach
7 Bay Area Discovery Museum
8 Conservatory of Flowers
9 Crissy Field
10 de Young Museum
11 Fort Baker
12 Fort Mason Center
13 Fort Point
14 Haines Gallery
15 Japanese Tea Garden
16 Lands End
17 Palace of Fine Arts
18 San Francisco Botanical Garden
19 SF Camerawork
20 Spire
21 St John Coltrane Church
22 Tunnel Tops
23 Wave Organ

ACTIVITIES
24 Batteries to Bluffs Trail
25 Coastal Trail
26 House of Air
27 Oceanic Society
28 Presidio Bowl

SLEEPING
29 Cavallo Point Lodge
30 HI San Francisco Fisherman's Wharf
31 Hotel del Sol
32 Lodge at the Presidio
33 Parsonage
34 Union Street Inn

EATING
35 Al6
36 Atelier Crenn
37 Borsch Mobile
38 Dalida
39 Greens
40 Izzy's Steakhouse
41 Kabob Trolley
42 Komeya No Bento
43 La Fromagerie
44 Lucca Delicatessen
45 Señor Sigsig
46 Warming Hut

DRINKING & NIGHTLIFE
47 Beach Chalet
48 Fort Point Beer
49 Round House Café
50 Travis Marina

ENTERTAINMENT
51 BATS Improv
52 Hardly Strictly Bluegrass
53 Magic Theatre
54 San Francisco Art Fair

SHOPPING
55 Fort Mason Outdoor Markets
56 Sports Basement

INFORMATION
57 Golden Gate Bridge Welcome Center
58 Presidio Visitors Center

Follow San Franciscan regulars to **Crissy Field** to stroll, jog, bike, skate or roll along scenic, flat, wheelchair-accessible paths. The strip where military planes once landed is now a reclaimed tidal marsh, where birders perch on strategically positioned benches. Puppies chase kite-fliers across Crissy Field's grassy lawn, and windsurfers skim bay waters along **East Beach**. Pick up the Bay Trail to reach **Fort Point** (1.6 miles from East Beach) and head over the Golden Gate Bridge (p350), or stop at certified-green cafe **Warming Hut** to browse California field guides and warm up with fair-trade coffee.

Showtime at Fort Mason Center

Watch talents launch in waterfront waterhouses

San Francisco takes subversive glee in turning military installations into civilian playgrounds. **Fort Mason** *(fortmason.org; free)* was an embarkation point for WWII troops, but today it launches cutting-edge theater and comedy. Pushing boundaries since 1967, **Magic Theatre** *(magictheatre.org; tickets sliding scale $35-75)* stages breakthrough works by provocative playwrights. The Magic houses stunning new murals and artistic residencies plus freeform jazz worship services for SF's legendary St John Coltrane Church.

Next door, Bay Area Theater Sports, aka **BATS Improv** *(improv.org; tickets adult/student $25/20)* dares you to suggest plot twists for raucous improvised comedy shows. Take center stage at improv workshops or weekend intensives

BEST WAYS TO SAIL AWAY

When the fog lifts and the sun shines, only one thing tops waterfront strolls: boating on the bay. These are our top picks for setting sail in San Francisco.

Oceanic Society: Naturalist-led Pacific whale-watching expeditions run during migration seasons. *(oceanicsociety.org; 7½hr; per person $300)*

Adventure Cat: Skim across the bay with the wind in your hair on catamaran trips, including 'Sail and Jail' getaways to/from Alcatraz. *(adventurecat.com; 90min cruise adult/child $75/35, Sail and Jail $125)*

Red & White Fleet: SF's original sunset bay cruises since 1892 – ring boxes keep popping. New triple-decker boats offer full bars and snacks. *(redandwhite.com; 1hr cruise adult/child $39/29, 2hr sunset cruise $58/38)*

ST JOHN COLTRANE

'There's music in his name,' proclaims the reverend at the African Orthodox **St John Coltrane Church**, a place of worship founded by passionate Bird fans and social activists Franzo and Marina King: Coltrane was posthumously made patron saint of the church in 1982. Mass kicks off with a joyous jam session Sundays at 11am in the Magic Theatre, and all are invited to participate – if you have an instrument to play or a groove in your soul, bring it. Over sessions that can run for five hours, liturgy is intermingled with fellowship and jamming. There's also a monthly meditation based around *A Love Supreme*, Coltrane's masterful 1964 album, which was recorded in one session. Even nonbelievers leave the church feeling Bird's sprit.

like improvised Shakespeare. Book in advance: classes fill quickly.

Make Art, Not War

Find artistic inspiration in military storehouses

During WWII, Fort Mason shipped out 23 million tons of wartime supplies – but now its storehouses supply artistic inspiration to 1.4 million visitors annually. Dockside nonprofit **SF Camerawork** *(sfcamerawork.org; free)* has showcased next-wave photographers since 1974, while **Haines Gallery** *(hainesgallery.com; free)* represents leading global contemporary artists like Andy Goldsworthy and Ai Weiwei. **Arion Press** *(arionpress.com; free)* showcases limited edition, letterpress art books featuring collaborations by leading poets and artists. The former pier warehouse, now known as Herbst Pavilion, includes arts-and-craft fairs among its arsenal of events, with annual highlights including spring's **San Francisco Art Fair**.

Brunch with Bridge Views

Chew the scenery at Greens

Since 1979, Fort Mason's ex-army mess hall has been commandeered by female star chefs, inventing flavor-bomb vegetarian dishes with organic ingredients from Marin's Buddhist Green Gulch Farm. Reserve ahead for bayfront tables at **Greens** *(greensrestaurant.com)* with breathtaking Golden Gate Bridge views, savor bar bites with Buddha-hand-infused cocktails at JB Blunk's reclaimed-redwood-stump tables, or get boxed lunches to enjoy on the docks of the bay.

Strike Poses at Palace of Fine Arts

Photobomb prom photos at SF's best backdrop

Like many a fine romance, the **Palace of Fine Arts** *(palaceoffinearts.com; free)* was a folly that wasn't expected to last. The California Arts and Crafts movement's leading architect Bernard Maybeck originally built this Greco-Roman ruin in plaster for the 1915 Panama-Pacific International Expo, but San Francisco decided to keep the palace after the fair, and eventually recast it in concrete. Join shy prom dates and shivering brides posing for photos under the Rotunda frieze, which shows art under attack by materialists.

EATING IN THE MARINA: FIVE-STAR PICNIC SUPPLIES

Lucca Delicatessen: Leave picnics to the pros at Lucca, makers of Italian deli classics since 1929. *9am-6pm* $

Komeya No Bento: Proper Japanese bento: sustainable salmon or duck breast, sushi rice, dashi broth and side salads. *11:30am-2:30pm & 5-6:30pm Tue-Sat* $

La Fromagerie: This sandwich board spoils you for choice – you can't lose with Toulouse, piled with duck, manchego and fig jam. *11am-6pm Mon & Tue, from 10am Wed-Sun* $

Fort Mason Outdoor Markets: Ex-shipyards host Sunday farmers markets, plus monthly (last Friday) night markets. *9:30am-1:30pm Sun & 4-9pm Fri* $

Musée Mécanique

Listen to the Wave Organ

Hum along with the bay

Follow a trail past yacht-club docks along a jetty poking into the bay, and you'll discover an aural oddity: the **Wave Organ** *(exploratorium.edu; free)*. Eerie sounds wheeze from repurposed SF cemetery marble statues and PVC plumbing parts, ingeniously reconfigured into acoustic sculpture by Exploratorium artists Peter Richards and George Gonzalez.

Game on at Fisherman's Wharf

Play vintage games at SF's Wild West arcade

The massive boatshed at Pier 45 can scarcely contain this sprawling, mind-blowing collection of 300-plus vintage mechanical amusements. Giant, freckle-faced Laughing Sal has freaked out kids for over a century, but don't let this deter you from the **Musée Mécanique** *(museemecanique.com; free)*. For less than a buck, you can battle Space Invaders, get your fortune told by an all-seeing wizard, peep at belly dancers through a vintage Mutoscope, or get hypnotized by a Ferris wheel made entirely from toothpicks.

PARTY OF THE CENTURY

San Francisco rebuilt from the ground up after the 1906 earthquake leveled almost everything – the city celebrated its comeback with an epic party in 1915: the **Panama-Pacific International Expo**. The northern shoreline was extended with landfill, then topped with a vast fairground. Across almost 400 square city blocks, the PPIE had it all: fanciful architecture crowned with the 435ft Tower of Jewels, glittering with 100,000 cut-glass gems; flashy technology, including a giant 14-ton Underwood typewriter; a huge Palace of Fine Arts lined with modern painting and sculpture; and forward-thinking events such as the International Conference of Women Workers to Promote Peace. The party was a smash – and technology, art and peace remain works in perpetual progress in San Francisco.

EATING IN MARINA: BEST FOR DINNER DATES

Dalida: Mediterranean flavors: Istanbul stuffed mussels, Aleppo roast chicken, Yemeni lamb stew, mmmm. *11:30-2pm & 5-9pm Fri-Wed, 11am-2pm Thu* $$

Atelier Crenn: Triple-Michelin-starred chef creates edible art inspired by SF's seafaring legends and her own farmstead. Reserve two months ahead. *5-9pm Tue-Sat* $$$

A16: Romance is assisted by award-winning wood-fired pizzas, house-cured salami and a deep Italian wine list. *5-9pm Mon-Thu, noon-9:30pm Fri & Sat, noon-9pm Sun* $$

Izzy's Steakhouse: SF's surest sign of commitment is sharing the Gomez, Izzy's plump prime rib with gooey au gratin potatoes. *5-9:30pm Mon-Fri, from 4pm Sat & Sun* $$$

SAN FRANCISCO'S FAVORITE SEA-LEBRITIES

Sea lions started taking over San Francisco's most coveted waterfront real estate in 1989 following the Loma Prieta earthquake, and have been making a glorious public display of themselves ever since. Night and day they canoodle, belch, noisily bark, scratch and gleefully shove one another off the docks, protected from predators and with plenty of herring and other bay fish to keep them full. Up to 2100 sea lions at a time converge on Pier 39's K dock between January and July, and whenever else they feel like sunbathing – California law requires yacht owners to relinquish valuable dock slips to accommodate them. Move aside, billionaires: San Francisco's sea mammal mascots are here to stay.

Seals, Pier 39

Meet Superheroes

Get up close and personal with comic legends

Founded with a grant from Bay Area cartoon legend Charles M Schultz of *Peanuts* fame, the **Cartoon Art Museum** *(cartoonart.org; adult/child $10/4)* showcases cartoon classics from Batman blockbusters to Calvin & Hobbes strips. But these curators aren't afraid of serious subjects either, showcasing Ukrainian political cartoons, SF feminist comics trailblazer Trina Robbins and Wahab Algarmi's stories of growing up Muslim by the Bay.

Family Fun on Pier 39

Choose your own bayside adventure

Sea lions aren't the only ones who enjoy sunny days out at **Pier 39** *(pier39.com; free)*. Families flock to this boardwalk for amusement-park atmosphere without the prohibitive entry fees. On the pier's bayside end, your chariot awaits at the antique **San Francisco Carousel** *(10am-8pm; $6 per ride)*, twinkling with 1800 lights and hand-painted with local landmarks.

EATING IN CHINATOWN: FAMILY-STYLE FEASTS

Good Mong Kok: Plump dumplings whisked from vast steamers into takeout containers. Takeout only. *7am-6pm* $

Hang Ah Tea Room: Families have converged here for generations – classics include spicy purse dumplings and creamy thousand-year-egg custard *bao*. *10:30am-8pm* $$

Dim Sum Bistro: Fresh, high-quality dim sum, including tender shrimp and chive dumplings, juicy pork and shrimp *siu mai*, and perfectly toasted sesame balls. Takeout only. *8am-3pm* $

Today Food: Watch pros rolling dough until translucent, loading in fresh veggies, shrimp and organic chicken to peak plumpness, then promptly pan-frying or steaming your meal. *8am-8pm* $

Celebrate Lunar New Year

Brighten winter nights with celebrations

Chase the 200ft dragon, legions of lion dancers, and local politicians on floats tossing lucky chocolate coins in red envelopes. The **Chinese New Year Parade** *(chineseparade.com)* is the highlight of San Francisco winters, complete with fireworks, drumlines and fierce troops of tiny-tot martial artists. By the end of the night, everyone's happy and hoarse from exchanging best wishes for prosperity.

Every 12 years or so, the lunar year's animal zodiac sign coincides with the animal zodiac sign of your birth year – which means you have an extra excuse to party. If you're not sure what your sign is, the red envelope-covered Chinese Zodiac Wall on **Jack Kerouac Alley** provides a handy summary of the animals, elements and character traits associated with your birth year.

Chinatown celebrates for a month, with special **night markets** *(bechinatown.weebly.com)* on lantern-lit Grant Ave supplying essential goods for an auspicious year ahead – including lucky bamboo, red envelopes and miniature mandarin trees. **Chinatown Kite Shop** *(chinatownkite.com)* sells two-person, papier-mâché lion-dance costumes.

Time-Travel at the Chinese Historical Society of America

Follow epic tales inside a living landmark

Built as Chinatown's YWCA in 1932 by Hearst Castle architect Julia Morgan, the **Chinese Historical Society of America** *(chsa.org; adult/student/child $12/10/5)* displays WWII Chinatown nightclub posters, Frank Wong's Chinatown miniatures, and Bruce Lee's martial arts costumes and extensive philosophy library. Exhibits trace anti-Asian hate speech from the Chinese Exclusion Act (1882–1943) to today, alongside 175-plus years of history-changing civil-rights activism.

Turn on the City Lights

Browse one of the world's most famous bookstores

Free spirits and free speech have found refuge at **City Lights Books** *(citylights.com)* since poet Lawrence Ferlinghetti founded the store in 1957. Wax poetic in the upstairs Poetry Room, load up on zines on the mezzanine and entertain radical ideas downstairs in the Pedagogies of Resistance section. On the main floor, City Lights publications include titles by Angela Davis, Diane di Prima and Noam Chomsky, proving the point on another of Ferlinghetti's signs: 'Printer's Ink Is the Greater Explosive.'

Telegraph Hill Stairway Hikes

Earn panoramic, romantic city views

In the 19th century, a ruthless entrepreneur began quarrying on the side of Telegraph Hill. City Hall eventually stopped the quarrying, but the view of the bay from the **Filbert Street**

CHINATOWN'S TECH TRAILBLAZERS

California's earliest high-tech adopters weren't 1970s Silicon Valley programmers – they were Chinatown switchboard operators c 1887 at the **Chinese Telephone Exchange** (today a bank at the corner of Washington and Grant Sts). Operators spoke six languages and memorized thousands of Chinatown residents by name, residence and occupation. Since people born in China were prohibited from entering the US during the 1882–1943 Chinese Exclusion era, the exchange provided Chinatown residents with their only family contact for over 60 years. A crew of women operators operated the switchboard seven days a week, with no holidays – until they unionized in 1943, and won a landmark victory for overtime back pay. Eventually private phone lines were installed citywide, and the exchange quietly closed in 1949.

EXPLORE THE WHARF'S WILD SIDE

Take photos of sea lions, stare down sharks, hop a submarine and swap stories with sailors.

START	END	LENGTH
Pier 39	Musée Méchanique	0.5 mile; 45 minutes

Take a selfie with the 1 **sea lions at Pier 39** but keep a safe distance – they may be adorable, but sea mammals can get territorial. Cross over to the east side of Pier 39 and head for dry land. Just before you reach it, your next stop is on the right-hand side. The sea lions were just a preview of what's ahead at the 2 **Aquarium of the Bay** – descend into underwater chambers lined with glowing jellyfish tanks, then step into glass tubes jutting deep into San Francisco Bay. Emerge from the deep and return to dry land. Head away from the tides of tourists strolling the Embarcadero and turn onto North Point.

3 **Bill Chester Longshoremen's Union Hall** is named for SF's trailblazing 1930s Black union leader. Behind the hall at the edge of the parking lot – the spot where the '60s psychedelic movement started – you'll spot Beniamino Bufano's serene statue of the city's patron St Francis. Turn right here.

Keeping a low profile on the east side of Pier 45 is the 4 **USS Pampanito**, a 1943 submarine that survived WWII to tell hair-raising tales of torpedo battles and deep dives in riveting onboard audio tours. Then head into the Pier 45 boatshed right next to the *Pampanito* for 5 **Musée Méchanique**, with its fully functional vintage games.

Steps is still (wait for it) dynamite. Climbing the steps to Coit Tower you'll have sweeping Bay Bridge vistas, and can peek at hidden cottages along Napier Lane's wooden boardwalk, and sculpture-dotted gardens in bloom year-round.

For more well-earned views, find the urban trailhead between 150 and 155 Francisco St to the **Francisco Street Steps**. Cross the courtyard, ascend to Grant Ave, and turn left to reach Jack Early Park, where you'll find scenic seats for two. Climb higher for Golden-Gate-to-Bay-Bridge panoramas, then descend via Grant Ave for a well-earned slice of pizza at **Golden Boy**.

Tarry in Union Square

Watch the cable cars turn

Union Square's image as a main tourist hub with shopping and hotels galore had been challenged by the pandemic, with major retailers and companies leaving the area. However, it's still a top place to stay while visiting – a great location for sights such as the San Francisco Museum of Modern Art (SFMOMA; p363) – and it's still home to the main cable-car turnaround – a part of classic San Francisco that remains steadfast.

Ride All Three Cable-Car Lines

Old-school San Fran

Cable cars almost disappeared in 1947, but the city came to its senses and eventually designated the system a National Landmark in 1964. Part of the city's **Muni system** *(sfmta.com/getting-around/muni/cable-cars; single $8, $13 1-day Muni passport recommended)* since 1944 (but here since 1873), SF's cable cars are the only operating cable-car system in the world, with more than 254,000 passenger trips per month. Ride north–south up and down the hills on both the Powell/Hyde and Powell/Mason lines, starting at the **Powell Street Cable-Car Turnaround**, which take riders between Downtown's skyscrapers, through culture-filled **Chinatown**, past Nob Hill's Fairmont Hotel and Grace Cathedral, ending at the tourist attractions of Fisherman's Wharf (p355). Most visitors stick to these lines, but there's a third line that tends to be less crowded – the east–west California line that runs between Van Ness Ave in Nob Hill and Davis St in FiDi. It passes many of the same landmarks, with the addition of Polk Gulch and more of FiDi.

THE TATTOOED LADIES OF NORTH BEACH

Back in the 1950s, Ringling Brothers Circus drew crowds just to see a 'tattooed lady' – meanwhile in San Francisco, Lyle Tuttle quietly opened a tattoo parlor that would inspire women worldwide to get tattoos. Over his 60-year career, Tuttle inked women across six continents and attracted celebrities to his shop – including Jane Fonda, Joan Baez, Janis Joplin and Cher. Tuttle credited his success to women's liberation, and was proud to assist women taking control over their own bodies and self-expression at his North Beach shop – and he made the process safer for everyone, championing sanitary tattooing practices with SF's Health Department. Tuttle has gone on to that great ink cloud in the sky, but you'll spot his Western Traditional designs around North Beach.

EATING IN NORTH BEACH: PANINI PICKS

Molinari: Massive panini loaded with buffalo mozzarella, sun-dried tomatoes, prosciutto and slabs of house-cured salami. *9am-5:30pm Mon-Fri, 9am-9pm Sat, 11am-3:30pm Sun* $

Palermo II Delicatessen: Try the irresistible signature sandwich: eggplant parmigiana with their own marinara and fresh mozzarella. *10am-5pm Tue-Sun* $

Fairuz Eatery: North Beach *nonnas* line up for falafel perfected over 20 years: crunchy yet fluffy, with nutty tahini and citrusy sumac in warm pita. *11am-8pm Sun-Thu, to 10pm Fri & Sat* $

Mario's Bohemian Cigar Store Cafe: Enjoy onion focaccia with meatballs, eggplant or grilled chicken, plus Chianti by the carafe and prime people-watching. *11am-9pm* $

AFFORDABLE OPERA

Yes, super cheap tickets for the **San Francisco Opera** *(sfopera.com)* still exist! For certain performances, they're available to everyone who creates an SF Opera account online and registers. The tickets are usually available from 11am to midnight the day before a performance, or until they're sold out. Check your email for notifications about ticket availability. There are also 200 standing-room tickets for most main-stage opera performances, which are for the rear orchestra or rear balcony. Tickets are only $10 each, but are cash only. They go on sale on the day of each performance, with a limit of two per person. Starting from 10am on the day, 150 tickets become available, whereas the remaining 50 are released two hours prior to the performance.

ACTIVITIES
1 Mission Cultural Center for Latino Arts
2 Potrero del Sol/La Raza Skatepark

DRINKING & NIGHTLIFE
3 El Rio
4 Jolene's
5 Mother
6 Wild Side West

ENTERTAINMENT
7 Bissap Baobab
8 Bottom of the Hill
9 Carnaval
10 Chapel
11 Red Poppy Art House
12 Verdi Club

Visiting a Storied Neighborhood

The Tenderloin Museum and its walking tours

In the **Tenderloin**, Muhammad Ali boxed, Billie Holiday sang, and LGBTIQ+ activists fought for their right to be served in cafeterias – and established America's first Transgender Cultural District. Historians from the Tenderloin Museum lead visitors on **tours** past these and other groundbreaking locales. You'll see the site of the Compton's Cafeteria Riot, plus some of the area's most iconic murals and public artworks. The museum also has robust programming, like a Compton's Cafeteria Riot play twice weekly at the annex space at 835 Larkin St.

The **Tenderloin Museum** *(tenderloinmuseum.org; adult/senior & student/12 & under $10/6/free)* itself takes about 45 minutes to peruse, showing visitors through photographs and

EATING NEAR DOWNTOWN MUSEUMS: OUR PICKS

Bini's Kitchen: Chef Bini Pradhan was the first in SF to serve Nepalese *momos* (dumplings). The turkey ones pop with a tomato-cilantro sauce. *11am-3pm* **$$**

Moya: This unassuming SoMa corner Ethiopian spot is known for mushroom and tofu *tib* (stew). *11am-2pm & 5:30-8:30pm Mon-Fri, 5:30-8:30pm Sat* **$$**

Estrellita's Snacks: A favorite La Cocina incubator alum brick-and-mortar spot dishing up huge Salvadorean pupusas. *10am-8pm Mon-Fri* **$**

Yank Sing: Upscale dim sum place with a daily rolling cart service – a rarity these days. *11am-3pm Tue-Fri, from 10am Sat & Sun* **$$$**

other information and ephemera covering the Tenderloin's long history, from the hopping nightclubs and brothels to an immigrant hub with affordable housing, to the fact that present-day Tenderloin has nearly more than 3500 children – the highest density of children in the city.

Municipal Magic

Astounding edifices

The **Civic Center** is anchored by the gold-accented dome of the beaux-arts **City Hall**. It's been the site of historic happenings, from the assassination of supervisor Harvey Milk and mayor George Moscone, to the first same-sex marriages. Neighboring the City Hall is the **San Francisco Main Library**, whose Larkin St entrance features a new Maya Angelou sculpture, *Portrait of a Phenomenal Woman,* by Berkeley artist Lava Thomas.

Experience the Theater District

Delve into musicals, plays, live music and more

SF's Theater District bursts with culture, from majestic old theaters to big concert venues to hoppin' new jazz clubs. For nationally touring smash-hit musicals like *Wicked* and *Hamilton*, look at the grand old **Curran** *(broadwaysf.com)*, **Golden Gate** *(goldengatetheatresf.com)* and **Orpheum** *(orpheumsanfrancisco.com)* theaters. The **Herbst Theatre** *(sfwarmemorial.org/herbst-theatre)* is a smaller, 900-seat venue inside the **War Memorial Opera House** that hosts performances such as string quartets and solo guitarists.

Go to the **American Conservatory Theater** *(act-sf.org)* for breakthrough shows that launch at this turn-of-the-century landmark. There are also smaller or experimental companies like **San Francisco Playhouse** *(sfplayhouse.org)*, **New Conservatory Theatre Center** *(nctcsf.org)*, **CounterPulse** *(counterpulse.org)*, **SAFEhouseARTS** *(safehousearts.org)* and **Phoenix Theatre** *(phoenixtheatresf.org)*.

Several jazz clubs pay tribute to past venues, where Miles Davis, Billie Holiday and Charlie Parker played underground. **Black Cat** *(blackcatsf.com)* is out to restore the laid-back, lowdown glory of the capital of West Coast cool with both a basement club and street-level bar. **Mr Tipple's Recording Studio** *(mrtipplessf.com)* hosts top local talent, plus a decent dumpling menu. The newest **Dawn Club** *(dawnclub.com)* revives a 1946 jazz venue, with top-rated cocktails.

FROM BAWDY TO BROADWAY

While the historic theaters of San Francisco all have rich history, the Golden Gate theatre on Taylor near Market St may have the most fun origin. It was originally built as a vaudeville house in 1922, hosting up to seven acts a night. As the theater evolved into a concert hall, stars like Frank Sinatra, Judy Garland and Nat King Cole graced its stage. During the theater's evolution, much of the gorgeous interior was torn down in favor of a more modern appearance. However, the late 1970s saw the Golden Gate restored to its art deco roots and it was reopened as a performing arts venue. The Golden Gate was added to the National Register of Historic Places in 1986.

TENDERLOIN BARS: OUR PICKS

HA-RA Club: Open since 1947, this classic dive with its iconic neon sign still has its original phone booth. *3pm-2am Mon & Tue, from noon Wed-Fri & Sun, from 3pm Sat*

Edinburgh Castle: Bagpiper murals on the walls, the *Trainspotting* soundtrack blaring and vinegary fish and chips until 9pm. *6pm-2am*

Bourbon & Branch: For award-winning cocktails in the liquored-up library, whisper the password ('books'). *6pm-midnight Sun-Wed, to 2am Thu-Sat*

Zombie Village: This reincarnation of a 1942 tiki bar is irresistible – the skull-lined bar serves potent rum. *5pm-midnight Wed, to 12:30am Thu, to 2am Fri & Sat*

BEST MISSION LIVE MUSIC VENUES

Chapel: Musical prayers are answered in a 1914 California arts-and-crafts landmark with heavenly acoustics for folk, indie artists and performance-art mayhem.

Bissap Baobab: Come for shareable Senegalese food, stick around for live acts and DJs after 9pm – bachata, Cuban jazz, Afrobeats, flamenco and jam sessions.

Red Poppy Art House: A snug Mission storefront doubles as a concert hall for international artists-in-residence, ranging from Armenian duduk virtuosos to Argentine tango quartets.

Verdi Club: Throwing swanky soirees since 1916 – check the calendar for bachata, queer two-stepping, Brazilian zou and swing-dance nights preceded by lessons – and bring cash for the speakeasy bar.

For other live music, **Rickshaw Stop** *(rickshawstop.com)* and **Bottom of the Hill** *(bottomofthehill.com)* are great small- to mid-size clubs for indie and underground acts. Larger concert halls like **Great American Music Hall** *(gamh.com)*, **Bill Graham Civic Auditorium** *(billgrahamcivic.com)*, **The Warfield** *(thewarfieldtheatre.com)*, **August Hall** *(augusthallsf.com)*, the Masonic and Regency Ballroom bring big touring acts. Don't forget the long-standing comedy club **Punch Line** *(punchlinecomedyclub.com)* in the Embarcadero, which local comedian Ali Wong graced during her rise to fame.

Toast Herstory at Lesbian Landmarks

Welcome home to Mission's legacy lesbian bars

Women have been making herstory in the Mission since the 1970s. After all that work, lesbians deserve somewhere to unwind – and the Mission provides lots of options.

Lesbian-owned since 1962, **Wild Side West** *(wildsidewest.com)* has stayed busy making herstory in the beer garden and making out on the pool table (Janis Joplin started it). You'll recognize femme-forward, cash-only corner bar **Mother** *(mothersf.com)* by its purple exterior and punk vibes. At women's watering hole **Jolene's** *(jolenessf.com)*, the neon sign announcing 'you are safe here' makes room for lesbian, trans, nonbinary and questioning partiers. Legendary lesbian-owned club **El Rio** *(elriosf.com)* started as a Brazilian gay bar, and today the full rainbow spectrum of colorful SF characters comes here to party.

Join Mission Cultural Festivals

Celebrate life to the fullest

SF is far from Rio, but you'd never know it during **Carnaval** *(carnavalsanfrancisco.org)*, when everyone shakes their tail feathers in Mission streets. On **Día de los Muertos** *(dayofthedeadsf.org)*, brass bands, dancing skeletons and Fridas galore meet in the Mission. Offerings line the processional route along Calle 24, culminating in moving outdoor community altars at **Potrero del Sol/La Raza Skatepark** *(sfrecpark.org)*.

Don't miss Día de los Muertos altar displays and epic mole tastings at **Mission Cultural Center for Latino Arts** *(MCCLA; missionculturalcenter.org)*, where celebrations of Latin culture range from gallery openings to documentary screenings.

EATING IN DOWNTOWN: POST-SHOW LATE-NIGHT EATS

Hinodeya Ramen Union Square: Wholegrain ramen in a light dashi-style broth made with bonito, kombu and scallops, and topped with *chashu* and soft egg. *10am-1:30am* $$

Tempest Bar & Box Kitchen: This favorite SoMa dive bar has a pool table, decades' worth of graffiti and satisfying bar food. *11am-2am Mon-Fri, from noon Sat & Sun* $

Pinecrest Diner: A (now mostly) 24-hour diner, family owned and operated since 1969. Dig into eggy breakfasts and big burgers anytime. *7am-11pm Sun-Tue, 24hr Wed-Sat* $

Dragon Horse: Cocktails, sushi, karaoke: say no more. *4-11pm Sun-Wed, to midnight Thu-Sat* $$

TOP EXPERIENCE

SFMOMA

At **San Francisco Museum of Modern Art** (SFMOMA), boundary-pushing modern and contemporary master works sprawl over seven floors. See the world-class photography collection, get an eyeful of Warhol's pop art and immerse yourself in cutting-edge contemporary installations. And see how SFMOMA began, with colorful characters worthy of SF by Frida Kahlo, Diego Rivera, Paul Klee and Henri Matisse.

Alexander Calder: Dissonant Harmony

The crowd-pleasing mobiles and metal sculptures of abstract artist Alexander Calder occupy part of the 3rd floor. Kinetic and whimsical, Calder's elements were actually always painstakingly thought-out. SFMOMA's collection includes the multicolored *Lone Yellow* and the spellbinding movements of *Quatrro Pendulati*. Outside the Calder gallery is the impressive *Living Wall*.

Afterimages: Echoes of the 1960s

The 5th-floor collection presents some of the greatest hits of pop art, including Andy Warhol's electrically colored prints of celebrities to Ellsworth Kelly's joined canvases of unevenly shaped, bold colors. The pieces push the idea that the consciousness-shifting art movements of the 1960s are still relevant today.

1900 to Now: SFMOMA's Collection

Rotating experimental works and masterpieces from its massive collection, SFMOMA encourages viewers to constantly re-examine the contradictions and interpretations of some of the greatest works of our time. Ponder the evolution of Diego Rivera's boldly colored works from cubist to postimpressionist and beyond, and Georgia O'Keefe's interpretations of nature and the feminine through her genre of combining fine charcoal lines with paint.

TOP TIPS

- Check your coat and bag for free.
- Up the stairs on the 2nd floor are the ticket booth and STEPS cafe, plus most of the free art on the walls, ceilings and floor below.

PRACTICALITIES

- sfmoma.org
- adult/senior/student/18 & under $30/25/23/free (special exhibits $10 extra)
- free first Thursday
- 10am-5pm Fri-Tue, noon-8pm Thu

TOP EXPERIENCE

Ocean Beach

At this blustery, atmospheric city beach, the sun sets over the Pacific – though fog banks may swallow it first. But fog doesn't keep hardy beachcombers, power-walkers and determined sandcastle architects away from this vast, serene stretch of pale golden sand. Standing at the water's edge you can watch the Pacific ebb and flow, with only a few surfers to remind you what century you're in.

BRYAN MIN/SHUTTERSTOCK

Lands End

TOP TIPS

- Break out your favorite costume or your most comfortable glitter thong for May's **Bay to Breakers** *(baytobreakers.com)*, a truly fun 7.5-mile run from the Embarcadero to Ocean Beach.
- The restaurant out back of Beach Chalet hosts raucous weekday happy hours, plus lazy brunches and live music at weekends.

PRACTICALITIES

- parksconservancy.org
- 24hr; parking lot closes at 10pm
- free

Walking Wild

San Francisco's 3.5 mile beach is not like the ones in Hollywood movies. Except for sunny spells in September and October, most days are too chilly for bikinis and clambakes here, and much better suited to meditative, windblown walks. Swimmers, beware riptides; walkers, mind sneaker waves. Keep an eye on the Pacific and you might spot brave surfers, passing ships and sea lions bobbing in the waves.

Sunset Dunes

By popular vote in 2024, San Francisco converted this section of highway to park trails for joggers, cyclists, skaters and walkers to enjoy. This section of the **Coastal Trail** connects **Fort Funston** to Ocean Beach and **Lands End**; stick to paths in areas undergoing habitat restoration, and keep dogs on leashes to protect wildlife. The dunes offer shelter for birdwatching – you might spot skittish snowy plover shorebirds taking cover here in winter.

Break for Art & Beer at the Beach Chalet

Take a break for food, drink, bathrooms and inspiration at an SF landmark. The Beach Chalet entryway is lined with splendid 1930s Works Project Administration (WPA) frescoes by Lucien Labaudt that celebrate the building of Golden Gate Park.

The Heart of Oakland

Downtown Oakland and Chinatown

Pedestrianized **City Center**, between Broadway and Clay St, 12th and 14th Sts, forms the heart of downtown Oakland. Enjoy a free noontime concert. Nearby **Oakland City Hall** is a beautifully refurbished 1914 beaux-arts masterpiece. Walking the streets, look for old gems such as the 1914 **Cathedral Building**, a Gothic Revival wonder on a triangular plot. It was a setting for Boots Riley's 2018 sublime dark comedy *Sorry to Bother You*.

Old Oakland, west of Broadway between 8th and 10th Sts, is lined with restored historical buildings dating from the late 19th century. The area has a lively restaurant and after-work scene.

East of Broadway and bustling with commerce, Oakland's workaday **Chinatown** centers on 8th and Webster Sts, as it has since the 1850s. Wholesale markets spill into the streets; check out the changing exhibits at the **Oakland Asian Cultural Center** (*oacc.cc; free*).

California's Museum

Dive into Oakland's history

The top draw is the **Oakland Museum of California** *(museumca.org; adult/child $19/free)*. Dedicated to the state, its permanent galleries range from California's diverse ecology and history to art – from traditional landscapes to reimagined cartography. Watch for blockbuster temporary exhibitions. It's open 11am to 5pm Wednesday to Sunday.

Visit the UC Berkeley Campus

Go Bears!

The Berkeley campus of the **University of California** *(berkeley.edu)*, called 'Cal' by both students and locals, is home to the oldest university in the state. It was founded in 1866, with the first students arriving in 1873. Today, Cal has more than 40,000 students, over 1500 professors and more Nobel laureates than you could point a particle accelerator at.

Officially called Sather Tower, the **Campanile** – as it is widely known – was modeled on St Mark's Basilica in Venice. The 307ft spire offers fine views of the Bay Area, and at the top you can stare up into the carillon of 61 bells. The Campanile is open from 10am to 4pm.

HISTORIC FORT BAKER

Fort Baker *(nps.gov/ goga; free)*, the 1905 army base with one of the world's best views, helped guard the entrance to the San Francisco Bay along with the better-known Fort Point on the south side. It was one of the last major forts built on the bay, and the army tried to stem its perennial problem of desertion by making the facilities here better than average. As you'll see from the buildings that still surround the parade grounds, there were porches, large windows and even indoor toilets.

Today the decommissioned fort fronts Horseshoe Cove, where there's still a Coast Guard station. Trails extend along the coast and you can spend the night in former officers' quarters at the luxe **Cavallo Point Lodge**.

EATING IN OAKLAND & BERKELEY: CASUAL DINING

Fentons Creamery: Everyone wants a scoop of luscious ice cream at this old-school Oakland parlor. Also old-fashioned lunches and snacks. A beloved classic. *11am-10pm* $

Arizmendi Bakery: Great for breakfast or lunch near Lake Merritt in Oakland. Bakery co-op not for the weak-willed: gourmet vegetarian pizza, chewy breads and gigantic scones. *8am-8pm* $

Acme Bread: Berkeley has one of the region's best bakeries, beloved for its take on classic sourdough bread. Memorable snacks like the ham and cheese croissant. *8am-4pm* $

La Note: Casual Berkeley cafe with a strong French accent. Popular at breakfast (goat cheese is an option); lunch brings salads and sandwiches. Sunny garden. *8am-2pm* $$

BERKELEY'S BEST BOOKSTORES

Moe's Books: New and used books in a vast store south of campus. Renowned for its knowledgeable staff; enjoy browsing across four floors.

Dark Carnival Imaginative Fiction Bookstore: One of the oldest science-fiction, fantasy and horror bookstores west of the Mississippi. It's all controlled chaos; lose yourself in the stacks.

Pegasus Books: Right on the Shattuck Ave commercial strip, Pegasus has great staff recommendations and daily specials on new and used titles.

Book Society: Browsing for books in this cozy, comfy space is all the better given the machines in back that dispense wine by the glass.

Sleepy Cat Books: You'll find the namesake felines dozing away as you browse the carefully curated selection of offbeat fiction and hard-to-find non-fiction. Also sells intriguing postcards.

BERKELEY

SIGHTS
1 BAMPFA
2 Bancroft Library
3 Campanile
4 Cathedral Building
5 Chinatown
6 City Center
7 Oakland Asian Cultural Center
8 Oakland City Hall
9 Oakland Museum of California
10 Old Oakland
11 University of California – Berkeley

EATING
12 Acme Bread
13 Arizmendi Bakery
14 Chez Panisse
15 Fentons Creamery
16 La Note

SHOPPING
17 Book Society
18 Dark Carnival Imaginative Fiction Bookstore
19 Moe's Books
20 Pegasus Books
21 Sleepy Cat Books

Inside a stainless-steel exterior, **BAMPFA** *(Berkeley Art Museum and Pacific Film Archive; bampfa.org; adult/child $18/free)* holds galleries showcasing artworks, from ancient Chinese to cutting-edge contemporary.

The **Bancroft Library** houses, among other gems, the papers of Mark Twain, a copy of Shakespeare's folios and a diary from the Donner Party. Public exhibits include the surprisingly small gold nugget that sparked the 1849 Gold Rush.

Berkeley's World-Famous Restaurant

Chez Panisse changed dining globally

California cuisine, farm-to-table, seasonal fare, sustainably sourced. These are just some of the food trends that **Chez Panisse** *(chezpanisse.com)*, open 5:30pm to 8:45pm Monday to Saturday, and its superstar proprietor Alice Waters can take at least some of the credit for. Pull out all the stops with a prix-fixe meal at the restaurant downstairs, which first opened in 1971. As always, the menu changes daily and is as good and popular as ever.

Walking Sausalito & the Golden Gate Bridge

Take a trip across the Golden Gate Bridge

One of the Bay Area's best walks begins and ends in San Francisco and features some of the region's best scenery.

Catch a mid-morning ferry to Sausalito, enjoying the views of Alcatraz and Angel Island. Stroll the town and get refreshments and a picnic. Follow East Rd south along the beautiful shoreline until you reach Fort Baker. Walk under the Golden Gate Bridge (p350) – which looms large and red overhead – and curve up the access road until you reach the popular viewpoint. Cross the bridge on the eastern walkway (the west side is for cyclists). Dress warmly! It's 1.7 miles across – take your time for the stellar views. It's 5 miles from Sausalito to the San Francisco side of the bridge, where you can stroll onwards to the Presidio and the Marina.

Enticing Fort, Seafront & Museum

Crab fishers and Bay ecology

Below the north tower of the Golden Gate Bridge, surprisingly uncrowded Fort Baker (p365) hides in plain sight. Stroll Horseshoe Bay, watch the winter-time crab fishers, and get a snack or lunch from one of several good outlets.

A highlight is the **Bay Area Discovery Museum** *(bayareadiscoverymuseum.org; $20)*, a child-centric, indoor-outdoor facility that introduces kids to the ecology of the bay.

Hit the Beaches at Point Reyes

Point Reyes' world-class coast

Virtually every strip of sand is a long drive from anywhere at Point Reyes, but every one is worth the effort. **Limantour Beach** is a great all-arounder with an array of wilderness

POINT REYES WILDLIFE

Point Reyes has an extraordinary range of wildlife, including 80 species of mammals and nearly 30 species of reptiles and amphibians. The largest animals here are the **elephant seals**, which number upward of 2000 on shore during late winter and early spring. As they rest after months of feeding non-stop at sea, you can see the adult males snoozing on the sand. Each weighs from 4400lb to 6000lb. Look for pups from January to March; August is the only month when you're unlikely to find any elephant seals at Point Reyes. Offshore, late December through mid-April is migration season for **gray whales**. You can often spot these behemoths from shore.

EATING & DRINKING IN SAUSALITO: OUR PICKS

Scoma's: Classics such as *cioppino* (a piquant seafood stew) and Crab Louie salad served on a pier. Sustainable seafood lineup changes daily. *11:30am-9:30pm* **$$$**

Venice Gourmet Delicatessen & Pizzeria: In the center; build a picnic with Italian sandwiches, prepared foods and baked goods or a crispy pizza. *9am-5pm* **$**

Barrel House Tavern: Waterfront tavern serving California cuisine like local cheeses and charcuterie. Good list of regional beer, wine and spirits. Book ahead. *11am-9pm* **$$**

Travis Marina: Fort Baker's near-secret bar welcomes everyone with incredible bay and bridge views. Regular live music. *4-8pm Fri, noon-8pm Sat, noon-6pm Sun*

BEST HIKES NEAR PALO ALTO

Stanford Dish Loop: The hilly 3.7-mile paved path is popular with runners, walkers and science nerds who want to see the 150ft-diameter radio telescope ('the Dish') that once communicated with NASA's *Voyager* spacecraft.

Baylands Observation Deck & Boardwalk: A hub for hiking trails that follow the bay shoreline through parks and wildlife-filled estuaries.

San Andreas Fault Trail: Learn all about earthquake geology on this gentle 1.5-mile self-guided path inside the Los Trancos Open Space Preserve.

Wunderlich County Park: Trails follow hillsides, gulches and streams under shady redwoods and oaks.

Windy Hill Preserve: Head west into the Santa Cruz Mountains. From this grass-covered hilltop trails radiate out into the redwoods.

hikes and stunning sunsets. **Drakes Beach** is backed by white sandstone cliffs and is arguably the most gorgeous of the main beaches. There's also the seasonal **Kenneth C Patrick Visitor Center**, which offers information, especially in elephant-seal mating season. West-facing **Point Reyes Beach** offers 11 miles of solitude. On many days – especially from late fall to spring – the sky turns an iridescent vermilion at sunset. Bring a blanket and enjoy the show.

Trails, Seabirds & Elk Reserve

Hiking the Point Reyes wilderness

Alluring trails crisscross Point Reyes over hillsides and along the shoreline. For views, the **Inverness Ridge Trail** heads for around 3 miles up to **Point Reyes Hill** (1339ft), affording spectacular vistas of the entire national seashore.

For wildlife, **Pierce Point Road** continues to the huge windswept sand dunes at **Abbotts Lagoon**, full of peeping killdeer and other shorebirds. At the end of the road is historical **Pierce Point Ranch**, the trailhead for the 9.4-mile round-trip **Tomales Point Trail** through the **Tule Elk Reserve**. The many elk are an amazing sight, standing with their huge horns against the backdrop of **Tomales Point**. The herd is one of the last in the lower 48 states of the US.

Exploring Stanford

An art and architecture tour

Stanford University *(stanford.edu)* is one of America's top universities academically, and among the most expensive. The faux California Mission Revival–style campus is a genteel place to stroll, with public artwork and murals. (Note: the rivalry with publicly funded UC Berkeley is intense.) Having been built on the site of the Stanford family's horse farm, the university maintains the humble-brag nickname The Farm.

Stop by the **Stanford Visitor Center** *(visit.stanford.edu)* off Galvez St for self-guided-tour info and maps. Many cover the multitudes of public art around campus. Download the Stanford Mobile app, which has walking tours.

Auguste Rodin's *Burghers of Calais* bronze sculpture marks the entrance to the **Main Quad** (begun 1887), an open plaza where the original 12 campus buildings – a mix of Romanesque and Mission Revival styles – are joined by the **Memorial Church** (1903). The church is noted for its beautiful

EATING NEAR POINT REYES: OUR PICKS

Saltwater Oyster Depot: Appealing chef-run bistro in Inverness with a sophisticated local seafood menu. Seasonal offerings include the famous oysters. *5-8pm Fri-Mon* **$$**

Tap Room: Inverness spot for sandwiches, burgers and noodle bowls alongside microbrews and top regional wines. A convivial mix of residents and visitors. *4-9pm Mon-Sat* **$$**

Bovine Bakery: The place to get breakfast and/or a picnic near the entrance to the peninsula. Organic treats, sandwiches, breads and good coffee. *7am-4pm* **$**

Cafe Reyes: Enjoy wood-fired pizza inside, on the patio or to go at this Point Reyes Station favorite. Great range of toppings. *noon-8pm* **$$**

Memorial Church

mosaic-tiled frontage, stained-glass windows and five organs with more than 8000 pipes.

Think Rodin

Stanford's masterpiece of a museum

Fronted by Ionic columns, the **Cantor Arts Center** *(museum.stanford.edu; free)* includes works from ancient civilizations to contemporary art, spanning the globe. The museum is renowned for its Rodin collection of over 200 works displayed both inside and out in a garden, including *The Thinker*. Rotating shows are eclectic in scope and include well-curated photography exhibitions.

Fun at Half Moon Bay

Get lost in the surf, sun and fog

Home to a long coastline, mild albeit foggy weather (bring layers!) and Mavericks, one of the biggest and gnarliest surf breaks on the planet, Half Moon Bay and neighboring Miramar and El Granada are prime real estate.

Although the shallowness of the bay means it should be called Quarter Moon Bay, the long stretches of sandy beach and coastal bluffs attract surfers, hikers and active-minded weekenders. The small downtown is architecturally historic and good for a stroll.

GREAT PUMPKINS

It's not just brussels sprouts and houseplants (that's what's in all those greenhouses) growing in Half Moon Bay. Starting early in the fall, fields are dotted with bright, nearly radiant pumpkins. The spectacle of rolling fields tightly speckled with orange stretching into the distance provides some of the only competition for attention with the views on the ocean side of the road. The best fields for the spectacle are south of Half Moon Bay.

Leading up to Halloween, pumpkin vendors line Hwy 1. The two-day **Half Moon Bay Art & Pumpkin Festival** *(hmbpumpkinfest.com)* in mid-October is famous for its pumpkin weigh-off, where beasts grown by fanatical cultivators (who zealously guard their secrets) can weigh more than 2500lb.

EATING & DRINKING IN PALO ALTO: OUR PICKS

Camper: In Palo Alto's symbiotic twin Menlo Park, a classic NorCal menu of locally sourced food prepared creatively. *10am-1pm Sat & Sun, 5-8:45pm Mon-Sat* $$$

Tamarine Restaurant & Gallery: Exquisite Vietnamese food in artful surrounds. Cocktails pair with small and large plates. *11:30am-2:30pm & 5-9pm* $$$

Palo Alto Creamery: A downtown institution, with sparkling chrome-and-red booths and a 1920s look; famous for breakfasts, milkshakes and pies. *8am-9pm* $$

Vino Locale: A wine bar in a Victorian house with an inviting terrace. Unpretentious by local standards, with a focus on regional foods and tasty bites. *3-9pm*

SUNDRY PHOTOGRAPHY/SHUTTERSTOCK

Half Moon Bay State Beach

Crescent-shaped and over 4 miles long, **Half Moon Bay State Beach** *(parks.ca.gov)* is a beautiful ribbon of sand along the Pacific. Much of it is nearly untrodden and it's easy to leave other visitors behind as you walk along the sandstone cliffs and dunes.

The 7.2-mile **Coastside Trail** runs the length of Half Moon Bay from the bluff above Manhattan Beach north to Pillar Point Harbor. Look for driftwood after storms and watch for whales offshore. When the bay is calm, get out and cruise water with **Half Moon Bay Kayak Co** *(hmbkayak.com; per hour from $30)*, which rents kayaks and SUP sets.

Wander the Town

Strolling downtown

Half Moon Bay's old **downtown** comprises six blocks of early-20th-century buildings dotted with cafes, boutiques, bookstores and more. It's good for an hour's stroll or more. Stop into the renovated **Half Moon Bay Coastside History Museum** *(halfmoonbayhistory.org; free)* for exhibits on local history, including surfing, and for a look inside the restored 1919 town jail.

EAT & DRINKING IN HALF MOON BAY: OUR PICKS

Jettywave Distillery: One of many fine choices near Pillar Point Harbor, serving locally caught seafood with Med and Thai accents. Welcoming patio. *noon-8pm Fri-Sun* $$

Old Princeton Landing Public House & Grill: Half Moon Bay's top venue for live music; an all-day bar near Pillar Point Harbor with elevated bar chow. *9am-11pm* $$

Ciya Mediterranean Cuisine: Superb uses of local ingredients and produce for dishes that capture flavors from around the Eastern Med, from Greece to Türkiye. *11am-9pm* $$

Hop Dogma Brewing Co: Top NorCal brewery serving hop-forward beers. Esoteric choices include Nintai, a Japanese-style rice lager, and their West Coast IPA 'Sincerely, Simcoe.' *2-8pm*

Northern California: Redwoods & Wine Country

WINE SIPPING | GIANT TREES | MOUNTAIN HIKES

California's wine valleys sparkle with a constellation of cool communities. In the Napa Valley, organic family wineries dare to make wines besides classic cabernets, while cyclists wave hello to sous-chefs weeding kitchen gardens. Head west to Sonoma County to wander thousand-year-old redwoods, pop open a bottle of bubbly with a saber in Healdsburg and visit farm-to-spliff dispensaries in Sebastopol. 'Wild' is the word that springs to mind when visiting the north coast and redwoods. The beaches are notably untamed, and the forests are called 'the redwood curtain' because the trees grow so tall and dense. In Eureka they've preserved a town's worth of Victorian-era architecture. In the northeastern corner of the state there are vast expanses of wilderness – some 24,000 protected acres – divided by rivers and dotted with cobalt lakes, horse ranches and alpine peaks. Even the two principal attractions, Mt Shasta and Lassen Volcanic National Park, remain relatively uncrowded.

TOP TIP

Wine tasting in California can be a pricey undertaking, especially in the Napa Valley. Keep in mind that some tasting fees are waived with a set bottle purchase. If Napa's fees are exorbitant for you, consider more reasonably priced wineries in the Russian River, Healdsburg and Alexander Valley regions, which also sometimes accept walk-ins.

GETTING AROUND

Napa and Sonoma Counties and their myriad valleys are surprisingly vast. They're easiest seen with your own wheels, but transit.511.org is a helpful resource to see the interlocking transit networks. Exploring the area around Mendocino means driving both north and south on Hwy 1, where rideshare services are scarce. I-5 divides the better-known mountain areas to the east from the lesser-visited forests, small towns and lakes to the west. Hwy 89 is the principal route to get around Mt Lassen.

NORTHERN CALIFORNIA: REDWOODS & WINE COUNTRY
0 50 km
0 25 miles
Grants Pass
Medford
Cape Sebastian
OREGON
CALIFORNIA
Smith River National Recreation Area
Siskiyou Wilderness
Crescent City
Klamath River
Marble Mountain Wilderness
Klamath
Redwood National & State Parks
Orick
Mt Shasta
Dunsmuir
Coffee Creek
Trinidad
Hoopa
Trinity Center
Shasta-Trinity National Forest
McKinleyville
Trinity Alps Wilderness
Trinity Lake
Shasta Lake
Manila
Arcata
Samoa
Arcata Bay
Mt Lassen
Eureka
Humboldt Bay
Weaverville
Whiskeytown-Shasta-Trinity National Recreation Area
Whiskeytown Lake
Redding
Fortuna
Ferndale
Scotia
Hayfork
Humboldt Redwoods State Park
Shasta-Trinity National Forest
Platina
Petrolia
Weott
Honeydew
Six Rivers National Forest
Red Bluff
The Lost Coast
Yolla Bolly-Middle Eel Wilderness
Shelter Cove
Paskenta
Leggett
Covelo
Mendocino National Forest
Black Butte Lake
Westport
Eel River
Snow Mountain Wilderness
Jackson Demonstration State Forest
Fort Bragg
Willits
Caspar
Lake Pillsbury
Mendocino
Mendocino Headlands State ParkForest
Albion
Upper Lake
Ukiah
Nice
Elk
Philo
Lucerne
Lakeport
Clear Lake State Park
Boonville
Manchester
Hopland
Kelseyville
Clearlake
Point Arena
Anchor Bay
Cloverdale
Gualala
Sea Ranch
Healdsburg
Lake Berryessa
PACIFIC OCEAN
Sebastopol
Sonoma
Napa

DAVID A LITMAN/SHUTTERSTOCK

Napa Valley Wine Train

Napa's Historic Streets & Tasting Rooms

Sample wines in the central city

Napa's buzzy 1st St is lined with indie wine-tasting rooms in historic storefronts. The most punk-rock tasting room is **Gamling & McDuck** *(gamlingandmcduck.com; tasting $35)*.

At **Brown Downtown** *(brownestate.com; tastings from $50)* find liquid courage with Duppy Conqueror, Jamaican folklore hero of Bob Marley songs. **Vintner's Collective** *(vintners collective.com; tastings from $50)*, housed in an 1875 former saloon, specializes in super small-batch wines. Or hit **Rebel Vinters** *(rebelvintners.com; tastings from $30)*, with board games and indie wines lining the bar.

Napa by Train or Gondola

Kick back, take it all in

Chug along in the **Napa Valley Wine Train** *(winetrain.com; ticket including dining from $223)* from downtown Napa to St Helena and back in a plush vintage dining car. If floating is more your speed, glide downstream with **Napa Valley Gondola** *(napavalleygondola.com; from $175)*.

NAPA WINE-MAKING HISTORY

Grapes have been grown on this 5-by-35-mile strip of farmland since the Gold Rush. But earthquakes and juice-sucking phylloxera bugs struck, followed by Prohibition and the Great Depression. Napa had 140 wineries in the 1890s, but by the 1960s only around 25 remained. In 1976 winemakers entered a few bottles into a blind tasting competition in Paris – and to much surprise, Napa wines took top honors. As Napa's reputation grew, global wine conglomerates moved in. With land now priced at up to $1 million an acre, independent, family-owned wineries work hard to stand their ground. Today, Napa wine tasting is not just famous, it allows you to get hold of many vintages only available on-site.

EATING IN NAPA: FINE DINING

Kenzo: Napa Michelin-starred Japanese magic paired with top wine and sake in chic minimalist harmony. Book ahead. *5:30-8:30pm Wed-Sun* **$$$**

Compline: This cozy, unpretentious bistro/wine bar offers a short, seasonal menu of hearty dishes. *5-11pm Wed & Thu, 11:30am-11pm Fri-Sun* **$$$**

Bistro Don Giovanni: With copper pans, garden fountains and black-vested waiters, the Don ladles on Italian charm. Weekends get packed and loud. *11:30am-9pm* **$$$**

Bear: Stanly Ranch's creative Californian fare spans Asian-dressed oysters to delicate handmade pastas. *7am-10pm* **$$$**

WINE TASTE LIKE A PRO

Swirl, sniff and swish Swirl your wine in the glass to release aromas, then have a good sniff to excite your salivary glands. Take a small sip and swish it around your mouth so all your taste buds get in on the action.

Sip and spit If you love what you're tasting, you'll want to try plenty – and that means pacing yourself. It's fair game to spit out your last sip, or even pour leftovers into the spittoon (aka 'chuck bucket').

Remember to eat Some wineries serve bites; otherwise snack in between.

Consider joining wine clubs carefully Your pourer may suggest joining their wine club (to buy discounted bottles annually). Don't feel pressured, especially if you're tipsy and fuzzy on the details.

NAGEL PHOTOGRAPHY/SHUTTERSTOCK

Mission San Francisco Solano

Sonoma's Plaza, Ringed by Monuments

Amble through California history

Sonoma's pride and joy is the plaza, with its venerable old theater, food and oh, yes, drinking options. **Tuesday night markets** are a tradition, May to November, with live music, food and artisan's wares. Bring a picnic for the free **jazz concerts** *(sonomavalleyjazzsociety.org)* from 6pm to 8:30pm every second Tuesday from June to September. Anchored by adobe **Mission San Francisco Solano** *(sonomaparks.org)*, the plaza's sights allow you to time travel across 200 years of California history.

Pair Local Art & Libations

Creativity for all the senses

Sonoma remains staunchly independent and proud of its creativity, which is on display at **Sonoma Valley Museum of Art** *(svma.org; adult/child/family $10/free/$15)* and the **Arts**

EATING IN SONOMA TOWN: RELAXED & DELICIOUS

Valley: Smack on Sonoma Plaza, this welcoming wine bar dishes up creative, seasonal offerings. *9am-3pm & 5-9pm Thu-Mon* $$

El Molino Central: Unforgettable Wine Country meals combine homegrown ingredients and Mexican culinary traditions. *11am-8pm Mon-Thu, from 9am Fri-Sun* $

Delicious Dish: Succulent burgers, fresh-catch fish sandwiches and salads with fries at a field-side diner with a patio. *10:30am-6:30pm Mon-Thu, to 2:30pm Fri* $

Sunflower Caffé & Wine Bar: The big back garden at this local hangout is a great spot for breakfast, a no-fuss lunch or an afternoon wine. *8am-3pm* $$

Guild of Sonoma *(artsguildofsonoma.org; free)*. Make an appointment to visit collective **La Haye Art Center** *(lahaye artcenter.com; free)*, located in a converted foundry, where you can tour its gallery and meet the artists.

In June join **Art at the Source** *(artatthesource.org; free)* and in October **Sonoma County Art Trails** *(sonomacounty arttrails.org; free)*, each two-week events that give you a chance to travel from studio to studio. Maps of the ateliers are available year-round.

Fantastical Sebastopol Sculptures

Art for art's sake

A cow rides a tractor, a rocket blasts off the lawn and a dinosaur grabs a red convertible for lunch: it's all happening on Florence Ave, in dozens of sculptures by **Patrick Amiot** *(patrickamiot.com)*, which are painted by Brigitte Laurent and made for neighbors' yards from recycled junk.

Around the corner at **Sebastopol Center for the Arts** *(seb arts.org; free)*, see the world from the perspective of Sonoma County's boundary-pushing artists. They organize excellent open-studio weekends county-wide, with Sonoma County Art Trails in October and Art at the Source in June.

Apples, Daisies & Good Times

Hearty horticulture and hard cider

Sebastopol had a reputation for boozy shenanigans long before Sonoma County's wine industry took off, because the heirloom-apple orchards that thrived here weren't originally intended for roadside bakery **Mom's Apple Pie** *(momsapple pieusa.com)*. They were used to make hard cider – a tradition upheld today at **Hopmonk Tavern** *(hopmonk.com)* and tasting room **Horse & Plow** *(horseandplow.com)*, and celebrated twice annually at the **Apple Blossom Festival** *(appleblossomfest.com)* in April and **Gravenstein Apple Fair** *(gravensteinapplefair.com)* in August.

About 150 years ago horticulturalist Luther Burbank cultivated fruit trees and daisies (like popular Shasta daisies) at **Luther Burbank's Gold Ridge Experiment Farm** *(wschs .org/farm; free)*, which is open to the public. You can also reserve ahead to taste namesake Gold Ridge Farms' organic apple and olive-oil products.

HOMEGROWN BOUNTY

Nicholas Izzarelli, Sebastopol native and owner-operator of **Goldfinch**, tells us his favorite ways to eat local. *goldfinch sebastopol.com*

We are lucky to be surrounded by farmers, ranchers, wineries, cheesemakers, foragers and fisher men and women, producing some of the best bounty available anywhere. Check out a farmers' market or winery (**Iron Horse** is my go-to), and meet incredibly talented and hardworking people showcasing what this county has to offer. As for restaurants, I *love* **Terrapin Creek** in Bodega Bay. Every dish is thoughtful, delicious and perfectly executed. **Khom Loi** offers locally sourced dishes with amazing Thai street-food flavors. On the coast, stop by **Hog Island Oyster Co** or the **Marshall Store** for the freshest seafood, beautiful scenery and chill Sonoma County vibes.

EATING & DRINKING IN SEBASTOPOL: INDIE FOODS & SWEET TREATS

Barlow: Two-acre village of indie food producers, ice creamers, artists, winemakers, coffee roasters and distillers. *hours & prices vary*

Screamin' Mimi's: Luscious homemade ice cream served by the ounce. Choose from a seasonal lineup of flavors. *11am-9:30pm Sun-Thu, to 10pm Fri & Sat* $

Sebastopol Cookie Co: Aromas entice at this indie bakery making restorative triple-chocolate cookies, snickerdoodles and more. *8:30am-5pm Tue-Sat, 9am-3pm Sun* $

Hardcore Espresso: Shambolic spot with quirky art around gardens and patios and crammed inside, plus top coffee and baked goods. *5:30am-5:30pm*

Sparkling Healdsburg

Parade of sensations

A stroll around Healdsburg's verdant central plaza, lined with cool boutiques, bookstores and tasting rooms, will quickly reveal why it's regularly listed among the top small towns in America.

Drink all along Northern California's coast from the comfort of your lounge seat at **Lioco** *(liocowine.com; tastings from $30),* specialist in coastal chardonnays and pinot noirs. At **Idlewild** *(idlewildwines.com; tastings $30),* especially fascinating Piedmontese wines are quietly made by fourth-generation winemaker Sam Bilbro. Also of Italian origin, the wines at **Portalupi** *(portalupiwine.com; tastings from $20)* include unexpected sparkling barbera. For eating, you can splash out at a gastronomic temple like **SingleThread** *(singlethreadfarms.com),* where edible Sonoma landscape is the first of 11 sensational seasonal courses. **Little Saint** *(littlesainthealdsburg.com),* with a delicious plant-based menu, lights up on its free music Thursdays. And what's not to love about **Noble Folk Ice Cream & Pie Bar** *(thenoblefolk.com)*?

Produce & Live Music Market Days

Tuesday and Saturday certified farmers markets

On sunny Tuesdays from May to September, Healdsburg's **farmers market** *(healdsburgfarmersmarket.org)* on the plaza begins with warm hellos from Sonoma County farmers and rolls into inspiring cooking demos and live music, plus seasonal events. Graze regional delicacies, such as Dry Creek peaches, steaming hot samosas, bean-to-bar chocolate, award-winning cheeses and organic Preston olive oil. On Saturdays (8:30am to 9pm from April to December) the **market** sets up in the West Plaza Parking Lot at North and Vine Sts, one block west of the plaza.

Mendocino: Timber Town

Step inside an 1860s house

Mendocino is the ultimate historic timber town. Transplants from New England founded the village along with a mill in 1852, bringing architectural influences that can be seen in the area's Victorian buildings today. The area's lumber industry thrived through the turn of the century, but when the mill closed in the 1930s the town's population and economic

HEALDSBURG'S ENTERTAINMENT & FESTIVALS

Tuesdays in the Plaza Concerts: In summer, join free Tuesday concerts; food vendors set up at 5pm, music plays from 6pm to 8pm. *(healdsburg.gov)*

Farmers Market Concerts: Check the website to see what's playing at Tuesday's market. *(healdsburgfarmersmarket.org)*

Healdsburg Jazz Festival: Jazz venues in June include wine-tasting courtyard Bacchus Landing. *(healdsburgjazz.org)*

Wine Road Barrel Tasting: In March, wineries throw open wine-cave doors to sample wine from the barrel. *(wineroad.com)*

Healdsburg Wine & Food Experience: In May, revel in local and international wine and farm-to-table food. *(healdsburgwineandfood.com)*

Wine & Food Affair: In November, 100 Sonoma County wineries offer a featured dish and wine pairing. *(wineroad.com)*

EATING IN HEALDSBURG: COOL BAKERIES & CAFES

Quail & Condor: The hot new kid on the block, with bakers from SingleThread making superb French-style pastries and bread. *8am-3pm Wed-Mon* $

Costeaux French Bakery & Cafe: Serving breakfasts since 1923, this bakery-cafe crafts quiches, omelets and pastries. *7am-3pm Sat-Tue, to 8pm Wed-Fri* $

Acorn Cafe: Stop in for coffee and breakfast or gourmet sandwiches, and end up people-watching on the plaza patio. *8am-3pm Mon-Fri, to 5pm Sat & Sun* $$

Troubadour Bread & Bistro: Classic boulangerie: sandwiches by day, pricey bistro with a set menu by night. *7am-4:30pm Tue-Sat, 8am-3pm Sun* $$$

CRUISING THE SONOMA COUNTY COAST TO MENDOCINO

Celebrate an uninterrupted stretch of coastal highway that skirts rocky shores, secluded coves and wind-sculpted beaches.

START	END	LENGTH
Bodega Bay	Mendocino	110 miles; 5 hours

Start alongside the fishing fleets of 1 **Bodega Bay**, cruising past the brilliant NorCal Pacific Coast scenery of Sonoma County State Park to the seal colony at the mouth of the Russian River at Goat Rock in 2 **Jenner**. As you cruise north again, you'll pass Jenner Headlands Preserve, which offers more walks, or continue straight to 3 **Fort Ross State Historic Park**, a reconstruction of a 19th-century Russian fur-trading fort.

From here, the road twists past the free 4 **Kruse Rhododendron State Natural Reserve**, with its rhododendron groves. One of the best reasons to spend the night around these parts is 5 **Salt Point State Park**, a 6000-acre stunner with sandstone cliffs dropping into a kelp-strewn sea and hiking trails crisscrossing windswept prairies and wooded hills. It's especially popular with mushroom foragers.

Weather-beaten but ritzy private community 6 **Sea Ranch** lines an ocean bluff, with five beaches open to the public. 7 **Gualala** is a hub for weekend getaways and sunny weather, with its arts center. Another half-hour up the coast, climb the 8 **Point Arena Lighthouse**, which has guarded the windy point since 1908. Slip a little further north to 9 **Elk**, a hamlet famous for its stunning clifftop views of towering rock formations. Wrap up by arriving at 10 **Mendocino** for an idyllic weekend.

WRECK OF THE FROLIC

In 1850 a ship retired from the opium trade – the *Frolic* – struck a reef near **Point Cabrillo**, about 3 miles north of Mendocino, and ran aground. Jerome Ford, who came from San Francisco to salvage the cargo, was too late as the Native Pomo (who had inhabited the region for some 10,000 years) had already recovered the Chinese luxury goods on board. But Ford took notice of the coast's real treasure: the enormous redwoods. He teamed up with entrepreneur Henry Meiggs, who bought a sawmill and had it transported to Big River. During the mill's 50-year run, it yielded a billion board feet of timber, used to build San Francisco and to rebuild it after the 1906 earthquake.

stability took a hit. Things turned around with the establishment of the Mendocino Art Center in 1959, revitalizing the town and infusing it with artistic charm: nearly two million travelers make a pilgrimage each year to shop at exquisite art galleries, dine at top-tier restaurants and soak up the views offered by a tiny town perched atop Pacific-kissed bluffs.

To get up close and personal with life in a 19th-century logging town, head to the **Kelley House Museum** *(kelleyhousemuseum.org; suggested $5 donation)*. William Kelley, a businessman who once owned almost all the land that would become Mendocino, built the historic house in 1861. Today, visitors can wander its bedrooms and see period furnishings and personal effects.

A Diamond in the Bluff

Stroll an extraordinary oceanside trail

If hiking trails were judged by ocean views, the path at **Mendocino Headlands State Park** *(parks.ca.gov)* would score an uncontested 10/10. For over 2 miles in one direction, the trail follows the edge of 70ft bluffs, meandering through wildflowers on land and past rock formations and dramatic arches in the water.

Experience Clear Lake State Park

Hiking trails and history

First things first: 'Clear Lake' is the body of water and 'Clearlake' is a town on its southeastern side. It's considered the oldest lake in North America, dating back one to two million years.

Dip your toe into Clear Lake, both metaphorically and literally, at **Clear Lake State Park** *(parks.ca.gov)*. Swim, fish, hike and bike, and get a feel for the lake's Indigenous history by hitting the half-mile **Indian Nature Trail**, which passes through what was once a Pomo village.

Summiting a Volcano

Hike Mt Konocti

The fact that Mt Konocti is a dormant volcano is only part of what makes hiking it so intriguing. Follow the 6-mile Wright Peak Summit Trail and you'll also spot an early 1900s cabin as well as the wreckage from a tragic 1970 plane crash.

The hike begins at the trailhead for **Mt Konocti County Park**. From here it's a steep climb to the top, gaining 1800ft

EATING IN MENDOCINO: OUR PICKS

GoodLife Cafe & Bakery: Starting the day with a blackberry Danish or biscuits smothered in sausage gravy – both served here – really is the good life. *7:30am-2pm* $

Mendocino Cafe: The eclectic menu at this lunch and dinner spot includes a Thai burrito, Indian-style curry and locally caught rockfish. *11am-4pm & 5-9pm* $$

Trillium Cafe: Swing by for fine dining focused on organic seasonal ingredients, or order a picnic basket to go. *11:30am-2:15pm & 5-8:30pm Fri-Tue* $$$

Fog Eater Cafe: This cozy vegetarian spot serves Southern-inspired recipes for dinner and a full brunch menu on Sundays. *4-8pm Wed-Sat, 10am-2pm Sun* $$

LORI A JONES/SHUTTERSTOCK

Mt Konocti

of elevation. You'll pass Downen Cabin, where the intrepid and peace-seeking Mary Downen lived solo in the early 1900s, about 2 miles into the hike. The mangled pieces of the white-and-turquoise Navion A aircraft, visible just to the right of the trail, sit just before the summit. At the top you'll get an eyeful of Clear Lake below, and on a good day you can also spot Mt Lassen and Mt Diablo. The downhill return is much easier on the muscles.

Panoramic Picnics on the Lost Coast

Enjoy a DIY outdoor meal

On your way into Shelter Cove, stop off at the **Shelter Cove General Store** *(sheltercovegeneralstore.com)* to grab sandwich supplies, snacks, locally brewed beer or a bottle of wine. Then, take your supplies to either **Abalone Point** or **Seal Rock** for a Pacific-view picnic. Both spots sit on a bluff overlooking the ocean and have picnic tables.

Urchins & Abalone Galore

Tide-pooling in Shelter Cove

Probably the most fascinating (and free!) Lost Coast activity for kids is to discover the diverse and wonderfully weird creatures living in the tide pools.

KELSEYVILLE PEAR FESTIVAL

Held on the last Saturday in September, Lake County's largest one-day event – the Kelseyville Pear Festival – is a real hoot and a showcase of the region's agricultural heritage, including the almighty pear. There are parades, live music and dancing on three stages, a giant decorative pear, a pie-eating contest, a scarecrow contest and plenty of street vendors. There are also special exhibits held all over town; for example, a tractor and engine show, or a display on the history of Kelseyville farming within the Pear Pavilion.

The event has grown from just 1500 attendees in 1993 to more than 10,000 in recent years. The festival's highly appropriate slogan? 'Catch the small-town magic.'

EATING AROUND CLEAR LAKE: OUR PICKS

Saw Shop Public House: A laid-back Kelseyville restaurant with superior farm-to-table California cuisine and delicious cocktails. *noon-8pm Tue-Sat, 11am-8pm Sun* $$

Park Place Restaurant: Lakeport's premier dining venue offers classic Italian and American dishes and lake views. *11am-7pm Sun-Thu, 11am-8pm Fri & Sat* $$

Blue Wing Saloon: Cozy up on the heated veranda with casual American fare and live music at this upper lake restaurant in the Tallman Hotel. *hours vary* $$

Catfish Coffee House: With a convenient drive-through window, this is the spot to grab coffee and bagels. *5:30am-6pm Mon-Fri, 6am-6pm Sat, 6:30am-6pm Sun* $

EUREKA'S BEST SHOPS

Humboldt Mercantile: Snag redwoods tees, hemp hand soap and locally made hot sauce at this souvenir hot spot.

Many Hands Gallery: Like visiting a few dozen artists' studios in one fell swoop; the gallery stocks ceramics, jewelry and particularly pretty leather journals.

Land of Lovely: Consider a visit here your personal invitation to luxuriate and pick up a new robe, bath soaks and botanical candles.

Eureka Books: Browse new, used and rare books, then have the Zoltar machine in front read your fortune.

Little Shop of Hers: Find an expertly curated collection of vintage clothes and accessories here for both him and her.

Start your tide-pooling adventure by parking at **Mal Coombs Park**, where you can't miss the **Cape Mendocino Lighthouse** *(capemendocinolighthouse.org; free)*. Originally located about 60 miles north of here, the lighthouse was moved in 1998 for preservation purposes. Today, it's maintained by the Cape Mendocino Lighthouse Preservation Society, who open it to the public as a museum each summer, from Memorial Day to Labor Day.

After giving the historic lighthouse a look, head down the set of stairs to the beach. At low tide, the area looks otherworldly, with rugged black rocks exposed. You may find treasures in the sand, like pieces of petrified wood or dried urchin shells, but climb the rock formations (always keeping an eye on the tide, of course), and peer into the puddles to an entire world of living aquatic critters.

Historic Crafts in Eureka

Get hands-on with historic traditional crafts

The word 'Eureka' expresses joyous discovery. It's also California's official state motto and the name of Humboldt County's capital – both fitting applications. In the city of Eureka, you're likely to find plenty of moments of joyful discovery.

Part museum, part professional woodworking studio, part center for learning traditional crafts, the **Blue Ox Historic Village** *(blueoxhistoricvillage.com)* houses a massive collection of Victorian-era woodworking machinery (still used today), a print shop, a craftsman's apothecary (for mixing stains, varnishes, paints and glues) and a textile atelier. And that's only what's inside the main building. Outside, guests can explore a skid camp – complete with a bunk house, cook shack and theater – and imagine what it was like to live in the area as a logger in the early 1900s. Keep walking the grounds and you'll also come upon working blacksmithing and ceramics studios. For the ultimate experience, book a **Blue Ox class** *(adult/child from $120/90)*, with activities such as blacksmithing, ceramics or stained-glass making.

Hiking 100 Feet High

Stroll the redwood canopy

At the **Redwood Sky Walk** *(redwoodskywalk.com)* inside Eureka's **Sequoia Park Zoo** *(redwoodzoo.org; adult/child $25/13)*, you can stroll up into a redwood grove and explore

EATING IN SHELTER COVE: OUR PICKS

Surf Point Coffee House: Find coffee, housemade pastries and wine pours to pair with lunch at this bistro with breathtaking views. *7:30am-4pm Fri-Wed, 7:30am-4:30pm Thu* $

Mi Mochima: From out of nowhere comes delicious and authentic Venezuelan cuisine: empanadas, arepas, *patacón* sandwiches. *hours vary* $$

Gyppo Ale Mill: California's most remote brewery serves its own lagers, pilsners and blondes, and knocks burgers and wings out of the park, too. *5-9pm Mon-Thu, noon-9pm Fri-Sun* $$

Mario's Marina Bar: This local hangout has killer ocean views from its patio and frequent live music. *hours vary* $$

the ancient giants from 100ft above the forest floor. The elevated trail is the longest of its kind in the western United States, with an ascent ramp, launch deck, accessible main loop, nine viewing platforms and an optional hanging bridge.

Discover Redwood National & State Parks

Unforgettable hiking and natural wonders

Waterfalls, fern-covered canyons, rugged ocean coastline and, oh yes, the world's tallest trees... In the upper reaches of California's Pacific Coast, the area is maintained by the National Park Service and California State Parks. In addition to **Redwood National Park**, this northern natural wonderland includes three state parks: **Prairie Creek Redwoods State Park**, **Del Norte Coast Redwoods State Park** and **Jedediah Smith Redwoods State Par**k. There isn't one main entrance to the area: the parks sit along a 50-mile driving route on Hwy 101.

For a quick hike, take the **Fern Canyon Loop** (southern): there's nothing quite like this 1-mile Prairie Creek canyon trail, which follows a stream surrounded by towering fern-covered walls (it served as a backdrop for *The Lost World: Jurassic Park*). Another option is **Simpson-Reed & Peterson Loop** (northern): hike two trails in under an hour at Jedediah Smith Redwoods. Combining these two short loop trails creates a 0.8-mile hike through a redwood grove that's suitable for just about any ability level.

If you have kids in tow, the **Lady Bird Johnson Grove** (southern), a 1.4-mile hike in Redwood National Park, is the ideal length for little ones, plus you'll find a number of benches for moments of rest. Another hike for kids is the **Stout Grove Loop** (northern): first-time hikers will feel a major sense of accomplishment when they dominate this 0.6-mile loop in Jedediah Smith Redwoods. The redwoods soaring above a lush forest floor will have kids hooked on the great outdoors.

For those hoping to see a waterfall, there's the **Trillium Falls Loop** (southern): at only 2.7 miles and with a trailhead that's right off Hwy 101, this Prairie Creek path could also qualify for the quick and kid-friendly categories. The scenic and soothing falls are located within the first half-mile of the walk. There's also the **Boy Scout Tree Trail** (northern): you'll have to put in a little more work to see the falls along this trail, located in Jedediah Smith Redwoods, but it's worth it. The total out-and-back hike is 5.6 miles and the waterfall, called Fern Falls, is the turnaround point.

YUROK COUNTRY

With 6500 enrolled members, the Yurok ('downriver people') comprise California's largest Native American tribe. Historically, they've been celebrated as expert basket weavers, canoe makers and fishers, and traditions continue to this day, including the **Klamath Salmon Festival** each August. In addition to supporting the tribe by hiring Yurok people as outdoor guides, consider purchasing their locally made handicrafts, especially the jewelry. You'll find dangly earrings made from pieces of abalone shell, and long beaded necklaces strung with pine nuts and white, tubular dentalium shells. Resembling miniature elephant tusks, dentalium shells were once used by the Yurok as currency. One great place to shop is the **Yurok Country Visitor Center** in Klamath, which has jewelry, in addition to T-shirts and hand-knit hats featuring tribal symbolism.

DRINKING IN EUREKA: BEST FOR BEER & COCKTAILS

The Shanty: Popular with young hipsters for its pinball, pool and sweet back patio, this is the coolest bar in town. *noon-2am*

Lost Coast Brewery & Cafe: Head to its restaurant on Fourth St for craft beers and burgers, or visit the brewery for a tour. *11:30am-9pm Wed-Sun*

Phatsy Kline's Parlor Lounge: Located inside the historic Eagle house, Phatsy's is the place for a fancy cocktail. *4-9pm Wed & Thu, 4-11pm Fri & Sat*

The Speakeasy: Squeeze in with the locals at this New Orleans–inspired bar with live blues and a convivial atmosphere. *4-11pm Sun-Thu, 4pm-2am Fri & Sat*

THE DAM AT SHASTA LAKE

On scale with the enormous natural features of the area, the colossal 15-million-ton **Shasta Dam** is second in size only to Grand Coolie Dam in Washington state and second in height only to Hoover Dam in Nevada. It was built between 1937 and 1949, with its 487ft spillway nearly three times as high as Niagara Falls. Woody Guthrie wrote 'This Land Is Your Land' here while he was entertaining dam workers. The **Shasta Dam Visitors Center** offers a 21-minute video shown on request, and self-guided walking tours across the vertiginous top of the dam are available from 6am to 10pm daily. It's located at the south end of the lake on Shasta Dam Blvd.

Hiking Mt Shasta

Woodland strolls, ambitious summit

At 14,179ft, Mt Shasta is only the fifth-highest mountain in California, but its beauty is unrivaled. The mountain has two cones: the younger, shorter cone on the western flank, called Shastina, has a crater about half a mile wide.

The moderate 3.5-mile out-and-back hike to the beautiful stone 1922 **Sierra Club Horse Camp hut** leaves from **Bunny Flat** (6940ft) and is open year-round, though you'll want snowshoes in winter. Bunny Flat is the starting place of the challenging **Avalanche Gulch**, the easiest route to the summit, best done between May and September. Although it's only about 10 miles round-trip, the vertical climb is more than 7000ft, so acclimatizing to the elevation is critical – many hikers overnight at **Helen Lake** (10,443ft). This route requires crampons, an ice axe and a helmet, all of which can be rented locally.

Crystal Shops & Vortex Tours

A mystical energy center

Mt Shasta is considered a power center, where mythical ley lines cross, producing a high concentration of electromagnetic energy. Within the town's tiny grid of streets you'll find six crystal shops, each different from the next. Our favorite is **Crystal Matrix** (*crystalmatrixgallery.com*), open 10am to 6pm Wednesday to Monday, which feels more like a rock-hound shop with a kind and intuitive owner who knows his stuff. Crystals in hand, sign up for a Vortex Tour. Ashalyn with **Shasta Vortex Adventures** was the first to introduce these types of tours but there are several operators around town.

Houseboating on Shasta Lake

Cruise a forested coastline

Shasta Lake is known as the 'houseboat capital of the world,' and with good reason: the water reaches 78°F (26°C) in summer and there are 365 miles of shoreline to putter along. All you need is a driver's license to rent a boat, and you'll get to pilot one of the many vessels gliding through the water at a reasonable 15mph. Pack your own supplies and enjoy lazy evenings cooking for yourself beneath the star-filled sky.

While some will be happy to float and swim at leisure, there are also several destinations to explore, including the famous

EATING IN THE MT SHASTA REGION: OUR PICKS

Bistro 107: Get excellent burgers and hearty hot sandwiches at this homey yet classy little joint. *11:30am-9pm Fri-Tue* $$

Hari On Shri Ram Indian Cuisine: The most authentic and delicious Indian food for hundreds of miles, served with a smile. *noon-3pm & 5-9pm Wed-Mon* $$

Lily's: Great American breakfasts plus Asian or Mediterranean-touched salads, fresh sandwiches and good, square meals. *8am-2pm & 4-8pm Wed-Sun* $$

Crave: Street tacos, sandwiches, barbecue, vegetarian...it's all good. The setting is basic but comfy and friendly. *11:30am-8pm Tue-Sat* $$

Mt Shasta

Lake Shasta Caverns, waterfalls like **Little Backbone Creek** (don't miss the natural waterslide), the Shasta Dam and any number of hiking trails.

This massive lake hosts the largest reservoir populations of ospreys and bald eagles in California. Ospreys are best seen between May and June, which is their nesting season. Look for bald eagles year-round.

Get Deep at Shasta Caverns

Underground geological wonderland

Located high in the limestone megaliths at the north end of Shasta Lake are the impressive **Lake Shasta Caverns** *(lakeshastacaverns.com; 2hr tours adult/child $44/26)*. Tours operate daily and include a boat ride across Shasta Lake. Once inside, it's a one-hour meander along lighted trails and some 600 steps, passing a wondrous array of formations, including waterfall-like curtains of limestone, impressively large stalactites and stalagmites, Jurassic fossils and coral-like helictites.

MT SHASTA'S BEST CAMPING

Lower Panther Meadows: Fifteen walk-in, summer-season tent sites are the highest on the mountain and have spectacular views.

Castle Lake Campground: Only six primitive, summer campsites are found here, about a quarter mile below the lake, but they are very special indeed.

Lake Siskiyou Beach & Camp: On the shore of Lake Siskiyou, this sprawling, family-friendly place has a summer-camp feel, with swimming and boat rentals.

Castle Crags State Park Campground: The campsites here are shady, pretty and have plenty of amenities.

McCloud Dance Country RV Park: With campsites under the trees and a small creek, this is a good option for families. The view of the mountain is breathtaking.

DRINKING IN REDDING: OUR PICKS

Fall River Brewing: Best beers around. Bring your kids if you have them and expect to mingle with locals. *noon-8pm*

Woody's Brewing Co: Open since 2015, with great beers plus a food menu – from burgers and salads to crunchy Tater Tots. *11am-9pm Tue-Sun*

Final Draft Brewing Company: Industrial-style brewpub with vats on display. Try beer styles you won't find elsewhere in Redding. *11am-9pm*

Westside Tap & Cork: Several wineries have tasting rooms in Redding but this is a good stop to sample a variety of them plus local beers. *4-9pm Tue-Sun*

A DRIVING TOUR OF LASSEN VOLCANIC NATIONAL PARK

This fiery landscape features roiling hot springs and crater lakes. Hiking stops can make it a multiday trip, but otherwise it takes a few hours.

START	END	LENGTH
Visitor Center	Manzanita Lake	28 miles; 3+ hours

Near the park's southwest entrance, the handsome 1 **Kohm Yah-mah-nee Visitor Center** is the perfect starting place, with educational exhibits, a gift shop, cafe and toilets. Turn north out of the parking lot and drive 1 mile. The best roadside place to see geothermal action, the 2 **Sulfur Works Hydrothermal Area** has bubbling mud pots, hissing steam vents, fountains and fumaroles. You can hike 1 mile to the Ridge Lakes from here.

The next 5 miles winds through some of the best vistas in the park. The big parking lot at the 3 **Brokeoff Volcano Scenic Vista** hosts a beautiful view of Brokeoff Volcano, Mt Conard and Diamond Peak.

In just over a mile turn into a parking lot for the 4 **Lassen Peak Scenic Vista**: the sight of the rocky slopes up close is awe inspiring. 5 **Hat Creek Meadow** is one of the best stops for fall foliage. It's a quick half-mile to your next stop on the right, the 6 **Devastated Area**, with a quarter-mile interpretive loop through a former eruption zone. The scenery becomes lusher over the next 7.5 miles.

7 **Chaos Crags** is a giant field of rock rubble, the result of a massive slide in the 1660s. It's about a mile through light forest to your final stop, 8 **Manzanita Lake**, where there are kayak rentals in summer.

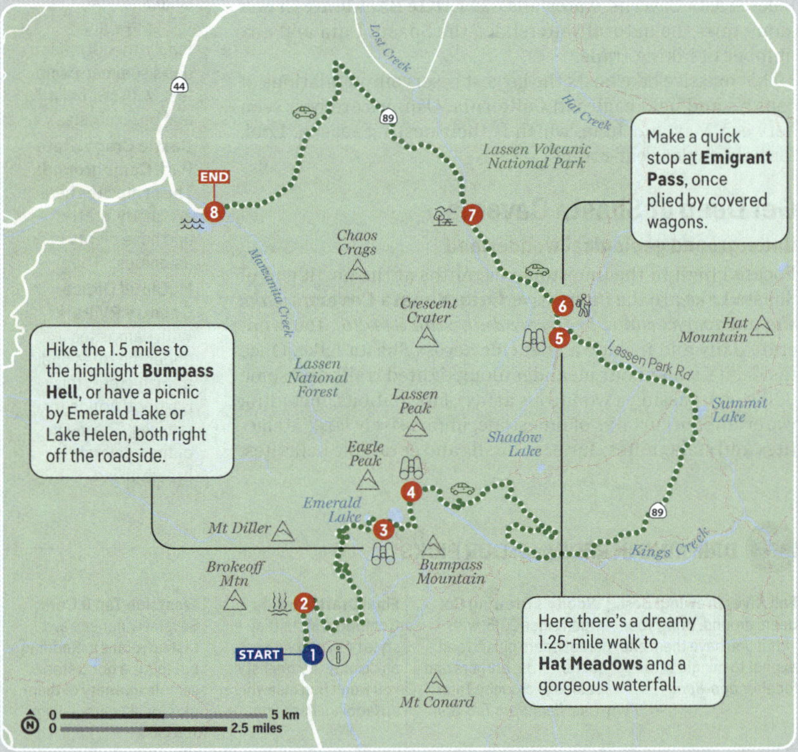

Make a quick stop at **Emigrant Pass**, once plied by covered wagons.

Hike the 1.5 miles to the highlight **Bumpass Hell**, or have a picnic by Emerald Lake or Lake Helen, both right off the roadside.

Here there's a dreamy 1.25-mile walk to **Hat Meadows** and a gorgeous waterfall.

Yosemite, Lake Tahoe & Gold Country

MAJESTIC DOMES | TURQUOISE WATERS | SPARKLING TOWNS

Yosemite, crown jewel of California's national parks, is defined by its plunging waterfalls, soaring trees, wildflower-dotted valleys and majestic domes. Carved by ancient glaciers, these stunning granite features have been gazed upon by devoted humans for some 8000 years.

Lake Tahoe sits more than 6000ft above sea level, straddling the California–Nevada border. The lake's almost unreal shades of blue and turquoise aren't found anywhere else in California, and the surrounding Sierra Nevada mountains frame the lake with dramatic peaks and dense pine forests. Winter brings deep snow and a flurry of activity at ski resorts.

A visit to Gold Country feels like traveling back in time. Historic buildings in their original glory, clapboard saloons, oak-lined byways and even the clip-clopping of horses all nod to the rich history of the area, famously known as the home of the Gold Rush of 1849.

GETTING AROUND

Driving is the most popular way to get around: in Yosemite this means traffic, smog and frustrating battles for spaces during summer. Tahoe Transportation District serves the south lake shore, and bike-rack-equipped Tahoe Area Regional Transit (TART) serves Truckee, the north shore and the Tahoe City area. The Gold Country is best enjoyed with your own vehicle, especially up Hwy 49. Distances are short, so fuel needs will be minimal (or do it all with only one charge).

Time Travel in Mariposa

Make a Gold Rush stop on your way to Yosemite

En route to Yosemite, this former Gold Rush town packs quite the cultural punch. The **Mariposa Museum & History Center** *(mariposamuseum.com; adult/child $10/5)* displays old menus, train tickets, photos and the like, and a Miwuk exhibit features expertly woven baskets, jewelry, arrowheads and

TOP TIP

Before driving to Yosemite, find out if you'll need a reservation for your visit and secure it through recreation.gov. If reservations are sold out, you can enter by booking lodgings within the park, taking a guided tour, obtaining a wilderness permit or Half Dome permit, or riding a YARTS bus.

YOSEMITE, LAKE TAHOE & GOLD COUNTRY
0 50 km
0 25 miles
Pyramid Lake
Plumas National Forest
Haskell Peak
Lake Oroville
Sierra Buttes
Bassetts
Sierra City
395
Reno
49
89
Middle Yuba River
Tahoe National Forest
Truckee
80
Nevada City
Grass Valley
Tahoe City
American River North Fork
Granite Chief Wilderness
Lake Tahoe
49
Auburn
Eldorado National Forest
NEVADA
CALIFORNIA
Coloma
Folsom Lake
Placerville
88
50
Apple Hill
Mokelumne River
Drytown
Volcano
Amador City
Sutter Creek
4
Stanislaus River
Jackson
Mokelumne Hill
Arnold
Camanche Reservoir
Cave City
Stanislaus National Forest
San Andreas
49
Murphys
108
Angels Camp
Yosemite National Park
Sonora
Jamestown
Stanislaus River
120
Chinese Camp
120
Yosemite Village
Patterson
Mariposa
Fish Camp

ROCKET GLASS/SHUTTERSTOCK

Lake Tahoe

more. Over at the county fairgrounds, rock hounds will dig the **California State Mining & Mineral Museum** *(parks.ca.gov; adult/child $4/free)*, where the 13lb 'Fricot Nugget' (the largest crystalized gold specimen from the California Gold Rush era) is proudly displayed.

Bouldering & River Rafting

River deep, mountain high

Climbing enthusiasts should pop over to the **Yosemite Climbing Museum** *(yosemiteclimbing.org/museum; suggested donation $5)*, which contains memorabilia stretching back to when the sport's pioneers were making their own gear. There's also the **Yosemite Boulder Farm**, a B&B with climbing and disc-golf on the town's outskirts. The property offers 6 acres of granite, with 20 boulders and climbs for every level. The owners spent three years clearing brush, leveling landings and power washing the boulders, and they operate the super-convivial B&B.

Declared a Wild and Scenic River by Congress in 1987, the **Merced** has twisting and tumbling white water that's best experienced on a raft. In spring, the exhilarating trip takes you down class III and IV rapids, whereas things get a lot more relaxed in summer after most of the snowmelt has run its course. **Zephyr Whitewater Expeditions** *(zrafting.com)* has been running trips on the Merced since 1973, and the large, reputable company has experienced guides and a seasonal office across from Yosemite Bug near Briceburg. Half-day trips cost $113 to $128; full-day trips range from $176 to $191 and include lunch.

If white water feels too extreme, head up the road to the **Merced River Recreation Management Area** *(blm.gov/visit/merced-river)* in Briceburg, where there's a **visitor center**, a picnic area, an extension bridge over the river, some campgrounds and a trail system. Depending on the time of year, it's an ideal spot for fishing, camping, hiking or just watching the rafts drift by.

BEST DAY TRIPS FOR HISTORY BUFFS

Hornitos: An old gold-mining settlement 30 minutes' drive west of Mariposa, with a still-operational bar, objects of intrigue and possibly ghosts.

Coulterville: Historic buildings line the streets of this charming former Gold Rush supply town 25 miles north of Mariposa.

Columbia State Historic Park: A mini Gold Rush theme park where volunteers dress in 19th-century garb and parade around blacksmith shops, theaters and saloons.

Hite Cove: Hike to a true ghost town on this 4.5-mile trail (one way) along the Merced River. Rock walls and heavy machinery remain.

Gold-Panning with Ira Estin: This longtime local (209-966-7262) takes you gold-panning along the Merced, teaching about the history and tools of the Gold Rush.

TOP EXPERIENCE

Yosemite National Park

Show-stopping Yosemite National Park is a UNESCO World Heritage Site, visited by millions of people each year. The original caretakers, the Ahwahneechee people, were violently displaced in the mid-1800s by white settlers. In 1864 President Abraham Lincoln ceded the land to California as a state park. This, paired with the efforts of conservationist John Muir, led to a congressional act in 1890 creating the national park.

SARAH_XIE7/SHUTTERSTOCK

Mariposa Grove

TOP TIPS

- Yosemite Village hosts the main visitor center, a museum, eateries and services.
- Curry Village is another valley hub with rooms, cabins, dining options and trailheads for popular hikes.
- Glacier Point can be reached on foot or with wheels and offers the park's most spectacular views.

PRACTICALITIES

- nps.gov/yose
- $20 per person, $35 per car to enter the park for three consecutive days

Touring Yosemite Valley

The **Yosemite Valley Loop Trail** generally follows Northside and Southside Drs, with some sections tracing the routes of former wagon roads. The most famous features you'll see are monumental 7569ft **El Capitan** (El Cap), one of the world's largest granite monoliths and a magnet for rock climbers, and 8842ft **Half Dome**, the park's spiritual centerpiece – its rounded granite pate forms an unmistakable silhouette. Meanwhile, Yosemite's waterfalls mesmerize even the most jaded traveler.

Climbing Half Dome

Just hold on, don't forget to breathe and – whatever you do – don't look down. A pinnacle so popular hikers need a permit to scale it, Half Dome is Yosemite Valley's coveted cocked-top jewel. The hike takes longer than an average work day, with an elevation gain equivalent to 480 flights of stairs and a near-vertical final stretch.

Mariposa Grove

In this cathedral of ancient trees, almost 500 hardy sequoias rocket to the sky. Early in the morning, explore Mariposa Grove in solitude and contemplate the thousands of years the trees have witnessed. Other highlights include walking through the heart of the still-living California Tunnel Tree and witnessing the girth of the Grizzly Giant.

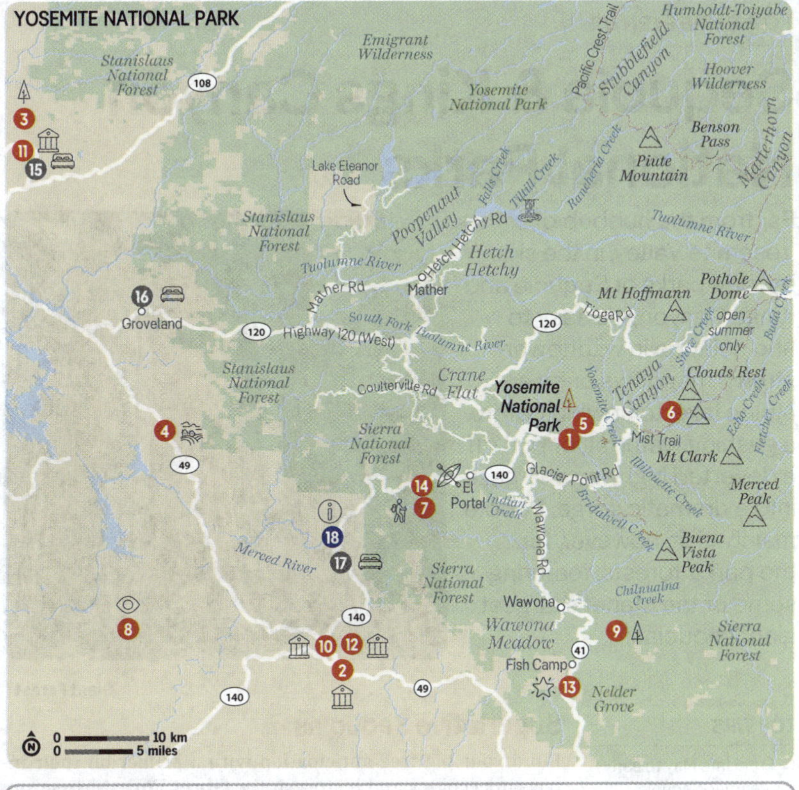

★ **HIGHLIGHTS**
1 Yosemite National Park

● **SIGHTS**
2 California State Mining & Mineral Museum
3 Columbia State Historic Park
4 Coulterville
5 El Capitan
6 Half Dome
7 Hite Cove
8 Hornitos
9 Mariposa Grove
10 Mariposa Museum & History Center
11 Tuolumne County Museum
12 Yosemite Climbing Museum

● **ACTIVITIES**
13 Yosemite Mountain Sugar Pine Railroad
14 Zephyr Whitewater Expeditions

● **SLEEPING**
15 Sonora Inn
16 Yosemite Basecamp
17 Yosemite Bug Rustic Mountain Resort

● **INFORMATION**
18 Briceburg Visitor Center

Riding the Sugar Pine Railroad

Steam train adventure

From mid-March through late November, the historic steam train of the **Yosemite Mountain Sugar Pine Railroad** *(ymsprr.com; per person from $31.80)* chugs from Fish Camp through Sierra National Forest on a 4-mile loop used for lugging lumber at the turn of the 20th century. It's a classic family adventure with some good history woven in. There's also a small museum, a gift store and a sandwich shop, plus gold-panning tours ($10/15 per person online/on-site) with a prospector.

TOP EXPERIENCE

Sequoia & Kings Canyon National Parks

Far from the hubbub of Yosemite Valley, in the side-by-side parks of Sequoia and Kings Canyon, it's easy to find solitude in wildflower-strewn meadows or by an alpine lake, to unwind before a gushing waterfall or pull off a deserted highway and gaze into a dramatic gorge. People mainly visit, however, for the parks' forests, featuring some of the planet's largest giant sequoias.

Giant Forest

TOP TIPS

- From late May to early September, Sequoia Shuttle runs buses four times daily between Visalia, Three Rivers and the Giant Forest Museum in Sequoia National Park.
- Campsites and wilderness permits must be booked on recreation.gov.
- Park-approved, bear-proof food canisters are mandatory for wilderness trips.

PRACTICALITIES

- nps.gov/seki
- $20 per person, $35 per car
- wilderness permit required for overnight backpacking

Superlative Sequoias

Build your big tree anticipation with a primer on their intriguing ecology and history at the **Giant Forest Museum**, housed in a historic 1920s building. Jump on the shuttle up the highway to **Giant Forest**, a 3-sq-mile grove that protects around half of the world's most gargantuan tree specimens. Among them is the world's biggest by volume, the **General Sherman Tree**, rocketing 275ft into the sky.

Hit the Trails

Moro Rock, just south of the Giant Forest, offers a quick ascent to the tippy-top of a granite dome and panoramic views, while Mineral King's Eagle Lake is a more secluded jaunt to a glacially carved tarn. The **High Sierra Trail**, a 49-mile stunner along a dramatic ridge, offers epic views and river crossings, concluding at Mt Whitney.

Spelunking

Crystal Cave *(visitsequoia.com/sequoia-national-park-attractions/crystal-cave; tour adult/child $20/10)* was carved over millennia by an underground river with marble formations estimated to be up to 100,000 years old. Stalactites hang like daggers from the cave ceiling, and milky-white formations take the shape of ethereal curtains, domes, columns and shields. Tickets for the 50-minute tour are only sold online in advance.

Skiing in Heavenly, Tahoe

Hit the slopes at Heavenly Resort

Tahoe is a year-round destination, with slow seasons a thing of the past. Winter brings deep snow at ski resorts like **Heavenly Mountain Resort** *(epicpass.com; Epic Pass single-day ticket adult/child from $94/48)* is perhaps the most well-known in California. It sits steps from the Lake Tahoe shoreline, with flabbergasting views plus trails that look like you're about to ski into the lake. With a base area at 6200ft above sea level and a summit above 10,000ft, it has the most skiable vert (vertical feet top-to-bottom) in Tahoe.

Follow the sun by skiing on the Nevada side in the morning for desert views, then moving to the California side in the afternoon. Snowboarders will want to carry speed on some flats to avoid hopping between states. Buy an Epic single-day ticket, rather than buying day-of at the ticket window, to save some dough.

High-Elevation Family Fun

Heavenly isn't just for winter

The **Heavenly Gondola** *(skiheavenly.com; adult/child from $79/39)* soars guests from the Heavenly Village in Stateline to Tamarack Lodge at more than 10,000ft above sea level. There's an observation deck at the halfway point with panoramic views of the entire Tahoe Basin, with summer activities like a zipline, a mountain coaster, tubing and hiking trails at the top. The gondola runs year-round for sightseeing, though the mountain may limit capacity for non-skiers on busy weekends.

Venture into Desolation Wilderness

Explore Tahoe's backcountry

Sculpted by powerful glaciers aeons ago, **Desolation Wilderness** *(fs.usda.gov)* covers 100 sq miles of high-elevation forest spread between the south and west shores. With no roads, the only way to visit is on foot, with dozens of hiking trails passing polished granite peaks and leading to deep-blue alpine lakes, glacier-carved valleys and resplendent pine forests that thin quickly at the higher elevations. It has exceptional wildflower hiking well into July.

Permits are required year-round for both day and overnight explorations, though day hikers can get them from self-issue stations at trailheads. Backpacking permits are available in

SEE ENVIRONMENTAL PROTECTION IN ACTION

Caroline Waldman, local expert and South Lake Tahoe resident, works for the Tahoe Fund, a nonprofit working to improve and protect Tahoe's environmental resources. *tahoefund.org*

The first stop on any sustainability success tour should be **Taylor Creek**. Walk along the interpretive trail to the viewing platforms and you may spot wildlife in action: kokanee salmon swimming, black bears napping or bald eagles soaring overhead. Next, head to Ski Run Blvd, where you'll find an empty lot transformed into the new **Ski Run Community Park**, complete with a climbing boulder. Head to Stateline, and in front of the **Tahoe Blue Event Center** you'll see a sculpture of a bald eagle holding a Lahontan cutthroat trout, crafted entirely from litter removed from Lake Tahoe by scuba divers.

EATING ON TAHOE'S SOUTH SHORE: ROMANTIC RESTAURANTS

Chart House: White-tablecloth dining a few miles from the tourist strip; lake views, and wildlife sightings aren't uncommon. *4-9:30pm Mon-Sat, to 9pm Sun* $$$

Edge Restaurant & Lounge: Tables are next to floor-to-ceiling windows. Check what time sunset is and reserve for 30 minutes beforehand. *hours vary* $$$

Wolf by Vanderpump: Arguably the most chichi casino restaurant in the area, with over-the-top decor and cocktails. *5-10pm Sun-Thu, from 4pm Fri & Sat* $$$

Evans American Gourmet Café: Reliably delicious and non-pretentious, with creative daily specials. *5-9pm Tue-Sat* $$$

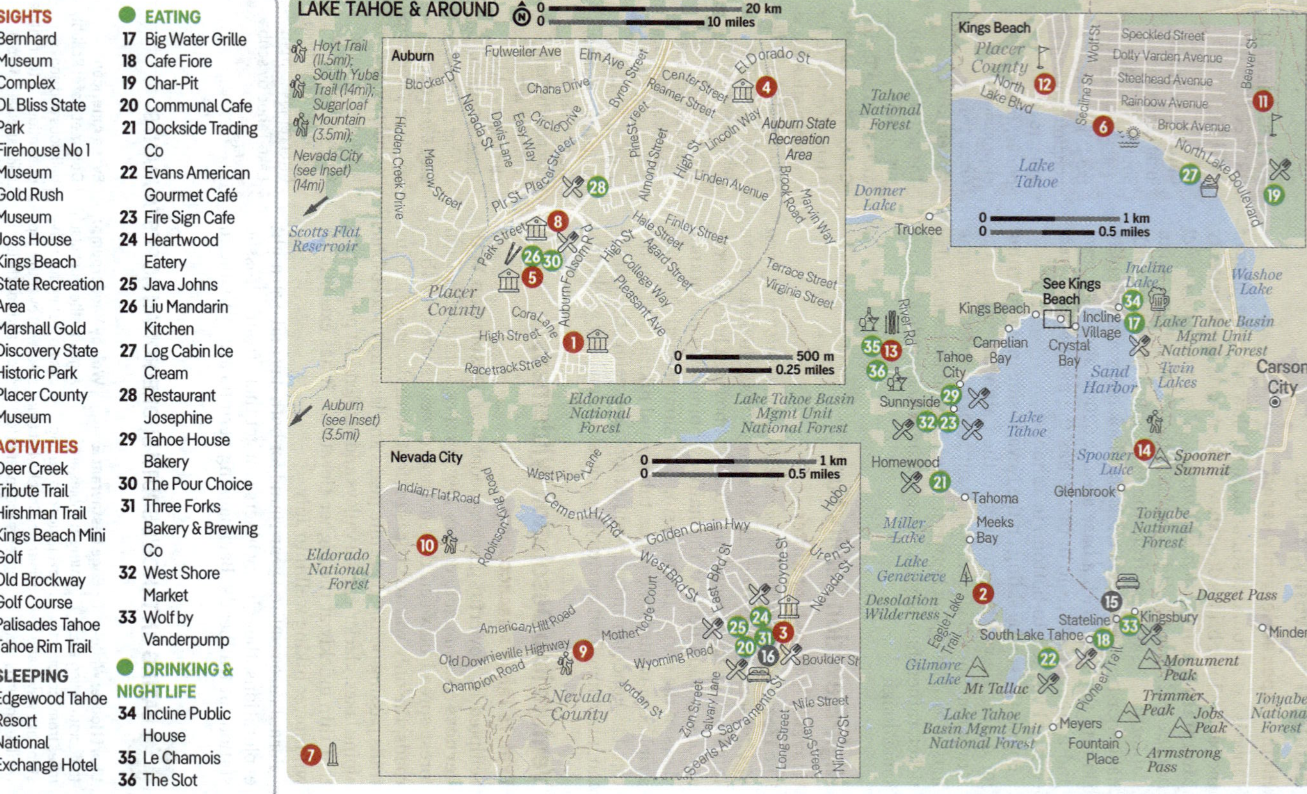

SIGHTS
1 Bernhard Museum Complex
2 DL Bliss State Park
3 Firehouse No 1 Museum
4 Gold Rush Museum
5 Joss House
6 Kings Beach State Recreation Area
7 Marshall Gold Discovery State Historic Park
8 Placer County Museum

ACTIVITIES
9 Deer Creek Tribute Trail
10 Hirshman Trail
11 Kings Beach Mini Golf
12 Old Brockway Golf Course
13 Palisades Tahoe
14 Tahoe Rim Trail

SLEEPING
15 Edgewood Tahoe Resort
16 National Exchange Hotel

EATING
17 Big Water Grille
18 Cafe Fiore
19 Char-Pit
20 Communal Cafe
21 Dockside Trading Co
22 Evans American Gourmet Café
23 Fire Sign Cafe
24 Heartwood Eatery
25 Java Johns
26 Liu Mandarin Kitchen
27 Log Cabin Ice Cream
28 Restaurant Josephine
29 Tahoe House Bakery
30 The Pour Choice
31 Three Forks Bakery & Brewing Co
32 West Shore Market
33 Wolf by Vanderpump

DRINKING & NIGHTLIFE
34 Incline Public House
35 Le Chamois
36 The Slot

AJ9/SHUTTERSTOCK

DL Bliss State Park

advance online. Be prepared to face hefty fines if you're not fire and bear aware.

YOU'RE IN THEIR HOME: BE BEAR AWARE

Black bears are cute from a distance, but leaving food and other items out brings them close to people – and when bears get too close to people, they face severe penalties. Help keep bears alive by following basic bear safety rules: never leave scented items unattended (or in your car), close kitchen doors and windows at night, and never leave trash outside next to a full dumpster. Bear canisters are mandatory for all overnight camping in the Tahoe basin. You can rent them from the Taylor Creek Visitor Center in South Lake Tahoe between June and October. If you see a bear in need of help, inform the **Tahoe Bear League** (*savebears.org*).

The West Shore's Best Beaches

Spend the day in Bliss

Just a few miles north of Emerald Bay State Park is **DL Bliss State Park** *(parks.ca.gov; parking $10)*, and while it's named for an early Tahoe tourism magnet, it could also be in honor of how you'll feel when you relax on its picture-perfect beaches. The park's Lester Beach and Calawee Cove are walk-in-only beaches tucked into small coves that somehow never seem too crowded. The park's Balancing Rock Trail goes past an oddity of nature that time seems to ignore, while the Lighthouse Trail heads to a historic lighthouse built by the Coast Guard in 1916. At 8600ft above sea level, it's the country's highest-elevation public lighthouse.

Romping Around Vintage Kings Beach

Hit the beach, 1960s-style

Few places in Tahoe are as untouched by recent development as Kings Beach. The humble and walkable town has a smattering of modest retro motels and a host of old-school dining establishments, from the vintage **Char-Pit** *(charpit.shop)* for burgers to family-owned **Log Cabin Ice Cream** *(logcabinicecream.squarespace.com)*.

EATING ON TAHOE'S WEST SHORE: CHEAPER PICKS

Tahoe House Bakery: A Swiss-style bakery and deli plus to-go breads, cheese and chocolate. *6am-3pm* $

West Shore Market: Fresh sandwiches and gelatos scooped lakeside at the deli. *7am-8pm, deli 10am-3pm or 3:30pm* $$

Fire Sign Cafe: A west-shore institution with constant crowds and wildly fluffy pancake stacks. *7:30am-2:30pm* $$

Dockside Trading Co: Grilled items, plus grab-and-go sandwiches and cheese-tastic burritos. *7am-7pm* $$

THE IMPRESSIVE TAHOE RIM TRAIL

The 165-mile-long **Tahoe Rim Trail** *(tahoerimtrail.org)*, or TRT, was first envisioned in the early 1980s, but wasn't completed until 2001. It encircles the lake, traversing its summits with an elevation gain/loss of about 24,000ft. In one go, it'll take an experienced hiker about 12 days to finish. Fortunately, there are 12 official trailheads throughout the basin, allowing hikers to explore select segments as day hikes or overnight trips. Mountain bikes are banned in designated wilderness areas and on sections that overlap with the Pacific Crest Trail. Bike-friendly segments include Brockway Summit to Watson Lake, Kingsbury Grade to Armstrong Pass, and Tahoe Meadows to Spooner Summit (allowed on even-numbered days). Be aware of wildlife and altitude risks while on the trail.

BILLY MCDONALD/SHUTTERSTOCK

Kings Beach State Recreation Area

In summer, all eyes are on **Kings Beach State Recreation Area**, a seductive 700ft-long beach that often gets deluged with sunseekers. The nostalgic 1920s **Old Brockway Golf Course** *(oldbrockway.com; green fees adult/child from $60/50)* will please golfers with its peekaboo lake views and a popular lakeview bar. Less-serious golfers can enjoy **Kings Beach Mini Golf** *(kingsbeachminiaturegolf.com; $15)*.

Winter at Palisades Tahoe

A hub for big-mountain winter sports

Combined, **Palisades Tahoe** *(palisadestahoe.com)* and Alpine Meadows (connected by lift and sharing one lift ticket) have 6000 skiable acres, making it the biggest ski resort in California. Though known for its expert runs and chutes, it has an expansive beginner area with a unique feature: it's near the top. That means beginners get expert-level views, even on their first day. Lift tickets are expensive, pushing $300 per day on winter weekends, so an all-season Epic Pass may be a better deal for repeat skiers. Parking reservations are required on winter weekends and holidays. If skiing isn't your thing, other winter draws include an all-ages snowtubing area, a year-round sightseeing gondola, and the 'Cushing Crossing' pond skim each May.

DRINKING ON TAHOE'S NORTH SHORE: BEST APRÈS-SKI

Big Water Grille: This lake-view restaurant near Diamond Peak is popular for sunset happy hours for deep-pocketed locals. *hours vary*

Incline Public House: Alibi Brewing's large location in Incline Village is a year-round favorite, with about a dozen local beers. *hours vary*

The Slot: An institution for cheap beer, loud music and '80s ski movies on repeat. *hours vary*

Le Chamois: Ski-in bar at Palisades Tahoe with Adirondack chairs, pizzas, an outdoor bar and plenty of post-ski sun in spring. *hours vary*

Touring Gold Country History in Auburn

History-rich museums

Often considered the heart of Gold Country, Auburn is the region's largest town and is steeped in Gold Rush charm. Stroll the Old Town for buildings dating to the 1850s – all with free admission. On the south side, the **Bernhard Museum Complex** *(placer.ca.gov)*, built in 1851 as the Traveler's Rest Hotel and later serving as the home of the Bernhard family, reflects 19th-century farm life.

Rebuilt by the Yue family in the 1920s after a mysterious fire, the clapboard **Joss House** *(auburnjosshouse.org)* stands on 'Chinese Hill,' one of many Chinese communities established during the Gold Rush, and gives an intimate look at what life was like for Chinese laborers back then. Tours run every Saturday between 10:30am and 2:30pm.

The 1st floor of the historic courthouse is home to the **Placer County Museum** (*placer.ca.gov*) and displays Native American artifacts, an 1877 stagecoach and huge unrefined gold nuggets. In the old Auburn train station, the kid-friendly interactive **Gold Rush Museum** *(placer.ca.gov)* includes a reconstructed mine and gold panning.

Gold Rush at Marshall Gold Discovery State Historic Park

Where the rush began

The **Marshall Gold Discovery State Historic Park** *(parks.ca.gov)* comprises a fascinating collection of buildings in a lovely riverside setting at the site of James Marshall's discovery. The museum tells the stories of some early settlers here, such as a group of African Americans who were once enslaved. Follow a short path along the south fork of the American River to the place where James Marshall made his fateful discovery and kickstarted the birth of the 'Golden State,' with its horrific consequences for the state's Indigenous people.

Gold Country's Star Town

Walking Nevada City

You can stroll around this charming town in just an hour if you're in a hurry, but it's best to take a leisurely stroll, stopping to eat, drink and shop along the way. Begin at **Firehouse No 1 Museum** *(nevadacountyhistory.org)*, a stately 1861 building and home to a small exhibit featuring curated

ALL THAT GLITTERS IS TRAGIC

John Sutter, who had a fort in Sacramento, partnered with James Marshall to build a sawmill on the swift stretch of the American River at Coloma in 1847. It was Marshall who discovered gold here on January 24, 1848, and though the men tried to keep their findings secret, prospectors from around the world stampeded into town. In one of the ironies of the Gold Rush, the men who made this discovery died nearly penniless. Many of the new immigrants who arrived seeking fortune were indentured, taxed and bamboozled out of anything they found. Meanwhile, the world of the local Native American Nisenan people was collapsing due to disease and displacement.

EATING & DRINKING IN AUBURN: OUR PICKS

The Pour Choice: Downtown coffee shop that also serves top-notch pastries, sandwiches and even cocktails. *7am-7pm Sun-Wed, to 9pm Thu & Sat* **$$**

Liu Mandarin Kitchen: Homemade dumplings and other northern Mandarin dishes tantalize the taste buds. *11am-9pm Thu-Tue* **$$**

Restaurant Josephine: A local go-to for a special occasion; dine on seasonal French cuisine in a handsome brick building. *5-9pm Tue-Thu, 4-10pm Fri & Sat* **$$$**

Maria's Mexican Tacos: Indulge in Maria's authentic tacos, burritos, tortas and fajitas right off the 80 at this local favorite. *Tue-Sat 10am-8pm* **$$**

NEVADA CITY'S BEST HIKES

Deer Creek Tribute Trail: Popular hike that starts in downtown and leads into the woods. Listen for rushing water and follow signs to the Angkula Seo Suspension Bridge or the Chinese Tribute Bridge.

Hirschman Trail: Tranquil 4.1-mile round-trip walk through wooded scenery leading to Hirschman's Pond. Especially stunning in the fall when the foliage changes colors.

Sugarloaf Mountain: Short 1.8-mile round-trip trail that offers stunning views of the town and surrounding landscape.

Hoyt Trail: Moderate 1.6-mile scenic river walk that leads to swimming holes along the South Yuba River and Hoyt Crossing.

South Yuba Trail: For the adventurous hiker or mountain biker, a portion of this quiet 20-mile trail takes you along the South Yuba River. Cell service is spotty.

WASIM MUKLASHY/SHUTTERSTOCK

Deer Creek Tribute Trail

items that tell the story of the local people, from stunning Nisenan baskets to preserved Victorian bridal wear. The prize exhibits are relics from the Chinese settlers who often built but seldom profited from the mines. It's open Wednesday to Sunday from May to October.

Follow Commercial St to numbers 309 to 316, the tiny survivors of the 19th-century Chinese Quarter. The South Yuba Canal Building (1855) is among the town's oldest. The renovated **National Exchange Hotel** *(thenationalexchangehotel.com)* welcomed its first guest in 1854 and is still the best place to stay in town – and to grab a craft cocktail. Take a break at Three Forks Bakery & Brewing Co, which serves beers and coffee, luscious baked goods and artisanal pizzas.

Untold Stories in Sonora

Historic nuggets

In the former 1857 Tuolumne County Jail, you'll find the great little **Tuolumne County Museum** *(tchistory.org; free)*, with a fortune's worth of gold displayed in the form of nuggets and gold-bearing quartz. Each of the former jail cells spotlights a different theme, one of which is the little-told story of African Americans during the Gold Rush. You can learn about former enslaved man William Suggs, who set up a leather harness business and successfully campaigned to overturn segregation in local schools.

EATING & DRINKING IN NEVADA CITY: COZY COFFEE SPOTS

Three Forks Bakery & Brewing Co: Come for the organic and fair-trade coffee, stay for the freshly baked pastries. *8am-8pm Mon-Thu, to 9pm Fri & Sat* $$

Communal Cafe: Hipster menu items like mushroom coffee and a vibrant butterfly pea matcha pair well with their farm-to-table fare. *7am-6pm* $

Heartwood Eatery: Signature latte, like their fragrant rose cardamom latte, nourishing bowls and farm-fresh salads make this a local go-to. *10am-4pm* $$

Java Johns: Homey family joint with an extensive coffee and tea menu. Prepare to wait during the weekends. *7am-2pm Mon-Fri, to 4pm Sat & Sun* $

Central California: The Coast & Sacramento

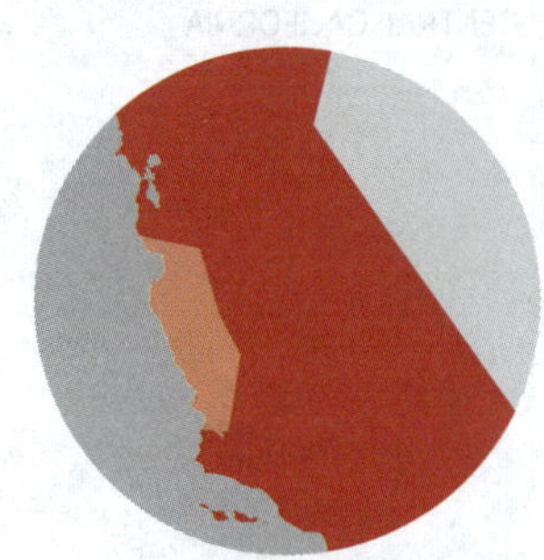

WILD SEAS | GREEN CAPITAL | VALLEY TOWNS

Santa Barbara has long been a weekend getaway for Angelenos, cozily nestled between the picturesque Santa Ynez Mountains and the Pacific Ocean, graced with Spanish Colonial architecture and chill, beach-town vibes. Along the coast from San Luis Obispo to Santa Cruz, savage landscapes are everywhere. Cliffs and sea stacks are smashed by the waves, redwood forests reach skyward and volcanic peaks defy all sense of time. With wind-buffeted hikes, white-knuckle road trips and a taste of the truly remote, nothing beats this coastline. The scent of sagebrush and salty sea air make you feel bracingly alive, while fog-diffused light adds an ethereal glow. Inland, attractive state capital Sacramento mixes history and culture with great food and drink, and every non-glitzy aspect of California is celebrated at the annual California State Fair. Wine is foundational to the valley's produce, and you can enjoy that and excellent craft beer at enticing university towns such as Davis and Chico.

GETTING AROUND

Though it's not the most scenic part of the route, the *Coast Starlight* train connects the Bay Area (Oakland and San Jose) with Salinas (near Monterey), Paso Robles, San Luis Obispo and Santa Barbara. Smaller towns can often be reached by bus but schedules are patchy; plan ahead. The Central Valley has an excellent train service. All the main cities of the San Joaquin Valley are linked to Sacramento and the Bay Area by fast and frequent Amtrak trains.

Classic Santa Barbara Landmarks

Architecture, gardens and natural history

Once you see the **Santa Barbara County Courthouse** *(sbcourthouse.org; free)*, you'll understand why couples plan weddings here. Taking up an entire city block, the Spanish Colonial Revival stunner is surrounded by inviting lawn and sunken garden. **Docent-led tours** *(weekdays at 10:30am, except for court holidays)* give details on the Moorish-style tile work and intricately painted Mural Room.

Founded in 1786, **Old Mission Santa Barbara** *(santabarbaramission.org; adult/youth $17/12)* is only one of two California missions that have continuously operated since their

TOP TIP

Check your feet after beach visits, as Santa Barbara shores have naturally occurring tar seeps that ooze up through the sand. If you've been tarred, give it a good dab of sunscreen and wipe with a paper towel.

CENTRAL CALIFORNIA
Boulder Creek
Henry Cowell Redwoods State Park
Santa Cruz
Aptos
Morgan Hill
Gilroy
Watsonville
Hollister
San Juan Bautista
San Luis Reservoir
Moss Landing
Salinas
Monterey
Carmel-by-the-Sea
Pinnacles National Park
Salinas River
Soledad
Los Padres National Forest
Big Sur
Santa Lucia Range
Ventana Wilderness
King City
San Ardo
Lucia
Jolon
Gorda
Silver Peak Wilderness
Lake Nacimiento
San Miguel
Cholame
San Simeon
Paso Robles
Cambria
Harmony
Atascadero
Cayucos
Los Padres National Forest
Morro Bay
Estero Bay
San Luis Obispo
Los Padres National Forest
Garcia Wilderness
Pismo Beach
San Luis Obispo Bay
Guadalupe
Santa Maria
PACIFIC OCEAN
Santa Barbara (27mi)
0 100 km
0 50 miles

establishment. If you're here during Memorial Day weekend, be sure to check out the chalk-painting festival **I Madonnari** *(@imadonnari)* as it transforms the Mission sidewalk into art.

Head a little further toward the foothills to the **Santa Barbara Museum of Natural History** *(sbnature.org; adult/child $19/14)* in its creekside nook amid oak habitat. Find natural context in exhibits ranging from Chumash culture, indigenous wildlife and geology, then complement it with forest bathing at the nearby **Santa Barbara Botanic Garden** *(sbbotanicgarden.org; adult/child $20/12)* – reservations required. The Channel Islands section offers spectacular views and native island flora.

Pacific Ocean Pleasures

Swim, surf, paddle, whale-watch

You could visit Santa Barbara without dipping a toe in the ocean...but why would you? Buffered from open ocean by the Channel Islands, the south-facing coastline offers a string of beautiful protected beaches. Novice surfers will appreciate the smaller swell of summer; most surf spots are best during the winter. **Leadbetter Beach** has a slow-rolling wave that makes it popular for lessons and beginners. Book surf lessons with **Santa Barbara Surf School** *(santabarbarasurfschool.com)* or **Surf Happens** *(surfhappens.com)*.

At the harbor, rent an SUP or a kayak at **Paddle Sports Center** *(paddlesportsca.com)*. Even within the breakwater, you'll encounter harbor seals, pelicans and rays on your paddle. Wildlife-watchers can book a whale-watching tour on the *Double Dolphin* of the **Santa Barbara Sailing Center** *(sbsail.com)* or with **Condor Express** *(condorexpress.com)*, to cruise the Santa Barbara Channel in search of over 30 species of cetaceans, including migrating humpbacks, blue or gray whales and orcas (depending on the season).

Spanish San Luis Obispo

On a mission

People who know San Luis Obispo can't utter its name without a faraway smile. SLO (pronounced 'slow') captures California's many charms in a petite package. Snuggled among volcanic peaks, the city is in easy reach of hiking trails, wine country and beach towns. Local architecture has a strong Spanish accent. SLO was founded by Spanish colonists in 1772 when the **mission** was built under orders of Junípero Serra, a key

BUILDING A CHUMASH CANOE

Alan Salazar, Ventureño Chumash and Tataviam Tribal Elder.

We established the Chumash Maritime Association in January 1997 to oversee construction of a *tomol* (plank canoe) for the Chumash community. We had to relearn the skills of building, paddling and navigating. In 1912 Fernando Librado Kitsepawit, whose family was of the *tomol* brotherhood, built one as a demonstration; our research relied on extensive notes taken by anthropologist JP Harrington from interviews with Librado.

In 1997 we built the first working *tomol* in modern times, with the help of the Santa Barbara Maritime Museum, and paddled it across the Santa Barbara Channel in 2001. Our goal was to revitalize the Chumash maritime culture, especially to involve our young people. Conditions permitting, we now do the channel crossing annually.

EATING IN SLO: BEST OUTDOOR DINING

Ebony: Sop up lentil stew with *injera* (teff flour bread) at this vegan counter-serve Ethiopian spot. *11am-8pm Thu-Sat, 10am-3pm Sun* $

Kiko: Tucked in the Central Market arcade, this colorful Peruvian place has a patio that is perfect for tangy ceviche and slow-cooked beef with a view. *5-9pm* $$

Novo: The tree-shaded patio is a place to fall in love...with your companion, or with pork carnitas and lamb shank. *11am-9pm Mon-Sat, from 10am Sun* $$$

Luna Red: Buzzing outdoor terrace. The menu travels from Mexico to Spain via mole tacos and seafood paella. *11am-9pm Sun-Thu, to 10pm Fri & Sat* $$

UNIQUE SHOPS & SOUVENIRS IN SLO

Blackwater: Nothing you need but everything you want: shirts, sarcastic greetings cards, needlepoint cushions and vintage signs.

Buen Dia Market: Grocery store or art gallery? Be amazed by meticulously curated delicacies, then shop for art prints at its sister store at 790 Higuera St.

Bizarre Antiques & Oddities: Rummage crystals and curios here.

Hands Gallery: Upscale boutique selling mosaic art, locally made jewelry and novelty socks.

Mama Ganache: Ethically sourced small-batch chocolate, including vegan truffles and cashew chews. Chocolate bark is durable enough for your journey home.

WYNN WYGAL/SHUTTERSTOCK

Madonna Inn, San Luis Obispo

player in the Spanish Empire's expansion. Exploring the city's mosaic of Spanish Mission style, art deco and the rosy-pink confection of the **Madonna Inn** is a sweet experience.

SLO's Highest Point

Hike to panoramic views at Bishop Peak

San Luis Obispo County's craggy beauty is a gift of the 'Nine Sisters,' a daisy chain of volcanic peaks stretching from Islay Hill, southeast of SLO, northwest to the coast at Morro Bay. The tallest is **Bishop Peak** (1559ft) and trails switchbacking up this volcanic plug start 2.5 miles northwest of downtown SLO.

To hike the **Summit Trail** (4 miles return; intermediate to advanced; 1180ft elevation) get over to Patricia Dr. There's a gentle incline after the **trailhead gate**, then take the left fork to follow the Summit Trail. Make your way up to the rocky summit for expansive views of SLO and the Santa Lucia Mountains beyond. Extend your ramble by adding the **Felsman Loop** (1.6 miles; easy to intermediate; 580ft elevation).

Cambria's Gem-Studded Moonstone Beach

Mosey along Cambria's multicolor shore

The jewel in Cambria's crown, Moonstone Beach glitters with colored pebbles. Walk down to the beach to admire smooth colorful gems washing ashore (look, don't take). The boardwalk

EATING & DRINKING IN CAMBRIA & CAYUCOS: LOCAL FAVORITES

French Corner Bakery: Cambria's croissant enthusiasts rave about the golden buttery goodies prepared at this casual cafe. *6:30am-6pm* $

Schooners: For sea dogs with discerning tastes (halibut with peanut slaw, rare ahi tuna), this friendly nautical boozer in Cayucos delivers. *11am-10pm Sun-Thu, to 11pm Fri & Sat* $$

Lunada Garden Bistro: Cayucos' enchanting garden sets the stage for elevated bistro dishes, from French-style duck to coffee-glazed pork. *11am-1:45pm & 5-8pm Tue-Sun* $$$

Salty Tiger: A secret speakeasy tucked into an upscale motel? We're in. Ask at Cayucos' Pacific Motel about its jauntily decorated one-room bar. *hours vary*

follows the shore for roughly 1.5 miles through coastal prairies. You'll see ground squirrels racing past and enjoy exhilarating views of the bluffs. Time your walk for late afternoon, when the sun casts a coppery glaze across the pebble beaches. Then you're just in time for dinner at the nautical-themed **Sea Chest Oyster Bar** *(seachestoysterbar.com; cash only; 5:30-9pm Wed-Mon)*, perhaps *cioppino* with a glass from their local-leaning wine list.

Improbable Hearst Castle

Venetian balconies and zebras

With a celestial hilltop setting and artworks to rival the Louvre, San Simeon's **Hearst Castle** *(hearstcastle.org; adult/child from $35/18)* is the jaw-droppingly opulent passion project of media mogul William Randolph Hearst (1863–1951). No expense was spared to build this 165-room hilltop estate, from Rapunzel-like towers to Italian marble monuments to a library crammed with priceless Greek urns. A menu of different guided tours lead you through the labyrinthine palace and its hidden corners. Ask staff where the zebras, descendants of Hearst's originals, were last spotted. The **Grand Rooms Tour** is ideal for first-time visitors but we love the **Upstairs Suites Tour**, which climbs to ornate guest rooms like the tower-top 'Celestial Bedroom' (there are 367 steps in total).

Art Until Sundown in Paso Robles

Immerse yourself in Paso Robles' art scene

Mission and now winery town Paso Robles has all the ingredients for an eclectic art scene: rolling hills that beg to be captured in watercolors and a collision of Native American, Spanish and cowboy aesthetics. **Studios on the Park** *(studiosonthepark.org; free; noon-4pm Sun-Thu, to 9pm Fri & Sat)* is an excellent porthole into the multifaceted scene. Step inside to muse at photography, pottery and glass art.

As the sun dips, see the hills sparkle at **Sensorio** *(sensoriopaso.com; adult/child $45/22)*, an outdoor art hub where Bruce Munro's *Field of Light* installation is in indefinite residence. Entranced by the light of more than 100,000 bulbs, you'll meander around fields turned multicolor. It's 5 miles northeast of Paso (Rte 46); book ahead. It's open 6:30pm to 10:30pm Thursday to Sunday from May through August, and 6pm to 10pm Thursday to Sunday in April.

NORTHERN CHUMASH MARINE PROTECTED AREA

When 156 miles of California's coast were designated a marine protected area in October 2024, there were many reasons to celebrate. The protected status of 4543 sq miles (south of Morro Bay to the northern edge of the Channel Islands) would allow whales, turtles, seabirds and more to thrive without the threats of pollution or natural gas extraction. It was also a victory for Northern Chumash Tribes, who comanage the reserve. They campaigned for decades for community control over the area's ocean management. The **Northern Chumash Heritage National Marine Sanctuary** *(sanctuaries.noaa.gov/chumash-heritage)* is also good news for visitors, who flock to these shores to witness the abundant marine life.

EATING IN PASO ROBLES: BUDGET OPTIONS

Paso Market Walk: Our picks at this mini food court: coffee from Common Grounds, vegan cheeses from the Vreamery and mini cupcakes from Just Baked. *hours vary* $

Paso Robles Farmers Market: Behold the local bounty! Grab-and-go food from tacos to gluten-free doughnuts, along with seasonal fruits and veggies. *9am-1pm Sat* $

Jeffry's Wine Country BBQ: Dry-rubbed and wood-fire smoked, the tri-tip and chicken are moreish. Veggie burgers and garlic mac 'n' cheese too. *11am-8pm Thu-Mon* $$

Aliyah's Kitchen: Want to feel full? Try seafood towers, heaped combo plates and $2 taco Tuesday. *10am-9pm Mon-Thu, to 1am Fri & Sat, 8am-9pm Sun* $

BEST FESTIVALS AROUND PASO ROBLES

Spring Release Month: March is for wine-lovers. A month-long program of winemaker dinners, talks, tours and more. *(pasowine.com)*

Art in the Park: Artists assemble in Paso's Downtown Sq to showcase their wares for a weekend (April and November). *(pasoroblesartinthepark.com)*

Paso Wine Fest: Let wine and live DJ sets wash over you at this mid-May celebration of good wine and good living. *(pasowine.com/winefest)*

Atascadero Lakeside WineFest: Wine, craft beer, live music and family-friendly fun at Atascadero's Lake Park in mid-June. *(atascaderolakesidewinefestival.com)*

Paderewski Festival: Concerts from late October to early November celebrate visionary composer Ignacy Paderewski (1860–1941), a Polish musician turned Paso rancher. *(paderewskifest.com)*

Urban Wine Tasting

Sip your way around Tin City

Less than 10 minutes by rideshare along Hwy 101 from Paso Robles, Tin City is a post-industrial cluster of friendly tasting rooms and distilleries. Start at **Union Sacré Winery** *(unionsacre.com; tastings $20)* where they have managed to make riesling cool again. Around the corner is **Field Recordings** *(fieldrecordingswine.com; tastings $25)*, which prides itself on sourcing exceptional grapes from underrated vineyards. At **ONX Wines** *(onxwines.com; tastings $25)*, the fruit-forward zinfandels slip down very easily at their terrace with a babbling fountain. All wine'd out? Close out the experience at **Tin City Cider Co** *(tincitycider.com; tasting paddle $20)*, where hand-harvested apples yield silky, not-too-sweet ciders.

The Life of Monterey's Marine Mammals

Spot sealife right from the shore

Some of Monterey's best beaches are VIP-only, and those VIPs are harbor seals. Just half a mile north of Monterey's famous aquarium is the **Harbor Seal Viewing Point**, where plump seals loll on a protected arc of pristine white sand. Further south, spy on sea lions from the pier at **San Carlos Beach** and **Old Fisherman's Wharf**. Along the way you'll spy playful sea otters and sea lions that belly-flop from the rocks.

Historic Cannery Row

Amble from overfishing to ocean conservation

On Monterey's Cannery Row, cacophonous fish factories have been replaced by a different kind of chaos: merry-making tourists! Formerly Ocean View Ave, the street was renamed in 1958 after author John Steinbeck captured this gritty neighborhood in his masterpiece *Cannery Row* (1945). Meandering along Cannery Row combines industrial history with the innocent pleasures of present-day Monterey. Make sure you idle through a souvenir store or slurp soft-serve along the way

Start a block northwest of the aquarium at the 1926 **American Tin Cannery** (when we passed through, it was destined to transform into a hotel). This powerhouse factory was one of the big players on Cannery Row in the 1930s and '40s, when the pungent tang of fish was heavy in the air.

Factories operated day and night, processing 250,000 tons of sardines annually. The Norwegian founder of Hovden Cannery

EATING IN MONTEREY: ECOFRIENDLY PICKS

Happy Girl Kitchen: An ecoconscious one-stop shop for coffee, every-grain avocado toast and deli food, just two blocks from Ocean View Blvd. *7am-5pm* $

Passionfish: Sustainably harvested seafood and local ingredients, from tomato-truffle scallops to 12-hour lamb. Beautifully presented with small-batch wine. *5-9pm* $$$

Fish Hopper: Dishing up sustainable fish since 1950, this bustling place has splendid views to accompany pasta, seared tuna or ribeye. *10:30am-9:30pm* $$$

Revival Ice Cream: Cold-brew coffee, honey and passion-fruit-mango are among the plant-based scoops. Dairy options too. *noon-9pm Sun-Thu, to 10pm Fri & Sat* $

WIRESTOCK CREATORS/SHUTTERSTOCK

Monterey Bay Aquarium

pioneered undersea pipes to vacuum tons of fish into his factory every minute. But cosmic balance has been restored: this site of voracious overfishing is now a bastion of ocean conservation, home to the **Monterey Bay Aquarium**.

A few steps south and across the street is the former **Wing Chong Company Grocery** (1918). Monterey's fishing industry was developed in the 1850s by Chinese fishers who established themselves at Point Ahlones. Wing Chong was also the inspiration for a similarly named grocery in Steinbeck's *Cannery Row*.

CARMEL'S REAL-LIFE DOLLHOUSES

There's a reason why **Carmel-by-the-Sea**, 9 miles south of Monterey, looks like it's from the pages of a fairy tale. More than two dozen buildings have steep gabled roofs, undulating lines and craggy stone chimneys, the design hallmarks of self-taught architect Hugh W Comstock (1893–1950). Their whimsical appearance was inspired by Hugh's wife, Mayotta Browne Comstock, who operated a successful business selling 'Otsy-Totsy' dolls. Mayotta wanted to create a suitably magical home for her rosy-cheeked ragdolls, and Hugh quickly went to work. First came the charming 'Hansel and Gretel Cottages,' then the 'Snow White Summer Palace.' Local demand for these quaint abodes boomed and the candy-colored houses remain some of the most coveted real estate in Carmel.

Surf's Up in Santa Cruz!

Learn to catch waves on Cowell's Beach

Between Silicon Valley and Monterey, the city of Santa Cruz is where students, dropouts and tech royalty all compete for the best surf breaks.

Even if your surfing experience goes no further than clinging to a bodyboard for dear life, that can all change in the gentle, predictable waves lapping **Cowell's Beach**. This sheltered cove on the west side of the **Santa Cruz Wharf** has excellent conditions for first-timers to stand up on a board, especially during the spring. Book a class with the venerable **Richard Schmidt Surf School** *(richardschmidt.com)*, teaching first-timers and improvers since 1978 (all equipment is included).

EATING IN SANTA CRUZ: OUR PICKS

Hanloh: Outstanding bar-restaurant with a short menu of well-spiced and slow-cooked Thai meals. Inside the Bad Animal bookstore. *5-9pm Wed-Sun* $$$

Abbott Square Market: Counter-serve choices galore: coffee, sushi, Venezuelan arepas and West African vegan stews. *8am-10pm Sun-Thu, to 11pm Fri & Sat* $

Chocolat: Eat more chocolate! Start with three types of mole, chocolate-BBQ pork and chocolate mezcal martinis. *noon-4pm Fri-Sun & 5-9pm Thu-Mon* $$

Penny Ice Creamery: Cult favorite for classic and outlandish flavors (blood-orange creamsicle, butter caramel). We're here for toasted marshmallow topping. *noon-11pm* $

Big Sur Road Trip

Surreally beautiful, Hwy 1 from Point Lobos to Ragged Point dances along fearsome cliffs and through forest groves. Don't rush: a day is doable but stay overnight to marinate in Big Sur's magic. Download maps (there's no cell service) and research online: when we last cruised through, a section of road south of Lime Creek Bridge remained closed due to a rock slide.

1 Painters Point

This cliff lookout is a breathtaking introduction to Big Sur. Prolong the views on a 1.5-mile return hike to inspiring Soberanes Point just south.

The Drive: Visitors are dazzled by their first views of Big Sur, so this section gets hectic with distracted drivers. Watch the road!

2 Garrapata Beach

Stroll the trail above the attractively rock-studded Garrapata Beach. It crosses a creek where white calla lilies burst into bloom (mid-February to mid-April).

The Drive: Along the next 4 miles to Bixby Bridge, you'll cross bridges and skirt bumpy headlands. Parking is a circus; only stop for photos if it's safe.

3 Bixby Bridge

This 1932 bridge clasps the devilishly steep Bixby Canyon, looping 260ft over the golden beach below. Castle Rock Viewpoint offers a picture-perfect vantage point.

The Drive: Ocean views are on show throughout this meandering, 8-mile stretch to Andrew Molera State Park.

4 Andrew Molera State Park

Meadows, beaches and bluffs make this tranquil state park a joy to explore. For big views of the rolling surf, take the Bluffs Trail (1.7 miles one way).

JON BILOUS/SHUTTERSTOCK

Garrapata Beach

The Drive: The road nudges inland and the next 4.5 miles are lined with redwoods, a precursor to rambles in the state park.

5 Big Sur Lodge

This lodge in Pfeiffer Big Sur State Park is a convivial place to grab coffee and baked goods before a heavenly forest hike; head high to Valley View (2 miles round trip; 200ft elevation).

The Drive: After 1.5 miles, take a sharp right (Sycamore Canyon Rd) to Pfeiffer Beach.

6 Pfeiffer Beach

This beach is renowned for sand that appears purplish when the light hits just right, the gift of manganese garnet from crumbling hills nearby. In winter you can catch sunset through Keyhole Arch... otherworldly.

The Drive: Rejoin Hwy 1: it twists and turns for 10 miles through forest and then along a serpentine stretch with Pacific views.

7 McWay Falls

Julia Pfeiffer Burns State Park is a beloved stop for 80ft McWay Falls, which cascades onto the beach. If the overlook trail is closed, viewpoints from Hwy 1 are signed from the road.

The Drive: If the road's open, 33 ocean-view miles extend to Ragged Point. In 2025, travelers had to turn around at Lime Creek, 4 miles south of McWay Falls.

8 Ragged Point

At this headland, toothy cliffs drop to deep-blue ocean. A short but steep walk descends to an ashen beach and the variable trickle of Black Swift Waterfalls. Celebrate journey's end at Ragged Point's inn-restaurant.

STORM-TOSSED SANTA CRUZ WHARF

Jutting out into the Pacific from the southern end of the beach boardwalk, Santa Cruz Wharf (p403) morphed from a potato-shipping outpost in 1914 into a big cog in Monterey Bay's sardine-canning machine, until the industry collapsed in the 1950s. It found a new identity for holidaymakers, who continue to pile into its bars and restaurants, or just peer through the portholes at sea lions, which can grow up to 8ft long. It lost its crown as the longest pier on the West Coast when violent waves in December 2024 caused an 150ft section to collapse, though you can't keep this venerable wharf down: the remainder was up and running again just two weeks later.

Beach Boardwalk Thrills

Get playful on roller coasters and a popular beach

Yelps of delight ring out from the Giant Dipper as it rattles along its tracks. Sugary air wafts from stalls selling funnel cakes and cumulonimbus-sized puffs of cotton candy. Families, groups of teens and wide-eyed visitors all pile onto the **Santa Cruz Beach Boardwalk** *(beachboardwalk.com; hours vary)*.

Founded in 1907, this palace of amusements, sprawled along a wooden boardwalk lining Santa Cruz Beach, is the oldest of its kind in the US. Don't skip a spin on the **Looff Carousel** (1911), with its original 1894 pipe organ, and the wildly popular landmark **Giant Dipper** (1924) wooden roller coaster. Tip: get garlic fries after the fast-rotating **Cyclone** and 125ft **Double Shot**, not before.

Explore Old Sacramento

Historic center with fascinating museums

The historic river port next to downtown, **Old Sacramento** *(oldsacramento.com; free)* is the city's top visitor draw: if you're walking here from town, enter the area on K St to avoid the deafening spaghetti junction of roads. The kitschy Gold Rush–era atmosphere makes it great for a stroll.

Join the underground tour run by the on-site **Sacramento History Museum** *(sachistorymuseum.org; adult/child $12/6, underground tour $30/25)*, which explores the tunnels that date from the time before everything was raised 18ft due to floods. The top sight is the **California State Railroad Museum** *(csrmf.org; adult/child $12/6)*, which has a huge collection of restored and notable locomotives and cars.

Sacramento's Colonial Origins

Dig into John Sutter's historic fort

Originally built by Swiss immigrant John Sutter, the mostly reconstructed site of **Sutter's Fort State Historic Park** *(suttersfort.org; adult/child $5/3)* was once the only white settlement for hundreds of miles. It was established in 1840 as part of the Mexican province of Alta California; today you can stroll within the fort's whitewashed adobe walls, where displays including furniture, medical equipment and a working blacksmith shop recreate life in the 1850s. A replica wagon illustrates the hardiness of pioneer families, who would load up their vehicles with belongings, then walk alongside, often for hundreds of miles.

EATING IN SACRAMENTO: OUR PICKS

Localis: A relaxed Midtown temple to Central Valley produce and California cuisine. Book ahead, especially for patio tables. *5-8:15pm Wed-Sat* $

Aioli Bodega Espanola: Spanish tapas in a garden near the capitol, plus a long wine list. *11am-10pm Mon-Sat, 3-9pm Sun* $$

Veg Café & Bar: Veg enchants with a modern space, and beautifully presented vegan dishes like cauliflower momo. *11:30am-9pm Tue-Sat, 11am-3pm Sun* $$

Tower Café: Best bet for big breakfasts, next to the iconic art deco movie theater. *8am-3pm Mon & Tue, 8am-8pm Wed, Thu & Sun, to 9pm Fri & Sat* $$

Sutter was an entrepreneur, con artist and itinerant debtor who enslaved the local Native American population to create his fortune, which was lost after gold-seekers swamped his lands. Visit the neighboring **State Indian Museum** *(parks.ca.gov; adult/child $5/3)* to learn about the culture that Sutter helped destroy.

Get Down in Davis

Bookstores, bikes, galleries and tree-lined streets

Much of Davis' energy comes from the free-spirited students who flock to the University of California, Davis (UC Davis), which boasts one of the nation's leading viticulture departments. Bikes outnumber cars two-to-one, and students make up half the population. Strolling the shady downtown, you'll pass family-operated businesses including some great book and thrift stores (the city council has forbidden any store over 50,000 sq ft – sorry, Walmart) plus public art projects.

The university is all about agriculture, and new types of produce that end up in your supermarket are developed here. The 100-acre **UC Davis Arboretum** *(arboretum.ucdavis.edu; free)* is a must-see for its well-marked botanical collections.

The campus has two notable cultural centers. The **Jan Shrem & Maria Manetti Shrem Museum of Art** *(manettishremmuseum.ucdavis.edu; free)* features contemporary artists working across a wide range of mediums in a dreamy modern space. The **John Natsoulas Center for the Arts** *(natsoulas.com; free)* is marked by an outsize mosaic cat on the way into town; the ceramic calico guards one of the state's most vibrant small contemporary art galleries.

The Original Farmers Market

Eat, drink and be merry

The **Davis Farmers Market** *(davisfarmersmarket.org)* is renowned for being one of the best in the country, and features over 150 food vendors; on Wednesday evenings bands play in the adjacent park.

Wander an Oak-Shaded Student Town

Good times in Chico

With its huge student population, **Chico** has the wild energy of a college kegger during the school year, and a lethargic hangover during summer. The oak-shaded downtown and lively

LIVE MUSIC IN SACRAMENTO

Jen Moore, owner of *@rivercitymarketplace*, introduces the city's music scene.

Midtown 's vibrant, eclectic music scene pulses with creativity and community. From soulful acoustic sets and indie rock to energetic funk, jazz and hip-hop, every genre finds a home in this lively urban hub. On any given night, music spills from cozy clubs, open-air patios and bustling taprooms, creating a rich tapestry of sound that reflects the city's diversity. The neighborhood's walkability makes it easy to explore multiple shows in one evening, whether you're catching a rising local artist or a surprise touring act. With events ranging from intimate performances to full-blown music festivals, the area offers an inclusive, ever-evolving experience that celebrates artistry and connection. It's more than music – it's the heartbeat of Sacramento.

DRINKING IN DAVIS: CRAFT BEER & COFFEE

Delta of Venus Cafe & Pub: Converted bungalow with a social, shaded patio, tons of veggie/vegan options, a bar and live music. *hours vary*

Davis Beer Shoppe: Mellow Davis beer hall with 650 varieties of craft beer, bottled and on tap. *11am-10pm Mon-Sat, to 8pm Sun*

Miskha's Cafe: A quintessential university cafe with a homey twist – the rose and lavender infused lattes are house favorites. *7:30am-6pm*

Three Mile Brewing Company: Microbrewery with a fantastic flight of crisp, hoppy beer made from local ingredients. *3-10pm Mon-Thu, from noon Fri-Sun*

WILD CHICO

It's not just the student parties that are wild in Chico. From the dense trees arcing over the streets to the rushing waters of Chico Creek, this city is intertwined with nature. Growing out of downtown, Bidwell Park stretches for 10 glorious miles northwest along the creek. Several classic movie scenes have been shot here, including from *Gone with the Wind* and *The Adventures of Robin Hood*.

The upper park is an untamed oasis, with miles of trails weaving along creek banks, between basalt rock formations and across meadows dusted in spring wildflowers. Bidwell is also full of swimming spots for hot Chico days. You'll find pools at One-Mile and Five-Mile recreation areas, and swimming holes in Upper Bidwell Park, north of Manzanita Ave.

BRYAN RAMSEY/SHUTTERSTOCK

Bidwell Park, Chico

California State University, Chico make it one of Sacramento Valley's most attractive hubs. Folks mingle late here in the restaurants and bars, which open onto patios when it's warm.

All ages will delight in **Shubert's Ice Cream & Candy** *(shuberts.com)*, a beloved old-time shop where five generations of Shuberts have produced delicious homemade ice cream, chocolates and confections.

Though the city – like the rest of the valley – wilts in the summer heat, the swimming holes in impressive **Bidwell Park** *(chico.ca.us)* offer an escape, as does floating down the gentle Sacramento River. The park stretches 10 miles northwest of downtown with lush groves and miles of trails.

Tour with a Brewmaster

Chico's iconic brewery

For many, Chico's top attraction has pilgrimage status: this is the home of the legendary **Sierra Nevada Brewing Company** *(sierranevada.com)*. Founded in 1979, the brewery was one of the pioneers of the craft-beer revolution. Today Sierra Nevada continues to try out new styles of beer at the various taprooms at its huge brewery complex near Hwy 99. Take a self-guided tour or go for one of the deep-immersion (not literally) sessions with a brewmaster. Soak up the suds in the excellent restaurant.

DRINKING IN CHICO: OUR PICKS

Secret Trail Brewing: Unassuming brewery away from downtown with a small, energetic taproom, live music Fridays and food trucks outside. *3-7pm Tue-Thu, noon-7pm Fri-Sun*

Roselle Bar & Lounge: Elegant cocktail bar in a nightlife area east of the center. Classy bar food and DJ nights. *4-10pm Wed-Fri, 11am-midnight Sat, 11am-4pm Sun*

Tender Loving Coffee: Craft-roasted coffee and big vegan breakfasts from this community hub near radical Pageant Theatre. *8am-2pm Tue-Sun*

Sierra Nevada Brewing Company: Hordes of fans gather at the birthplace of Sierra Nevada Pale Ale and Schwarber, a Chico-only black ale. *11am-4pm Sun-Thu, to 5:30pm Fri & Sat*

Los Angeles & the Deserts

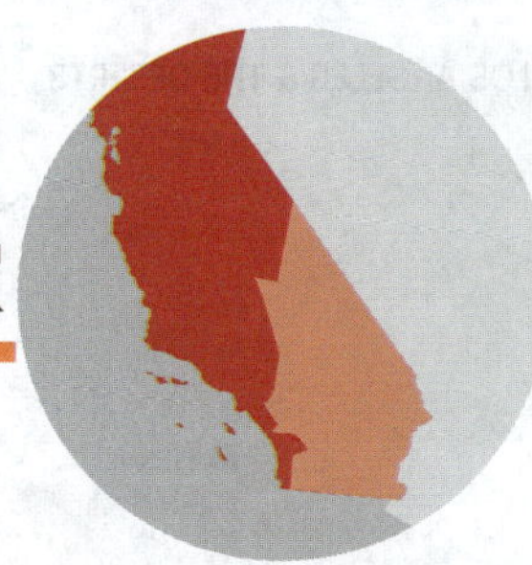

CINEMATIC CITY | OUTSTANDING ART | DESERT DREAMS

Los Angeles means many things to many people. It is a city of dreams but has too much traffic. It enjoys perfect weather but there are so many mountain fires. It has the best golden-hour sunsets but the smog is terrible. All these things ring true about this enormous city in Southern California, and one thing is absolutely for sure – nothing beats the pulsating, vivacious flair of Los Angeles. LA is also a kaleidoscope of cultures from around 140 countries, with nearly 220 languages spoken, creating an intricate web of diversity that connects deep beneath the surface. It is a place of acceptance, and what makes LA truly shine is the diversity of its people, who uniquely come together as one. Beyond the City of Angels, California's vast desert landscapes await adventurous souls with geologically diverse trails, environmental art, dark starry skies and the ever-sunny culture of Palm Springs.

GETTING AROUND

Los Angeles is vast and not walking-friendly, so traveling by car or public transportation – Metro buses, DASH buses and Metro Rail trains – is recommended, though avoid the freeways between 5pm and 7pm. Dockless scooters with Lime and Bird are also a great way to buzz around. A car or recreational vehicle (RV) is the best way for getting around the deserts; the parks encompass thousands of square miles and are not served by public transportation.

Hollywood's Galaxy of Stars

Follow the Walk of Fame

Jennifer Lopez, Bob Hope, Marilyn Monroe and Aretha Franklin are among stars being sought out, worshipped, photographed and stepped on along the **Hollywood Walk of Fame** (*walkoffame.com*). Or, in the case of many names, pondered over, since production staff and writers are also honored. They've been adding the brass and pink-terrazzo stars since 1960.

Follow the galaxy along Hollywood Blvd between La Brea Ave and Gower St, and on Vine St between Yucca St and Sunset Blvd. At least 30 new stars are added a year and the ceremonies often draw famous faces. Check the website for the schedule.

TOP TIP

Los Angeles is known for perpetual sunshine. But come the evenings the temperatures can dip dramatically. Pack a pullover for your nocturnal LA adventures.

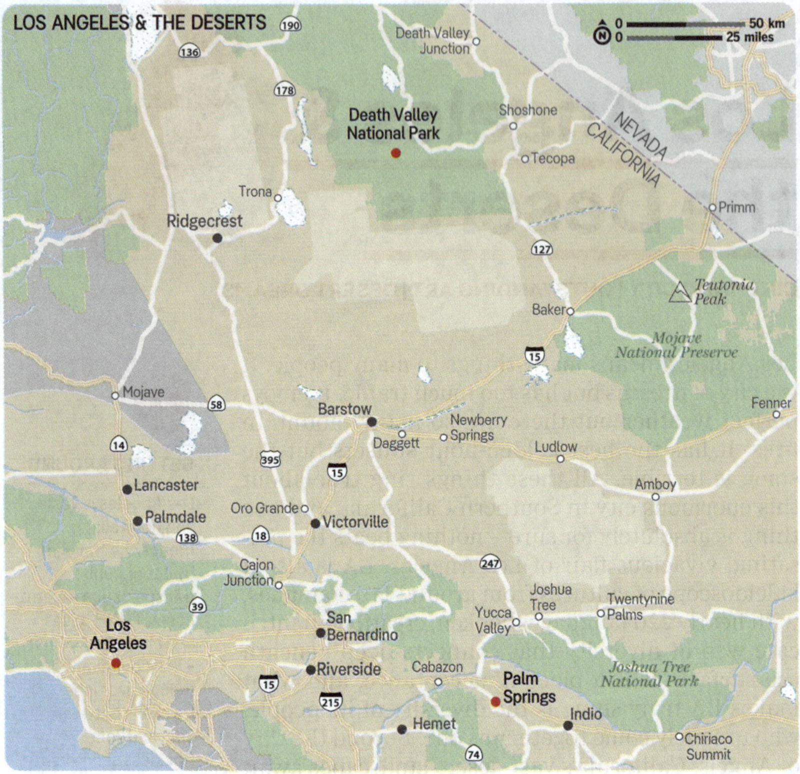

LOS ANGELES & THE DESERTS

Death Valley Junction
Death Valley National Park
Shoshone
Tecopa
NEVADA
CALIFORNIA
Primm
Trona
Ridgecrest
Teutonia Peak
Baker
Mojave National Preserve
Mojave
Barstow
Newberry Springs
Daggett
Fenner
Ludlow
Amboy
Lancaster
Palmdale
Oro Grande
Victorville
Cajon Junction
Joshua Tree
Twentynine Palms
Yucca Valley
San Bernardino
Los Angeles
Riverside
Cabazon
Palm Springs
Joshua Tree National Park
Indio
Hemet
Chiriaco Summit
0 50 km
0 25 miles

An Icon Was Born

Spot the Hollywood Sign

Perched at the top of Mt Lee in the Hollywood Hills is the iconic **Hollywood Sign** *(hollywoodsign.org)*. The story goes that *Los Angeles Times* publisher and real estate developer Harry Chandler erected the sign in 1923 (back then it said 'Hollywoodland') as a way to advertise luxury homes in the hills. What was only supposed to be there for 18 months became a permanent landmark that has come to symbolize a place, an industry and a mythology.

Three hiking trails lead to the sign: Brush Canyon Trail, Mt Hollywood Trail and Cahuenga Peak Trail.

DRINKING IN HOLLYWOOD: OUR PICKS

Frolic Room: Anything goes at this dive that's served everyone from Judy Garland to Charles Bukowski. Toast the fabulous cartoon mural. *11am-2am*

Harvard & Stone: Lures partiers with bands, DJs and burlesque troops working their saucy magic. It's ski lodge meets steampunk factory, with a rockabilly soul. *9pm-2am*

Bar Lis: Hollywood's all around the rooftop lounge of the hip Thompson Hollywood. There's a bit of a posh Med vibe (Cannes, anyone?). *6pm-midnight*

Tabula Rasa Bar: Away from the glitz, this unpretentious wine bar gets everything right with well-picked tunes and regular live gigs. Rear terrace. *2pm-midnight*

Hollywood's Last Great Studio

Tour Paramount Studios

Indiana Jones, *The Godfather* and the *Ironman* series are among the blockbusters that originated at **Paramount Pictures**, the country's second-oldest movie studio (1914) and the only major one still in Hollywood proper. Two-hour **golf-cart tours** *(paramountstudiotour.com; from $69)* of the studio complex are offered year-round, taking in the back lots and sound stages. Passionate, knowledgeable guides offer fascinating insights into the studio's history and the movie-making process in general.

Observe LA!

And the universe from the Griffith Observatory

The universe aside, the rooftop viewing platform of the **Griffith Observatory** *(griffithobservatory.org; free)* offers unparalleled views of LA and the Hollywood Hills. The art deco observatory has made cameos in numerous movies and TV shows, among them *La La Land*, *Terminator*, *24* and *Alias*. The film it's most associated with, however, remains *Rebel Without a Cause*, commemorated with a bust of James Dean on the west side of the observatory lawn. Inside, there's a planetarium and all sorts of unmissable exhibits on the cosmos.

Finding parking can be akin to finding life on another planet. It's best to arrive on a weekday before noon. Otherwise, especially on weekends, try hiking up the hillside from Los Feliz (it *is* a great trail). Or, take the DASH Observatory/Los Feliz shuttle bus from the Vermont/Sunset metro station.

Famed Film Locations in Griffith Park

Hike to Bronson Caves

With more than 50 miles of trails, Griffith Park is LA's great hub of hiking, accessible from all directions and offering all types of experiences. A good start is the family-friendly short (0.7 miles one way) jaunt up **Bronson Canyon** off Canyon Dr to **Bronson Caves**. The latter are legit stars: among many appearances, they were the Bat Cave in the old *Batman* TV series and were the climactic location in the still-relevant *Invasion of the Body Snatchers* (1956). From here, more challenging trails lead to sights like the Hollywood Sign.

BEST FILMS ABOUT HOLLYWOOD

Sunset Boulevard (1950): Director and screenwriter Billy Wilder at his best, plumbing the dark side of fame and Hollywood's delusions.

The Player (1992): Robert Altman brings decades of experience on the front lines to this biting satire about the moral rot at the heart of studio execs.

La La Land (2016): Timeless musical of plucky kids hoping to make it big in Hollywood.

The Artist (2011): Won the Oscar for Best Picture for its story of the often-brutal late-1920s transition from silent pictures to talkies.

A Star Is Born: Pick your version (1937, 1954, 1976, 2018) of the classic drama about fame and tragedy.

EATING & DRINKING IN LOS FELIZ: OUR PICKS

Figaro Bistrot: A culinary ménage à trois involving a boulangerie, bistro and lounge, Figaro channels Paris with heavy mirrors, sidewalk tables and Gallic-inspired fare. *8am-midnight* **$$**

House of Pies: Indomitable survivor of a chain that once swept California, the House serves top diner fare plus its namesake desserts in myriad flavors. *7am-1am* **$$**

Covell: Over 150 wines by the glass, showcasing interesting producers, unusual grapes and lesser-known regions. Barkeeps are generous with tastings. *4pm-midnight*

Tiki-Ti: Channeling Waikiki since 1961, this tiny tropical tavern packs in everyone from stylish slummers to 'non-ironic' partiers in Hawaiian shirts. *6pm-midnight Wed-Sat*

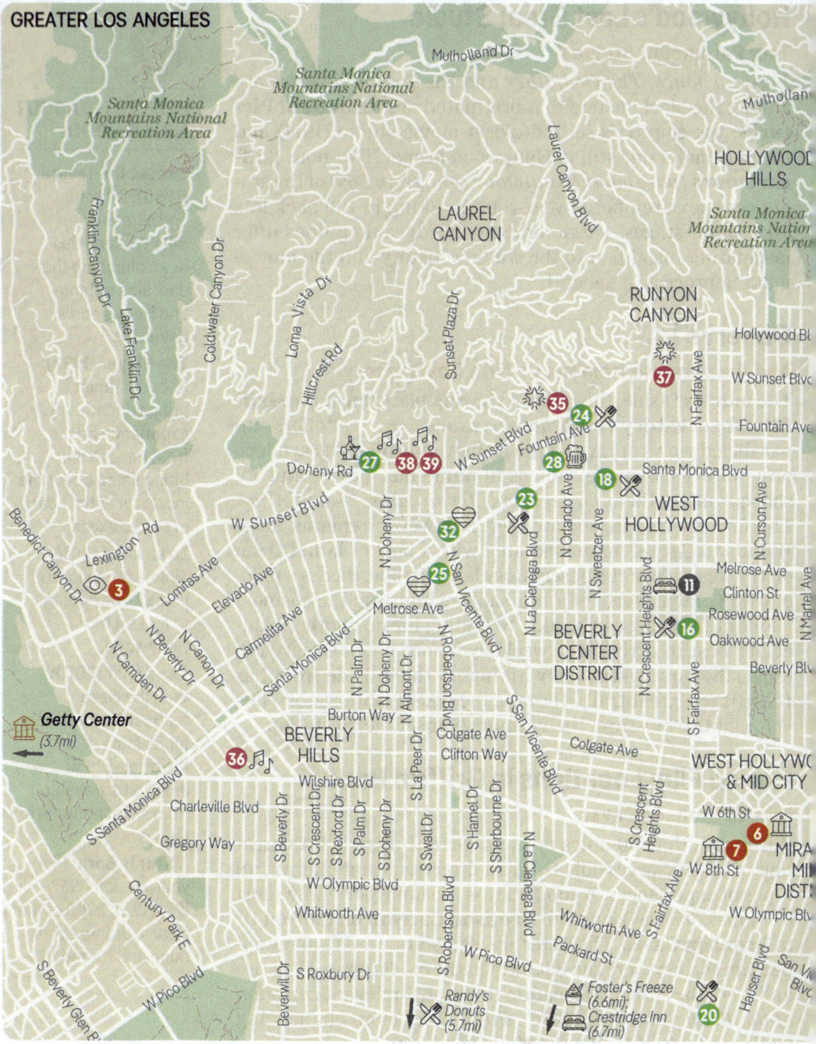

GREATER LOS ANGELES

Mulholland Dr
Santa Monica Mountains National Recreation Area
Santa Monica Mountains National Recreation Area
Mulholland
HOLLYWOOD HILLS
Santa Monica Mountains National Recreation Area
LAUREL CANYON
Laurel Canyon Blvd
Franklin Canyon Dr
Lake Franklin Dr
Coldwater Canyon Dr
Loma Vista Dr
Hillcrest Rd
Sunset Plaza Dr
RUNYON CANYON
Hollywood Bl
W Sunset Blvd
N Fairfax Ave
Fountain Ave
Doheny Rd
W Sunset Blvd
Fountain Ave
Santa Monica Blvd
WEST HOLLYWOOD
W Sunset Blvd
N Doheny Dr
N Orlando Ave
N Sweetzer Ave
N Curson Ave
Benedict Canyon Dr
Lexington Rd
Lomitas Ave
Elevado Ave
Carmelita Ave
N La Cienega Blvd
N San Vicente Blvd
Melrose Ave
Melrose Ave
Clinton St
Rosewood Ave
Oakwood Ave
Beverly Blv
N Crescent Heights Blvd
N Martel Ave
BEVERLY CENTER DISTRICT
N Beverly Dr
N Canon Dr
N Camden Dr
Santa Monica Blvd
N Palm Dr
N Doheny Dr
N Almont Dr
N Robertson Blvd
S Fairfax Ave
Getty Center (3.7mi)
Burton Way
BEVERLY HILLS
S La Peer Dr
Colgate Ave
Clifton Way
S San Vicente Blvd
Colgate Ave
WEST HOLLYWOOD & MID CITY
Wilshire Blvd
S Santa Monica Blvd
Charleville Blvd
Gregory Way
S Beverly Dr
S Crescent Dr
S Rexford Dr
S Palm Dr
S Doheny Dr
S Swall Dr
S Hamel Dr
S Sherbourne Dr
N La Cienega Blvd
S Crescent Heights Blvd
W 6th St
W 8th St
MIRA MI DIST
W Olympic Blvd
W Olympic Blv
Century Park E
Whitworth Ave
S Robertson Blvd
La Cienega Blvd
Whitworth Ave
S Fairfax Ave
W Pico Blvd
Packard St
S Beverly Glen Bl
W Pico Blvd
Beverwil Dr
S Roxbury Dr
Randy's Donuts (5.7mi)
Foster's Freeze (6.6mi); Crestridge Inn (6.7mi)
Hauser Blvd
San Vi Blvd

HIGHLIGHTS
1 Griffith Observatory
2 Paramount Pictures

SIGHTS
3 Beverly Hills Hotel
4 Disney's First Studio
5 Hollywood Walk of Fame
6 La Brea Tar Pits & Museum
7 LACMA
8 Snow White Cottages

ACTIVITIES
9 Bronson Canyon
10 Bronson Caves

SLEEPING
11 Banana Bungalows Hotel & Hostel West Hollywood
12 Highland Gardens Hotel
13 Hollywood Roosevelt
14 Hotel Normandie LA
15 Silver Lake Pool & Inn

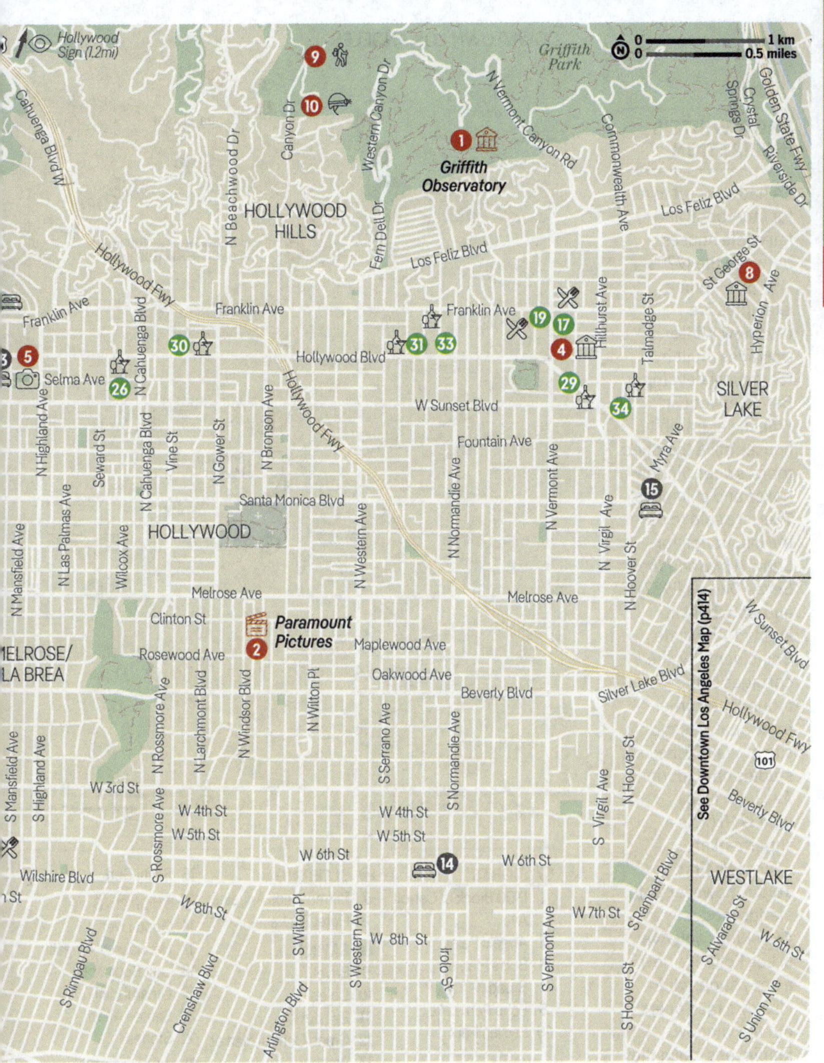
Hollywood Sign (1.2mi)
Griffith Park
Griffith Observatory
Paramount Pictures
HOLLYWOOD HILLS
HOLLYWOOD
SILVER LAKE
MELROSE/ LA BREA
WESTLAKE
Los Feliz Blvd
Franklin Ave
Hollywood Blvd
W Sunset Blvd
Fountain Ave
Santa Monica Blvd
Melrose Ave
Beverly Blvd
Wilshire Blvd
Hollywood Fwy
Silver Lake Blvd
See Downtown Los Angeles Map (p414)

EATING
16 Canter's
17 Figaro Bistrot
18 Hamburger Mary's
19 House of Pies
20 My 2 Cents LA
21 Pink's Hot Dogs
22 République
23 Tail O' the Pup
24 Tower Bar
DRINKING & NIGHTLIFE
25 Abbey
26 Bar Lis
27 Bar Next Door
28 Barney's Beanery
29 Covell
30 Frolic Room
31 Harvard & Stone
32 Micky's WeHo
33 Tabula Rasa Bar
34 Tiki-Ti
ENTERTAINMENT
35 Comedy Store
36 Jazz Café at Cipriani Beverly Hills
37 Laugh Factory
38 Roxy Theatre
39 Whisky-a-Go-Go

SNOW WHITE'S INSPIRATION

LA had a secret love for storybook and fairy-tale houses between the 1920s and '30s – prime examples are the **Snow White Cottages**. Built by fantastical developer Ben Sherwood in 1931, the eight white houses have thatched roofs, sweet window boxes and chimneys. They are said to be the inspiration for *Snow White and the Seven Dwarfs* (1937) and were built in ersatz Tudor style. Coincidentally, the cottages stand just around the corner from what was the site of Walt Disney's studios on Hyperion Ave from 1926 until 1940 (now a supermarket).

Disney's first studio, however, still stands modestly at 4647 Kingswell Ave in Los Feliz. It's now a copy shop, where Mickey's face peers out the window. Employees claim they sense the ghost of Walt every day.

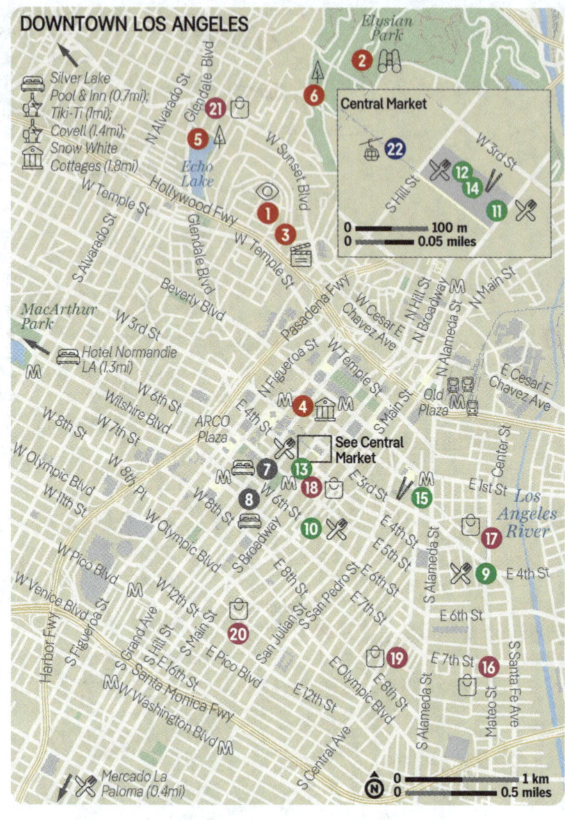

SIGHTS
1 1300 Block of Carroll Ave
2 Angels Point
3 Bob's Market
4 Broad
5 Echo Park Lake
65 Elysian Park

SLEEPING
7 Biltmore Los Angeles
8 Hotel Per La

EATING
9 Bavel
10 Cole's
11 Eggslut
12 Grand Central Market
13 Perch
14 Sticky Rice
15 Sushi Gen

SHOPPING
16 Good Liver
17 Hennessey + Ingalls
18 Last Bookstore
19 Omami Mini
20 Santee Alley
21 Stories

TRANSPORT
22 Angels Flight

EATING IN DOWNTOWN: BEST HIGHER-END PLACES

Sushi Gen: Grab a lunch seat in Little Tokyo; chefs carve slabs of the freshest fish. Dinner is less frenetic. *11am-2pm & 5-8:30pm Tue-Sat* **$$**

Perch: Two elevators get you to this French rooftop bar-restaurant on the vintage Pershing Square Building. Bewitching Manhattan-esque views. *4pm-1am* **$$**

Bavel: Sleek, loud and showered in cascading vines, come here for phenomenal, modern takes on Middle Eastern classics. Fine cocktails. *5-11pm* **$$$**

Cole's: Dark, time-warped tavern, claims progeny (with Philippe) of the French dip sandwich. Great time-warp bar area and cocktails. *3pm-midnight* **$$**

Downtown's Striking Museum

Be dazzled at the Broad

Rapidly evolving, DTLA (Downtown LA's preferred moniker) is the city's most intriguing patch, where cutting-edge architecture and killer modern-art museums contrast sharply with blaring mariachi tunes. The **Broad** *(thebroad.org; free)* is a must-visit for contemporary-art fans ('Broad' rhymes with 'road'). It houses the world-class collection of local philanthropist and billionaire Eli Broad and his wife, Edythe, with more than 2000 postwar pieces by dozens of heavy hitters, including Cindy Sherman, Jeff Koons, Andy Warhol, Roy Lichtenstein, Robert Rauschenberg, Keith Haring and Kara Walker. The striking museum is popular, so secure your free entrance time online.

Taste Grand Central Market

A global culinary feast

Designed by prolific architect John Parkinson and once home to an office occupied by Frank Lloyd Wright, LA's beaux-arts **Grand Central Market** *(grandcentralmarket.com)* has been satisfying appetites since 1917 and today is DTLA's always-busy hub of food culture (opening hours vary). Lose yourself in its bustle of neon signs, stalls and counters, peddling everything from fresh produce and nuts, to sizzling Thai street food at **Sticky Rice**, hipster breakfasts at **Eggslut** and modern deli classics, artisanal pasta and specialty coffee.

For a digestive interlude, exit and cross S Hill St for a quick ride on **Angels Flight** *(angelsflight.org; $1)*, the famous, short funicular up to Bunker Hill and yet another local star of many a production.

Soaring Folk Art

Marvel at the Watts Towers

The three 'Gothic' (or is it Gaudí-esque?) spires of the fabulous **Watts Towers** *(wattstowers.org; tour adult/child $7/3)* rank among the world's greatest monuments of folk art. In 1921, Italian immigrant Simon Rodia set out to 'make something big' and then spent 33 years cobbling together this whimsical free-form sculpture from concrete, steel and a motley assortment of found objects: from green 7Up bottles to seashells, tiles, rocks and pottery. The towers reach up to 99.5ft in height, just below the city's legal limit of 100ft.

DOWNTOWN'S BEST SHOPPING

Last Bookstore: LA's largest new-and-used bookstore. Rare tomes, terrific vinyl, good prices and staff recs. *(lastbookstorela.com)*

Omami Mini: In Row DTLA, fashion-forward clothing for under-12s (though it's really aimed at parents). Lots of comfy cottonwear. *(omamimini.com)*

Hennessey + Ingalls: Arts District new-and-used bookstore focusing on design, from architecture and landscaping to photography and fashion. Good set design section. *(hennesseyingalls.com)*

Good Liver: Carefully curated space with beautiful objects you're unlikely to find elsewhere, each displayed with its story. *(good-liver.com)*

Santee Alley: Scores of alley vendors with bargains in clothing and eyewear between Santee St and Maple Ave from Olympic Blvd to 12th St.

EATING IN SOUTH LA: TOP CHOICES FOR A QUICK BITE

Mercado La Paloma: A quick walk under I-110 from Expo Park, fabulous food hall has everything from Yucatan cuisine to Thai. *9am-9pm* $

Patria Coffee Roasters: Only a block from Compton's City Hall, this art-filled coffeehouse is a standout for top-end coffee drinks. Next to a park. *8am-3pm* $

Foster's Freeze: Time-warp Inglewood ice cream emporium that hasn't changed in decades. Order a hot fudge sundae and enjoy it at a picnic table. *10am-8pm* $

Randy's Donuts: Famously excellent doughnuts are your first or last memory of LA going to/from LAX. Simplest flavors, like glazed old-fashioned, are best. *24hr* $

DISPLAYING ART IN A NEW WAY

LACMA's new building is the bold vision of Swiss architect Peter Zumthor, who is known for his works on cultural and social service institutions. The curvaceous, airy, cantilevered galleries straddle Wilshire Blvd. Floor-to-ceiling windows will make the most of LA's natural beauty, highlighting its hills and celebrated natural light.

Inside, LACMA's curators have challenged themselves to utterly rethink how their huge and rich collection is displayed. They want to dispense with the Eurocentric and chronological narrative that dominates art museums and instead show how works spanning mediums, cultures and time interrelate. As they readily admit in interviews, this new paradigm is a 'challenge.' Debate about their efforts will undoubtedly be vigorous, beginning with the new building's opening in 2026.

Compton's Anthem

See the site of 'Not Like Us'

West Coast rap and hip-hop have been part of Southern California since NWA's 1988 album *Straight Outta Compton* launched the careers of Eazy E, Ice Cube and Dr Dre, and established gangsta rap.

Jump ahead and Compton remains relevant as megastar Kendrick Lamar showed in 2024 with his music video for 'Not Like Us.' Viewed millions of times, it features scenes shot at the striking modernist **Martin Luther King Memorial** on the wide open plaza at **Compton City Hall**.

Lamar invited Compton to show up for the shoot and they did. The results are joyous, vivacious. It's worth visiting the location while watching the video on your phone. After, cross S Acacia Ave and see what's on at the **Compton Art & History Museum** *(comptonmuseum.org; adult/child $5/3)*.

A Stunning New Home for Art

Take in the wealth at LACMA

Soaring across Wilshire Blvd, the new **LACMA** *(Los Angeles County Museum of Art; lacma.org; adult/child $28/13)* is set to open for visitors by mid-2026. The $720 million David Geffen Galleries will replace the museum's four aging buildings.

As well as millennia worth of stunning global treasures, permanent collection highlights include Chris Burden's outdoor installation *Urban Light* (a surreal selfie backdrop of hundreds of vintage LA streetlamps). Two other works are iconic LA: *Mulholland Drive* by David Hockney and *105 Freeway* by Catherine Opie.

LACMA's Zen-like Pavilion for Japanese Art houses pieces ranging in origin from 3000 BCE to the 21st century.

Smell the Ice Age

Get stuck on the La Brea Tar Pits

Mammoths, saber-toothed cats and other critters roamed LA's savanna in prehistoric times. The **La Brea Tar Pits & Museum** *(tarpits.org; adult/child $18/7)* preserve a trove of skulls and bones and are one of the world's most famous fossil sites. Generations of young dino hunters have come to learn about paleontology in the museum.

Outside, the smell of asphalt permeates the air as the tar pits still bubble away, and beloved models show mammoths stuck in the gooey crude oil bubbling up from deep below

EATING IN MIRACLE MILE & FAIRFAX: OUR PICKS

République: Artisan bakery, light-filled cafe and buzzing bistro with daily-changing French-accented dishes. Great desserts. *8am-2pm & 5:30-10pm* $$

Canter's: This veteran deli isn't closed despite appearances. Legendary pastrami and other standards. Comfy booths, knowing servers and parking. *6am-11:30pm* $$

My 2 Cents LA: The acclaimed restaurant of TV chef Alisa Reynolds has a loyal, A-lister following for Southern fusion fare. Book ahead. *11:30am-9:30pm Thu-Sun* $$$

Pink's Hot Dogs: Famous doggeria (since 1939) with slow-moving lines thanks to the droves who descend for garlicky all-beef frankfurters drenched in chili. *9:30am-midnight* $

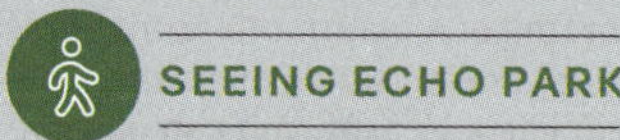

SEEING ECHO PARK

From old Victorians to an iconic lake, Echo Park is a star on screen and off. Its shops and views are bonuses.

START	END	LENGTH
Bob's Market	Angels Point	3.1 miles; 3 hours

Begin at ❶ **Bob's Market** (1913), aka Toretto's Market & Deli, owned by Vin Diesel's character in the *Fast & Furious* franchise. Look for the shelf of merch. It was also in *LA Confidential*.

Walk uphill to Angelino Heights, established in the mid-1880s as one of LA's first suburbs. Its most charming street is ❷ **1300 Block of Carroll Ave**, home to the city's largest concentration of Victorian-era homes. A few house numbers of note: 1300 is the grandest on the block; 1316 captures the look of the 1880s with its old-style drapes; 1329 is the most original and was Halliwell Manor in the TV series *Charmed*; 1330 has Asian details like the lion dogs below the arch; and 1337 is the oldest house on the block (1872).

Walk down via Bellevue Ave to ❸ **Echo Park Lake**, anchor of the lovely, namesake park. Rent a swan-shaped pedal boat. One block of Sunset Blvd has a thicket of cool retail like the literature-rich ❹ **Stories** and the indescribable Time Travel Mart. You won't regret a minute you spend inside.

Walk north up Portia St and use your map app to wander through leafy ❺ **Elysian Park** and up to ❻ **Angels Point**. Under towering public art, you'll enjoy uncommon views of LA, including Dodger Stadium, Downtown and Hollywood.

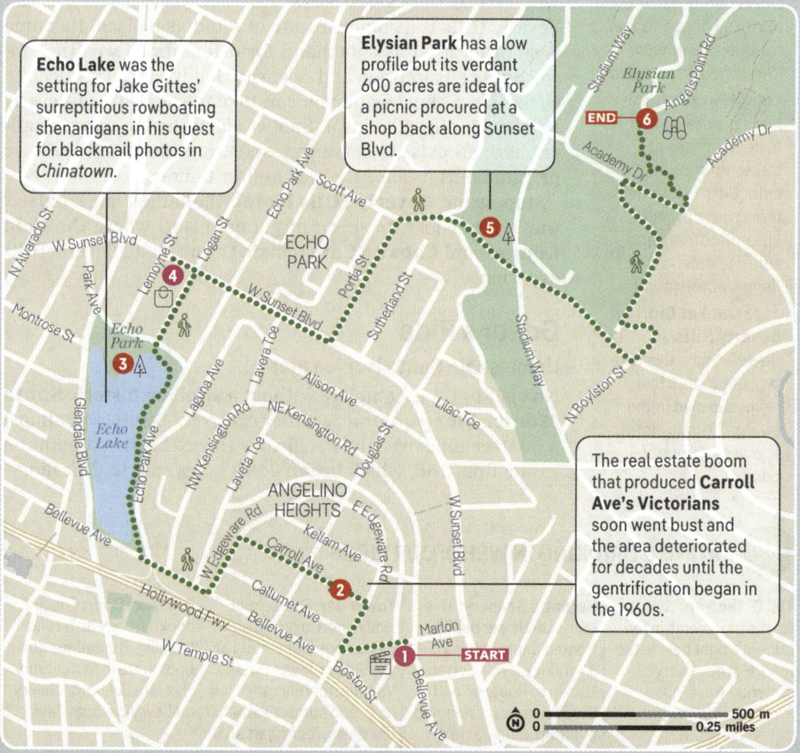

Echo Lake was the setting for Jake Gittes' surreptitious rowboating shenanigans in his quest for blackmail photos in *Chinatown*.

Elysian Park has a low profile but its verdant 600 acres are ideal for a picnic procured at a shop back along Sunset Blvd.

The real estate boom that produced **Carroll Ave's Victorians** soon went bust and the area deteriorated for decades until the gentrification began in the 1960s.

WEHO'S BEST LIVE PERFORMANCES

Whisky-a-Go-Go: The Whisky trades on its legend status when the Doors were the house band and go-go dancing was invented here back in the '60s. *(whiskyagogo.com)*

Roxy Theatre: A Sunset Strip fixture since 1973, this small venue puts you close to the bands. The lineup varies, with some big-names. *(theroxy.com)*

Comedy Store: The club with cred. Richard Pryor, George Carlin, Eddie Murphy, Robin Williams and David Letterman were nurtured here and the tradition continues. *(thecomedystore.com)*

Laugh Factory: The Marx Brothers used to keep offices at this long-standing club. Gets big names trying out new sets, up-and-comers and surprise celebs. *(laughfactory.com)*

Jazz Café at Cipriani Beverly Hills: In Beverly Hills, this luxe jazz bar caters to a refined crowd in the swank Cipriani Hotel. Top acts. *(cipriani.com)*

Wilshire Blvd. A life-size diorama of a mammoth family dramatizes the cruel fate of countless thousands of animals between 50,000 and 10,000 years ago. Nearby, you can observe pits where fossils are still being discovered.

Do the West Hollywood Walk

A neighborhood like no other

Santa Monica Boulevard is the main drag of West Hollywood (WeHo) and bar-hopping its length is one of the LA region's great joys. The LGBTIQ+-centric bars and clubs heave through the weekends, with Sunday brunch being a must, while weeknights are busy as well.

Central to WeHo is one of the most iconic gay nightclubs on the West Coast today, the **Abbey**, which serves the community as much as a cultural center as a bar and nightclub. With over three decades in the game, it's been called the best gay bar in the world. It's open from 11am to 2am daily.

The boulevard abounds with choices like the iconic **Micky's Weho**, with long-running drag shows. It's open noon to 2am. **Hamburger Mary's** is the Sunday afternoon brunch go-to; it's open from 11am to 10pm.

If You Were Rich & Famous

The Beverly Hills experience

Beverly Hills is as much a state of mind as a place. Its name is so often used as shorthand for ostentatious wealth, conspicuous consumption and celebrity that it can get reduced to cliché. On a short walk, you can take in the heart of Beverly Hills, including Rodeo Dr. Spoiler alert: the big-name retailers here all exist to serve free-spending tourists; they have private boutiques for the rich and/or famous.

Stop at the **Beverly Hills Hotel**, the famed 'pink palace' that's never lost its sheen of glamour and where the **Polo Lounge** and **Cabana Cafe** remain the ultimate Beverly Hills experience.

Go for a Ride

Unmissable Santa Monica Pier

No visit to LA is complete without a stroll on historic **Santa Monica Pier** *(santamonicapier.org; free)*. Stretching almost a quarter-mile over the Pacific, it's the exclamation point on iconic Route 66, which began 2400 miles east in Chicago.

EATING & DRINKING IN WEHO: OUR PICKS

Tail O' the Pup: Look for the big weenie in the bun – it's right beside the road. Hot dogs served in myriad ways. *noon-10pm* $

Barney's Beanery: This burger and beer bar has fronted Santa Monica Blvd since it was better known as Route 66 and Studebaker cars steamed out front. *11am-2am* $$

Tower Bar: Old-school Hollywood luxury in an indoor-outdoor setting at the Sunset Tower Hotel. Vaunted martinis and high-end burgers to match the views. *7am-10pm* $$$

Bar Next Door: Enticing cocktail bar with a solid backlist of creations going back more than a century. Has rare libations; cheery, mellow vibe. *5pm-2am*

NORTHSKY FILMS/SHUTTERSTOCK

Venice Boardwalk

Dating to 1908, the pier is the city's most compelling landmark. Every angle is dominated by **Pacific Park** *(pacpark.com; rides from $8)* amusement park and its family-friendly arcades, carnival games, soaring Ferris wheel and tame roller coaster. Nearby is a vintage 1922 carousel and an aquarium. The pier is most photogenic when framed by California sunsets and when it comes alive with free concerts and outdoor movies in the summertime.

Living Life on the Sand

Venice's beach and boardwalk

Prepare for a sensory overload on the **Venice Boardwalk**, one of LA's essential experiences. Buff bodybuilders brush elbows with street performers and sellers of sunglasses, ribald underwear, Mexican ponchos and cannabis, while cyclists and in-line skaters whiz by on the bike path, and skateboarders and graffiti sprayers get their own domains.

BEACHES FROM SANTA MONICA TO MALIBU

El Matador State Beach: Park on the bluffs and stroll down to sandstone towers rising from emerald coves. Dolphins breach the surface beyond the waves.

Zuma Beach: Easily accessed from the PCH (and Metro bus), with parking and long stretches of sand. Find privacy in the southeast at Pirate's Cove.

Malibu Lagoon State Beach: Where Malibu Creek meets the ocean, migratory birds proliferate, attracting human spotters. To the north are popular surf breaks.

Will Rogers State Beach: The quiet alternative to the famous strands to the south. This is the beach used for *Baywatch* and dozens of other productions.

Santa Monica State Beach: There are endless ways (volleyball's big!) to enjoy this 3.5-mile stretch of sand, running seamlessly into Venice Beach in the south.

EATING IN SANTA MONICA & VENICE: OUR PICKS

Bay Cities Italian Deli & Bakery: In Santa Monica, this is LA's best Italian deli, period. Signature sandwich: the spicy Godmother. *9am-6pm Wed-Sun* $

Santa Monica Farmers Markets: Explore one of Santa Monica's outdoor farmers markets stocked with a vast bounty. *8am-1pm Wed & Sat* $

Café Gratitude: Cutting-edge Venice vegan dishes are paired with an open patio and sea breezes. It's sustainable, locavore, organic and always surprising. *10am-9pm* $$

Gjusta: A very local bakery, cafe and deli behind a nondescript storefront on a hidden Venice side street. Great patio. Food to go is ideal for picnics. *7am-4pm* $$

TOP EXPERIENCE

Getty Center

Straddling a hilltop in the Santa Monica Mountains off the 405, the palatial Getty Center offers an irresistible feast of art, design and botanical beauty. Ponder the myths and landscapes of Dossi, Van Gogh and Cézanne, gaze out over the City of Angels and kick back in a verdant wonderland of gurgling water, lush lawns and world-famous sculptures.

TOP TIPS

- Visit early morning or mid-afternoon. Sunsets create a remarkable alchemy of light and shadow. Saturday nights are usually less crowded.
- Get the essential GettyGuide app. Free audioguides are available in the lobby. Bring photo ID.
- Consider bringing a picnic lunch to enjoy on the beautiful grounds.

PRACTICALITIES

- getty.edu
- free, timed entry reservation
- parking $25

Artistic Highlights

The Getty's collections focus on European art, with a concentration on works from the 19th and 20th centuries. There are genuine treasures here. In the east pavilion, seek out Gentileschi's *Danaë and the Shower of Gold* and Rembrandt's self-portrait, *Rembrandt Laughing*. In the west pavilion, look for Van Gogh's *Irises*, Monet's *Wheatstacks, Snow Effect, Morning*, Manet's *Jeanne (Spring)* and Turner's *Modern Rome – Campo Vaccino*. The south pavilion's outdoor terrace is home to Marino Marini's excitable bronze *Angel of the Citadel*, while the grounds themselves are studded with prized sculptures, including three works by Henry Moore.

Fossils & Gardens

The 16,000 tons of travertine cladding the Getty came from the same Italian quarry used for Rome's ancient Colosseum. Look closely to spot fossilized shells, fish and foliage. Don't miss the lovely Cactus Garden on the remote South Promontory for breathtaking city views.

Unmissable Events

Concerts, lectures, films and other cultural events for grown-ups keep the space buzzing with locals. Most are free, but some require reservations (or try standby). On Saturday evenings in summer, the center hosts Off the 405, a popular series featuring top progressive pop and world-music acts in the Getty courtyard.

VENICE & SOUTH COAST BEACHES

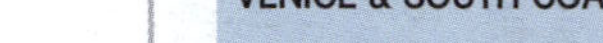

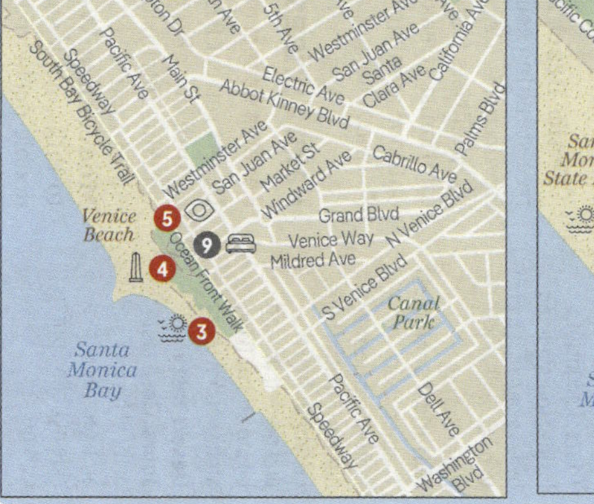

HIGHLIGHTS
1 Santa Monica Pier

SIGHTS
2 Santa Monica State Beach
3 Venice Beach
4 Venice Beach Art Walls
5 Venice Boardwalk

SLEEPING
6 Crestridge Inn
7 Georgian Hotel
8 HI Los Angeles Santa Monica Hostel
9 Samesun Venice Beach

EATING
10 Bay Cities Italian Deli & Bakery
11 Café Gratitude
12 Foster's Freeze
13 Gjusta
14 Randy's Donuts
15 Santa Monica Farmers Markets

ENTERTAINMENT
16 Pacific Park

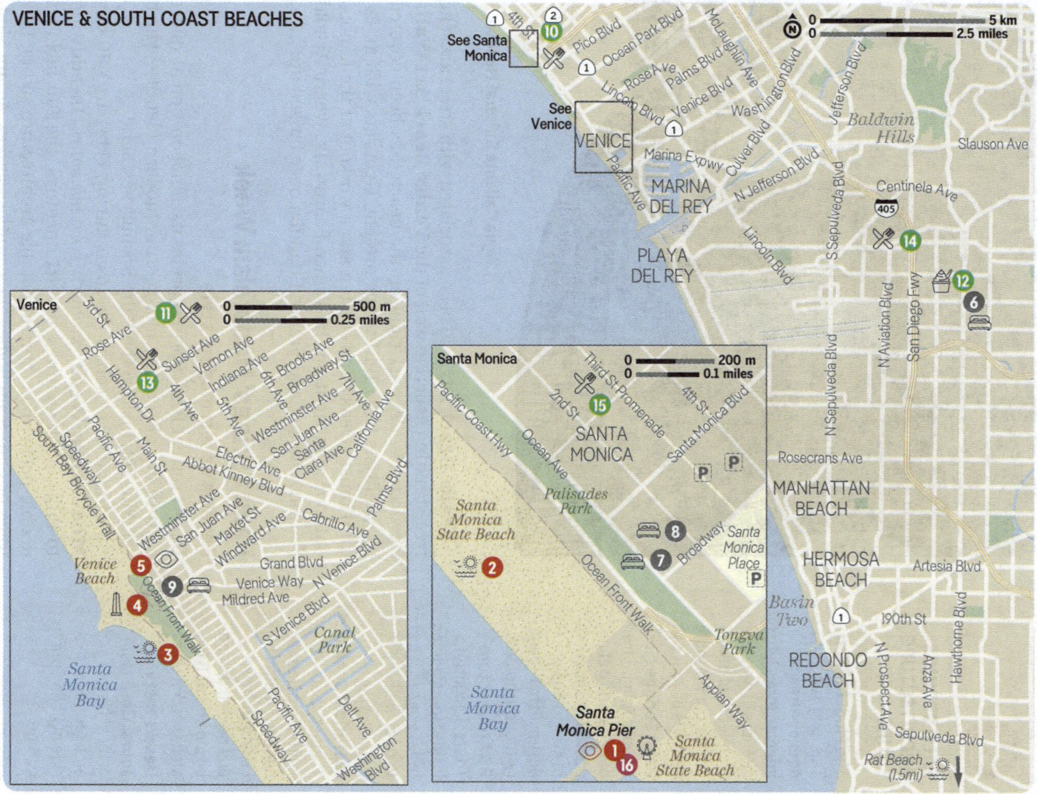

PALM SPRINGS ARCHITECTURE TOURS

The Modern Tour: This long-running agency arranges intimate looks into the interiors of notable architectural gems, in their comfortable vehicles or your own.

Palm Springs Mod Squad: Admire from outside, and get a peek at the interiors of meticulously designed mid-century-modern homes.

PS Architecture Tours: Insightful, insider tours guided by bike or car; it's best to book well ahead.

Palm Springs Historical Society: Themed tours featuring celebrity homes (Sinatra, Elvis, Elizabeth Taylor), and guided driving, biking and walking architectural tours.

Desert Tasty Tours: Get a taste of local history and architecture with a side of Palm Springs cuisine.

STEVE CUKROV/SHUTTERSTOCK

Agua Caliente Cultural Museum

Venice Beach has long been associated with street art. The free-standing concrete wall of the **Venice Beach Art Walls** *(veniceartwalls.com)*, right on the beach, has been covered by graffitists from 1961 to the present. Gym rats with an exhibitionist streak can get a tan and a workout at the famous outdoor gym right on the Venice Boardwalk, where Arnold Schwarzenegger and Franco Columbu once bulked up.

Palm Springs' Modernism Week

Revel in desert modern style

Desert retreat Palm Springs prides itself not only on its queer culture but also on its mid-century-modern identity, which remains intrinsic to the Palm Springs aesthetic.

Mid-mod fever seizes the town during February's 10-day **Modernism Week** *(modernismweek.com)*. In addition to talks, book signings and art openings, the fun includes double-decker bus tours of notable architecture sights, rare tours of significant homes and countless soirees. A mini Modernism Week pops up in October over a long weekend.

EATING IN PALM SPRINGS: OUR PICKS

Farm: Buzzy, relaxed, French-style simplicity. Breakfast and lunch are walk-in only; expect a wait. Reserve a table for prix-fixe dinner. *8am-2pm daily & 5:30-9:30pm Fri-Tue* $$

Rooster & the Pig: No reservations; arrive before opening and come hungry for Vietnamese fusion. Cocktails incorporating Asian twists perfectly complement the cuisine. *5-9pm Wed-Sun* $$

El Mirasol: Family-run Mexican restaurant whose mole and *pipián* make a spicy change of pace from your favorite standbys. *9am-9pm* $$

Barn Kitchen: Locally sourced ingredients prepared beautifully for fresh American cuisine, enjoyed in open-air elegance. *11am-9pm* $$

Otherwise, look out for the cantilever-roofed **Palm Springs Visitors Center**, the Mountain Station of the **Palm Springs Aerial Tramway** and the **Palm Springs Art Museum**.

Agua Caliente Cahuilla Culture

Explore Agua Caliente Cultural Museum

A wonderful way to learn about the history and culture of the Agua Caliente Band of Cahuilla Indians is at the **Agua Caliente Cultural Museum** *(accmuseum.org; adult/senior $10/5)* on North Indian Canyon Dr. Historical photographs, interactive displays and audio components bring to life the Indigenous experience of colonialism and its effect on the culture, but also spotlight living traditions and the natural history of the area.

The 'Agua Caliente' in the tribe's name speaks to one of its ancestral land's sacred treasures: the mineral hot springs known as Séc-he. In the larger plaza complex, the **Spa at Séc-he** *(thespaatseche.com)* welcomes guests to partake in these thermal waters. Book ahead for luxury spa treatments or relax with a day pass that includes a 15-minute private soak.

Remnants of Joshua Tree's Human History

Rock art and ruins

At the **Joshua Tree National Park** *(nps.gov/jotr; 7-day pass per car $30)*, the mostly flat, rewardingly varied **Barker Dam Loop Trail** journeys into this wonderful park's natural history: a little spur leads to a shallow cave full of petroglyphs.

An easy walk takes you to the well-preserved **Wall Street Mill**, passing ore-crushing ruins, the headstone of the unfortunate loser of a shootout and the **Desert Queen Well**, and continues to the crumbling pink ruins of **Wonderland Ranch**.

The ruins of **Ryan Ranch**, an easy half-mile walk from the road, are worth a look as the Ryan brothers incorporated gold dust into the adobe. At the park's southern end, it's a quarter-mile walk beyond the coolness of **Cottonwood Spring** to some trailside *metates* (grinding stones) left by the Cahuilla.

Hiking Joshua Tree's Varied Terrain

Follow classic JTree trails

If you're hiking with children, the **Discovery Trail** offers a bit of scrambling and informative interpretive signs and is a great park intro for grown-up kids as well. For

PLAN & PREPARE

All of the principles of **Leave No Trace** *(lnt.org/why/7-principles)* apply when visiting Joshua Tree National Park, but it's particularly important to plan ahead and prepare. Once you enter the park, there are zero services aside from vault toilets at trailheads and campgrounds, and running water only at the park entry points. Cell-phone service is nonexistent inside the park. Bring everything you'll need: plenty of water (at least a gallon per person for the day), salty snacks to keep your electrolytes balanced and layers so you can adjust to sudden weather changes. Have all of the survival basics so you can fully enjoy the spectacular desert environment.

EATING IN JTREE: PICNIC PROVISIONS

Campbell Hill Bakery: Superb pastries, soups, pizza and a line out the door in Twentynine Palms; check IG for current hours and arrive early. *6-9pm Thu-Sat* $

The Dez: Grab-and-go sandwiches, salads, charcuterie and coffee in Joshua Tree for your national park picnic. *6:30am-4pm* $

Desierto Alto: An excellent bottle shop with a well-rounded selection of picnic goodies and gift-worthy edibles. *7am-7pm* $

Joshua Tree Farmers Market: Both Twentynine Palms and Joshua Tree hold Saturday farmers markets. *8am-1pm* $

THE FIRST PEOPLE OF DEATH VALLEY

Timbisha Shoshone people lived in the Panamint Range for centuries, visiting the valley every winter to gather acorns, hunt waterfowl, catch pupfish in marshes and cultivate small areas of corn, squash and beans. After the federal government created Death Valley National Monument in 1933, the tribe was forced to move several times and was eventually restricted to a 40-acre village site. Years of protests and lobbying by tribal activists resulted in President Clinton signing the Timbisha Shoshone Homeland Act in 2000, transferring 7500 acres of land back to the tribe and creating the first Native American reservation inside a US national park. Today, a few dozen Timbisha live in the **Indian Village** near Furnace Creek.

classic bouldery Joshua Tree scenery, the 2.5-mile **Split Rock Loop** is another easy one, with a short spur leading to **Face Rock**.

Hikers wanting to gain elevation can head to the lesser-trafficked northwestern corner of the park, where the 6.5-mile **Panorama Loop** takes you through Joshua trees before rising into piñon-and-juniper forest atypical to most of the park. You'll find panoramic views of the Coachella and Yucca Valleys along the 1200ft climb.

Rambling & Scrambling in Death Valley

Day hiking in Death Valley

True, it's the lowest place in North America, at 282ft below sea level, the hottest place in the world, when it hit 128°F (53°C) in the summer of 2022, and the driest of the US national parks – but **Death Valley National Park** *(nps.gov/deva; 7-day pass per car $30)* is an amazing place to hike. Because of its brain-melting extremes, it's best to hike before 10am and after 4pm during the hottest seasons.

Flash floods are the reason that sinuously winding slot canyons like **Mosaic Canyon** even exist, and hikers have them to thank for this canyon's beautifully exposed layers of juxtaposed Noonday dolomite and Mosaic Canyon breccia (mudflow carbonates studded with inclusions of rock fragments).

A quite differently spectacular gallery of wondrous geology is **Golden Canyon**, off the northern end of Badwater Rd. Take the Golden Canyon–Gower Gulch loop that starts in a narrow slot and climbs along a towering golden wall before dropping you into the badlands visible from **Zabriskie Point**.

Desolation Canyon is another stunner, with splashes of pink, green and purple from iron oxides and chlorite, and the payoff of a beautiful view at the end. Some minor scrambling is involved. Finally, at **Ubehebe Crater**, a 1.5-mile hike around the rim gives you a fascinating look at the remains of a maar volcano, in which the meeting of magma and groundwater causes a steam explosion. In spring, desert flowers bloom in the pyroclastic pebbles.

Hiking Anza-Borrego Desert State Park

Nature trails and route-finding adventures

Many visitors to Anza-Borrego Desert State Park wind up hiking the **Borrego Palm Canyon Nature Trail** *(day use $10)*, but it's popular for good reason. The fun, easy trail ends

EATING IN DEATH VALLEY: OUR PICKS

Panamint Springs Resort: An inclusive, sunny saloon ambience and good food; this spot is a welcome stop on the park's western end. *7am-9pm* $$

Toll Road Restaurant: Buffet breakfasts and square meals at Stovepipe Wells, with a bar next door and a convenience store across the road. *7-10am & 11:30am-9pm* $$

Ranch 1849 Buffet: At the Ranch plaza in Furnace Creek, the buffet spread won't wow you, but the plentitude will satisfy. *6-10am, 11am-2pm & 5-9pm* $$

Last Kind Words Saloon: Burgers and pasta in Wild West–bedecked environs, complete with taxidermied critters and hammered-tin ceilings. *5-9pm* $$

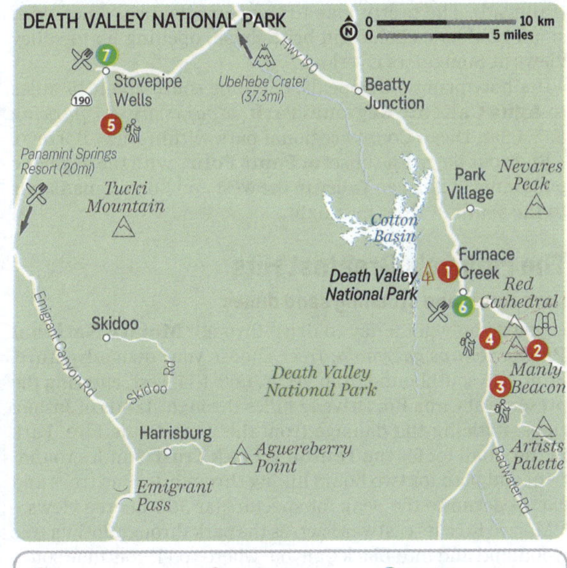

HIGHLIGHTS
1 Death Valley National Park

SIGHTS
2 Zabriskie Point

ACTIVITIES
3 Desolation Canyon
4 Golden Canyon
5 Mosaic Canyon Trail

EATING
see 6 Last Kind Words Saloon
6 Ranch 1849 Buffet
7 Toll Road Restaurant

at the Borrego Palm Canyon Oasis, named after its native California fan palms.

A longer alternative to Borrego Palm Canyon is the nearby 5-mile **Hellhole Canyon Trail**, taking you from the open desert to lush oases with little waterfalls and maidenhair ferns.

Anza-Borrego South to North

Petroglyphs, hot springs and diverse landscapes

Pack a lunch and start early for your drive south, through the park's Pinyon Mountains and beautiful higher-elevation piñon and juniper country. From the junction of Hwy 78 and County Rd S2, drive 6 miles to the Blair Valley turnoff, a dirt road at Mile 22.9. A map there shows the way to the **Pictograph Trail** (a high-clearance vehicle recommended to the

GREAT HIKES NEAR BORREGO SPRINGS

Robin Halford, author of *Hiking in Anza-Borrego Desert, Volumes 1–3*, suggests hikes located within 25 minutes of Borrego Springs.

Cannonball Run
In addition to the cannonball formations embedded in the mudstone here, you can also see the uplifting that occurred eons ago that's almost like natural rock art.

Cool Canyon
A wonderful meandering canyon at a higher elevation, with different vegetation and cooler temperatures than on the desert floor.

Bill Kenyon Trail
This out-and-back isn't difficult, with wonderful cacti and other desert flora along the trail. You end up with a really nice view across Hwy 78 to a *bajada*, where several alluvial fans come together.

EATING & DRINKING IN BORREGO SPRINGS: OUR PICKS

Kendall's Café: Friendly, relaxed, nostalgic little diner with a patio on the strip mall, serving typical American breakfast and Mexican options at lunch. *7am-2pm* $

Carmelita's Mexican Grill & Cantina: Down-home Mexican favorites tucked away in a corner of the mall, with shaded patio seating. *10am-8pm* $

Red Ocotillo: Crab-cake eggs Benedict for breakfast, lamb shanks for dinner. A lovely garden spot with a cute patio. *7:30am-8:30pm* $$

Carlee's: With hearty American food, a wraparound bar (open later) and pool tables after food service has ended, this is the best evening hang in town. *11am-9pm* $$

DESERT TORTOISES

The desert tortoise is a threatened species found in the Mojave Desert Preserve as well as California's larger desert regions. Though the species has been around for millions of years, its populations have declined over the past several decades. Stressors include rising temperatures from climate change, disease, human encroachment on desert habitats and even ravens, which prey on baby tortoises. Consider it a blessing if you see a desert tortoise in the wild. In fact, always check under your parked car before driving away, and watch out for tortoises trundling across roads.

trailhead). The pretty hike to the petroglyphs is lined with small boulders, cholla and brittlebush, opening up to valley views at Smugglers Overlook.

If a hot-spring dip appeals, continue south about 15 miles to **Agua Caliente Regional Park** *(sdparks.org; $5, parking $5)*, a San Diego County regional park within Anza-Borrego.

End your day with sunset at **Fonts Point**, with the dramatic panorama of Borrego Valley to the west and Borrego Badlands to the south in their best light.

The Mojave's Greatest Hits

Lava tubes and stunning sand dunes

If you've only got a day to drive through **Mojave National Preserve** *(nps.gov/moja; free)*, choose your own adventure. From I-15 southbound from Vegas, take I-15 west, entering the preserve at Cima Rd. Drive 12 miles through stands of Joshua trees, noticing the damage from the 2020 Dome Fire. Park in the small lot for the **Teutonia Peak Trail** (3 miles round-trip) and plan for two hours hiking through Joshua trees and cactus scrub to the peak for spectacular 360-degree views.

Mojave Rd cuts eastward across the park through Joshua tree woodland and into Black Canyon, where you'll continue south again through remote ranchlands between Mojave mountain ranges. About 10 miles south along Black Canyon Rd, stop at **Hole-in-the-Wall Visitor Center** and walk the flat, one-mile **Rings Loop Trail** clockwise (south from the parking lot). The walls on this fun hike include steep sections featuring bolted rings for handholds. Exit to I-40 along Essex Rd.

Alternatively, head 24 more miles westward along I-15 to Baker to take Kelbaker Rd south into the park. At the Aiken Mine Rd turnoff 19 miles in, drive another 5 miles through lava-bed landscape to the hilltop **lava tube** spotlit on one end by natural skylights. Look for the ladder descending into the cave.

Continue south on Kelbaker Rd, stopping at the **Kelso Depot Visitor Center** to learn a bit of preserve history. Around 7 miles further south, turn off toward the magnificent **Kelso Dunes**. Allow two to three hours for the round-trip hike, then onward to I-40.

Mitchell Caverns Detour

Geological salons of Mojave history

A little pocket of a California state park surrounded by Mojave National Preserve, **Providence Mountains State Recreation Area** *(parks.ca.gov; $10)* is a high-altitude encapsulation of the Mojave. The isolated mountains here support distinct species like rock squirrels. The main draw is **Mitchell Caverns** *(reservecalifornia.com; tour including day-use fee $20)*, a protected chain of stalactite- and stalagmite-laden chambers.

Southern California: Disneyland to San Diego

DISNEY MAGIC | WINERY-HOPPING | LAID-BACK CITY

Today, Disneyland Resort®, which comprises the Disneyland Park and newer Disney California Adventure theme park, remains a magical experience for the more than 14 million kids, grandparents, honeymooners and international tourists who visit every year. At alluring Newport Beach you'll find the largest recreational harbor on the West Coast, with 10 miles of waterfront offering boating and fishing, water sports and endless views. En route to San Diego, Temecula features fine wineries, while small beach communities like La Jolla have cultures uniquely their own.

San Diego is a city unlike any other in California. The second-largest in the state by population, it has everything you could ask for in a metropolis: vibrant arts and culture, diverse and varied neighborhoods, incredible food and more entertainment than you could ever see yourself. But even with all that, the city manages to always feel relaxed. Chill coastal vibes are ingrained in every corner of this Southern California paradise.

TOP TIP

San Diego shares an international border with Tijuana, and it's easy for US citizens with passports to head south and explore one of the world's most-visited cities. There's even a Cross Border Xpress skybridge connecting the Tijuana International Airport to San Diego.

GETTING AROUND

Newport Beach lies an hour's drive south of Downtown LA. Amtrak or Metrolink trains from LA are fast and scenic and stop at Anaheim's ARTIC transit center, a short shuttle ride to Disneyland by bus (routes 14 or 15). For San Diego, take Amtrak's *Pacific Surfliner* train, which travels daily between Santa Barbara, Los Angeles and the city, with stops in between.

Disney California Adventure Park

TOP EXPERIENCE

Disneyland Resort®

Walt Disney's creation is the self-dubbed 'Happiest Place on Earth.' The streets of the Disneyland Resort are always clean, employees always upbeat and parades happen daily. Since opening in 1955 Disneyland has delighted hundreds of millions. Disneyland Park is the original and most famous area, Disney California Adventure Park (DCA) the newer theme park, and Downtown Disney District comprises an outdoor pedestrian mall with restaurants.

DON'T MISS

- Star Wars: Rise of the Resistance
- Space Mountain roller coaster
- New Orleans Square
- Indiana Jones Adventure
- Grizzly River Run
- World of Color fireworks

Disneyland Park

From the entrance of Disneyland Park, you leave SoCal behind and enter **Main Street USA**, an idealized turn-of-the-20th-century town fashioned after Walt's hometown of Marceline, Missouri. Hop the steam **Disneyland Railroad** for a great intro to the park as it circles the perimeter. Controversially in 2025, *Great Moments with Mr Lincoln*, the 15-minute audio-animatronic show with Honest Abe spouting bromides, has been partially replaced by *Walt Disney – A Magical Life*, in which a robotic Walt (who died in 1966) talks about his vision for Disneyland and sings a song.

PRACTICALITIES

● disneyland.disney.go.com

Star Wars: Galaxy's Edge

Inside Disneyland's largest 'land' (14 acres), the mega-popular **Star Wars: Rise of the Resistance** puts you in an immersive adventure where you must escape from a Star Destroyer. Nearby are opportunities to make your own lightsaber or droid, or drink adult beverages or blue milk at Oga's Cantina, modeled after the inside of Jabba's Palace. Fans of the movies will enjoy just wandering around, marveling at Disney's fanatical attention to detail.

Tomorrowland

The 1950s Imagineers' vision of the future could now be called Mid-Century Land. Venerable **Space Mountain** remains one of the USA's best roller coasters, hurtling you into complete darkness at great speed. For retro high-tech, the **monorail** glides from Downtown Disney and the hotels to its stop in Tomorrowland.

Fantasyland & Frontierland

Fantasyland is best known for 'It's a Small World,' a boat ride past hundreds of audio-animatronic international children singing an earworm of a theme song. After a revamp, it reopened in 2025 with even more tiny characters, including ones from *Coco*.

Thrills are provided by **Big Thunder Mountain Railroad**, a mining-themed roller coaster.

New Orleans Square & Bayou Country

Honoring Walt's favorite city, New Orleans Square captures a slice of French Quarter charm. The ever-wonderful **Pirates of the Caribbean** is the second-longest ride in Disneyland (17 minutes) and provided inspiration for the popular movies. The water ride **Tiana's Bayou Adventure**, inspired by *The Princess and the Frog*, opened in 2024. **Tiana's Palace** is popular for its authentic New Orleans cuisine.

Adventureland

Among the attractions here, the hands-down highlight is the safari-style **Indiana Jones Adventure**. Cool down on the purposely hokey **Jungle Cruise**. The classic **Enchanted Tiki Room** features a campy show of singing, dancing birds and flowers. Skip the overhyped Dole Whips.

Disney California Adventure Park

Across the plaza from Disneyland, DCA is an ode to the state with an overlay of Disney intellectual property. It feels less crowded than Disneyland Park and has excellent rides and attractions. The superb **Grizzly River Run** takes you 'rafting' down a faux Sierra Nevada river – you will get wet. Kids can tackle the **Redwood Creek Challenge Trail**, with its 'Big Sir' redwoods. If you're hungry, the **Corn Dog Castle** has a grab-and-go hot link corn dog that's the best in the parks.

PARADES, FIREWORKS & LIVE ENTERTAINMENT

There are daily parades in Disneyland and DCA, with floats accompanied by Disney tunes and costumed characters. Don't miss DCA's premier show, the 22-minute **World of Color** nighttime spectacular, with fireworks over the lagoon.

TOP TIPS

- Buy your tickets in advance online at disneyland.disney.go.com. Many Disney vacation planning sites offer discounted tickets.
- On busy days, waits for the most in-demand rides can range from one to two hours, but the Lightning Lane Multi-Pass ($35 per day per person) allows priority access on many rides. For the most popular rides there's an additional Individual Lightning Lane cost per ride – you can purchase these without having to buy a Multi-Pass.
- Bring a power bank for your smartphone. The Disneyland app is a must-have to keep track of wait times, book Lightning Lane passes, order food, make dining reservations and lots more.

SOUTHERN CALIFORNIA: DISNEYLAND TO SAN DIEGO

Make a Splash at Newport Beach

If you don't get on the water, you didn't visit Newport

For an adventure by sea – or just to see the superyachts docked nearby – head to Mariner's Mile. This is where you'll disembark for water excursions like harbor tours, gondola rides and sailing lessons. Or rent your own **Duffy boat** *(duffyofnewportbeach.com)* and cruise around the harbor on your own. There are even **sunset dinner cruises** *(citycruises.com)* where you can enjoy dinner and drinks as you take in Orange County's singular sunset.

EATING IN NEWPORT BEACH: WATERFRONT RESTAURANTS

21 Oceanfront: In Doryman's Oceanfront Inn, this fine-dining seafood and steak restaurant serves up unparalleled beach views. *4pm-late* **$$$**

Nobu Newport Beach: Outpost of the legendary Japanese with two floors of water views. *noon-3pm Fri-Sun, Tanoshi 5-7pm Mon-Thu, dinner from 5pm* **$$$**

Rusty Pelican: An institution in Mariner's Mile since 1972, this harborside restaurant serves creative fish preparations with a robust wine list. *11am-10pm* **$$$**

Crystal Cove Shake Shack: Serving burgers and shakes on the beach since 1945; eat them on picnic tables and head straight back to the sand. *7am-9pm* **$$**

To enjoy the water from land, head to **Lido Marina Village** *(lidomarinavillage.com),* a waterfront shopping and dining area with its own cinema, boutiques and an array of restaurants from casual to fine dining. Mariner's Mile and Lido Marina are also where you'll see boats decorated for the holidays.

Fun on Four Wheels

Moke Cruising

A quintessentially SoCal experience is cruising around in a Moke. It looks a bit like a miniature Jeep, with an open top and a roll bar, but it's an electric vehicle that tops out at 25mph. It's perfect for cruising along the shore or any low-speed road, especially on a sunny day. Rent one from **Newport Beach Moke** *(newportbeachmoke.com),* or **Adventure OC** *(adventureoc.com)* in Huntington Beach. Rentals are available by the hour, day or week.

Wandering Old Town Temecula

Step into the past

The heart of Temecula Valley was an important location in the Old West: after Mexico ceded California to the United States, Temecula served as a stagecoach stop and was also home to California's second-ever post office, after San Francisco. Following the Civil War, the town saw an influx of settlers from the East. In 1882 the area saw the establishment of the Pechanga Reservation and the construction of a train station. The **Temecula Valley Museum** *(temeculavalley museum.org)* explores local history, from the Native Luiseno tribe to Mission San Luis Rey (1798), with a miniature street scene for kids to play in.

Walking into Temecula's Old Town today recalls the late 1800s: there are still plenty of historic Old West buildings along Front St, but now they're home to antiques stores, boutiques, craft breweries and restaurants. **Temecula Olive Oil Company** *(temeculaoliveoil.com)* grows its own olives and presses them into robust olive oils; tastings are free in the shop. **Old Town Spice & Tea Merchants** *(spiceandteamer chants.com)* sells 350 spices and 100 loose-leaf teas. **Temecula Lavender Co** *(temeculalavernderco.com)* sells products made from flowers grown on its own local lavender farm. One block on Fourth St holds several antiques shops, like **Old Town Antique Faire** and **RECLAIMED @ Main St Market**,

NEWPORT BEACH'S BEST BEACHES

Crystal Cove State Park: Unique destination with three beaches, campsites, cabins and an underwater park for snorkeling and diving.

Corona del Mar State Beach: Known as Big Corona, this beach is family- and pet-friendly. If it looks familiar, you might recognize the beach from *Gilligan's Island.*

Newport Beach Pier: The stretch of sand on Balboa Peninsula around the Newport Beach Pier has fine sand and views, and proximity to many shops and cafes.

Little Corona del Mar Beach: Calm beach known for snorkeling and tide pools, with no steps down to the sand.

The Wedge: This scenic beach's waves make it popular with surfers. In the summer, boards are prohibited between 10am and 5pm.

DINING IN TEMECULA: OUR PICKS

Bolero Restaurante: Serves Spanish tapas with a gourmet sensibility. Chef Hany Ali trained and cooked throughout Europe before arriving in California. *8am-9pm* $$

Small Barn: This farm-to-table restaurant and boutique winery evolved from the owners' backyard winemaking operation. *5-9pm Tue-Thu, 11am-10pm Fri, 10am-10pm Sat, 10am-8pm Sun* $$

Espadín Mezcal + Cocina: When you need a break from wine, this spot serves inspired regional Mexican food with agave-based cocktails. *11am-9pm Sun-Thu, 11am-10pm Fri & Sat* $$

The Goat & Vine: This stone-hearth kitchen might be casual, but its approach to food is not: everything (pizza dough, sauces etc) is made in-house daily. *11am-9pm* $$

PECHANGA RESORT CASINO

One of the largest casinos in the country is in Temecula, just minutes from Old Town. Pechanga, owned by the Pechanga Band of Indians, has 200,000 sq ft of gaming – and a lot of reasons to visit, even if gambling isn't your thing. The AAA Four Diamond property (named the best casino in the country by *USA Today*) has a large luxury hotel with an enormous pool complex and spa, a concert venue that brings in acts like the Beach Boys and comedian Kevin James, and more than a dozen restaurants including a fine-dining steakhouse and an upscale sushi bar.

EKAM/SHUTTERSTOCK

which refurbishes vintage furniture. The largest country music venue on the West Coast, the **Stampede** *(thetemeculastampede.com)* has line dancing, bull riding and live music every weekend. It's located in the Old Town.

Winery-Hopping in the Temecula Valley

Enjoying wineries and much more

Because the weather is dry and hot, similar to a Mediterranean climate, Temecula is especially well-suited to growing Spanish, French and Italian grape varietals. Expect to sip sangiovese and syrah – though vineyards farm more than two dozen different grapes locally. At **Doffo Winery**, Marcelo Doffo channels his Argentine and Italian heritage to make outstanding zinfandel and red blends, and also has a collection of vintage motorcycles at the winery. **Miramonte Winery**, another standout, focuses on Spanish- and Portuguese-influenced styles like tempranillo and medium-bodied red blends.

La Jolla's Public Art

Natural beauty and creative vibes

The natural beauty of the hilly coastal city isn't the only thing worth looking at in La Jolla. A massive public-art program has been working on beautifying the city since 2010. Today, there are 15 large-scale murals on display, and more than 40 total pieces of public art, which are always a pleasant surprise to stumble on in your explorations.

Grape vines, Temecula Valley

BEST BEACHES OF LA JOLLA

Directly below Scripps Park in La Jolla Village is **La Jolla Cove**, one of the most famous beaches in Southern California. The cove is great for swimming or just lounging in the sand. This is also the beach where you're almost guaranteed to spot sea lions. Remember to keep your distance; some days there are ropes in place to ensure the sea lions have enough space on the beach.

Families love **La Jolla Shores**, **Windansea Beach** and **Torrey Pines State Beach** for their mild surf and expansive sand. Surfers love **Black's Beach** and **Tourmaline Surf Park**, which is better for beginners because of its milder surf.

The **Murals of La Jolla website** *(muralsoflajolla.com)* details the art and the artists, includes YouTube videos, and offers a self-guided walking tour to see them for yourself. If you can't get enough of the vibrant works, take them home with you in *The Murals of La Jolla* coffee-table book, a work of art in itself that supports the project.

Fine Art in La Jolla

Art walk and galleries

The city has a robust art scene, especially in the number of nationally renowned artists whose works are on display in galleries. On the **La Jolla Village Art Walk** *(lajollabythesea.com)*, find Martin Lawrence Galleries as well as LIK Fine Art, the showroom of the artist who sold the world's most expensive photograph: Peter Lik's *Phantom* sold for $6.5 million in 2014. The Museum of Contemporary Art San Diego, which also has a location in downtown San Diego, showcases works created since 1950 and has strong collections of pop art, Latin American art and works by San Diego and Tijuana artists.

Exploring the Heart of San Diego

Downtown, the Gaslamp District and the Embarcadero

San Diego is a large city, packed with so many fascinating sights that you'll want to give yourself a good amount of time to explore. The Gaslamp District downtown was named for the gas streetlights installed in the area in the late 1800s.

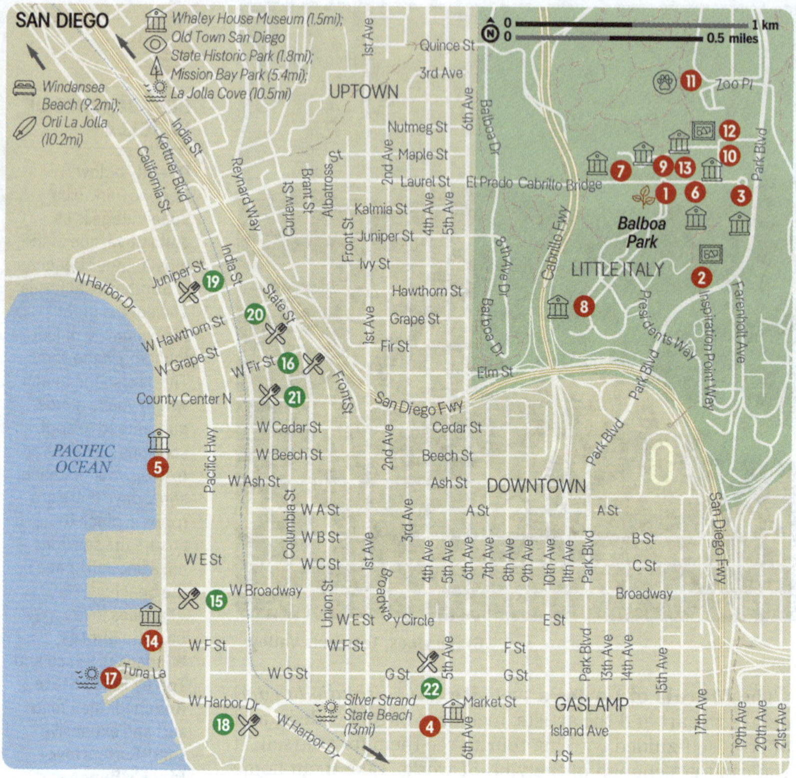

SAN DIEGO

Whaley House Museum (1.5mi); Old Town San Diego State Historic Park (1.8mi); Mission Bay Park (5.4mi); La Jolla Cove (10.5mi)

Windansea Beach (9.2mi); Orli La Jolla (10.2mi)

Silver Strand State Beach (13mi)

UPTOWN · LITTLE ITALY · Balboa Park · DOWNTOWN · GASLAMP · PACIFIC OCEAN

HIGHLIGHTS

1 Balboa Park

SIGHTS

2 Centro Cultural de la Raza
3 Fleet Science Center
4 Gaslamp Museum at the Davis-Horton House
5 Maritime Museum
6 Museum of Photographic Arts
7 Museum of Us
8 San Diego Air & Space Museum
9 San Diego Museum of Art
10 San Diego Natural History Museum
11 San Diego Zoo
12 Spanish Village Arts Center
13 Timken Museum of Art
14 USS Midway Museum

EATING

15 Animae
16 Civico 1845
17 Fish Market
18 Headquarters at Seaport
19 Juniper & Ivy
20 Mona Lisa Italian Foods
21 Morning Glory
22 Werewolf

EATING IN SAN DIEGO: LITTLE ITALY

Juniper & Ivy: One of the most decorated restaurants in San Diego, with a seasonally driven fine-dining menu. *5-9pm Sun-Thu, to 10pm Fri & Sat* $$$

Mona Lisa Italian Foods: This grocery and restaurant is like the local version of Eataly. *deli 9am-10pm, restaurant 11am-9:30pm Mon-Sat, from noon Sun* $$

Civico 1845: In addition to freshly made pasta and Calabrian cuisine, this restaurant has a full slate of vegan offerings. *4-9pm Sun-Thu, to 10pm Fri, noon-10pm Sat & Sun* $$

Morning Glory: Whimsical brunch restaurant with a roving Bloody Mary cart and breakfast carbonara and chilaquiles. *8am-3pm Mon-Fri, to 4pm Sat & Sun* $$

There are more than 100 places to eat, drink, shop and dance in Gaslamp's 16 square blocks. This is where to head if you're looking for nightlife in San Diego, or to have a cocktail on a rooftop lounge. Rumors of ghost sightings swirl throughout the neighborhood, especially at the **Gaslamp Museum at the Davis-Horton House** *(gaslampfoundation.org; entry $8)*, which offers ghostly walking tours.

At the waterfront area of downtown San Diego, Embarcadero, tour the **USS Midway Museum** *(midway.org; adult/child $39/26)*, a decommissioned aircraft carrier that served for 47 years, and explore the **Maritime Museum** *(sdmaritime .org; adult/child $24/from $12)*, a collection of historic ships that includes the 150-year-old *Star of India*, the oldest active sailing ship.

Discover Old Town San Diego

A true step back in time

Old Town San Diego State Historic Park *(oldtownmarket sandiego.com)* is a stretch of 19th-century buildings where people lived and worked nearly 200 years ago. Tour an old schoolhouse, or see the spot where the first American flag was raised in San Diego, in 1846. Shops in the park represent a simpler way of life. You can make your own candles or buy penny candy. Bazaar del Mundo, in the center of the historic area, translates to 'marketplace of the world' and brings together merchants selling everything from jewelry to pottery.

Arguably the most iconic of Old Town's historic buildings is the **Whaley House Museum** *(whaleyhousesandiego.com; adult/child $13.30/9.50)*, constructed in 1856 on the site where public hangings once took place. Today, it's rumored to be so haunted that it's been featured on many ghost-hunting TV shows. At night it offers ghost tours and after-hours paranormal investigations.

Cruising the Coast

San Diego's varied coastal communities

The sparkling beach on **Coronado Island** is praised as one of the best in the country, while the southernmost beach town in California is in **South Bay**, only a few miles from the Mexico border. **Imperial Beach** is popular for fishing, surfing, bird-watching and cycling. **Mission Bay Park** is the place to go for water sports, or to charter a fishing or sailing excursion.

SAN DIEGO'S BEST BIKE PATHS

San Diego has over 1800 miles of bikeways – use the **San Diego Regional Bike Map** *(sandag. org)* to find your route.

Bayshore Bikeway: A 24-mile loop from Coronado to Chula Vista, but you can stick to the beachside **Silver Strand** for a bike-path-only route.

Mission Bay Bike Loop: Mission Bay, between SD and La Jolla, has a flat 12-mile bike path with gorgeous views.

Balboa Park Loop: Cruising around the park on two wheels offers a new perspective.

San Diego River Bike Path: This 20-mile car-free path follows the San Diego River from Mission Valley to Ocean Beach.

Los Peñasquitos Canyon: This mountainous area has hiking and biking paths for all levels.

EATING IN SAN DIEGO: GASLAMP & EMBARCADERO

Headquarters at Seaport: Village San Diego's old police HQ now houses with food stalls, fine dining and shopping. *10am-9pm Mon-Sat, to 8pm Sun* $$

The Fish Market: Freshly caught fish goes straight from the sea to your plate at this Embarcadero restaurant. *11am-8:30pm Sun-Thu, to 9pm Fri & Sat* $$

Animae: Steakhouse infused with Japanese and Filipino influences from chef Tara Monsod. Chic, art-filled dining room. *5-9pm Sun-Thu, to 9:30pm Fri & Sat* $$$

Werewolf: This lively brewpub in the Gaslamp is a high-energy destination serving brunch and elevated bar food. Nightly karaoke. *8am-2am* $$

VISITING MEXICO

As San Diego shares an international border with Tijuana, US citizens with passports can easily travel south to explore the Mexican border town. A Cross Border Xpress skybridge connects the Tijuana International Airport to San Diego. International visitors can also cross the border, but need a valid passport as well as a valid I-94 form or multiple entry visa or visa waiver, which can be managed through the US Customs & Border Patrol's CBP One app.

In TJ, as locals call it, you can shop duty free, eat Mexican food and explore the city's sights, like the Tijuana Cultural Center, which combines art galleries with a botanical garden, performance stages and an aquarium.

OLGA SHUSTERS/SHUTTERSTOCK

Flamingos, San Diego Zoo

Museum-Hopping in Balboa Park

Art, history and science museums

The nickname for **Balboa Park** *(balboapark.org),* 'the Smithsonian of the West,' isn't hyperbole. San Diego's version of New York's Central Park is home to 17 museums and performance venues, Spanish Renaissance architecture and the **San Diego Zoo** *(sandiegozoo.org; adult/child $76/66).*

For fine-arts appreciation, try the **Museum of Photographic Arts** *(mopa.org; entry by donation)* for its vast photography collection, the **San Diego Museum of Art** *(sdma.org; adult/child $20/free)* for its rotating international exhibits and the **Timken Museum of Art** *(timkenmuseum.org; free)* for works by European Old Masters.

The **Centro Cultural de la Raza** *(centrodelaraza.com; free)* is an arts center highlighting Mexican, Indigenous and Latino culture; at the **Spanish Village Arts Center** *(villageartscenter.org)* a community of more than 200 artisans show their works.

To learn about the world, try the **Museum of Us** *(museumofus.org; adult/child $19.95/16.95),* dedicated to human history. The **San Diego Air & Space Museum** *(sandiegoairandspace.org; adult/child $35/22)* has the real Apollo 9 Command Module and artifacts from Amelia Earhart and Charles Lindbergh. The **Fleet Science Center** *(fleetscience.org; adult/child $24.95/19.95)* features 100 interactive science exhibits and the **San Diego Natural History Museum** *(sdnhm.org; adult/child $24/14)* displays a T rex skeleton.

Places We Love to Stay

$ Budget $$ Midrange $$$ Top End

San Francisco

p346

HI San Francisco Fisherman's Wharf $ Get million-dollar waterfront views in an ex-army barracks that's now SF's top hostel. Choose private rooms or dorms (some co-ed), all with shared bathrooms and a communal kitchen offering free breakfasts.

Green Tortoise Hostel $ North Beach's hostel encourages bonding with pool, ping-pong, games, co-working stations and weekly live music shows in the sunny ballroom. Perks include a sauna, free breakfast, good wi-fi, on-site laundry and communal kitchen. Dorm rooms have generous lockers.

Pacific Tradewinds Hostel $ San Francisco's smartest all-dorm hostel has a fully equipped kitchen (free coffee, tea and PB&J sandwiches), spotless showers, sturdy bunk beds, laundry (free sock wash), luggage storage, no lockout time and, best of all, fun staff. No elevator.

Hotel del Sol $$ With splashy beach-ball color schemes, a palm-lined courtyard and heated outdoor pool, the Marina's mid-century motor lodge is SF's top choice for families.

Lodge at the Presidio $$ The officers' post turned ecolodge has dashingly handsome guest rooms with pillowtop beds, historic photos and commanding views – request a room overlooking the Golden Gate Bridge.

Orchard Garden Hotel $$ SF's first LEED-certified green hotel is surprisingly affordable and conveniently located just outside Chinatown, with a gym, rooftop deck and optional breakfast at the sustainable Roots restaurant.

Hotel Bohème $$ The quintessential North Beach inn has smallish rooms named after Beat writers, with wrought-iron beds, original artwork and small bathrooms. Some rooms face noisy Columbus Ave and there's no elevator – but novels practically write themselves here.

Union Street Inn $$$ Live like a Victorian socialite at this grand B&B with six antique-filled guest rooms, afternoon tea in lush gardens and generous breakfasts in the parlor.

Fairmont San Francisco $$$ Magnificent marble lobby, opulent mosaic penthouse suite – plus San Francisco eccentricity, including the tiki Tonga Room and the circus-mural Cirque Bar. Guest rooms have business-class comfort. For historic appeal, reserve in the original 1906 building; for jaw-dropping views, go for the tower.

Parsonage $$$ At this 1883 Italianate Victorian, with original Carrara-marble fireplaces, rose-brass chandeliers and period furnishings, the antique-adorned rooms are named after San Francisco's grand dames. Architect Julia Morgan gets the best views. Two-night minimum.

Bay Area

p365

B-Love's Guest House $ Artist Traci 'B-Love' Bartlow rents out rooms in her West Oakland house, which includes a garden. The shared bathroom has Bartlow's photography on the walls.

Dinah's Garden Hotel $ South of the university campus and downtown in Palo Alto, with great rates, oversized rooms, balconies and garden-filled grounds and an outdoor pool.

Graduate Berkeley $$ Only a block from campus at Berkeley, this seven-story 1928 hotel plays up its ties to the university. Collegiate-inspired details throughout.

Gables Inn Sausalito $$ Tranquility, style and peace in Sausalito. The inn includes a historical 1869 home, and has 13 rooms, four cottages and three apartments, some with grand views.

Mill Rose Inn $$ Right near the center of Half Moon Bay on a large plot with private gardens filled with flowers. Traditional style with luxe details.

North Coast & Redwoods

p371

Mattole Campground $ At the northern point of the Lost Coast Trail, this campground is just steps from the beach and has 27 sites.

Jedediah Smith Redwoods Campground $ Stay in the main loop, outer loop or redwoods cabin area, with cabins that sleep up to six.

Inn at 2nd & C $$ This glorious historic hotel in Eureka has been tastefully restored to combine Victorian-era decor with every possible modern amenity.

Historic Requa Inn $$ Every room at this 100-year-old inn has a Klamath River view – and one room is the town's former post office.

Mendocino Grove $$ This glamping gem by the sea in Mendocino has safari-style tents and elegant bathhouses.

Camellia Inn $$$ Cheery pink 1871 mansion in Healdsburg, with camellia-filled gardens, sociable parlors and upbeat, helpful innkeepers.

Napa & Sonoma p373

Sonoma Creek Inn $ Quirky 16-room motel in Sonoma with retro-Americana decor, including vintage California travel posters and postcard lamps.

An Inn 2 Remember $$ Steps from Sonoma Plaza, this vintage 1910 charmer offers warm welcomes and private, comfortable lodgings.

Inn at Occidental $$ Escape the ordinary at this 16-room Victorian inn in Occidental, with heirloom quilts for getting cozy in the redwoods.

Blackbird Inn $$$ In Napa, relax in a ruggedly handsome 1902 California Craftsman cottage with eight plush rooms.

Mt Shasta p382

LOGE Mt Shasta $$ Dorms, gear lockers, shared bathrooms and covered campsites geared toward social, active folks.

Bidwell House B&B $$ Near Mt Lassen, the historic summer home of pioneers John and Annie Bidwell has classic accommodations that come with all the modern amenities.

Sequoia, Yosemite & Lake Tahoe p385

evo Tahoe City Hotel $ An adventure-focused hotel in Tahoe City with modern rooms and lots of communal social spaces, plus a sauna and cold plunge.

Yosemite Bug Rustic Mountain Resort $ Budget-friendly oasis with eclectic accommodations, a beloved restaurant and a spa. Near Mariposa.

Yosemite Basecamp $$ An 'adventure loft' and 'basecamp bunkhouse' in Groveland with boot dryers and soaking tubs.

John Muir Lodge $$ A stone-and-timber retreat in Grant Grove Village with homespun rooms, a cozy fireplace and tent cabins (Sequoia and Kings Canyon National Parks).

Granlibakken Resort $$ A 74-acre historical resort at Tahoe City with on-site activities, where vintage cabin meets modern wilderness lodge.

Village at Palisades Tahoe $$ Hotel rooms up to multiroom condos lofted above the shops of the Palisades Village.

Gold Country p395

Foothills Motel $ Good-value retro-modern motel in Auburn with an on-site bowling alley with 24 lanes, a bar, and a diner. It's a five-minute drive to Old Town.

Two Room Inn $$ Sweet two-room Victorian cottage with stained-glass lattice windows and a prime spot on Broad St, Nevada City, just steps away from all the action.

Sonora Inn $$ A historic 1896 hotel in Sonora, redone for modern times. Rooms and suites are pet-friendly for an added fee. The rooftop pool is a beloved respite on hot days.

The Central Coast p397

Apple Farm Inn $ A whimsical tree-shaded complex surrounding a century-old millhouse in San Luis Obispo.

Fogcatcher Inn $$ Elegant and plush, the design is all earth tones and driftwood at this inn on Cambria's Moonstone Beach.

Fernwood Resort $$ Stay in woodsy rooms with outdoor hot tubs or snug glamping tents at this friendly, few-frills resort with a cozy tavern in Big Sur.

Martine Inn $$ Old-fashioned elegance in Pacific Grove, Monterey, with 25 antique-dotted rooms filling an early-20th-century estate.

Pine Inn $$$ Leaning into its 1889 origins, this elegant hotel in Carmel-by-the-Sea has rooms with baroque prints and barrel armchairs. Splurge on an ocean-view room.

Pacific Blue Inn $$$ Between downtown and the boardwalk in Santa Cruz, this courtyard B&B with earth-tone rooms prides itself on a light carbon footprint.

El Encanto $$$ An enchanting 1920s classic in the Riviera neighborhood looks out over the city from its foothill perch, a real Santa Barbara refuge.

Allegretto Vineyard Resort $$$ Old-world elegance, on-site wine tasting and spa treatments in Paso Robles. The rooms are adorned with velvet and chandeliers.

Sacramento p406

HI Sacramento Hostel $ This hostel in a magnificent Victorian mansion offers good trimmings at rock-bottom prices. It's within walking distance of Old Sac.

Family Laundry & Spa $ Named for its neon sign, this B&B is located in a 1920s Craftsman-style home with three comfortable suites.

Delta King $$ It's a kitschy treat to sleep aboard the *Delta King*, a 1927 paddle wheeler docked on the river in Old Sacramento.

Citizen Hotel $$ This 1924 beaux-arts tower features luxe linens, an atmospheric reception and an upscale farm-to-fork restaurant on the ground floor.

Davis & Chico p407

Vine Inn $$ Located right in the beating heart of Davis, this modern motel-style inn has simple, comfortable rooms.

Goodman House $$ Delightful B&B in a 1906 home on a tree-lined Chico esplanade. Features include claw-foot baths, French antique beds and a Viennese grand piano.

Hotel Diamond $$$ This 1904 building is the most luxurious place to lay your head in Chico, with a high-thread count, a swanky bar and a top-notch restaurant.

Los Angeles p409

HI Los Angeles Santa Monica Hostel $ Near the beach and promenade, budget-friendly digs that rival facilities at properties costing many times more. Single-sex dorms and private rooms.

Highland Gardens Hotel $ Famous landing spot for future celebs. Motel-style accommodations are only one block from the first star on the Walk of Fame.

Banana Bungalows Hotel & Hostel West Hollywood $ Budget digs in a primo location. Private rooms are a great deal, especially those with full kitchens.

Crestridge Inn $ A good indie motel in Inglewood that's convenient to the SoFi Stadium area and LAX. Basic, budget-friendly rooms.

Samesun Venice Beach $ In a refurbished 1904 building with spectacular rooftop views of Venice Beach. Dorms, private rooms and a cool travelers' vibe.

Hollywood Roosevelt $$ Hollywood lore lives large at its most famous hotel (tip: get a pool room). Celebrity stories abound.

Biltmore Los Angeles $$ Grand old dame awash with history, grandeur and legend. The Academy Awards were founded in the Crystal Ballroom in 1927.

Hotel Normandie LA $$ Dating to 1926, the Normandie has vintage luxuries and a famous bar.

Hotel Per La $$$ Vintage interiors and a rooftop pool in a restored Downtown palazzo that was once the grand digs of the Bank of Italy. Plush rooms.

Silver Lake Pool & Inn $$$ Channeling Palm Springs, effortlessly hip, chilled and awash in SoCal light; the design credentials include locally produced art and bright rooms.

Georgian Hotel $$$ Across the street from Palisades Park and the Pacific beyond, this eye-catching 1933 art deco landmark has a snug ocean-view veranda.

Palm Springs & the Deserts p422

Jumbo Rocks Campground $ There's classic bouldery JTree landscape at this popular campground with over 100 sites.

Panamint Springs Resort $ A spacious, family-run campground and rustic motel rooms at Death Valley National Park's western end, with sweeping views across the Panamint Valley.

Mid Hills Campground $ This tranquil campground in Mojave National Preserve is set amid trees.

Drift Palm Springs $$$ The airy rooms and suites have a spare, desert-inspired design; located in downtown Palm Springs on Indian Canyon Dr.

Southern California p427

Resort at Pelican Hill $$$ This sprawling Newport Beach oceanside resort has five restaurants and two golf courses. Accommodations go up to four-bedroom villas.

Orli La Jolla $$$ In a historic building in La Jolla, this 13-room boutique hotel has thoughtful touches and a fun vibe.

San Diego p433

Wayfarer San Diego $$ On Pacific Beach, this newly renovated hotel has suites and rooms with gorgeous ocean views.

Kona Kai Resort & Spa $$ A Shelter Island hotel with a private beach – a rarity in San Diego – and a tropical island feel.

Guild Hotel $$$ A boutique hotel in a century-old building that was once a YMCA, with original architectural details.

Hotel del Coronado $$$ One of the most historically significant and beautiful hotels in California, located directly on the beach.

Researched and curated by Sarah Etinas

Pacific Northwest

AN UNBEATABLE NATURE ESCAPE

Innovative cities and gorgeous natural landscapes come together in the Pacific Northwest.

As much a state of mind as a geographical region, the northwest corner of the US is a land of subcultures and new trends, where evergreen trees frame snow-dusted volcanoes and inspired ideas scribbled on the back of napkins become tomorrow's start-ups. You can't peel off the history in layers here, but you can gaze wistfully into the future in fast-moving, innovative cities such as Seattle and Portland, which are sprinkled with food carts, streetcars, microbreweries, green belts, coffee connoisseurs and quirky urban sculptures.

Before the Pacific Northwest (PNW) became the unconventional, tech-forward region that we know today, it was home to several long-established Native American communities, including the Chinook, the Salish, the Nez Percé and the Yakama, to name just a few. Western contact didn't occur until the 18th century, and from there, it was a snowball effect of changes – native populations were wiped out, city infrastructure began to develop, and the landscape was transformed by new industries like logging and mining.

These changes formed the basis for what is now the modern-day Pacific Northwest – a region more diverse than its regional generalizations depict. The urban hubs of Seattle and Portland serve as emblematic cities, with their progressive politics and tech industries, but head east into the region's drier and less verdant interior, where the cultural affiliations become increasingly more traditional and where raucous rodeos, peaceful fly-fishing and small-town values are still very much alive.

DANITA DELIMONT/SHUTTERSTOCK

THE MAIN AREAS

SEATTLE
A city surrounded by natural beauty.
p446

WASHINGTON
Stunning landscapes, fresh seafood, picturesque wineries.
p456

PORTLAND
Unconventional and quirky from the start.
p471

OREGON
Beaches, waterfalls, and snowcapped mountains.
p481

For places to stay in the Pacific Northwest, see p494

NICHOLAS J KLEIN/SHUTTERSTOCK

Multnomah Falls (p486), Oregon

Find Your Way

Washington and Oregon are the two states at the heart of the Pacific Northwest. The major cities of Seattle and Portland are west of the Cascade Mountains but they're still a couple of hours' drive from the Pacific Ocean.

CAR

Like much of the US, traveling around the greater Pacific Northwest region requires a car. Parking can sometimes be tricky and pricey in big cities, but overall, a car is still the most convenient transportation option.

LIGHT-RAIL

Portland, Oregon; Seattle, Washington; and Tacoma, Washington, all have convenient light-rail systems that make it easy to get around the main metro areas sustainably. These light-rail routes don't currently expand beyond the major cities.

BUS

Buses offer affordable intracity and intercity transportation options. While not typically the speediest option, they can be great for travelers on a budget or looking to travel more sustainably.

Seattle, p446
Incredible museums, sprawling parks and a global dining scene are just some of the things to experience in this lively city.

Portland, p471
Flavorful restaurants and gorgeous parks will compete for your attention in Oregon's unabashedly quirky big city.

Oregon, p481
Wineries, waterfalls, mountains and beaches are just the beginning of the classic Pacific Northwest beauty found in greater Oregon.

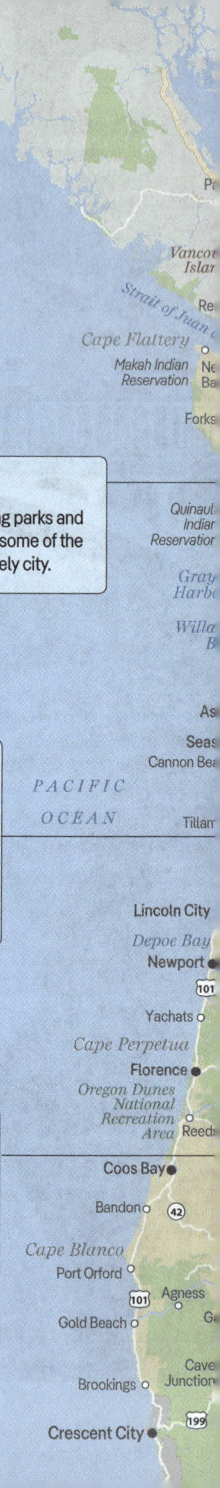

PACIFIC OCEAN
Cape Flattery
Makah Indian Reservation
Forks
Lincoln City
Depoe Bay
Newport
Yachats
Cape Perpetua
Florence
Oregon Dunes National Recreation Area
Coos Bay
Bandon
Cape Blanco
Port Orford
Agness
Gold Beach
Brookings
Crescent City

0 — 200 km
0 — 100 miles

Washington, p456
From peaceful islands in the west to wine regions in the east, greater Washington State is fantastic for a calm, nature-filled escape.
CANADA
Vancouver
Castlegar
North Cascades National Park
Strait of Georgia
Bellingham
Fidalgo Island
Anacortes
Newhalem
Skagit River
Victoria
Whidbey Island
Port Angeles
Port Townsend
Winthrop
Colville Indian Reservation
Columbia River
Colville
Stehekin
Lake Chelan
Lake Roosevelt
Spokane Indian Reservation
Newport
Olympic National Park
Puget Sound
Everett
Mukilteo
Cascade Range
Coulee Dam
Chelan
Seattle
Bremerton
Space Needle
Leavenworth
Spokane River
Coeur d'Alene
Spokane
Snoqualmie Pass
Coulee City
Tacoma
Wenatchee
Puyallup
Olympia
WASHINGTON
Moses Lake
Mt Rainier National Park
Mt Rainier (14,411ft)
Ellensburg
IDAHO
Colfax
Ashford
Pullman
Moscow
Packwood
Columbia River
Snake River
Yakima
Lewiston
Toppenish
Blue Mountains
Yakama Indian Reservation
Kennewick
Walla Walla
Mt St Helens (8363ft)
Mt Adams (12,276ft)
Benton City
Grande Ronde River
Columbia River
Umatilla
Vancouver
Hood River
Umatilla Indian Reservation
Arlington
Pendleton
Imnaha
Enterprise
Dundee
Estacada
Mt Hood (11,240ft)
Joseph
La Grande
Wallowa Mountains
Salem
Warm Springs Indian Reservation
John Day River
Halfway
Oxbow
Mt Jefferson (10,495ft)
Kimberly
Albany
Baker City
Cascade Range
Madras
Mitchell
McKenzie Bridge
Sisters
John Day
Eugene
Prineville
Three Sisters (10,363ft)
Bend
Seneca
Broken Top (9175ft)
Ontario
Mt Bachelor (9065ft)
OREGON
Burns
Malheur River
Lake Owyhee
Steamboat
Diamond Lake
Crane
Harney Lake
Malheur Lake
Crater Lake National Park
Summer Lake
Summer Lake
Steens Mtn (9773ft)
Jordan Valley
Burns Junction
Shady Cove
Lake Albert
Frenchglen
IDAHO
Upper Klamath Lake
Warner Lakes
Alvord Desert
Medford
Klamath Falls
Crump Lakes
Ashland
Mt Ashland (7533ft)
Lakeview
McDermitt
CALIFORNIA
Goose Lake
NEVADA

Plan Your Time

The Pacific Northwest covers a lot of ground. You'll want to prioritize what's most important to you – whether it's bustling city life, hiking adventures or peaceful winery visits.

A Weekend Getaway

- Start at Seattle's **Pike Place Market** (p450), getting lost, browsing, tasting and bantering with the producers. Don't miss the gum wall or the salmon tossing. Take the monorail to Seattle Center, where you'll spend the afternoon admiring the views at the top of the **Space Needle** (p446) and the art at **Chihuly Garden and Glass** (p447).

- Explore the best of North Seattle, with a kayaking adventure at the **Washington Park Arboretum** (p454) or a few hours at the **Ballard Locks** (p454). Dive into Belltown's nightlife scene, catching a performance at the **Pacific Northwest Ballet** (p452) or a jazz act at **Dimitriou's Jazz Alley** (p452). If time allows, watch the Seattle Kraken taking to the ice of the **Climate Pledge Arena** (p451) or the Seahawks racing down the lengths of **Lumen Field** (p455).

IAN DEWAR PHOTOGRAPHY/SHUTTERSTOCK

Lumen Field (p455)

SEASONAL HIGHLIGHTS

There's always something new happening in the Pacific Northwest. Plan your visit around the seasonal activities that catch your eye or be surprised by the festivities on arrival.

MARCH

Much of the region is still overcast. Lower-elevation hikes have thawed from winter snow, while higher elevations still have prime snowshoeing conditions. The **Penn Cove Musselfest** (p461) takes place on Whidbey Island.

APRIL

With April showers, the US' largest tulip festival comes to life. Tiptoe through a rainbow of beautiful blooms at the **Skagit Valley Tulip Festival** (p463) in Mt Vernon, Washington. Stick around the region for rummage sales and locally made ice cream.

MAY

In McMinnville, Oregon, the **UFO Fest** (p484) puts on a whole weekend of alien-themed events, with the highlights being the Alien Pet Costume Contest and the Alien Costume Parade.

A Weeklong Trip

- Experience the best of Western Oregon, starting with the Portland highlights, like **Washington Park** (p477) and **Powell's City of Books** (p471). From there, buckle in and get ready to hit a few noteworthy Oregon towns: **Astoria** (p490), a beautiful coastal city where *The Goonies* was filmed; **McMinnville** (p481), for charming wineries and a space-themed water park; and **Eugene** (p485), for its hippie-esque atmosphere and lively Saturday market.

- Round out your week in Oregon with a visit to **Crater Lake National Park** (p482), the only national park in Oregon and home to the deepest, bluest lake in the US. Drive around to stop at the many viewpoints, or lace up your hiking shoes to tackle the challenging but rewarding 3.5-mile **Garfield Peak** hike.

Two Weeks to Explore

- With two weeks, you have time to tackle the aforementioned Oregon road trip, journey up to Seattle to hit the previously noted highlights and add Washington's best national parks to the itinerary too. Start with **Mt Rainier National Park** (p458), where you can take in the awe-inspiring mountain views from **Ricksecker Point** and tackle the beloved **Sourdough Ridge Trail**.

- Once you've got your fill of one national park, venture to the next: **Olympic National Park** (p459), where the diverse array of landscapes serves as a playground for nature-lovers. Hike around the accessible **Hurricane Ridge**, soak in the healing mineral waters of **Sol Duc Hot Springs**, admire the sea stacks at Rialto Beach and bask in the greenery of the **Hoh Forest**, just to start.

JUNE

The popular **Portland Rose Festival** (p477) harkens in summer with carnival rides, live entertainment, dragon boat races, and daytime and after-dark parades. June is also when several types of salmon will start 'running' from saltwater to freshwater.

JULY

July is peak season in the region, thanks to the ideal temperatures and sunshine-filled skies. It's when hikes are at their greenest, wild berry bushes are at their fullest and waterways come alive with kayakers and paddleboarders.

SEPTEMBER

There are quite a few annual events that take place in the PNW each September, but **Bumbershoot** (p450), Seattle's premier arts and music festival, may be the best of the bunch.

OCTOBER

While you can forage at every time of year, October is a favorite, thanks to the abundance of mushrooms that pop up. (Be sure to go only with an experienced forager.)

Seattle

STUNNING VIEWPOINTS | LGBTIQ+ HANGOUTS | ELECTRIC SPORTS GAMES

GETTING AROUND

The layout of Seattle is fairly straightforward, tucked between Puget Sound on one side and Lake Washington on the other, with I-5 running straight down the middle. Most of the main neighborhoods are reachable by the city's Link light-rail train. Otherwise, buses, cars, streetcars or bikes - depending on where you're staying - are options.

As the home of big-name technology giants like Microsoft and Amazon, Seattle is often thought of as the height of innovation. Each of the city's approximately 1500 tech start-ups - from pioneers of advanced artificial intelligence to innovators working on sustainable space travel - seems on the verge of its big breakthrough.

And while much of the city is now filled with towering glass skyscrapers to house these innovators, the surrounding nature serves as a beloved juxtaposition. With sparkling Puget Sound to the west, the snowcapped Cascade Mountains to the east and urban green spaces dotted all throughout town, it's easy enough for Seattleites to escape the urban hustle.

All of that said, at its core, Seattle is a city of kindness and acceptance. Cultural communities share the flavors of their ancestry in family-owned restaurants, rainbow flags fly proudly over LGBTIQ-owned businesses and local bookstores stock their shelves with accessible titles. It's safe to say, Seattle is a city more than worth exploring.

TOP TIP

To ride the easy-access Link light-rail system, opt to use either the Transit Go app or an ORCA card to make your experience as seamless as possible.

To the Top of the Space Needle

Views from a UFO-inspired landmark

If there's one attraction that comes to mind when you think of Seattle, it's undoubtedly the **Space Needle** *(spaceneedle.com; adult/child from $35/30)*. Standing proudly in Seattle Center at 605ft tall, this UFO-inspired tower was originally built for the 1962 World's Fair and continues to welcome about a million visitors every year. Head to the upper observation deck for an open-air deck showcasing some of the best views of the city, Puget Sound and Mt Rainier. Then, venture to the lower Loupe Level, where a revolving deck spins guests around during a leisurely 30-minute circumnavigation.

JOSEPH SOHM/SHUTTERSTOCK

Space Needle

Feel Inspired by Whimsical Glass Art

Visit Chihuly Garden and Glass

An exquisite exposition of the life and work of dynamic local sculptor Dale Chihuly, **Chihuly Garden and Glass** *(chihulygardenandglass.com; adult/child $32/free)* is possibly the finest collection of curated glass art you'll ever see. It shows off Chihuly's creative designs in a suite of interconnected rooms and an adjacent garden in the shadow of the Space Needle.

Dive into Pop Culture

Architecture meets entertainment

The **Museum of Pop Culture** *(mopop.org; adult/child from $25/19)* – or MoPOP – is an inspired marriage between super-modern architecture and legendary rock-and-roll history. Inside its avant-garde frame, you can tune in to the famous sounds of Seattle or attempt to imitate the rock masters in an interactive 'Sound Lab.'

EATING NEAR THE SPACE NEEDLE: OUR PICKS

Maiz Molino: Get your Mexican food fix at Maiz Molino, where the brunch chilaquiles and dinner duck mole chalupas are both sure to please. *hours vary* $$

Paju: A small and simple space that serves modern takes on beloved Korean dishes. *hours vary* $$

Toulouse Petit: Cajun-Creole restaurant with New Orleans–inspired food, decor and ambience. Get the perfectly puffy buttermilk beignets. *hours vary* $$

Tilikum Place Cafe: Savor French onion soup and Dutch baby pancakes at this seasonal, European-style cafe. Make reservations. *hours vary* $$

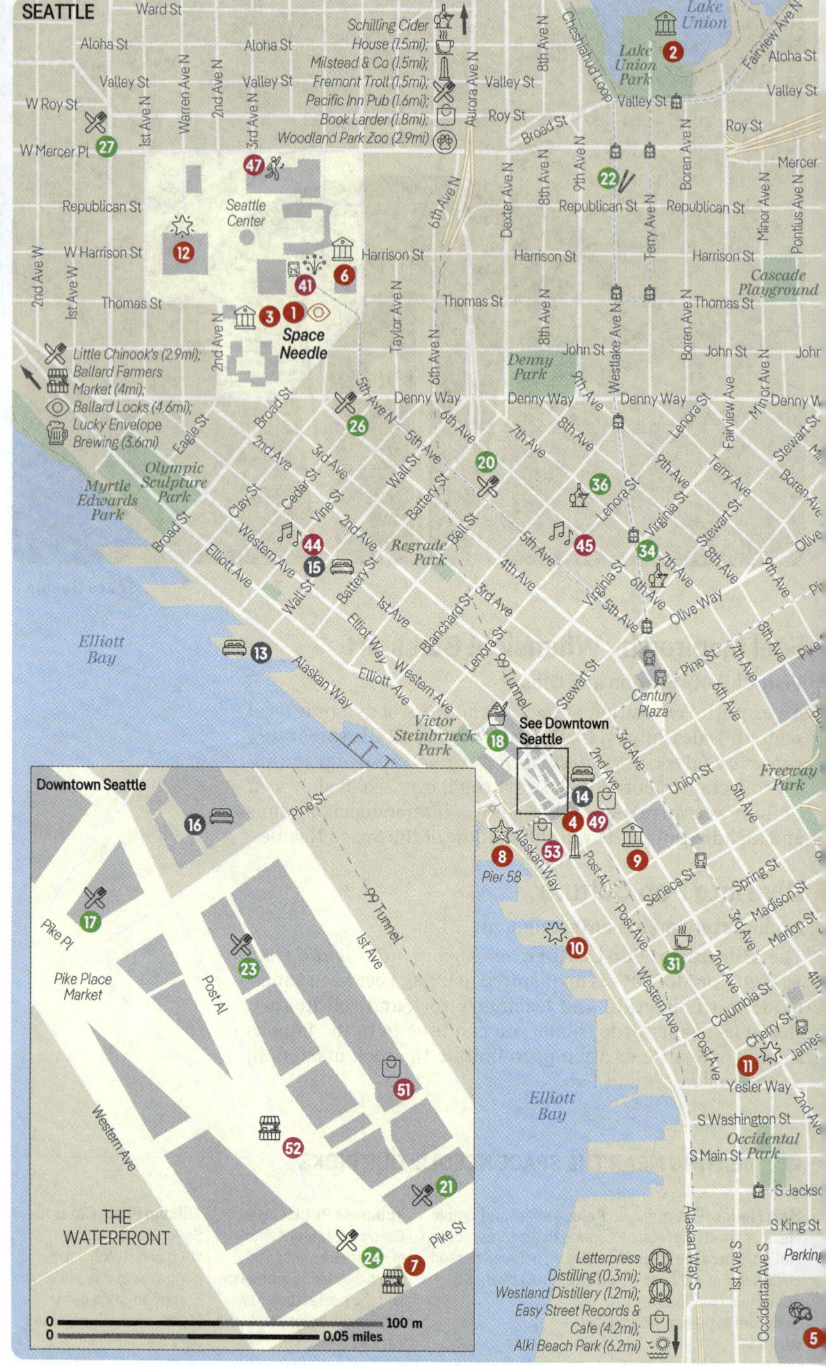
SEATTLE
Schilling Cider House (1.5mi);
Milstead & Co (1.5mi);
Fremont Troll (1.5mi);
Pacific Inn Pub (1.6mi);
Book Larder (1.8mi);
Woodland Park Zoo (2.9mi)
Lake Union
Lake Union Park
Seattle Center
Space Needle
Little Chinook's (2.9mi);
Ballard Farmers Market (4mi);
Ballard Locks (4.6mi);
Lucky Envelope Brewing (3.6mi)
Olympic Sculpture Park
Myrtle Edwards Park
Denny Park
Regrade Park
Cascade Playground
Elliott Bay
Victor Steinbrueck Park
See Downtown Seattle
Century Plaza
Freeway Park
Pier 58
Occidental Park
Letterpress Distilling (0.3mi);
Westland Distillery (1.2mi);
Easy Street Records & Cafe (4.2mi);
Alki Beach Park (6.2mi)
Downtown Seattle
Pike Place Market
THE WATERFRONT
0 100 m
0 0.05 miles

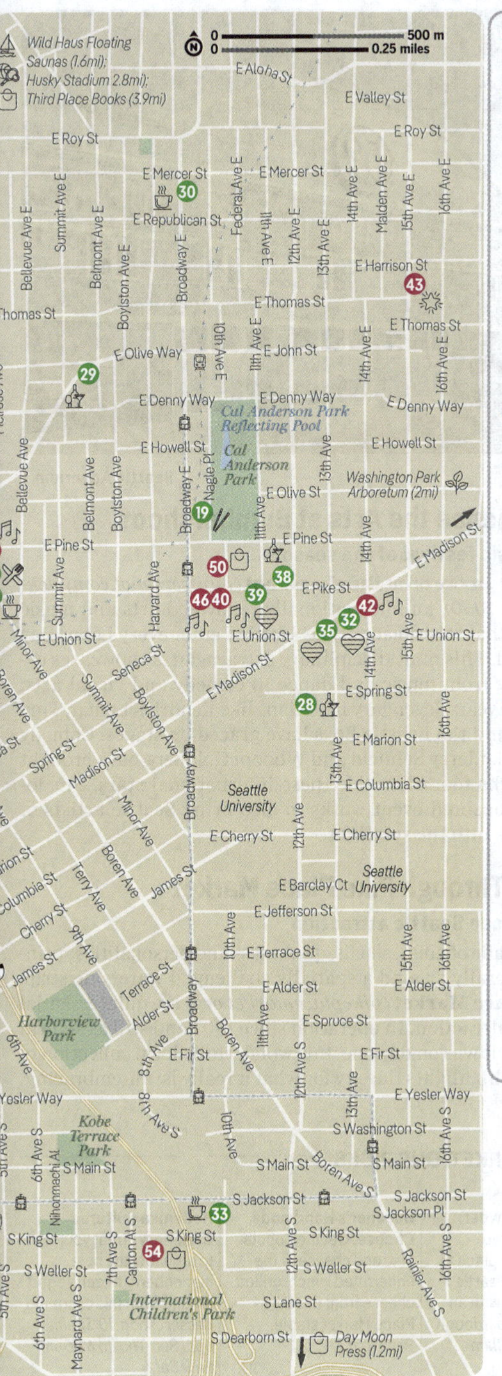

HIGHLIGHTS
1 Space Needle

SIGHTS
2 Center for Wooden Boats
3 Chihuly Garden and Glass
4 Gum Wall
5 Lumen Field
6 Museum of Pop Culture
7 Public Market Sign
8 Seattle Aquarium
9 Seattle Art Museum

ACTIVITIES
10 Argosy Cruises
11 Bill Speidel's Underground Tour
12 Climate Pledge Arena

SLEEPING
13 Edgewater
14 Green Tortoise Seattle Hostel
15 Hotel Crocodile
16 Inn at the Market

EATING
17 Beecher's Handmade Cheese
18 Hellenika Cultured Creamery
19 Ltd Edition Sushi
20 Maiz Molino
21 Matt's in the Market
22 Paju
23 Pike Place Chowder
24 Pike Place Fish Market
25 Taylor Shellfish Oyster Bar
26 Tilikum Place Cafe
27 Toulouse Petit

DRINKING & NIGHTLIFE
28 Canon
29 Doctor's Office
30 Espresso Vivace
31 Futurebean by Storyville Coffee
32 Madison Pub
33 Phin
34 Phocific Standard Time
35 Pony
36 Rachel's Ginger Beer
37 Starbucks Reserve Roastery
38 Unicorn
39 Wildrose

ENTERTAINMENT
40 Barboza
41 Bumbershoot
42 Chop Suey
43 Club Comedy Seattle
44 Crocodile
45 Dimitriou's Jazz Alley
46 Neumos
47 Pacific Northwest Ballet
48 Vice Seattle

SHOPPING
49 Eighth Generation
50 Elliott Bay Book Company
51 Metsker Maps
52 Pike Place Market
53 Seattle Waterfront Market
54 Tsue Chong Retail Store

MAKE A REAL CHANGE

As of 2024, it was estimated that around 16,000 people were experiencing homelessness in Seattle. And while the city's large population of unhoused people may give some visitors pause, it's important to keep in mind that they are citizens of the neighborhood the same as anyone else, and pose no more a threat than their housed neighbors. One way to contribute to the solution is by buying the weekly newspaper *Real Change*. You'll see vendors, many of them unhoused people, selling it on the street for $2 (vendors buy the paper for $0.60 a copy and keep the profit). The paper, founded in 1994, generates over $1 million a year for homeless causes.

DARRYL BROOKS/SHUTTERSTOCK

Seattle Aquarium

Experience the Arts at Bumbershoot

The music festival of the season

Get your groove on at **Bumbershoot** *(bumbershoot.com; tickets from $150)*, an internationally renowned arts and music festival that takes place at the Seattle Center every Labor Day weekend. This multidisciplinary extravaganza showcases everything from music and dance to comedy and visual arts. Over the years, legendary musicians like Kendrick Lamar, Tina Turner and the Beastie Boys have graced its stages. Comedy giants like Jerry Seinfeld and Whoopi Goldberg have brought the laughs too. Alongside these international stars, this locally sponsored event works to also bring Seattle artists of all kinds into the spotlight.

Shop Through Pike Place Market

A must-see Seattle attraction

A cavalcade of noise, smells, quirkiness and personalities sprinkled liberally around a spatially challenged waterside strip, **Pike Place Market** *(pikeplacemarket.org)* is a quintessential Seattle attraction. In operation since 1907 and still as soulful today as it was on day one, this wonderfully local collection of vendors highlights the city for what it really is: all-embracing,

EATING IN PIKE PLACE MARKET: OUR PICKS

Matt's in the Market: The menu at Matt's features ingredients that come from the famed market down below. *11:30am-2:30pm & 5:30-10pm Mon-Sat* $$$

Pike Place Chowder: This counter-serve restaurant is the place to get some fresh Seattle clam chowder – with an optional fresh sourdough bread bowl too. *11am-5pm* $

Beecher's Handmade Cheese: Get the popular mac and cheese or the underrated kimchi grilled cheese from this Pike Place Market staple. *9am-7pm* $

Hellenika Cultured Creamery: Treat yourself to arguably the best marionberry frozen yogurt around from this charming dessert shop. *10:30am-6pm Sun-Thu, to 6:30pm Fri & Sat* $

eclectic and proudly unique. Be sure to snap a picture with the neon **Public Market sign**, watch the fishmongers at the **Pike Place Fish Market** stall toss massive salmon around, press your own sticky addition to the **Gum Wall**, pick up a blooming flower bouquet, and snack on a cheesy meal from **Beecher's Handmade Cheese**, just to start.

Make Marine Animal Friends

The new and improved Seattle Aquarium

More than 10,000 underwater creatures call the **Seattle Aquarium** *(seattleaquarium.org; adult/child from $34/22)* home, including otters, seahorses, rays and even a giant Pacific octopus. Most recently, the aquarium has added a state-of-the-art Ocean Pavilion, which includes a 360,000-gallon tank housing animals from the Indo-Pacific.

Sail Puget Sound

Stunning water views await

The stunning Puget Sound is a highlight of any visit to Downtown Seattle. Want to experience it firsthand? **Argosy Cruises** *(argosycruises.com; adult/child $45/29)* provides the perfect opportunity with multiple daily cruises departing from Pier 55. The popular Harbor Cruise is one hour of delightfully informative narration and lovely city skyline views.

Stroll Through the Seattle Art Museum

Spotlighting Native art

The collection at the **Seattle Art Museum** *(seattleartmuseum.org; adult/child from $30/free)* feels uncommon, intimate and extraordinary. Its sterling selection of contemporary and antique art of the Indigenous peoples of the Pacific Northwest alone makes this a required stop on any city getaway.

Catch a Game at Climate Pledge Arena

Sustainability meets sports

The **Climate Pledge Arena** *(climatepledgearena.com)* is an incredibly cool venue, in more ways than one. First off, the arena officially became zero carbon-certified in October 2023 – and it required a whole lot of sustainable plans to get there. It's powered by 100% renewable energy, implements on-site

BEST LITERARY FINDS IN SEATTLE

Elliott Bay Book Company: Pop into arguably the best-known bookstore in the city. Located in Capitol Hill, this literary haven has over 150,000 titles and an incredibly inclusive selection.

Third Place Books: Find your next read – new or used – at Third Place Books. Then, settle in to read it at the on-site cafe or pub.

Day Moon Press: A cozy, family-owned letterpress print shop with loads of old-school printmaking gear and a small retail section.

Book Larder: Experience the best of books and bites at Book Larder, a North Seattle gem with shelves stocked to the brim with cookbooks.

Metsker Maps: Get equipped for your next travel adventure at Metsker Maps. This nearly century-old shop is filled with maps, globes and travel guidebooks.

DRINKING IN SEATTLE: BEST COFFEE SHOPS

Futurebean by Storyville Coffee: The cozy yet modern coffee shop serves impeccable breakfast sandwiches, cinnamon rolls, salted caramel cookies and, of course, coffee. *8am-2pm*

Espresso Vivace: Widely regarded as the best espresso in the city. The founder David Schomer is also credited with bringing latte art to the US. *6am-7pm*

Milstead & Co: This fabulous Fremont coffee bar meticulously selects its beans with sommelier-level skill and has a 'bean menu' that changes daily. *7am-4pm*

Phin: Venture to Little Saigon in the International District, where the baristas at Phin brew fantastic condensed milk-drizzled Vietnamese coffee drinks. *8am-3pm Mon & Wed-Fri, to 5pm Sat & Sun*

SEATTLE: THE BIRTHPLACE OF GRUNGE

Grunge emerged in Seattle in the 1980s as a reaction against the perceived excesses of 1980s hair metal and mainstream rock. Bands like Green River, Mudhoney and the Melvins blended the raw energy of punk rock with the heavy, distorted sounds of metal, often played at a slower tempo, creating the gritty, sludgy sound that grunge is known for. Initially many artists disliked the 'grunge' label, (accurately) viewing it as a marketing term. However, as the genre gained mainstream popularity in the early 1990s with bands like Nirvana, Pearl Jam, Soundgarden and Alice in Chains, the term became widely accepted, even if begrudgingly by some, as a descriptor for this unique 'Seattle Sound'.

waste sorting to prioritize zero waste initiatives and uses captured rainwater to make the Kraken's ice rink, just to start.

While these sustainable features are fantastic in their own right, the venue's two sports teams bring even more excitement. First, there's the Seattle Kraken, a pro hockey team that officially joined the NHL in 2021 and soon after qualified for the Stanley Cup playoffs in 2023. Then, there's the Seattle Storm, a legendary WNBA team that has garnered 16 playoff appearances and four championships under their belt since their establishment in 2000. Both teams have amassed thousands of die-hard fans, making the game atmosphere absolutely electric.

Visit the Birthplace of Grunge Music

Welcome to the Crocodile

Seattle is considered the birthplace of grunge music, and the **Crocodile** *(thecrocodile.com)* is one of the main venues that made that musical renaissance happen. Grunge greats like Nirvana, Pearl Jam, Soundgarden, Alice in Chains and Mudhoney have all performed at the Crocodile, and to this day, you can still see incredible live music acts – grunge or otherwise – at this legendary Seattle institution.

Listen to Live Music at Dimitriou's Jazz Alley

A legacied jazz hub

Not a lot of people know it, but Seattle was a hive of jazzy creativity in the 1940s and '50s. Some of the legacy remains at **Dimitriou's Jazz Alley** *(jazzalley.com/www-home)*, where national and international jazz acts take the stage. It's a holdout in the face of the area's gentrification and a local institution for more than four decades. It's worth noting that this intimate space is a seated venue, but dining is optional.

Spend an Evening at the Ballet

A dance performance to remember

Founded in Seattle in 1972, the **Pacific Northwest Ballet** *(pnb.org; tickets from $5)* is a leading American ballet company. Under the artistic direction of Peter Boal since 2005, the PNB presents over 100 annual performances at McCaw Hall, featuring a diverse repertoire of classical and contemporary works including their renowned *Nutcracker*. Even better, they're forward thinking regarding who can be a ballet

EATING IN SEATTLE: BEST SEAFOOD

Taylor Shellfish Oyster Bar: Arguably Seattle's best oyster spot, with several locations around the city. Capitol Hill is the flagship. *noon-8pm Sun-Thu, to 9pm Fri & Sat* **$$**

Ltd Edition Sushi: Splurge on a seasonally inspired omakase (chef's choice) experience at this Michelin-worthy restaurant. *5-9:30pm Mon-Fri* **$$$**

Pacific Inn Pub: Amidst all the competition, Pacific Inn Pub's expertly spiced, panko-crusted fish and chips are some of the best in town. *11am-2am* **$$**

Little Chinook's: This casual eatery is known for its fish and chips, with both crisp panko-breaded and lighter tempura options. *11:30am-6pm* **$**

NICHOLE PARK/SHUTTERSTOCK

Red panda, Woodland Park Zoo

dancer, with exceptionally talented BIPOC, nonbinary and transgender dancers taking to their stage.

Swap Tailgating for Sailgating

At UW's Husky Stadium

You've heard of tailgating, but what about sailgating? Since the University of Washington's **Husky Stadium** *(gohuskies.com)* is right on Lake Washington, the most avid football fans charter boats, join sailgating cruises, or even take out their own vessels, dropping anchor a little ways away from the shore and reveling in pregame food, drinks and fun. To reach the stadium, flag down the shuttle boat service – they start getting crowded an hour before kickoff – and they'll get you where you need to go.

Find the Fremont Troll

Aptly hidden under the bridge

Beneath the Aurora Bridge sprouts the *Fremont Troll*, a 13,000lb steel and concrete sculpture of a troll crushing a Volkswagen Beetle. It was made by four artists – Steve Badanes, Will Martin, Donna Walter and Ross Whitehead – and was the winner of a 1989 competition to design thought-provoking public art.

Meet the Animals at Woodland Park Zoo

Running semi-free

The **Woodland Park Zoo** *(zoo.org; adult/child from $27/16)* is consistently rated as one of the top 10 zoos in the country. It was one of the first in the nation to free animals from their restrictive cages in favor of ecosystem enclosures, where animals from similar environments share large spaces designed to replicate their natural surroundings. Say hello to the beloved red pandas and Humboldt penguins!

WHERE TO SHOP LOCAL IN SEATTLE

Ballard Farmers Market: Experience the local tradition of a weekend farmers market visit with a trip to Ballard Farmers Market, home to more than 100 vendors.

Eighth Generation: Admire Native American artistry first-hand at Eighth Generation, a new addition to Seattle's downtown owned by the Snoqualmie Tribe.

Seattle Waterfront Market: Support local artists at this collective selling everything from watercolor paintings to floral soaps.

Tsue Chong Retail Store: Get yourself some 'unfortunate' (misshapen) fortune cookies from the family-owned Tsue Chong Retail Store.

Easy Street Records & Cafe: Purchase a record from a new-to-you artist at arguably the city's most multifarious record store.

SEATTLE ON THE WATER

Washington Park Arboretum: Kayak your way around Washington Park Arboretum for beautiful blooms and unbeatable water views.

Wild Haus Floating Saunas: Heat your worries away as you sail on Lake Union via a wood-fired sauna boat, courtesy of Wild Haus Floating Saunas.

Center for Wooden Boats: Enjoy a completely free boat ride on Lake Union each Sunday with the Center for Wooden Boats, departing from Lake Union Park.

Kenmore Air: Take to the water and to the skies with Kenmore Air's Seattle Scenic Seaplane Tour.

Alki Beach Park: Soak up the sun on Seattle's most popular shoreline, tucked away from the hustle and bustle in West Seattle.

ARTCHEMY LABS/SHUTTERSTOCK

Starbucks Reserve Roastery

Experience the Ballard Locks

A feat of engineering

The **Ballard Locks** *(ballardlocks.org)*, a popular attraction that allows boats to move between the Puget Sound and the Ship Canal, travel a 22ft rise from saltwater to fresh. The fish ladder here is open to the public and offers a unique opportunity to watch salmon migrate upstream.

Tour the Starbucks Reserve Roastery

Behind the coffee curtain

While most Starbucks fans will venture to the first Starbucks in Pike Place (p450), the **Starbucks Reserve Roastery** *(starbucksreserve.com/locations/seattle-roastery)* in Capitol Hill may be time better spent. At the roastery of this Seattle-grown chain, you can sip on coffee-tasting flights ($13 to $19), take a behind-the-scenes look at the roasting area ($45) or take an espresso martini-making class ($95), just to start.

Experience Capitol Hill's Nightlife Scene

Bars, clubs and comedy

Capitol Hill comes to life after dark. Looking to dance the night away to DJ sets or live music performances? Pick your venue based on music genre. **Vice Seattle** *(viceseattle.com)* is known for EDM, **Neumos** *(neumos.com)* leans toward punk and hip-hop, **Barboza** *(thebarboza.com)* has an eclectic but pop-heavy line-up, and **Chop Suey**'s *(chopsuey.com)* bookings are as mixed as the dish it's named after.

Still yet, there are loads of LGBTIQ+ hot spots. **Pony** *(ponyseattle.com)* has reached a level of popularity where most denizens either love or loathe it, while circus-themed **Unicorn** *(unicornseattle.com)* has made its mark with jello shots and pinball games. Let's not forget **Madison Pub** *(madisonpub.com)*, a gay sports bar, and **Wildrose** *(thewildrosebar.com)*, a longtime lesbian bar.

Alternatively, swap bass drops for punch lines with a show at **Club Comedy Seattle** *(clubcomedyseattle.com)*, which features both national headliners and up-and-coming local artists.

Catch a Game at Lumen Field

Feel the energy of the crowd

While **Lumen Field** *(lumenfield.com)* is best known as the home of the Seattle Seahawks (NFL), this iconic sports arena also lays claim to the Seattle Reign (NWSL) and the Seattle Sounders (MLS). All of these teams have won multiple titles in their respective sports and divisions. Even better, they boast some of the most enthusiastic fan bases in the country; book tickets far in advance – especially for Seahawks games – as they often sell out quickly.

Explore Seattle's Hidden City: the Underground

A subterranean adventure

Believe it or not, the original 1800s Seattle was built on unstable, sandy ground. Over time those buildings began to sink. When the Great Seattle Fire of 1889 decimated a 30-block radius, much of the city needed to be rebuilt. Today, visitors can explore these sunken streets and structures – reminiscent of an abandoned construction site crossed with a Hollywood movie set – through **Bill Speidel's Underground Tour** *(undergroundtour.com; adult/child $22/10)*. Mix in a little humor and history and you have a recipe for a fun and educational activity.

LOOKING FOR MORE TROLLS?

If you thought the greater Seattle area could only have one troll sculpture, well, you'd be wrong. Besides the Fremont Troll, there are a handful of others spread around, all made by Danish environmental artist Thomas Dambo. Find these trolls in Ballard, West Seattle, Bainbridge Island, Vashon Island and Issaquah (with the final one in the Pacific Northwest series in Portland, Oregon; p478), tucked amidst the trees or standing proudly in front of museums. Learn more about these incredible sculptures and the artist behind them at *nwtrolls.org*.

DRINKING IN SEATTLE: OUR PICKS

Letterpress Distilling: Travel to Italy at Letterpress Distilling for liqueurs like amaro and limoncello. *noon-6pm Sat, to 4pm Sun*

Westland Distillery: Sip on some of the finest whiskey in town – straight or in cocktails – at Westland Distillery. *hours vary*

Lucky Envelope Brewing: Sample beers with fun flavor notes, from gingerbread to citrus, at Lucky Envelope Brewing. *hours vary*

Schilling Cider House: Enjoy the crispness of Pacific Northwest apples in drink form. *3-9pm Wed & Thu, 1-10pm Fri, noon-10pm Sat, to 8pm Sun*

Phocific Standard Time: Chase a pho-fat-washed shot of Jameson with pho broth at this Vietnamese-inspired speakeasy. *5-11pm Tue-Thu, to midnight Fri & Sat*

Rachel's Ginger Beer: The zingy, ginger-based drinks pack a punch – both in the original non-alcoholic form and mixed into fun cocktails. *11:30am-8pm Mon-Sat*

Canon: Frequently listed as one of the best bars in the world, with innovative cocktails as tasty as they are artful. *5pm-1am Sun, Wed & Thu, to 2am Fri & Sat*

Doctor's Office: Way more fun than your usual doctor's visit, here your 'prescription' is a masterfully crafted cocktail of your choice. *4pm-1am*

Washington

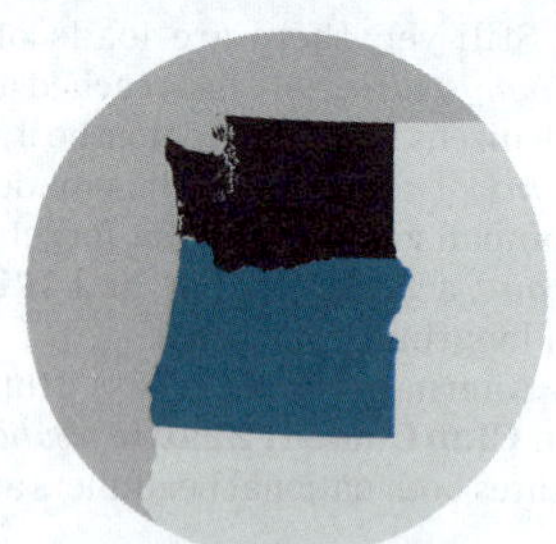

STUNNING LANDSCAPES | FRESH SEAFOOD | PICTURESQUE WINERIES

Places

Aptly nicknamed the 'Evergreen State,' Washington is arguably the heart of the Pacific Northwest. With that title comes everything you'd hope for, from the lush, green Olympic Peninsula to the wild, white peaks of the Cascade Mountains and the relaxed, kayaker-friendly San Juan Islands. Head east and you'll see another side of the state: aridly beautiful, with upscale wineries and cowboy-style breakfasts in equal measure, plus orchards, wheat fields and pioneer history.

Outside of the big urban jolt of Seattle, there are a few other main population centers – Spokane, Bellingham, Olympia – each with its own sort of charm. Still, to get the most out of visiting Washington, you'll want to leave the cities behind and lose yourself in the mountains and the woods, along the coast or on the islands. The state's three national parks are incredible in their own rights, while the lesser-known nature spots offer equally rewarding experiences. Safe to say, the best experiences here are mostly unmediated.

TOP TIP

Make time for Washington's beautiful national parks. While this may require planning ahead (timed entry passes, transportation logistics etc), these landscapes are more than worth the extra effort.

GETTING AROUND

To keep it simple, a car is by far the best option for getting around Washington. There are bus routes and Amtrak train routes crisscrossing the Evergreen State, but they're not the most convenient for traveling lengthy distances. Ferries are also an important part of Washington's transportation infrastructure, shuttling people and cars across the Puget Sound; when taking a vehicle aboard a ferry, be sure to give yourself quite a bit of buffer time, as the ferries often get filled to capacity, meaning you'll have to wait for the next sailing.

BRITISH COLUMBIA
CANADA
MONTANA
IDAHO
OREGON
PACIFIC OCEAN
0 100 km
0 50 miles
1
Vancouver Island
Lake Cowichan
Neah Bay
Strait of Juan de Fuca
Lake Ozette
Forks
Lake Crescent
Port Angeles
Sequim
Port Townsend
Deer Park
Clearwater River
Olympic National Park
Lake Quinault
Lake Cushman
Hood Canal
Aberdeen
Westport
Ocean Park
Long Beach
Seaview
Cape Disappointment State Park
Astoria
Young River
Tillamook Bay
Bellingham
San Juan Islands
Fidalgo Island
Whidbey Island
Mt Vernon
Bainbridge Island
Vashon Island
Seattle
Tacoma
Olympia
Centralia
Castle Rock
Silver Lake
Longview
Columbia River
Vancouver
Camas
Mt Baker
Baker Lake
North Cascades National Park
Ross Lake
Skagit River
Skagit Valley
Everett
Washington Cascades
Cascade Pass
Sauk River
Glacier Peak
Jack Mtn
Mt Logan
Carbon River
Mt Rainier
Paradise
Mt Rainier National Park
Nisqually River
Riffe Lake
Mt St Helens National Volcanic Monument
Mt Adams
Hood River
The Dalles
Maryhill
Goldendale
Remmel Mtn
Harts Pass
Rainy Pass
Stehekin
Pyramid Mtn
Lake Chelan
Lake Wenatchee
Stevens Pass
Leavenworth
Mt Stuart
Ellensburg
Yakima Valley
Selah
Yakima
Wapato
Granger
Toppenish
Grandview
Winthrop
Okanogan
Twisp
Omak
Omak Lake
Methow River
Tonasket
Republic
Lake Roosevelt National Recreation Area
Columbia River
Grand Coulee
Grand Coulee Dam
Ephrata
Moses Lake
George
Potholes Reservoir
Sunnyside
Prosser
Benton City
Richland
Pasco
Lake Wallula
Ione
Northport
Kettle Falls
Colville
Metaline Falls
Priest Lake
Cusick
Chewelah
Lake Pend Oreille
Deer Park
Spokane River
Spokane
Cœur d'Alene Lake
Davenport
Cheney
Ritzville
Lind
Palouse
Colfax
Pullman
Palouse Falls State Park
Connell
Lewiston
Pomeroy
Dayton
Waitsburg
Walla Walla
5
104
90
97
2
410
82
12
84

TOP EXPERIENCE

Mt Rainier National Park

As the most glaciated peak in the contiguous US, Mt Rainier (pronounced ruh-*neer*) boasts unsurpassed beauty around every twist and turn. Visible from up to 300 miles away, the mystical peak has been the grounding soul of Western Washington for millennia. Its original Puyallup name – Tahoma – means 'mother of all waters.'

MICHAEL CARNI/SHUTTERSTOCK

TOP TIPS

- At the time of writing, Mt Rainier National Park required timed entry reservations for the Sunrise Corridor during peak season (July 11 to September 1). Reservations are released in batches and get snatched up quickly, so be sure to set a reminder.

PRACTICALITIES

- nps.gov/mora/index.htm
- $30 per vehicle
- open 24/7

Mt Rainier from Paradise

The **Paradise District** may be the most popular part of Mt Rainier National Park – and the most easily accessible, via the Nisqually entrance. Here, gape in awe at the 188ft **Narada Falls**; take in particularly stunning views of Mt Rainier from the **Ricksecker Point** road cutout; or tackle the wildlife-dotted 1.2-mile **Nisqually Vista Trail**.

Mt Rainier from Sunrise

The Sunrise area is secretly the favorite of many Washingtonians, and entered via the forested drive from the White River entrance (closed to cars for the long winter). The view from the **Sunrise Point Lookout** is of not only Mt Rainier but of the whole Washington Cascade chain, from Mt Baker to Mt Adams.

Want to see the largest glacier in the continental US? Take a quick stroll to **Emmons Vista** – or a longer hike along the **Sourdough Ridge Trail** or **Glacier Basin Trail** – to marvel at Emmons Glacier. If you're feeling particularly hardy, try waking up at 3am for the 5.6-mile hike to the **Fremont Fire Lookout** to take in the sunrise.

TOP EXPERIENCE

Olympic National Park

Olympic National Park is one of the most ecologically diverse places on earth. The terrain gets in your bones (and that's not just the dampness). You could wander the moss-draped trails of the Hoh Rainforest, discover the Pacific Ocean in a colorful tide pool, ski on one of the National Park System's only ski lifts, and camp under stars you haven't seen in decades.

Hurricane Ridge

In the winter, the 10-mile drive to the top of the accessible Hurricane Ridge leads to a wintertime ski treat, where snowshoeing, tubing, cross-country skiing, downhill skiing and snowboarding opportunities abound. (Note: bring your own food, supplies and rental gear.) In the summer months, wildflowers, hiking and stargazing are at their peak.

Sol Duc Hot Springs

Three healing mineral water pools are fed by a constant stream of the Sol Duc hot springs (there's also a conventional pool). Plus, just across the way, there's a delightful 0.8-mile trail to **Sol Duc Falls**.

Rialto Beach

Rialto Beach's coastline is wild and cinematic, filled with crashing waves, timeless driftwood and a raft of offshore sea stacks. Seals, bald eagles and gray whales make appearances, and in low tide, tide pools reveal starfish, anemone and urchins.

Hoh Rainforest

After years of listening to nature, sound recording expert Gordon Hempton found the quietest place in the lower 48: a mossy log in the Hoh Rainforest. While the secret is out and the forest isn't quite as quiet, admire the Tolkien-like magic of the details: old-growth cedar and spruce, Jurassic ferns and noise-swallowing moss, lichens and fungi.

TOP TIPS

- Download the National Park Service app before you go for maps. Internet coverage is spotty (at best).
- Gas up and load up on supplies in Port Angeles.
- With only five restaurants in the entire park, plan ahead or dine in Forks or Neah Bay.

PRACTICALITIES

- nps.gov/olym/index.htm
- $30 per vehicle
- open 24/7

TOP EXPERIENCE

North Cascades National Park

Protected by sharp mountain peaks with frightening names – Mt Fury, Mt Terror and Desolation Peak – North Cascades National Park has only one access road (Hwy 20, aka the North Cascades Scenic Hwy), which is closed in winter. But once you make it inside, there's a whole host of breathtaking nature sights: 300 glaciers, 200 types of birds and countless hikes are just the beginning.

PHOTO VOLCANO/SHUTTERSTOCK

Diablo Lake

Glacial Waters Run Deep

One of the few sights in North Cascades National Park that's generally accessible year-round, **Diablo Lake** is also among the most stunning. Its shocking turquoise color comes from reflective 'glacial flour' in the water. Though glacier-fed, the lake is actually an artificial reservoir, a result of the 1920s-era Skagit River Hydroelectric Project. You can easily gaze upon Diablo Lake from your car at a viewpoint along Hwy 20, but it's worth taking time for a closer look. Kayaking the lake is otherworldly; if you didn't bring your kayak, the educational **North Cascades Institute** *(ncascades.org; adult/child $50/30)* offers informative three-hour boat tours.

Stay in Stehekin

What, no road access? Cut off from the rest of Washington's highway network by craggy mountains, Stehekin is that rarest of modern American settlements: it's unreachable by car. Getting here is largely the point of a visit, although being here is also wonderful, as the remoteness makes the village impossibly peaceful and quiet. The only thing resembling stress here is making sure you get to the **bakery** on time.

TOP TIPS

- To reach Stehekin, take the **Lady of the Lake ferry** *(ladyofthelake.com; one way $25-45)* across Lake Chelan, either as a day trip or for an overnight stay (book well ahead for both ferry and lodgings).

PRACTICALITIES

- nps.gov/noca/index.htm
- free
- open 24/7

Bellingham & Around

Saltwater adventures in Fairhaven

Perched above Bellingham Bay, the southside district of Fairhaven is Bellingham's unofficial outdoor adventure hub – and an epicenter for bioluminescent activity. Both the **Community Boating Center** *(boatingcenter.org; $100)* and **Moondance Sea Kayak Adventures** *(moondancekayak.com; $105)* offer summer bioluminescence paddles to see this neon-colored phenomenon, and should be booked well in advance.

Wind down Chuckanut Drive

This 24-mile road winds along the coastline from Bellingham to Skagit County's **Bow**, with the Cascade Mountains and Bellingham Bay framing each side. Be sure to stop at **Larrabee State Park** *(parks.wa.gov/find-parks/state-parks/larrabee-state-park; $10)* along the way for gorgeous hikes and marine-creature-filled tide pools. Need to refuel? **Taylor Shellfish Farm** *(taylorshellfishfarms.com)* isn't far, and the salty, fresh oysters make for a particularly delicious waterside meal.

Whidbey & Fidalgo Islands

Connecting the islands

Linked by the iconic Deception Pass bridge, Fidalgo and Whidbey islands are home to the sprawling **Deception Pass State Park** *(parks.wa.gov/find-parks/state-parks/deception-pass-state-park; $10)*. On the Fidalgo (Anacortes) side, stop by **Rosario Head** for a short walk to epic sea cliffs. Hike or drive from Rosario to the busy boat launch and sprawling lawn at **Bowman Bay**. Trekking south from Bowman Bay leads to **Lottie Point** and **Lighthouse Point** – scenic sea bluff trails through evergreen forest and Pacific madrone.

Sustainable seafood in Coupeville

Whidbey Island's Coupeville is home to **Penn Cove Shellfish** *(penncoveshellfish.com)*, a sustainable seafood farm famous for its mussels. Countless island restaurants serve Penn Cove mussels, clams and oysters, and you can see the beds just west of town along Madrona Way. Stop by local grocery stores (like Prairie Center Market) to purchase and cook your own, or attend **Penn Cove Musselfest** (March) to tour and dine on the property.

ANACORTES' BEST TOURS

Outer Island Excursions: Whale-watching tours (May to September) launch from Anacortes' Skyline Marina. *(outerislandx.com)*

Anacortes Kayak Tours: Kayak outings from 1½ to five hours, plus bioluminescence tours and multiday trips. *(anacorteskayaktours.com)*

Maritime Heritage Center: Free museum detailing Anacortes' maritime history. Take a self-guided tour of the WT *Preston* sternwheeler. *(anacorteswa.gov/422/Maritime-Heritage-Center)*

Skagit Guided Adventures: Walking and hiking tours from a six-hour ecotour to a three-hour guided hike. Both include transportation. *(skagitguidedadventures.com)*

Self-guided tours: Anacortes offers free self-guided tours on its website. *(anacorteswa.gov)*

DRINKING IN NORTHWESTERN WASHINGTON: BREWERIES

Chuckanut Brewery: This celebrated lager brewer operates a barn-red production facility and sunny beer garden at the Port of Skagit. *1-8pm Mon-Thu, noon-8pm Fri-Sun*

Terramar Brewstillery: Sip Skagit-made beer, spirits and non-alcoholic options from Terramar's sprawling beer garden with views of the Chuckanut Mountains. *11:30am-9pm*

El Sueñito Brewing: Super-satisfying tamales and tacos complement sessionable brews at this LGBTIQ- and Mexican-owned brewery. *11am-10pm*

Anacortes Brewery: One of the oldest breweries in Washington (established in 1994) with time-tested beers, a robust food menu and live music. *11am-8pm Sun-Thu, to 10pm Fri & Sat*

ANNUAL EVENTS AT MT BAKER

Mt Baker hosts two big annual events during the snow season. In January or February, snow-sports enthusiasts flock to the ski area to witness the **Legendary Banked Slalom** race. Started by 16 snowboarders in 1985, it's one of the sport's longest-running events and draws world-class competitors.

Every Memorial Day Weekend in May, the **Ski to Sea** race – a multisport team relay – begins at **Mt Baker Ski Area** and ends 93 miles away at Bellingham Bay. Racers compete in cross-country skiing and downhill ski/snowboard legs at Mt Baker before running and road biking down Mt Baker Hwy. First run in 1973, Ski to Sea is the largest one-day event in Whatcom County.

BILL PERRY/SHUTTERSTOCK

Picture Lake

Mt Baker

A scenic drive to Mt Baker's Artist Point

Summer at the 10,781ft Mt Baker is spectacular. Subalpine trails lead through forests and wildflower meadows to glacier-clad mountain views. The 57-mile **Mt Baker Scenic Byway** *(bellingham.org/drive-and-hike-mt-baker-scenic-byway)* is ideal for road-trippers, quickly leaving the city behind and transitioning from blueberry fields to old-growth forests.

Most visitors make a beeline for **Picture Lake** – and for good reason. Pull off the road for an iconic shot of 9131ft **Mt Shuksan** reflected in the waters. Sometimes called the most photographed mountain in North America, Shuksan's rugged appeal is undeniable.

The first 55 miles of Mt Baker Hwy are open year-round. To drive the final 2.5 miles from Heather Meadows to **Artist Point** – by far the road's most spectacular stretch – visit between July and September.

The road ends at Artist Point. There's no road through these mountains – just miles of national forest and the Mt Baker

EATING & DRINKING ALONG MT BAKER HWY

Wake 'N Bakery: 'Get sconed' at the go-to spot for baked goods, breakfast burritos, coffee and trail snacks in Glacier. *7am-5pm* $

The North Fork Brewery: Locals drive from Bellingham for the North Fork's pizza and beer in Deming. Always packed, but worth the wait. *noon-9pm* $$

Chair 9: Unpretentious, all-ages après-ski bar and pizza place boasting the 'first cocktail' on the way back from Baker. *hours vary* $$

Graham's Bar & Restaurant: Old-fashioned pub in a 1906 building, serving Glacier off-and-on since the 1970s. *hours vary* $$

Wilderness. Walk south on the short, paved Artist Ridge Trail, where Mt Baker dominates the western skyline and Mt Shuksan rises to the east. Stay after dark for incredible stargazing.

Heaven for hikers

Hikers can experience everything from a joyous jaunt to epic, multiday backpacking trips during summer hiking season at **Mt Baker** *(fs.usda.gov/r06/mbs/recreation; $5)*. **Horseshoe Bend Trail** is a forested, 3-mile round-trip trek along the Nooksack River. At the end of Mt Baker Hwy, the 1-mile round-trip **Artist Ridge Trail** is the most popular hike on the mountain, climbing gently to Huntoon Point for incredible views of Mts Baker and Shuksan.

Then there's the moderate **Chain Lakes Loop**, which gains 1800ft of elevation and showcases a series of picturesque lakes along its 6.5-mile route. The nearby, strenuous **Lake Ann Trail** (8.2 miles round-trip, 2100ft elevation gain) leads to a stunning lake and close-up views of Mt Shuksan.

Trails around Mt Baker are typically accessible between July and early October. Check with the **Forest Service** *(fs.usda.gov/mbs)* for road and trail conditions before setting out. Always dress in layers, check the forecast and plan accordingly. A Northwest Forest Pass is required for parking at national forest trailheads.

Skagit Valley

Farms, food and flowers

Between La Conner and Mt Vernon, the lower **Skagit River Valley** *(visitskagitvalley.com)* thrives in every season, especially spring and summer. During the former, flowers reign supreme in Skagit Valley. The season kicks off in March with **La Conner Daffodil Festival**, a celebration of bright yellow blooms. In April, the famous **Skagit Valley Tulip Festival** draws massive crowds. The ticketed **Roozengaarde** and **Tulip Town** experiences burst with colorful tulip fields and offer endless photo opportunities.

And during the latter, Skagit Valley farms produce abundant fruits and veggies, with over 90 different crops grown in the region. Taste your way across the valley with farm visits – from produce stands to pumpkin fields. Don't miss an essential stop at **Snow Goose Produce** *(snowgooseproducemarket.com)*, an open-air country market overflowing with local produce, flowers and 'immodest' ice-cream cones.

WHY I LOVE THE SKAGIT VALLEY TULIP FESTIVAL

Sarah Etinas, Lonely Planet writer

When I first heard about the Skagit Valley Tulip Festival, I wasn't sure what to make of it. I wasn't sure if there were really fields of colorful tulips stretching on and on, or if the photos I was seeing were all camera angles primed to perfection. So I bought my ticket and drove my way up.

A bit of traffic later, and my doubts were proven gloriously wrong. At just one of the farms, colorful rows of tulips in a dozen shades spread far and wide, with the snowcapped Cascade Mountains providing an even more beautiful backdrop. Cozy swings, tucked-away daffodils and an adorable gift shop completed the visit – one that I hope I get to repeat sometime soon.

EATING IN WASHINGTON: WORKING OYSTER FARMS

Goose Point: Right on Willapa Bay, Goose Point has been family-run since 1975. Enjoy oysters at a rustic picnic table or take oyster shooters to go. *9am-5pm* $

Taylor Shellfish Farms Shellfish Market: With three restaurants in Seattle, Taylor Shellfish Farms' market next to its Hood Canal processing plant offers fresher-than-fresh oysters. *10am-6pm* $

Brady's Oysters: A family-run oyster farm just west of Aberdeen with a couple of picnic tables, an authentic Pacific Northwest vibe, and oysters harvested feet away. *9am-6pm* $$

Oysterville Sea Farms: The most 'full service' of the bunch, with elegant picnic tables and a dozen menu options. *11am-6pm Thu-Mon* $

ROCHE HARBOR HISTORY

At the north end of San Juan Island, seaside Roche Harbor was once the largest lime producer in the Pacific Northwest. The company town was built by Tacoma and Roche Harbor Lime Company founder John S McMillin in 1886 to support his enterprise. The lime kilns, hotel, and historic structures still stand today, restored and transformed into the stylish **Roche Harbor Resort**. Brick-lined paths lead to three unique eateries – from casual, dockside Lime Kiln Cafe to formal McMillin's Dining Room.

The McMillin family is memorialized north of Roche Harbor at the **McMillin Memorial Mausoleum** (also known as Afterglow Vista). This otherworldly open-air rotunda features six chairs surrounding a limestone table, each containing the remains of a McMillin.

CLAUDIA G COOPER/SHUTTERSTOCK

Billy Frank Jr Nisqually National Wildlife Refuge

San Juan Islands

Whale-watching by land and sea

Near the top of every Pacific Northwest bucket list are the San Juan Islands, an emerald archipelago made up of 172 named isles and reefs. The most populous and developed of the islands, **San Juan Island** *(visitsanjuans.com/san-juan-island)* is ground zero for whale-watching.

The most environmentally friendly way to see whales and other sea mammals is from land. **Lime Kiln Point State Park** *(parks.wa.gov/find-parks/state-parks/lime-kiln-point-state-park; $10)*, also known as 'Whale Watch Park,' is one of the best places in the world to view orcas from land. Though sightings are never guaranteed, visiting between May and September (and bringing binoculars) increases your chances of seeing southern resident orcas offshore.

Consider joining a responsible whale-watching tour to significantly increase your orca-spotting odds. **Western Prince Whale & Wildlife Tours** *(orcawhalewatch.com; adult/child $155/145)*, the San Juans' oldest whale-watching company, specializes in adventurous open-air excursions.

Take a hike on Orcas Island

The largest and most mountainous of the San Juan Islands, rugged **Orcas Island** *(visitsanjuans.com/orcas-island)* is beloved for its natural beauty. Rural roads connect seaside hamlets, with parks and preserves taking up much of the island's 57 sq miles. **Moran State Park** *(moranstatepark.com)* alone is home to over 30 miles of forested trails leading to lakes, waterfalls, and island views that will leave you gaping in awe.

Bainbridge Island

Visit the Bloedel Reserve

A poetic juxtaposition of untamed Pacific Northwest forest and manicured English gardens, **Bloedel Reserve** *(bloedelreserve.org; adult/child $26/9)* is a 140-acre sanctuary at the north end of Bainbridge Island. It includes meadows, reflection pools and the original Bloedel family's French-style home. In summer, Bainbridge Performing Arts puts on a not-to-be-missed Shakespeare performance. Reserve timed tickets online.

Sequim

Looooong walks on Dungeness Spit

The longest sand spit in the US at 5.5 miles long, **Dungeness** *(fws.gov/refuge/dungeness; $3)* is also the namesake of the famous crab. . Washingtonians consider walking this Sequim trail a rite of passage. Brave souls kayak to the lighthouse, and adventurers can spend a week there as volunteer keepers. (Thankfully, you get driven.)

Olympia

Boardwalk stroll through wildlife

Stroll below bald eagles, hummingbirds and kestrels in the **Billy Frank Jr Nisqually National Wildlife Refuge** *(fws.gov/nisqually; $3)* in Olympia. The peaceful and picturesque estuary park was established in 1974, and is the protective home of hundreds of migratory birds, steelhead trout and salmon and seals. As you traverse the accessible 4 miles of boardwalk and gravel path, keep an eye out for mammals, too, including beaver, mink, muskrat and coyote. (You can even rent binoculars from the visitors center.) Arrive early, as parking fills up quickly.

Seaview

Digging razor clams

Razor clamming on **Long Beach** is just about the most Washingtonian activity imaginable. All you need to razor clam are three things: a shellfish license, a clam gun or small shovel and to go during razor-clam season. (Many hotels and guesthouses offer shovels and clam guns to guests, or you can buy one locally.) Show up about an hour before low tide and look for 'clam shows': dimples, doughnuts or keyholes in the wet

TWILIGHT TIME IN FORKS

When *Twilight* series author Stephenie Meyer searched for the rainiest, grayest town to set her vampire novel, she landed on Forks, WA, sight unseen. Several books and movies later, this remote Olympic peninsula logging town has become a global *Twilight* pilgrimage site. While the movies weren't filmed there, there are now *Twilight* tours, *Twilight*-themed shops and the Forever Twilight Festival (annually in September).

Bonus: Forks has many affordable motels, and is perfectly situated for a night's rest between the northern highlights and the western beaches.

EATING & DRINKING IN LONG BEACH

Seaview Biscuit Company: Flaky, airy biscuit perfection with Southern classics like fried chicken, pimento cheese and homemade jam. *7am-1pm, Thu-Tue* $

The Pub at Shelburne Hotel: Inside a 100-year-old hotel, a cozy, wood-paneled spot serves pub fare with charm and local flair. *noon-10pm Sun-Thu, to 11pm Fri & Sat* $$

Adrift Distillers: Celebrate the region's signature cranberry with a sweet-tart liqueur at this relaxing beachside tasting room. *10am-5pm Mon & Tue, 11am-7pm Wed-Sun*

Ilwaco Cider Company: Rustic wood tables, small-batch ciders, Nordic-leaning flavors like elderberry and cardamom – and, of course, local cranberries. *noon-8pm*

THE SALMON'S IMPOSSIBLE JOURNEY

Every year, salmon return from the open Pacific Ocean to the exact river where they were born – often making impossible leaps to complete their mind-boggling journey. Scientists still don't fully understand these feats, but the salmon seem to rely on chemical cues and magnetism. Their lifecycle is brutal: many fish die mid-jump, battered by rocks or snatched by bears, eagles or mountain lions. If they 'succeed,' they spawn (laying or fertilizing eggs), then die, nourishing their native forested ecosystems. You can spot these salmon doing these death-defying stunts in waterways throughout the Pacific Northwest between July and November.

sand. Center the clam gun, twist, pull the plug, and grab fast – razor clams are shockingly speedy for mollusks and can dig up to 1ft per minute.

Check wdfw.wa.gov for dates and locations, typically announced a few days or weeks in advance. Fall season runs September to December; spring is March through May. Open dates depend on tides, toxins, algae and clam population health.

Follow in Lewis and Clark's windswept footprints

Cape Disappointment State Park *(parks.wa.gov/find-parks/state-parks/cape-disappointment-state-park; $10)* feels like an Olympic National Park in miniature, with dramatic coastlines, isolated beaches and grand lighthouses (with a fraction of the tourists). The rugged headland marks the end of Lewis and Clark's journey, as well as the confluence of the Columbia River and Pacific Ocean (also known as the Graveyard of the Pacific, with over 200 shipwrecks in its churning waters).

The fortress-like **Lewis & Clark Interpretative Center** *(parks.wa.gov; adult/child $5/2.50)* was built to withstand the same battering weather the explorers faced. From the center, you can see (or walk to) the **Cape Disappointment Lighthouse**, the Pacific Northwest's first, built in 1856. For dramatic, misty cliffs, head to **North Head Lighthouse**.

Kite condition perfection

With wide beaches and steady winds, Long Beach is now home to one of the US' largest concentrations of world-class kite fliers. The **World Kite Museum** *(worldkitemuseum.com; adult/child $6/4)* celebrates this heritage with kites from around the globe, including traditional designs from Asia, as well as military kite history. The museum sponsors the annual Washington State International Kite Festival in the third full week of August. Want to try it yourself? Its shop sells kites, conveniently across the street from one of the best kiting beaches in the world.

Washington Cascades

Brats, brews and music

It's hard to resist the Bavarian act put on by **Leavenworth** *(leavenworth.org)*, even if it's a little over the top. The town is small (about 2400 people) but crammed with shops, restaurants and hotels – every last one decorated like something out of a community theater production of *The Sound of Music*. Leavenworth's cute schtick goes down smoother with beer and sausages – easy to find in this pedestrian-friendly town. As you stroll along Front St, consider **Gustav's Grill & Beer Garden** *(gustavsleavenworth.com)* for the faux-Alpine facade, or **München Haus** *(munchenhaus.com)* for outdoor seating and Icicle Brewing beer. Suitably primed, make your way to the gazebo at Front St Park, where most days you'll find a Bavarian-themed event going on: an expansive Christmas market, accordion concert or the annual **Leavenworth International Alphorn Festival** *(leavenworthalphorns.org/alphorn-festival)*.

ULF NAMMERT/SHUTTERSTOCK

Mt St Helens National Volcanic Monument

Volcanic adventures

On May 18, 1980, at 8:32am, Mt St Helens erupted with a violence that blew off the mountain's entire north face and melted several glaciers. It was the most destructive volcanic eruption in US history. Hundreds of sq miles of surrounding forest and thousands of wild animals were obliterated in its wake, and 57 people died.

The volcano and the zone of devastation around it are now preserved as **Mt St Helens National Volcanic Monument** *(fs.usda.gov/visit/national-monuments/mount-st-helens)*, dotted with viewpoints and visitor centers that offer an up-close way to witness both the destructive and the restorative forces of nature. You can peer at the blast zone from access roads, paddle a lake formed in the eruption, hike through millennia-old lava tubes, or even trek all the way to the summit.

Hike hundreds of miles of trails

There are literally hundreds of miles of hiking trails crisscrossing the **North Cascades**. Even just covering the best-known routes would take years. (We speak from experience.) So how do you decide where to go? The good news is, there are no bad choices.

Icicle Ridge Trail *(wta.org/go-hiking/hikes/icicle-ridge-1)* is a 6-mile round-trip trek with epic views over Leavenworth. **Lake Valhalla** via the Smithbrook Trail *(wta.org/go-hiking/hikes/lake-valhalla)* is a 7-mile round trip that would be a good first backpacking trip for kids or beginners. The pretty lake has a sandy beach, and a short side trip to Mt McCausland offers views of Glacier Peak. And **Cascade Pass and Sahale Arm** *(wta.org/go-hiking/hikes/sahale-arm)* is one of the top hikes in the North Cascades National Park area for good reason. You'll see carpets of blueberry bushes in the meadows, friendly marmots sunbathing, outrageous fall colors and maybe a bear.

MAKING A HIKING PLAN

Planning a few months in advance will help you get the most out of any hike in the North Cascades. Some popular trails require permits, so that's step one: make sure they're available for the area you want to visit on the dates you want to go. If permits aren't an issue, you have greater flexibility.

For the most up-to-date information, seek out recent trip reports for the places you want to hike. Start with the Washington Trails Association's excellent database *(wta.org)*. As your trip gets closer, contact the land manager responsible for that area, usually National Park headquarters or a US Forest Service ranger station. They'll have details on trail conditions, road closures, weather and any unexpected concerns, like fire danger.

TRACKS IN TIME

Visitors to Yakima might be surprised to see a rolling anachronism on the city's streets: trolley cars from the early 1900s, still in operation. The cars are part of the Yakima Valley Transportation Company's interurban electric railroad, which originally stretched for 44 miles. Trains have operated on the rail line every year since 1907. Today, 5 miles of track between Yakima and Selah are kept running as a tourist attraction, using the original powerhouse and the 'car barn' built in 1910 to store the trolleys. Trolleys run north along 6th Ave; learn more at **Yakima Valley Trolleys** *(yakimavalleytrolleys.org)*.

Yakima Valley

Floating the Yakima River

It's hard to beat a lazy summer day floating along the mellow **Yakima River**. The water is calm enough to be beginner-friendly (class I-II), and there are multiple road-access points and campsites along the 27-mile stretch through the Yakima River Canyon, so you can customize the length of your trip. It's perfect for zero-stress river camping. You can rent rafts and arrange a car-shuttle service through **Red's Fly Shop** *(redsflyfishing.com; from $129)*.

Unpretentious wine tasting

The Yakima Valley is home to more than 90 wineries and encompasses five AVAs (American Viticultural Areas) in a compact area. These vineyards grow more than half the wine grapes produced in Washington State. The broad range of different wines, plus the famous lack of stuffiness in these farm-country vineyards, makes this an ideal place to learn about wine tasting or to introduce a hesitant friend to its pleasures.

A few places to seek out include the fifth-generation **Gilbert Cellars** *(gilbertcellars.com; tastings $20)*; **Treveri Cellars** *(trevericellars.com; tasting prices vary)* for its sparkling wines and Sunday brunch; **Bonair** *(bonairwine.com; tastings $10)*, one of the valley's oldest winemakers; and **Terra Blanca** *(terrablanca.com; tastings $20)*, whose Red Mountain tasting room looks like a Tuscan villa.

Walla Walla

Tour the local tasting rooms

The Walla Walla Valley became Washington's second AVA in 1984. Today there are nearly 3000 acres of vineyards in the AVA and more than 120 wineries. Conveniently, around 30 of these wineries have tasting rooms right downtown, so you can visit several at once without needing a designated driver. For star-powered sips, don't miss **Pursued by Bear** *(pursuedbybearwine.com; tastings $25)*, the winery owned by *Twin Peaks* actor Kyle MacLachlan, a Yakima local. Other downtown stops to seek out include the friendly, family-owned **Kontos** *(kontoscellars.com)*; locally recommended **Time & Direction** *(timeanddirectionwines.com)*; and **Seven Hills** *(sevenhillswinery.com)*, one of the first wineries in the area.

EATING IN THE YAKIMA VALLEY: OUR PICKS

Red Pickle: This fun place inside an old filling station in Ellensburg serves creative tacos and fried chicken. *3-9pm Tue, 11:30am-9pm Wed-Sat, to 7pm Sun* $

Los Hernandez: It's not every day a tamale place wins a James Beard award, but this one in Yakima has. *11am-6pm* $

Essencia Artisan Bakery: Head to this homey bakery for creative sandwiches (think ginger roast beef), soups, salads and panini. *6am-4pm Tue-Fri, 7am-1pm Sat* $

Crafted: A farm-to-table restaurant in Yakima that makes the most of the surrounding agricultural bounty with an ever-changing menu. *5-9pm Thu-Mon* $$$

Yakima River

A dark chapter in history

With several paved walking trails and an informative museum, the **Whitman Mission National Historic Site** *(nps.gov/whmi/index.htm; free)* commemorates a grim event known as the Whitman Massacre, the result of a conflict in 1847 between white missionaries led by Marcus Whitman and the local people of the Cayuse Nation. Part of the complicated story of the Oregon Trail, the 138-acre park is best explored with the 90-minute self-guided audio tour available on the National Park Service app.

Palouse Falls State Park

A waterfall wonder

An hour north of Walla Walla, the thunderous 198ft **Palouse Falls** *($10)* is the kind of natural wonder that seems to appear out of nowhere. Since 2014, it has been the official state waterfall of Washington.

For the most dramatic experience, visit in spring when the water level is highest. The park offers several good viewpoints overlooking the falls. For safety, all trails to the base of the falls have been closed. Warning signs along the edge of the cliffs are very emphatic, for good reason – people have fallen to their deaths, so stay alert and obey posted closures.

HOORAY FOR HOPS

The Yakima Valley grows about 75% of the hops in the US. You'll see them as you drive around – tall green walls of climbing vines. (No wonder the air smells vaguely like a hazy IPA.) It's the female hop cone that's used in brewing; the flavor in its oils and acids balances out the malty taste and helps preserve the beer. Hops are harvested toward the end of August and into September. In October, keep your eyes peeled for local fresh-hop beers on tap. Harvesting and stripping out the cones from the hop plants is an intense, complicated process. Then they're dried, baled and sent on their way to be distributed to breweries, where, through science and magic, they reach their final form.

DRINKING IN WALLA WALLA: OUR PICKS

Coffee Perk: A comfy hangout with friendly service, good lattes and drip coffee, croissant sandwiches and free wi-fi. *7am-5pm Mon-Sat, to 3pm Sun*

Sleight of Hand Cellars: One of the most fun wineries to visit in the valley, with rock and roll on vinyl and a laid-back atmosphere. *11am-5pm*

Public House 124: Balance out all the wine with a craft cocktail or microbrewed beer at this upscale pub. *4-10pm Tue-Thu, 3-10pm Fri & Sat*

Marc Bar: Sleek cocktail lounge inside the landmark historic Marcus Whitman Hotel. *4-11pm*

IAN DEWAR PHOTOGRAPHY/SHUTTERSTOCK

SMOKEJUMPING & WILDFIRE AWARENESS

The wildfire-fighting technique known as 'smokejumping' was invented in the Methow Valley. In 1939 the Forest Service started training firefighters to jump out of planes as a way of getting them to otherwise inaccessible areas quickly. It turned out to be both effective and efficient. In 1945, the Forest Service established a base outside Winthrop, which still operates today as the **North Cascades Smokejumper Base**. The location is no accident: wildfire activity is on the rise in the region and across the state. Fires can cause sudden closures and unexpected changes to travel plans. Keep tabs on your planned routes with the Watch Duty app, the WTA Trailblazer app, recent trip reports and the Washington Department of Transportation's road status updates.

DENNIS MACDONALD/SHUTTERSTOCK

Grand Coulee Dam

Spokane

An education in regional art

Spokane's **Northwest Museum of Arts & Culture** *(northwestmuseum.org; adult/child $15/9)* occupies a sleek building in the beautiful Browne's Addition neighborhood, the oldest part of town. It has a fantastic collection of art, artifacts and historical documents from around the Pacific Northwest, including Vanessa Helder's watercolor series on the Grand Coulee Dam, and a particularly good collection of Native American artwork.

Grand Coulee Dam

An engineering masterpiece

While the more famous Hoover Dam (p263) gets around 1.6 million visitors per year, the four-times-larger and arguably more significant **Grand Coulee Dam** *(usbr.gov/pn/grandcoulee/visit/index.html)*, inconveniently located far from everything, gets only a trickle of tourism. If you're in the area, don't miss it – it's one of the country's most spectacular displays of engineering and you'll get to enjoy it crowd-free.

The **Grand Coulee Dam Visitor Center** details the history of the dam and surrounding area with movies, photos and interactive exhibits. Free guided tours of the facility run regularly in summer, leaving from the visitor center, and involve taking a glass-walled elevator 465ft down into the Third Power Plant, where you can view the generators from an observation deck. Laser light shows on summer evenings tell the story of the dam's construction.

Portland

QUIRKY ART | FABULOUS FOOD | URBAN GREENSPACES

Portland started out as a port city, but its name has nothing to do with its position on the Willamette River and everything to do with a coin toss. The city's two founders wanted to name the city after their respective hometowns. While the man from Maine won, Portland could have just as easily been called Boston. This 1843 penny toss was just the beginning of an unconventional way of doing things.

In the early 2000s, people caught wind of a little city in the Pacific Northwest where housing was affordable, beer was good and nature was everywhere. What once felt like a small town in disguise emerged as a destination in its own right. The culinary scene boomed and Portland began showing up on 'best places to live' lists. Portlanders no longer had to clarify that they were from Oregon, not Maine, when on vacation elsewhere in the US. While growth has slowed recently, Portland has managed to hold onto its reputation as a bastion for hipsterism, natural beauty and exceptionally tasty food.

GETTING AROUND

Portland is compact and well planned. It's divided on an east–west axis by the Willamette River and between north and south by Burnside St. Street names are preceded by cardinal and intercardinal prefixes (eg N, S, NW, SE), making it easy to orient yourself.

The city has a robust and bicycle-friendly public transportation network that includes buses, a light-rail network known as the MAX and modern streetcars (trams). The MAX is a convenient way to get between Portland International Airport (PDX) and Downtown. You can also drive around the city, and you'll need a car for most day trips.

Explore One of the World's Largest Bookstores

A block of books

If you're big on books, the chance to visit **Powell's City of Books** *(powells.com)* may have played a role in your decision to visit Portland. Occupying three floors and a full city block, Powell's touts itself as the largest independent new-and-used bookstore in the world. Books (and a smattering of gifts) are

Continued on p474

TOP TIP

Portland is one of the most sustainability-focused cities in the US. Do your part during your visit by using public transportation, carrying a reusable water bottle and tote, and shopping local or secondhand.

PORTLAND

HIGHLIGHTS

1 Portland Japanese Garden
2 Powell's City of Books

SIGHTS

3 Council Crest Park
4 Forest Park
5 Governor Tom McCall Waterfront Park
6 Hoyt Arboretum
7 International Rose Test Garden
8 Mt Tabor Park
9 OMSI
10 Oregon Zoo
11 Pittock Mansion
12 Skidmore Fountain
13 Vietnam Veterans of Oregon Memorial
14 Washington Park
15 Wishing Tree
16 Witch's Castle
17 World Forestry Center

ACTIVITIES

18 Cascada Thermal Springs + Hotel
19 Last Thursday on Alberta

SLEEPING

20 Heathman Hotel
21 Hotel deLuxe
22 Inn at Northrup Station
23 McMenamins Kennedy School

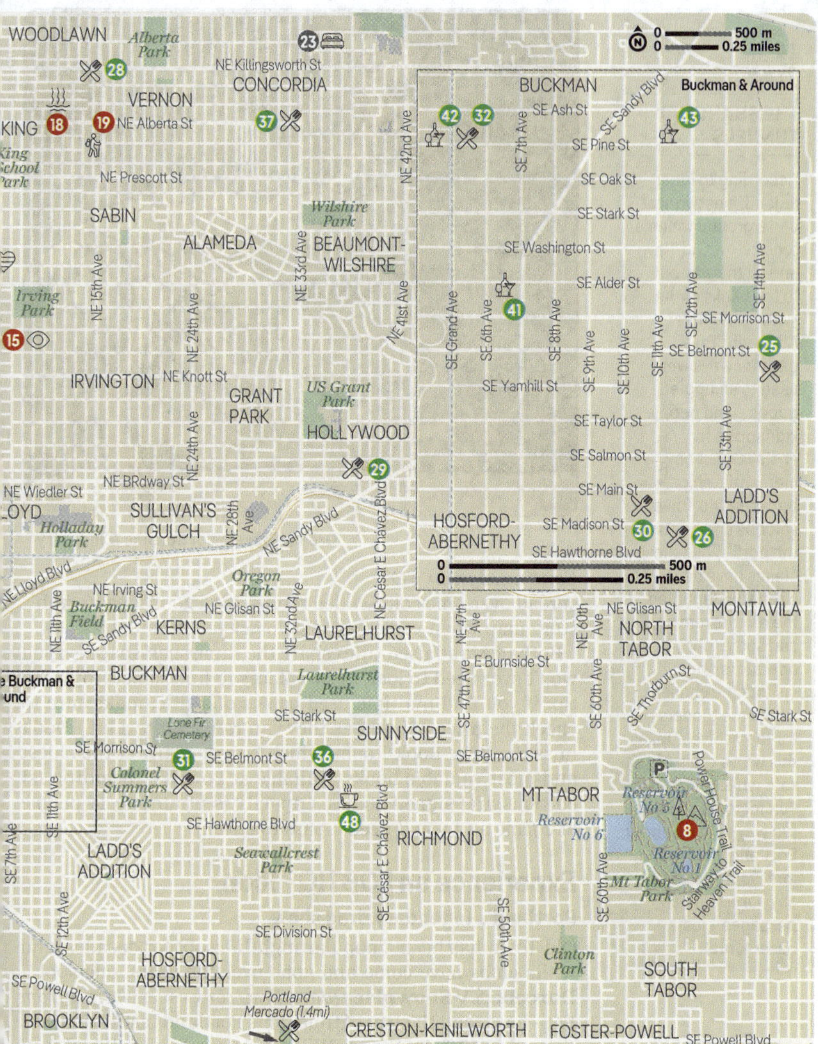

EATING
- 24 Andina
- 25 Astera
- 26 Cartopia
- 27 Escape from NY Pizza
- 28 Feral
- 29 Gado Gado
- 30 Hawthorne Asylum
- 31 Jade Rabbit
- 32 Kann
- 33 Kayo's Ramen Bar
- 34 Langbaan
- 35 Mediterranean Exploration Company
- 36 Paradox Cafe
- see 26 Potato Champion
- 37 Urdaneta
- 38 Voodoo Doughnut

DRINKING & NIGHTLIFE
- 39 Back2Earth
- 40 CC Slaughters
- 41 Creepy's
- 42 Doc Marie's
- 43 Hungry Tiger
- 44 Kell's Irish Pub
- see 25 Nectaris
- 45 Raven's Manor
- 46 River
- 47 Shanghai Tunnel Bar
- see 32 Sousòl
- 48 Tōv Coffee II

ENTERTAINMENT
- 49 Darcelle XV Showplace

SHOPPING
- 50 Always Here Bookstore
- 51 Portland Saturday Market
- 52 Portland Skidmore Market

THE SHANGHAI TUNNELS

According to local legend, a network of underground tunnels runs below Old Town and all the way out to the banks of the Willamette River. Allegedly, these passageways were used to smuggle goods – and people kidnapped for enslavement on mercantile ships – between Old Town saloons and boats in the port. While these claims have never been substantiated, the rumors remain, and some tour operators offer visitors the chance to see the tunnels for themselves. Take this with a grain of salt: while Shanghai Tunnel tours can be a fun way to learn about Portland history and lore, you won't see any subterranean passages – just basements.

ANTARES_NS/SHUTTERSTOCK

Oregon Museum of Science & Industry

Continued from p471

spread over nine color-coded rooms. It's a good idea to grab a store map when you enter to help get you oriented.

Both new and used titles share the same shelf space, so you won't ever need to look in two places to find something. (Pro tip: if you find multiple used copies of a title, make sure to check the price of each, as they can range quite a bit.) Don't miss the Rare Book Room, which houses many of the oldest and most valuable books available at Powell's, including 1st editions and signed copies. Capacity is limited to 14 people at a time and you'll need a pass to enter.

Experience an LGBTIQ+ Icon

Portland's legendary drag show

Old Town has been a popular nightlife spot for decades, and while clubs have come and gone over the years, one spot – **Darcelle XV Showplace** *(darcellexv.com; cover charges from $5)* – has stood the test of time. This Portland institution was opened in 1967 by Walter Willard Cole, a local cultural icon and LGBTIQ+ rights activist who performed as Darcelle. At the time of his death in 2023, Cole was the Guinness World

DRINKING IN OLD TOWN: OUR PICKS

Raven's Manor: Celebrate the macabre at this spooky spot offering Halloweenesque cocktails and interactive experiences. *hours vary*

River: Laid-back sports bar with video poker, pool tables and TVs playing sports games. *noon-2:30am*

Shanghai Tunnel Bar: Descend into this subterranean bar with pinball and pool tables, cocktails and beer on tap. *5pm-2am Wed-Fri, noon-2am Sat, 5pm-midnight Sun-Tue*

Kell's Irish Pub: This brewpub offers a solid whiskey list plus a cigar lounge (a rarity in Portland). *4-10pm Wed & Thu, noon-midnight Fri & Sat*

Records-certified oldest drag performer in the world. Although Darcelle is no longer with us, her memory is kept alive at the club through multiple drag performances per week – including a Sunday drag brunch.

Visit OMSI

Science is for everyone

Oregon Museum of Science & Industry *(omsi.edu; adult/child $20/15)* is a spacious science and technology museum that offers hands-on permanent and special exhibits designed to get visitors of all ages excited about science. Check out the interactive labs focused on physics, chemistry, paleontology and insects or head to the **Natural Sciences Hall** to see displays on everything from geology to climate science. Visitors of all ages love the **Turbine Hall**, where an earthquake simulator allows you to experience the quake sensation, while young'uns can head to the **Curium**, a special area for those eight and under. Don't miss a tour of the decommissioned **USS Blueback Submarine**, the US Navy's final diesel-electric submarine, or take a trip into the night sky through a **Kendall Planetarium** show.

While children certainly are OMSI's target audience, visitors of all ages are welcome. If you feel awkward being the biggest kid around and you just want to enjoy the exhibits without worrying about stepping on tiny toes – and maybe have a drink – you can check out one of the themed monthly **OMSI After Dark** sessions, exclusively for the 21-and-over crowd.

Portland's Doughnut Obsession

Good things come in pink boxes

If you see a late-night line around the block in most cities, you'll probably assume that people are waiting to get into an exclusive nightclub. In Portland, when people line up it's almost always for food, especially at hot spots such as **Voodoo Doughnut**. Founded in the early noughties, Voodoo gained early notoriety for selling doughnuts laced with NyQuil and Pepto-Bismol, and although health authorities put a quick stop to their shenanigans, many of the doughnuts are still far from conventional. Try the Voodoo Doll – a vaguely human-shaped jelly doughnut with a pretzel stake driven where its little heart would be – or the Diablos Rex, a simple chocolate-cake doughnut adorned with a frosted pentagram.

THE BEST PARKS IN PORTLAND

Fernhill Park: Sprawling park with a splash pad and a mix of grassy lawns and forested areas.

Forest Park: Gargantuan 5200-acre wooded park with over 80 miles of trails.

Laurelhurst Park: Grassy park with paved paths for walking and jogging, picnic tables and plenty of green space.

Mt Tabor Park: Take in sunset views from the summit of this dormant, wooded cinder cone.

Oaks Bottom Wildlife Refuge: This 163-acre park near the Willamette River provides a safe haven for birds and aquatic creatures.

Washington Park: Perched above Downtown Portland, this huge park is home to the Portland Japanese Garden.

EATING IN NORTHWEST PORTLAND

Andina: This long-standing spot in the Pearl District is known for offering seasonally inspired Peruvian fare and tasty pisco sours. *5-9pm* **$$$**

Langbaan: This intimate Nob Hill restaurant serves Thai tasting menus crafted from seasonally available ingredients. *5:30-8:15pm Wed-Sun* **$$$**

Escape from NY Pizza: Order New York-style pizza by the slice at this no-frills favorite on 23rd Ave in Nob Hill. *11:30am-11pm* **$**

Mediterranean Exploration Company: Pearl District spot with outdoor seating showcases flavors of Greece and the Levant through meze and grilled-meat dishes. *4-10pm* **$$**

JAPANESE GARDEN DESIGN 101

Hugo Torii, garden curator at Portland Japanese Garden, introduces Japanese garden design.

Japanese gardens have evolved over the course of 1000 years, with each iteration reflecting the needs of a given time. This evolution has created a rich diversity of garden styles, all of which offer something unique to be appreciated. However, the quintessential factor that elevates landscapes such as Portland Japanese Garden is that they allow the visitor to experience Japanese culture and its emphasis on respecting nature and being in harmony with it. Whether a space is decorative like a raked gravel garden or more rustic like a tea garden, it provides a place to confirm our connection and find our distance with nature, and in this, the opportunity to heal.

SARAH QUINTANS/SHUTTERSTOCK

Portland Japanese Garden

Street Food Central

Outdoor dining at food-cart pods

While Portland has plenty of great restaurants, the city is equally known for its food carts (aka food trucks). Most can be found in food-cart 'pods,' converted parking lots with common picnic-table dining spaces that house anywhere from four to upwards of 20 carts. While you'll find food-cart pods all over Portland, Southeast has a particularly high concentration. Two of the largest are **Cartopia** – famous for the poutine at long-standing food cart **Potato Champion** – and **Hawthorne Asylum**, a couple of blocks away. Just up the road, **Tōv Coffee II** serves up Egyptian-style coffee, tea and sweets in a converted double-decker London bus. If you want to try food from across Latin America, head to the **Portland Mercado**, a hybrid market and food-cart pod that showcases food from across the region.

EATING IN SOUTHWEST PORTLAND

Chart House: Take in some of the best views in Portland from the massive windows at this long-standing steak and seafood restaurant. *hours vary* $$$

Salvador Molly's: See just how much heat you can handle by trying the famed Great Balls of Fire (habanero cheese fritters). *11:30am-9pm Sun & Tue-Thu, to 10pm Fri & Sat* $$

Seasons & Regions: Head to this neighborhood seafood spot to try out fresh seafood cooked in a range of styles. *4-9pm* $$

Verde Cocina: This suburban spot blends Mexican and Pacific Northwest ingredients and flavors with excellent results. *11am-9pm Mon-Fri, from 10am Sat & Sun* $$

Down by the River

Walk along the Willamette

Stretching for 1.5 miles along the western banks of the Willamette River, **Governor Tom McCall Waterfront Park** (referred to simply as 'Waterfront' by most locals) is a great place to stroll if you want to experience Portland's greenery without having to leave Downtown. It hosts some of the city's biggest spring and summer events in the city, including the Portland Cinco de Mayo Fiesta, the **Waterfront Blues Festival** and **Portland Pride**.

It's also one of the main venues of the **Portland Rose Festival**, an annual community celebration that features multiple parades and a carnival – known as the CityFair – which takes over a section of the park for roughly two weeks.

Explore Washington Park

A park of many gardens

Just west of Downtown Portland (and a short MAX ride away), sits Washington Park, a hilly, 410-acre park characterized by tree-lined trails, grassy open spaces and some of Portland's top attractions. If you come by light-rail, you'll end up at the southwestern corner of the park where three popular sights – the **Oregon Zoo** *(oregonzoo.org; adult/child $26/21)*, **Vietnam Veterans of Oregon Memorial** and **World Forestry Center** *(worldforestry.org; adult/child $8/5)* – are located. If you have to pick one, make it the Forestry Center, which features two floors of exhibits that cover topics ranging from the future of forests to forest fires to the logging industry.

A short walk (or a one-stop ride on the park's free shuttle) will take you to the **Hoyt Arboretum**, a 'living museum' with around 2300 species of trees from around the world. From the arboretum, you can take a shuttle ride or hike along the Wildwood Trail to the **International Rose Test Garden**, where you'll have the chance to wander among over 10,000 blooming rose bushes representing more than 600 varieties, all while taking in fabulous views of the city. Up a small hill from this floral delight, the **Portland Japanese Garden** *(japanese garden.org; adult/child $22.50/16.50)* is considered one of the most authentic Japanese gardens outside of Japan and features bridge-crossed ponds, a teahouse, numerous stone features and lots of beautiful foliage – including cherry trees.

MAY YOUR WISHES COME TRUE

Portlanders love to set up whimsical displays in their front lawns. Some tether toy horses to sidewalk horse rings (loops found in sidewalks throughout town that were used in the pre-car era to hitch horses). Others build fairy gardens, or free libraries. However, the most enchanting of Portland's sidewalk treasures is the **Wishing Tree** on the corner of NE 7th and Morris. At this interactive display, pedestrians are invited to write their wishes on tags (provided) and tie them to the tree. For an extra dose of magic, anyone making a wish should also read someone else's and hope that it comes true.

EATING IN SOUTHEAST PORTLAND: OUR PICKS

Astera: Locally foraged and farmed dishes steal the show at this upscale plant-based restaurant that strives to keep waste to a minimum. *hours vary Thu-Sun* $$$

Jade Rabbit: Dine on dim-sum classics and hearty Filipino dishes, or try a cocktail (come with tiny plastic bunnies instead of umbrellas). *hours vary Wed-Sun* $$

Kann: See what the fuss is about at Kann, a wood-fired Haitian restaurant under the helm of celebrity chef Gregory Gourdet. *4-10pm Tue-Thu, to 11pm Fri & Sat* $$$

Paradox Cafe: This old-school diner on Belmont St has been serving up huge breakfasts and sandwiches for decades. *9am-2:30pm Thu-Mon* $

LGBTIQ+ PORTLAND

Always Here Bookstore: A NE Portland bookstore that focuses on books written by LGBTIQ+ authors and with LGBTIQ+ themes.

Back2Earth: Welcoming Northeast Portland bar with a solid sound system, dance floor areas and a few arcade games.

CC Slaughters: An Old Town LGBTIQ+ nightclub and lounge with karaoke nights, dance parties and drag shows that's been around since the 1980s.

Darcelle XV Showplace: (p474) A Vegas-style drag cabaret that was launched in 1967 by Portland's beloved drag queen, the late Walter Cole (aka Darcelle).

Doc Marie's: Billing itself as a 'lesbian bar for everyone,' this Southeast Portland spot offers regular trivia nights, karaoke and dance parties.

Stroll Through Alberta Arts District

Celebrate Last Thursday

The stretch of NE Alberta St between NE 12th and 32nd Avenues known as the Alberta Arts District is one of Northeast Portland's biggest draws, and for good reason. This walkable stretch is loaded with cute boutiques, bars, restaurants and galleries, and is home to **Cascada**, a hotel and thermal-spa complex with a glorious subterranean soaking circuit. Black heritage markers tell an important piece of the story of this historically African American neighborhood and many businesses are decorated with colorful large-scale murals.

While the Alberta Arts District attracts crowds pretty consistently, its biggest draw is the monthly **Last Thursday on Alberta** celebration, which emerged in the late 1990s as a countercultural alternative to the long-running First Thursday art walk in the Pearl District. During this monthly event, artists and other vendors set up street-side tables to hawk their wares, street performers entertain the masses and local businesses keep their doors open late. Although Last Thursday happens throughout the year, it's far busier in the summer, when the street is also closed from traffic.

Don't Feed the Troll

A visit to Ole Bolle

Head to the wooded gardens of **Nordic Northwest** (*nordicnorthwest.org; free*) cultural center in Southwest Portland's Garden Home neighborhood to find one of the city's largest residents: **Ole Bolle**. This 19ft troll was fashioned by Danish artist Thomas Dambo, who's celebrated for using upcycled materials to create massive trolls around the world. Ole Bolle is one of six of his kind found across the Pacific Northwest as part of Dambo's *Northwest Trolls: Way of the Bird King* project. After spending time with Ole Bolle, it's worth stopping inside the cultural center's main building, **Nordia House**, to grab a Swedish snack at on-site cafe **Broder Söder** or do a bit of shopping at its gift shop.

City Viticulture

Urban wine culture

Portland's proximity to Oregon's celebrated Willamette Valley wine country makes it tempting to take a day out of your schedule for a bit of wine tasting, but thanks to **Amaterra**

DRINKING IN SOUTHEAST PORTLAND: OUR PICKS

Creepy's: If you're scared of clowns, this harrowing bar will give you the ick...or have you in a fit of nervous laughter. *4pm-1am Sun-Thu, to 2:30am Fri-Sat*

Hungry Tiger: Punk-rock music and vintage tiger-themed decor add to the DIY aesthetic of this hip dive bar with pool, pinball and stiff drinks. *hours vary*

Sousòl: The subterranean sister bar of Kann serves tropical cocktails, mocktails and some seriously tasty cuisine inspired by Caribbean flavors. *4-1pm Thu-Sat*

Nectaris: Sample a wide range of wines from Oregon and around the world at this cozy neighborhood wine spot. *hours vary Thu-Sun*

QUIGGYT4/SHUTTERSTOCK

Portland Saturday Market

(amaterra.com), you can get a sense of the wine country experience without venturing far. Straddling a vine-covered hillock in the West Hills, this winery feels very much like it's in the countryside, despite being less than 5 miles from Downtown. Drive up to the top of the hill where you'll have the option to dine on Pacific Northwest fare at the restaurant or do a wine tasting on a lower-level patio. Both spots offer fantastic views for miles. There's just one catch – you'll have to purchase a 'social membership' for $25, which you can apply to the purchase of two or more bottles of wine during your visit.

Getting Crafty

The hippiest markets in the land

Before farmers markets were all the rage, many Portlanders would spend their Saturdays checking out the handicrafts and food booths at the **Portland Saturday Market**

PORTLAND'S BEST VIEWS

Council Crest Park: A quick drive from Downtown via the posh West Hills will take you up to this small park. At 1073ft above sea level, it's the highest point in the city.

George Himes City Park: This wooded park is just one of many spots along SW Terwilliger Blvd where you can get great views of Portland.

International Rose Test Garden: Head to this bloom-filled spot and take in quintessential postcard views of the Portland skyline, with Mt Hood in the distance.

Mt Tabor: Stand atop Southeast Portland's own active volcano to take in Portland views for miles.

Pittock Mansion: Hike (or drive) up to this historic home on the edge of Forest Park for fantastic views of Downtown and beyond.

EATING IN NORTH & NORTHEAST PORTLAND: OUR PICKS

Gado Gado: James Beard Award–nominated spot serving Indonesian-inspired dishes, including a chili crab dinner on Sundays and Mondays. *5pm-9pm* **$$$**

Feral: Upscale plant-based restaurant with inventive dishes made primarily from locally farmed and foraged ingredients. *5-9pm Wed & Thu, to 10pm Fri & Sat* **$$**

Kayo's Ramen Bar: This spot serves hearty bowls of clear-broth ramen (rather than the better-known tonkotsu-style). *hours vary* **$$**

Urdaneta: Come to this intimate spot for tasty tapas and other Spanish classics and an excellent wine and vermouth menu. *5-10pm Tue-Sun* **$$$**

DEE BROWNING/SHUTTERSTOCK

Forest Park

(portlandsaturdaymarket.com). Founded in 1974, it's the largest continuously operating open-air craft market in the United States, with booths extending from just next to the circa-1888 Skidmore Fountain on SW 1st and Ankeny all the way across to Governor Tom McCall Waterfront Park where live music performances are frequently staged. A second market, the **Portland Skidmore Market** (*portlandskidmore market.com*) occupies an entire city block east of the **Skidmore Fountain**. While everything sold at the Saturday Market must be handcrafted, vendors at the Skidmore Market have a bit more liberty – and many sell imported goods from Central America and South Asia.

A Nature Escape in the City

Portland's urban forest

If you want to experience the grandeur of Oregon's forests but don't want to drive out to the nearby Columbia Gorge (p486), you're in luck: Portland has its own urban forest, just a few minutes' drive from the Pearl District. With over 80 miles of trails spread out over 5200 acres, **Forest Park** is big enough to rarely feel crowded, even if you hit up the popular **Wildwood Trail**, a 30-mile footpath that runs the entire length of the park, past an abandoned stone structure known as the **Witch's Castle** and into nearby Washington Park. While ambitious hikers and runners might brave the entire trail, most people just hike shorter segments.

Oregon

CRAFT BREWERIES | PEACEFUL WINERIES | WATERFALL WONDERS

It's hard to slap a single characterization onto Oregon's geography and people. Its landscape ranges from rugged coastline and thick evergreen forests to barren, fossil-strewn deserts, volcanoes and glaciers. As for its denizens, you name it – Oregonians run the gamut from pro-logging conservatives to tree-hugging liberals. What they have in common is an independent spirit, a love of the outdoors and a fierce devotion to where they live.

It doesn't usually take long for visitors to feel a similar devotion. Who wouldn't fall in love with the spectacle of glittering Crater Lake, the breathtaking colors of the Painted Hills in John Day or the hiking trails through deep forests and over stunning mountain passes? And then there are the towns: you can eat like royalty in McMinnville, go Saturday-market shopping in Eugene or sample an astounding number of brewpubs in Bend.

Places

GETTING AROUND

Like much of the US, a car is by far the best option for getting around Oregon. If for whatever reason a car isn't feasible, there are bus routes and train routes winding their way through the state. POINT, Oregon's public intercity bus service, has routes between popular towns and cities, like Portland, Eugene, Bend and Astoria. Alternatively, Amtrak's train network nearly exclusively runs through the Cascades, with Eugene, Salem and Portland all along the way. Do note that both buses and trains have limited frequency and routes.

TOP TIP

Much of the appeal of Oregon is its natural beauty. Do your part to keep the landscapes as stunning as they are by picking up after yourself, following fire-use restrictions, and making sustainable choices.

TOP EXPERIENCE

Crater Lake National Park

The only national park in Oregon, Crater Lake National Park was created by a cataclysmic volcanic eruption 7700 years ago. The collapsed caldera then filled with glacial melt and rainwater to form the deepest, bluest lake in the US. The resulting landscape is wondrous to behold – from the old-growth forests to the lake itself.

STAS MOROZ/SHUTTERSTOCK

An Iconic Hike

To fully grasp the size, colors, and surrounding landscape of the otherworldly Crater Lake, most visitors will hike up to higher elevations on multiple trails. Head to the east end of Rim Village and follow the paved path to the trailhead for **Garfield Peak**, a moderately challenging 3.5-mile hike up switchbacks with excellent valley views. You'll pass patches of snow almost year-round as you gaze at the jewel-blue water in one direction and mountains and valley in the other. It packs a great reward for just a two- to three-hour adventure.

Family-Friendly Trails

For a shorter but still substantial jaunt, the **Watchman Peak Trail** is short and steep, leading you to a fire tower with panoramic views. For a quick loop, check out **Sun Notch Trail**, just off Rim Drive. This family-friendly trail is just 0.8 miles, with a great view of Phantom Ship. In the winter, this is a popular spot for snow-shoeing. Remember that the temperature can change quickly with elevation changes so pack layers and plenty of water for all your hikes. Dogs are not allowed on most trails in the park.

TOP TIPS

- Rim Drive, the 33-mile road circumnavigating Crater Lake with dozens of viewpoints and trailheads along the way, is getting some upgrades. The five-year project began in 2023, closing portions of the road each year. Most of the road will remain drivable, but check for closed sections before departing.

PRACTICALITIES

- nps.gov/crla/index.htm
- per car $20-30 (varies by season)
- open 24/7

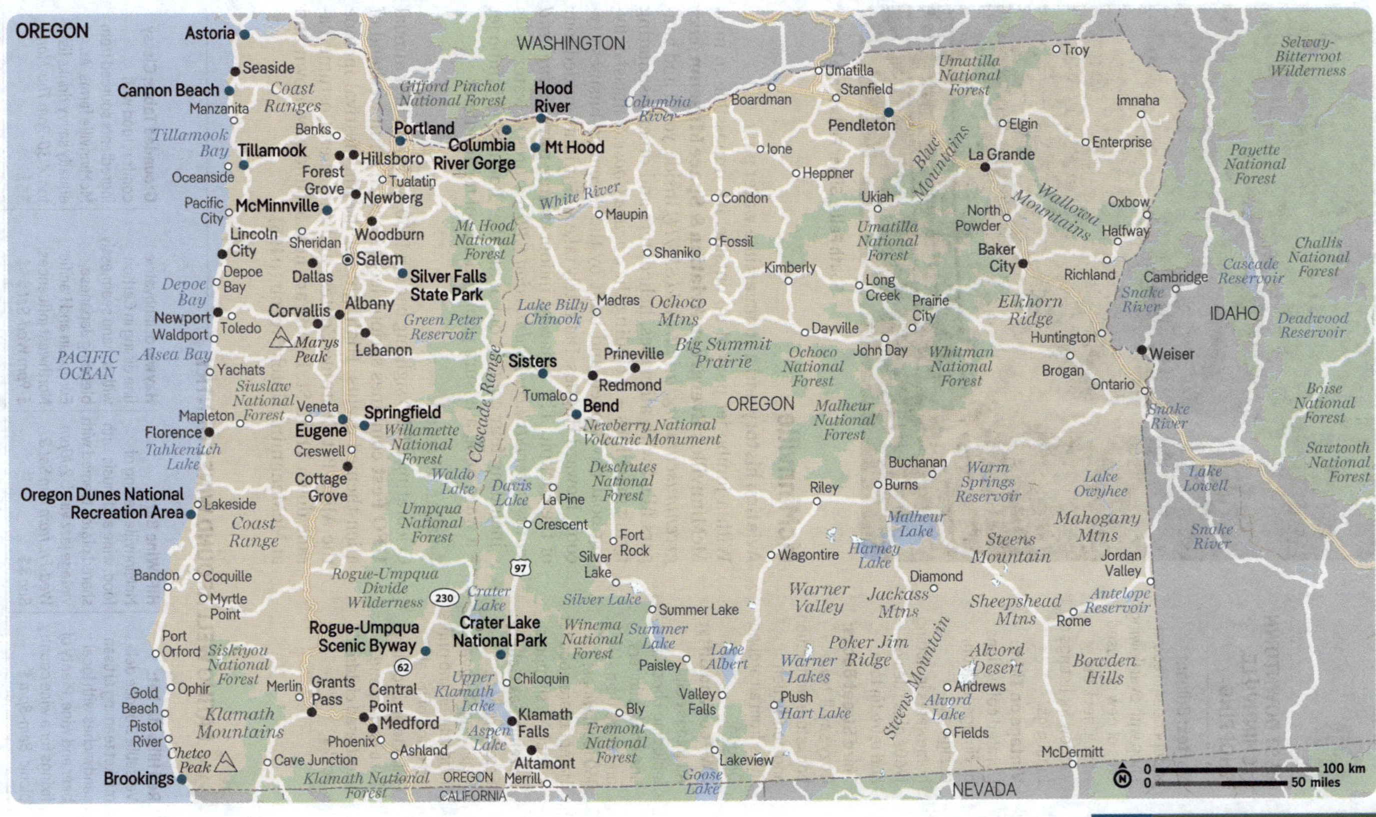
OREGON
WASHINGTON
IDAHO
NEVADA
OREGON
CALIFORNIA
PACIFIC OCEAN
Astoria
Seaside
Cannon Beach
Manzanita
Coast Ranges
Tillamook Bay
Tillamook
Oceanside
Pacific City
McMinnville
Lincoln City
Depoe Bay
Newport
Waldport
Toledo
Alsea Bay
Yachats
Siuslaw National Forest
Mapleton
Florence
Tahkenitch Lake
Oregon Dunes National Recreation Area
Lakeside
Coast Range
Bandon
Coquille
Myrtle Point
Port Orford
Siskiyou National Forest
Ophir
Gold Beach
Pistol River
Chetco Peak
Brookings
Klamath Mountains
Cave Junction
Klamath National Forest
Banks
Hillsboro
Forest Grove
Tualatin
Newberg
Sheridan
Woodburn
Salem
Dallas
Silver Falls State Park
Corvallis
Albany
Marys Peak
Lebanon
Green Peter Reservoir
Veneta
Eugene
Springfield
Creswell
Cottage Grove
Willamette National Forest
Portland
Gifford Pinchot National Forest
Hood River
Columbia River Gorge
Mt Hood
Columbia River
White River
Mt Hood National Forest
Maupin
Shaniko
Lake Billy Chinook
Madras
Ochoco Mtns
Cascade Range
Sisters
Prineville
Redmond
Tumalo
Bend
Newberry National Volcanic Monument
Waldo Lake
Davis Lake
La Pine
Deschutes National Forest
Crescent
Fort Rock
Silver Lake
Umpqua National Forest
Rogue-Umpqua Divide Wilderness
Crater Lake
Crater Lake National Park
Rogue-Umpqua Scenic Byway
Chiloquin
Upper Klamath Lake
Grants Pass
Merlin
Central Point
Medford
Phoenix
Ashland
Klamath Falls
Aspen Lake
Altamont
Merrill
Silver Lake
Summer Lake
Winema National Forest
Paisley
Lake Albert
Bly
Fremont National Forest
Valley Falls
Lakeview
Goose Lake
Boardman
Umatilla
Stanfield
Pendleton
Ione
Heppner
Condon
Fossil
Kimberly
Ukiah
Umatilla National Forest
Long Creek
Dayville
Big Summit Prairie
Ochoco National Forest
OREGON
Malheur National Forest
John Day
Prairie City
Whitman National Forest
Blue Mountains
La Grande
North Powder
Baker City
Elgin
Enterprise
Imnaha
Troy
Wallowa Mountains
Oxbow
Halfway
Richland
Elkhorn Ridge
Huntington
Brogan
Ontario
Weiser
Cambridge
Snake River
Cascade Reservoir
Payette National Forest
Selway-Bitterroot Wilderness
Challis National Forest
Deadwood Reservoir
Boise National Forest
Sawtooth National Forest
Lake Lowell
Buchanan
Burns
Riley
Warm Springs Reservoir
Lake Owyhee
Malheur Lake
Harney Lake
Wagontire
Steens Mountain
Mahogany Mtns
Jordan Valley
Diamond
Warner Valley
Jackass Mtns
Sheepshead Mtns
Antelope Reservoir
Rome
Poker Jim Ridge
Warner Lakes
Plush
Hart Lake
Alvord Desert
Andrews
Alvord Lake
Fields
Bowden Hills
McDermitt
97
230
62
0 100 km
0 50 miles

BEST DOWNTOWN MCMINNVILLE SHOPPING

Vortex: Brilliant independent record shop with overflowing bins of new and used vinyl. Check the window for listings of local gigs.

Vintage on Third: Curated collections of vintage fashion, design and homewares including 1960s glass design and retro tin toys.

Third Street Books: Cozy small-town bookstore with fiction and non-fiction titles from all around Oregon.

NW Food and Gifts: All things edible including chocolate and confectionery, and more than 160 local wines. Hampers are good for indecisive shoppers.

Artemis Fox Gallery: Screen prints depicting Oregon landscapes and prints on wood of local wildlife and scenery. Also jewelry and illustrated children's books.

BOB POOL/SHUTTERSTOCK

South Falls, Silver Falls State Park

McMinnville

Aviation history and a summertime water park

With a jumbo jet parked up outside, it's impossible to miss McMinnville's **Evergreen Aviation & Space Museum** *(evergreenmuseum.org; adult/child $24/14)*.Inside, you'll find hangars filled with airplanes, helicopters and other fascinating flying machines – including the *Spruce Goose*, a massive flying boat envisioned and built by the eccentric business tycoon, Howard Hughes. Definitely take a 15-minute guided tour of the cockpit. The adjacent indoor **water park** *(wingsandwaveswaterpark.com; admission $39)* features 10 waterslides – including four coming out of another Boeing 747 jumbo jet – a wave pool, a leisure pool and a pool for toddlers.

An alien invasion

Celebrating a UFO sighting back in 1950, McMinnville's annual **UFO Fest** combines serious lectures with a fun weekend of alien-themed events. Highlights of the May festival include the Alien Pet Costume Contest and the Alien Costume Parade down Third St. Events are held around downtown and at McMenamins Hotel Oregon (p495).

EATING WELL AROUND WINE COUNTRY

Red Hills Market: Versatile Dundee deli-market teaming artisan sandwiches with local beer and wine. Plenty of fixings for a wine country picnic. *8am-8pm* $

HiFi Wine Bar: McMinnville pairing of food, wine and music with shared plates teamed with vintage jazz vinyl. *2-10pm Wed-Fri, from 1pm Sat & Sun* $$

Hayward: Innovative fine dining in Carlton with a menu seamlessly blending Japanese, European and Pacific Northwest influences. *5-9pm Wed-Sat* $$$

Grounded Table: Classy comfort food with ingredients sourced from McMinnville farms. An equally savvy drinks list, too. *4:30-9pm Thu-Mon* $$$

Willamette Valley wineries

Fostering delicate pinot noir grapes as well as pinot gris, chardonnay and riesling, the climate of the northern Willamette Valley make the region Oregon's most bountiful wine-growing area. Centered on McMinnville and nearby towns including Dayton, Carlton, Newberg and Dundee, the broader Willamette Valley AVA incorporates more than 700 wineries across 11 different sub-region AVAs.

Among the hundreds of wineries, some stand out. **Ken Wright Cellars** is a well-established winery with impeccable pinot noir credentials. **Soter Vineyards** serves seven-course lunch tasting menus with biodynamic pinot noir and chardonnay. Reservations are essential. **Stoller Family Estate** is the world's first LEED-Gold Certified winery guaranteeing sustainability and eco-friendly design, and it features a spectacular hilltop tasting room. **Remy Wines** – founded by a former McMinnville mayor – is known for its single-vineyard, single-varietal Italian-style wines crafted from sangiovese, dolcetto and nebbiolo.

Silver Falls State Park

Short walks for stunning views

Just east of Oregon's capital city of Salem, find the cascade-filled **Silver Falls State Park** *(stateparks.oregon.gov; $10)*. This 9000-acre escape is filled with countless waterfalls, many of which are accessible by easy to moderate hikes. The **North Falls Lookout trail** is a 1-mile return walk for views of the 136ft-high waterfall. Don't miss continuing behind the falls. At the even more spectacular **South Falls**, water thunders over a mossy ledge to a rocky pool 177ft below. The best view is on the gentle trail, down which also continues behind the falls. Last but certainly not least, the popular **Trail of Ten Falls** is a spectacular 7.2-mile moderate loop trail with natural swimming pools and, as its name implies, nearly a dozen waterfalls.

Eugene

Great weekend market and colorful street art

Primarily known as a hippie-esque college town, downtown Eugene is easily explored on foot – particularly during the popular **Saturday Market** *(eugenesaturdaymarket.org)*. Folk from around the Willamette Valley sell locally made products from food and drink to arts and crafts, and there's live music from Americana and country to jazz and classic rock. Food-cart flavors straddle the globe.

Springfield

Hang with everyone's favorite cartoon family

Oregon-born Matt Groening, creator of *The Simpsons*, confirmed in 2012 that Homer's hometown was indeed named after Springfield, Oregon. Visit the **Emerald Art Center** for a photo op with the yellow-hued clan on the famous couch, a promotional prop from 2007's *The Simpsons Movie*. Ask for a free map showing the location of more than 40 other Simpsons murals and street-art locations around downtown Springfield and the greater Eugene-Springfield area.

GETTING ACTIVE IN EUGENE

Gary Tepfer, a Eugene-based photographer, shares his favorite ways to stay active in Eugene. *(@garytepfer.com)*

Eugene's foresighted city planners preserved natural areas that can now be accessed on foot or by bike. To the east, the **Howard Buford Recreation Area** offers hiking and horseback-riding trails, and its hillsides burst with wildflowers in spring. Northwest of Eugene is **Fern Ridge Reservoir**, a large lake and marshland with the region's richest bird habitat. There are also running trails through city parks and along the river, a basalt climbing cliff on **Skinner Butte**, and a canoe path near the Willamette River. Definitely not to be overlooked is **Spencer Butte** for hiking. From the top it has unsurpassed views of the High Cascades to the east, and miles of trails and acres of old-growth forests.

BEST HOT SPRINGS IN THE CASCADE MOUNTAINS

Bagby Hot Springs: Ninety miles east of Salem. Clothing-optional hot springs with wooden tubs in semi-private bathhouses. Accessible via a 1.5-mile forest trail.

Terwilliger Hot Springs: Located 55 miles east of Eugene. Terraced outdoor pools framed by large rocks, accessed via a 500yd walk.

Breitenbush Hot Springs: More developed with spa and massage services on offer; 70 miles east of Salem.

Belknap Hot Springs: Spring-fed pools located 5 miles east of McKenzie Bridge. Also camping and a lodge.

McCredie Hot Springs: Eight miles east of Oakridge in the Willamette State Forest. Natural, undeveloped and clothing-optional.

Hood River

Brilliant display of aviation and automotive history

For fans of classic airplanes, cars and motorcycles, a visit to the **Western Antique Aeroplane & Automobile Museum** *(WAAAM; waaamuseum.org; adult/child $23/12)* on Hood River's south side is highly recommended. Most of the airplanes can still fly, and many are from pioneering American manufacturers now lost to the mists of time. In early September, the museum's annual **Fly-in** sees pilots arrive in their lovingly preserved aircraft. To fully appreciate the collection of more than 300 planes and vehicles, allow at least two hours.

Riding the rails on the Mt Hood Railroad

The scenic **Mt Hood Railroad** *(mthoodrr.com; adult/child $37/27)* is a family favorite. The railroad once transported timber and fruit from the Upper Hood River Valley, but now shuttles visitors past rivers and through fragrant orchards. Look forward to Mt Hood views en route. After 45 minutes, there's an hour-long stop at the **Fruit Company**, a gift store, orchard and heritage museum, before trundling back to Hood River. Runs from April to October. Book ahead online.

A spirited brace of tasting rooms

In a city famous for brewing beer, two Hood River tasting rooms are presenting a spin on distilling, Columbia Gorge-style. Highlights of **Hood River Distillers**' tasting room are mini-cocktails and curated flights of the award-winning gin, whiskey, vodka and bourbon, while the focus at **Wilderton Aperitivo Co** is on non-alcoholic versions of traditional Italian *aperitivo* spirits.

Columbia River Gorge

Experience Multnomah Falls

At 620ft, **Multnomah Falls** is the tallest waterfall in Oregon. A 1-mile trail leads to the top with a stop at picturesque **Benson Bridge** along the way. Since the falls are such a major attraction, you'll need to buy a timed-use permit ($2) online at recreation.gov for visits between from late May to early September. Want to continue the adventure? From the top of Multnomah Falls, trail 420 is a loop route continuing to **Wahkeena Falls**.

DRINKING IN HOOD RIVER: CRAFT BEER FAVORITES

pFriem Family Brewers: Superb beers, including barrel-aged specials, at a waterfront location. The upscale pub dining menu showcases ingredients from around the gorge. *11:30am-9pm*

Ferment Brewing Company: Ferment's sleek taproom combines gorge views with precisely crafted beers, cocktails and non-alcoholic tipples. *11am-9pm Mon-Fri, from 10am Sat & Sun*

Spinning Wheels Brewing Project: A perfect Pacific Northwest mashup of vinyl listening bar and neighborhood nano-brewery. *4-9pm Mon-Fri, from 2pm Sat & Sun*

Full Sail Brewing Company: Hood River's pioneering brewpub partners salads, sandwiches and burgers with river views. An outdoor patio is a bonus on sunny days. *11am-9pm*

NICHOLAS J KLEIN/SHUTTERSTOCK

Multnomah Falls

Visit the Bonneville Dam

On the Columbia River lies a powerful 20th-century feat of engineering: the Bonneville Dam. This Depression-era project generates enough electricity for 900,000 homes. After passing through security, drive slowly into the massive site – soundtracked by the spillway's thundering waters – and visit the **Bradford Island Visitor Center** *(nwp.usace.army.mil/bonneville)*. Ascend to the roof terrace for spectacular views. Downstairs is a fish ladder where lamprey and salmon journey past the dam from August to October. Just west of the dam, massive sturgeon – including Herman, a hulking 500lb octogenarian – can be seen amid the leafy grounds of the **Bonneville Fish Hatchery** *(myodfw.com)*. Visit in September and October to see spawning Chinook and Coho salmon.

Mt Hood

Snow sports on the mountain

Mt Hood offers the longest snow-sports season in the US, with the **Timberline Lodge Ski Area** *(timberlinelodge.com; day passes from $95)* usually opening early to mid-November, and sometimes staying open until late May. To the east, **Mt Hood**

HOOD RIVER'S CENTENARIAN BRIDGE

Celebrating its centenary in 2024, the 4418ft-long Hood River–White Salmon Interstate Bridge could be the gorge's least-loved thoroughfare. Each of the two lanes is just 9.5ft wide – there's no room for bicycles or pedestrians – and the surface is a vehicle-shaking iron grid. Planning to replace the bridge is ongoing (Washington State committed $50 million in May 2025), and in April 2025 payment for the bridge ($3.50) went strictly electronic. Locals can sign up for a transponder giving a discounted rate of $1.75, and if you're driving a rental car, the toll will probably be added to your hire costs. Otherwise, you have 14 days to pay online *(portofhood river.com)* before getting charged an additional $3 administration fee.

EATING IN HOOD RIVER: CAFES TO FINE DINING

Broder Øst: A cozy option adjacent to the Hood River Hotel with Scandinavian-inspired breakfast dishes. Try the Pytt i Panna (Swedish-style hash). *8am-3pm* $

Solstice Woodfire Cafe: Wood-fired pizzas, cocktails and good beer near the waterfront. Order the Coho Salmon pizza with local gorge salmon. *11.30am-8pm Wed-Sun* $$

Votum: Hood River's fine dining frontrunner combines a hushed space with a seafood-focused degustation menu often including salmon, oysters and king crab. *5-10pm Thu-Mon* $$$

Celilo Restaurant & Bar: Tender steaks and perfectly cooked fish dishes partner with a wine list featuring Oregon and Washington varietals. *5-9.30pm Tue-Sat* $$$

BEST TRAILS NEAR BEND

Phil's Trail: On Bend's west side, this is one of Oregon's best networks of mountain-biking trails. Young riders will love the skills course.

Pilot Butte: A 1.8-mile out-and-back trail ascends the 4142ft-high peak of this volcanic cone just east of downtown.

Tumalo Falls: Central Oregon's most photographed waterfall (97ft) has trails leading to several smaller cascades upstream.

Shevlin Park: A locals' favorite spot for hikes along Tumalo Creek. Trails of up to 6 miles explore old-growth ponderosa forest.

Deschutes River: South of town, start at **Lava Island Falls** from where it's 2.5 miles to **Dillon Falls**, a great spot for a picnic.

Meadows *(skihood.com; day passes from $99)* also opens early November and closes around early May. Courtesy of the Palmer Snowfield, it's even possible to tackle the Timberline Lodge Ski Area in summer, an alpine thrill mainly reserved for experienced and professional skiers.

Near Government Camp, **Mt Hood Skibowl** *(skibowl.com; day passes from $72)* is the closest ski area to Portland, and it's popular for night-skiing with Portlanders driving out for an evening on the slopes. On the northeastern slopes of the mountain, **Cooper Spur Ski Area** *(day passes from $52)* caters mainly to beginners and families.

Cross-country skiers and snowshoers can try **Trillium Sno Park** or the **White River West Sno Park**, while just off Hwy 35, **Teacup Nordic** has around 15 miles of groomed trails.

A Sno-Park **parking permit** *(1 day/3 days/annual $4/9/25)* is required for most Mt Hood snow sports areas from November to April.

Hiking around Oregon's highest peak

While Mt Hood is great for winter sports when the temps are chilly, it's equally as fantastic for hiking during the warmer months with its miles of trails ($5). The 7-mile loop trail passing by the 120ft **Ramona Falls** may be the most popular of the bunch, though the shorter, 4.2-mile trail to pretty **Mirror Lake** draws its fair share of crowds too. Another kid-friendly trail is the **Old Salmon River Trail**, which is 4 miles, out and back. Look forward to towering trees draped in moss and a shimmering pool that's perfect for a dip on a hot day.

For a more rigorous challenge, the **Timberline Trail** is a 42-mile trail circumnavigating Mt Hood, and passing by waterfalls and alpine meadows. Check ranger stations on track conditions, as parts of the trail get washed out.

Bend

Tubing the Deschutes River

Floating along the Deschutes River through town is the quintessential Bend experience. From mid-June through Labor Day, **Tumalo Creek Kayak & Canoe** *(tumalocreek.com; 2hr including shuttle $27)* operates a tube rental and shuttle service that is bookable online. Book well ahead.

Beginning at **Riverbend Park** in the Old Mill District and ending in Drake Park near downtown, the float route – plan on 60 to 90 minutes – is gentle most of the way except for a

EATING & DRINKING AROUND MT HOOD: OUR PICKS

Glacier Public House: In Government Camp with menu options including salmon cakes and a warming cheese fondue. Definitely a good option in cooler weather. *9am-9pm* $$

Mt Hood Brewing Co: Government Camp's brewpub combines a relaxed ambience with hearty fare including pizzas, sandwiches and short ribs. *11am-9pm* $$

Barlow Trail Roadhouse: Century-old rustic and unpretentious restaurant and bar near Zigzag. Serves big-portioned diner-style meals. *8am-8pm Thu-Sat, to 4pm Sun* $$

Blue Ox Bar: The coziest of the eating and drinking options at Timberline Lodge (p495). Mt Hood Brewing beers, mountain-inspired cocktails and flatbread pizza feature. *11am-8pm* $$

Deschutes River, Bend

short stretch of rapids dubbed the Fish Ladder. If you're tubing with younger family members, it's possible to bypass these rapids with a short on-the-land portage detour. Sunblock, a hat and river shoes are all essential.

The last Blockbuster

In Bend, you don't need a DeLorean to travel back in time 30 years. Just visit the corner of Revere Ave and Third St where you'll find the world's last **Blockbuster** *(bendblockbuster.com)* video store. Inside, the DVD racks, blue-shirted employees and packages of microwave popcorn will instantly transport you back to the '90s. There are also racks of VHS tapes for sale.

Visit Newberry National Volcanic Monument

South of Bend, the Newberry National Volcanic Monument is a sprawling landscape of lava flows, tubes and dormant craters. Stop at the visitor center to get the lay of the land, before continuing to the **Lava River Cave**, a mile-long lava tube under the forest. Tours are self-guided, but timed permits from recreation.gov are mandatory.

Don't miss the **Newberry Caldera**, a massive crater 5 miles in diameter. Both **Paulina Lake** and **East Lake** are located inside the caldera. Most visitors start their exploration at **Paulina Falls** (80ft), where a short trail (150yd) leads from the parking lot to the top of a twin waterfall, before heading back to the lakes for fishing, hiking, campgrounds and hot

HIKING PERMITS IN THE CASCADES

Central Cascades Wilderness Permits *(per person $1)* are required on 19 of the 79 trailheads in the Mt Jefferson, Mt Washington and Three Sisters wilderness areas from June 15 to October 15. A Forest Service employee is usually at the trailhead to check permits and provide trail information. The permits are also needed for overnight stays (per group $6) in all three wilderness areas. In addition to the hiking permits it's also a good idea to have a Northwest Forest Pass, which allows parking in the national forest parking areas. Printable day passes ($5) are available online. Several retailers in Bend also sell the passes. Some (but not all) trailheads have parking ticket machines.

DRINKING IN BEND: CRAFT BEER

Deschutes Brewery & Public House: Est. 1988 as Bend's first craft brewery; classics are Black Butte porter and Mirror Pond pale ale. *11am-9pm Sun-Thu, to 9:30pm Fri & Sat*

Crux Fermentation Project: A five-beer tasting flight is the best way to experience this Bend favorite with beautiful Cascade views. *11am-9pm Sun-Thu, to 10pm Fri & Sat*

Boss Rambler Beer Club: There's a quirky, aprés ski ambience at this Westside taproom with refreshing hazy IPAs. *noon-8pm Sun-Thu, to 9pm Fri & Sat*

Ale Apothecary: Wild-fermented, sour and spontaneously fermented beers are the fascinating highlights of this rustic taproom. *2-8pm Wed-Sat, to 6pm Sun*

MINDFUL TIDE-POOLING

Marine Science educator **Alanna Kieffer**, who runs foraging, clamming and coastal explorations through her company Shifting Tides, shares advice on responsible tide-pooling. *(@shifting_tides_nw)*

It's important to be careful about walking on rocks. When the tide goes out, you'll see rocks covered in species that aren't moving. While these species don't appear to be alive, they often are. So it's best to walk on bare rocks or stick to the sand. While one person stepping on things that may be alive might not be that harmful, when everyone at the beach does it – which happens in the spring and summer – there's a big impact.

springs. Alternatively, there's the **Paulina Lakeshore Trail**, a 7.5-mile loop trail that takes around 2½ hours, while mountain bikers can tackle the 21-mile-long **Crater Rim Trail** encircling both lakes.

Sisters

Take advantage of Central Oregon's dark skies

With more than 300 days of clear skies per year, minimal pollution and higher elevations, Central Oregon is ideal for stargazing. In 2025 the town of Sisters was awarded International Dark Sky Place status. A good pair of binoculars and a stargazing app like SkySafari makes a fine combo for a DIY night sky encounter. Alternatively, visit the Hopservatory at **Worthy Brewing** *(worthygardenclub.org; donation $5)* and observe the heavens through the research-grade telescope. **Wanderlust Tours** *(wanderlusttours.com; $130)* also offers stargazing experiences at Fort Rock on selected nights from late May to October. Book well ahead.

Drive the Cascade Lakes Scenic Byway

Usually open from late May to October, the 66-mile Cascade Lakes Scenic Byway begins in Bend and travels south through volcanic highlands and the Deschutes National Forest. Day trips visiting spring-fed lakes surrounded by snowcapped peaks are possible, but campsites and resorts make overnighting easy.

Start with the 9065ft **Mt Bachelor**, a ski resort on a dormant stratovolcano that has epic summer hiking, mountain biking and zip-line opportunities. Past Mt Bachelor, the highway only opens in late May, after the worst of winter. Four miles on is the **Todd Lake Trailhead** (permit required), offering a family-friendly 1.7-mile hike around **Todd Lake**. Experienced hikers should consider venturing to spectacular glacier-fed **No Name Lake** (permit required), only thawing in late July to reveal its turquoise-green color.

Continue 6 miles southwest to **Elk Lake**, a family destination with a rustic resort, while the twisting shoreline of nearby **Hosmer Lake** is popular with kayakers. Atlantic salmon, rainbow trout and brook trout are easily spotted (fly-fishing only). Round out the drive with a few more stunning lakes, including **Lava Lake**, **Cultus Lake** and **Twin Lakes**.

Astoria

In the footsteps of Lewis and Clark

Although the land now known as Astoria has been inhabited for millennia, its current incarnation started at the turn of the 19th century, when explorers and fur traders began taking an interest in the region. Among them were Captain Meriwether Lewis and Second Lieutenant William Clark who, under the auspices of the US Army's Corps of Discovery, journeyed to the West, ultimately ending their journey just 6 miles south of downtown Astoria. It was here that the Corps built **Fort Clatsop**, where they lived from December 1805 until March 1806.

CASCADE DRONE PHOTOGRAPHY/SHUTTERSTOCK

Todd Lake

Today, the Fort Clatsop area is protected as part of the **Lewis & Clark National State and Historical Park** *(nps.gov/lewi/index.htm; free),* which has a collection of 12 different spots across Oregon and Washington related to the Lewis and Clark expedition. Although the original fort is no longer standing, there's a fully furnished replica in its place. When you're done exploring the compact fort, head to the visitor center's exhibit hall to check out displays featuring everything from old weapons to a model canoe.

The Hollywood of Oregon

If you've ever watched the 1985 kids' film *The Goonies*, then you've seen Astoria, at least on a screen. Start your *Goonies*-themed adventure with a visit to Mikey's house, known locally simply as the Goonies House, located at 368 38th St – just note that you can only see it from the outside. From here, it's a 2-mile drive to the **Flavel House Museum** *(astoriamuseums.org/explore/flavel-house-museum; 20adult/child $7/2),* where Mr Walsh (Mikey's dad) worked in the movie.

Cannon Beach

Picture-perfect

The coastal town of Cannon Beach is a popular day trip amongst Portlanders, especially in the summer. Start at the main thoroughfare, **Hemlock St**, a boutique-dotted drag

WILDFIRE AWARENESS

Southern Oregon has seen devastating wildfires become stronger and more frequent in recent years, largely due to climate change. In 2020, record-breaking wildfires across the state burned over a million acres and killed 11 people. You'll see evidence of that fire and more recent ones as you drive around the region. As dry summer months and ongoing drought persist, visitors should be aware that wildfires can impact travel plans. If you are camping in the summer, check on fire restrictions at ranger stations – by late summer, campfires are typically banned. Check Southern Oregon air quality at aqi.oregon.gov if smoke is a concern. An AQI over 100 is considered unhealthy, and you may want to reconsider outdoor activities.

EATING IN ASTORIA: OUR PICKS

Bowpicker Fish & Chips: A converted boat turned food cart serving breaded albacore and British-style fries. *11am-6pm Tue-Sat, to 4pm Sun* $

Daphne: High-end farm-to-table spot with an extensive wine list and menu that evolves with the season. *5-9pm Tue-Sat* $$$

Fedé Trattoria: Upscale Italian spot with hearty meals made mostly from locally sourced ingredients, including seafood. *3:30-9pm Tue-Sat* $$$

Himani Indian Cuisine: No-frills North Indian restaurant with large portions and an even larger selection. *noon-8pm Sun-Thu, 9am-4pm Fri* $$

FINDERS KEEPERS

If you spend much time browsing antique shops on the Oregon Coast, you'll probably notice round glass balls of all sizes in shades of soda-bottle green. While there are some replicas out there, many of these balls are Japanese fishing floats that were traditionally used to keep fishing nets afloat. They used to be a common beachcomber's find on the Oregon Coast; today, you'll mostly find the floats in local shops.

These floats were also the inspiration for Lincoln City's Finders Keepers in which around 3000 blown glass floats per year are hidden on the beach for lucky visitors to find. If you find one of the colorful baubles, it's yours to keep – you can even register it online for a certificate of authenticity.

that is among the best places in the region to pick up fine art and higher-end souvenirs. Book-lovers can easily spend hours poring over the tomes in the **Cannon Beach Book Company** *(cannonbeachbooks.com)*. Once you've had your retail fix, head to the beach to see **Haystack Rock**, a 17-million-year-old Oregon icon. If you've got binoculars, bring them: this frequent star of Oregon Coast postcards is around 235ft tall and provides refuge to all sorts of seabirds, including fluffy tufted puffins. The area around the monolith is particularly fun during low tide, when the waves recede to reveal lots of little tide pools.

Tillamook

A different type of tasting room

The city of Tillamook is a very cheesy place – literally. The city's biggest draw is the **Tillamook Creamery** *(tillamook.com/visit-us/creamery; free)*, where you can take a self-guided walk through Oregon's best-known cheese-and-dairy-product factory or get a closer look at what goes into making Tillamook products with a guided cheese or ice-cream tour. Expect plenty of free samples.

Oregon Dunes National Recreation Area

The dunes that inspired Dune

Extending for around 40 miles from just south of Florence all the way to Coos Bay, the **Oregon Dunes National Recreation Area** *($5)* is the largest expanse of coastal sand dunes on the continent. It was these very dunes that provided the inspiration for Pacific Northwest author Frank Herbert's eco-sci-fi novel *Dune,* which was later adapted into film versions.

The dunes are popular for off-highway vehicle adventures, though if you'd rather approach the sands with a little less adrenaline, take a hike along the **Oregon Dunes Loop Trail**.

Brookings

A gorgeous stretch of coastline

The **Samuel H Boardman State Scenic Corridor** might just be the prettiest stretch of an already gorgeous coastline. Start your sightseeing at **Arch Rock**, where a small path leads to a couple of benches that look out over gorgeous sea stacks, including the aptly named Arch Rock itself. From here, continue south to the not-so-secret **Secret Beach** and **Thunder Rock Cove**. Take in views from the parking lot or head down a ¾-mile trail to the beach – just don't attempt this during high tide when most of the beach is submerged. Make **Natural Bridges** your next stop to see bridge-like rock formations as they're lapped by frothy sea spray. By now, you've probably spent enough time looking at the beach that you'll actually want to head down to the seashore. Continue south over the **Thomas Creek Bridge** until you reach **Whaleshead Beach**. Drive right down to the beach or park at the **Whaleshead Viewpoint** and follow a steep trail down to the shore.

NICHOLAS J KLEIN/SHUTTERSTOCK

Umpqua Hot Springs

Rogue-Umpqua Scenic Byway

Chasing eye-catching cascades

The second half of the Rogue-Umpqua Scenic Byway heads south, past Crater Lake, to follow the waterfall-dotted Rogue River. The 1.5-mile **Susan Creek Falls Trail** is a good place to start; it offers informational placards to get you acquainted with the local flora, including vine maples, Pacific dogwoods and grand firs.

Further down Hwy 138, **Fall Creek Falls** is a sparkling cascade over a rock wall into a shallow pool that's great for swimming on hot days. **Toketee Falls** is a popular stop where the parking lot is often full, but people move in and out quickly as the trail is only 0.8 miles long. Keep driving past Toketee Falls to **Umpqua Hot Springs**, an iconic Oregon spot to soak where cascading pools invite you to soak and relax in the mossy forest. Unfortunately, it's also well known for being overused and attracting litterbugs. Hopefully, those before you will leave it better than they found it, and you can do the same.

Pendleton

A spectacle of Western culture

For the second full week of September, the Eastern Oregon town of Pendleton is transformed into a rollicking Western celebration. The very first round-up took place in 1910 and exceeded all expectations for attendance and festivity – and the enthusiasm has held strong since. From bull riding and Indian relay racing to the Happy Canyon Pageant, a dramatic enactment of the settling of the American West, every day is action-packed. The nightlife can get a little rowdy, but there are plenty of activities for families, too. Plans for the round-up should be made well in advance.

DARK SKY SANCTUARY

Have you met ALAN? (You definitely have.) Artificial light at night (ALAN) is pervasive in most places thanks to lightbulbs, traffic lights, glowing screens and all the ways humans have found to illuminate darkness. ALAN impacts navigation, hunting and sleep patterns for many animals, including humans. DarkSky International is a leading organization in promoting natural darkness by encouraging the reduction in ALAN and designating certain places as distinctly dark – making them destinations for stargazing. In 2024 the Oregon Outback was named a Dark Sky Sanctuary. Thanks to the vast desert and low population of this 1.5-million-acre swath of Lake County – along with collaboration and public education on reducing light pollution – Oregon is now home to the largest Dark Sky Sanctuary in the world.

Places We Love to Stay

$** Budget **$$** Midrange **$$$ Top End

Seattle p446

Green Tortoise Seattle Hostel **$** Meet new people and make easy trips to Pike Place Market when staying at this affordable hostel.

Hotel Crocodile **$$** Settled above the city's famed grunge venue, the Crocodile, this boutique hotel has 17 rooms, each with a unique mural from a local artist.

Inn at the Market **$$$** Located within Pike Place Market, this boutique hotel is in the middle of the excitement but still manages to be surprisingly quiet within the rooms.

The Edgewater **$$$** This high-end, over-water hotel balances classy and rustic design styles – and has epic Puget Sound views.

Olympic Peninsula & Washington Coast p459

Sol Duc Campground **$** Reserve early on recreation.gov for the best campsites, including quiet Sol Duc, or check out mossy Hoh Rainforest, seafront forested Mora, or the isolated vistas of Deer Park.

Sol Duc Hot Springs Resort (p459) **$$$** Cozy cabins surround the lodge and hot springs. Guests can soak an hour before the public. Kitchenettes available.

Northwestern Washington & the San Juan Islands p461

Deception Pass State Park **$** Even with over 300 camping spaces across several wooded loops, the views mean you need to book now. Mix of tent and RV sites with hookups.

San Juan County Park Campground **$** Situated on San Juan's western shoreline, these 20 campsites are in high demand. Reserve in advance.

Doe Bay Resort **$$** A true wellness retreat, serene Doe Bay offers camping, yurts and cabins, plus outdoor soaking tubs. On-site Doe Bay Cafe grows organic ingredients and serves elevated locavore food.

Hotel Bellwether **$$$** Bellingham's premier waterfront hotel, located in a park-like marina setting. Its bay-view suites offer touches of luxury, including jetted tubs and fireplaces.

Washington Cascades p466

Stehekin Valley Ranch **$$** All kinds of activities, including cycling, horseback riding, kayaking and hiking, go on at this well-organized place in North Cascades National Park.

Paradise Inn **$$** Designed to blend in with the environment and constructed almost entirely of local materials, the historic (1916) Paradise Inn was an early blueprint for National Park–rustic architecture.

Ross Lake Resort **$$$** The floating cabins at this secluded resort in Stehekin (near North Cascades National Park) were built in the 1930s. Reached by ferry from the parking area near Diablo Dam.

Walla Walla p468

Columbia River Inn **$$** Opposite the visitor center in Grand Coulee is this clean, comfortable inn, with some hot-tub rooms, a fitness center and a sauna. It's the best place in town.

Freehand Cellars **$$$** If staying *near* wine country isn't good enough, you can book one of two apartments or the luxury Airstream trailer right on the grounds of this Wapato vineyard.

The Inn at Abeja **$$$** Historic farmhouse and winery set in the foothills of the Blue Mountains, 4 miles east of Walla Walla. Luxury accommodations are in impeccably restored self-contained houses that played a historical role at the farm (hayloft, mechanic's shed etc).

Portland p471

Hotel deLuxe **$** Longtime hotel just west of Downtown near the Goose Hollow neighborhood featuring vintage Hollywood-inspired decor and elegant brunches at on-site restaurant Gracie's, a long-time Portland institution.

Heathman Hotel **$$** A classic Portland hotel with elegant rooms, great on-site dining and a library full of books signed by past-guest authors.

Inn at Northrup Station **$$** Colorful, all-suites hotel within a short jaunt of the shops and restaurants on NW 23rd Ave.

McMenamins Kennedy School **$$$** Sprawling concept hotel occupying a converted elementary school, complete with rooms that were once classrooms (with the cloakrooms and chalkboards to show for it), multiple pubs and a hot soaking pool.

Willamette Valley p481

Timbers Inn $ This recently renovated 1958 motel celebrates a super-convenient downtown Eugene location. Retro design touches partner with modern rooms.

McMenamins Hotel Oregon $$ Eclectic artwork enlivens this McMinnville outpost of McMenamins' Pacific Northwest hospitality empire. In warmer months, don't miss drinks at the rooftop bar.

Atticus Hotel $$$ Luxurious downtown McMinnville hotel with ultra-modern decor and large rooms. Bikes are available for guest use, while the hotel's Cypress restaurant channels the best of the Mediterranean.

Gordon Hotel $$$ Downtown Eugene boutique hotel with bars and restaurants including a Prohibition-style speakeasy, a Mexican-themed rooftop bar and a modern American tavern.

Columbia River Gorge p486

Hood River Hotel $$ This characterful and historic hotel was built in 1912 and retains its early-20th-century character. Eclectic design touches abound and the downtown location is very convenient.

Timberline Lodge $$$ A gorgeous lodge oozing with history and charm, Timberline offers a variety of cozy rooms from dorms to deluxe. Ski-field access in winter, and elevated alpine hiking in spring and summer.

Columbia Gorge Hotel & Spa $$$ A historic Spanish Mission–style hotel set amid lush gardens with its own natural waterfall. The hotel's lounge bar is exceptionally cozy on a cooler day. Around 2 miles west of downtown Hood River.

Central Oregon & the Cascades p488

Bunk + Brew Hostel $ In a historic house near downtown Bend, this social hostel with mixed dorms and private rooms also features a sauna and regular events including live music.

Oxford Hotel $$$ The most upscale accommodation in Bend with super-spacious rooms, an understated and elegant ambience, and Modern American fine-dining onsite at ROAM restaurant.

The Oregon Coast p490

Norblad $ Hip, century-old hotel offering budget-friendly rooms in Astoria's city center.

Crater Lake Lodge $$ Sleep next to Crater Lake in this historic lodge whose exterior is featured in 1980 horror film *The Shining*. Amenities are basic but the location makes up for any shortcomings.

Stephanie Inn $$$ Romantic, upscale inn with close-up Haystack Rock views plus a spa and a fine-dining restaurant with great wine.

Bowline Hotel $$$ Astoria boutique hotel in a former fish-processing plant with maritime-themed rooms, many overlooking the Columbia River.

Eastern Oregon p493

Pendleton House Historic Inn $$ A pink 1917 mansion built in the Italian Renaissance style with beautiful vintage decor.

The Lodge at Hot Lake Springs $$$ Soak in the natural hot springs right outside a historic lodge. Pub and movie theater make it hard to leave this La Grande accommodation.

ANDRIANA SYVANYCH/SHUTTERSTOCK

Portland streetscape, including the Heathman Hotel

TOOLKIT

The chapters in this section cover the most important topics you'll need to know about in the Western USA. They're full of nuts-and-bolts information and valuable insights to help you understand and navigate the Western USA and get the most out of your trip.

Boynton Canyon (p283), Arizona

BRANNON_NAITO/SHUTTERSTOCK

Arriving

Many of the largest airports in the United States are in the western part of the country, including Dallas-Fort Worth (DFW), Denver (DEN), Los Angeles (LAX) and Las Vegas (LAS). Train service is also available from other parts of the country, but it's much quicker to fly between major destinations.

Visas

The US Visa Waiver Program (VWP) allows passport holders from 42 countries to stay up to 90 days in the US without a visa. Pre-authorization is available via the Electronic System for Travel Authorization (ESTA).

Cell Phones

US cell plans usually work nationwide, and plans typically include texting, calling and data. It's easiest to buy a digital SIM online before your trip.

Wi-Fi

Wi-fi is free, fast and widely available at most airports, hotels, restaurants and other public spaces across the Western US.

Clothing

The West has a huge variety of microclimates, from hot deserts to cool mountains and parks. Layers are a must, no matter when you visit.

From Airports to Popular Destinations

FROM	TO	DURATION
ALBUQUERQUE	GRAND CANYON	6HRS
ALBUQUERQUE	SANTA FE	1HR
BOZEMAN	YELLOWSTONE NP	1½HRS
DALLAS-FORT WORTH	AUSTIN	3½HRS
DENVER	ROCKY MOUNTAIN NP	1½HRS
LAS VEGAS	GRAND CANYON	4½HRS
LAS VEGAS	ZION NP	4½HRS
LOS ANGELES	DISNEYLAND	1½HRS
LOS ANGELES	JOSHUA TREE NP	4HRS
PHOENIX	GRAND CANYON	3½HRS
SAN FRANCISCO	YOSEMITE NP	4HRS
SAN FRANCISCO	NAPA VALLEY	2HRS

FROM LEFT: FUSE/GETTY IMAGES, GEORGE MDIVANIAN/EYEEM/GETTY IMAGES

Getting Around

Driving is the standard way to get around in most of the Western US, and having your own car or rental vehicle makes traveling between destinations much easier.

TRAVEL COSTS

Car rental
from $50/day

Gas
$4-6 per gallon

EV charging
$0.35-0.60/kWh

Bicycle rental
approx $40/day

Renting a Car

Unless you plan to stick to the cities, renting a car is a smart move. Rentals are widely available at airports, and most major companies offer the choice of electric or gasoline-fueled cars. Most rental companies require drivers to be at least 25 years old, but some will rent to younger drivers for an additional fee.

Road Conditions

Road conditions vary quite a bit, and many forested areas are accessible via bumpy, gravel roads. It's worth considering renting an all-wheel-drive vehicle if you plan to spend much time on backroads or out in the wilderness. All national parks and many state parks have excellent infrastructure, with roads that are suitable for small vehicles.

TIP

Many parts of the West lack adequate cell phone service, so make sure to download offline maps before you head off the beaten path.

ROAD RULES

The rules of the road vary between states, so it's a good idea to familiarize yourself with the rules of each. For example, U-turns at traffic lights are illegal in Oregon (except when there's a posted sign permitting them), but are allowed in other western states. It's legal to turn right on a red light in all 50 states, except when a sign indicates otherwise.

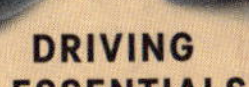

DRIVING ESSENTIALS

Drive on the right

Speed limits vary considerably, maxing out at 70mph in Oregon and California and up to 85mph in parts of Texas

.08

Blood alcohol limit is 0.08%, except in Utah, where it's 0.05%

Train & Bus

Trying to get around the American West while relying only on trains and buses is quite the challenge, though not impossible if you have a lot of time on your hands. Long-distance bus operators such as Greyhound and FlixBus offer service between major cities, while Amtrak runs the trains in this part of the country.

Bicycle

Hardcore cyclists will find a lot of ground to cover in the Western US, with bike-friendly roads and special campsites for cyclists and hikers in many state parks. Still, long-distance cycling in this part of the country is no easy feat, and rapid changes in elevation and climate in some areas require serious preparation.

Plane

The easiest way to get between major cities in the West is to fly, but for people who are big on road-tripping, this method takes some of the magic out of the experience. Still, flying is the best way to go if you want to see a lot and don't have months to do it.

Money

CURRENCY: UNITED STATES DOLLAR ($)

Credit & Debit Cards

Most businesses in the Western US accept credit cards, debit cards and contactless phone payments, and it's easy to travel through much of the region without any cash. However, some convenience stores charge a fee (either a percentage or a set fee, usually around $0.50) to use a card for a purchase under $5.

Cash

Cash is used by some people in the Western US, especially for tipping hotel and valet staff and for smaller purchases. Pennies are being phased out (production stopped in 2026). If you plan to use cash, it's smart to keep some small notes on hand, as not everyone will have change.

HOW MUCH FOR A...

City bus fare
$1.50-3

Road toll
$2.50-10

State park parking
$5-10

ATM fee
$3

HOW TO... Save on National Park Fees

If you plan to visit more than two national parks in one year, it's worth picking up an America the Beautiful pass *(store.usgs.gov/2025-annual-pass; vehicle with up to four adults $80; US resident or citizens 62 or over $20)*. Passes are valid for one year and give you unlimited access to over 2000 national parks, wildlife refuges, forests and more.

Sales Tax

All states in the western US have sales tax, except for Oregon and Montana. Rates typically fall between 6% and 9%, and are added on after the advertised price. Hotel taxes are common, even in destinations where there's no sales tax, and are typically levied on top of the advertised room rate.

SPLITTING THE TAB

In the US, groups of friends dining together typically pay for whatever they consumed rather than splitting the tab down the middle.

TIPPING CULTURE

The US service industry is heavily fueled by tips, and a growing number of establishments – from bakeries to cannabis dispensaries – now have tipping options on their payment screens. In some states, restaurant servers make less than minimum wage with the assumption that their tips will supplement the difference. In other states, servers get minimum wage, but still expect tips. A minimum of 20% is standard at restaurants (although 15% for take-out is acceptable).

Rideshare and taxi drivers are tipped similarly, while it's customary to leave $5 a day for hotel cleaning staff.

Accommodations

Vacation Rentals

For a live-like-a-local experience – and access to a kitchen – a vacation rental may be your best option. Options run the gamut, from private rooms in local homes to multiroom mansions that can accommodate large groups. While prices can run slightly higher than typical hotel room rates, you can save a lot of money by cooking for yourself.

Camping

Camping options abound in the Western US, both in state and national parks and on private property. States and counties typically have their own reservation systems, while reservable campsites in national parks and forests can be booked up to six months in advance at *recreation.gov*. Camping on land managed by the Bureau of Land Management (BLM) is typically free and doesn't require permits.

Boutique Hotels & Inns

Boutique hotels and independently owned inns are good options if you want the creature comforts of a hotel without the sterile vibes. Rooms and common areas at these properties tend to have a bit more character than what you'd likely find at your average business hotel, and often still have hotel-style perks such as breakfast buffets and daily housekeeping.

Revamped Motels

Don't let the exteriors deceive you: many traditional motor hotels have been revamped from tired old digs to sleek, neo-mid-century stays loaded with retro glamor. While these glowed-up motels are most often found in destinations that lean heavily into their vintage appeal (think Palm Springs), you'll find them in popular vacation spots across the region.

HOW MUCH FOR A NIGHT IN...

A campsite **$0-75**

A hostel dorm **$40-80**

A hotel **$90+**

Cabins, Yurts & Glamping

If you love the outdoors, but aren't keen on the idea of pitching a tent or sleeping on hard ground, you have options. Many state and national parks have cabins or yurts for rent, but reservations typically fill up well in advance. Glamping – a portmanteau of camping and glamor – is more often available at private properties and nature resorts. Glamping tents are typically equipped with beds and often have electricity.

FIRE-LOOKOUT TOWERS

Forest fires have always been part of life in the Western US, and for many years, officials used one-room fire-lookout towers to keep an eye out for blazes. Today, these towers are more often used for elevated camping. Most fire-lookout towers are on federal land and can be reserved on *recreation.gov*. Because of their popularity, these towers are often snapped up the second they become available (typically six months in advance at 7am Pacific), so you'll need to be ready to pounce if you want a chance at a stay.

FROM TOP LEFT: RUSLAN IVANTSOV/SHUTTERSTOCK, 279PHOTO STUDIO/SHUTTERSTOCK, CORY WOODRUFF/SHUTTERSTOCK

Family Travel

The Western US is a prime destination for family travel, thanks to its mix of beaches and forests, theme parks and science museums. Cities are full of activities for kids of all ages, while the great outdoors offers ample opportunities for camping, hiking, winter skiing, summer swimming, and simply slowing down and enjoying time as a family.

Strollers & Car Seats

Most public buildings in the Western US are suitable for strollers, but baby carriers are a better option for hiking outside of short, accessible trails in some public parks. Car seats are required for infants and most children, but height, weight and age requirements vary by state. Many states require booster seats for children who are under 57in (145cm) tall.

Breastfeeding

Breastfeeding in public places is more common on the West Coast than in more conservative states, and some Americans find the practice controversial. US airports are required to have designated lactation spaces outside of bathrooms thanks to the Friendly Airports for Mothers Act; in other areas, mothers often cover up with a blanket (but this is by no means required).

Kids Menus

Kids menus are common in chain restaurants and at many hotels, some of which allow children under 12 to dine for free (at least at breakfast) with a paying adult. Menu options typically include blander dishes such as mac and cheese and chicken nuggets.

Baby-Changing Tables

Baby-changing tables are found in most women's restrooms, and in a growing number of men's and all-gender/family restrooms. In multi-stall restrooms, tables are typically either found in the main area or in larger wheelchair-accessible stalls.

BEST ATTRACTIONS FOR KIDS

Dinosaur National Monument (p205) Touch real dinosaur skeletons at this prehistoric spot on the Colorado–Utah border.

Disneyland (p428) Meet Mickey Mouse or go on a ride in this California classic, nicknamed the 'happiest place on earth.'

Maquoketa Caves State Park (p96) Kids can don headlamps and try out some easy spelunking at this Iowa attraction.

Oregon Museum of Science & Industry (p475) Try out an earthquake simulator or descend into a submarine at this hands-on museum in Portland.

NATIONAL PARK JUNIOR RANGERS

The National Park Service's Junior Rangers program gets kids excited about natural history and the environment through a range of special activities, typically presented to families in an activity book (available for free at visitor centers). Kids who complete the activities in each booklet then pledge to protect and respect national park lands. They are then rewarded with a special badge and the title of Junior Ranger from the park that they're visiting. Some parks also offer special Junior Ranger programs that range from guided plant walks to immersive astronomy experiences under the night sky.

RED HERRING/SHUTTERSTOCK

Health & Safe Travel

INSURANCE

It's always a wise idea to take out travel insurance, even if you don't plan to participate in adventure sports or other high-risk activities. The US medical system is such that hospital bills can easily run into the tens of thousands of dollars, and overseas visitors are not exempt from paying. Some travel-insurance policies also cover lost luggage and trip cancellations.

Wildfires

Wildfires are part of a typical summer in much of the Western US, often starting to flare up as early as June and continuing through October in some areas. Risks associated with wildfires go beyond just flames themselves; wildfire smoke can cause severe health issues for both people and their pets.

Safe Hiking

It's best not to hike alone, but if you do want to hit the trail solo, always let someone know where you're going and when you'll be back. Never go off designated trails and carry a compass, a whistle, a fully charged phone, a flashlight and plenty of water.

CANNABIS

Recreational marijuana is legal for adults 21 and over in much of the Western US, but some states ban it outright (even for medical use).

AIR QUALITY INDEX

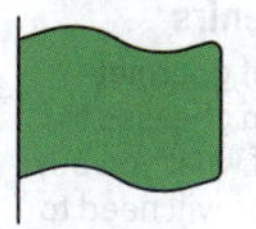

GREEN Good

YELLOW Moderate

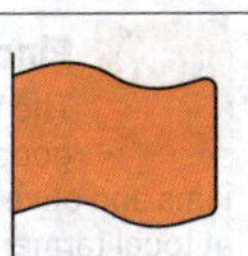

ORANGE Unhealthy for Sensitive Groups

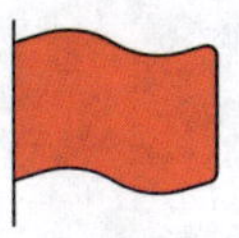

RED Unhealthy

PURPLE Very Unhealthy

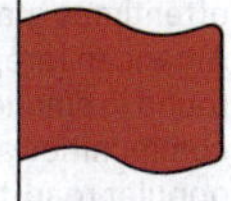

MAROON Hazardous

Staying Cool & Hydrated

High temperatures and glaring sun put you at risk of serious health issues, including heatstroke and dehydration. In hotter destinations, keep yourself safe by drinking water at regular intervals, and don't forget a sun hat and sunscreen. If possible, limit outdoor activity between 10am and 4pm, when sunlight is at its most brutal.

HOUSELESSNESS

Homelessness is a major issue in much of the Western US, and while it's particularly noticeable in larger cities, you may see unhoused people in smaller communities, too. Mental health issues – including substance abuse disorders – are major contributors to this issue. Other people are simply down on their luck, a side effect of the US' relatively limited social safety net.

Food, Drink & Nightlife

When to Eat

Breakfast Usually between 6:30am and 10:30am. Can range from a pastry or a smoothie to a hearty meal of pancakes, bacon and eggs.

Lunch Served between 11am and 2pm, and often consists of one-item dishes such as sandwiches, burritos or burgers.

Dinner Mostly eaten between 6pm and 9pm. Restaurant dinners are typically heavier than lunch offerings and are often complemented with appetizers and desserts.

MENU DECODER

Biscuit A type of neutral or slightly salty quick bread, similar to a scone, that's typically served with gravy at breakfast. Not to be confused with a cookie.

Chef's table A dining experience where guests are seated at a table or counter near the kitchen and get to interact with the chef.

Corkage The fee a restaurant charges to patrons who bring in a bottle of wine from elsewhere to enjoy with their meal.

Entrée The main course.

Gluten-free Does not contain any gluten, but may be prepared in shared spaces or using shared equipment such as fryers.

Pairings Wines selected specifically to match dishes. Wine pairings are often offered as an optional add-on to tasting menus.

Vegan Does not contain any animal products, including dairy, eggs and honey.

Where to Eat

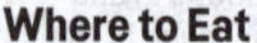

Brewpubs Restaurants anchored on breweries, often serving elevated takes on burgers and other bar food.

Diners Casual restaurants with oftentimes greasy American fare; often found in smaller communities and on popular road-trip routes.

Fine-dining restaurants Found in larger cities and in wine countries and often showcase locally grown and foraged ingredients.

Food trucks Also known as 'food carts' in some areas, food trucks typically offer limited menus and quick service. Taco trucks are particularly popular in southwestern regions.

HOW TO... Find Gourmet Souvenirs

The Western US is full of gourmet goodies, from wines and cheeses to jams and olive oils. While much of what you buy at local farmers markets and shops will need to be consumed within days, there are plenty of shelf-stable treats that make great souvenirs. Nuts are a great choice, and many states have their own specialties, including pecans in Texas and hazelnuts (also known as filberts) from Oregon. Salsa is huge in the Southwest – make sure to pick up the hatch-chile variety if you're in New Mexico. In Arizona, there's candy made from prickly pears, a type of cactus that abounds in the state. As you get closer to the southeastern US, you'll find plenty of barbecue sauce options (and just as many people with strong opinions about barbecue sauce). Texan and Kansas City–style are two dominant varieties.

FROM TOP: ETORRES/SHUTTERSTOCK, ANDREI KUZMIK/SHUTTERSTOCK

HOW MUCH FOR A...

Coffee
$3-6

Pint of craft beer
$5-8

Glass of wine
$6-10

Cocktail
$7-18

Slice of pizza
$5-6

Scoop of ice cream
$4-5

Taco
$3-4

Food-cart meal
$9-15

HOW TO... Go Wine Tasting

Wine tasting is hugely popular in the Western US, but there are a few things to know before you set out. First, many wineries require reservations for tastings. While some do allow drop-ins, they often fill up during the summer and on weekends. Some wineries also close their tasting rooms during the winter, especially those in cooler climates. Most wineries offer a standard tasting menu, and many offer additional tasting menus and wines by the glass. While free tastings were once standard, most wineries charge fees ranging from $15 to $30 per person. Fees are usually waived with a minimum purchase (often two or more bottles).

Wines are typically served in the same glass, one pour (tasting) at a time. Once your tasting is poured, swirl it to open up the flavors – a good way to do this is by setting your glass on the table to stabilize it before swirling. Bring the glass up to your nose and inhale slowly to take in the aroma, then taste a small sip, allowing the wine to cover your mouth so you can taste and feel it on different parts of your tongue. Swallow and exhale, noting any lingering flavors and fragrances. If you like what you've sampled, you may want to finish your glass. If not (or if you're driving), pour out the rest in the provided spit bucket.

Wine Regions

While the bulk of US wineries are concentrated on the West Coast in regions such as Napa, Sonoma and the Willamette Valley, you'll find vibrant wine scenes across the region, notably in Colorado, Texas and even Arizona.

REGIONAL CUISINE

There's a lot of debate around what 'American food' actually is. Some define it as hamburgers and fries, but most agree that American cuisine is better exemplified by a range of culinary styles and ingredients that reflect the country's cultural and geographical diversity. This variety is evident in the American West, where culinary practices and traditions vary significantly, both between regions and across state lines.

Midwestern food is perhaps closest to the meat-and-potatoes vision of the standard American diet, and dishes from some parts of the region evolved from German and Scandinavian traditions. Missouri has barbecue traditions all its own, as does Texas, which is also the birthplace of Tex-Mex fare, known for its ample use of yellow cheeses and cumin. Today, it's one of the more popular cuisines in the Western states, and many dishes that people assume are from Mexico – including nachos and chimichangas (deep-fried burritos) – are actually Tex-Mex in origin. New Mexico puts its own spin on Mexican and Tex-Mex dishes, and popular dishes such as chilaquiles and burritos are served with sauce made from the state's celebrated Hatch chiles. You can order dishes with red or green salsa or go for 'Christmas' stye and get a mix of the two.

On the West Coast, California cuisine puts a heavy emphasis on fresh, locally sourced ingredients that are often prepared using less oil and fats than elsewhere in the country. Pacific Northwest cuisine is similarly locavorian, emphasizing the use of mushrooms, seafood and other ingredients that are abundant in Oregon and Washington.

Responsible Travel

Climate Change & Travel

It's impossible to ignore the impact we have when travelling; Lonely Planet urges all travelers to engage with their travel carbon footprint, which will mainly come from air travel. While there often isn't an alternative, travelers can look to minimise the number of flights they take, opt for newer aircrafts and use cleaner ground transport, such as trains. One proposed solution – purchasing carbon offsets – unfortunately does not cancel out the impact of individual flights. While most destinations will depend on air travel for the foreseeable future, for now, pursuing ground-based travel where possible is the best course of action.

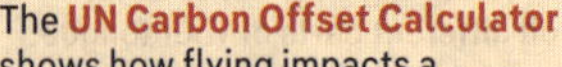

The **UN Carbon Offset Calculator** shows how flying impacts a household's emissions

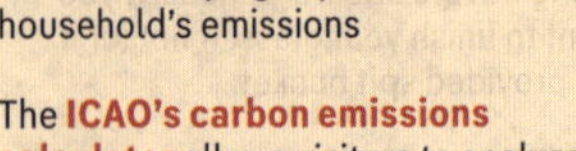

The **ICAO's carbon emissions calculator** allows visitors to analyze the CO2 generated by point-to-point journeys

Go Vegan

Animal agriculture is one of the major drivers of climate change. Reduce your impact by choosing plant-based meals and materials when you can, or by going vegan altogether.

Deposit Your Bottles

California and Oregon have container deposits on most cans and bottles, in which you pay $0.10 extra per container on select beverages. You can claim it back at area recycling kiosks (often found at supermarkets).

Learn about Indigenous American history and culture at the **First Americans Museum** (p80) in Oklahoma, **Museum of the Plains Indians** (p234) in Montana and the **Seattle Art Museum** (p451) in Washington.

Hike, cycle or ski through the mountains, spending the night in off-grid huts en route. Options include the 10th Mountain Division Hut Association, San Juan Huts and **Summit Huts Association** (p195).

CARRY CUTLERY

When ordering takeout, ask the restaurant to skip giving you cutlery. Instead, carry a travel set with a knife, fork, spoon and chopsticks, or go ultra-minimalist and just carry your own spork (spoon-fork combo).

WATER WISE

Droughts are common in much of the Western US, particularly in California. The state's Department of Water Resources has a dedicated website with more details on how you can conserve water *(saveourwater.com)*.

On Leash

Many state parks and natural areas have leash laws in place. While these rules can help keep people safe (and trails poo-free), they also help protect local wildlife from getting chased by excited pups.

Invasive Species

Invasive species are a problem across Western US natural areas, often hitching rides on hiking boots or firewood. Always use boot brush stations at parks and never bring firewood from other regions. Learn more about how you can prevent spreads at *naisma.org/programs/playcleango*.

Buy Local

Locally grown and made products use fewer fossil fuels to transport, and buying them helps keep dollars in the communities where you're visiting. Farmers markets, natural-health-food stores and craft bazaars are all great places to shop.

Stargazing opportunities abound in the West. Check DarkSky International *(darksky.org)* for more info.

Seattle's **Climate Pledge Arena** (p451) is powered entirely by renewable energy.

Western snowy plovers are a threatened species of bird that breed and nest on sand spits and salt lakes throughout much of the West. Watch where you walk, especially in the spring-fall nesting season.

RESOURCES

happycow.net
Find vegan and vegetarian restaurants and options easily.

Nature Conservancy Carbon emissions calculator

Alternative Fuels Data Center
Electric vehicle charging station map.

CLOCKWISE FROM BOTTOM LEFT: RYH STUDIO/SHUTTERSTOCK, TOMMASO LIZZUL/SHUTTERSTOCK, HANNATOR/SHUTTERSTOCK

LGBTIQ+ Travelers

In many parts of the Western US, LGBTIQ+ travelers will feel welcomed, especially in progressive West Coast cities such as San Francisco and Portland. Things can feel different in rural areas, especially those in states with more conservative populations, such as Texas and Nebraska, where some travelers may not feel safe expressing themselves or showing affection to their partners in public.

Pride

Most major (and plenty of smaller) cities in the Western US have Pride celebrations. While the majority take place in June, some cities hold their celebrations in alternate months (typically in spring, summer or early fall).

Noteworthy events include San Francisco's **Pride Celebration** *(sfpride.org)*, which has been running since 1970, and **Pride Houston** *(@pridehoustontx)*, which launched back in '79. Other major Pride festivities include **Seattle Pride** *(seattlepride.org)*, **Portland Pride** *(portlandpride.org)*, **LA Pride** *(lapride.org)*, Salt Lake City's **Utah Pride** *(utahpride.org)* and **Denver Pride** *(denverpride.org)*. For a comprehensive list of Pride events, visit *gaypridecalendar.com*.

VEGAS WEDDINGS

Same-sex marriage has been legal in Nevada since 2014, opening Vegas's huge wedding industry up to all couples. Now, you can get an express wedding with an Elvis impersonator to do the honors at one of Sin City's numerous chapels, including the **Gay Chapel of Las Vegas** *(gaychapeloflasvegas.com)*, which specializes in LGBTIQ+ weddings and vow renewals.

LGBTIQ+ California

While many cities and neighborhoods in the Western US are LGBTIQ-friendly, there are a few areas that are destinations for queer travelers. Unsurprisingly, many are in California, including Palm Springs, San Francisco's Castro District and Guerneville in Sonoma County.

QUEER HISTORY

In 1966, the Compton's Cafeteria riot erupted in San Francisco's Tenderloin neighborhood as a response to police harassment against transgender people and drag queens. Less than 50 years later, part of the Tenderloin became the world's first official transgender district. Learn all about the area's history and its role in the LGBTIQ+ rights movement at the **Tenderloin Museum** (p360).

LGBTIQ+ Resources

International Gay and Lesbian Travel Association *(iglta.org)* An extensive resource with guides and travel information for LGBTIQ+ travelers.

LGBT National Help Center *(lgbthotline.org)* Resources and support for community members in need.

Out Traveler *(outtraveler.com)* Online magazine with travel and lifestyle articles and reviews.

NITO/SHUTTERSTOCK

Accessible Travel

Larger cities and public buildings typically have good accessibility infrastructure in place, thanks largely to requirements put forth by the Americans with Disabilities Act (ADA). Natural areas can provide challenges, though many do have wheelchair-friendly trails.

National & State Parks

Many state parks and most national parks have a mix of inaccessible and wheelchair-friendly trails, and most have accessible tent and RV campsites. Check individual websites for details.

Airport

All US airports must comply with ADA regulations, which translate to accessible restrooms, step-free access to gates, and airplanes and wheelchair assistance (which is best to request in advance).

Accommodations

Most larger hotels have multiple accessible rooms. Features include wider doors and adapted bathrooms with roll-in showers and grab bars, braille signage, and visual emergency alarm and doorbell systems.

IN COLOR

Some museums and visitor centers offer loaner pairs of EnChroma's color-blindness-correcting glasses to visitors who need them. including the **Boise Art Museum** (p239) and Spokane's **Northwest Museum of Arts and Culture** (p470).

Trains

Commuter trains are typically wheelchair-friendly and often have audio announcements and visual signals. Amtrak passenger trains can accommodate wheelchairs with advance notice, but chair size and clearance requirements apply.

Park Access for All

The America the Beautiful access pass grants US citizens and permanent residents with disabilities free lifetime access to over 2000 national parks and recreation sites. Many state parks also offer discounted parking or admission.

PICTURE THIS

Held annually in Austin, the **Cinema Touching Disability Film Festival** *(@ctdfilmfestival)* uses film as a way to change perspectives on disability through documentaries, short films and more, created by filmmakers from across Texas.

RESOURCES

AccessibleGo *(accessiblego.com)* Book accessible hotels, vehicles and equipment or join the community forum for tips and advice.

Curb Free with Cory Lee *(curbfreewithcorylee.com)* Award-winning travel blog by a wheelchair-using traveler.

Society for the Accessible Tourism & Hospitality *(sath.org)* Accessibility tips and disability-centered destination guides.

TravelAbility *(travelability.net)* Accessibility resources listed by state.

TSA Cares *(tsa.gov/travel/tsa-cares)* Flight security information for travelers with disabilities and access needs.

Many travelers have hidden disabilities, meaning it's not always apparent that they need support. The Hidden Disabilities Sunflower program offers lanyards that travelers can wear to discreetly alert others that they may need a bit of extra help. Learn more at hdsunflower.com.

WONWOO LEE/GETTY IMAGES

Cable cars (p359), San Francisco, California

Nuts & Bolts

OPENING HOURS

Banks 8:30am-5pm Mon-Fri (many have additional shortened morning hours on Saturdays)

Gas stations 6am-11pm (many are open 24 hours but only accept credit cards when unstaffed)

Restaurants 11am-9pm (hours vary, check in advance)

Bars to 2am (1am in Utah and parts of Nebraska, 2:30am in Oregon, 3am in parts of Illinois)

Movie theaters matinees start as early as 10am with last screenings around midnight on weekends

Clothing stores 10am-9pm, typically with shorter Sunday hours

Supermarkets 7am-11pm, some open 24/7

GOOD TO KNOW

Time zones
Pacific, Mountain, Central (GMT/UTC -8, -7, -6 hours, respectively)

Country Code
+1

Emergency Number
911

PUBLIC HOLIDAYS

New Year's Day January 1

Martin Luther King Jr Day Third Monday of January

President's Day/ Washington's Birthday Third Monday of February

Easter Sunday March or April

Memorial Day Last Monday of May

Juneteenth June 19

Independence Day July 4

Labor Day First Monday of September

Indigenous Peoples' Day and Columbus Day Second Monday of October

Veterans Day November 11

Thanksgiving Day Fourth Thursday of November

Christmas Day December 25

Weights & Measures

The US uses the imperial system, except bottled water and soft drinks are often sold by the liter. Temperatures are measured in Fahrenheit.

Smoking

Banned indoors in most states; looser restrictions in Idaho, Nevada, Texas and Wyoming.

Electricity 120V/60Hz

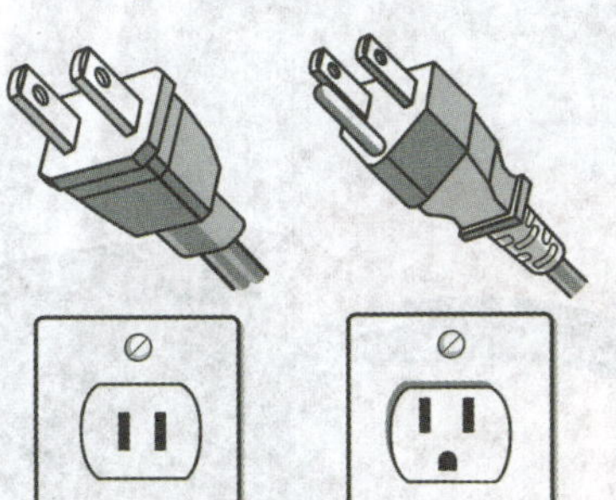

Cellular Data

Mobile internet coverage is excellent in cities, but can be poor to nonexistent in many rural and wilderness areas.

ROUTE
66

STORYBOOK

Our writers delve deep into different aspects of Western life

Route 66 (p22), California

ARTUR DEBAT/GETTY IMAGES

A HISTORY OF WESTERN USA IN 15 PLACES

The western United States is often described in terms of its natural wonders, from vast prairies and deserts to snowcapped mountains and evergreen forests. While this massive region is certainly a geographic wonderland, to understand it is to know its backstory. By Margot Bigg

WHEN PEOPLE SPEAK of the West, there's often a sunset involved. Tropes range from cowboys riding off into the sunset to stereotypical surfer dudes catching the final waves before the sun sinks into the Pacific. This could be because the idea of the West – at least in the American imagination – initially took form in the minds of American imperialists from 'back East,' many of whom felt compelled, whether by greed or by so-called 'Manifest Destiny' (a prevalent 19th-century belief that westward expansion was providential), to conquer whatever they could, from the Mississippi River to the Pacific Ocean. For the Native people who had lived in these lands for thousands of years, however, what we now know as the West was not an idea. It was simply home.

The story of the West didn't begin with the Lewis and Clark expedition, nor did it take root when European fur traders and Jesuit priests began setting up settlements on the Pacific Coast. But the story also didn't end with the Oregon Trail, the Gold Rush or the arrival of railways. The western US developed tremendously in the 20th century, thanks to immigration and technological advances, and is now a hotbed of creativity and innovation. And while it's certainly a land of many tales – some rather tragic – the story of the West is still being written.

1. San Juan Islands, Washington

THE PIG WAR

Although the last time the US and the UK went to war was in 1812, there was a dispute known as the Pig War that happened a little later, in 1859. At the time, San Juan Island, in what is now Washington State, was claimed by both countries. Here's what happened. An American farmer saw a pig digging up potatoes on his land and shot it dead. The pig's owner, an Irishman, learned of the fatality and demanded compensation. The two men butted heads and their dispute was soon politicized, catalyzing a land dispute that dragged on until its peaceful resolution in 1872.

For more on the San Juan Islands, see p464

2. Fort Clatsop, Oregon

A LIFE-SIZED TIME CAPSULE

In December 1805, an expedition led by Meriwether Lewis and William Clark of the US Army's Corps of Discovery – aided by Sacagawea, a Lemhi Shoshone teenager – landed just 6 miles south of what is now downtown Astoria. Here they established Fort Clatsop, the first US military structure west of the Rockies, where they would spend the final winter of their expedition before returning east. Although the original fort no longer exists, a replica with period displays (and, if you come in the summer, costumed interpreters) stands in its place. There's also a large visitor center displaying documents, weapons and a model canoe.

For more on Fort Clatsop, see p490

3. Monterey's Custom House, California

WHERE THE US TOOK CALIFORNIA

Built in 1827 and then rebuilt in 1841, Monterey's Custom House is the oldest government building in the state. It was constructed when California was part of the newly independent country of Mexico, and importers bringing goods into the Monterey Bay port had to stop at the building to pay duties to the Mexican government. While the building's age is noteworthy, it's more significantly known as the spot where – in 1846 – Commodore John Drake Sloat raised the American flag during the Mexican–American War, effectively claiming California as part of the US. Today, it's protected as part of the Monterey State Historic Park.

For more on Monterey, see p402

Neon Museum (p261), Nevada

ANTARES_NS/SHUTTERSTOCK

4. Little Bighorn Battlefield National Monument, Montana

CUSTER'S LAST STAND

Little Bighorn Battlefield National Monument preserves the spot where the Battle of the Little Bighorn, or Custer's Last Stand, took place in 1876. The battle was part of the Great Sioux War, which erupted after the US settlers, hungry for gold that had been discovered in the Black Hills, began encroaching on Native lands. A battle ensued, led by George Armstrong Custer, who – along with his men – succumbed to Lakota and Cheyenne forces. This battle was considered a catalyst for the US to double down on their efforts to conquer Native land and force Native Americans onto reservations.

For more on Little Bighorn Battlefield National Monument, see p236

5. Minidoka National Historic Site, Idaho

AN AMERICAN CONCENTRATION CAMP

In 1942, mere months after the attack on Pearl Harbor, President Franklin D Roosevelt signed an order that led to the internment of over 120,000 people of Japanese descent, the majority of them US-born citizens. Ten camps were set up in remote locations, including the Minidoka War Relocation Center in southern Idaho. This concentration camp, now preserved as the Minidoka National Historic Site, had more than 13,000 captives at its peak. Some of the structures remain, and there's a visitor center with exhibits and a bookstore. Ranger-led tours take place on summer weekends.

For more on Minidoka National Historic Site, see p245

6. Neon Museum, Nevada

LET IT SHINE

Neon signs have been an integral part of the Las Vegas cityscape for nearly a century, but many of the pieces that once illuminated Downtown and the Strip are long retired. Instead of being sent to scrapyards, however, these civic icons were put on display at the Neon Boneyard, part of the city's Neon Museum. Today, the museum has over 250 signs on display, including a massive one from the Flamingo Las Vegas Hotel & Casino, the longest-running casino hotel on the strip. Visit on a night tour to see them at their illuminated best.

For more on the Neon Museum, see p261

7. Grand Canyon, Arizona

DEEP HISTORY

Millions of years of geological history are on full display at the Grand Canyon, perhaps the best-known natural wonder in the country. Pay attention to the bottom layers of Zoroaster granite and Vishnu schist, which are counted among the world's oldest exposed rocks. The geology and vistas alone inspire awe and humility in many visitors, but there's much more to this Arizona wonder. Stop by the Village Historic District, which was founded in 1901, when the first steam-powered train arrived at the Canyon's South Rim. Here you can see eclectic turn-of-the-century buildings designed by architect Mary Colter, including the pueblo-inspired Hopi House.

For more on the Grand Canyon, see p273

8. Los Alamos, New Mexico

WEAPONS THAT CHANGED THE COURSE OF HISTORY

In the early 20th century, the US developed the world's first atomic bombs in what was dubbed the Manhattan Project, which took place across three sites. Plutonium was manufactured in rural Washington State, uranium was enriched in Tennessee and the bombs themselves were created at Los Alamos. Today, the three locations comprise the Manhattan Project National Historic Park, which is now managed by the National Park Service. Visitors can learn more at the visitor center or at Los Alamos History Museum, stop by Oppenheimer's former home, or join a 'behind the fence' tour of the site, available thrice yearly by reservation.

For more on Los Alamos, see p330

9. Fort Worth Stockyards, Texas

WILD, WILD WEST

In the late 1800s, Fort Worth was a key stop on the Chisholm Trail, which was used by cowboys to drive cattle from the south of Texas to Kansas. Today, it's a lively historic district jam-packed with historic buildings from its Wild West heyday, many of which now house Western apparel shops, barbecue restaurants and country music dancehalls. The Old West vibe is at its most apparent during the twice-daily cattle drive, complete with real cowboys dressed in duds that make them look like they were plucked straight out of the 19th century.

For more on the Fort Worth Stockyards, see p154

10. Dinosaur National Monument, Utah & Colorado

JURASSIC PARK

On the northern end of the Colorado Plateau on the Utah–Colorado border sits one of the best collections of fossils in the United States, preserved as the Dinosaur National Monument. The monument's gargantuan Quarry Exhibit Hall invites visitors to see – and touch – the fossilized remains of dinosaurs embedded in a 'Wall of Bones.' Although the dinosaur bones are the start of the show, the park also draws in those interested in human history. They come to see a multitude of petroglyph and pictograph sites that have been attributed to the Fremont people, who lived here between the 4th and 14th centuries.

For more on Dinosaur National Monument, see p205

11. Yellowstone National Park, Wyoming

THE USA'S FIRST NATIONAL PARK

In 1872 President Ulysses S Grant signed the Yellowstone National Park Protection Act, thereby establishing Yellowstone as the nation's first national park. The idea to preserve the area's cultural and natural history spurred the formation of the National Park Service, which now has over 2000 sites. Today, Yellowstone is home to many historic structures, including the grand Old Faithful Inn. Yellowstone's thermal waters and vast swaths of land had been used by humans long before it became a park, however, and many Native communities, including the Bannock, Crow, Nez Percé and Shoshone people, spent time on the land for centuries before European occupation.

For more on Yellowstone National Park, see p218

12. Homestead National Historical Park, Nebraska

HOME ON THE RANGE

The Homestead Act of 1862 changed the course of the western US significantly. It

MICHAEL GORDON/SHUTTERSTOCK

Quarry Exhibit Hall, Dinosaur National Monument (p205), Colorado

spurred American settler colonial expansion by taking public land (that had been Native land until the Indian Removal Act of 1830) and granting private citizens – including single women and formerly enslaved people – 160-acre plots to farm. The first of these plots is now Homestead National Historical Park, which tells the story of American homesteading and its impact on shaping the country. The park has a large Heritage Center where you can learn about this era in history before heading to the nearby Palmer-Epard Cabin, an example of a typical homesteader dwelling.

For more on Homestead National Historical Park, see p90

13. Deadwood, South Dakota

EUREKA!

Popular among fans of the HBO series of the same name, Deadwood admittedly feels a bit cheesy at first glance, with its proliferation of casinos and monster truck rallies. However, if you give it a chance, you'll see that this National Historic Landmark is doing a mighty fine job of preserving its history as a former Gold Rushush town. The casinos and the tourism dollars that they bring in mean that its 1870s buildings are in great shape, and there's still plenty to experience if you want to learn about the Gold Rush, including history-themed tours that cover everything from archaeology to Deadwood's Chinatown.

For more on Deadwood, see p121

14. Gateway Arch, Missouri

GO WEST, YOUNG MAN!

Nicknamed the Gateway to the West, the Gateway Arch is a symbol of both St Louis and of westward expansion, despite having only been erected in the 1960s. This massive arch stands at 630ft at its highest point and was conceptualized as a tribute to Thomas Jefferson's vision of a continental United States. While the four-minute tram ride to the top of the arch is a highlight, it's equally worth stopping by the Museum under the Gateway Arch, where six exhibits delve into topics in 19th-century American history, from the Lewis and Clark expedition to the idea of Manifest Destiny.

For more on the Gateway Arch, see p60

15. Route 66, Multiple States

THE MOTHER ROAD

Stretching from Chicago to the California Coast, Route 66 has served as a main road to the West for many generations. Established in 1926, it was considered the easiest way to get to California from the Midwest, and many Dustbowl migrants traveled the road during the Great Depression, as chronicled in *The Grapes of Wrath*. Although Route 66 was officially decommissioned in 1985, many nostalgic drivers continue to retrace the route every year, often taking a slow approach, stopping along the way to see the many historic signs, roadside attractions and natural wonders that flank the so-called Mother Road.

For more on Route 66, see p22

HOW THE WEST IS NOW WON

Get to know what makes the people and places of the West tick, based on some of the region's top industries. By Amelia Mularz

GOLD! LAND! OPPORTUNITY! Unfortunately, the gold mining spree of the 1850s has come and gone, and available land is hard to come by, unless you first scoop up a lucrative job in tech or entertainment. But the West is lush with crops, innovations in artificial intelligence, blockbusters and energy – including the future of clean energy.

Agriculture

Farmers markets are certainly bustling across the West. Often called 'America's breadbasket,' the Great Plains region is blessed with fertile soil and high-producing wheat and corn farms. Kansas and North Dakota regularly duke it out for top wheat producer in the country, and Iowa ranks first for corn. Then there's California, where crops include everything from avocados to tomatoes to pistachios and walnuts. And while the Golden State is the country's top agricultural earner overall, Texas has the most farms. But don't count out the Pacific Northwest, which could be called the Peppermint Northwest. Washington is the top mint-producing state in the nation, and when combined with

Soy and corn fields in Iowa

Oregon and Idaho, the area grows 93% of the mint in the whole country.

Tech

It's no secret that California – the birthplace of the iPhone, a pioneer in artificial intelligence and HQ for tech titans like Apple, Google, Meta and Nvidia – is a major player in tech. So are its neighbors to the north. Oregon has its own version of Silicon Valley, an innovation epicenter called Silicon Forest, and Washington is home to Microsoft, Amazon and Expedia. Texas has also gained a reputation as a tech hub, with Dell, Apple and Amazon each having a major presence in Austin – aka Silicon Hills.

CALIFORNIA LEADS THE US IN NEW BUSINESSES, VENTURE CAPITAL, MANUFACTURING, TECH AND AGRICULTURE. WITH A GDP OF $4.1 TRILLION, CALIFORNIA BECAME THE FOURTH-LARGEST ECONOMY IN THE WORLD IN 2024, EDGING OUT JAPAN AND INDIA.

Entertainment

Southern California still has a major grip on the world's TV and film offerings, and yes, it continues to draw scores of Hollywood hopefuls who come to LA pursuing their dreams of acting, writing and directing. But the industry landscape is changing, much to the despair of many Angelenos who work in entertainment.

According to a recent report, the film and TV industries made up 64% of LA County's entertainment industry in 2013, but that portion had dropped to only 52% by the end of 2024. Due to a combination of factors, including high production costs and competition for tax incentives from other states, filming has gone elsewhere, including to New York and Georgia. But keeping within the West, New Mexico and Texas have also been luring production companies with sizable tax incentives.

Energy

Film may be a burgeoning industry in Texas, but fossil fuels are anything but – the Lone Star State leads in the US in both crude-oil and natural-gas production. Fellow Western states New Mexico, North Dakota and Colorado are no slouches in the energy department either. Together, they make up four of the top five crude-oil producers in the country (Alaska, which ties with Colorado, is the fifth).

When it comes to clean energy, the West is also making its mark. Texas leads the charge in wind energy, which contributes about $1.7 billion a year to the state's GDP. By 2031 the industry is projected to expand by 44%, creating thousands of new jobs. Behind Texas, Iowa, Oklahoma and Kansas rank second, third and fourth, respectively, for wind production in the US.

California is the country's top state for solar energy, and Texas comes in second. The Golden State also generates the most geothermal electricity, with three times the capacity of the second-largest producer, Nevada. But when it comes to real movers and shakers in the renewable energy space, don't forget South Dakota. In terms of the overall percentage of a state's electricity sales that come from renewable energy, the Mt Rushmore State wins with a whopping 92%.

Wind turbines in Texas

FROM LEFT: JMURPHPIX/SHUTTERSTOCK, KRISTI BLOKHIN/SHUTTERSTOCK

WHERE THE BUFFALO ROAM

Sacred to the Sioux. An icon of the West. A symbol of unchecked capitalism. The American buffalo carries a lot of meaning on its big, shaggy shoulders. By Amy C Balfour

IMAGINE A LOW-ROLLING plain. Prairie grass brushing against your knee. A few grasshoppers. A butterfly. All's quiet. Tranquil. But then...a low rumble just off the horizon. Dust rises from a nearby hill. In moments, the earth is rattling beneath your feet, the rumble rolling into a thundering roar. Grass and dirt explode beneath a herd of racing buffalo. Surprisingly graceful. The ground quakes. Dirt scatters. And controlled chaos pounds past in one poetic, ephemeral moment.

It's a compelling sight, and one America almost lost thanks to rampant overhunting. But today, the American buffalo is back and basking in the glow of celebrity. Bison were named America's official national mammal pursuant to the National Bison Legacy Act in 2016, while director Ken Burns shared their story in his 2023 documentary *The American Buffalo.*

What's in a Name?

Is there a difference between buffalo and bison in the US? Nope, they refer to the same animal. The word buffalo derives from *le boeuf,* the French word for buffalo. French fur trappers likely introduced this name by mistake, thinking that American buffalo were the same species as African and Asian buffalo. They aren't, but the name stuck. Bison is the short version of the scientific name *Bison bison*. Tribes had their own names too; perhaps the best known is *tatanka*, used by the Lakota. The Cheyenne identified the animals by sex, age and developmental characteristics – and ended up with 27 different names!

Buffalo Beginnings

Bison bison roamed what is now the United States at least 12,000 years ago, surviving the wave of extinctions that killed off mastodons, woolly mammoths and sa-

 Above: Buffalo in Custer State Park (p120)

ber-toothed tigers. With few predators, bison flourished, and they may have numbered anywhere from 30 million to 60 million. Their territory stretched from Canada south to Mexico, and southeast from the Great Plains to many of the original British colonies. Some made their way west of the Rockies.

For thousands of years bison anchored the spiritual lives of many Native American tribes. Plains tribespeople in particular considered buffalo sacred and were grateful that the animals sacrificed themselves to provide the necessities of life, including tools, food, clothing and hides, which were used in tipis.

From Conquistadors to Capitalists

Spanish colonists were the first Europeans to see American buffalo, and their recorded encounters date back to the mid-1500s. Colonists in America's mid-Atlantic and Southeast regularly saw buffalo – even in Florida! – in the 1600s and 1700s. By the early 1800s, however, the eastern herds had been killed off or driven away.

Thanks to the scientific observations of the Lewis and Clark expedition, which followed the Missouri River west toward the Pacific in the early 1800s, we know bison continued to thrive in the Great Plains. In 1806, after one memorable sighting near today's Chamberlain, South Dakota, Meriwether Lewis wrote: 'From this eminance I had a view of a greater number of buffalow than I had ever Seen before at one time. I must have Seen near 20,000 of those animals feeding on this plain.'

But this heyday was not to last. Buffalo robes, known for their warmth, and salted buffalo tongues became 'must-haves' for the East Coast smart set. New railroad lines soon dropped hunters and their increasingly efficient rifles directly onto the plains. Destructive overhunting ensued, and bison herds were decimated in the 1870s and 1880s. By some estimates their numbers dropped from 30 million at the start of the century to fewer than 1000 by 1889!

The US government allowed this wasteful destruction, and miles and miles of carcasses – stripped only of their valuable hides and tongues – were left rotting on the plains. Why the disregard? The government understood that if buffalo were eliminated, the plains tribes people – starving and utterly devastated – would be easier to relocate onto federal reservations.

In subsequent years, thanks to the efforts of a few ranchers and conservationists, including President Theodore Roosevelt and Comanche chief Quanah Parker, small bands of surviving herds grew in number and eventually flourished. Today there are about 450,000 bison in the United States.

Do Not Touch the Buffalo!

Buffalo are the largest land mammal in the country. Males weigh up to 2000lb, while females max out at 1000lb. And though they look cumbersome, buffalo can reach speeds of 35mph. They are typically brown, have two small horns and are marked by pronounced shoulder humps.

In Yellowstone National Park visitors must stay at least 25yd (23m) from buffalo while Custer State Park in South Dakota recommends 100yd (91m). As some national park visitors have painfully learned, buffalo can charge you if angered, and can cause severe bodily harm. The safest place to observe is from a car on a roadside pull-off. Do not feed them and never touch calves, even if they look abandoned.

Where Buffalo Stampede Today

Buffalo stampedes were actually rare, typically only occurring when herds were hunted or spooked. But they were a remarkable sight. Today, you can witness a controlled stampede during the annual Buffalo Round-Up at Custer State Park (p120). During this one-day event, held the fourth Friday of September, buffalo wranglers herd the park's 1450 buffalo into corrals where they are sorted, branded and vaccinated before the fall buffalo auction. This annual sale keeps the park's herd at manageable levels. The round-up began in 1965 as a low-key affair, but today more than 25,000 people come to watch the action.

Some critics argue that the round-up puts the animals under undue stress, but on the flip side the herd is vaccinated that day, which protects their long-term health. You can also immerse in the excitement of a buffalo stampede at Custer State Park's Bison Center, where oversized videos drop you into the frenzy.

Navajo woman, Navajo Nation
SERGII FIGURNYI/SHUTTERSTOCK

VISITING THE NAVAJO NATION: A GUIDE TO RESPECTFUL TRAVEL

To appreciate and get more out of your visit to the Navajo Nation, you should arrive prepared to be a respectful visitor. By George Joe, a Navajo writer with his own travel guide, NavajoGuide.com.

THE NAVAJO NATION is the largest American Indian reservation in the United States, spanning three states – New Mexico, Arizona and Utah – and covering an area nearly the size of West Virginia. In many areas of the reservation, there is no electricity, running water or cell phones, residents 65+ do not speak English, and centuries-old ceremonies are still conducted.

The very first thing first-time visitors ask is: 'Is it similar to a Tony Hillerman novel?' You can get a sense of Navajo culture by reading Hillerman's mystery novels, but they are fictional and many things he writes about are not entirely accurate, which he does so as not to give away tribal secrets. Watching the TV series *Dark Winds* can also offer a glimpse into Navajo life in the 1970s.

Visiting Sites & Attractions

When visiting the Navajo Nation, it's crucial to follow local rules, such as staying on designated roads and trails. For example, in Monument Valley, visitors must remain on Valley Dr and not wander into areas where Navajo families live. The only authorized hiking trail without a guide is the 3.9-mile Wildcat Trail.

- Always check if a guide is required before visiting specific locations. A list is usually available on the tribe's discovernavajo.com website.
- Avoid off-road driving or causing damage to natural areas.
- Do not drive too fast as it stirs up dirt.
- Respect restrictions like 'no bicycles' in certain areas like Monument Valley.

Forrest Gump Hill near Monument Valley is at Mile 13 on Hwy 163. It's famous as the place where Forrest Gump ended his run in the movie. The view is stunning, but be

mindful of oncoming traffic when taking photos.

If visiting the Navajo Nation Council Chambers, be quiet inside and turn off your cell phone, especially if a meeting is taking place. If attending a chapter meeting, also be quiet. Since you are an outsider (not tribal member), you do not need to sign in.

Attending Public Events & Ceremonies

If you attend a Navajo Council meeting inside the Navajo Council Chambers, remember that food is not allowed, and attendees are expected to remain silent. Similarly, if you attend a chapter meeting, which is public, treat it like attending a city council meeting.

When visiting sacred sites or attending ceremonies, like the Kinaaldá (a coming-of-age ceremony for girls), it is crucial to observe with respect and silence. Modest attire is recommended, and guests should bring a gift of food if invited. For ceremonies like the Yei Bi Chei (a traditional nine-day ceremony), it's best to attend with a Navajo companion to ensure you follow proper protocols.

While traveling on reservation roads, you might see signs for cultural events such as 'Ndaah' or 'Squaw Dance.' These events are often for Navajo community members and should be treated with the same respect as a church service. Confirm whether visitors are welcome before attending, and remember that certain ceremonies are private, unless a Navajo invites you.

During prayers, songs and talks, one should not interrupt and should remain respectfully silent and out of the way when inside the ceremonial hogan or home site area. Appropriate attire means dressing modestly – covering your skin is recommended. If you are uncertain, you may ask for guidance on how to proceed or act.

If you meet a medicine man, be respectful of their time and purpose. Many are elderly and may not speak English. Avoid pressing them with questions, as they may be engaged in important cultural responsibilities.

National Parks & Archaeological Sites

When visiting national parks within the reservation, follow these guidelines.

- Do not enter or alter archaeological sites.
- Avoid entering private property without permission.
- Do not deface rock walls or structures.
- Ask permission before photographing Navajo people, their homes or their animals.

Photography Etiquette

If you are taking photos for personal use, no permit is needed. However, for any commercial photography or video, you must obtain a permit from the Navajo Parks & Recreation Department in Window Rock. Certain events, like ceremonies or Native American Church gatherings, are off-limits for photography.

Respectful Behavior & Attire

While visiting the Navajo Nation, maintain modest dress and avoid clothing that is revealing or tight. Avoid loud and boisterous behavior, as it can be considered disrespectful. Displays of affection, such as hugging or touching, should only be done with permission.

Direct eye contact can be considered impolite in some contexts.

Navajo people often have a reserved demeanor, especially around strangers.

Navajo tacos

TIM M LANTHIER/GETTY IMAGES

Respect their space and limit unnecessary conversation.

How to Respectfully Purchase Authentic Navajo Arts & Crafts

When buying Navajo arts and crafts, it's important to be courteous. Avoid questioning craftspeople aggressively about the authenticity of their silver or stones because it is a big concern. Most are dedicated artisans, and there is a strong tradition of self-regulation among them. Refer to reputable guides like *navajo guide.com* for tips on where to find authentic goods and how to buy directly from the source. Many well-established trading posts and stores offer genuine items both on and off the reservation.

- Do not raise your voice or make accusations.
- Learn how to distinguish quality artisanship, but trust that most sellers operate with integrity.

WHEN VISITING SACRED SITES OR ATTENDING CEREMONIES, IT IS CRUCIAL TO OBSERVE WITH RESPECT AND SILENCE.

Turquoise jewelry
GRANDRIVER/GETTY IMAGES

Handling Panhandlers

If you plan to spend time on the reservation, you might encounter individuals asking for money, similar to city life. Often, such requests may be related to purchasing alcohol, which the tribe disapproves of but cannot fully control. If you feel uncomfortable, a polite 'no' usually suffices. In some cases, it may be best to walk away to avoid confrontation.

To avoid further interactions, offering a small amount of change can sometimes deter continued requests.

Avoiding Stereotypes

There are common misconceptions about Navajo life. For instance, Navajos do not live in tipis; traditional homes include hogans - eight-sided structures with the entrance facing east - or modern housing. While most Navajos speak English, older residents in remote areas may be more comfortable speaking in Navajo, and an interpreter may be needed. It is worth noting that fewer than 0.5% of Navajo children today enter school speaking the language.

Navajo Cultural Taboos

Navajo culture includes many taboos, and it's helpful to be aware of a few, for example, do not look at an eclipse or eat or sleep during one. If a convenience store suddenly closes at noon with a sign that says 'Reopens after Eclipse,' you will know why. Respect these traditions, as they are deeply meaningful to many Navajo people.

- Don't point at a rainbow with your index finger. You might lose it. Instead, use your thumb.
- Don't throw objects at a dust devil (whirlwind). Don't curse at a whirlwind or run into one, because it will affect your heart.
- Do not touch trees or rocks struck by lightning.

Navajo Cuisine: What to Expect

There are many safe and delicious dining options throughout the reservation, from restaurants in larger towns to roadside stands offering traditional Navajo dishes. For those curious about authentic flavors, the Window Rock Food Pavilion is a great place to try Navajo cuisine.

Roadside stands and food booths must have a permit, and tribal health workers frequently inspect them. Usually, they post their permit. Please do not make disparaging comments about the smell of the food or how it is cooked.

Be respectful when trying traditional foods, like mutton stew or frybread, even if they seem unfamiliar.

By following these guidelines, you can enjoy a respectful and enriching visit to the Navajo Nation, while appreciating the rich history, culture and traditions of the Navajo people.

SAVING THE NEW MEXICO CHILE

The state's beloved spicy fruit is under threat. Jade Bremner asks the experts how we can help to save it.

FOR NEW MEXICANS chile is more than just food – it connects the people with the state's history, culture and land. Chile has become an emblem of the Land of Enchantment and the state produces the majority of the spicy fruit in the US. On any visit to New Mexico you're likely to see chile garlands, or ristras, hanging from shops, see the spicy fruit logo on license plates and taste it on everything from burritos and burgers to smoothies and ice cream. But the future of the New Mexico chile is unknown.

The Significance of the New Mexico Chile

Growing chile in New Mexico dates back to the Pueblo people, who planted heirloom seeds. Chile farming here is still done using traditional methods, as the pods are not easily farmed by machinery. Instead, they are picked by hand so they're whole. Their red pods are then air-dried the original way, hung on ristras, creating brightly colored garlands in public spaces.

Some 30,000 visitors make the pilgrimage to the small town of Hatch, 40 miles north of Las Cruces, every year to experience what has been dubbed the 'Chile

Pictured clockwise from top left: Chile farmer, Hatch Valley; Red-green chiles, Hatch Valley; Chile harvest, Hatch Valley; Drying chiles, Albuquerque Old Town (p325)

Capital of the World'. Here every business sells the local crop in some form, most of them display the pods out front and some even roast chile in the street to tempt customers in with the sweet smell. The annual two-day extravaganza, Hatch Chile Festival, takes place every September celebrating the spicy fruit.

A Sought-After Chile

'It's the climate,' says Chantel Wagner, daughter of Jim Wagner of Big Jim Farms in Los Ranchos, on why New Mexico chile is so delicious. 'It's perfect for growing chile.' Chantel's family has been growing the organic fruit for four generations, perfecting the art since the early 1900s. Along with the climate, the soil and water are also just what the crop needs, she explains: 'this combination just creates really flavorful chile... which you can add to everything.' Her dad Jimmy is one of many locals who eat green and red New Mexico chiles with every meal.

There's 'a sweetness and earthiness and, bit of smokiness to it,' agrees New Mexico resident and scientist, Holly Brause.

Problems the Spicy Crop Faces

'When late summer and fall come, you start really looking forward to the chile roasters on the sidewalks,' says Holly. 'The smell of chile kind of permeates the towns, and everyone is so happy to get it fresh.' But behind the scenes, there's a chile crisis brewing. Holly's recent study, titled *The Uncertain Future of New Mexico Chile: Can a Heritage Crop Adapt to Water Scarcity?* looks at the sharp decline in production since the 1990s, due to a number of contributing factors including climate change, labor shortages and foreign competition.

Before 1994 there were around 34,000 acres of chile planted and harvested, but by 2023 there were only 8500. One reason for this is that chile farming is incredibly hard work. 'The harvest starts in August, when it's typically over 100°F. The sun is scalding so really difficult work, it's really physically demanding and it's seasonal work,' explains Holly.

'With farming you only get paid basically once a year, so it makes it really difficult to make a living and be sustainable,' says Chantel. There are also environmental factors threatening the future of chile production, which are linked to climate change. 'Severe droughts make it really really difficult to access water,' says Chantel. Chile farming is 'super high risk, it's hard work, and you don't make a whole lot of money.'

What Travelers Can Do to Help

Chantel's family business, Big Jim Farms, sees a responsibility to keep chile-growing traditions alive. But their 9-acre farm has had to diversify to create other revenue streams. They now offer 'U-Pick' immersive experiences for visitors, plus tours and chile workshops, including salsa- and tamale-making cooking classes. 'This helps us be sustainable, make money to keep farming, and it also brings awareness to plant preservation and supports farming and local agriculture,' says Chantel, who believes there are not only health benefits to eating chile (which is packed with vitamin C) but in the physical process of growing it. This grounding activity gets folks away from their computers and phone screens and offers a fun day outdoors. 'It's a very therapeutic experience as well as being a great contribution to the community...people can also volunteer to plant and harvest chile. We continue the traditions of chile farming to teach the next generation.

Travelers can also choose to buy New Mexico produce to support local farmers, instead of buying Mexican or Chinese imports. Choose restaurants serving local products or offering farm-to-table experiences with an emphasis on low food miles, or buy local chile from stores. Holly explains that it's worth considering the packaging before you put items in your basket. 'Some products do carry the New Mexico certified label or the Hatch certified label,' she says.

A Possible Alternate Future

Big Jim Farms irrigates water from the Rio Grande River, but water levels are diminishing as a result of climate change, and an over reliance on groundwater. Big Jim Farms is considering other water sources including building wells, but this will come at a cost of millions of dollars. Holly says help from the authorities could help: 'There are definitely policy issues that have to be addressed so that we can maintain our water resources for the future without losing our agricultural production, and I think that there are creative ways to get there.'

Mariachi musician
SCHARFSINN86/GETTY IMAGES

LA PASIÓN DEL MARIACHI

From San Antonio's 'finest female mariachi' to the Rio Grande Valley's high school mariachi competitions, Mexican Americans in Texas are showcasing their roots through this storytelling tradition.
By Priscilla Totiyapungprasert

MARIACHI BANDS CAN be found performing at special occasions all over Texas, carrying string and brass instruments, and dressed in elegant cowboy-inspired suits. While traditional groups perform folk songs, dramatic rancheras and soulful corrido ballads, modern mariachi ensembles play with genres, with bands performing a fusion of cumbias, Tejano, and even punk and hip hop. The diversity of mariachi speaks to the diversity of Mexican Americans and the multifaceted, multiracial modern American identity

You can find a mariachi band at weddings, quinceañeras, Catholic church bazaars, restaurants and birthday parties. In April, San Antonio's annual **Fiesta** *(fiestasanantonio.org)* celebrates the city's history, culture and heritage, and visitors can enjoy mariachi bands as they perform along the River Walk.

In the El Paso area, the large Catholic parishes often invite mariachi and other regional bands to their kermés, or annual church bazaar. The bazaars are held from July through mid-October. Grab a deep-fried gordita and enjoy the tunes at St Ignatius of Loyola Parish in El Paso's historic Segundo Barrio.

The Origin of Mariachi

Mariachi style of folk music was first documented in the 19th century and possibly originated in or around the Mexican state of Jalisco. The music blended indigenous oral tradition with Spanish instrumentation, such as the five-stringed vihuela. African enslaved people brought syncopathic beats and polyrhythmic patterns while Austrian Emperor Maximilian brought polka bands that added brass instruments to the mix.

While early mariachi musicians were day laborers who wore plain workmen's clothes, modern musicians are known for their iconic charro outfit consisting of long, tight pants or a long skirt, a bolero jacket, a silk tie and a sombrero, all embroidered with decorative motifs. Certain instruments, such as the bright trumpet and deep guitarrón, help give mariachi music its signature, festive sound.

Regional styles of music developed over the years, but mariachi songs share common themes. They tell the tales of the brave and the betrayed, of those who have loved and longed and lost. In the ranchera *Volver, Volver*, Vicente Fernández crooned about an old flame and the torture of not being able to turn back time.

Sometimes that love doubled as love for a woman and love for homeland. In *Caminos de Michoacán*, Federico Villa sang of searching through all the cities of Michoacán for the lover he left behind.

Pedro de Lille's *Corrido de Chihuahua* captures the desert spirit by paying tribute to sun-kissed, sotol-drinking Chihuahua. A jaunty accordion melody introduces this ode to the largest state in Mexico, which once stretched into present-day West Texas before the US claimed the northernmost territory in 1848, the spoils of the Mexican–American War.

Lille grew up in Chihuahua, but crossed the border to live in El Paso from 1910 to 1917 during the Mexican Revolution. El Paso, like many cities along the southern border of Texas, has a binational community with shared history and culture. It was through Mexican immigrants, as well as these border communities, that the tradition of mariachi spread in Texas.

The Revolution Comes to Texas

Mariachi experienced a boom after the Mexican Revolution as Mexican folk music and regional music became points of patriotism. Songs of revolutionary heroes such as Pancho Villa and Mexico's natural beauty stirred feelings of pride that traveled north as mariachi made its way to the American Southwest.

The grito, a high-pitched yell sometimes interjected in mariachi songs, is used as an impassioned battle cry to mark the start of Mexican Independence Day celebrations. In Austin and other cities in Texas, the Mexican consulate will typically lead a grito to commemorate September 16 when the Grito de Dolores kickstarted the Mexican War of Independence in 1810.

Mexican Americans have embraced the sociopolitical aspects of mariachi in other ways. During the Chicano Movement of the 1960s, Mexican American civil rights activists saw mariachi as a way to connect to their roots and as a form of resistance, according to the book *Mariachi Music in America: Experiencing Music, Expressing Culture* by Daniel Sheehy.

Community leaders have taught mariachi in schools and churches. After Texas passed the Bilingual Education Act in 1968, which allocated funds for bilingual programs in public schools, the San Antonio Independent School District began offering mariachi classes. Mariachi also reached the university level.

In 1977, graduate students at the University of Texas at Austin founded Mariachi Paredes de Tejastitlán, named in honor of their Mexican American studies professor and border historian Américo Paredes. Some mariachi performers described their art as an unapologetic declaration of existence following the 2016 election of President Donald Trump, who described Mexican immigrants as criminals.

The historic tie between the US and Mexico is featured in *El Milagro de Recuerdo*, a mariachi opera performed at Houston Grand Opera, that tells the story of a family spending their last Christmas in Mexico before moving to the US.

Music also became a part of collective grief and healing in 2019, when a white supremacist shot and killed 23 people at a Walmart store in El Paso. Local musician Josue Rodriguez wrote and sang his corrido *El Llanto de El Paso, Texas* for a community in shock and mourning. At vigils, mariachi ensembles performed *Amor Eterno* by beloved, borderland singer Juan Gabriel. In 2022, mariachis traveled to Uvalde

Vicente Fernández (p528)

VALERIE MACON/AFP VIA GETTY IMAGES

to perform *Amor Eterno* after tragedy struck again and a gunman killed 21 people at Robb Elementary School in Uvalde.

Mariachi Evolves without Machismo

While mariachi is associated with machismo, a certain image of Mexican masculinity, the rise of female mariachi ensembles buck the convention. In 1968, the all-female Las Rancheritas from Alamo in South Texas visited US troops in Vietnam and became the first mariachi group to travel to a war zone to perform, the *Los Angeles Times* reported.

While Las Rancheritas are no longer around, other groups continue to break through gender stereotypes in the male-dominated arena, such as Mariachi Rosas Divinas and Mariachi Amor a Mexico, the first and only all-female mariachi groups in Dallas and Houston, respectively. In San Antonio, Mariachi Las Alteñas has been performing since 2002 and bills itself as 'Texas' finest female mariachi.'

PETER LARSEN/WIREIMAGE/GETTY IMAGES

Mariachi Rosas Divinas

WHILE MARIACHI IS ASSOCIATED WITH MACHISMO, A CERTAIN IMAGE OF MEXICAN MASCULINITY, THE RISE OF FEMALE MARIACHI ENSEMBLES BUCK THE CONVENTION.

In recent decades, mariachi sensations have made it to TV specials. The Fort Worth brothers who founded Mariachi Real de Alvarez went from playing for tips at restaurants to performing a scene in the Netflix series *Queen of the South*.

Netflix focused again on mariachi, this time on a youth culture in its 2023 documentary *Going Varsity in Mariachi* – a look at the competitive world of high school mariachi in South Texas. The Rio Grande Valley boasts of some of the most competitive varsity mariachi teams and the slice-of-life documentary follows the Mariachi Oro band from Edinburg North High School as it competes for the state championship.

Mariachi competitions are a big deal in the Lone Star State, with youth ensembles traveling to compete in statewide and national showdowns.

But for young, next-generation musicians, mariachi is more than a hobby – it's a tie to their family roots and a declaration of Texas' Mexican American heritage.

Mariachi Events in Texas

Mariachi Extravaganza (San Antonio; *mariachimusic.com*): This decades-old festival is also a national competition, featuring multiple days of performances and culminating in a final showdown on the last day and a concert with the competition winners. Expect a mix of professional mariachi groups and school-aged performers.

Festival de Mariachi en la Isla (Corpus Christi): Said to be one of the largest mariachi gatherings in the world, this multiday event started at Texas A&M University-Corpus Christi. The lineup typically features women-led performances and discussions, as well as regional high school ensembles and many local groups.

Mariachi Festival (Houston; *mariachifestival.com*): This nonprofit promotes mariachi and ballet folklórico programs in schools. The multiday festival generally kicks off with a Mariachi Mass, blending mariachi music with Catholic tradition.

Sombrero Festival (Brownsville; *sombrerofestival.com*): Not exclusive to mariachi, but if you feel like watching competitors attempt their best grito, head to this binational, pre-Lenten event on the border. Full of family-friendly activities, this long-standing festival is known for its popular grito competition, where men and women compete to deliver the greatest grito.

All-year occasions: Plenty of sit-down, Tex-Mex and Mexican restaurants in the state showcase a mariachi band, typically on the weekends. Check restaurant websites or call ahead to find out specifics.

Colorado River
MAREK ULIASZ/ALAMY

COLORADO'S CHANGING CLIMATE

In the parched Rocky Mountains, water is everything. How is climate change impacting the region's long-term prospects?
By Christopher Pitts

THE MOST VISIBLE indication of the effects of climate change in Colorado are not in the state itself, but further downstream along the Colorado River. In 2022 water levels at Lake Mead, the massive reservoir formed by the Hoover Dam outside Las Vegas, fell to their lowest level ever, at just one-fourth of its capacity.

The infamous bathtub ring, a chalky white coating on the reservoir's cliffs, is a reminder of just how far the water's surface has dropped in the past two decades. At its all-time low in 2022, the ring extended 150ft down to the water's surface – or 26.63% capacity. Even after two historically wet winters, in 2024 the reservoir had only risen to 34% capacity. If the water in the Colorado River continues to be used at the same rate as today, the US Bureau of Reclamation concluded that the water level in the reservoir will soon drop so low that Hoover Dam will no longer be able to generate electricity. And after that? There remains the possibility that one day, the reservoir could reach 'dead pool,' when the level in the dam drops so low that the river stops flowing entirely, and Arizona, Nevada, southern California and northwestern Mexico will be cut off from their main source of water.

The Colorado River

But what does all this have to do with Colorado? In a word: snowpack. The Colorado River, whose headwaters lie on the western slope of Rocky Mountain National Park and whose tributaries are scattered across the Rockies, is largely fed by snowmelt. Approximately 90% of all the water in the river comes from the mountains of Colorado, Wyoming and Utah, with the lion's share coming from Colorado watersheds. The equation is simple: the less snow that falls in the Rockies, the less water there is in the river, and less water that's available for one of the most important agricultural regions in the country – not to mention the 40 million people who live in the Colorado River basin (including Los Angeles, San Diego, Las Vegas and Phoenix).

Of course, as any skier will tell you, snowpack varies from year to year. Some years may be above average, others below. But data from the Environmental Protection Agency (EPA) indicates that overall, there has been a downward trend over time: across the West, snowpack has declined an average 23% since 1955. More importantly, the date of peak snowpack has been moving steadily backward. That is, the largest amount of snow in the Colorado

Rockies used to be measured in mid-April; over the past decade, that date has been inching toward March.

What does that tell us? That because of climate change, winters are slowly getting shorter. Meanwhile, summer temperatures in the Southwest have risen faster than in any other part of the United States. In Colorado, they've risen by 2.5°F since the beginning of the 20th century. Higher temperatures mean increased aridity and higher rates of evaporation throughout the landscape. Soils in particular have dried out to such an extent that when the spring runoff begins, much of that snowmelt is sucked straight into the ground, leaving increasingly less water that makes it into the river system – even in years when snowpack is average.

Factor in the 20-plus-year megadrought that is currently gripping the region (the worst in 1200 years), and a flawed seven-state compact that draws more water from the Colorado River than there is annual flow, and you have all the ingredients for what has become a monumental crisis – albeit in slow motion. At this point, it seems highly unlikely that nature will replenish the Lake Mead or Lake Powell (on the Utah–Arizona border) reservoirs on its own. Barring an end to the drought, the only other way to avoid dead pool is to reduce consumption.

Wildfire-fighting efforts in Boulder (p188), 2022

MICHAEL CIAGLO/GETTY IMAGES

Considering that roughly one-half of all the water that flows out of the spigots in Los Angeles, San Diego and Phoenix comes directly from the Colorado River (in Vegas it's upwards of 90%), drastically reducing consumption in what is one of the fastest-growing regions in the US may seem like a tall order. But city dwellers aren't even the primary consumers. That would be agriculture, which sucks up 80% of the allotted river flow. And yet, reducing agricultural demand for irrigated water is easier said than done. With only 3in of annual rainfall, Yuma (Arizona) and the Imperial Valley (southern California) might seem like some of the world's most improbable farmland, but they're actually the nation's primary producer of winter fruit and vegetables. When farmland in the rest of the nation is on winter vacation, 90% of all the carrots, lettuce and other greens you find at the supermarket are being grown in the always-sunny desert, irrigated directly with Colorado River water.

Climate change is not the only reason the Southwest's most important water source is drying up. Flawed planning, stubborn special-interest groups, outdated water rights and a naturally occurring drought cycle all play their own role. But as in so many other situations, climate change makes an already serious problem that much worse. As the Colorado snowpack continues to decline and summer temperatures continue to rise, eventually, there can only be one outcome. And sure enough, in 2023 an agreement on the first round of water restrictions was finally reached: the three Lower Basin states agreed to cut 3 million acre-feet of water use per year through 2026, in return for $1.2 billion in payments from the federal government. A critical first step in establishing a permanent agreement when the temporary deal expires.

Wildfires

Beyond the consequences for all the people who live downstream, climate change has a direct impact on Coloradans as well.

Colorado's mainstay of the tourism economy, skiing ($5 billion in annual revenue), seems to be headed for a day of reckoning, though the impacts of warming weather are less immediately visible for high-altitude ski resorts in the Rockies than in lower-elevation resorts in the Alps or along the East Coast, where winter rainfall is already commonplace. While Colorado ski resorts are nonetheless preparing for shortened seasons and less natural snowfall, there is another less obvious threat on the near horizon: wildfire.

In 2021, just miles from the residential sprawl around Lake Tahoe, California, the Caldor Fire raced through the mountains with such startling speed and ferocity that it's a miracle that firefighters were able to stop the blaze before it reached the lakeside settlements. One of the casualties of the fire, however, was the Sierra-at-Tahoe ski resort, where roughly 80% of the terrain was burned; the shocking photos of empty ski lifts being swallowed up by a raging orange inferno seemed to encapsulate all fire-mitigation challenges the West is currently facing.

THE LESS SNOW THAT FALLS IN THE ROCKIES, THE LESS WATER THERE IS IN THE RIVER, AND THE LESS WATER THAT'S AVAILABLE FOR ONE OF THE MOST IMPORTANT AGRICULTURAL REGIONS IN THE COUNTRY.

FRANCISCO BLANCO/SHUTTERSTOCK

While California's fires may get more coverage in the media, this is a region-wide phenomenon. Over the past decade, unusually hot and dry conditions have led to an increase not only in the number of wildfires per year, but also in their intensity. Warming conditions have stressed forests, making them more susceptible to disease and infestations of spruce, fir and pine beetles. Huge stands of dead trees – anyone who drives up Trail Ridge Rd in Rocky Mountain National Park will spot the gray- and rust-colored stands of deadwood – combined with exceptionally dry grasses, low humidity and high winds have resulted in increasingly massive fires. Of the 20 largest fires in Colorado history, 16 occurred after 2011, and the other four took place in the 2000s. The three largest ever, Cameron Peak, East Troublesome and Pine Gulch, all took place in 2020, filling the skies outside several major cities with raining ash and a terrifying red glow.

Another change is that there is no longer a wildfire season. What used to be a late-summer event might now happen at any time of year, as evidenced by the most destructive fire in Colorado history, the Marshall Fire, which sprang up at the edge of Boulder on December 30, 2021. Fueled by 115mph gusting winds and a complete absence of snowfall that year, the grassland fire swept through a dense residential community in a matter of hours, completely destroying over 1000 homes and businesses, taking two lives and causing $2 billion in damages.

There's no question that decades of overly aggressive fire suppression on public lands is partially to blame for the blazes, as the Smokey the Bear strategy resulted in the accumulation of huge amounts of fuel and dense understory vegetation throughout the West. While no one wants unplanned fires to happen (campfires are off-limits in many places throughout Colorado), local officials today are passing on a different sort of message. It's no longer one of fire suppression, but fire adaptation. As the Boulder City Wildfire Preparedness Guide reminds its residents: 'We live in a location where the wildfire threat is real. Wildfires happen frequently. A wildfire that threatens your home is not a matter of if, but when.' Residents in the West are learning to be prepared, because they are now living in an environment where people have to accept wildfires and mandatory evacuations as an inevitable part of their lives.

BREAD CULTURE IN THE BAY AREA

A bevy of bakers is drawing people from near and far to revel in the rich culture around artisanal bread. By Lisa Park

HEAD OVER TO Acme Bread Company in Berkeley any day of the week and you'll find a line of customers that's sometimes 30-plus deep, eagerly waiting to get inside. Hand-drawn signs touting savory creations such as 'hella wet levain' and 'multigrain spelt' border the bakery's picture window, which offers a tantalizing glimpse of the arts-and-crafts loaves that have earned Acme accolades and a devoted following. Meanwhile, the yeasty aroma of freshly baked bread keeps customers enthralled until it's their turn to pick and choose from crusty baguettes, buns, rounds and rolls – like a kid in a candy store.

Not too shabby for a bakery that's been around for over 40 years. But Acme's not alone when it comes to getting this kind of steadfast attention. Artisanal bakeries across the San Francisco Bay Area are drawing big crowds and fostering communities keen on indulging their appetite for – and love of – handcrafted, high-quality bread.

Artisanal Bread's Ups & Downs

Bay Area breadmaking goes back to the mid-1800s when Isadore Boudin of Boudin Bakery used a sourdough starter given to him by a gold miner to create his classic French bread. While the rest of the country moved toward ultra-processing bread post WWII (using commercially made cake yeast and chemicals such as emulsifiers to speed up production), Boudin Bakery resisted. Staying true to old-world traditions, it still makes bread with just flour, water and salt, using the same starter or mother dough from 176 years ago.

Even as Boudin flourished, many artisanal bakeries gave way to large, industrial operations mass-producing cheap, bland, chemically enhanced white bread. It wasn't until the 1970s when a new breed of bread makers, including Zen monks, hippies and counterculture kids, decided they'd had enough of Wonder Bread. They started making bread the old-fashioned way – kneaded and shaped by hand then baked in wood-fired ovens – fusing classic techniques focusing on texture and flavor development with modern values emphasizing good, clean and nourishing food.

Over the next few decades, bakers at Tassajara, Cheeseboard Collective, Acme, Semifreddi's and the San Francisco Baking Institute (SFBI) each had a hand in 'laying the groundwork for people to enjoy arts-and-crafts style bread,' says Miyuki Togi, SFBI baking instructor. Their success helped elevate people's appreciation for, as Togi explains, 'handmade bread that takes time and is made with care.' And it also helped make artisanal bread accessible – via storefronts, restaurants and grocery outlets – throughout the Bay Area.

Tartine's Outsize Impact

Then along came Tartine in the early aughts. Its novel bakes experimenting with longer fermentation, higher hydration, whole grains and a super-dark crust blew the Bay Area bread scene wide open. The now-famous brand snagged the ultimate endorsement from New York Times food writer Mark Bittman who called Tartine his 'favorite bakery in the United States.'

Artisanal bakeries inspired by Tartine's spirit of innovation and excellence started popping up all over the Bay, each investing the time and resources toward creating delicious, nutritious bread. Consider San Francisco favorite the Mill, whose owner and head baker Josey Baker specializes in freshly milled (in house, no less) wholegrain sourdough breads that need up to 40 hours to complete – 'because good things take time,' according to Baker on his website.

At Fournée Bakery in Berkeley, the mission is to 'make the best possible product consistently using the best possible ingredients sourced from local farms and purveyors.' Meanwhile, Mountain View–based the Midwife and the Baker is all about cultivating 'craft and community,' baking only with organic flour and seeds from sustainable farms to create quality products for its customers.

"THERE'S A REAL SYMBIOTIC RELATIONSHIP BETWEEN MAKING BREAD THAT'S BEAUTIFUL AND HAVING PEOPLE WHO VALUE YOU AND THE ART OF BAKING." AZIKIWEE ANDERSON, RIZE UP BAKERY FOUNDER

Tartine Bakery
GADO IMAGES/ALAMY

Love for Craft & Community

With Tartine's meteoric rise, 'customers got more serious about what they were looking for in bread,' says Togi. In addition, 'people in the Bay Area are more open to paying more for better quality food. So they don't mind paying more for a loaf of really good bread from a small bakery.'

Theo Dolarian, fellow SFBI baking instructor and Mill alumnus, agrees and adds that 'people are also more open to new flavor profiles. They will try different things... The wonderful thing about the San Francisco Bay Area is that if there's a style of bread you're interested in, there's a place that does it and probably does it really well.'

Case in point: home-based-project-turned-growing-commercial-operation Rize Up Bakery, whose inventive sourdough breads – ube, masala and K-pop (aka gochujang) – have struck a resounding chord. Says founder Azikiwee Anderson (who was previously a chef), 'the only reason I get to innovate is because I have customers who care enough to support what I'm doing. There's a real symbiotic relationship between making bread that's beautiful and having people who value you and the art of baking.'

Adds Anderson, Rize Up is a reflection of the San Francisco Bay Area, 'where there's a lot more we than I. Breadmaking is about being part of a community of different cultures. It's about representing and including those cultures so that they feel seen and cared about.'

'When you ask me what makes bread culture in the Bay Area special, I really do think it's the community. We're part of something bigger. And when you're surrounded by people who care and are down to do the hard work, that makes our bread untouchable.'

Baking is a labor of love for the craft and for the community, says Anderson, whose North Star questions include things like: 'Would you stand in line for our bread? Would you buy it special to share at a dinner? When you bite into it, do you do a little happy dance? Does it talk to your soul?'

Yes, yes and so much yes.

STORYBOOK

A HISTORY OF SEATTLE'S TECH INNOVATION

A quick peek at how Seattle became the tech-forward city it is today. By Sarah Etinas

OVER THE PAST half a century or so, Seattle has developed a reputation for churning out tech giants, like Microsoft, Amazon and Boeing. But the city wasn't always a hub of innovation. Dive into Seattle's roots and learn what historic, economic and cultural factors transformed it into the future-facing city that it is today.

The Beginnings

While technology as we know it today revolves around big-time innovations like planes and computers, Seattle's roots weren't quite that complex. As a matter of fact, when Seattle was first settled by Westerners in the late 19th century, things were very far from the skyscrapers of today. The original buildings sunk into the sandy soil, and one of the earliest mayors, Henry Yesler, plundered the city's finances via a dubious lottery system, nearly causing Seattle to fall into bankruptcy. To top it all off, the Great Seattle Fire of 1889 completely decimated all 29 blocks of the city's downtown.

A handful of years later, Seattle finally had an opportunity to pick itself up, brush itself off and try to rebuild: the Klondike Gold Rush. Between 1896 and 1899, tens of thousands of gold prospectors stopped in Seattle to stock up on food, clothing, mining equipment and other essentials before making their way up to the Klondike River in Canada to pan for gold nuggets. It's estimated that this brought about $64 million dollars of revenue into the city – approximately $2.53 billion in today's money – in just those few years. Needless to say, this gold rush gave the city a much-needed

 Above: Boeing Dreamliner

CLOCKWISE FROM TOP LEFT: MINH K TRAN/SHUTTERSTOCK, STEFANO POLITI MARKOVINA/SHUTTERSTOCK

economic boost and set it down a path of growth once again.

Boeing Steps on the Scene

At the turn of the 20th century, Seattle's advancements continued, with the expansion of train lines and the creation of shipping companies like UPS. This little Pacific Northwest frontier town truly began to bloom, and it was here that Detroit-born Bill Boeing took a chance in 1916. His company, originally known as the Pacific Aero Products Company and renamed Boeing shortly after, became Seattle's first modern-day tech company.

Just a year after Boeing was established, the US officially entered into WWI. The aerospace pioneer promptly stepped up, securing contracts to build critical aircraft for the US Navy. Surprisingly, even after the war was over, the payment from these planes wasn't enough for the company to secure its fate and survive the Great Depression. To keep the company afloat, Bill Boeing had employees build nearly whatever clients were asking for – from furniture to boats – all the while searching for ways to break into the cargo shipping and commercial airline industries. But it wasn't really until WWII – when the US needed another influx of military aircraft – that the aerospace giant finally found its footing. As this wartime surge transformed Boeing into a manufacturing powerhouse, it reshaped Seattle along with it, bringing nearly 50,000 jobs to the area and laying the groundwork for the city's future growth.

Microsoft Makes Its Mark

Now, technically, Microsoft was started by Bill Gates and his business partner Paul Allen in Albuquerque, New Mexico, in 1975, but the two soon decided to relocate to Seattle in 1979, probably to be back in their home city. Initially focused on developing programming languages like BASIC for early personal computers, the company's big break came with the creation of MS-DOS, the operating system for IBM's revolutionary PC in the early 1980s. This success paved the way for the groundbreaking Windows operating system and later the Microsoft Office software.

As Microsoft grew, so did the surrounding greater Seattle communities of Bellevue and Redmond. The company became an enormous job creator, drawing in technical talent and skilled professionals from around the globe. This influx of high-paying jobs spurred massive economic development, driving demand for housing, services and infrastructure, effectively transforming the eastern side of Lake Washington into a bustling technology hub and further cementing Seattle's reputation as a leader in innovation.

Amazon Arises

Two decades later, in 1994, the soon-to-be-ubiquitous Amazon made its debut. Founded by Jeff Bezos in his garage in Bellevue – just outside Seattle proper – the company began as an online bookstore, rapidly expanding its offerings to become the 'everything store' it's known as today. Amazon's revolutionary e-commerce model transformed retail and, like Boeing and Microsoft before it, dramatically reshaped Seattle's urban landscape. The once-industrial South Lake Union neighborhood in particular got a facelift, with Amazon setting up its urban campus there in 2010. The area now has dozens of Amazon office buildings, including the eye-catching architectural marvel known as the Amazon Spheres, as well as a couple of no-checkout Amazon Go stores and a pair of company-owned Community Banana Stands (grab a free banana when you pass!). Beyond the Amazon-owned spots, the neighborhood also now has countless modern high-rise apartment buildings, bustling restaurants and a thriving retail scene, largely thanks to the job potential this international giant has provided through the years.

The Tech Startups of Today

But Seattle's technological innovations didn't stop back in the '90s. As a matter of fact, as of 2025, it's estimated that there are between 1400 and 1800 startups in Seattle, the majority of which are in tech. They're pioneering everything from advanced artificial intelligence and cutting-edge biotechnology to sustainable space travel and immersive gaming experiences. And with the deep well of talent brought over by the big companies before them, it's only a matter of time before one of these ventures becomes the next Boeing, Microsoft or Amazon.

INDEX

Map Pages **000**

E

Map Pages **000**

Map Pages **000**

Map Pages **000**

"The Grand Canyon lives up to the hype: its immensity, its grandeur, its beauty and its very age, all scream for superlatives."

"With sparkling Puget Sound to the west, the snow-capped Cascade Mountains to the east, and urban green spaces dotted throughout town, it's easy for Seattleites to escape the urban hustle."

Mapping data sources:
© Lonely Planet
© OpenStreetMap http://openstreetmap.org/copyright

FROM LEFT: ANTON_IVANOV/SHUTTERSTOCK, CDRIN/SHUTTERSTOCK

THIS BOOK

The 7th edition of Lonely Planet's Western USA guidebook was written and researched by Amy C Balfour, Margot Bigg, Sarah Etinas, Anthony Ham, Lauren Keith, Amelia Mularz, Liza Prado, Helena Smith and Regis St Louis. This guidebook was produced by the following:

Destination Editor Caroline Trefler

Production Editor Kate James

Image Editor Catalina Aragón

Cartographer Valentina Kremenchutskaya

Coordinating Editor Michael MacKenzie

Assisting Editors James Appleton, Janet Austin, Imogen Bannister, Nigel Chin, Peterjon Creswell, Kate Mathews

Cover Researcher Katelyn Perry

Thanks Saralinda Turner

Paper in this book is certified against the Forest Stewardship Council™ standards. FSC™ promotes environmentally responsible, socially beneficial and economically viable management of the world's forests.

Published by Lonely Planet Global Limited
CRN 554153
7th edition – Feb 2026
ISBN 978 1 83758 424 6

10 9 8 7 6 5 4 3 2 1
Printed in Malaysia